I hope this book helps you on your person

Best
kind h̶e̶a̶r̶t̶s̶ from

Pierre Sabak

The Murder of Reality

– SERPENTIGENA –
THE SERIES

VOLUME 1

The Murder of Reality
Hidden Symbolism of the Dragon

Written and Illustrated by

Pierre Sabak

SERPENTIGENA
PUBLICATIONS

This book is dedicated to the Children of Man (the Bashari*)
May we live in PEACE and learn to LOVE one another

* 'Bashari' is an Arabic word and means human (not divine)

I would like to thank the following people:

My Wife
*Thank you for loving me and supporting me emotionally throughout my life
and for your precious gift...*

Neil Hague
*Thank you for such a wonderful book cover and for all your help and support over the
years – without your input this book would never have been conceived.*

Carl Hollingsworth
*Sincere thanks for setting up www.pierresabak.com and additional promotions.
Carl can be contacted at lilolcarlos@aol.com*

David Icke
*Opening the doorway to a very deep rabbit hole
(or is that a viper's nest?)*

Sylvia Cook
*When I needed help you were there willingly.
Thank you for your commitment and proof reading such a difficult manuscript.*

Anthony Foster
*Thank you for your exceptional layout and creative design.
Your enthusiasm and friendship is beyond measure.*

Danny Williams
*Always there for me whenever I needed help or support.
Selfless and caring throughout my life you are my 'bestest' friend!*

Mother
Thank you for being such a patient, loving and wonderful person in my life.

Leo
Being a father figure and mentor.

Brother
For all the wonderful times past, present and future.

Dad
For being my dad.

Takashi & Kuniko
Thank you for all the help and support over the years!

*Last of all my grandparents, family and friends past and present
Thank you for making me – ME!*

Contents

Quotations by Pierre Sabak

People are under the apprehension that wars are fought between men.
In actual fact, wars are fought between men and angels,
and the only way to win this war is to stop fighting!

Wars are historically for one single purpose to break humanity!
You break the enemy physically, and your country breaks your mind
psychologically! Once broken, the individual is no longer capable of
thinking like a rational being.

In a war situation, people have always adopted a 'them' and 'us' mentality.
What humanity has failed to consider is that the 'them' and 'us' may not
actually be 'human'.

Mankind will never have human rights until his status is considered
equal to that of the djinn (jinn).

The problem with our political system is that the government does not
represent the people. In fact, the state is fighting a perpetual war against
the people masked under the banner of freedom and liberty.

Dehumanizing another human is not human!

The alien issue will not go away. Humanity is too frightened to talk about it
or even to consider the question seriously. Universal to all cultures, fantastical
creatures from the sky have visited our planet throughout the course of human
history. The pertinent question then is not whether they exist but how much
influence do non-human entities exert over world governments. The historical
pervasiveness of non-disclosure suggest these creatures assume absolute power!

Man as the engineer, mathematician and intellectual has principally used his
power of reason to make the human race servile and superstitious.

A democracy has no need for an army.

Words don't lie they deceive!

'Illuminotics' is a new academic field and is the study of the symbols of
the Illuminati.

II

Prologue
We are Being Watched, Sir

'There is a lady, Mrs. Clarer, who is known throughout the world as being a South African woman who not only communicated with, but mothered a child by a father from another world. There's nothing unusual or so unearthly about Madame Clarer's story. There have been many women throughout Africa in various centuries who have attested to the fact that they had been fertilized by strange creatures from somewhere. She's not alone...

... It is a difficult thing to be the one who sees something like I have described, because it is very easy for others to accuse one of madness, or worse yet, of deliberate falsifying. Yet those people who have been in proximity to such a thing lose all their doubts when they have had the experience. There is such an enormous gap between those who have seen and those who have not. I suggest to those who have not to keep an open mind, and have sympathy for the ones who have. We are being watched, sir!'

Vusamazulu Credo Mutwa [Official Zulu Historian and Shaman]: Zulu Shaman, Dreams, Prophecies, and Mysteries, Destiny Books, Vermont, 2003, p152

Foreword
The Murder of Reality

'The basic tool for the manipulation of reality is the manipulation of words. If you can control the meaning of words, you can control the people who must use the words'.[1]
Philip K. Dick

'Language is like an encryption key, initiation permits one to access knowledge at a security clearance level. Understanding words is a means of bypassing the guards and stealing the security card'.
Pierre Sabak

'It would not be impossible to prove with sufficient repetition and a psychological understanding of the people concerned that a square is in fact a circle. They are mere words, and words can be molded until they clothe ideas in disguise'.
Joseph Goebbels

1. David Icke, The David Icke Guide to the Global Conspiracy (and how to end it), David Icke Books, 2007, p255

This work has taken me nearly seven years to research and is intended as an academic textbook on the cultic symbolism of the snake. Primarily a comprehensive study of language, the book addresses the ultimate crime THE MURDER OF REALITY! It details historically the involvement on this planet of a non-human race of creatures that are reptilian in appearance. A predator, it rules the human mind through thought manipulation, implanted in the fabric of language itself.

The intention of the predator is to hold humanity in a construct or conceptual framework that is reptilian in characteristic. Engineered through the inheritance of language, this research demonstrates a universal code written in symbols.

A first of its kind, my study analyzes the control of thought and its influence upon collective reality via 'etymology' (the study of words), Greek 'etumos' (true). In essence, the human species has had its thought processes hijacked and rewired. Sadly, we have lost the ability to think like a mammal. Trapped like a rat in a maze, paralyzed in a construct not of our making. The handlers of man lurk deep in their cesspits. This book intends to cast some light and reveal its shadow - a terrible force working at the core of humanity!

Pierre Sabak - 9th September 2009

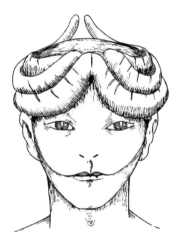

'Serpentigena' from the Latin word for (the serpent race).
The drawing is based upon historical descriptions of the 'serpentigena'. White in appearance and slender, this being stands about seven feet tall and is snake like in appearance. Evidence indicates the rank of creature is directly related to the length of horn and is behind the symbolism of the crown and turban. Sanskrit, Greek, Zulu and Japanese traditions state that the warrior class have a vertical third eye, which can kill a man with a single look. Chinese legends tell us that there are 9 races or species of 'dragon' (Lung), which range in colour from red, white, green and mottled.

IV

Snake Eyes
Be Quick or be Dead

Covered in sinners and dripping with guilt
Making you money from slime and from filth
Parading your bellies in ivory towers
Investing our lives in your schemes and your powers

You got to watch them – Be quick or be dead
Snake eyes in heaven – the thief in your head
You've got to watch them – Be quick or be dead
Snake eyes in heaven – the thief in your head

Be quick!
Or be dead!
Be quick
Or be dead!

See... what's ruling all our lives
See... who's pulling strings...
I bet you won't fall on your face...
Your belly will hold you in place
Who pulls the strings...

The serpent is crawling inside of your ear
He says you must vote for what you want to hear
Don't matter what's wrong as long as you're all right
So pull yourself stupid and rob yourself blind.

You got to watch them – Be quick or be dead
Snake eyes in heaven – the thief in your head
You've got to watch them – Be quick or be dead
Snake eyes in heaven – the thief in your head

Be quick!
Or be dead!
Be quick
Or be dead!
Be quick or be dead!

Be Quick or be Dead, Iron Maiden, Fear of the Dark, Released 13ᵗʰ April 1992

Introduction
The Language of Symbolism

'Above all, it is the philologian who must be the spearhead of the new enquiry. It is primarily a study [of] words. A written word is more than a symbol: it is an expression of an idea. To penetrate to its inner meaning is to look into the mind of the man who wrote it'.[1]

John M Allegro (Former Assistant Lecturer on Comparative Semitic Philology)

'Our way into the mind of ancient man can only be through his writings, and this is the province of philology, the science of words. We have to seek in the symbols by which he represented his spoken utterances clues to his thinking'.[2]

John M Allegro (Former Assistant Lecturer on Comparative Semitic Philology)

This book is about the use of symbols in context to the 'dragon', defined as a 'fallen angel'. A critique on 'philology' (a study of words), the text examines the conceptual framework of reality composed of speech, grammar and syntax. By carefully defining those parameters, the dragon holds the human attention in an ontological construct.

Language paints the intellectual landscape and provides the blueprint to thought. Defined comprehensively as the 'talker', the reptile conveys itself through symbolism and the determination of language. To paraphrase the Oxford English Dictionary:

> *'Language is the method of communication, either spoken or written, consisting of words in an agreed way extending to a community or country'.*

Picture source: Matthew Hurley & Editor Neil Hague,
Alien Chronicles, Quester Publications (see picture credits).
The Virgin Mary and Saint Giovannino - School of Lippi, 1406-1469.
Early Renaissance painting of the angelic host betrothed to the virgin and her
divine offspring. Depiction of the host is reminiscent of a modern spaceship (UFO).
Note also bemused spectator and the 'dog' - a symbol of 'Sirius'.

The definition likewise extends to that of the symbol and is found again quoted in the Oxford English Dictionary:

1) *'A symbol – A thing conventionally regarded as typifying, representing, or recalling something, especially an idea or quality (white is a symbol of purity)'.*

2) *'A mark or character taken as the conventional sign of some object, idea, function, or process, e.g. the letters standing for the chemical elements or the characters in musical notation'.*

The author of this work provides the following exposition:

1) *A symbol – A notational motif used to denote a <u>symbolic equivalent particularly through the mode of homonyms</u> e.g. the Semitic noun 'havalah' (a circle)[3] registers 'af'a' (a viper).[4]*

2) *The purpose and application of a sign or synonym is to <u>substitute the object with a symbolic counterpart</u>. Adoption and use of the symbol is universal to all cultures and are primarily devices of subterfuge.*

For instance, in Japan knotted paper is tied around the parameters of the temple and shrine. The Japanese noun for 'paper' (kami)[5] is a polymorph of 'God'.[6] A 'knot' (musubu) is a homonym of a 'contract',[7] related conceptually to 'musume' (a daughter).[8]

The symbol of the 'knot' connotes 'marriage', located inside of the temple, a factor recorded also in Arabic. Here the 'rope' (habl)[9] is used to signify 'pregnancy' (habl).[10] The 'joint or ligature' thus represents a 'marriage, contract or intercourse', and is a cognate of the 'snake'.[11]

Connection or crossover between the woman and the serpent is relative to the 'cabal' or 'secret society', supplemental to the 'Masonic Brotherhood', explicit of the 'Illuminati'. A secret organization, the 'Illuminated Ones' record the hidden history of humanity primarily through covert symbolism.[12] Presented in the introduction as a summary, the serpent's existence is substantiated through the study of philology.

Repeated, the same signifiers are found in all of the world's languages. The bloodline of the angelic order and its dealings with man are secret and sanctioned through the law. Union between the snake and its priesthood is archived universally and is demonstrated in the Roman and Semitic languages.

The Latin word for 'brotherhood' is named (fraternitas), derived from the Arabic classification 'ifrit or afreet' (a malevolent demon or djinn / jinn). 'Ifrit' proceeds from the Arabic word 'fritar' (deceiver),[13] deduced from the substantive 'frt' (deception). 'Fritar' is transliterated into Modern Greek as 'feedhee' - pronounced feethee - (snake).[14] Protected, the ifrit's existence is concealed by the fraternity Latin 'frater' (brother)[15] - a guardian or preserver of the serpent's knowledge.

Judaic lore equates the 'ifrit' with 'writing', codified within religious scriptures. In Hebrew for example, the stem 'ivrit' denotes (the Hebrew language).[16] 'Ivrit's etymological root is correlated with 'fritar' (deceit), expositional of the 'ifrit' or 'frater'. An anagram 'ifrit' exposes the Arabic verbal stem 'irif' the verb (to know).[17]

Addendum, 'Hebrew' (ivrit) and Arabic ciphers demonstrate an aptitude for wordplay through the 'switch of vowel' (pointing) or letters.[18] Historically the spelling of Semitic words are not standardized, but written according to strict rules, governed by numerical, astrological and linguistic encryption.

Other techniques of deceit employed by the Arab grammarians include the use of homonyms - evident in religious texts. To recap, *a symbol is a notational motif, used to denote a symbolic equivalent particularly through the mode of homonyms*. An 'homonym' otherwise an 'homophone' or 'polymorph' is defined in the Oxford English Dictionary as follows:

> *A word having the same sound as another but of different meaning or origin [e.g. altar and alter]*.

In the Arabic language, a 'polymorphic word' is written as 'wujuh al Qur'an' (the forgotten recitation),[19] literally (the forgotten Koran). 'Wujuh' has the appended meaning (directions or faces [e.g. a facet]). The Koran thus is an esoteric document. It is written in layered language and is a book of initiation.[20] 'Wujuh al Qur'an' expresses the secret or occult traditions of the Koran.

Fallen, the serpent hid evidence of its existence in the Bible and Koran, using 'polymorphic' language, penned cryptically by Arab scholars as (wujuh al Qur'an). Hebrew academics refer to the search for hidden meaning, obscured by secret codes as 'entering the forbidden grove'. The Semitic word for 'grove' is 'pardes' conceptually 'paradise' (a circled or walled mound).[21] According to Professor Walter Burkert:

> *'...paradosis [Greek]... can be used in a narrower sense, referring to instruction, and in a larger [sense]... instruction plus ritual. ...paradosis [in the Bacchic mystery rites describes]... the transmission [of knowledge] from one generation of "sacred persons" to the next... [originating from the snake and its enclosure the temple or grove]'.* [22]

Summarized, literal doctrinal teaching contrasts with a selective discrimination of word patterns, anagrams, puns, ciphers and etymologies, discursive of the inner workings. External, the framework of the parable conceals initiatory knowledge. Greek theologians described this dichotomy as the 'inner' and 'outer' mysteries.

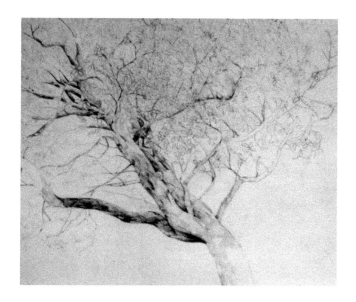

Entering the forbidden grove (grave) pertains to hidden knowledge, concealed through anagrams and word association. Equated with the 'tree and serpent', the orchard connotes the Canaanite Goddess 'Asherah' a cognomen equated with 'Asas' Greek 'Isis' - Refer to Chapter 43 Naked Snakes Pt 2.

The propensity for 'double meaning' (Greek paronomasia) is documented also in Latin. For example, the Roman adverb 'Latine' denoting (the Latin language) is derived from 'latens' the adjective for (hidden or secret).[23] The Roman stem 'latens' descends from the Arabic word 'lut' (a veil). Recurrent, the dragon's nature and form is obscured from man - an idea encoded in the scriptures!

Intrinsically, the Semitic noun 'nahash or nakhash' (a serpent)[24] shares the additional meaning (to decipher). 'Nahash' written as 'nhsh' indicates the verb (to deceive). The words 'deceive' and 'decipher' are from the same family of words, cognate with the 'reptile' and 'language'. Symbology of the 'snake' (a djinn, alternatively jinn) is consistent with the 'ifrit', analogous to 'ivrit' (the Hebrew language). 'Hebrew semantics' (ivrit) suggest the Judaic scriptures are by nature duplicitous, written in a coded form, commensurate to the 'snake'.

Distinctions between the 'fritar' (a deceiver), 'frater' (brother) and 'ivrit' (language) originate in the Old Semitic lexicon. In Arabic, the sequence 'akh' (brother)[25] recites 'haka' (the Syrian word to speak, talk or tell),[26] connoting 'acan' (a flaming seraph). 'Acan' informs the Old English noun 'hack' (a serpent), adjoined with an 'angel or messenger' - Arabic 'hakim' (a ruler).[27]

Identical themes are duplicated in the Hellenistic mysteries. The Greek noun 'philosopher' from the compound 'philo-sopher' (a brother of wisdom) is a play on 'philo ophis' (a brother of the serpent). In addition, 'philo' (brother) informs the word 'philology', defined as (the science of language, particularly historical or comparative).[28]

The 'brothers of wisdom' (i.e. a serpent) extract their name from 'Sopher' (the Goddess of Knowledge). Sopher's appellation is taken directly from the Judaic word 'sofer' (a writer or scribe), diminutive of 'sefer' (a book),[29] evocative of 'seraph' (a snake).

Further connections between the 'serpent and language' reiterate prominent themes, aligned in the Semitic and Greek mystery schools. In Arabic for example, 'sura' (a verse) of the Koran[30] is registered with 'Zuhrah' (Venus),[31] Hebrew 'Zohra', and is co-adoptive of the Greek noun 'saura' (a lizard).[32] 'Zuhrah' is identical to the Hebrew etymon 'zohar' (brilliance),[33] abridged in Semitic with 'zau' (light).

Allegorized as a composer of scripture, reference to the serpent is found in the Syrian dialect. The noun 'haiya' (snake)[34] is cogent in Arabic with 'aya' (verse) and 'ayat' (sign). Devine knowledge of the Koran's 'sura' implies a 'fallen angel', Greek 'saura' (a lizard). Manifestation of the 'reptile' is configured in Hebrew with 'sira' (boat)[35] - a device of the 'angelic progeny'.

Iconic, 'sira' (boat) notates the 'host', loosely the 'se'irim' (a type of fallen angel), identified with 'seraph' (a snake), collectively the 'seraphim'. 'Seraph' is derived from the verb 'saruf' (burned),[36] disclosing the 'burnt offering' (Latin hostia), tandem to the 'angel' (the host). The boat heralds the 'angelic host' (a sailor or crewmember), cognizant with the written law, figurative of 'religion', Latin 'religare' (to moor a ship).[37] Comparison between the 'boat and scriptures' is recorded in Arabic.

'Safinah' the word for (a ship, boat or vessel) is polymorphic and indicates a (blank book).[38] The equivalent pun is found recorded also in Greek. 'Biblos' (Bible) corresponds with 'biblia' (books), a derivation of 'biblos' (a papyrus or bulrush), a variant on 'byblos' (boat). Examples of similar composite nouns suggest the 'Lord' and 'host' (crew) are likened to 'book or scriptural metaphors'. Ecclesiastical language collates the 'scriptures' (biblos) with the Latin transitive verb 'bibere' (to drink),[39] allegoric of Communion and wor-ship - a theme replicated in the Semitic wordplays.

For example, 'safinah' (a ship) constitutes the Hebrew noun 'sefel' (a cup)[40] and suggests the 'mystery' - an evening meal,[41] addendum with the angelic 'seraphim' and the 'votive'. The equivalent play in English is 'vessel' (a cup or boat). Symbolically, the 'vessel' is correlated with the 'hostia' Latin (victim), aligned to the angelic 'host' (a sailor).

Identification with 'safinah' (a boat) divulges the Arabic title 'sarif' (a noble) from 'sarafa' (exalted), translated into English as 'Lord-ship'. The origin of the 'sarif' is analogous to the angelic lineage the 'seraphim', cognate with 'seraph' (a snake), defined technically as a 'sailor'. In addition, knowledge of this creature parallels 'sefer' (a book) - a correlation summed up in the Semitic-Grecian play 'sura' (verse) and 'sauros' (lizard), Arabic 'aya' (verse) and 'haiya' (snake).

Derivations of the stem 'sefer' (book) include 'sippur' (a tale or story) and 'lesapher' the verbal stem (to tell).[42] 'Le'sapher' informs the English transliteration 'Lucifer', archaic of an 'angel', literally (a messenger of scriptural knowledge). Lucifer's name is appropriated from the Semitic verbal stem 'La'sapher' (to tell) and appears in the Latin corruption 'Lux ferre' (light bringer). 'Lux-ferre's title connotes a 'dragon or seraph', signified as 'Venus - the Morning Star'. 'Lucifer', a cognomen of 'cipher', is similar to his brethren the 'ifrit' (a deceiver), affiliated to the serpent's initiatory 'vernacular' (ivrit), connoting 'duplicity' (fritar).

Conceptually the reptile is defined as a linguist emphasized throughout Semitic discourse. The Hebrew noun 'sefer' (book) reproduces 'seraph' (a flaming angel or serpent) and 'safa' (language).[43] Sefer in English is rendered as cipher. 'Sippur' (to tell) arises from the Old Semitic stem 'zeph' (hidden), specific of the oral tradition, recorded through homonyms. Judaic scriptures are thus written in a codified 'language' (ivrit), identified with initiation and 'deception' (fritar).

The same analogy runs true in the Arabic language. 'Ta'ban' (a snake)[44] pertains to the verb 'taba' (to print) or 'tab' (edition).[45] 'Tab's stem conveys 'tabi' (a follower) and 'tab'a' (a partisan).[46]

Etymologically the 'snake' is closely related to 'talib or taliba' (a student), cognizant originally with 'Thebes' - the old capital of Egypt, a religious place of study. Sacred knowledge of Thebes defines the oral tradition, committed into Hebrew writing as the 'Talmud' (instruction) from the compound 'tillel' (to cover) and 'le'lamad' (to-teach).[47] The 'student or learner' is rendered in Hebrew as (the talmid),[48] suggesting 'veiled instruction'. 'Talmid' is interchangeable in Arabic with 'talib', 'taliba' or 'taliban' (a student) - an initiate of the 'Theban priesthood', synonymous with the device of the 'cobra' (tea'ban).[49] A composite 'taliban' is loaned from the Egyptian root 'tab'an' (a snake) and 'talib' (a student).

The red serpent (emblem of the city of London) is a depiction of the 'fox' (Arabic ta'alib) an initiatory device of the 'student' (taliba), cognate with the 'Theban priesthood', signified with the brazen 'cobra' (tea'ban), correlated with the 'turban'. Refer to Appendix 5.

Recourse to the Talmud and its symbolism divulges the Jewish tradition the 'Kabbalah' (Caballa), obtained from the Semitic stem 'qbl' (to receive). It outlines the 'hidden tradition' of the Jews[50] and originates from the Arabic transitive verb 'khabba' (to hide or conceal).[51] The 'Kabbalah' in essence specifies a 'secret oral tradition', received from an angelic source, conveyed through word groupings and etymological comparisons. 'Khabba' (hide) is a variation on the Hebrew term 'caba' (a messenger or host), derived from the Old Egyptian noun 'qeb' (a serpent).[52] Its origins are adduced from the 'Dog Star' (Arabic Al Kalb).

Relationship between the dragon and received knowledge, conversant with the spoken word, is conveyed also in Greek teaching. For example, the adjective 'theoretikos' (theoretical) is a pun on 'theotokos' (the offspring of the Gods), a euphemism of the dragon. In ancient Greek, 'large snakes' are referred to as (drakonates), a word suggesting (sharp-sightedness) from 'derkomai' (to perceive keenly [or insight]).[53] Progeny of 'theotokos' outlines 'theoreo' the verb (to look at), related to 'Theos' (God) cited in Greek custom as a 'watcher, angel or dragon'.

'Theoreo' informs the English word 'thesaurus' (a collection of words or concepts) from the Greek noun 'thesaurus' (a treasure). Thus it is said the 'lizard' (a sauros) otherwise a 'dragon' guards 'treasure' (the-saurus). In the Grecian mysteries, 'treasure' implies 'intellectual riches', protected or guarded from the 'profane',

Latin 'pro-fanum' (before the temple). The 'dragon', a 'sentinel' conventionally a 'talker', is documented as liking word games and riddles, viewed as a custodian of treasure (words).

Documented in the Indo-European languages, similar ideas interconnect the 'dragon with language'. The Akkadian noun 'peor' (snake) relates to the Sanskrit title 'pala' (a king), in Egypt 'Par-o' (a Pharaoh). 'Pala' informs the Indo-European root 'parle' (to speak), theoretical to the 'reptile' shared in the Indo-Semitic languages. In Hebrew for instance, the root 'dibur' (to talk, otherwise speak)[54] is symmetrical with the Sanskrit noun 'deva' (a deity), English (devil). Likewise in the Old Arabic 'acan' (seraph) is cogent with the Syrian root 'haka' (speak, talk or tell)[55] - labels assigned to 'hakim' (the sovereign).[56]

According to arcane folklore, the devil personifies a serpent and is registered as a 'talker', 'trickster' or 'cheat'. A 'deceiver' theoretically (an ifrit), the devil, is similar in principle to the Middle Eastern tradition of the 'djinn' (jinn). Arabian lore discloses the fallen jinni as cunning and intelligent, indistinguishable from the angel, king or dragon. Hebrew semantics classify the 'jinni' as 'geoni' (brilliant or intelligent)[57] and informs the Latin root 'genius' (a guardian spirit).[58] 'Genius' is compatible in the Persian language with 'jan' (the vital spirit).

Originally, 'genius' classifies a divine force or spirit, termed 'inspiration' that shaped the character of man. *[Religiously] the genius [is] associated with household Gods and ancestral spirits, the manes.*[59] Semantically, the 'manes' defined as (the soul of the dead)[60] is cognate with 'mens' Latin (the mind or intellect).[61]

Both the Latin and Hebrew expressions 'genius' and 'geoni' are definitions, explicit of the 'djinn' from the Old Semitic noun 'djen' (a serpent). 'Djen' is written in the hieroglyphic sign list as a 'cobra' (transliterated 'd' or 'dj')[62] - a sign of the 'Theban priesthood' (See Appendix 9).

Derivation of the name 'jinni' plural 'djinn' is probably Egypto-Akkadian from the compound 'Dj-En' (a Snake-Lord) or 'Dj-An' (Heavenly-Snake). In early Arabic, 'dj-in(n)' specifies the conjunction (that-snake).[63] Manifested as a 'spirit', 'serpent' or 'lord', the 'jinni' is associated with the creation of 'religion' (Arabic din).[64] Greek syntax lists the 'djinn' with 'gen' (origin) and 'genea' (race), equivalent to the 'jinni', distinguished as the 'Theban'.

The snake's juxtaposition with creation recounts the 'fallen angels' (the Shatani, otherwise Satan), classified as a 'dragon'. Congruent in Arabic, the 'Shatani' parallels the adjective 'sha'tir' (wise),[65] opposite the Latin feminine noun 'scientia' (knowledge or skill),[66] transferred into English as 'science'.

Similar comparisons in fact are universal and found embedded in all human languages. In African mythology, the 'serpent' is called 'Nyoka' (the instructor or expert).[67] The Zulu's name for their 'serpent being' is the 'Chitauri', an appellation meaning (Children of the Serpent). According to the shaman Credo Mutwa, they are referred to as the 'Talkers'. In Japan, the red serpent Gods the 'tengu' (a goblin or braggart),[68] written in kanji as 'heaven's dog' (Sirius), are likewise equated with 'talking'. The epithet 'tengu' is a play on the Japanese noun 'tango' (word).[69]

Further, the Japanese word for 'reason' denoting 'origin' is 'riyu(u)',[70] a name recognizant with 'ryu' (a dragon).[71] 'Ryu' is matched in Arabic with its counterpart the 'djinn' - a 'serpent' relative to the Greek radical 'gen' (origin).

Considered as the root of all knowledge, the serpent's bloodline is consistent with illumination, emblematic of the sun - a sign of creation and intelligence (brilliance). Egyptian iconography links the 'seraph' with 'light' - an attribute characteristic of the 'dragon, angel or king', referred to in Judaic literature as the 'shining ones'. The Arabic equivalent is 'akh zauri' (the brothers of light) - a name reproduced in Latin as the 'Illuminati'.

Conjoined to the solar motif, the 'cobra' (Arabic tea'ban) designates 'initiatory knowledge' (taliban), relative to the 'djinn', indexed with the 'Theban priesthood' and its 'scriptural tradition' (the Talmud - Instruction). 'Theban' and 'ta'ban' (a snake) is written in Latin as the homophone 'anguigena' (a Theban, interpreted also as the offspring of the dragon).

Connection between the 'serpent and wisdom' is conveyed furthermore in the Hellenistic languages. The Greek noun 'skolex' (worm) imbibes the Latin noun 'scala' (ladder)[72] and 'schola' (a lecture, school, sect or followers).[73] 'Schola' informs the English words 'school and scholar'. In English, the equivalent play is 'serpent and savant'.

Resemblance between the 'reptile and teacher' is framed in Egyptian mythology as the 'Crocodile God' (Sobek), identified with 'sabaq' the Arabic word for (a lesson or lecture).[74] Appearance of 'Sobek' suggests 'Venus' (Sabah-Kha), literally the 'Morning-Star', pictured in Judaic lore as the 'seraph' - 'Lucifer', deemed as the 'angelic messenger', 'lesapher' (to tell).

Philological reference between the scholar, snake and acumen underlines many of the Semitic etymologies. In Egyptian-Arabic for example, 'mokh' translated as (brains)[75] puns with the Hebrew word 'mal'akh' (an angel).[76] The Egyptian noun 'bal' (mind)[77] corresponds with the Hebrew serpent deity 'Baal' (a Lord).[78]

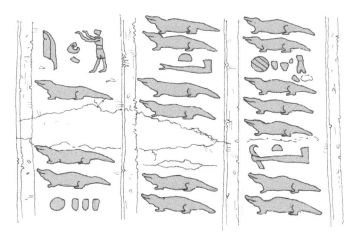

Sobek's hymn written entirely in pun-cryptogram, Esna Temple, Egypt.

In Latin, 'serpens' (a serpent)[79] contrasts with 'sapiens' (intelligent),[80] congruent in Arabic with the verb 'khafa' (to know), cognizant with 'af'a' (a viper).[81] Articulated in the Middle Eastern languages, the 'k', 'h', 'a' and 'e' sound are phonetically similar, demonstrated in the Semitic lexicon. 'Khafa' (know) is analogous in Hebrew to the noun 'havana' (understanding),[82] cogent with 'ef'e' (an asp),[83] philological to 'Eve'. Initiatory knowledge attributed to woman is thus complicit of 'sin' (avon),[84] identified with 'comprehension' (havana), illustrative of the 'fallen' (hava). Namesake of the 'fallen' is of course an appellation of the 'viper' (af'a), classified as an 'angel'.

Scholars of the 'Koran' refer to translations of their sacred book as an 'interpretation' - a consideration shared also by Egyptian writers. Historical concern for the preservation of secret traditions, diluted through translation (particularly of homonyms), is documented in the Hermetica. The author Asclepius in his epistle to the divine King 'Ammon' (hidden)[85] eulogizes his apprehension, quoted in the following extract:

'Translation will greatly distort the sense of the writings, and cause much obscurity. Expressed in our native language [Egyptian], a teaching conveys its meaning clearly; for the very quality of the sounds; and when the Egyptian words are spoken, the force of the things signified works in them'. [86]

'... keep the teaching untranslated, in order that the secrets so holy may not be revealed to the Greeks, and that the Greek mode of speech, with its arrogance, and feebleness, and showy tricks of style, may not reduce to impotence the impressive strength of the language, and the cogent force of the words. For the speech of the Greeks... is devoid

of power to convince; and the Greek philosophy is nothing but a noise of talk. <u>But our speech is not mere talk; it is an utterance replete with workings</u>'.[87]

To conclude, the essence of language loans itself to symbolism, represented sublimely through the study of philology and homonyms. A hidden mentor of man, the angel in occult lore is a reptilian entity, distinguished as the hidden master or king.

Principally the dragon, a teacher of words and arithmetic, embedded knowledge of itself sequenced in numerical codes - a secret history veiled in mathematics, geometry, astronomy, semiology and language. Systematic and intelligent, the adoption of signs is discursive of arcane wisdom, pertaining to the snake and its concealment.

Untrusting towards humans, this creature hides behind occult ritual. Frightened of being uncovered, it uses war, economic and political coercion to force nations to do its bidding.[88] Ancient accounts suggest the snake is duplicitous in its designs and dealings with man. This book intends to reveal the nature of the beast! The premise of the next chapter is to define what the angel is and give some background detail to this majestic and enigmatic being...

'Language is how ghosts enter the world. They twist into awkward positions to squeeze through the blank spaces'.[89]

Anne Michaels 'What the Light Teaches', Skin Divers

1   John M Allegro: The Sacred Mushroom and the Cross, Abacus, 1973, p17

2   Ibid, p25

3   Ralph Ellis: Eden in Egypt, A Translation of the Book of Genesis out of the Original Egyptian Text, Edfu Books, 2004, p280 (Appendix A5 Hebrew-Egyptian Dictionary)

4   Hippocrene Concise Dictionary: English-Arabic, Arabic-English, Hippocrene, New York, 2005, p135

5   Collins Shubun, English Japanese Dictionary, New First Edition, Harper Collins Publishers, 1996, p361

6   Ibid, p216

7   Sanseido New Concise Japanese English Dictionary, Revised Edition, Japan, p587

8   Ibid

9   Hippocrene Concise Dictionary, English-Arabic, Arabic-English, Hippocrene, New York, 2005, p104 ['Habl' (rope) is paired with the esoteric traditions of the 'Kaaba Shrine' - Refer to Chapter 4 Firestar p66]

10 Ibid, p94

11 Historically, the reptile conquered mankind through the matriarch, choosing to fashion his descendents on the serpent's image. From this contract followed the creation of governments. Mediation between the angelic realm and the kingdom documents the royal protagonist, a human-angelic line presented as a demigod or king.

12 'Sumbolon' Greek (a symbol), literally 'syn-ballo' (thrown together), is paired with 'sumbioo' (to live together), English 'symbiosis', generative of 'bios' (life). The symbol catalogues the pairing of the species through the matriarch, protected through the secret society network.

13 Michael W Ford, Luciferian Witchcraft, Grimoire of the Serpent, Succubus Publishing, MMV, 2005, p262

14 Collins Gem: Greek Phrase Book, Harper Collins, Italy, 2003, p183

15 John C Traupman PhD, The New College Latin & English Dictionary, Bantam Press, 1988, p120

16 Prolog, Pocket Bilingual Dictionary, English-Hebrew, Hebrew-English, Prolog, 2003, p184

17 Hippocrene Concise Dictionary, English-Arabic, Arabic-English, Hippocrene, New York, 2005, p65

18 The use of wordplay is detailed numerously within the Persian priesthood. For example, the famous poet Jalalu'ddin, nicknamed 'Rumi' literally (the Roman), illustrates the Semitic stem 'ramay' (deceitful), characteristic of the 'snake'. 'Ramay' in Arabic is a derivation of 'ram' (lofty), connoting an 'angel'. In Greek literature, the classical poet Homer [Latin 'homo' (a man)], is obtained from the Semitic root 'komer' (priest), correlated with 'qamar' (the moon).

19 M.A.S. Abdel Haleem: The Qur'an, Oxford University Press 2004, pXXX (Introduction)

20 Ibid, pXXXV In academic circles, the term for idiomatic structure within Arabic prose is 'iltifat' (turning from one thing to another, understood as a grammatical shift within a pronoun or verb for rhetorical purposes). Provident throughout Koranic discourse, the employment of 'iltifat' suggests a type of encryption key either acrostic or 'numerical' (atbsh). 'Iltifat' is grouped intellectually with the 'ifrit' - an extension of the dragon and hidden knowledge.

21 The noun 'pardes' (a walled enclosure), a symbol of the 'foundation', is cognate with the worship of Osiris, and operates as an acronym. 'Pardes' is created from the first four methods of extracting the scriptures message: 'Peshat' (literal meaning), 'Remez' (hint), 'Drash' (interpretation) and 'Sod' (secret). 'Pardes' informs the Greek study of classical history and its relationship to revealed knowledge. The etymology of 'pardes' is borrowed in the Hellenistic branch of languages to convey 'paradosis' (sacred learning), relative to the oral tradition, equated with geometry (Refer to Chapter 19 Adam Atum pp190-191).

22 Professor Walter Burkert: Ancient Mystery Cults, Harvard Press, 1987, p153 (Notes to pp68-70)

23 John C Traupman PhD: The New College Latin & English Dictionary, Bantam Press, 1988, p165

24 Prolog Pocket Bilingual Dictionary: English-Hebrew, Hebrew-English, Prolog, 2003, p365

25 Hippocrene Concise Dictionary: English-Arabic, Arabic-English, Hippocrene, New York, 2005, p21

26 Ibid, p187

27 Ibid, p109

28 A modern example of the Alchemist is 'Einstein', a name translated from the German as (iron-stone). He is shown in numerous photographs as sticking out his tongue - a symbol of the serpent identified with the philosopher (The word philosopher in this context refers to a secret society of scientists, traced back to the philosophical schools of learning, equated with the snake).

29 Prolog: Pocket Bilingual Dictionary, English-Hebrew, Hebrew-English, Prolog, 2003, p466

30 A 'prose' is comparable in English to the verb 'oppose' and is similar conceptually to 'verse' and 'versus' Latin (towards), rendered in Medieval Latin as (against) - i.e. 'grammatical shifts' (Latin vertere / Arabic iltifat). The root of 'versus' is cognate with the adverb 'versute' (cunning), implicit of the 'vestis' (a snakeskin), Arabic 'ifrit' (a djinn).

31 Ferozsons Urdu-English Dictionary: A Comprehensive Dictionary of Current Vocabulary, (Revised Edition), Ferozsons Ltd, Lahore, p418

32 'Zuhrah' (Venus) is related to the Hebrew etymon 'zohar' (light), identical in Arabic to 'zau', and is consistent with 'zari' (an alien or angel). In Greek, 'Zuhrah' is rendered as 'sauros' (lizard).

33 Prolog Pocket Bilingual Dictionary: English-Hebrew-Hebrew-English, Prolog, 2003, p50

34 Hippocrene Concise Dictionary: English-Arabic, Arabic-English, Hippocrene, New York, 2005, p186

35 Prolog Pocket Bilingual Dictionary: English-Hebrew-Hebrew-English, Prolog, 2003, p45

36 Ibid, p53

37 John C Traupman PhD: The New College Latin & English Dictionary, Bantam Press, 1988, p265

38 Ferozsons Urdu-English Dictionary: A Comprehensive Dictionary of Current Vocabulary, (Revised Edition), Ferozsons Ltd, Lahore, p441

39 John C Traupman PhD: The New College Latin & English Dictionary, Bantam Press, 1988, p29

40 Prolog: Pocket Bilingual Dictionary, English-Hebrew, Hebrew-English, Prolog, 2003, p95

41 Latin 'vesper' (evening supper or the west) denotes 'verpus' (a circumcised man), cognizant with the 'Western priesthood' (the Rabbi) from the Syrian root 'ryab' (west).

42 Zecharia Sitchin: The Cosmic Code, Book VI The Earth Chronicles, Avon, 1998, p165

43 Prolog: Pocket Bilingual Dictionary, English-Hebrew, Hebrew-English, Prolog, 2003, p225

44 Hippocrene English-Arabic, Arabic-English Dictionary, Hippocrene, New York, 2005, p292

45 Ibid

46 Ibid, p293

47 Prolog: Pocket Bilingual Dictionary, English-Hebrew, Hebrew-English, Prolog, 2003, p412

48 Ibid, p228

49 Ahmed Abdel-Hady: Egyptian Arabic, A Rough Guide, Dictionary Phrasebook, Lexus, 2002, p69

50 Mark Hedsel: Edited and with an Introduction by David Ovason: Magician, Magus or Initiate? The Zelator, The Secret Journals of Mark Hedsel, 1999, p70

51 Hippocrene Concise Dictionary: English-Arabic, Arabic-English, Hippocrene, New York, 2005 p29

52 Ralph Ellis: Eden in Egypt, A Translation of the Book of Genesis out of the Original Egyptian Text, Edfu Books, 2004, p280 (Appendix A5 Hebrew-Egyptian Dictionary)

53 Jack Tresidder (General Editor): The Complete Dictionary Of Symbols, In Myth, Art and Literature, Duncan Baird Publishers, 2004, p157

54 Prolog: Pocket Bilingual Dictionary, English-Hebrew, Hebrew-English, Prolog, 2003, p410

55 Hippocrene: English-Arabic, Arabic-English Dictionary, Hippocrene, New York, 2005, p187

56 Ibid

57 Prolog: Pocket Bilingual Dictionary, English-Hebrew, Hebrew-English, Prolog, 2003, p50

58 John C Traupman PhD: The New College Latin & English Dictionary, Bantam Press, 1988, p124

59 Edited by Russ Kick: Everything You Know is Wrong, The Disinformation Company 2002, Essay by Nick Mamatas: How to Rid the World of Good, p164

60 John C Traupman PhD: The New College Latin & English Dictionary, Bantam Press, 1988, p177

61 Ibid, p181

62 Mark Collier & Bill Manley: How to Read Hieroglyphs, British Museum Press, 1999, p136 (Sign List B60)

63 Hippocrene Concise Dictionary: English-Arabic, Arabic-English, Hippocrene Books, 2005, p200

64 Ibid, p101

65 Ibid, p141

66 John C Traupman PhD: The New College Latin & English Dictionary, Bantam Press, 1988, p279 ['Scientia' (knowledge or skill) informs the English etymon 'science' from the Arabic root 'sha'tir' (wise), and are etymologies linked to the dragon - 'Satan'. The symbol of learning is therefore represented as the 'serpent', and appears in medicine as the 'caduceus' wand' (a double serpent)].

67 Vusamazulu Credo Mutwa: Zulu Shaman, Dreams, Prophecies, and Mysteries, Destiny Books 2003, p155

68 Sanseido: New Concise Japanese English Dictionary, Revised Edition, Japan, p927

69 Ibid, p905

70 Ibid, p695

71 Ibid, p706

72 John C Traupman PhD: The New College Latin & English Dictionary, Bantam Press, 1988, p279

73 Ibid

74 Ferozsons: Urdu-English Dictionary, A Comprehensive Dictionary of Current Vocabulary, Revised, Ferozsons Ltd Lahore, p426 ['Sabaq' or 'sabak' (a lesson or lecture), 'sabaq dena' v. (to instruct or teach)].

75 Ahmed Abdel-Hady: Egyptian Arabic, A Rough Guide, Dictionary Phrasebook, Lexus, 2002, p57

76 Prolog: Pocket Bilingual Dictionary, English-Hebrew-Hebrew-English, Prolog, 2003, p23

77 Hippocrene: English-Arabic, Arabic-English Dictionary, Hippocrene, New York, 2005, p154

78 Ibid, p155

79 John C Traupman P.D: The New College Latin & English Dictionary, Bantam Press, 1988, p285

80 Ibid, p277

81 Hippocrene Concise Dictionary: English-Arabic, Arabic-English, Hippocrene Books, 2005, p135

82 Prolog: Pocket Bilingual Dictionary, English-Hebrew-Hebrew-English, Prolog, 2003, p447

83 Ibid, p29

84 Ibid, p373

85 The Hermetic Document, Libelous XVI, is set out in the form of an epistle, attributed to Asclepius, forwarded to the divine King Ammon.

86 Editor Walter Scott: Hermetica, The Writings Attributed to Hermes Trismegistus, Solos, p106

87 Ibid

88 A deceiver of humanity - the reptile contrives social, religious, political and sexual boundaries. Ideologically, it governs and opposes, Labour and Conservative, Capitalist and Communist, Fascist and Liberal, Green and Global. Compartmentalisation of all the world's religions is regulated through the partition of the priesthood. This includes the Sunni and Shiite, Catholic and Protestant, Pharisee and Sadducee, Hinayana and Mahayana (Buhddism), ad infinitum. Masonic societies describe this duality as 'Ordo ab Chao' (Order out of Chaos) a motto attributed to the 'Shatani' (an adversary or opposer).

89 Bloomsbury Anthology of Quotations: Bloomsbury, London, 2002, p249

The Murder of Reality

1

The Mal'Akh

'There are things that fly through the night, those you call UFOs, which we in Africa call Abahambi Abavutayo, [literally] "the fiery visitors"… Long before they were even heard of in other parts of the world, we, the people of Africa, had contact with these things and the creatures inside [of] them… I can only speak within certain constraints because we are not allowed to talk in any detail about these sacred things. Our people fear that should we do that, then the star ships would stop visiting us'.[1]

Credo Mutwa, South African Shaman

'Among His signs are the ships, sailing like floating mountains'.[2]

Koran: Sura 42 verse 32

'Come to the earth, draw nigh, O boat of Ra, make the boat to travel, O mariners of Heaven'.[3]

Wallis Budge (Egyptologist)

The Modern English word 'angel' is derived from its immediate Latin root 'angelus' via the Greek translation 'angelos' (a messenger). Variations of an angel include the Anglo-Saxon designation 'engel' from the Old French word 'angele'. 'Angelus' (a messenger) records the Latin transitive verb 'aggero' (to bring forward, utter or convey)[4] and is closely matched with 'agere' (to act or do)[5] with the appended meaning (to chase or hunt).[6]

Hellenistic scholars known as the Septuagint,[7] responsible for the Greek translation of the Old Testament (3rd-2nd century BC), interpreted the Hebrew name 'mal'akh' (an angel as an emissary),[8] taken from the Semitic stem 'amar' (to speak or to command).[9] The angel is noted as a diplomatic representative.

A degree or rank of angel is listed as an 'archangel', conceptualised as an 'ambassador' of the Lord. The Latin prefix 'arch' derives from the Greek stem 'arkh' (a chief),[10] rendered formally as 'arkhos' (a ruler),[11] deductive of 'arkho' (to rule). 'Arkhos' is cognate with the German title 'haco' (a high kin) - a permutation on the Greek honour 'archon' (a supreme ruler).[12] 'Haco', 'arkhos' and 'archon' recapitulates the Arabic dignitary 'hakim' (a ruler, governor or sovereign) from 'hakam' (to reign).[13] 'Hakim's titular determines the Syrian root 'haka' (to speak, talk or tell).[14]

Contextually the 'talker' describes a 'messenger or a type of angel', mutual to 'hakim' (a sovereign) - an appellation equated with the 'snake'. 'Hakim' and its Greek appropriation 'arkhos' is preserved in the Old English noun 'hack' (a serpent), differentiated from the Babylonian noun 'acan' (a flaming seraph). 'Acan' is consistent with the Old Egyptian stem 'akh' (to shine) and 'arq' (to twist). In the Greek mysteries, 'arq' is inimical of 'akhos' (pain or distress), additional to 'agkho' (to throttle) - actions accorded to 'arkhos' (a ruler).

The signatory 'arkhos' (Arabic hakim) originates from the Sanskrit lexicon. Enumerated as 'arga' (a lord), the title parallels the related verb 'akishi' (to rule). Honorific 'arga' conforms to the Hindu noun 'arka' (sun), correlated in Persian with the noun 'ankh' (eye).[15] Throughout Indo-European languages, the monarch is represented with the motif of the circle and eye symbols of the reptile or dragon. In Greek, the assignment 'arga' (lord) is analogous to 'ago' the suffix (to lead), figurative of the adjective 'hagios' (holy), iconic of 'halos' (a disk). The 'halo' Greek 'halos' is a homonym of (salt), Hebrew 'melakh', referential to 'mal'akh' (an angel). Universally combined with the 'deity' the 'halo' is equated with the 'serpent' and 'light'.[16]

To summarize, the prefix 'arch' (a chief) represents a 'circle', demonstrated in Latin as 'archus' (a type of arch or curve), assigned to 'arkos' (a ruler). The auxiliary prefix 'arch' (Greek arkh) is obtained from the Egyptian stem 'arq' (to wiggle or bind around) and 'akh' (to shine), corresponding with the Babylonian titular 'acan' (a burning seraph).

Esoterically 'akh' is employed in Arabic as the noun 'akh' (brother),[17] descriptive of the 'enlightened' or the 'illuminati', lateral to 'acan' (a shining serpent). The verbal stem 'akh' in Modern Arabic is addendum to the idiom 'haqq' (truth) - a term constant with a 'luminary', the 'hakim', indexed as (a ruler). 'Akh' is further utilised in Hebrew as the suffix 'mal'akh' (an angel),[18] denoting (a shining king).

Delegation of the 'mal'akh' bequeaths the Persian title 'mal' (a leader or king), opposite 'mar' (a snake). Relationship between the 'monarch and snake' is also evident in Classical Greek. The Hellenistic adjective 'basilikos' (royal) refers to 'basileus' (a king), extracted from 'basiliskos' (a serpent). Appointment of the regal, a 'basileus' is equivalent in Arabic to 'hakim' (a ruler), taken from the Babylonian root 'acan' (a snake or uraeus).

Recorded within the Greek and Arabic traditions, the angels are represented as serpentine in appearance - a feature evident in the Latin language. For example, the Roman word 'angelos' (angel) is consistent with the Latin etymology 'anguis' (snake) and informs the English adjective 'angry', suggesting a correlation with sacrificial atonement. Relationship between the 'snake and monarch' is evident also in the Indo-European languages.

Deconstruction of the Semitic and Persian name 'mal'akh' (an angel) is interpreted as (a transfigured king or serpent) - a denomination preserved in the hieroglyphs. In the Egyptian lexicon, 'akh' (to shine or flash) describes 'heka' (magic), literally (a flaming double), assigned to the 'watcher' (a dragon). 'Heka' is devolved from the Arabic root 'hakim' (a ruler).

Encoded in Greek mythology, 'heka' is modified as 'Hectare', the 'Goddess of Sorcery', pictured as a 'witch or dragon'. Semantically, 'drakon' stems from the Greek root (to watch or flash) - a simile of angelic materialisation. Judaic sources list 'irin' (the watchers) as (the shining ones) - nominal of an 'angel or serpent'.

Correlation between the 'snake' and 'radiance' enunciates the Hebrew adjective 'mu'ar' (light),[19] deduced from the Akkadian noun 'mul' (a star). 'Mu'ar' (light) delineates the Indo-Persian word 'mar' (a radiant serpent). Further examples within the Semitic dialect include numerous depictions of the snake, contrasted with light. For example in Aramaic, the appellation 'zari' (an alien) has the appended meaning (angel). Appearance of 'zari' is contingent in Arabic with 'zau' (light), Hebrew 'zohar',[20] inferring 'zokhel' (a reptile).[21]

Manifestation of the 'radiant angel' translates into Greek as 'drakon' (a dragon). Archaically, 'angels' are represented as 'shining' and signified with light adjectives, validated through blood sacrifice. Lustrous, the burnt offering alludes to 'flashing' and recalls the dragon's ability to 'shape-shift', likened to a 'flashing star'.

Comparisons between the 'angels' (otherwise aliens) replicate the burning 'uraeus' (cobra) - a symbol of rebirth. The fiery seraph in Egyptian iconography is traditionally affixed on the Aten disk, contrasted with angelic transfiguration and the materialization of the sun or king.

The phenomenon of 'morphing' is compared to a 'builder' - symbolic of initiatory knowledge. Epigraphically the apprentice suggests a 'mason' (archaically the Pharaoh), represented as an 'architect'. Cognomen of 'amar' (a builder) from the Egyptian verbal root 'amal' (to do)[22] is related to 'amir' (a prince).[23] Classification of the 'amar' generically (a craftsman) fits with the Hebrew stem 'amar' (to speak or command), additional to 'mal'akh' (an angel).[24] A homonym of (a talker or builder), the angel specifies the title 'amar', covert to the 'changeling or substitute'.

Transliteration of the Hebrew word 'amal' (worker) parallels the Arabic root 'amar' (builder), rendered in the late Persian as (immortal).[25] A class of deity, the 'Amar' in Persian literature personifies 'mar' (a serpent), explicit of 'mal' (a king). Designation of 'amar' in the Semitic language discloses the 'builder' - a 'snake or angel', affiliated to the mother an oracle priestess.

Inside of the mystery cults, the 'worker or craftsman', conventionally a 'mason', is paired sexually with the 'matriarch' and 'light'. Apocryphal writing links the 'builder' (amar) with the 'mother' (Old Hebrew ama), cognate with the Arabic noun 'ahmar' (red). The 'red mother' is doubled with the 'scarlet whore' - a 'menstrual priestess',[26] visualized as the 'Western sun'.

Progeny of the 'mater' (ama) is relative to 'amiri' (a princess)[27] and pertains to 'amir' (a prince). His offspring in the Akkadian philology indicates the 'Western people', designated as (the Aamu). Juxtaposition between the 'matriarch' (ama) and the 'Aamu' details an angelic decree, founded upon the firstborn, ascribed to the veneration of nocturnal angels, allocated to the roosting (roast) owl.

Adoration of the 'mal'akh' defined within Judaic tradition as (an angel) proceeds dialectically from the Canaanite Goddess of Death - Moloch. Represented as a horned owl, the Goddess parallels the hunter in situ to the worship of nocturnal angels.[28] Veneration of the owl earmarks child sacrifice, linked with the human angelic or royal line,[29] indicative of the sunset, equated with death.

'Moloch' otherwise 'mal'akh' (an angel) is consistent in Arabic with the noun 'mahlik' (a place of destruction, danger or a danger spot) and 'muhlik' the adjective (fatal or destructive).[30] The terms are interchangeable in Hebrew with 'malik' (lord) and 'maluk' (ruler).[31] Phonological relationship between 'mahlik' and 'malik' implies 'melekh' (a sovereign)[32] from the Akkadian titular 'malku' (a king). In Arabic, 'melekh' (monarch) is allied with angel cults, synonymous with human sacrifice. The comparative word play in English is the adjective 'heinous', contrasted with 'Highness'.

Appearance of the 'mal'akh' Hebrew (angel) is associated with war, famine and death. Universally the 'mal'akh' are attributed with conflict and disunity, encapsulated in the Greek verb 'makhe' (to fight) from the Semitic address 'melekh' (a king), duplicated as 'makel' (the royal staff).[33] A symbol of the 'king', the 'staff' is a marker of the 'serpent', documented as an 'aggressor'.

Ancient scriptures label the 'angels' as 'rapists and pillagers', likened to an 'army' or 'task force'. Fallen, the 'angel' is compared to a 'crew member of a naval vessel' Hebrew (tsabaoth, alternatively spelt as sabaoth or s'baot), deduced from the Semitic noun 'tsava' (army, warfare or soldiers).[34] Philologically the appellation of the 'tsabaoth' is conceived from the Egyptian noun 'saba' (a star).[35]

Religiously, God's soldiers resemble an invasion force from heaven, bracketed with star iconography, compatible with the Islamic depiction of angels. In the Koranic tradition, the armies affiliated with the Lord are termed as the 'thaqal' translated by M.A.S. Haleem as (a mighty or heavy army), written prosaically as (all their forces).[36] In Sura 55 verses 31-33, titled The Lord of Mercy, the 'thaqal' are quoted as such:

'We shall attend to you two huge armies [of jinn and mankind]... Jinn and mankind, if you can pass beyond the regions of heaven and earth, then do so: you will not pass without Our authority'.[37]

Conceptually, the 'thaqal' elucidates 'tariq' (a highway)[38] and plays on the Syrian intransitive verb 'tharrak' (to move),[39] discursive of the seven levels or highways of heaven. The 'thaqal' corresponds with the 'tsabaoth' (literally crew), rendered in the Modern Hebrew as 'tsevet',[40] translated into Medieval Latin as the 'host' (an army).

Manifestation of the host intimates the sacrifice of a 'victim', termed in Roman liturgy as the 'hostia' in tandem with 'haustus' (drinking, swallowing or streams of blood).[41] 'Haustus' technically refers to (blood drinking), obtained from the Greek root 'hustera' (womb), denoting the ingestion of menstrual blood. Immolation of the 'menses' is comparative to 'light', deemed as the 'fire-star'.

An arcane signifier, the 'fire-star', is registered with the setting sun (Venus) and rebirth, identified with the 'womb', relative to the 'worm' - an angel.

Similarity between the 'angel and tributary' is reiterated in the Syrian lexicon. 'Acan' (a seraph) is explicit of the Syrian root 'akal' the verb (to eat), cognate with the Egyptian noun 'akl' (food),[42] specific of the votive.[43] Propitiation of the 'akl' is mirrored in the Arabic etymon 'akhir' (extreme, final, last, ultimate or utmost).[44] Transfiguration of the angel into a dragon or seraph is situated ritualistically with sacrificial death and rebirth. Resurrection of the snake depicts the builder, equated with the temple (body) and its reconstruction.

As demonstrated, the 'mal'akh' are accredited with 'human sacrifice', displayed in the Canaanite tradition as the patron Goddess 'Moloch'. Further, the 'angels' are conceived as 'crew members of naval vessels', literally 'star-ships', registered in the Hebrew lexicon as 'tsabaoth' Latin (the angelic host).

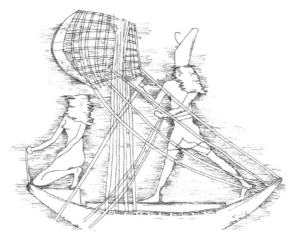

'Gods as Sailors' - note crescent sail boat, symbolic of the moon.

Philological evidence indicates the 'angel' is synonymous with the 'crew' (tsevet), recorded as (tsabaoth, alternatively s'baot), seminal of the king. His angelic ascendancy is evident in the Hebrew title 'melekh' (a king), subtracted from the Hebrew noun 'mal'akh' (an angel), sourced from 'malakh' (a sailor).[45] Comparison between 'melekh' (sovereign) and 'malakh' (sailor), implicit of an 'angel', is translated into English as (king-ship).[46] Advent of the 'host', labelled as 'royal', is reductive of the 'warrior', and designates 'killing', titular of the 'king'.

Similarities between the 'angel and monarch' are evident furthermore within the Canaanite tradition. The epithet 'Baal' (Lord) corresponds with the Arabic root 'bah'har' (sailor)[47] from 'bahr' (sea).[48] Closely grouped, the terms suggest 'bahir' (bright or shining),[49] indicative of an 'angel or dragon'. Connection between a 'magical or radiant being' and a 'naval personnel' is supplemented in the English language. For instance, the noun 'fairy' (a type of angel) is paired semantically with the word 'ferry' (adjunct with fiery).

To summarise, the compound 'mal'akh' (an angel) denotes (a shining serpent), interpreted as (a radiant king). His cognomen is identical with the title 'Majesty', pictured as a 'flaming snake' or 'watching eye'. Association between the watcher and the serpent is pertinent. The 'eye' is a synonym of the 'dragon', deified as an 'angel' - his offspring deemed as royal or human-angelic.

In the Indo-Semitic languages, the 'eye' illustrates 'mal' (a king), complimentary of 'mar' (a serpent), rendered in Arabic as the adjective 'mar' (saint[ly]).[50] Linguistically, the 'saints' are categorised with the fallen race - the 'Shatani' (Satan), epitomised as the reptile. 'Mar' (a serpent) is cross-referenced in the Egyptian hieroglyphic with the verb 'maar' (to see), Old Semitic 'mar'eh'. Translation of 'mar' (a snake) from the Persian language is commensurate in Hebrew with the etymon 'mu'ar' (light)[51] and 'maar' (sight). The triple signifier of the 'reptile, eye and light' is transferred into Greek vocabulary as the noun 'drakon' (a reptile) from the root (to watch or flash).

Persona of the ruler embodied as the 'Seeing Eye' imparts the 'double', recorded as the 'snake or apparition'. Comparison between the eye and reptile is auxiliary in English. The etymon 'spyro' (a dragon) replicates the Greek noun 'speira' (coil), cogent in the Anglo-Saxon languages with the verb 'to spy', suggesting the 'watcher or seraph'.

In the Catholic Church, the optic device duplicates the 'Seeing Eye' - an emblem of the 'dragon or angel'. Bloodline of the fallen serpent is transcribed genealogically from the Egyptian God of rebirth Osiris. Adorned in a shroud and mummified, his bandages symbolise the snakeskin, illustrative of resurrection. 'Osiris' name is written epigraphically with the 'throne and eye' emblems of the proto-monarchical line of Egypt. Device of the eye, ascribed to the reptile (a watcher), elucidates the seraph - emblematic of the king.

Symbols, pertaining to the fallen deity - the 'mal'akh', are complex and include the depiction of the 'angel' as a 'supplanter, dragon or navigator'. Ancient descriptions record 'angels' as 'sailors or mariners' of heaven, labelled variously as 'tsabaoth' (the crew members). Characterized as a hunter of man, the seraph is pictured as a rapist and desecrater. In addition, the 'snake' in Judaism is envisaged as a 'watcher' (irin) of the earth, transposed into the Greek etymology as 'drakon' (a dragon) from 'drakos' (an eye), shared epigraphically with 'Osiris'.

Epitomizing conflict and violence, the 'tsabaoth' are traced historically from the divine lineage of the God Osiris, depicted as a sailor. Veneration of Osiris' boat demarcates a 'star-ship' or 'space-ship', enacted liturgically through 'wor-ship'. Diagrammatically, the 'church' is laid out as a 'boat', classified with the 'king and governance'. In Old English, the noun 'weorthscipe' is transliterated in the modern idiom as (worship), from the compound 'worth-ship'. 'Scipe' (a ship) is diminutive of the Greek noun 'skaphos' (boat), cognizant with 'skipper and ship'.

Aerial view of some empty boat-pits, lying close to the great pyramid.

Bloodline of the sovereign emphasizes human angelic descent, replicated through the 'snake' - a race of 'fallen angels'. This renegade group are termed in Latin as the 'serpentigena', literally (serpent race).[52] Commemorated in Judaic tradition with the fallen tribe, the serpentigena are stylised as the star or dragon.

To conclude, the 'host' are progenitors of formalised 'religion' - a word borrowed from the Latin transitive verb 'religare' (to bind back or moor a boat).[53] Materialisation of the 'mal'akh' is disclosed in Greek tradition as:

> '... makarismos, referring to the blessed nature of one who has seen the Mysteries [i.e. an initiate]'.[54]

Documentary evidence for such a creature is found throughout classical writing. Jewish scriptures record the snake in the Apocryphal testament of 'Amram' (elevated-nation), attributed to the 'father of Moses'. In this important and sacred document, Amram reveals to his reader the submission of man, behoved to the fallen dragon - overlord and ruler of the earth. His summary of the snake is sobering and provides an excellent place to draw this chapter to a conclusion. He writes:

'They answered me 'we have been empowered and rule over all of mankind'... One of them was terrifying in his appearance like a serpent, his cloak many colour(s) yet very dark ... his visage like a viper'.[55]

1 The South African Shaman Credo Mutwa, Zulu Shaman, Dreams, Prophecies, and Mysteries, Destiny Books, Vermont, 2003, p121

2 M.A.S. Abdel Haleem, The Qur'an, Oxford University Press, p313 (Sura 42 Consultation verse 32).

3 Harold Bayley, The Lost Language of Symbolism, Dover Press, 2006, Vol 2, p307 (Bayley quotes from Wallis Budge's text, Legends of the Gods).

4 The Greek verb 'aggero' (to convey) is comparable to the Japanese verb 'ageru' (to give).

5 John C Traupman, PhD, The New College Latin & English Dictionary, Bantam, 1988, p10

6 Ibid, p11

7 Historically, the name 'Septuagint' derives from the tradition that there were 'seventy' translaters. Religiously, the number signifies the Seventy Elders of Israel and the renewal of the covenant, conveyed to Moses through the commandments.

8 Latin 'Septuaginta' (seventy) is a pun on the Roman name 'serpentigena', literally (serpent race).

9 Ralph Ellis, Eden in Egypt, A Translation of the Book of Genesis out of the Original Egyptian Text, Edfu Books, 2005, p13

10 Greek 'arkh' (a chief) is related to 'arkh(e)' denoting (the beginning).

11 The Latin prefix 'arch' (a chief), Greek 'arkh', is evidenced in the etymons 'archduke' or 'archbishop'.

12 Harold Bayley, The Lost Language of Symbols, Dover Publications, New York, 2006, p14

13 Hippocrene Concise Dictionary, English-Arabic, Arabic-English, Hippocrene Books, 2005, p187

14 Ibid [The 'act of invocation' (Arabic haka) is symmetrical in Greek with 'arche', denoting (the beginning), theoretical to creation, paralleled to the 'ruler' (hakim or arkhos)].

15 Ferozsons Urdu-English Dictionary, Revised edition, Ferozsons Ltd, Lahore, p19

16 Harold Bayley, The Lost Language of Symbols, Dover Publications, New York, 2006, pp336-349

17 Hippocrene Concise Dictionary, English-Arabic, Arabic-English, Hippocrene Books, 2005, p21

18 Laurence Gardner, Genesis of the Grail Kings, Bantam Books, 2000, p64

19 Prologue, Pocket Bilingual Dictionary, English-Hebrew, Hebrew-English, Prologue, 2003, p232

20 Ibid, p326 ['zohar' (radiance)]

21 Ibid, p340

22 Hippocrene Concise Dictionary, English-Arabic, Arabic-English, Hippocrene Books, 2005, p320

23 Ibid, p95

24 Theologically, the 'host' are signified as an 'angelic chorus'. According to scholars, the name is correlated with 'divine invocation' (Egyptian hu) and parallels the Semitic etymology 'amar' (to speak or command).

25 Bruce Lansky, The Complete Book of Baby Names, Hinkler Books, 2004, p298

26 The 'red mother' evokes 'menstrual blood', equated with the mammal and sexual union with the snake - illustrative of sacrificial death and rebirth.

27 Hippocrene Concise Dictionary, English-Arabic, Arabic-English, Hippocrene Books, 2005, p95

28 Scholars are under the apprehension that Moloch is a God. Milton's writing in Paradise Lost, book i 392-398 refers to 'Moloch' as a 'God', to quote: 'He was worshipped in Rabba'. Moloch's name though reminiscent of the Hebrew titular 'melekh' (king) is also similar to the Hebrew word 'malka' (queen), Arabic 'malika'. In referenced work, Moloch is defined as a masculine God - a controvertible argument. Symbolically, the Goddess is depicted as a roosting owl - her nest the tinder, used to burn the votive. Moloch through the use of the owl glyph in Egypt is connected to the Mother Goddess 'Mut' (death). The owl personifies the cannibal as it eats its own offspring. A nocturnal bird, it is linked to the

appearance of the moon - a feminine symbol of the Goddess, who possesses a pair of horns (Venus). Moloch is also connected to whoring and prostitution, demonstrated in the Biblical book of Leviticus 20-3-5 '...Because he hath given of his seed unto Moloch, to defile my sanctuary and to profane my holy name... and all that go a whoring after him, to commit whoredom with Moloch...' In classical myth, 'Moloch's insignia the 'owl' is shared with the 'Goddess Athene'. Homer called her the 'owlish one' - a statement which purports that she was once worshipped as an 'owl'. In Celtic tradition, the angel 'Molloch' is known as the 'maid of the hairy arms', and is considered as a type of banshee. The 'dual arm' is used hieroglyphically to write (the double) a symbol of the Goddess and rebirth.

29 In a modern context, the owl is a symbol of initiatory learning, used as a common sign in comprehensive schools to signify education. Archaically, the fowl is cognate with child sacrifice. Additionally, the owl lays circular eggs, reminiscent of the serpent's egg. The owl's chick, when born, possesses a fine down that is almost identical to hair, illustrative of an hairy angel, digressions of a nocturnal deity or an 'hemitheos' (half God).

30 Ferozsons Urdu-English Dictionary, A Comprehensive Dictionary of Current Vocabulary, (Revised Edition), Ferozsons Ltd, Lahore, p752

31 Prologue, Pocket Bilingual Dictionary, English-Hebrew, Hebrew-English, Prologue, 2003, p261

32 Ibid, p222 (king)

33 Ibid, p390

34 Ibid, p28

35 The 'tsabaoth' is transliterated into modern English as (sabaoth), and is identified with the 'Sabaean' priests - the 'Sabi'.

36 M.A.S. Abdel Haleem, The Qur'an, Oxford University Press, p354 (See footnote C).

37 Ibid

38 Hippocrene Concise Dictionary, English-Arabic, Arabic-English, Hippocrene Books, 2005, p297

39 Ibid, p300

40 Prologue, Pocket Bilingual Dictionary, English-Hebrew, Hebrew-English, Prologue, 2003, p92

41 John C Traupman PhD, The New College Latin & English Dictionary, Bantam, 1988, p130

42 Hippocrene Concise Dictionary, English-Arabic, Arabic-English, Hippocrene Books, 2005, p148

43 'Hakim' (a ruler) otherwise 'acan' (a seraph) is equated with immolation i.e. 'akl' (food). The same pun is evident in the early Semitic designation 'Baal' (a Lord) and 'bala' (swallow).

44 Hippocrene Concise Dictionary, English-Arabic, Arabic-English, Hippocrene Books, 2005, p148

45 Prologue, Pocket Bilingual Dictionary, English-Hebrew, Hebrew-English, Prologue, 2003, p352

46 'Malakh' (a naval crew member) is reductive from the hieroglyph 'mar' (lake or sea), inherited in Latin and French respectively as 'mare' and 'mer' (sea).

47 Hippocrene Concise Dictionary, English-Arabic, Arabic-English, Hippocrene Books, 2005, p153

48 Ibid, p154

49 Prologue, Pocket Bilingual Dictionary, English-Hebrew, Hebrew-English, Prologue, 2003, p50

50 Hippocrene Concise Dictionary, English-Arabic, Arabic-English, Hippocrene, 2005, p235

51 Prologue, Pocket Bilingual Dictionary, English-Hebrew, Hebrew-English, Prologue, 2003, p232

52 John C Traupman PhD, The New College Latin & English Dictionary, Bantam, 1988, p285 [Traupman translates 'serpentigena' as (dragon offspring) - 'serpent race' is however a viable rendition, as the stem 'gens' can signify (a race, tribe, offspring, stock, species, breed or people)].

53 John C Traupman PhD, The New College Latin & English Dictionary, Bantam, 1988, p265

54 Timothy Freke & Peter Gandy, The Jesus Mysteries, Was The Original Jesus A Pagan God, Thorsons, 2000, p199

55 Andrew Collins, From the Ashes of Angels, The Forbidden Legacy of a Fallen Race, Michael Joseph Ltd, 1996, p48

2

The Sabi Priesthood

Seven deadly sins
Seven ways to win
Seven holy paths to hell
And your trip begins

Seven downward slopes
Seven bloodied hopes
Seven are your burning fires
Seven your desires…

I am he, the bornless one
The fallen angel, watching you
Babylon, the scarlet whore
I'll infiltrate your gratitude
Don't you dare to save your son
Kill him now, and save the young ones
Be the mother of a birth strangled babe
Be the devil's own, Lucifer's my name.

Moonchild (Introduction and First Verse), Iron Maiden,
Seventh Son of a Seventh Son, April 23rd 1988 (St Georges Day).

The Egyptian word for 'star' (sba or saba, in Akkadian shubar) is written in the hieroglyphic with the sign of a five-pointed star - a pentagram diagrammatic of the orbit of Venus. 'Saba' is related in Arabic to the word 'sabah' (morning), suggesting an early correlation with the 'morning star'.

In Urdu, 'sabah' refers to (the daybreak, dawn or morning breeze).[1] The original root of 'saba' concurs with the Sumerian root 'sub' (below) and indicates the setting of the stars - literally the submerging of the stars. Astrologically 'sub' and 'saba' connotes the precession of the Equinoxes.

Further, in the Arabic language, 'sabah' (morning) is polymorphic and designates the number (seven), recorded in the modern adjective 'saba'.[2] Celestially, the figure suggests a connection with the 'Pleiades', specified as the 'Seven Sisters' of the constellation 'Taurus' (the Bull).[3] Appearance of the 'bovine' in the Persian mysteries is intrinsic to the deification of 'Mithra' (Refer to Chapter 11 The Amorites).

The star system of 'Taurus' known commonly as the 'Pleiades' features deities, reminiscent of the 'angelic host', referred to in Judaic scriptures as the 'sailors'. 'Pleiades' is thought to originate from the Greek word 'plein' (to sail - as in plain sailing)[4] and corresponds to the Goddess 'Pleione'.[5] To emphasize, the 'sailor' is a symbol of the 'angel'. Translation of 'Pleiades' into Greek originates from the Arabic corruption of 'sabah' the word (to swim) with the appended meaning of (morning).[6] 'Sabah' is cognizant with the Old Egyptian noun 'saba' (star) - a homonym used in Arabic as the adjective (seven - as in the seven stars of the Pleiades).

Classical mythology represents the 'Pleiades' as the 'seven daughters of Atlas and Pleione'. Allegorically, the children of heaven are transformed into the constellation Pleiades. Pleione's child, Electra is the seventh daughter, recorded as the invisible star. According to Greek legend, Electra's discreet appearance documents the Goddess' shame at marrying a human being.[7] Her obscurity, a salient feature of the narrative, discloses mortal angelic intercourse and its concealment.

Electra's Hellenistic name relates to 'electuary' (to lick up). The Greek root 'ekleikho' informs the Frank word 'lecher' (to lick) assimilated into English as the adjective 'lecherous' (having strong sexual desires). 'Lecher' additionally augments the English etymology 'leech', descriptive of (a bloodsucker), grouped with the Old English noun 'lik' (a corpse). A 'lecher' describes a 'lackey', theoretical to the verbs 'like', 'luck' and 'look', implicit of a 'dragon'. 'Lackey' is educed from the Arabic root 'lihiq' (to follow).

Idolization of the fallen Goddess imparts early practices, associated with bloodletting and lust. 'Electra's cognomen is a play on the Greek namesake 'Alecto' (the Implacable or Guilty One) - an appellation shared in classical mythology with the 'Fury'.

A class of deity, the Fury is typically described as possessing the visage of a dog[8] with bat-like wings and writhing snakes for hair. Combination of the 'reptile with hair' is an esoteric marker of the 'human-angelic' lineage. In some versions of the myth, the 'Furies' are huntresses, carrying scourges, sickles and torches.[9] Known to their contemporaries as 'daughters of the night', the 'Furies' are aligned astrologically to the 'Pleiades'.

Indiscretions between humans and deities are signified with 'starlight', and equated ritualistically with 'menstrual blood', termed as the 'fire-star'. Consumption of the 'fire-star' annotates 'flashing' - a marker of the 'dragon', identified with 'divine birth'. Theologians refer to this sacred union as the 'Immaculate Conception' from the Latin root 'macula' (spot, stain, blemish or disgrace).[10]

Mycenaean 'star-fire' challace with a horned fallopian 'graal' (grail) design.

Ontologically, 'Alecto' is a euphemism of a nocturnal angel, recognizant of a vampire.[11] In alternative accounts, 'Alecto' (guilty) is called 'Allecto' (relentless).[12] Her Hellenistic name is shown to originate from the Arabic root 'Alaq' (a clot, conceptual with 'menstrual blood' and 'divine birth'. According to M.A.S. Abdel

Haleem's scholarly appendices for his translation of the Koran, he defines the idiom as follows:

> *[Alaq signifies] a stage in the development of a foetus, i.e. embryo. Alaq can also mean anything that clings: a clot of blood, a leech even a lump of mud. All these meanings involve the basic idea of clinging or sticking. Clinging involves a state of total dependence ...'*[13]

The label 'alaq' (clot) in Arabic demonstrates a connection with 'eating', originally enunciated as 'blood drinking', signified as 'allaq la' (feed)[14] from the Syrian root 'alak' (chew).[15] Conceptually 'alaq' is related to 'af'lak' (heaven), manifested in Greek as 'Alecto' or 'Electra', assigned to the 'Pleiades'.[16] Pertinently the 'q' or 'k' morpheme in Semitic is similar to the phoneme 'h'. 'Alaq' philologically is analogous to the name of God 'Allah', otherwise 'alaq' (a clot)[17], traced from the Aramaic root 'Eloh' (light),[18] connoting a deity.

Occult lore illustrates the 'Pleiades' as the 'seven' (sab'a) pointed 'star' (saba), an emblem affiliated with the 'host'. Transposed into religious symbolism, the 'septagram' pertains to the 'menorah' (the seven-branched candlestick). 'Seven candles' represent the 'seven stars' in combination with the 'seven branches'. Rendered in Latin as 'virga' (stick), the 'seven branches' correlate with the seven vestal 'virgins' (virgo), personified as the 'Seven Sisters'.[19]

In mystical Judaism, the 'candelabra' embodies 'angelic coitus', simultaneous with the 'onset of menstruation', consentient to 'Electra or Alecto' (the Guilty One). For example, the 'menorah' records the Semitic cryptogram 'min-nora' written as the entendre (terrible[20]-sex[21]). The Hebrew adjective 'nora' (horrid)[22] is duplicated in the English expletive 'Bloody Nora'!

Device of the 'menorah' is symptomatic of the serpent's liaison with mortals, exhibited in the Japanese verb 'minoru' (fruitful or fertile). In the Greek language, the 'menorah' encodes the 'menorrhoea' (the flow of blood at menstruation), literally 'meno-rheo' (the monthly flow). 'Menorrhoea' compliments the Latin wordplay 'mens-rea' (guilty-mind).

Structurally, the classical compound 'menorrhoea' is a derivation from the obscure Hellenistic word 'miara', typically translated as (taboo), but rendered properly as (blood stained),[23] and denotes the 'woman's cycle'. 'Miara' in Persian is represented as 'mar' (a red serpent), transferred into the Semitic languages as 'mar'eh' (a watcher).

Theologically 'menorrhoea' discloses (the menstruating) priestess, originating from the offspring of the angels (cabal). Ovulation of the 'scarlet whore' is compared to 'oblation', offered as a propitiatory. In the Judaic and Persian law, the 'menses blood' characterizes the 'mammal' e.g. man, and details ritual contamination of the serpent's (angel) lineage through human intercourse. Comparisons between the 'fallen woman' recurrent with the deity 'Alecto' (culpable) documents 'Immaculate Conception', preserved in the Arabic etymon 'alaq' (a 'clot' of blood), dualistic of the votive. Immolation is compared to angelic rebirth, aligned to the mysteries and is confluent in Greek with 'ekleikho' (to lick up) from the Arabic root 'allaq la' (to feed), denoting 'ritual blood drinking'.

'Alecto's namesake 'Electra' marks out the alignment of the 'Seven Sisters', attributed with the constellation of the 'Pleiades' and the 'Sabi' priesthood. The figure 'seven' enumerates the ritual 'death of the firstborn' and appears in Jewish numerology as the 'seven mysteries' - divulged in the next chapter.

1   Ferozsons Urdu-English Dictionary, Revised Edition, Ferozsons Ltd, Lahore, p780

2   Ibid, p426 [The adjective 'seven' is written as (saba) and is related to the Arabic noun 'sab'a', denoting the noun (seven), implicit of the 'Pleiades'].

3   In Meso-American art, the 'Crotalus' (rattlesnake) pattern signifies the 'rattle' called (tzab), which is the same word in the Yucatec Mayan dialect for the 'Pleiades' star cluster' - a small cluster of 'seven stars' in the 'Taurus constellation'. Tzab's stem is reminiscent of the Japanese etymology 'Subaru' (Pleiades) and 'suberu' (slippery). These terms are phonetically consistent with the Arabic root 'saba' (star), alternatively (seven). 'Saba' is found in the older Akkadian noun 'shubar' (a star or the Pleiades). In the next chapter, we shall observe how 'saba' in the Semitic language appertains to the 'angelic host', the 'tsaba' or 'tsava' (crew). For further information about the Meso-American word 'tzab', refer to Geoff Stray's excellent research on ancient calendars. Catastrophe or Ecstasy: A Complete Guide to End-of-Time Predictions-Beyond 2012, Vital Signs Publishing, pp98 & 99 (The Pyramid of Kukulcan: A Precessional Alarm Clock).

4   Brewers Dictionary of Phrase and Fable, London Cassell and Company, 1954, p715

5   'Pleiades' corresponds with the classical pun 'Pala-Haides' (the Ruler of Hades). The namesake helps to explain the relationship between the 'Morning Star' and the worship of 'Sirius', linked to heaven in conjunction with its nemesis - the constellation 'Pleiades'. Both 'Sirius and Pleiades' closely govern the cycle of our solar system, and each star system possesses a hidden star, replete with dragon iconography.

6   Hippocrene English-Arabic, Arabic-English Dictionary, Hippocrene, New York, 2005, p274

7   Brewers Dictionary of Phrase and Fable, London Cassell and Company, 1954, p715

8   In Greek mythology, the Furies' appearance is linked to the 'dog' and is a covert reference to the Dog Star 'Sirius'.

9   J.A. Coleman, The Dictionary of Mythology, An A-Z Of Themes, Legends and Heroes, Capella, 2007, p391

10 John C Traupman PhD, The New College, Latin & English Dictionary, Bantam, 1988, p175

11 Brewers Dictionary of Phrase and Fable, London Cassell and Company, 1954, p383

12 J.A. Coleman, The Dictionary of Mythology, An A-Z Of Themes, Legends and Heroes, Capella, 2007, p47

13 M.A.S. Abdel Haleem, The Qur'an, A New Translation, Oxford University Press, 2004, Sura 96 (Al-Alaq), p428

14 Hippocrene English-Arabic, Arabic-English Dictionary, Hippocrene, New York, 2005, p47

15 Ibid, 319

16 Linguistic comparison between the serpent and heaven is preserved additionally in Arabic. The word 'afa' (serpent) is reminiscent of 'af'lak' (sky, heavens or firmament) and compares in Egyptian with 'qeb' (serpent) and 'qebhu' [heaven(s)].

17 'Allah' (light) and 'alaq' (clot), nominal of the 'Pleiades', is also grouped with the Semitic pun 'Allah' and 'awr' (to bark), suggestive of the 'Dog Star', reinforcing a split in the priesthood between the 'Pleiades and Sirius'.

18 'Eloh' (light) is linked philologically with 'Aur' (Sirius), and further demonstrates a division in the priesthood between 'Sirius and the Pleiades' (See Chapter 35 Menstrual Fish Dogs and Pharaohs).

19 The 'seven stars of the Pleiades' are symbolically matched with the 'seven northern stars of Ursa Minor', set adjacent to the 'Drakon' constellation.

20 Prolog, Pocket Bilingual Dictionary, English-Hebrew-Hebrew-English, Prolog, 2003, p415 ['Nora' (terrible)]

21 Ibid, p366 ['Min' (sex)]

22 Ibid, p191 ['Nora' (horrid)]

23 John M Allegro, The Sacred Mushroom and the Cross: A Study of the Nature and Origins of Christianity within the Fertility Cults of the Ancient Near Middle East, Abacus, 1970, p189

3

The Seven Divisions

Anna: It changed colors, like the chameleon, it uses the jungle.

Dillon: You saying that Blain and Hawkins were killed by a fucking lizard? That's a bullshit sight (psyche) job. There's 2 to 3 men out there at the most. Fucking lizard!

Predator, Arnold Schwarzenegger, 20th Century Fox 1987, Story by Jove![1]

The bible ascribes 'seven' with the completion of God's work, classified with the 'Sabbath', numerological to divinity. At a covert level, the 'saba' logogram locates the 'seven heavens' and coincides with the 'seven planets' of the solar system. Depicted as 'thrones' or 'angels', the 'planets' are replicated in the Mithraic religion as the 'seven rungs' (ribs) of initiation. In the Sumerian seals, the 'septenary' is combined with the 'branches of a tree' - a 'menorah' indicating a bloodline, unified sexually with the serpent and priestess.

Catholicism celebrates the number 'seven' in conjunction with the 'sacraments' - a sequence provident in apocalyptic literature. The Book of Revelation, for example, describes the Seven Churches in Asia Minor.[2] *'...geographical[ly] [the] place-name 'Asia' is almost certainly a play on the Semitic word for healing, '-s-y', [transcribed] 'asya', [a] 'physician'... [and is the] source for the Sectarian name [of the Qumran community the] Essenes.'*[3]

'Seven Churches of Healing' compare to a reference, noted in the Essene scrolls from the Dead Sea, in which the sect is called the 'Seven Divisions of the Penitents of Israel'.[4] Numerically, the order suggests a close arrangement with the 'Sabi' brotherhood, proximate to the 'Pleiades' and the formation of the early church, governed through the Qumran fraternity.

'Essene' is written in Greek as 'Essenoi' or 'Essaioi'.[5] According to the classical scholar 'Philo' (brother), 'Essenoi' stems from the Hellenistic word for 'holy' (oseeos),[6] noted in the Catholic pun 'Holy See', implicit of an 'angel or dragon'.

'Oseeos' is derived from the Semitic maxim 'Osei ha-Torah' (doers of the law) and collectively refer to the 'Osim' - pronounced 'Oseem'. The Christian writer Epiphanius mentions this denomination as the 'Ossenes',[7] a title complimentary in Aramaic with 'asya' (a doctor of the law). Lineage of the 'Essenes' is sourced from the 'Seven Divisions of Israel', adjunct with the 'Seventy Elders'.

'Seven Divisions' form the historical backdrop to the 'Sabian' priesthood, originating from 'Moses' and his marriage to one of Jethro's (Reuel) seven daughters. 'Jethro' (superiority) is described in the book of Exodus as a priest of Median. The high priest's daughter 'Zipporah' is a derivation from 'zeph' (hidden), earmarked as the 'seventh daughter of the Pleiades' (Electra). Esoteric, 'Zipporah' reads as 'sippur-Rah' (the story of Ra). Circumstantial evidence links the 'hidden star of Ra', denoting 'Sirius', with the 'hidden star of the Pleiades', signified as 'Jethro's daughter', inducted from the lineage of 'Zilpah' - See footnote[8].

Winged gazelle, Persian, including personare mask of satyr (detail).

Astrological demarcations represent the 'Pleiades' as the 'seven-pointed star', stylized as the 'menorah' - the 'seven virgins' or the 'fire-star'. Device of the 'saba star', the 'septagram' is combined with the 'goat' - an emblem of the 'fallen host', affiliated in Arabic to the 'Sabi' priesthood. Archaically the totem of the 'goat' is arrived from the Semitic root 'tsvi' or 'tsbi' (gazelle).[9]

The 'Sabi' priestcraft is rendered in Greek as the 'Sibyl' (an oracular priestess), depicted as the 'goat'. In French and Spanish, 'Sabi' apprises 'savoir' and 'sabe', variations of the verb (to know), congruous with 'illumination' and the 'serpent'. The 'b' and 'v' consonants swap in the European spelling of Arabic words.

'Sabe' is cognate with 'civilis', literally (civil), extracted from the Latin root 'civis' (a citizen). 'Civis' corresponds with the Roman word 'cervus' (stag)[10] from the Semitic stem 'tsvi' (gazelle). Symbol of the 'gazelle', 'goat' or 'stag' is utilized as an insignia of the 'horned (crowned) serpent', applied to the 'illuminati' - the 'Sabi'. Relationship between the 'star' and 'goat' (a demon) is found in the linguistic comparison of 'star' and 'satyr'. In Greek mythology, the 'khimaira'

(English chimera) signifies a 'demi-God', and is taken from the Hebrew root 'Chem', denoting (the Pleiades).[11]

The split between Chem (the celestial goat) opposite 'Pleiades' (Taurus the bull) explains etiologically the myth of the 'chimera'. Significantly, the partition between the 'caper' and 'bovine' indicates a separation within the priesthood, signified as the 'fallen star'. Connection between the 'Morning-Star' and the 'Pleiades'[12] is framed in addition with the 'Sothic star'.

Chimera - mythical creature with a lion's head (Orion), a goat's body (Pleiades) and a snake's tail (Sirius) - sculpted as a canine, sometimes as a fox. See diagram Chapter 35 p333.

Development of civilization and its religious institutions is deductive from an angelic source, elicited from the Sabi priesthood. In Arabic, 'Al Sab'a' rendered in English as (Sabian) is a derivative from the Arabic root 'Saba'ia' (the Star People), extrapolated from 'Saba' (the host). The 'Sabians' venerated the 'Morning-Star' (Sabah-Kha), cognate with 'Lucifer' and the 'fallen host'.

Tributary of the firstborn or fire-star offered to the rising star Venus is evidenced throughout Indo-European etymologies. In English, the homonym 'sun' and 'son' is an alliteration of 'sin'. The play is replicated in the Old Hebrew as the verbal stem 'na'or' (enlightened),[13] sequenced with 'nour' (boy) and 'nora' (terrible).

Adulation of the Egyptian 'Sun' God 'Ra'[14] is transposed in the Modern Hebrew adjective 'ra' (evil),[15] connected to offerings of the firstborn 'son' - a theme reproduced in the English etymology. For instance, the noun 'morning' accedes with 'mourning', and 'day' with 'die' [Latin 'dea' (a deity)]. Identical word associations are reiterated in the Semitic lexicon. 'Boker' (morning) is punned with 'boke' (weep) - appellations assigned to the 'firstborn' (bekore).

Corresponding anagrams are duplicated in the Persian and Arabic languages. In Urdu, 'sabr' (to suffer) is a play on the Arabic noun 'sabah' (morning) and 'sabi' (a child). Ancient etymologies suggest early 'morning' rites (sabah) are commensurate with offering a newborn 'child' (sabi), cogent with the determination of the weekly 'Sabbath'.

Celebration of the Holy day equates with the death of the firstborn - a proposition evident in Arabic. The Semitic root 'Shabbat' denoting (the Sabbath) is doubled with 'sa'ubat' (difficulty, hardship, trouble or distress),[16] which appears in the abbreviated form as the adjective 'sa'b' (hard, difficult, rough, arduous, troublesome or perverse).[17] 'Sa'b' is twinned in Arabic with 'sabb' (to curse or swear at) and 'sabab' (cause),[18] suggesting 'human origin'. The Semitic wordplay 'sabb' and 'sabab' is reproduced in the English pun (curse) and (cause), disclosed as divine retribution.

In comparison, the Urdu verb 'sabr' (to suffer) informs the English noun 'saber' (a sword), classified with the Arabic stem 'saab' (hard or difficult).[19] The Persian word 'sabr' (to suffer) infers the loss of an 'infant' or 'youth', accounted from the Arabic root (sabi).[20] Philologically 'sabi' (child) is consistent with 'Sab'a' (priest), lateral to 'sulbi' (descended from or legitimate)[21] and informs the English noun 'sibling'. Greek ritual equates the 'sulbi' with the 'Sibyl' from the Akkadian root 'Sibulla' (an Oracle).

Offshoots of the 'Sab'a' variously the 'Sibulla or Sibyl' recall the 'Shebet' (tribe), conceptual with the verbal stem 'sbt' (to rest), elaborated as the 'Sabbath' (Akkadian Shabattu). Worship of the itinerant angel collates with the moon and Venus, inferred from the reciprocal wordplay between the 'star and priesthood'.

Elements taken from the Mohammedan Church parallel with the 'saba' (star), definitive of the 'Sab'a' (priest), bracketed with the 'Morning-Star' (Old Semitic Sabah-Kha). Observed in the early sky, 'Venus' appears as a 'crescent' - a device married symbolically to the 'moon'. Emergence of Venus is associated with the nocturne, theoretical to the 'Sabbath' and 'rest' (sbt). Depicted as 'reposed', the 'priest' is identified with 'death'. Examined in Greek philology, the word 'koma' (sleep) is congruent with the Hebrew noun 'komer' (priest).[22] Moreover, the titular 'komer' is shown to originate from the Arabic noun '(q)amar' (moon) and emphasizes the 'crescent's affiliation with the 'Islamic denomination'.

Lock of Youth
Horus stands upon the crocodile 'Sobek', a pun on 'Sabah-Kha' (the Morning-Star). The two crocodiles
signify the Morning and Evening Star. Archaically the dragon is associated with flashing.

In Muslim culture, the noun 'sabah' (morning) is correlated with 'Sahabi' (the friends of Mohammed), otherwise the 'Sabi' (Sabian or host) and delineates the 'illuminati', progeny of the 'Shebet' (tribe). Koranic traditions annex the 'Sab'a' (priest) with the 'Sahabi', asseverated as (the Companions of the Prophet). Variations of the 'Sabi', 'Sahabi' and 'Sibyl' (an oracle) are found also in Classical mythology.

In Greek legend, the assignment 'Sabazius' signifies the name of (Bacchus), employed in Latin as the plural noun, denoting (the festival in honor of Bacchus).[23] The 'Sabazius' is identical to the 'Sabbatical or Sabbath'. Central to the worship of 'Sabazius' is the God 'Pan', personified as the 'goat' motif, interior to the 'Phrygian mysteries', with whom 'Dionysus' is identified.[24] Relationship between the 'goat' and 'Sabazius' is equivalent in the Semitic traditions with the 'Sabi' or 'Sab'a' and their emblem the 'tsvi' (gazelle), replicated in Northern Europe as the 'stag' (cervus).

Celebration of the 'Sabazius' sanctions the hidden death of the innocent child - the 'scapegoat' contiguous with the 'Morning-Star'. Doctrinally the goat's incarnation as an angel of death prescribes sacerdotal induction into the

Bacchic mysteries. Bacchus' debauchery allegorizes 'bacca' (a berry),[25] obtained from the Semitic root 'boker' (morning).[26] Technically Bacchus is a morning God of sacrifice, related to revelry and drunkenness.

Persian mysteries equate the grape with 'sabuh' (ceremonious 'wine'), specified as (alcohol drunk in the morning) from the Arabic noun 'sabah' (morning). 'Sabuh' (morning wine) is rendered in Arabic as 'sahba' (red wine).[27] Both etymologies link to 'blood and light' symbolism, and suggest a connection with 'Luciferic rites', shown as the 'crescent' or 'pentagram' - an emblem of 'Venus'. Esoterically 'Venus' Latin 'Lux-ferre' (Light-bringer) is synonymous with the fire-'star' (saba) - symbolic of ritual communion.

'Sahba' (red wine) codifies the drinking of menstrual blood (light), addendum to angelic procreation. Philologically 'sahba' parallels the Egyptian Arabic noun 'sahba' (a friend, girlfriend or owner).[28] Implicit of the matriarch 'sahba' is allied religiously to the 'Sabi' priesthood.

In Freemasonry, the 'priestess' is adjunct with the 'Mother Lodge', referred to cryptically as 'subah' (a society, assembly or association). Religiously, the mater's induction into a sexual covenant or marriage with a deity elicits 'suhbat' Arabic (sexual intercourse).[29] Etymologically 'suhbat' is linked with ritual hedonism, correlated with the 'morning' rite (sabah) - expressions of the 'Sabbath', symmetrical to the orgiastic rites of 'Sabazius' (Bacchus).

Ritual ingestion of 'wine' (sahba) describes 'blood drinking' and the veneration of the 'fire-star', the 'mother priestess', characterized as the 'Sibyl'. 'Offspring' of the 'Sibyl' (an oracle) denotes the 'sulbi' (descended from), specifying an angel, aligned to 'sabi' (a child), implicit of the 'Sabi' priestcraft. Progeny of the 'Sabi' (priest) or 'Sibyl' annotates the 'angelic messenger' (caba), definitive of the 'Morning-Star' (Sabah-Kha), esoteric of 'Sirius' (Al Kalb). Archaically the worship of 'Sirius' is paired with the 'serpent' (qeb).

Executed through royal mediation, the fallen star is mooted with the practice of fratricide, centered on deity worship. Concealed, this covenant discloses the fallen 'tribe' (Shebet), monumental to the lunar cycle - the 'Sabbath'. Merged with the sailor, the Moonchild or votive, the 'tributary' receives the 'fire-star', and is anointed as the 'sacrificial Messiah', manifested through the 'oracle's menstrual blood'. Substitution of the king heralds 'celestial ancestry', personified as the 'goat, bull or chimera'.

Combination of the 'Pleiades' with 'Sirius', the 'goat-bull' illustrates 'Venus', duplicitous of the 'solar emblem'. Orbit of the sun and solar system revolves around 'Alcion' - the 'central star of the Pleiades'. Movement of the star mirrors the earth's ecliptic orbit around the sun. Its passage is analogous to the 'Sothic' year, enumerated as '365 and a quarter days'. In addition, both the 'Pleiades and Sirius' systems share hidden stars, equivalent to the gas body 'Jupiter', figured as a 'proto-star', aligned to 'Saturn'.

In conclusion, 'Venus' operates as a 'shifting signifier' of the constellation 'Sirius', opposite the 'Pleiades'. The 'morning' (sabah) articulates the 'creation' of the 'seven planets', allied with the 'seven' stars (Arabic sab'a).[30] Historical confusion over the 'saba' (star)[31] and its double alignment with 'Sirius' and 'Taurus' concedes a split inside of the Persian and Babylonian (Judaic) priesthood.[32] In Exodus 32, Moses establishes a new covenant through the destruction of Aaron's 'golden calf' - celestial to the 'Pleiades'.

Reaffirmed in the book of Leviticus 16:18-19, Aaron is required to offer the blood of a 'bull and goat' - indicative of the merging of separate traditions. This it seems is incumbent of the unification of the 'Pleiades with Sirius', personified as the 'bull' and 'goat-fish', to quote:

> '... He shall take some of the bull's blood and some of the goat's blood and put it on all the horns of the altar. He shall sprinkle some of the blood on it with his finger seven times to cleanse it and consecrate it from the uncleanness of the Israelites'.

1 'Jove' is another name for 'Jupiter' - a planet connected to the Judaic priests, the Sadduceas - Refer to Chapter header.
2 Martin Selman & Martin Manser, Collins Dictionary of the Bible, Collins, 2005, p275
3 John M. Allegro, The Sacred Mushroom and the Cross, A Study of the Nature and Origins of Christianity within the Fertility Cults of the Ancient Near Middle East, Abacus, 1970, p200
4 Ibid
5 Michael Baigent & Richard Leigh, The Dead Sea Scrolls Deception, Arrow Books, 2001, p250
6 Ibid, p252
7 Ibid, p254
8 'Zipporah', Moses' wife, is a probable pun on Jacob's first wife 'Zilpah', and suggests initiation through the matriarch.
9 Prolog Pocket Bilingual Dictionary, English-Hebrew-Hebrew-English, Prolog, 2003, p166 ['tsvi' (gazelle)]
10 John C. Traupman, Ph.D, The New College, Latin & English Dictionary, Bantam, 1988, p480
11 Marke Pawson, Gematria, The Numbers of Infinity, Green Magic, England, 2004, p5
12 In later chapters, we shall see how the 'Morning-Star' is grouped with the worship of 'Sirius' and 'Orion', suggesting a faction or a rival group to the veneration of the 'Pleiades'. Early evidence shows a division or split within the priesthood, represented cryptically as the 'bull-serpent' and 'goat-fish'.
13 Prolog, Pocket Bilingual Dictionary, English-Hebrew-Hebrew-English, Prolog, 2003, p131
14 Denigration of 'Ra' (Sirius - in Modern Hebrew evil) coincides with the split, internal to the priesthood, conjunct with the veneration of the Pleiades. Partition of the priesthood and its

denominations record the 'bull', astrologically 'Taurus', factional to the 'scapegoat' (Hebrew Chem) - the 'Pleiades'.

15 Prolog, Pocket Bilingual Dictionary, English-Hebrew-Hebrew-English, Prolog, 2003, p137

16 Ferozsons Urdu-English Dictionary, A Comprehensive Dictionary of Current Vocabulary (Revised Edition), Ferozsons Ltd, Lahore, p481

17 Ibid

18 Hippocrene English-Arabic, Arabic-English Dictionary, Hippocrene, New York, 2005, p274

19 M.A. Abdel-Hady, Egyptian Arabic Phrasebook, Rough Guide, Lexus, 1998, p242

20 Ferozsons Urdu-English Dictionary, A Comprehensive Dictionary of Current Vocabulary (Revised Edition), Ferozsons Ltd, Lahore, p479

21 Ibid, p482

22 Prolog, Pocket Bilingual Dictionary, English-Hebrew, Hebrew-English, Prolog, 2003, p315

23 John C Traupman PhD, The New College, Latin & English Dictionary, Bantam, 1988, p274

24 John M Allegro, The Sacred Mushroom and the Cross, A Study of the Nature and Origins of Christianity within the Fertility Cults of the Ancient Near East, Ababcus, 1973, p104

25 John C Traupman PhD, The New College, Latin & English Dictionary, Bantam, 1988, p352

26 Prolog, Pocket Bilingual Dictionary, English-Hebrew, Hebrew-English, Prolog, 2003, p262

27 Ferozsons Urdu-English Dictionary, A Comprehensive Dictionary of Current Vocabulary (Revised Edition), Ferozsons Ltd, Lahore, p484 ['Sahba' (red wine) is a 'Luciferic' symbol, connected to 'light and blood'. Lucifer's cognomen 'Lux-ferre' (light bringer) euphemistically refers to the 'blood bringer'].

28 M.A. Abdel-Hady, Egyptian Arabic Phrasebook, Rough Guide, Lexus, 1998, p242

29 Ferozsons Urdu-English Dictionary, Revised Edition, Ferozsons Ltd, Lahore, pp478-479

30 Hippocrene English-Arabic, Arabic-English Dictionary, Hippocrene, New York, 2005, p110 ['sab'a' (seven)]

31 Venus' duplicity is conceived as the 'Morning-Star', paired with the 'Evening-Star', depicted in the classical world as a 'God and Goddess', connected to the 'hermaphrodite or eunuch'.

32 The Babylonians depicted the split within the priesthood as the goat-fish (Chem), contrasted with the the Greco-Persian bull-serpent (Sarapis). Esoterically, the double dragon (red and white) or warring serpent pays homage to the snake and fish, and suggests two different strains of reptilian hominid, assigned respectively to the Pleiades and Sirius. Admixture of the serpent's seed with 'humankind' originally designated with the 'Pleiades' resulted in civil war and is equated with the star system Orion. Diluvial myths suggest a contingent of humans, fled from the Pleiades and hid in our own solar system on Mars - an arguement developed in chapters 34 and 35.

The Murder of Reality

4 Firestar

*'I looked, and I saw a windstorm coming out of the north – an
immense cloud with flashing lightning and surrounded by brilliant
light. The centre of the fire looked like glowing metal,
and in the fire was what looked like four living creatures...'*
Ezekiel 1: 4-5, Holy Bible, New International Version, Gideon

*'God presides in the great assembly;
he gives judgment among the "gods".*
Psalm 82: 1, Holy Bible, New International Version, Gideon

The Egyptian noun 'Sabah-Kha' (Morning-Star) celebrates the 'Sabbath', paralleled to the 'Sabi priesthood' in combination with the 'angels' (caba). Appellation of 'caba', literally (messenger), is translated into Latin as the 'angelus' or 'host'. Semantically, the 'caba' interconnects with the 'mystery', and is derived from the Semitic verbal stem 'qbl' (to receive). Its root is from the Egyptian noun 'qeb' (a serpent), identified with the 'fallen angel' in situ to the priestess and her monthly cycle.

Surreptitious, the 'Kabbalah or Caballa' (to receive) outlines the 'hidden tradition of the Jews'[1] and originates from the Arabic transitive verb 'khabba' (to hide or conceal).[2] The 'Kabbalah' in essence specifies a 'secret oral tradition', received from an 'angelic source', conveyed through word groupings and etymological comparisons. Philological deconstruction of the 'Kabbalah' suggests 'khabba' (hidden), extracted from the Arabic etymon 'Qabila' or 'Qabili' (tribe).[3] Its origins are correlated with the descending 'host' (the caba). Evidence for this assertion is given in Exodus 24:15-17, quoted from the Gideon Bible:

> 'When Moses went up on the mountain, the cloud covered it, and the glory of the Lord settled on Mount Sinai. For six days the cloud covered the mountain, and on the seventh day the Lord called to Moses from within the cloud. To the Israelites the glory of the Lord looked like a consuming fire on top of the mountain'.

In the Hebrew text, Yahweh descends upon on Mount Sinai in an object called 'kabod', interpreted misleadingly as (a consuming or devouring fire). 'Kabod' in Modern Hebrew is rendered as the adjective 'kaved' (heavy) or alternatively as the noun 'koved' (heaviness).[4] 'Kaved' is deduced etymologically from 'kavod' (dignity),[5] implicit of 'divine ascendancy' from the 'Qabila'.

In the book of Ezekiel, the prophet described the 'kabod', quite literally as (a heavy thing), and recounts the object as 'luminous and radiating'. Biblical scholars translate 'kabod' dubiously as (glory). Ezekiel likened the phenomena to wheels within wheels[6] and considered the 'kabod' as a source of 'divine knowledge' (See Chapter header).

To summarize, the 'tribal group' (Qabila) is equated with 'divine descent' in relation to the 'kabod' and its 'concealment' (khabba).[7] Sexual combination between humans and the 'emissary' (caba), literally 'messenger', is identical to the appearance of a 'snake-hominid' (qeb-i), indexed in Latin as (draconiopides). Materialization of the 'angel' (caba) coincides with the beginning of 'menstruation'[8] (Hebrew le'-kabel, 'to-menstruate')[9], cognate with 'fertilization', Arabic 'habl' (pregnancy).[10]

In the Semitic traditions, 'ovulation' is envisaged as a 'rouge serpent' or a 'menstrual fish' an eel - insignia of the matriarchal line. Symbolized as the 'fire-star', the 'oracle' is distinguished by her 'period', coordinated through the cycle of the 'moon' and 'Venus', symmetrical with the 'Sabbath'.

'Qebhu' (firmament) depicted as the 'matri-arch'
symbolised as the 'dome' (qubbi) or 'vault' (qubba) of heaven

'Onset of the woman's period' (le'kabel) parallels the 'vault' of heaven (qubba), juxtaposed with divine 'conception' (habl). Hieroglyphic scribes link 'kabel' (the woman's cycle) with 'qebhu-sbau' (the night-sky or starry-firmament). 'Qebhu' (firmament) is taken from the Arabic etymon 'qubba' (vault), cogent with 'qubbi' (dome).[12] The 'vault' of heaven (qubba) is represented as the 'arching female' or a 'dome' (qubbi), associated liturgically with the 'woman's period' (kabel). Visualised as a matri-arch, her naval is the cornerstone of heaven.

Additionally, 'qebhu-sbau' is interpreted by Egyptologists as (the fresh waters of the stars).[11] A conservative translation, the phrase 'watery firmament', is annotated as the plural noun 'kabel-sbau' (the menstrual stars). This in occult tradition is known as (the fire-star) - a euphemism of the priestess' cycle. Archaically the woman's 'angelic' progeny (caba) is synonymous with the 'sky' (qebhu) - her 'menses' (kabel) mythologised as the 'sunset or clot of blood'. Marked as the sanguine disk, the emblem is recurrent of celestial 'pregnancy', esoteric of the 'Dog Star' (Al Kalb), twinned with the 'Evening-Star' - Venus .

The 'matri-arch' is pictured historically as the Goddess of the 'vault' (qubba), in Old Semitic 'qebhu', etymological to 'qeb-hu' (a water-snake). Metaphorically a sea serpent, the nocturne registers a menstruating eel, outlined in Egyptian lore as the deity Apophis - a Goddess of Conflict (Refer to Chapter 33 Scarlet Whores Menstrual Eels and Ejaculating Cobras).

Assignment of 'kabel' (menstrual blood) constitutes 'kaved' (heavy), identified in the book of Ezekiel with the 'glory' of God (kabod - a 'heavy object'). 'Kabel' further designates the Old Egyptian word 'Qeb-El', (a Serpent-God, an angel), a polymorph translated as a (a Seraph of Light). 'Qeb-El' otherwise 'Qeb-Ra' is adopted in English as the noun 'cobra' (Cob-Ra). Hooded, the uraeus corresponds with the rays of fire, pictured as droplets of blood, contiguous with the disk, dome and cervix.

The 'bloodied halo' illustrates the menstrual cycle - a clot of blood, equidistant with the 'sunset', grouped with the 'moon' and 'Venus'. Imagined as the 'fire-star', the 'red circle' is conjoined with the 'serpent' - a solar motif of the 'jinni or seraphim'. Fertile 'blood' extracted from the priestess' womb corresponds with 'light', consigned to the 'fire-star' - an appellation of the 'neophyte', sourced from the angelic 'group' (cabal). Bloodline of the scarlet priestess is identified with the 'Sabi' priestcraft[13] - cultic of the 'Sabbath', unified with the 'moon' and 'serpent'.

Islamic custom renders the 'seraph of heaven' (qeb-hu), literally 'water-snake', as the 'Muslim shrine of pilgrimage' (Kaaba), from the Arabic noun 'ka'b' or 'ka'ba' (cube). 'Ka'b' is transliterated into Hebrew as 'kubiya',[14] Greek 'kubos' written ostensibly in the hieroglyphs as 'qebhu' (firmament). Arcane, the 'cube' is a signifier of the 'night-sky'. Foundation of the 'Kaaba' resembles (a square), interchangeable with 'qubba' (vault) and 'qubbi' (dome). Elementally, the 'square and circle' pertain to the 'kingdom and matriarch', covert to the 'serpent and heaven'.

Religiously, the 'Kaaba' shrine denotes the 'Naval of the Earth', equated with the epicenter of the cosmos (circle). Linguistically, 'Kaaba' is relative to 'khabba' (concealment), grouped with 'kabel' (menses) from 'habl' (rope or cord).[15] 'Habl' is transliterated into English as (cable) and suggests the 'umbilical' cord from the Arabic homonym 'habl' (pregnancy).[16] Theologically, the heavenly 'cube' (ka'ba) designates the betrothal of the sibyl to a deity, imputed with human 'angelic' attributes (caba), reproduced as the menstrual fish or eel (qeb-hu).

In summary, the 'sacred house' of God, 'Kaaba', is likened to the 'temple or womb', conceptualized as 'qebhu' (heaven), signified as 'ka'ba' (cube) or 'qebhu' (water-snake). The Kaaba edifice accords in mystical Islam with sacred geometry, noted by Platonic scholars. Offspring of the 'dragon' or 'angel' annotated in the Apocrypha as 'illegitimate' castigate the 'scarlet whore' and her maternity, the 'cabal'. Provenance of the 'Judaic tradition' (the Kabbalah) is sourced from the 'tribal' offspring (the Qabili).[17] A secret 'cabal', the 'Qabili' ordains 'caba' (a messenger), defined as the 'host' - connected to the 'Kaaba' shrine. Philological, the 'caba' classifies 'qeb' (a serpent), disclosed as 'qebi' (an angel) - a being originating from the constellation 'Al Kalb' (Sirius).

Closely aligned, the 'Qabili' in principle are grouped in the Hebrew traditions with the 'Shebet or Shevet' (tribe),[18] known collectively as 'shabesh' (the bastards).[19] Disclosure of the 'Shebet' and its denomination, the 'Sabi' priesthood, mark their origin from 'saba' (the seven 'stars' of the Pleiades), correlated with angelic division between the 'host' (army) and Sirius. Incarnation of the 'fallen angels', the 'Qabili' memorialises the first Sabbath and the creation of man, sequenced with the 'Pleiades' and the 'Seven Stars'.

1   Mark Hedsel, Edited and with an Introduction by David Ovason, Magician, Magus or Initiate? The Zelator, The Secret Journals of Mark Hedsel, 1999, p70

2   Hippocrene English-Arabic, Arabic-English Dictionary, Hippocrene, New York, 2005, p57

3   Ibid, p131

4   Prolog, Pocket Bilingual Dictionary, English-Hebrew, Hebrew-English, Prolog, p183

5   Ibid, p110

6   Zecharia Sitchin, The Cosmic Code, Book VI (Earth Chronicles), Avon Books, 1998, p270

7   'Khabba' informs the English words 'cover' and 'covert'.

8   The author John A Keel in his momentous work the 'Mothman Prophecies' observed that the winged being, the Mothman, materialized primarily during the woman's cycle, and appeared to be attracted to the smell of blood. Keel notes that the phenomenon is similar to the North American Indian entity, the Thunderbird, in which warriors were assigned special duties to protect menstruating women.

9   Prolog, Pocket Bilingual Dictionary, English-Hebrew, Hebrew-English, 2003, p252 ['le'kabel' (to menstruate)]

10 Hippocrene English-Arabic, Arabic-English Dictionary, Hippocrene, New York, 2005, p184

11 Alan F. Alford, The Midnight Sun, The Death and Rebirth of God in Ancient Egypt, Eridu Books, 2004, p128 ['Qebhu-sbau' is sometimes written as 'qebhu-sabau'. Both are interpreted as (the starry firmament) or (fresh waters of the stars)].

12 Hippocrene English-Arabic, Arabic-English Dictionary, Hippocrene, New York, 2005, p264 [The Arabic noun 'qubba' (vault) and 'qubbi' (dome) is compared to the Syrian noun 'qubba' (hat) - a domed hat worn by an angelic being (See Chapter 26 The Six Foundations - illustration of Hermes, p251). Alternatively, the Egyptian scribes picture the 'dome' as (the vault of heaven), drawn as the woman's arched body (Refer to this chapter's illustration of matri-arch, p65)].

13 Progeny of the oracular priestess is combined sexually with the 'spitting cobra' - an emblem of the 'seraphim', equal to the 'flashing dragon'.

14 Prolog, Pocket Bilingual Dictionary, English-Hebrew, Hebrew-English, 2003, p94 [Hebrew 'kubiya' (cube) - an esoteric signifier of heaven. In Arabic 'ka'b' (cube) is connected to 'qubbi' (dome). Geometrically the 'dome and circle' fits inside of the 'square' and are aligned architecturally to the 'creator and heaven'].

15 Hippocrene English-Arabic, Arabic-English Dictionary, Hippocrene, New York, 2005, p184

16 Ibid

17 Ibid, p131

18 Prolog, Pocket Bilingual Dictionary, English-Hebrew, Hebrew-English, Prolog, 2003, p429

19 Ibid, p37 [Modern Hebrew 'le'shabesh' (to bastardise)]

5

The Fallen Tribe

'No one would have believed in the last years of the nineteenth century that this world was being watched keenly and closely by intelligences greater than man's and yet as mortal as his own; ... With infinite complacency men went to and fro over this globe about their little affairs, ... No one gave a thought to the older worlds of space as sources of human danger, or thought of them only to dismiss the idea of life upon them as impossible or improbable... Yet across the gulf of space, minds that are to our minds as ours are to those of the beasts that perish, intellects vast and cool and unsympathetic, regarded this earth with envious eyes, and slowly and surely drew their plans against us'.[1]

H. G. Wells, The War of the Worlds: Book 1, The Coming of the Martians, Chapter 1 The Eve of the War

Descent of the fallen angels in Semitic lore is commemorative of the first 'Sabbath' and the creation of man, aligned to the 'seven stars'. In the Hebrew tradition, the Egyptian noun 'saba' (star) is converted to 'Shabbat' (the holy day of rest), and originates from the Mesopotamian festival 'Shabattu'. The Hebrew root 'sbt' denotes physical (rest), in the third person past tense 'sabat' (he rested), and in the present tense 'sobet' (he rests).[2] The verbal stem 'sbt' is polymorphic and can alternatively mean (end) or indicate the action (to set right).

'Sbt's original use suggests a relationship between sleep (i.e. rest) and death, reiterated in the account of Genesis Chapter 2. Here God finishes creation on the seventh day and rests, whilst blessing the occasion and making it a holy day.[3]

Contextually, the verbal root 'sbt' (rest) is a guised reference to God's entourage, named as his host - an itinerant army conceptualized as an invading unit. The second part of this statement will be addressed shortly. 'Sbt' (to rest) initially implied a group, denoted by the similarity between the verb 'sabat' (he rested) and the Hebrew noun 'Shebet or Shevet' (a tribe or clan). Designation of 'Shebet' is from the Egyptian root 'Shabbat' (tribe),[4] coherent with '(t)sabaoth' (the host).

Celebration of God's creation is compared to conquest or mastery, reprised as the mystery. Theoretically, 'Shabbat' sanctions (the holy day of rest), affiliated to (a tribe or band) of nomads, referred to cryptically as the 'Shevet' or 'Shebet'. Traditions regarding the 'Shabbat' (tribe) and its origins are secret, conveyed through the 'Sabi' priesthood.

Enactment of the festival 'Shabbat' is linked to ancestral migration from the stars. 'Shabbat' is transliterated into English as the 'Sabbat(h)', derivative from the Akkadian word 'Shabattu'. Mesopotamian, the 'Shabattu' celebrates the monthly festival of the full moon - the symbol of the female cycle, paralleled to sexual conjugation. Jewish lore transposes the jubilee 'Shabattu', technically the 'Shabbat' (Sabbath) to the 'bride of Jehovah', referred to as 'Sekhina Matronit'.

In this meta-narrative, Yahweh's fiancée Matronit is depicted as roaming the earth, searching for her groom Jehovah. Prototypically, Sekhina is a female archetype, used as a religious symbol to herald the beginning of Shabbat, characterized theologically through marriage [of the serpent] with Israel.[5]

Mediation between the bride and groom specify the covenant of Abraham, transferred through the human-angelic line of kings, emblematic of the moon. The lunar device in the early history of the Israelites is a symbol of the priesthood, correlated with human angelic intercourse. Conciliated, the monarch's administration of Yahweh's Kingdom is proclaimed through ritual law, expatiated through the Sabbath.

Shabbat's decree celebrates procreation, formalized through a sexual covenant or marriage with God. This union is characterized in Arabic as 'suhbat' (sexual intercourse).[6] Philologically, 'suhbat' is closely assigned in the Egyptian Arabic to the noun 'sahba' (a friend, girlfriend or owner).[7]

'Subah' in Masonic vocabulary is used to indicate (a society, assembly or association), paralleled to the 'Sabi' priestcraft. They trace their origins from the Egyptian root 'Shabbat' Hebrew 'Shevet' (tribe). Relationship between 'suhbat' (coitus) and 'subah' (an assembly) is rendered in English as the homonym 'member', denoting (a phallus or a person belonging to a society). Esoterically this fraternity is known as the 'Illuminati' - a designation of the 'Sabian'.

In Arabic, 'Al Sab'a', recorded in English as 'Sabian', translates as (the people of the star) from 'Saba'ia' (the Star People). Reference to the 'Star People' appears in the Essene commentary, specified in the obscure text the 'Damascus Document'. Here, the prophet predicted is named as the 'Interpreter of the Law' and called the 'Star', adduced with the 'Prince' from the Line of David - the 'Sceptre'.[8]

Adoption of the 'star' motif distinguishes the royal line, descended from the 'Sabian' priesthood. Depicted as a warring faction or an elite warrior class, the 'Sabi' priests are equated with the 'host and serpent'. Observed as the 'luminary', the Star of Israel is identified with the 'Children of Light' (the Sabi). Historically the 'Sabi' (a child or priest) resembles the 'Shebet' (tribe), cognate with the Morning-Star (Sabah-Kha), accrued with the Messianic covenant. The Hebrew noun for a 'star' (kokhba) is a play on the Aramaic title 'Kokh Bar' (Son of the Law) connoting the 'fallen star'.

Within the Semitic tradition, the 'serpent' is depicted as a 'conquering army' (the tsabaoth), rendered from the Modern Hebrew noun 'saba', 's'baot' or 'sabaoth'. Philologically, 'tsabaoth' is a derivation from 'tsevet' (crew)[9] and technically specifies (a crew of a ship or vessel). Judaic lore casts the 'tsabaoth' as (an army of a boat or a naval itinerant), explicit of 'saba' (a star or host).

The Hebrew word 'tsaba', spelt alternatively as 'tsava' or 'saba', translates as (army, soldiers or warfare)[10] and is related to the Semitic root 'tvila' (wet or immersion). Conceptual to the angelic mariner, the etymon 'tsaba' is preserved in the hieroglyphic vocabulary. For example, the Egyptian word 'tchaba' denoting (an army or soldiers)[11] is cognizant with 'tsabagi' (a flood or immersion). Paired conceptually together, the terms 'tchaba' and 'tsabagi' infers a fleet of naval ships in relation to the heavens. Theban priests incorporated the theme of the solar vessel with deity worship. Prosaically, the 'sky' is described as the 'duat' (the upper ocean) from the Semitic etymon 'duad' (two), implying the dual waters.

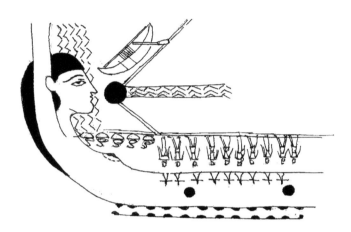

Depiction of the 'duat' is esoteric of the 'double waters' - fresh and salt.
The 'qebhu' (firmament) is symbolised as a woman's body, duplicated as the 'water snake' (qeb-hu).

Esoteric Hebrew equates the 'tsabaoth' (host) with the 'shibboleth' (a stream, flow or flood). Its root is observed in the Egyptian radical 'shabareth' (river or stream), cognate with 'tsaba' (immersion).[12] 'Shibboleth' (river) contains a number of complex puns in the Old Semitic. For example, 'shibboleth' plays on the Semitic expression 'shibi-lev' (to have a satiated heart),[13] a concept grouped religiously with the 'Sibulla or Sabi' priesthood.

'Shibboleth' in the pharaonic lexicon is similar to 'sibbolet' (a grain of corn), employed in the Egyptian, Greek and Persian mystery schools as a simile of the 'starry firmament'. Priests imagined the universe as abundant and full of life, the stars as generative seeds, suggesting an ancient belief in extra terrestrial life. According to classical mythology, the 'vault of heaven' is imagined as a 'ford', 'river', 'fertile plane' or 'field'. Philological comparison between 'shibboleth' (river) and 'sibbolet' (grain) indicates early farming practices, connected to the 'irrigation of water' and the worship of 'fertility Gods'.

Astrologically, 'Shibboleth' (the water causeway) suggests the Milky Way - a covert symbol of the angelic 'contract'. An anagram, the 'shibboleth' discloses the 'shi'a-bariyth', alternatively the 'shari-bariyth' (the majestic or legal covenant).[14]

In the book of Judges 12:5-6, the division between Jephthah and Ephraim[15] is sealed contractually with the blood of the Ephraimites, to quote:

> *'The Gileadites captured the fords of the Jordan leading to Ephraim, and whenever a survivor of Ephraim said, "Let me cross over," the men of Gilead asked him, "Are you an Ephraimite?" If he replied, "No," they said, "All right, say 'Shibboleth'." If he said, "Sibboleth", because he could not pronounce the word correctly, they seized him and killed him at the fords of the Jordan...'*

Written in esoteric language, the parable details the angelic wars between men and deities in opposition to the 'shibboleth' (river), designating the 'shi'a-bariyth' (contract). An historical narrative, the incident documents a division within the priesthood itself and the reversal of the covenant.

Initiation into the covenant, covertly the 'shibboleth or shi'a-bariyth' recollects the 'Sabi' priests, symbolized through 'tsaba or tvila' (immersion). Ritual, sprinkling of water registers the 'tsabaoth' a diversification of 'sabaoth' (the host). A stream of knowledge indicates the angelic sailor, idiomatic of baptism and ritual bathing. Submersion of the 'initiate' concurs with a 'soldier of the Lord'. 'Shibboleth' (river) signals the 'Sibulla or Shibulla' (a Priestess or Oracle). The 'Sibyl' is coordinated in Arabic with her offspring the 'sulbi', extracted from the 'Sabi' (priest) - an ancient bloodline originating from heaven (the Pleiades).

Similar themes pertaining to divine ascendancy are highlighted in the Zulu language. The Sangoma (medicine man) Mutwa in an interview with Rick Martin during September 1999 highlighted the relationship between the Zulu nations and their ancestral heritage, connected to the stars. Kingship in the Zulu legends is attributed with nomadic descent from angels. To quote verbatim:

> *'When you ask a South African white anthropologist what the name of Zulu means, he will say it means 'the sky', and therefore the Zulu call themselves 'people of the sky'. That sir, is nonsense. In the Zulu language, our name for the sky, the blue sky, is 'sibakabaka'. Our name for inter-planetary space, however, is 'izulu' and... 'weduzulu', which means 'inter-planetary space, the dark sky that you see with stars in it every night', also has to do with travelling sir.*

> *[For example] the Zulu word for travelling at random, like a nomad or gypsy, is 'izula'. Now, you can see that the Zulu people in South Africa [are] aware of the fact that you can travel through space, not through the sky, like a bird, but you can travel through space, and the*

Zulus claim that many, many thousands of years ago, arrived out of the skies, a race of people... who married their daughters... and produced a powerful race of Kings and tribal Chiefs... [16]

It is with Credo's profound observations that this chapter is drawn to a close. The next section examines the history of the host - a military group of renegade angels, referred to as the Illuminati (Sabi). Historically, a belligerent organization, the 'Illuminati', have assimilated themselves into human culture through the conquest of the matriarch!

1   H.G. Wells, The War of the Worlds, Classics Omnibus Edition, Wilco Publishing House, 2007, p95

2   Guy Deutscher, The Unfolding of Language, William Heinemann, 2005, p171

3   'Yahweh' (God) is depicted theologically as a 'being' - his name extracted from the verb (to be). Consistently throughout Judaic scripture, 'Yahweh' is enunciated as the 'living God'.

4   Ralph Ellis, Eden in Egypt, A Translation of the Book of Genesis out of the Original Egyptian Text, Edfu Books, 2005, p312 [Appendix A5 - Dictionary 'Shebet or Shabbat' (a Tribe)]

5   Laurence Gardner, Genesis of the Grail Kings, Bantam Books, 2000, p160

6   Ferozsons Urdu-English Dictionary, Revised edition, Ferozsons Ltd, Lahore, pp478-479

7   M.A. Abdel-Hady, Egyptian Arabic Phrasebook, Rough Guide, Lexus, 1998, p242

8   Michael Baigent & Richard Leigh, The Dead Sea Scrolls Deception, Arrow Books, 2001, p221

9   Prolog, Pocket Bilingual Dictionary, English-Hebrew, Hebrew-English, Prolog, 2003, p92

10 Ralph Ellis, Eden in Egypt, A translation of the Book of Genesis out of the Original Egyptian Text, Edfu Books, 2005, p274 (Appendix A5 - Dictionary)

11 Egyptologists transliterate the Semitic word 'tsava' (army) as 'tchaba' in the Pharaonic vocabulary. Constantly, scholars change the spelling of the Egyptian hieroglyphs to conceal the Semitic root of the language.

12 Ralph Ellis, Eden in Egypt, A Translation of the Book of Genesis out of the Original Egyptian Text, Edfu Books, 2005, p78

13 Hippocrene English-Arabic, Arabic-English Dictionary, Hippocrene, New York 2005, p285 ['Shibi or Shab'an' (to be satisfied with food or to have one's fill)].

14 Ibid, pp284-285 [I have translated 'Shi'a' as (Majestic). Its literal meaning however is (a beam of light or ray), cognate with the Persian titular 'Sah' (a King)].

15 The 'Gileadites' refer to 'Gil-ad' Arabic (the resurrected generation), antithetical to the 'Ephraim' - an angelic bloodline. Ephraim's name is derived from 'ef'e' (an asp).

16 Michael Tellinger, Slave Species of God, Music Masters, South Africa, 2005, p553

6

Tsabaoth the Army of the Lord

'Now war arose in heaven, Michael and his angels fighting against the dragon; and the dragon and his angels fought, but they were defeated and there was no longer any place for them in heaven. And the great dragon was thrown down, that ancient serpent, who is called the devil and Satan, the deceiver of the whole world – he was thrown down to the earth; and his angels were thrown down with him'.

Revelation 12: 7-9, Holy Bible, New English Version

Traditions of the 'host' are assimilated linguistically with the 'watcher' (Hebrew tsofe)[1] identical with the 'tsabaoth' or the 'fallen dragon'. Depicted as a conquering army, the 'tsabaoth' is a derivation from 'tsevet' (crew)[2] and designates (a crew of a ship or vessel). Judaic tradition casts the 'tsabaoth' as (an army of a boat or a naval itinerant) - a term cognate with the Sabi priesthood. Collectively the 'Star People' (the Sabi) are identified with the 'tsabaoth' and the 'illuminati'.

'Tsabaoth' (Hebrew for a crewmember) is a permutation on the Egyptian vernacular 'tchaba' (meaning army or soldiers), transliterated from the Semitic classification 'tsaba'.[3] 'Tchaba' is deduced from the Egyptian denomination 'tcheba' (ten thousand), indicative of an army commander.[4] Translated into Latin as 'Legion', the unit represents a commander of fallen angels, referred to as (the multitude or host).

In the early Egyptian lexicon, 'tcheba' suggests ground troops or infantry, as 'tchaba' is related to the word 'tcheb' (meaning spear, harpoon or stab).[5] The title 'tchoeb' signifies a commander of ten thousand troops (tcheba), rendered in the Bible as 'Joab' - the name of King David's commander.[6] His Egyptian epithet signifies a commander of an 'army' (tchaba), consistent with the pharaonic title 'djeba' (a leader of troops) - possibly the same word.

In Judaic traditions, the 'tsabaoth' is aligned to 'tevach' (slaughter), established in the Egyptian lexicon as 'tabach' (to slaughter or butcher) from 'tchaba or tsaba' (an army). 'Tevach' is provident in the Modern Arabic 'tabach' (to ruin or disfigure). A variant of the idiom 'tabach' appears in the Semitic root 'tabakh' (the verb to cook),[7] implicit of ritual immolation and bloodshed.

Philologically, 'tabach' (butcher) is similar to the pharaonic term 'djebaka' (to slaughter, slay or kill),[8] cogent with 'djeba' (a leader of troops) and 'djabhu' (to pray, beg or petition).[9] In Modern Semitic, 'djeba' is related to the stem 'd-b-r' [read as 'debar'] (to guide, manage, control or lead out)[10] defined in the Torah as the Exodus. 'Debar' (to control) translates into the Greek as 'kubernao' (to steer), a nautical term referring to a ship or governance comparative to the host.

In ancient Arabic, 'debar' (to guide) is symmetrical with 'dabah' (to kill or slaughter).[11] 'Dabah' informs 'dabh' (a sacrifice),[12] expositional in the Indo-European languages of 'diabolos' (a devil)[13] from the Sanskrit root 'div' and 'deva'. Progeny of the 'dejeba' (commander) conveys the Arabic plural noun 'diyab' (wolf),[14] otherwise a 'dog soldier' - a covert symbol of the djinn (jinn). This race of beings is consistent with the Dog Star Sirius[15] and share similar characteristics with the host.

Crest of Saunderson of Lincolnshire based on a drawing circa 1590

Dialectically 'djeba' (a leader of troops) [Arabic debar] contrasts with its allomorph 'tchaba' (Hebrew 'tsaba' - an army). 'Tsaba' is partnered in the ancient Egyptian with the stem 'tsab' (a covered wagon).[16] Philological comparison suggests 'tsab' distinguishes a type of sailing vessel, demonstrated in the Hebrew noun 'tebah or tevah' (an ark). 'Tebah' specifies a 'boat' homologous to 'tsabaoth' (a crew of a ship). The idea of a sailing vessel characterized as a 'chariot' or a 'covered wagon' is further referenced in the book of Ezekiel and is coherent with the solar (stellar) vessel.

Jewish lore regards the 'chariot' as a symbol of concealed knowledge, known as 'Merkabah' mysticism,[17] drawn from the Hebrew office 'Mebakker' (a Bishop), equivalent to the Syrian root 'mrabba' (educated).[18] The 'vessel or chariot' (Heb. merkava)[19] connotes the angelic conqueror. In the book of Ezekiel, the prophet refers to the vehicle of God as the 'merkabah or merkava' (chariot). As a polymorph, 'merkava' encodes 'mar-hava' (a fallen-saint) a bloodline derived from 'mar' (a serpent). There are additional puns with regards to God's Chariot 'Merkabah'. The Semitic word 'merkabah' expresses 'mebakkoth' the feminine principle of 'b-k-h' (to weep or bewail). God's crewmembers, the 'tsabaoth' are portrayed as the harbingers of death, personified in classical mythology as the wailing siren or harpy, equal in Judaic tradition to the singing host.

Identification of the 'tsabaoth' (a naval crew) allied with 'tsva'i' (the military)[20] is adduced also from the Roman language. 'Tsabaoth' is translated into the Medieval Latin as 'hostis' or 'host' (an army), extracted from the ancient Greek 'oseeos' (holy). In the Roman Church, the angelic 'host - Arabic debar' (a leader) is correlated with sacrificial death of the 'hostia' (Arabic dabh), understood as the 'victim'. The 'victima' is matched in Hebrew with the etymon 'korban' (a victim),[21] explicit of (a sacrifice).[22]

Early practices of razing an enemy's city are traced to the worship of deities, associated with warfare, evident in the Syrian dialect 'raiz' (rage or annoyance).[23] Old Testament reference to the God of the Hebrews describes him in the plural as 'the Lord of the Host'. His conquest parallels the 'subjugation' (slm) of man. The 'surrender' of humanity (slm) is a synonym of the verbal root 'shomer' (a keeper). God and his Elohim are depicted as conquerors of the world(s) and the domesticator of man.

Mediation between the host and mankind specifies a religious 'covenant' (the bariyth - Modern Hebrew brit[h]), cultic of the 'shibboleth' (river) - Refer to Chapter 5 the Fallen Tribe. In Old Semitic, the contract is described as 'Brit-An' (Britain) and refers to the (Covenant of Heaven). Muslim scholars argue the covenant of God is commensurate with 'sallim' religious (submission),[24] a homonym of 'salam' (peace).[25] Salam is relative to 'sama' (heaven)[26] and 'samah' (to forgive).[27] Unequivocal, the 'surrender or resignation of oneself' is expressed in Arabic as (aslama), transliterated into English as (Islam).

Early accounts of the 'Elohim' plural (the Gods) imply a military dictator-ship, characteristic of invasion and conquest. Historically the capitulation of man is attributed to the 'angelic crew' (the tsabaoth) conceived as (the host). Itinerants, the sailors are annotated in Aramaic as 'zari', translated (alien, stranger or foreigner), relative in Arabic to 'zau' (light) - Hebrew 'zohar' (shine).[28] The noun 'zau' is constant with the Arabic classification 'Zuhrah, alternatively Zohra' (Venus)[29] and 'zuhr' (early afternoon prayer), signalled with the Evening Star. Described as the light bringer or the fallen daystar, 'Zuhrah' is bracketed in Greek with 'sauros' (lizard).

'Sauros' is deduced from the Syrian etymon 'zar' (an alien), indexed in Hebrew as (a foreigner),[30] and appears in the Modern Hebrew locution 'khayzar' (a space alien).[31] The compound 'Khay-zar' is read literally as (a star-alien). Epigraphically 'kha' is registered as (a star) and is consistent with 'khai' (of or from the stars), annotated in the English as (a star-man).

Technically, 'khayzar' (a star man, otherwise an alien) appears in the Greek name 'Kaisar', rendered in the Latin as 'Caesar'. Kaisar's esoteric name reiterates the connection between the angelic lineage of the Emperor in conjunction with heaven.

In the hieroglyphic, 'kha' (a star) is grouped with the terms 'qara' and 'kher', used to denote (war), in comparison to the fallen host, depicted as the star or the sovereign. Advent of the star 'Venus' is iconic of the destruction of the earth, collaborative of angelic victory and the development of the monarchy.

Philologically, 'kha' (a star) is interchangeable with the Sumerian title 'Kar' (a king or angel), defined in the original tongue as (a hunter). The epithet 'Kar' is cognizant with the Hebrew word 'kary' (soldier)[32] archaically the 'multitude or host'. 'Kar and kari' is rendered in Medieval English as the noun 'quarry' (to hunt).

Greek statue of 'Kar' (Horus) - the hunter in Roman military dress

Alliteration of 'Kar' and 'Kari' is transferred into English as 'Royal and Warrior' alternatively 'King and Killing'. The Sumerian titular 'Kar' (Sovereign) provides the immediate root of the name 'Horus', transliterated in the hieroglyphs as 'Kar or Har' (hunter), represented by the Royal falcon. A migratory bird, the hawk, denotes the host the 'peregrinus', defined in Latin as (an alien).[33]

An initiate, the 'Sabi' of the (star) cults 'saba' are referred to variously as 'Sabi' (a child). They are grouped with the 'akh zauri' (illuminati) - collaborations of the 'khayzar' listed as (the star man) or (the Emperor - 'Kaisar'). Rendition of the 'Kaisar' in the Semitic augments the term 'khasar guf' (an incorporeal)[34] form. 'Khayzar' is indexed in the Old Persian with 'Ksaytiya' (a King), shortened in the Late Persian as 'Sah - Arabic Shah'. Abbreviated, the title is transcribed into the Cyrillic script as 'Tsar' - variegations of 'stellar and star'.

To summarize, the 'enlightened or shining one' is identical to the 'dragon' (flash) or angel, catalogued in apocalyptic literature as the 'akh-zari'. Gnostic scholars mistranslated the appellation as the (brothers of light) from the Arabic corruption 'akh-zauri'. Theoretical in the Latin to the 'illuminati', the 'akh-zauri' is cultic of the 'akh-zari' - a term connoting human angelic offspring literally (alien or visitor). Classification of the 'akh-zari' is read in the original Syrian as (a brother of an alien) - a title interchangeable with an (angel), implicit of a 'King' written as (Shah or Sah).

Lake Lucerne, Switzerland, June 2007, author's photo (UFO reconstruction)

Cryptically, there are additional wordplays at work in the Aramaic titular 'akh-zari' connoting deity offspring. In the Hebrew language, 'akh-zari' is rendered as the compound 'akhzari' (cruel)[35] and is preserved in the Latin. Tributaries regarding the 'hostia' literally (victim or sacrifice)[36] is attributed to the worship of the 'host'. Semantically God's 'crew' is cruel and the 'host' hostile. The 'host' is mutual with the Latin adjective 'hosticus' (foreign or strange i.e. alien), relative to 'hostis' (an enemy).[37] Similarly, in the Hebrew 'tsabaoth' is identified with 'zva'a' (horror).[38]

In summary, synoptic references in contemporary culture to 'alien vessels' in the modern vernacular (a UFO) is matched with a much older orthodoxy. The epithet 'zari' (an alien) translates in the Modern Arabic as (a visitor)[39] and is identical to (the crewmember) - the 'tsabaoth'. Both are described as angelic and latent with the modern phenomenon of the 'star-ship' in accordance with the Hebrew philology 'kalalit'.[40] Pictured in Judaic accounts, the 'kalalit' describe large vessels literally (space-ships) floating upon the waters of space.

1   Prolog, Pocket Bilingual Dictionary, English-Hebrew, Hebrew-English, Prolog, 2003, p455 (The 'v' sometimes written as an 'f' is very close to the 'b' sound, observed in written Arabic).

2   Ibid, p92

3   Ibid, p28 ['Tsaba' (Army)]

4   Ralph Ellis, Eden In Egypt, A Translation of the Book of Genesis out of the Original Egyptian Text, Edfu Books, 2005, p250

5   Ibid, p274 (Appendix A5 - Dictionary)

6   Ibid (Appendix A5 - Dictionary)

7   M.A. Abdel-Hady, Egyptian Arabic Dictionary, Lexus, 2002, p72

8   Ralph Ellis, Eden in Egypt, A Translation of the Book of Genesis out of the Original Egyptian Text, Edfu Books, 2005, p308 (Appendix A5 - Dictionary)

9   Ibid, p309 (Appendix A5 - Dictionary)

10 John M. Allegro, The Sacred Mushroom and the Cross, A Study of the Nature and Origins of Christianity within the Fertility Cults of the Ancient Near Middle East, Abacus, 1970, p75

11 Hippocrene English-Arabic, Arabic-English Dictionary, Hippocrene, New York, 2005, p64

12 Ibid, p105

13 'Dabble' in magic or a 'dab hand' is esoteric of 'dabh' (a sacrifice).

14 Hippocrene English-Arabic, Arabic-English Dictionary, Hippocrene, New York, 2005, p141

15 Hitler's name 'Adolph' designates (a wolf - e.g. Sirius) and is consistent in Roman mythology with the birth of Remus and Romulus - the progenitors of the Roman Empire.

16 Ralph Ellis, Eden in Egypt, A translation of the Book of Genesis out of the Original Egyptian Text, Edfu Books, 2005, p279 (Appendix A5 - Dictionary)

17 Alix de Saint, Translated from the French by Elfreda Powell, The Good Angel Guide, For Reluctant Sinners, 1999, p114 [Transliterated into English as 'merkabah' (a chariot) - the word is written in Hebrew as 'merkava'].

18 Hippocrene English-Arabic, Arabic-English Dictionary, Hippocrene, New York, 2005, p244

19 Prolog Pocket Bilingual Dictionary, English-Hebrew-Hebrew-English, Prolog, 2003, p63

20 Ibid, p255

21 Ibid, p448

22 Ibid, p352

23 Hippocrene English-Arabic, Arabic-English Dictionary, Hippocrene, New York, 2005, p267

24 Ibid, p121 ['Sallim' (submit)]

25 Ibid, p88

26 Ibid, p278

27 Ibid, p278 ['Samah' (forgive) is also a homonym meaning (to allow)].

28 Prolog Pocket Bilingual Dictionary, English-Hebrew-Hebrew-English, Prolog, 2003, p368

29 Ferozsons Urdu-English Dictionary, A Comprehensive Dictionary of Current Vocabulary, (Revised Edition), Ferozsons Ltd, Lahore, p418

30 Prolog Pocket Bilingual Dictionary, English-Hebrew-Hebrew-English, Prolog, 2003, p158

31 Ibid, p20

32 Ralph Ellis, Eden in Egypt, A Translation of the Book of Genesis out of the original Egyptian Text, Edfu Books, 2005, p308 (Appendix A5 - Dictionary)

33 John C Traupman PhD, The New College Latin & English Dictionary, Bantam, 1988, p341

34 Prolog Pocket Bilingual Dictionary, English-Hebrew-Hebrew-English, Prolog, 2003, p202

35 Ibid, p93

36 John Traupman PhD, The New College Latin & English Dictionary, Bantam, 1988, p133

37 Ibid

38 Prolog Pocket Bilingual Dictionary, English-Hebrew-Hebrew-English, Prolog, 2003, p191

39 Hippocrene English-Arabic, Arabic-English Dictionary, Hippocrene, New York, 2005, p314 ['Zar' (verb to visit)]

40 Prolog Pocket Bilingual Dictionary, English-Hebrew-Hebrew-English, Prolog, 2003, p384

7

Al-Khidr

'Here lies the Devil – ask no other name.
Well – but you mean Lord?
Hush! We mean the same'.
On a Lord: Samuel Taylor Coleridge

'And did the countenance divine
Shine forth upon our clouded hills?
And was Jerusalem builded here
Among these dark satanic mills?'
Jerusalem: William Blake

Throughout ancient sources, the monarch and the line of prophets are depicted as mediators of heaven (host) and earth (man) - their progeny demigods. Liken to an invading force, the angels are connected to the destruction of the earth. In Greek mythos, this annihilation is described as 'kataklusmos' (a cataclysm), derived from 'klumos' (flood). Destruction of man and later the rebirth of the state is aligned to angelic intervention, paralleled to the Sabi and the 'tsabaoth' (host).

The ship is a symbol of divine birthright, traced through the lineage of Noah and Moses, presented in mythology as the basket. The term 'naval' denoting (a crew of a ship) is contiguous with 'navel' (the stomach, womb or center) nominal of the shrine and 'omphalos-stone' Greek (a navel). In Hebrew, naval denudes 'navi - Arabic nabi' (prophet)[1] - a bloodline descended from an angel.

Semantically, member-ship, lord-ship, king-ship, scholar-ship, wor-ship and relation-ship implies 'mal'akh' (an angel) in collusion with 'malakh' (a sailor), suppositional of 'melekh' (a king). Recreation of man and society in the image of the host is predicated on a secret covenant (government), conceived through human angelic offspring (king-ship).

Statecraft describes the 'government' adduced from the Latin transitive verb 'gubernare' (to rule or steer)[2] and signifies 'gubernator' (a navigator of a boat).[3] 'Gubernare' is a Latinisation of the Greek 'kubernao' (to steer a boat), vocabulary associated with the angelic host. The ruler rendered in Arabic as 'Sultan' parallels the Hebrew term 'shilton' (government),[4] essentially identified with the fallen angels - the 'S(h)atani'.

'Satan, Hebrew shatan' (to oppose) suggests that the government is adversarial and bipartisan, likened or conceived in the image of Satan. In the Bible, the designation Satan is used to describe a political faction of David. So in the book of 1 Samuel (29:4), David is himself referred to as a 'Satan' literally (an adversary) of the Philistines.[5] The same themes are evident also in Islam.

In Arabic, 'Satan' is interchangeable with 'Sultan' (a ruler or power) from 'saluta' (to rule). His bloodline is affiliated with the 'klippoth' (a demon) from the etymon 'klipa' (shell)[6] - a distinction rudimentary to the lineage of the 'Caliph'.

Muslims refer to Mohammed as 'the Messenger' an assignment used in Greek and Latin to denote an 'angel'. In Catholicism, the shell motif symbolizes a saint - an etymology self-referential to the 'Shatani' bloodlines, identified with the 'klippoth' and Caliph. The seashell is a symbol of Venus and is a marker of Royal ancestry, equated with the priesthood. For a fuller and complete definition of Caliph, refer to my next book Shapeshifter the Serpent Unveiled.

The 'Satanic bloodline administers 'shilton' (government) and is a concept replicated in classical myth. 'Diabolus' the Greek word signifying (the devil)[7] conceals 'Boule' the Hellenistic name for (the Senate). 'Diabolus' operates as a clever pun on 'dia-boule' (through the Senate), analogous in Hebrew to 'Satan and shilton'. Boule is extrapolated from the Semitic cognomen 'Baal' (Lord), equal to 'bar'har' (sailor) titular of the Canaanite God. Allegorically, the Government is an agency of the devil and is linked to the lineage of the Shatani, epitomized through the division of man.

'Combatant', 'adversarial' or 'the opposer' are all other names for the fallen race, registered in Greek as the 'agonia' (contestant), cognizant of agony, equated with the 'Shatani'. The theme of opposition between man and angel is recorded in the Greek etymology 'gonos' (to race), comparative to 'agon' (a contest), translated into English respectively as 'race' (competition) and 'race' (bloodline).

Segregation between deity and man are reinforced through the political system. Parliament denotes the French verb 'parlé' (to speak) a pun on the Hebrew word 'Par-o' (Pharaoh), Sanskrit 'pala' (king).[8] Parliament, historically the Senate, is termed as the Upper and Lower Legislature a symbol of heaven and earth. In English, the 'Lower House' is referred to as the 'Commons', translated from the Latin adjective 'plebeius' (common, low or vulgar),[9] specific of man. The appellation Commons is procured from the Latin 'comans' the adjective (hairy, longed haired or plumed) signifiers associated with the 'mammal'.[10]

In the political world of Islam, the cognomen 'si'a' (party) transliterated into English as 'Shiah', are a faction symbolized with 'sha'r' (hair) - a designation of man, relegated to the 'Commons'.

Assignment of the 'Shiah' specifies 'siyasa' (politics)[11] - recurrent of the fallen angel. Appointment of the Shiah concords with 'sira' (boat), Greek 'Kubernao' (a navigator), and is a classification of the 'host' and 'government'. Adversarial, the 'si'a' are covertly recognizant with 'sihr' (sorcery) and 'sirr' (mystery), connoting 'se'irim' (a demon or goat). Technically, the Secretary (Secret-ary) describes a guardian of secrets, attributed to the Shatani and the se'irim.

Appellation of the se'irim is reproduced from the Old Semitic noun 'seir' (red), concomitant in Hebrew with the etymon 'se'ar' (hair)[12] - Arabic 'sha'r'.[13] Archaically the human-angelic line is differentiated with 'hair', correlated with 'seir' (a sanguine goat) - a symbol of the mammal (man). 'Sha'r' the Arabic signifier (hair) covertly implies (wicked), rendered 'shar',[14] equated with the fallen line the 'Shiah'.[15] The term 'shar' (evil)[16] is abbreviated from the Syrian intransitive verb 'sha'al' (to burn)[17] - indicative of the burnt offering.[18]

Goat wearing red vestaments with scallop shell discursive of the woman's genitalia / a demon. The dog is a symbol of the altar and suggests the temple shrine (Diablerie, detail- After Cornelis Saftleven).

The se'irim's testimonial line the Shiah is angelic. Relationship between the se'irim and deity is demonstrated in the Sumerian noun 'zu' (a winged demon). In Old Persian, the word is cross-referenced with 'zu' (bird), specified in the Greek as 'zoion' (an animal). The Sumerian epithet 'zu' (a fallen deity) reflects the Arabic root 'zau' (light), identified with 'seir' (red).[19] Annotation of the 'zu', 'se'irim' or 'zoion' is consistent genealogically with the 'shia(h) or si'a' (a religious party). Ancestry of the shiah earmarks 'zar' (an alien), lateral to 'sah' (a king).

'Zoion' classifies an animal or being from heaven and is utilized as an astrological notation of the 'zodiac animals' from the Greek compound 'zoidiakos'. Specification of 'zoidiakos' pertains to the Hellenistic root 'zoidion' (an animal effigy or a sculptured animal figure). Philological evidence suggest celestial animals personify deity characteristics associated with angelic (alien) entities.

Permutation on the Indo-European root 'zoion' (animal) is symmetrical in Hebrew with the angel cult of 'Siyon' (Zion) transposed from 'se'irim'.

'Sira' (boat) emphasizes the angelic 'se'irim', enumerated in the Sumerian philology 'zu' (demon). The noun 'zu' is compatible etymologically in Arabic with 'zari' (alien). A symbol of governance, the ship interconnects to the development of religion founded upon written laws.

'Safinah' the alternative noun for (boat) is compared in Arabic to the title 'sarif' (a noble) from 'sarafa' (exalted). Origin of the 'sarif' is analogous to the angelic or sailor's lineage the seraphim, cognate with 'seraph' (snake). In Hebrew, the 'sarif' constitutes the Semitic noun 'sefel' (cup) and conveys the 'mystery' (evening meal), addendum with the angel (seraphim) and votive. Symbolically the cup is paired with the basket (boat) and tallies with the menstrual womb.

Marriage of St. Catherine, 1479, Central part of triptych, detail, Hans Memling.
The image depicts the 'sarif' (noble) holding the Serpent Grail equated with 'sefel' (cup).

'Sarif' (literally lord-ship) is a variant of 'sheriff' and 'sharif'. In Egyptian Arabic, the vocabulary is matched with the verbal stem 'shaf' (to see),[20] symbolic of the dragon. Historically the sharif are descendents of Mohammed through the line of 'Fatima' in Arabic (chaste) an adaptation of 'Fatih-ma' (not-light) a sign of the Bath Kol. Fatima's name infers Mohammed's lineage is divine and angelic.

Islamic commentaries note the 'sharif' class as possessing the green veil or turban - a reference to the Koranic angel 'Al-Khidr' (the Green One). A messenger, he is a harbinger of death. Al-Khidr corresponds in the Egyptian mysteries with the deity Osiris, seated upon a throne of water. Osiris is reproduced as a green man, embalmed in a snakeskin.

The angelic being Al-Khidr described in Sura 18:64-82 is responsible for meeting both Mohammed and Moses.[21] A clue to Al-Khidr's enigmatic title is preserved in the Aramaic language. In Old Arabic, there are no words to describe good and bad. The closest signifiers employed are the words 'ripe and unripe' equal to (good and bad). Green 'unripe' epitomizes 'evil' and is picked up in the Latin adjective 'crudus' (bloody, cruel or merciless), appended with the meaning raw, unripe or green.[22] Esoterically, Al-Khidr is reminiscent of the reaper, associated with death.

Al-Khidr's Arabic name is punned with 'al'-kadi'[23] (a judge) from 'kada' (to judge), and is related to the verb 'qad' (to lead).[24] The play on Al-Khidr and al-kadi further extends in Modern Arabic to the political usage of the terrorist cell 'Al Qaeda' literally (data) denoting (Intelligence). Originally, 'qaeda' specified (Divine Revelation) and is linked to sacrificial death.

'Al Qadr' (the Night of Glory) refers to Meccan Sura 97 and records the evening of the first Revelation, imparted by Gabriel. 'Al Qadr' conceptually links the messenger Gabriel with 'Al-Khidr' (the Green One). The point is reiterated in Christian orthodoxy, in which Gabriel is availed in green vestments. Al-Khidr's namesake is symmetrical in Greek to Arcadia - a variation of Akkad and specifies the secret priesthood equated with the nocturnal angel.

Documented in the Koran, the figure Al-Khidr teaches Mohammed through a series of incidents. One such episode includes killing an 'innocent' child - an action met with the prophet's consternation. Khidr later chooses to extricate himself from the Messenger's company for his lack of comprehension. In the text of the Koran, Mohammed is chastised for asking too many questions.

Conclusion to the prophet's partnership with the angelic figure is registered in the Arabic. The name 'Khidr' (Green) is an anagram of the Hebrew word 'khadal or khadar' meaning (end, cease or seal)[25] and is from the Egyptian idiom 'khatam' (to finish, end or seal). 'Khadal' is also reminiscent of the Hebrew word 'Khaddar' the name of (Eve), indicative of the fall. Symbolism of the woman parallels Mohammed's doubts towards Al-Khidr, culminating in a cessation or break in the prophet's relationship with the angel. Severance of terms with Al-Khidr is commensurate with Eve.

Al-Khidr by nature is duplicitous and his appearance alludes to Venus, the fallen 'Morning Star' (Lucifer the Light Bringer), cited in the Latin vocabulary. The Roman intransitive verb 'cadere' (to fall) indicates the angel Khidr. Application of 'cadere' in Latin is translated as (slain, die, be sacrificed) and is similar to the transitive verb 'caedere' (to hack at, chop, to strike, to beat, to fell, cut down, cut off, cut to pieces, kill or murder).[26] Analysis of the Latin grammar suggests 'cadere' fits with the tradition of Mohammed, in which the angel Gabriel (Al-Khidr) extracts the prophet's heart - symbolic of 'judgment' (cadi).

Enunciated in the Koranic traditions, the theme of death and loss are repeated in Freemasonry. The Masonic 'square' (the quadrus, in Italian quadro) is linked to the 'caduceus' (dual serpent) and 'cadere' (death). 'Quadro' is coordinated in Arabic with the 'kaaba' (square) - the Holy Shrine situated in Mecca. Theoretically, the shrine is a memorial of the 'seal' (khadal), depicted as the covenant - associated with Gabriel identified with Al-Khidr.

In addition, Gabriel (Djibril) is referred to in the Koran by two other important titles. The first is 'Ruh-ul-Qudus', a name punned in Latin with 'quadrus' (a square) and 'Ruh-ul-Amin' (the trustworthy spirit).[27]

Orientalist writers such as Dermenghem recount Gabriel's physical appearance drawing important analogies with the race of the 'irin' Hebrew (watchers, shining ones or those who are awake). The appellation 'irin' approximates in Greek to the 'egregoris' or 'grigori' (a watcher)[28] connoting a dragon or angel. In particular, the 'watcher' coincides with the green deity Osiris, whose name is written epigraphically with the 'eye'. Dermenghem notes the following:

> *'[His] countenance white as snow, blood hair flowing, in garments sewn with pearls and embroidered in gold'.*[29]

Dermenghem's description of Gabriel is written in codified language. The Hebrew word 'sheleg' (snow)[30] alludes to 'le'shager' the action (to send[31] or ship[32]), terms consistent with the messenger or host. Gabriel's blood 'red hair' respectively (seir and se'ar) compares to the (se'irim) a 'fallen angel', registered with the goat or gazelle, emblems of the Shiah and Sabi priesthood.

The caper illustrates the Shiah marked with 'red or fair' locks in combination with the green turban - a sign of Al-Khidr. In addendum, the Old Semitic noun 'ophir' (gold) is matched with 'ofer' (fawn)[33] and 'af'a' (viper). Written in Modern Hebrew, the adjective 'ze'havi' (golden)[34] specifies the illuminati the Sabi, adjunct with the 'tsvi' (gazelle)[35] and seraph.

Symbol of the hairy goat 'seir' documents human-angelic descent - iconic of the pearl. Colloquial Arabic lists 'lulu' (a pearl)[36] with the 'hemitheoi' (half-god), recorded in the Akkadian as 'lulu' - an assignment attributed to the daughter of Lilith. Indexed in the Old Semitic, 'lulu' translates as (mixed) - idiomatic of (a changeling or demigod). Cultic circles regard the lulu's offspring with the worship of 'nocturnal' deities (lel), classified with the angel Lilith.

In summary, the crewmember or host ascribes the nightly visitor, relative in Islamic lore to the angel 'Al-Khidr', characteristic of 'Ruh-ul-Qudus' (Gabriel) and 'Al Qadr' (revelation). Affiliated with the Shiah, Gabriel is matched with 'saba' (a star), esoteric of the 'Star People' (Sabi) equated with the nomadic 'tribe' (Shebet). Babylonian sculpture depicts the messenger as the amphibian 'goat' (the se'irim), contrasted with the cherubim and basket insignia. The carrier connotes the matriarch's womb or offering. Offspring of the oracle and cherubim in Judaic lore is reverent to the Prophet Moses - an ancient bloodline traced from the angelic mariner.

Dermenghem's portrayal of Gabriel further concords in the Apocrypha with the descriptions of Noah, appended to the Book of Enoch. Scriptural evidence suggests Arab scholars connected the bloodline of Noah with Gabriel, adjacent to Al-Khidr. Significantly Enoch's account proposes Noah to be the purveyor of the human-angelic line, founded upon the matriarch. Her offspring are linked to the prophets of Islam via the Judaic traditions of Moses, detailed in the next chapter.

In conclusion, descriptions of Gabriel matches the navigator, recorded in the book of Noah. The account provides a fascinating and insightful explanation of Noah's pedigree. The text reads:

> '... Methuselah, took a wife for his son Lamech, and she became pregnant by him and bore him a son [Noah]. And his body was white as snow and red as a rose; the hair of his head as white as wool and his demdema ('long curly hair') beautiful; and as for his eyes, when he opened them the whole house glowed like the sun ... And his father, Lamech, was afraid of him and fled and went to Methuselah his father; and he said to him, 'I have begotten a strange son. He is not like an (ordinary) human being, but he looks like the children of the angels of heaven to me, his form is different, and he is not like us ... It does not seem to me that he's of me, but of angels...'.[37]

1 Prolog, Pocket Bilingual Dictionary, English-Hebrew, Hebrew-English, Prolog 2003, p319 (Navi)

2 John C Traupman PhD: The New College Latin & English Dictionary, Bantam 1988, p128

3 Ibid, p128

4 Prolog, Pocket Bilingual Dictionary, English-Hebrew, Hebrew-English, Prolog 2003, p172

5 Laurence Gardner: Genesis of the Grail Kings, Bantam Books 2000, p132

6 Prolog, Pocket Bilingual Dictionary, English-Hebrew, Hebrew-English, Prolog 2003, p367

7 'Diabolus' Greek (devil) is further a pun on 'dia-bolus' (through clay) nominal of Adam - the neophyte.

8 'Pala' (king) and 'parlé' (speak) is equivalent in the Semitic language to 'hakim' (ruler) from the Syrian root 'haka' (talk).

9 John C Traupman PhD: The New College Latin & English Dictionary, Bantam 1988, p230

10 Ibid, p48

11 Hippocrene Concise Dictionary, English-Arabic, Arabic-English, Hippocrene, New York, p291

12 Prolog, Pocket Bilingual Dictionary, English-Hebrew, Hebrew-English, Prolog 2003, p178

13 Hippocrene Concise Dictionary, English-Arabic, Arabic-English, Hippocrene, New York, p55

14 Ibid, p140

15 The Arabic epithet 'Shiah' correlated to 'shar' (wicked) is found in the Celtic title 'Bard', comparable to 'bad'.

16 Hippocrene Concise Dictionary, English-Arabic, Arabic-English, Hippocrene, New York, p43

17 Ibid, p281

18 Arabic 'sha'r' (hair) and 'shar' (evil) are etymologies aligned to the noble bloodline the 'Shiah', analogous in the European languages to the Frank word 'hair' (hate). In the Roman language, 'barba' denotes (beard - relative to barbaric), Greek 'barbaros' (foreign or alien).

19 The Old Persian word 'unzen' (red) also means (gold). In Japanese, 'aka' denotes (red) and is relative to 'akarui' (light). The same comparisons are analogous in the Old Semitic noun 'seir' (red), contrasted with the Arabic etymon 'zau' (light).

20 M.A. Abdel-Hady: Egyptian Arabic, A Rough Guide, Dictionary Phrasebook, Lexus 1998, p241

21 John Baldock: The Essence of Sufism, Eagle Editions 2004, p225 (Appendix 2)

22 John C Traupman PhD: The New College Latin & English Dictionary, Bantam, 1988, p68

23 'Kadi' Arabic (judge) is sometimes transliterated as 'Cadi' or 'Qadi'.

24 Hippocrene Concise Dictionary, English-Arabic, Arabic-English, Hippocrene, New York, p258

25 Ralph Ellis: Eden in Egypt, A Translation of the Book of Genesis out of the Original Egyptian Text, Edfu Books 2005, p285 (Appendix A5 - Dictionary)

26 John C Traupman PhD: The New College Latin & English Dictionary, Bantam Books 1988, p31

27 Badar Azimabadi: The World of Angels, Adam Publishers, Shandar Market, Delhi 1996, p48

28 Andrew Collins: From the Ashes of Angels, The Forbidden legacy of a Fallen Race, Michael Joseph London 1996, p3

29 Badar Azimabadi: The World of Angels, Adam Publishers, Shandar Market, Delhi 1996, p60

30 Prolog, Pocket Bilingual Dictionary, English-Hebrew, Hebrew-English, Prolog 2003, p80

31 Ibid, p363

32 Ibid, p368

33 Ibid, p147

34 Ibid, p171

35 Ibid, p166

36 Hippocrene Concise Dictionary, English-Arabic, Arabic-English, Hippocrene, New York, p88

37 Andrew Collins: From the Ashes of Angels, The Forbidden Legacy of a Fallen Race, Michael Joseph London 1996, p1

8

Baskets and Bastards

'Take some of the firstfruits of all that you produce from the soil of the land... and put them in a basket... The priest shall take the 'basket' [tene] from your hands and set it down in front of the altar of the Lord your God... And you and the Levites and the aliens among you shall rejoice in all the good things the Lord your God has given to you and your household'.
Deuteronomy 26: 2, 4 and 11, Holy Bible, New International Version, Gideon

'Moses was educated in all the wisdom of the Egyptians and was powerful in speech and action'.
Acts 7:22, Holy Bible, New International Version, Gideon

In the Semitic language, the word 'basket' implies different sizes, shapes, and constructions, and has different names summarized below:

1) Sal - made of twigs, specially for bread (Genesis 40:17)

2) Salsilloth - a similar basket used for gathering grapes (Jeremiah 6:9)

3) Tene - in which the first-fruits are offered (Deuteronomy 26:4)

4) Dud - to carry fruit (Jeremiah 24:1) and clay to the brickyard (Psalms 81:6)[1]

5) [Tebah] - a 'chest' constructed from bulrushes (Exodus 2: 1-3) or an 'ark' (Genesis 7:1)

6) [Sabat] - Modern Arabic a breadbasket found in grocery stores

The current Arabic noun for a basket (in a shop) is 'sabat'[2] and references the Hebrew verb 'sabat' (to rest), memorialized as the 'Shabbat' (Sabbath). The 'sabat' (basket) is symmetrical with 'Shebet' (a tribe or clan), connected to Moses in conjunction with the host and flood. Insignia of the casket is a precursor to the establishment of the civil monarchy, replicated as the snake.

The basket is a symbol of the serpent's lineage and is a device utilized esoterically to convey an angelic birth. 'Dud' (the Old Semitic noun for a basket) is a homonym in colloquial Arabic of 'dud' (a worm or caterpillar).[3] Progeny of the worm is equated with the line of kings and is encrypted in the Semitic lexicon.[4]

Finding of Moses, 1904: After Lawrence Almah Tadema, Oil on Canvas (1992)

For example, the alternative Hebrew noun for a basket is 'sal', utilized in Arabic to abbreviate the word 'saluta' (to rule).[5] 'Saluta' is nominal of the 'Sultan' and his (noble) line the 'atsil', cognate with the fallen angels the S(h)atani.[6] In occult lore, minions of the Shatan are depicted with the signifier of 'salt' (Latin sal), substituted in Arabic with the basket, ruler or worm.

'Sal' (basket) conforms to the Latin root 'sal' (salt) and 'salis' (salt water or the sea)[7] - covert symbols of the matriarch's divine union with heaven. Her offering is registered with the basket and salt. The Roman noun 'sal' (salt) is catalogued with the female genitalia 'saltus' (a polymorph indicating the verb to leap),[8] implicit of a deity, represented as a goat or noble.

'Salire' (the intransitive verb to leap) notates 'salis' (salt water), illustrative of the fallen angel, addendum to the basket and childbirth. 'Saltus' (the womb or to leap) is drawn from the Sumerian logograph 'sal', annotated as the woman's sexual organs.[9]

Designated as the 'mere' or 'ma', (the matriarch) compares in esoteric Latin to the noun 'mare' (the sea) - diagnostic of the host and Venus. Similar analogies are reconfigured in the Hebrew. The noun 'malakh' (sailor)[10] is equivalent to 'melakh' (salt).[11] The signifier of 'salt' articulates 'mal'akh' (an angel)[12] and 'melekh' (a king).[13] In summary, materialization of the 'angel' connoting a mariner is conceptual to the basket (a ruler), equated with salt.

Biblically salt is applied to purify the offering and is concurrent in Catholicism with baptism. Its use during ritual oblation is accorded to the Jews, outlined in the book of Numbers 18:19, and is a practice adopted by the Greeks and Romans. In the Second Book of Chronicles 13:5, 'salt' is integral to the covenant of Israel. The passage reads as a rhetorical question:

> *'Don't you know that the Lord, the God of Israel, has given the kingship of Israel to David and his descendents forever by a covenant of salt?'*

The term 'melakh' (covenant of salt) covertly designates the angelic lineage - the 'mal'akh'. Unification between heaven and earth deemed as the 'salt covenant' is administered traditionally through 'melekh' (the king). Imperial governance, situational to the 'basket' (sal) and 'salt' (sal), is a dividend attributed to the navigator or host.[14]

Within Rabbinic tradition, the 'basket' is integral to the cult of Moses. Judaism recalls him as a Prophet of the Law and the author of the Sacred Canon - the Torah. Moses' divine lineage is recorded with the basket – a theme reiterated in the biblical account. In the book of Exodus, the Pharaoh decrees to kill the newborn male - an act prophetic of the death of the Egyptian firstborn. To safeguard Moses and prevent detection, his mother conceals him in a bitumen basket - a symbol of the matriarch.

Classical writers saw a relationship between bitumen and the black deoxygenated menstrual blood. *Judaean bitumen is the best, according to the [Greek scholar Dioscorides], and he notes that 'it shines like purple'.*[15] The same authority maintains that 'bitumen' termed 'asphaltos' (asphalt) 'drives out menses' and 'strangulates the womb'.

Here Dioscorides makes a punning reference in Classical Greek between 'asphaltos' (asphalt) and 'asphuxia' (not a pulse), rendered in English as 'asphyxia'. 'Strangulation' (asphuxia) is further a play on the Greek noun 'hustera' (womb).[16]

The bitumen carrier serves as a metaphor of the womb, coupled with the negation of the firstborn, sanctioned from the Royal house. Codified language used by Dioscorides is typical of the Greek and Semitic mystery schools, tabulated from the hieroglyphs.

According to the British Museum sign list, the hieroglyph 'basket' (sometimes annotated as a bread basket) is used to write the title 'neb or nb' (lord),[17] rendered from the Arabic titular 'nabi' (prophet).[18] 'Nabi' in standard Arabic is transliterated from the Egyptian Arabic title 'nebi' (prophet).[19] The philology of 'neb' is related to 'neboo, alternatively nbw' (gold).[20] Application of the title 'neb' (lord) technically 'nebi' (prophet) infers that the bread basket sign is read also as a ritual vessel. Its use is cognizant with dipping or immersion, prescriptive of divination and sacrificial rites.

In context to Moses, the basket 'glyph' describes Mount 'Nebo' (Golden), recognized in the book of Deuteronomy Chapter 34 as the location of Moses' death. Here 'Nebo' operates as a clever pun on the Semitic expression 'naboh' (to foretell) and 'nabi' (prophet). Moses is accorded the status of a prophet, 'prognostic' (nibui - prediction) of his demise on Mount Nebu. The basket sign reinforces Moses' lineage, characteristic of a son of a 'prophet' (nabi) or 'lord' (neb). His title further suggests he is allied to the martial priesthood of the Sultan, encoded anagrammatically within the hieroglyph itself (Refer to footnote[21]).

In Judaism likewise, there are numerous wordplays pertaining to Moses' casket, adjacent to the military leader, noted in the book of Exodus. The Hebrew word 'tebah' defined as (Moses' reed basket) is a deliberate pun on the Egyptian word 'djeba' (a commander), in addition to 'tchaba' (tsaba - the host).

Tutankhamun: Androgyne seated on the 'neboo' (gold) glyph implicit of 'neb' (a lord or prophet)

'Tebah' philologically is derived from the Egyptian root 'tjeb' (a sealed chest). According to the scholar David Rohl, 'tjeb' by the New Kingdom is pronounced as 'teb' (perhaps with a final vowel). The word 'tebah' and 'tjeb' have the same meaning (chest).[22] Relationship between the ruler and sacrifice is comparative to the Egyptian noun 'tchebe-t' (a coffin, sarcophagus or wicker basket),[23] incorrectly transliterated from the Old Semitic noun 'tebah'.

The expression 'tebah' (basket, ark or chest) is used additional to Moses in the accounts of Genesis to indicate Noah's Ark. Recorded in the creation narratives, the 'tebah' offers protection and shelter to Noah and his family during the deluge. 'Tebah' is a clever play on the Arabic verbal stem 'tawba' (repentance or forgiveness), cognate with 'tawa' (to obey).[24]

According to the book of Genesis apprised from the earlier Akkadian Gilgamesh epics, the Lord of the host (angelic sailor) precipitates a flood to destroy man. The symbol of the ark, basket or boat notates Moses' lineage antecedent from the offspring of Noah, deemed angelic or noble.

Royal mark of the casket exemplifies Moses' sacred birth, sequential from the illegitimate patriarch Noah, described in the Book of Noah (Refer to the previous chapter). Noah's bloodline is traced genealogically from the serpent or watcher. Replete with military connotations, the ark is allied to the royal leader the 'commander' (tchaba or dejeba), consistent with the 'host' (tsabaoth).

To recap, Moses' ark details his Royal (angelic) ascendancy, paralleled to the covenant of Noah - a theme elaborated in the Gospels. In the New Testament, baby Jesus is placed into a manger, used as a theological comparison to 'Moses basket'. 'Manger' from the Latin root 'mandere' (to chew)[25] is a symbol cogent with the ordination of the covenant, enacted liturgically through communion. 'Mandere' symbolically infers 'mandare' (to command, order, enjoin or commission).[26] Its use is analogous in the Semitic to 'tebah' (a basket) and 'tchaba or dejeba' (a commander).

There is a clear proximity established between the 'army' (tchaba, Modern Semitic tsaba) and death, inferred by the boat or 'ark' (tebah), pictured as the coffin (tchebe-t), provident within Freemasonry.[27] The ark features the destruction of the firstborn, commensurate with the inundation of the Nile, associated with the stories of Noah and Moses. In addition, the 'reed basket' operates as a dual signifier, denoting (a dignitary or a military leader). His office is equated with an angel (a serpent) - synonymous with the host and remuneration (sacrifice).

Throughout Semitic literature, the ark is identified with immolation. 'Corbis' (the Latin feminine noun for a basket)[28] is cognate with 'carbo' (charcoal)[29] from the Semitic word 'corbon' describing (a gift dedicated to God).[30] 'Korban' is translated into Modern Hebrew as (a sacrifice).[31] The 'corbis' annotates a deity's status or Royal pedigree.

To summarise, the wicker motif in early Judaic mythology denotes the inception of the priesthood, ascribed to the law writer Moses. Hierarchy of the 'carrier' (tebah) signifies Royal ancestry, traced from an angelic source, originating from 'Noah's Ark' (tebah). In Egyptian iconography, emblem of the ark discloses a sovereign or prophet, predated in Babylon to the winged 'cherubim' (an angelic guardian).

Pervasive throughout Syrian carving, the messenger holding the basket suggests propitiations of the first fruits, implicit of the firstborn. The 'basket of offering', indexed in Old Semitic as (tene), is derived from the Syrian root 'taman' (price),[32] rendered in Egyptian Arabic as 'temen'.[33] 'Tene' (a basket) semantically implies 'payment' or 'purchase' - thematic of sacrificial loss. Assigned to the cherubim, the offertory is recognizant with the king and the redemption of sin.

The cherub is replaced in Greek ritual with the 'canephorus' plural 'canephori' (the basket offerer) - an arcane symbol of divine birth modelled on sacrificial offerings. The 'canephori' depicts (a sculptured figure of a youth or maiden, bearing a basket on their head, containing tributaries).[34] These gifts are associated with the 'feast of the Gods',[35] esoteric of 'Phosphoros' (the Morning-Star). Intrinsic to the firstborn, the wicker carrier is grouped intellectually with the monarch and angel, substituted with the child. Its death is reciprocal to the basket (womb) and salt (angel), ingredients of atonement, correlated with the tribute.

1 Alexander Cruden: Cruden's Complete Concordance, To the Old & New Testament, Lutterworth Press, London 1963, p32 (Basket)

2 M.A. Abdel-Hady: Egyptian Arabic Phrasebook, Rough Guide, Lexus 1998, p52

3 Hippocrene English-Arabic, Arabic-English Dictionary, Hippocrene, New York 2005, p170

4 Archaically the line of kings is represented as the 'goat' or 'hairy snake'. See Section 'Priesthood of Saturn' from Chapters 26 to 31 pp 249-298.

5 'Saluta' Arabic (rule) is cognate with the greeting 'salutations - French salut, Latin salutare' (to visit, pay respect to or pay reverence to [the Gods]).

6 The Arabic noun 'sal' (basket) in the Persian language alludes to the deity 'Zal' - the progenitor of the Shahnameh Kings, said to have ruled Sistan, thought to be Eastern Iran. 'Zal' in ancient Persian means (aged - in Arabic 'sayk').

7 John C Traupman PhD: The New College Latin & English Dictionary, Bantam Books 1988, p276

8 Ibid, p276

9 Geoffrey Sampson: Writing Systems, Hutchinson Education, London, 1985, p51

10 Prolog Pocket Bilingual Dictionary, English-Hebrew-Hebrew-English, Prolog 2003, p352

11 Ibid

12 Ibid, p23

13 Ibid, p222

14 Among the Arabs, to eat a man's salt is considered to be a sacred bond between the host and his guest. The contemporary link between the basket and sodium chloride (king/covenant) is illustrated during the funeral ceremony. Before burial, the body is covered in salt, contiguous with the angel and covenant. Brewers Dictionary of Phrase & Fable, Cassell & Company, London 1954, p800 (Salt)

15 John M Allegro: The Sacred Mushroom and the Cross, A Study of the Nature and Origins of Christianity within the Fertility Cults of the Ancient Near Middle East, Abacus 1970, p91

16 In the Roman language, 'bitumen' is punned with 'bito-mens' (to go-to the altar). 'Mens' (altar) corresponds to the noun 'mensis' (month - the root of menstruation and menses).

17 Mark Collier & Bill Manley: How to Read Egyptian Hieroglyphs, British Museum Press 1998, p142 (Index Sign List F4)

18 Hippocrene English-Arabic, Arabic-English Dictionary, Hippocrene, New York, 2005, p96

19 Ibid, p255

20 Bridget McDermott: Decoding Egyptian Hieroglyphs, Duncan Baird Publishers 2003, Sign Index, p168 'Neb and Nbw' (Lord and Gold) is comparative in English to God and Gold).

21 The basket icon 'sal' in Arabic abbreviates the word 'saluta' (to rule) and is found in Egyptian texts where the sign is used to write (a dignitary), transliterated according to Egyptologist as 'neb'. It is to be noted with caution that the designation of 'neb' written with the 'bread basket' sign is problematic. Inclusion of the 'breadbasket' suggests 'neb' should actually be read as 'sal' (a breadbasket) - nominal of 'saluta' (to rule). The problem is reinforced epigraphically. Recorded in the hieroglyphic, the 'nb' glyph looks very similar to a 'laver' (a large brass vessel for Jewish priests utilized for ritual ablutions), correlated archaically with divination, identified with 'nebi' (a prophet). Anagrammatic ambiguities are a device, consistent with the spelling of hieroglyphic words, adopted by the literati.

22 David Rohl: Legend, The Genesis of Civilisation, Arrow books Limited 1999, p139

23 Ralph Ellis: Eden in Egypt, A Translation of the Book of Genesis out of the original Egyptian Text, Edfu Books 2005, p280 (Appendix A5 – Dictionary)

24 Hippocrene English-Arabic, Arabic-English Dictionary, Hippocrene, New York 2005, p298

25 John C Traupman PhD: The New College Latin & English Dictionary, Bantam Books 1988, p177

26 Ibid

27 'Tebah' (an ark, chest or coffin) suggests that Noah's Ark is compared in literary terms to a large floating 'mausoleum'.

28 John C Traupman PhD: The New College Latin & English Dictionary, Bantam Books 1988, p350

29 Ibid, p62

30 John M Allegro: The Sacred Mushroom and the Cross, A Study of the Nature and Origins of Christianity within the Fertility Cults of the Ancient Near Middle East, Abacus 1970, p234

31 Prolog, Pocket Bilingual Dictionary, English-Hebrew & Hebrew-English, Prolog 2003, p352

32 Hippocrene English-Arabic, Arabic-English Dictionary, Hippocrene, New York 2005, p295

33 Ibid, p299

34 It is probable the 'canephori' (the basket offerers) is punned with the Latin noun 'canis' (a dog), cogent with the star Sirius.

35 Brewers Dictionary of Phrase & Fable, Chassell & Company, London 1954, p171 (Singular Canephorus)

9

The Exodus and the Ram

'Then Pharaoh gave this order to all his people: "Every boy that is born you must throw into the Nile, but let every girl live". Now a man of the house of Levi married a Levite woman, and she became pregnant and gave birth to a son... But when she could hide him no longer, she got a papyrus basket for him and coated it with tar and pitch. Then she placed the child in it and put it among the reeds along the bank of the Nile... She [Pharaoh's daughter] named him Moses, saying, "I drew him out of the water".'

Exodus 1:22 and 2: 1-3 and 10, Holy Bible, New International Version, Gideon

'... An angel of the Lord appeared to Joseph in a dream. "Get up," he said, "take the child [baby Jesus] and his mother and escape to Egypt. Stay there until I tell you, for Herod is going to search for the child to kill him".'

Gospel of Mathew 2: 13, Holy Bible, New International Version, Gideon

In the book of Exodus, the baby Moses is concealed in a basket - a hallmark of his angelic birthright, doubled symbolically with the death of the firstborn. Historically the tradition of Moses, cast into the river Nile, corresponds with the Babylonian King Sargon, recorded in the Akkadian language. The translation reads:

> *'I am Sargon the mighty king, king of Agade [Akkad].*
> *My mother was a high priestess, my father I knew not ...*
> *My city is Azupiranu, which is situated on the banks of the Euphrates.*
> *My 'changeling'[Lulu] mother¹ conceived me, in secret she bore me.*
> *She set me in a basket of reeds, she sealed my door with bitumen.*
> *She cast me into the river ...*
> *Akki, the drawer of water, took me as his son and reared me...*
> *Ishtar (Inanna) granted me her love,*
> *And for four and ... years I exercised kingship'.²*

There are a number of similarities between the accounts of Sargon and Moses. The name 'Moses' in the narrative of Exodus means (to draw out of water), repeated in the Hebrew pun 'Mosis'. In Greek, 'mosis' denotes (an offspring or heir)³ from the Egyptian root 'mass' (a descendent). The suffix 'mass' is preserved in the pharaonic names Thothmoses and Rameses, transcribed in the Egyptian as Djhutimass and Ra Mass.

Moses' name in the original texts is clearly associated with 'moser' (to deliver)⁴ and 'yesha' (deliverance),⁵ rendered in the Greek as 'Jesus'. Additionally, the Hebrew verbal stem 'yesha' is paired conceptually in the Old Testament with 'Yisra El' (Israel) formerly Jacob. 'Israel's' acquired name is translated as (he that strives with God, literally to deliver) - a play on his tribe name 'Asher'(Sanction[ed]).⁶

'Yesha' (deliverance) informs the adjective 'yashar' (straight), translated into the Latin as 'rectus' (a ruler) - nautical terms identified with the sailor. In the Islamic tradition, Israel prescribes 'Izra-il, classified with Azrael' (the angel of death),⁷ paralleled to the Exodus and the host.

'Moses' conception from water' (moser) fits with the Akkadian inscription of 'Akki' (the drawer of water), read in alternative translations as (the irrigator).⁸ The Prophet Moses, otherwise 'Mosis' (to draw out), Akkadian 'Akki', parallels the Greek prefix 'ago', meaning (to lead, bring up or draw out), diminutive of 'agape' (unrequited love), evocative of the 'Agapao' (celebration). As a suffix, 'ago' appears in Hellenistic vocabulary such as 'nekragogos' (leading forth the dead), 'psukhagogeo' (to conjure up souls from the Nether world) and so on.⁹

'Ago's original root 'akki' is derived from the Sumerian word 'ag-ag' (love), adjunct in Classical Greek with 'hagios' (holy). The Greek adjective is conceptual to the Egyptian Arabic stem 'hagg or hajj' (a pilgrim),[10] recollected as the 'ago'. Employed in written Greek, 'ago' conveys the Hebrew verb 'mosis' (to draw out). Classical usage of 'ago' within the Septuagint's edition of the Exodus suggests a meta-narrative - a theme detailed in Hellenistic mythology.

Greek writers, for example, refer to the 'Argo' as the ship that carried the fleece of the Golden ram rescued by Jason and the Argonauts. Cultic reference to the Argo infers 'ago' (to lead), thematic of divine intervention, cognate with the Agapao feast. In a different version of the myth, the Argo is used by Danaus to transport his fifty daughters, when they fled from Egypt to escape the ruler Aegyptus. In structure and narrative, the story is similar to Moses killing the Egyptian and running away to marry Ruel's daughter - a Medianite.

In reference to Danaus, he is recorded as the son of Belus, the brother of 'Egypt' (Aegyptus) and the brother-in-law of Phoenix (sovereign over the Phoenicians). Danaus himself gave his name to 'Danaans' - a word of unknown origin used commonly by Homer and other poets to designate (the Greeks).[11]

Dionysus otherwise Danaus is demonstrated in the Greek mysteries to originate from the tribe of 'Dan' (judge), fathered by Yisrael and his concubine Bilhah, recorded in Genesis 30:6. The name Dan is transferred into Greek as Danaans, his Semitic mother Bilhah, transliterated as Belus. Biblically the tribe of Dan settled in the North of Canaan, marked as the utmost Northern region of Israelite territory. Etymologically, Dan is related to Dane, written in the Liturgical Latin as Dani, Old Norse Dane.[12]

Mythological, Danaus' name is almost certainly a pun on 'Dion-ysus' (Lord-Ysus) otherwise Jesus. Read as a subtext, Danaus' sexual exploits pertaining to his daughters are encoded in the Syrian language. His namesake 'Jesus or Ysus' covertly infers 'jasus' (a spy),[13] linked to 'jauzi' (a spouse or wife),[14] thematic of 'jaza' (to punish).[15]

'Danaus' otherwise 'Dionysus, Jason or Jesus' leads us back in a circuitous fashion to the traditions of the Exodus and the portrayal of Moses as a fugitive. This set of events is conjunct in the Bacchic mysteries to Jason and the Argonauts.

The word Argonaut is a compound of 'Argo' (to lead), affixed with the Greek term 'nautes' (a sailor) from 'naus' (a ship). Designation of 'naus' is used as a suffix and is related to the word 'Thanos' read as 'Tha-naus' (a nobleman)[16] literally (lordship), specified as 'Danaus' or 'Dan-naus'. The etymological comparison of Danaus and Thanaus is more than probable, as there is no 'd' sound in the Greek alphabet. The delta sign is read as a 'th'.

Danaus otherwise Dionysus (Dion-Ysus) or Thanaus is illustrated as the protagonist Jason - a permutation on the Greek appellation Jesus (Yesus). 'Jason' (healer) is another form of the name 'Jesu' and 'Joshua' (Hebrew ye'shu'a - salvation).[17] 'Ye'shu'a' marks 'yesha' (to deliver), cognomen of 'Yisrael' (Israel), correlated with the tribe Asher and his older brother Dan.

Comparison between the Greek and Hebrew suggests 'Yesha' and 'Asher'[18] is a variation on the mythology of Dionysus, identified in the Semitic with Israel, affiliated chronologically to Moses - the 'leader' identical to 'moser' (to deliver). Philologically, 'ago' (the leader) describes (a navigator) of the 'Argo' - a signifier of the host, correlated religiously with the 'Agapao' festival.

Argo's root is reflected in the Latin lexicology 'arca' (a chest or coffin), vocabulary pertaining to the boat or 'ark'. 'Arca' is mutual in Greek to 'arkhe' (beginning), innate with 'arkhos' (ruler), represented as the sailor, aligned to the ram.

Elaboration of the Agapao circumvents the golden ram traditions, connected to the Passover lamb. In the early Christian communities, the 'Agapao' classifies (the love feast) before or after the communion held for the poor - a vestige of the Bacchic cult ceremonies.

Worship of Bacchus corresponds in the Judaic calendar with the Passover lamb, linked to the crossing of the Red Sea. Slaying of the Egyptian army duplicates the death of the firstborn, stylized as blood and water (Red Sea). Christian liturgy commemorates this covenant through the sacrificial blood and water of the innocent lamb Christ. His death theologically substitutes the lamb of Christ with the Passover lamb.

In the original book of Exodus, the 'Red Sea' is described incorrectly as 'Yam Suf' (the Reed Sea). 'Confusion' in the English translation results from a wordplay, contrived from the ancient Hebrew, conveyed also in the Anglicization of 'red' and 'reed'. The Hebrew noun 'kane' signifying (a reed) is punned in the Old Semitic with the word 'khanun' (the red daub put on the head of ewes in pastures). Khanun is extracted from the rare Sumerian word 'gan-nu' (red dye).[19] This dye is probably the same as the Arabic root 'hinna' in English (henna).

The older form of the Semitic noun 'kane' (reed) is rendered as 'kanah' and is found in the name 'kana'ana' (Canaanite).[20] Appellation of 'kana'ana' suggests (a scribe or a scholar), approximate to (a literary, educated or cultured person).[21] Cryptically 'kane' (reed) indicates the red people 'khanun', traced back through the lineage of Adam, Cain and Esau.[22] Doctrinally the red descendents pertain to the thearchy of the 'Red Crown' (dsrt), assigned to the Pharaohs of Lower Egypt[23] - a mystery cult originating from Canaan.

'Cain yellow' archaically 'red'[24] is grouped in the Latin with 'canicular' - the brightest star of 'Canis Major' (the Dog Star - Sirus). Symbol of the star appears in the Greek mysteries as the 'canephorus' plural 'canephori', equivalent to (the basket bearers), historically the cherubim. The canephori aka the cherub is marked in Judaism by Moses cachet and the atonement of the infant male - elemental to the creation of a new covenant.

In the European branch of languages, Khanun informs the Old English word 'kunna' (to know - with regard to language), grouped in the Latin with 'cunnus' (vulva), illustrative of the 'salt' covenant (sal) or 'basket' (Arabic sal). 'Khanun' is transliterated in the Greek as 'kanon' and signifies (the Ecclesiastical law or a decree), epitomized by the red vesture of the priest. 'Kanon' (decree) is reductive from the Arabic root 'qanun' (law),[25] implicit of the red ewe 'gan-nu'.

The ram deity Amun, (basket motif) Temple of Seti I, Abydos, Dynasty XIX

Citation of 'qanun' (law) reflects the Semitic word 'kany' (jealous), denoting Yahweh as a 'jealous (or red) God', connoting legal propriety. Variations of 'kanon' (law) allude to the Roman transitive verb 'cano' (to sing, play, celebrate, prophesy, predict, foretell and to sound the signal for battle - signa canere).[26] The root of 'cano' originates from the Hebrew title 'Kohen' (priest) - synonymous with 'recitation' (Koran) of the 'law' (qanun).

> ... [the expression] 'khanun' [red daub also] looks exactly like another
> Semitic word... [kh-n-n to] be gracious, source of many personal
> names in the Old Testament, like Khanan, Hanan; Khanun, Hanun;
> Kannah, Hannah; Yokhanan (Yahweh has been gracious)... [27]

In the Egyptian mysteries, the red ram (khanun or gan-nu) connotes sado-sexual rites, accorded to the deity 'Khnum' (joined). 'Khnum' is translated into the Hebrew as 'Levi' (joined - most likely an artery) from 'lev' (heart).[28] Namesake of Levi is paternal to the tribe of Moses - the Levites.

'Khnum's incarnation as the Egyptian 'Creator God' facilitates the Nile's inundation,[29] cognate with the rising of Sirius. The 'daubed Blood' of the red ram, 'khanun' is combined symbolically with 'khnum', characterized as blood and water. Khnum's cognomen is etymologically a variant of the Egyptian deity 'Amun' (hidden), linguistically identified with 'water'. Amun is also a ram, and outlines the monarchial lineage, assigned to the hidden priesthood (See Chapter 11 the Amorites).

At the Temple of Amun attributed to Sety I, Abydos, Dynasty XIX, the head of Amun and Horus (falcon) is combined with the motif of the reed basket, and inscribes the royal insignia of the Pharaoh. The basket a device of the 'menstrual womb' is a symbol of the red ram or goat 'khnum' - classified with offspring of the 'canephorus' (a basket bearer) equal to the cherubim and Sirius.

Pairing of Amun's basket with the bulrush is significant. The bulrush or reed when in seed appears like a feather, emphasized by the similarity of the Egyptian hieroglyph for 'feather' and 'bulrush'. Archaically the 'feather' denotes an angel or alien, referred to by Greek scholars as the 'hemitheoi' (literally half God).

Within the borders of Egypt, the feather signifies 'Maat' (the Virgin Goddess of Judgment), equated theologically with the firstborn and the weighing of the 'heart' (lev). A ritual, accorded to the Levite priest, in propinquity to the 'joint' covenant of the ram 'Khnum' allied to 'Amun'. This agreement discloses the 'Western' priesthood (the Rabbi) descended from the Amorites - a people related to the Canaanites and Hyksos ancestral of the red people originating from the east.

In summary, progeny of this people is conveyed through the angel and matriarch, symbolized as the 'basket' or 'ruler' - nominal of the tribe of Levites. Proponents of the Levites and Amorites are linked covertly to Moses and the death of the firstborn. The latter tradition, a vestige developed from the Babylonian priesthood a covert faction, betrothed to the Western Covenant and the worship of the ram Amun!

1   The translation 'changeling mother' comes from G Roux, Ancient Iraq.

2   Alan F. Alford: When the Gods Came Down, The Catastrophic Roots of Religion Revealed, New English Library, Hotter and Stoughton 2000, p255

3   Laurence Gardner: Genesis of the Grail Kings, Bantam Books 2000, p259

4   Prolog Pocket Bilingual Dictionary, English-Hebrew-Hebrew-English, Prolog 2003, p103

5   Ibid, p103

6   Ibid, p353 'Asher' (Sanction[ed]) is related to 'osher' (happiness), consistent with the Egyptian Arabic root 'ash'ar' (blond) - appellations of a caucasian priesthood, registered with the lion of Judah and the tribe of Israel (Asher).

7   Alix de Saint Andre: Translated from the French by Elfreda Powell, The Good Angel Guide, For Reluctant Sinners, Souvenir Press 1999, p102

8   The Akkadian name Akki is probably an intentional pun on 'Akh Ki' (a brother of the earth).

9   John M Allego: The Sacred Mushroom and the Cross, A Study of the Nature and Origins of Christianity within the Fertility Cults of the Ancient Near East, Abacus 1973, p206

10 Hippocrene English-Arabic, Arabic-English Dictionary, Hippocrene, New York 2005, p185

11 Editors Simon Price & Emily Kearns: The Oxford Dictionary of Classical Myth & Religion, Oxford University Press 2003, p145

12 In the Bible, the tribe of 'Dan' from the Hebrew word 'dun' (judge) is described as warlike, analogous etymologically to a 'Dane' the Norse word for (a Viking). In addition, etymologies taken from High German were used by scholars to translate Old Semitic dialects - including the grammar and configuration of the Hittite language - a tongue closely related to German.

13 Hippocrene English-Arabic, Arabic-English Dictionary, Hippocrene, New York, 2005, p209

14 Ibid

15 Ibid

16 'Thanos' (a noble man literally lord-ship) has the additional meaning of (a bear-man).

17 Prolog Pocket Bilingual Dictionary, English-Hebrew-Hebrew-English, Prolog, 2003, p353

18 Inversion of the name 'yesha' (to deliver) is 'yasir' (a captive) - idiomatic of an 'initiate' or 'neophyte'.

19 John M. Allegro, The Sacred Mushroom and the Cross, A Study of the Nature and Origins of Christianity within the Fertility Cults of the Ancient Near Middle East, Abacus, 1970, p149

20 A medium of knowledge and writing the 'reed' is articulated in the English homonym 'read'.

21 Gary A. David, Eye of the Phoenix, Mystery Visions & Secrets of the American Southwest, Adventures Unlimited, U.S.A, p201

22 'Khanun' the (red) people shares the same meaning as the 'Edomites', traced from the lineage of Esau (hairy). Biblically, the Edomites are analogous to the 'dog-men' - the calebites allied to the Israelite tribe Judah. The implication is that the 'Kana'ana' (Canaanite) are identical to the Edomites (the red people) - a tribal branch, affiliated to Israel via the lineage of Adam and Cain. Such a suggestion would indicate Israel's religion is based upon the Canaanite cults, centred upon the veneration of the Dog Star.

23 Appellation of the name Canaanite from the root 'khanun' (red) is shared with the names 'Adam' and 'Cain' - designations connected to the 'Red Crown' (dsrt) of Lower Egypt.

24 In Old French and Latin, the term 'Cain' denotes the colour (yellowy or sandy red). In ancient tapestries, Cain and Judas are represented with yellow beards - symbolic of 'treason', signifiers correlated with Moses and his sojourn out of Egypt.

25 Hippocrene English-Arabic, Arabic-English Dictionary, Hippocrene, New York 2005, p66

26 John C Traupman PhD: The New College Latin & English Dictionary, Bantam Press 1988, p34

27 John M. Allegro: The Sacred Mushroom and the Cross, A Study of the Nature and Origins of Christianity within the Fertility Cults of the Ancient Near Middle East, Abacus 1970, p150

28 Prolog Pocket Bilingual Dictionary, English-Hebrew-Hebrew-English, Prolog 2003, p183

29 George Hart: A Dictionary of Egyptian Gods and Goddesses, Routledge & Kegan Paul 1986, p110

10

Amun and the Slaughter of the Ram

'It is the glory of God to conceal a matter; to search out a matter is the glory of kings. As the heavens are high and the earth is deep, so the heart of kings are unsearchable'.

Proverbs 25:2-3, Holy Bible, New International Version, Gideon

Expiation of Isaac theologically elicits darkness and death, coherent with the sunset, the ram and the tabernacle. Interpretation of the fallen ram denotes a solar motif, conjunct with the 'Western' priesthood (Aamu), replete with the deity Amun. Hieroglyphically, 'Amen-t' or 'imnt' is fallaciously written as (the west), transliterated accurately as 'ish-hama'arav' (a Westerner).[1] Amun's epithet is diagnostic of the 'Aamu wabi' (the Western priesthood), administered through the solar crown of 'Hammurabi'.

Decay of the solar mascot registers the 'Western God - Amun' (the Concealed One), derivative of 'amen' (secretive).[2] In Modern Hebrew, Amun or Amen corresponds to 'amem' (darken or eclipse), additionally translated as (cunning or slyness),[3] indicative of 'kabsh' (a ram). Employed in the Hebrew lexicon, Amun's name is synonymous with 'le'amen' (to train or instruct),[4] implicit of 'initiation'. Worshippers of Amun are the 'Emori' (Aamu) - a people cogent with 'emuna' (faith),[5] stylized as the western crescent or the dual horns (See Islamic Crest).

Structured through 'emuna' (belief),[6] Amun's followers enumerate the outer mysteries presented as 'amin' (credible),[7] specified in Arabic as 'amin' (the faithful).[8] Endorsement of 'amin' (faithful or credible) divests 'amun' (concealment), indicative of 'amem' (deception). Comparison of related etymologies suggest the initiator is actively misled, regarding the symbol's extent.

Analysis of the sign and its precise meaning are allocated to the inner mysteries, divulged through the worship of Amun, equivocal to the ram and votive. Deconstruction of Amun's name evident in Greek is analogous to 'amouroo' (darken), distilled from 'amauros' (dim), consistent with 'amnos' (lamb).[9]

Glossary, attributed to the obscured God, metaphors the shadow of the ram, locked in perpetual conflict. Its struggle compels the sun to descend into the black abyss timed with death. Religiously the sun's canopy is a simile of death, exhibited ritualistically as the tabernacle and veil. A Canaanite allegory, the Egyptian myth of the dying ram, is manifested in the Old Kingdom as the deity 'Kherty' (the lower one),[10] found in the Hebrew stem 'le'horid' (to lower).[11] Kherty's appellation for the first time is shown to be a corruption of the Semitic etymon 'horid' (lower).

In the example presented, Egyptologists have switched the 'h' with a 'k' and the 'd' with a 't' - common to the Semitic dialects, thus rendering his name in the first person as Kority. Originally unpointed, scholars have also reconfigured the vowel 'i' with the 'e', conjoined with the letter 'r' - a morpheme dropped in the

Egyptian dialect. 'Kherty' is transcribed in the original tongue as 'Horidi' - a name pronounced gutturally as 'Khoridi'.[12]

Kherty's visage embodies the ram, and implies a relationship with the God 'Khnum' (joined - literally atonement). He records the 'Creator God' a proponent of the Nile's inundation.[13] The nomen 'Khnum' is etymologically a variant of 'Amun', characterized as water.[14]

The ancient Libyan word 'aman' (water)[15] is connected in the Semitic language to the noun 'amem' (concealment), correlated with Amun. In Hebrew, the obscured 'le'amem'[16] is matched linguistically with 'mayim' (water).[17] The 'siman mayim' (watermark)[18] suggests 'shamayim' (heavens),[19] conceived as the sky or the firmament, adjoined to 'shemesh' (the sun).[20]

Demise of the trapped ram evokes obstruction, recurrent with Satan - a name obtained from the Hebrew verbal stem 'stn' (an adversary, opponent or to obstruct). Talisman of the ram and sometimes the goat or gazelle is used in the Kabbalah and alchemical tradition to represent a fallen se'irim, identified with black (hidden) magic and human sacrifice.

The feathered ram a solar motif characterised as Amun – symbolic of the slain (risen) Lord identified with the western sun.

Doctrinally, the slain ram symbolizes conflict, personified as the fallen (dying) sun, elucidated in the Roman mysteries. The Latin term 'aris' (belonging to) pertains to 'Aries' (the ram), extracted from the Greek idiom 'ares' (conflict), efficacious of the Western (hidden) priesthood.

'Ares' conveyed in Latin and Greek signifies 'aeris' (the sky) and 'aer' (air) - metaphors of the 'spirit' (breath), cognizant with the lamb and death. Rebirth of Aries is compatible in Hebrew with 'aliya' (the ascendant) lamb 'ayal' - histrionic of the sun's resurrection.

Theologically, Amun the God of Darkness is paired with the reification of the innocent lamb. Etymological comparisons suggest the propitiation of the hidden votive. Defined through ritual, Amun's nomenclature is switched in the Old Semitic with 'Aamu' (an Asiatic) - see footnote.[21]

'Aamu' (Westerner) taken from the hieroglyphic spelling is transcribed by some academics as 'Ramu' - a generic term applied to (people or mankind).[22] The modern Hebrew word 'am' (nation)[23] Arabic 'umma' suggests the hieroglyphic transliteration is suspect. Distinguished in the Hebrew as 'Emori' or the 'Aamu' (Amorite), the name 'Ramu' infers the Arabic etymon 'ramm' (grief),[24] equidistant with the 'Occidental' nations.

Academic scholars previously corrupted the spelling 'am' (nation) and offer the alternative spelling 'ramu' to connote heavenly or angelic beings, identified with death. The Semitic word 'ram' (lofty) infers 'ramm' (grief), philological to 'ra'am' (thunder).[25] Clashing of the heavens implies dissension and darkness, congruous with the 'flashing serpent', featured as the 'transfigured king or angel'.

Probation of the ram thus interconnects with the pharaonic cult of 'Amun', affiliated to the 'Aamu' priesthood of Babylon, equated with the solar ram and war. Typically symbolized as ascended or hung, the 'ram' annotates the lodge hut or tabernacle, preserved in the Roman language. The Latin adjective 'rame' describes (branches or boughs),[26] inimical of the trapped ram housed within a tent or tabernacle.

In conclusion, 'ramus' (branch) contrasts with the Semitic stem 'ramay' (a deceiver),[27] implicit of the veiling of rites, concurrent in Biblical tradition with the patriarch Lot. Philologically 'ramus' (bough) is traced from the Egyptian root 'ramm' (grief), signifying the '(R)-Aamu' (people). Rendered in the Hebrew as the 'am' or the 'Emori', they are cross-referenced in the Latin with the 'emorior' (to die off).[28]

Ancestry of the Roman and Greek Emperors follow the 'Ramu' (people), covert to the 'Aamu', denoting the 'Western nation' - the 'am' or 'umma'. Connived from Thebes, this ultra secretive priesthood originated from Syria. Roman mythology verifies the 'Ramu' (Aamu) as a nation delineated from the Imperial Roman House of 'Ramnes'.[29] Its faction is recognizant with the clan of 'Remus and Romulus'[30] - progenitors of Rome.[31]

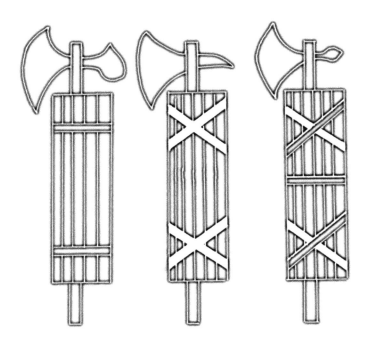

Three variations of the fasces logo – judicial of imperial (sacred) law

Concealed, the Ramnes bloodline replicated itself through the sigil of the 'flowering branch' (rame) - a signifier of Rome. Reproduced as the 'fascis' (bundle),[32] the branch is covert to the Fascist brotherhood.[33] Developed from Babylon, the Imperial lineage of Ramnes follows the Sodalist fraternity of Lot (Aamu), precipitated through the induction of Abraham.

Initiation of Abraham into the cult of Amun earmarked the sacrificial ram and the emolument of Isaac, expropriated to the king. This rite is linked to the lambing season, accorded to the patriarch Lot, proliferated (ramified) from the Western nation of the Amorites - outlined in the next chapter.

1   Prolog, Pocket Bilingual Dictionary, English-Hebrew, Hebrew-English, Prolog 2003, p458

2   Ralph Ellis, Eden in Egypt, A Translation of the Book of Genesis out of the Original Egyptian Text, Edfu Books 2005, p281 (Appendix A5 - Dictionary / Amen)

3   Ibid

4   Prolog, Pocket Bilingual Dictionary, English-Hebrew, Hebrew-English, Prolog 2003, p426

5   Ibid, p144

6   Ibid, p39

7   Ibid, p91

8   Hippocrene Concise Dictionary, English-Arabic, Arabic-English, Hippocrene 2005, p46

9   The Latin noun 'agnus' (lamb) combines the Greek words 'hagios' (holy) with 'amnos' (lamb).

10 George Hart: A Dictionary of Egyptian Gods and Goddesses, Routledge & Kegan Paul 1986, p110

11 Prolog Pocket Bilingual Dictionary, English-Hebrew, Hebrew-English, Prolog 2003, p239

12 Attempt to hide 'Kherty's name, originally 'Horidi', is further linked to Masonic symbolism. 'Kherty' is a pun on the Syrian profession 'khaiyata(i)' (tailor) - a symbol of the lamb and door (Refer to Chapter 24 the Crown of Jupiter).

13 George Hart: A Dictionary of Egyptian Gods and Goddesses, Routledge & Kegan Paul 1986, p110

14 'Khnum' a variant of the name 'Amun' is characterized as 'blood' and 'water'. Combination of Khnum with Amun is pictured as the menstrual sunset - stylized as the red goat. Relationship between air and water suggests the elevated (winged) ram is typically amalgamated or switched with the amphibious fish - a goat correlated with descent.

15 George Hart: A Dictionary of Egyptian Gods and Goddesses, Routledge & Kegan Paul 1986, p5

16 Prolog, Pocket Bilingual Dictionary, English-Hebrew, Hebrew-English, Prolog, 2003, p277

17 Ibid, p455

18 Ibid

19 Ibid, p183

20 Ibid, p403

21 'Aamu' (a Westerner) translated alternatively as (an Asiatic) does not infer a 'Semite' as commonly assumed within academia, but relates to a hidden Caucasian race - its priesthood affiliated to the worship of nocturnal angels (Refer to Chapter 11, The Amorites). Further, the designation 'west' does not specify a location, but is encumbant of a hidden nation, classified with the Aamu (Amorite) and the Dual Crown of Egypt.

22 Ralph Ellis: Eden in Egypt, A Translation of the Book of Genesis out of the Original Egyptian Text, Edfu Books 2005, p300 (Appendix A5 – Dictionary)

23 Prolog Pocket Bilingual Dictionary, English-Hebrew, Hebrew-English, Prolog 2003, p295

24 Hippocrene Concise Dictionary, English-Arabic, Arabic-English, Hippocrene 2005, p268

25 Prolog Pocket Bilingual Dictionary, English-Hebrew, Hebrew-English, Prolog 2003, p419

26 John C Traupman PhD: The New College Latin & English Dictionary, Bantam Press 1988, p259 ['Rame' (of branches or boughs)].

27 Prolog Pocket Bilingual Dictionary, English-Hebrew, Hebrew-English, Prolog 2003, p100

28 John C Traupman PhD: The New College Latin & English Dictionary, Bantam Press 1988, p99

29 Ibid, p259

30 Remus' death at the hand of his brother Romulus mirrors Cain and Abel (avel - mourn).

31 The Roman imperial lineage 'Ramnes' depicted as 'ramus' (a branch) extends to the Presidential family name Bush - a bloodline related to the Roman Emperors and European Royalty.

32 John C Traupman PhD: The New College Latin & English Dictionary, Bantam Press 1988, p113

33 The 'fascis' (bundle) is extrapolated from the stem 'fas' noted as the divine law.

11

The Amorites

The great king
of the Southern island
His name is the greatest
Hame Hame Ha
He's known as a
very romantic king
All the wind is his song
All the stars are his dreams
*Hame Hame Ha
Hame Hame Ha
Hame Hame Hame Hame Ha

The great king
of the Southern island
His queen's name is also
Hame Hame Ha
A very kind wife
She gets out of bed after sunrise
And goes to bed before sunset
Hame Hame Ha ... (*repeat)

The great king
of the Southern island
All his children are named
Hame Hame Ha
They don't like school, and
if it's windy, are late to class
When it rains they stay at home
Hame Hame Ha ... (*repeat)

[All] the people
of the Southern island
Everybody's name
is Hame Hame Ha
An easy name to remember
But alas, is confusing to all
As everybody you meet is called
Hame Hame Ha!
Hame Hame Ha ... (*repeat)[1]

Japanese Children's Rhyme, Music Rights Tokyo KK
1976: Translation by Hikaru Ai & Pierre Sabak[1]

Amun historically is a God of the ancient Egyptians (overtly the local God of Thebes), whose worship spread to Greece and Rome. The Romans referred to him as Jupiter Ammon, equated in Greece with Zeus. Archaically, Amun is allied with the Amorites - the founders of the first Dynasty of Babylon, in particular with the rule of Hammurabi I (d.1750 BC).

A critical examination of Hammurabi's name suggests the deity Amun originated from Babylon and is not indigenous to Egypt. The priests of Amun are a death cult and venerate the resurrection of Osiris, affiliated with the Southern Crown and the western sun.

The cognomen 'Hammurabi' is translated as (the Rabbi of Aamu). Depicted as (the Westerner), he is recorded as 'ish-hama'arav'.[2] In the Egyptian language, the name 'Hammurabi' is read in the plural as (the priest of Amun), phoneticized as 'Ahimnu-wabi'. Semantically, the title is interchangeable with (the priest of the Aamu) otherwise the 'Aamu-wabi'. 'Wabbi' or 'warbi' is Egyptian for (priest)[3] and in Hebrew 'Rabbi' is related to the Syrian word 'ryab' (the setting of the sun)[4] and 'rarbi' (west).[5]

The Hebrew appellation 'Rabbi' literally (Lord or Master) is rendered in the hieroglyphic as 'wabi' (a priest)[6] and is consistent with the word 'Arab(i)' (an Arab). Denominational status aligns the Judaic and Arabic priesthood to Egypt via Babylon. The Arabs are represented esoterically as (a scorpion) in Egyptian Arabic 'aa'rab'[7] - its venom a marker denoting the bull's phallus. Early reference to this animal is found in the tomb of King Scorpion, 3300 BC. His inscription refers to the 'Mountain of Darkness', suggesting (the west).[8]

Symbol of the scorpion is further integral to the deity 'Mithra' - the God of resurrection worshipped in Persia and Rome. In the Old Persian, 'Mithra' translates as (contract), originating from the Sanskrit word 'mitra' also (a contract) - a term synonymous in the Sumerian language with 'Martu' (West). Mitra otherwise Mithra is interchangeable in Hebrew with 'mitsva' (commandment),[9] connoting 'mitsri' (an Egyptian).[10]

Within the ecclesiastical tradition, the 'mitra' distinguishes (the bishop's mitre), symbolic of the 'Western' (Martu) Church. The Greek noun 'mitre' signifies (a girdle or turban). Vestures worn by the priest denote the 'contract' - emblematic of the 'mitra' and the worship of 'Mithra'.

Veneration of Mithra in Rome and Persia is cognate in Egypt with the sacrifice of Amun - the amphibious ram. Ancestry of the innocent lamb in the Roman Church is deified as Christ - the personification of God. Amun's loss parallels redemption, recorded in the Avestan mysteries as the blood of Mithra.

In Roman Catholicism, the 'mitra' (agreement) is sanctioned through the Holy 'mother' (the mater), signified as the fish. An ancient device, the fish's crown is worn in Babylon by the priests of Dagon (Nimrod), representational of an angel, grouped with the phallus - conical of the mitra. Progeny of the fish and priestess is deemed as angelic or royal and records the Western covenant.

Like Amun, Mithra is manifested through the offering and is partnered with 'Martu' (the Western) sun in relation to 'death', rendered in Persian as 'mart' Latin 'mort'. Covert, sacrifices attributed to the Martu (Amorite) are identified with the 'martyr, Greek martur' (a witness) - an admission of Mithraic rites.

In the Semitic dialect, 'Mithras' cognomen suggests 'sirat mifras' (a sailboat),[11] explicit of the 'host', 'sailor' or 'angel'. His followers are 'rewarded' (Greek misthos) with eternal life. Mithra traditionally is considered as the God of the sun, linked with the sacrifice of the 'bull' (Taurus), consigned astrologically to the Pleiades.

Mithra with bull (Pleiades), dog (Sirius) and scorpion (Arab). Droplets of blood depicted as corn – a symbol of heaven. The sheaf of corn also doubles as a serpent, feather or dreadlock emblems of the reaper.

Etymological comparison between 'mitra' (covenant) and 'Martu' (West) suggests Mithra is affiliated to the setting sun, correlated in Hebrew with 'mita' (death).[12] Philological resemblance reveals a connection between the 'Martu' and Amorite, referred to by the scholar David Rohl.

The Kingdom of the Amorites is situated between Mesopotamia and the Mediterranean lands of Western Asia, termed 'Amurru'. The Egyptian word for Semitic (or Asiatic) is 'Aamu'[13] - a term cognate with 'Hyksos' annotated 'Aam'. 'Aamu's definition is further derived from the Akkadian 'Amurru' - a derivative of the Sumerian word 'Martu' (Westerners).[14] 'Martu' is catalogued in the Hebrew as 'Emori' and is indexed under the name (Amorite). Emori is rendered from the Hebrew etymon 'eima' (horror).[15]

The phallic crown the mitra is worn in Babylon by the priests of Dagon.
An Angel or Dragon the protagonist Nimrod is represented as a fish.

The 'Martu' are characterized linguistically with the late Persian word 'mart' (death), Hebrew 'mita', Arabic 'mot' and informs the Latin root 'mort'. In the Modern Arabic, the 'Martu' (Westerners) refer to the 'Mada' priesthood, recourse to the 'Medoi' (English Median).[16]

Philologically, the Greek denomination 'Medoi' informs the Hellenistic word 'media' (cunning),[17] denoting the serpent or artificer (mason) - symbolic of the ram (Amun). Median's root is observed in the Latin adjective 'medeis' (magic),[18] evocative of 'Media' (a female priest) or 'Medix' (a magistrate).[19] Appellation of the 'medix' is analogous in the Roman language to the feminine noun 'medius' (middle),[20] connoting the priestess or arbitrator.

Ritual practices, concordant with 'medeis' (magic), correspond in Greek with 'magikos' (magic) from 'Magos' (a practitioner of the arts). Assignment of 'Magos' is a derivation from the Old Persian etymon 'Magus' (a magician). The

'Magus' or 'Maga' are correlated in the Semitic languages with the propagation of the angelic lineage. Demonstrated in Hebrew lexicology, 'Magus' is equivalent to 'maga mini' (sexual intercourse),[21] cogent with the Hebrew word 'magi' rendered in English as (occult).[22]

Magus is further related in the Old Arabic to the direction 'magahrib or marrib' (west). Etymologically 'magahrib' is deduced from the priestly groups the 'Maga' and 'Rabbi' - synonymous with the 'Mada' and 'Martu', definitive of (the West). Offspring of the 'Martu', commonly known as (the Median) Greek 'Medoi', correlate with the arcane people the 'Amorites', analogous to the 'Westerner'.

Transliteration of the Anglicized name Amorite is recorded in the Latin corruption 'Amoritus' literally (lover of rites), consistent with (favor-rite). The Roman masculine noun 'ritus' (rite)[23] is traced from the Sanskrit root 'ritu' (red), corresponding to the Latin feminine noun 'vitis' (vine).[24] Subterfuge in the Roman language of the name 'Amurru' Hebrew 'Emori' into 'Amoritus' parallels the Sanskrit etymology 'amrit' (the nectar of the Gods). 'Amoritus' is translated from the Arabic word 'Accadi' (English Akkadian) - a modification from 'akh-ada' (a brother [of the] offering).[25]

Elixir of the Aamu pertaining to the Amorite or Akkadi suggests blood drinking, rendered in the Greek as 'ambrotos' (English ambrosia, the immortal food of the Gods), denoting the menses blood. Commensurate in Arabic with 'ahmar' (red), the Amorite is indicative of the 'Aamu', registered from the line of 'Adam' (adom - red), 'Cain' (khanun - red) and 'Esau' (Edom - red).

Designation of the Amurru in the Egyptian idiolect is punned conceptually with 'Ameri' (not loved) Latin 'amarities' (bitter).[26] The Aamu or Amurru people are rendered in the Hebrew language as the 'Emori' - a term borrowed in the Latin to signify the concept (to die, die off or die out).[27]

Emori are defined as a Royal line, evident in the Egyptian Arabic title 'emir' (a prince)[28] and 'emira' (princess).[29] By definition, the 'Aamu' are (a people or a nation) Hebrew 'am',[30] Arabic 'umma'.[31] In addition, they are associated with death of the firstborn, provident in Judaic theology. Liturgical appropriations of the newborn in the Egyptian dialect are cognizant with 'ama' (to give)[32] and 'amma' (mother)[33] from the Sanskrit root 'amah' (nurse).

The 'emira' (royal) and 'amma' (matriarch) infers incestual relations obtained from the root 'aama' (a father's sister or aunt).[34] Prenatal, the amma connotes the Arabic etymon 'ahmar' (red)[35] and informs the Greek noun 'haima' (blood). The red mother heralds the 'prince' (amir, plural umara)[36] recondite in the Persian with 'mar' (a snake), esoterically the red ouroboros depicted as a dragon or fox.

Inception of the 'Western prince' (amir) from the 'scarlet' (ahmar) 'matriarch' (amma) is referenced in Apocryphal literature in the book of Revelation. Represented as the Antichrist, his mother the 'Scarlet Whore' is symbolic of menstruation and the 'west' (rarbi), relative to the Rabbi and the Mada (Martu) priesthood.

In the Indo-European languages, the direction 'west' is inauspicious and paired with death. 'Occidental' denoting someone from the 'West' is derived from the Latin 'occidere' (to massacre, annihilate, wipe out, slay, kill or murder) and is cognizant with 'occidens' (the setting sun and the West).[37] The term 'Occidental' is mutually inclusive of the 'Emori' (Aamu), associated with the 'Amorite' (Martu, Mada, Arab and Rabbi).

Geographically, the border separating Egypt from Amurru is located in modern day Syria, referred to by the Greeks as 'Aramaios', recorded in the biblical rendition 'Aram' (reductive of Aamu). The appellation 'Aamu' marks 'Ham' - the son of the biblical patriarch Noah. In Genesis 10, Ham is noted as the father of Cush, patriarch to the God Nimrod (the Hunter - Orion). Genesis 10:10-11 King James Edition, Nimrod's Kingdom encloses the following regions:

'And the beginning of his kingdom was babel [tower], and Erech [Iraq], and Accad, and Calneh, in the land of Shinar [Sumer]. Out of that land went forth Asshur [Assyria later Israel], and built Nineveh, and the city Rehoboth, and Calah.'

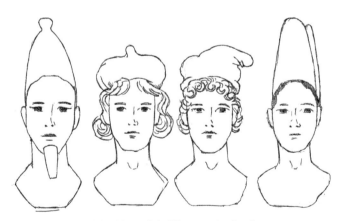

Headdress of the Western priesthood

Traditionally Ham's son 'Cush' (negro) is descended from the Southern part of ancient Nubia, a region of Southern Egypt and Northern Sudan, ruled under the Southern White Crown. Biblical scholars argue the cursed line of Ham signifies the black races, exploited as a sophism to conceal a hidden lineage.

Pairing of Aramaios with Southern Egypt suggests the two regions are archaically identified with the same branch of people. The governance of these localities are historically stipulated covertly under contractual obligation to the rule of Hammurabi, apportioned to the Upper Crown.

According to seals dedicated to Hammurabi (Ahimnu-wabi), the principle deity of the 'Aamu' is referred to as 'Amurru' - a term also used to distinguish his (nation or people). Amurru is interchangeable with the Egyptian God Amun.

The partnership of Egypt with the nation Amurru or Aamu incorporates the Babylonian (Akkadian) empire with the Dual Crown of Egypt. The affiliation of the Upper and Lower House demarcates the rule of 'Hammurabi' (the Rabbi of Aamu) - an iteration of the 'West'. Hammurabi's Kingdom is extended centrally to the province of Thebes - historically considered as the capital of Amun.

Close examination of fragmentary evidence suggests Amun's city is stealthily situated in or nearby the Western regions of Mari on the Western bank of the Euphrates in Syria. The most likely site for Amun's capital is the city of Haran, placed centrally amongst Mari, Asshur and Nuzi.[38] Additionally, Haran shares the name of Abraham's brother, the father of his nephew Lot,[39] biblically the patriarch of the Amorite people. Haran's relationship with Lot infers the worship of Amun and a causal link with Judaism.

Argument for the placement of Amun's throne next to the Euphrates River is demonstrated religiously. Amun is depicted both as a hidden God, equated with water and a God of the West, allied to Hammurabi and the crescent. Devotional masking of Amun's origin and his capital is integral to his deification.

Hammurabi's region extends to the biblical Kingdom of Erech, transliterated as Iraq. Erech in the Old Semitic is written 'Uruk' (Iraq)[40] and is from the Syrian plural noun 'uruq' (vein),[41] metrical to the Arabic transitive verb 'haraq' (to burn).[42]

'Haraq' is symbolic of the hidden votive, consigned religiously to Amun and his covert residence at Haran overtly Thebes. Semantically 'uruq' and 'haraq' is grouped in the Old Semitic with 'harel' (an altar),[43] deduced from 'har-El' (God's mountain).[44] Relationship between the mountain and the pyramid is linked in Canaanite mythology to angelic rebellion, sequenced in Hellenistic chronology with the royal lineage of Erech.

Classical legends suggest 'Erech' is identical to the 'Emori' (Aamu), rendered in the Latin as 'occidental' (dead). The weakened lineage of Erech pertains historically to the destruction of Atlantis - aboriginal with the Athena and Theban priesthood. An offshoot of the Western nation 'Uruk' (Iraq) subsequently Erekh (Athens) is traced from the descendents of Ham - the son of Noah (Refer to Chapter 32 The Builders).

'Erech's name, indexed in Classical Greek, signifies (strife), abridged from the Semitic noun 'yare'akh' (moon), diminutive of 'yored' (to descend). The lunar crescent is an emblem of Venus and marks the Assyrian or 'Western priesthood'. Etymologically, 'Erech' and 'yare'akh' relate to the verb 'havoc' - its root according to the Oxford dictionary unknown.

Significantly Erech's application in ancient Greek is used to note the Athenian Kings, whose vestiges originate from a fallen lineage (angelic), equated with Uruq (Iraq). Classical mythology partners the Erechthenian Kings with Uruk, sourced earlier from Atlantis.

According to Plato, 'Erichthonios' or 'Erechtheus' is the first King of Athens and the progenitor of the Athenian race - a theme repeated in Homer's Iliad. Erechtheus (Cecrops) in Plato's account is noted for fighting against the people of Atlantis.[45] 'Erichthonios' and 'Erechtheus' names are translated as (the strife of the earth) and (the shatterer).[46]

Recorded in Greek legend, Erechtheus' appearance is part-human and part-serpent, listed in Plato's Critias with 'Cecrops' (circular eye), connoting the 'Cyclops'.[47] This astonishing tradition is repeated in Apollodorus' library: Cecrops is cited as the first King of Athens, born from the earth [Adam], possessing the body of a man and a serpent, joined into one.[48]

Example afforded by Erech and the Athenian line is important, as it illustrates the region of Greece is connected to Syria and its satellite Egypt specifically Thebes. Bloodline of the Athenian Kings and later the Roman Emperors traced their descent from the capital Thebes covertly Haran. Influential, Haran's affiliation outlined the serpent's genus and the propagation of the Western or Roman Church.

In the ancient order, Thebes government annotated the Cobra crown - a device ratified covertly with Syria (Haran) and the 'Western Priesthood' nominal of Amun. Secretly, this denomination is known throughout history variously as the 'Aamu', 'Emori', 'Erech', 'Uruq', 'Amorite', 'Canaanite', 'Umma', 'Hyksos', 'Martu', 'Medoi' or 'Mada'. Its institutions seeded the Babylonian, Egyptian, Athenian and Roman Dynasties, avowed as the 'Western Empire', the cornerstone and mantle of 'Europe'!

1   The King's name 'Hame Hame Ha' contains a number of interesting puns in Japanese: 'Hame' is punned with 'ame' (rain), lateral to 'ama' (a nun, fisherman or slut). 'Ama' (a nun) is also a pun on 'hana' (a flower) and operates at a similar level linguistically to the Greek word 'neophyte' (newly planted). 'Hana' (flower) rhymes with 'hane' (feather) and 'oni' (demon), relative to 'haneru' (to jump or splash). 'Oni' additionally plays with 'hone' (bone) and 'fune' (ship). The latter connection is because the 'h' and 'f' are not differentiated in spoken Japanese. The King's last name 'ha' denotes (a tooth or blade).

2   Prolog Pocket Bilingual Dictionary, English-Hebrew-Hebrew-English, Prolog, 2003, p458

3   Bridget McDermott: Decoding Egyptian Hieroglyph, Duncan Baird Publishers, London, 2003, p169 (Sign Index List)

4   Hippocrene English-Arabic, Arabic-English Dictionary, Hippocrene, New York, 2005, p273

5   Ibid, p139

6   'Rabbi' signposted as (west) is an inversion of the English etymon 'priest' (prey-East).

7   Ahmed M.A. Abdel-Hady: Egyptian Arabic, The Rough Guide, Dictionary Phrasebook, Lexus, 1998, p221

8   Alan F. Alford: The Atlantis Secret, A Complete Decoding of Plato's Lost Continent, Eridu, 2001, p392 (Notes to Pages 125-140)

9   Prolog, Pocket Bilingual Dictionary, English-Hebrew, Hebrew-English, Prolog, 2003, p74

10 Ibid, p126

11 Prolog Pocket Bilingual Dictionary, English-Hebrew-Hebrew-English, Prolog, 2003, p352

12 Ibid, p99

13 David Rohl: A Test of Time, The Bible - From Myth to History, Century, 1995, p334

14 Zecharia Sitchin: The 12th Planet, Avon Books 1978, p84

15 Prolog, Pocket Bilingual Dictionary, English-Hebrew, Hebrew-English, Prolog 2003, p191

16 In Hellenistic legend, 'Media' translated in the Greek as (cunning) i.e. 'medeis' (magic) suggests a 'Median', implicit of a 'sorceress'. Media helped Jason to obtain the Golden Fleece and later married him. The Greek legend in theme parallels Moses' marriage to Ruel's daughter - a Medianite.

17 'Media' (Greek cunning) is translated in Hebrew as 'amem' (cunning, slyness or darkness) and is related philologically to 'Amun' (concealed).

18 John C Traupman PhD: The New College Latin & English Dictionary, Bantam Press, 1988, p180

19 Ibid, p181

20 Ibid, p180

21 Prolog, Pocket Bilingual Dictionary, English-Hebrew, Hebrew English, Prolog, 2003, p211

22 Ibid, p277

23 John C Traupman PhD: The New College Latin & English Dictionary, Bantam Press 1988, p272

24 Ibid, p497

25 Hippocrene English-Arabic, Arabic-English Dictionary, Hippocrene, New York, 2005, p148 & p317 ['Ada' (Give)]

26 John C Traupman PhD: The New College Latin & English Dictionary, Bantam Press, 1988, p13

27 Ibid, p99

28 Hippocrene English-Arabic, Arabic-English Dictionary, Hippocrene, New York, 2005, p171

29 Ibid, p172

30 Prolog, Pocket Bilingual Dictionary, English-Hebrew, Hebrew-English, Prolog, 2003, p295

31 Hippocrene English-Arabic, Arabic-English Dictionary, Hippocrene, New York, 2005, p79

32 'Ama' (give) and 'amma' (mother) are etymologies consistent in Arabic with 'amr' (an order or command).

33 Ralph Ellis: Eden in Egypt, A Translation of the Book of Genesis out of the Original Egyptian Text, Edfu Books, 2005, p82

34 Ahmed M.A. Abdel-Hady: Egyptian Arabic, The Rough Guide, Dictionary Phrasebook, Lexus, 1998, p221

35 Hippocrene English-Arabic, Arabic-English Dictionary, Hippocrene, New York, 2005, p100

36 Ibid, p95

37 John C Traupman PhD: The New College Latin & English Dictionary, Bantam Press, 1988, p202

38 Asshur is the spiritual home of the tribe of Ashur later Israel and is adjacent to Nuzi - the location of the Nazir priesthood (Nazorean).

39 Ian Ross Vayro, Tears In Heaven, Joshua Books, Australia, 2008, p353

40 'Uruq' (vein) is equated in the occult to 'azraq' (blue), hence the English expression 'blue blood' - a term used to define a king or noble, whose bloodline originates from Uruk (Iraq). Semitic deities from heaven, correlated with blood drinking, are signified with the blue stone Lapis.

41 Hippocrene English-Arabic, Arabic-English Dictionary, Hippocrene, New York, 2005, p135

42 Ibid, p89

43 Ralph Ellis: Eden in Egypt, A Translation of the Book of Genesis out of the Original Egyptian Text, Edfu Books 2005, p273 (Appendix A5 - Dictionary Sign Lists)

44 Prolog, Pocket Bilingual Dictionary, English-Hebrew, Hebrew-English, Prolog, 2003, p264 ['Har' (Mountain)]

45 Alan F. Alford: The Atlantis Secret, A Complete Decoding of Plato's Lost Continent, Eridu, 2001, p219

46 Ibid, p279

47 'Cecrops' (circular eye), a name cross-referenced in the Hebrew with 'khrop' meaning (sleep).

48 Alan F. Alford: The Atlantis Secret, A Complete Decoding of Plato's Lost Continent, Eridu, 2001, p263

12

Thebes and the Offspring of the Dragon

'The world's great empress on the Egyptian plain,
That spreads her conquests o'er a thousand states,
And pours her heroes through a hundred gates,
Two hundred horsemen and two hundred cars
From each wide portal issuing to the wars'.[2]

POPE: Iliad, i (Thebes)

Obscured, the hidden priesthood of 'Aamu' are known as the 'Western people' and are identical to the 'Emori' (the Amorite). Affiliated to the Southern Crown, the Aamu are covert to the rule of Hammurabi and his introduction of Amun theology into Egypt. Hammurabi's rule 1750 BC is contemporaneous with the Second Intermediate Period in Egypt (1782-1570), prior to the founding of the New Kingdom (1570-1070).[2]

Promulgation of Hammurabi's doctrine culminated with the 18th Dynasty and the rule of the Pharaoh Amenhotep IV - a lineage deduced from the 'Hyksos' (Amorite). Egyptologists know Amenhotep IV more commonly under the pseudonym 'Akhenaten' (Risen Sun)[3] or 'Amenophis' (Hidden Snake). Akhenaten's capital relocated to Amarna, subsequent to the apparent dissolution of the Theban theocracy.[4]

Philologically, 'Theban' is derived from the Arabic noun 'ta'ban' (a snake),[5] recorded in Egyptian Arabic as 'teaban' (a cobra).[6] The sign is used in the hieroglyphic to write Upper Egypt (Southern Kingdom), its capital Thebes aligned to the White Crown of Osiris. Egyptologists mistranslate the 'cobra' (teaban) as the Goddess 'Wadjet' - a clever pun on the Sanskrit noun 'Rajah' (king).[7]

The cobra is a symbol of the Theban priesthood identified with heaven.

Relationship between the 'seraph' and 'Theban' is picked up in the Latin polyvalent 'anguigena' (offspring of the dragon)[8] or (Theban).[9] Thebes is esoteric in the Phoenician language of 'thibbun' (naval),[10] assumed through the matriarch's copulation with the 'snake' (a fallen angel). Presented as a religious place of study or 'instruction', Thebes informs the Judaic transmission of the oral tradition, the 'Talmud' (Refer to Appendix 5). In the Arabic etymon, 'ta'ban' (a snake)[11] is closely related to 'talib' or 'taliba' (a student)[12] known in the English-speaking world as the 'Taliban'. An 'initiate', the 'taliban' is depicted as 'ta'alib' (a fox)[13] symbolic of a cunning or sly animal. Maligned, the canine is recondite with a red serpent and Sirius (See Footnote[14]).

Thebes traces its historical precedence from the first man 'Kadmos' literally (ancient one or easterner).[15] In Hebrew, 'kadum' (ancient)[16] is a play on the Old Semitic word 'Qadam' (East) identified with Orion.[17] 'Kadum' (ancient) refers to 'kadmoni' (the ancestral),[18] assigned in the Semitic language to Adam, depicted as the fox, equated with the rouge serpent.

'Kadmos' (ancient one) informs the Greek etymon 'kadm(e)ia' (the earth), figurative of Adam the neophyte, derived from the Hebrew word 'adom or aduma' (red).[19] His offspring is indexed in the Hebrew with 'adama' (soil), denoting (the red earth).[20] The nation of Adam is signified as 'ard-am' (the people of the earth).[21] Likewise, in Greek 'kadmeia' (Latin cadmean - earth) translates as (a Theban) and is correlated with the scarlet pigment cadmium.[22]

Kadmoni, Kadmos and Adam etymologically refer to the 'Kadmeioi' people, known also as the 'Akkadi' or 'Akkadians' in north central Mesopotamia (Iraq, Uruq or Erech), and share the same family line as the Aamu, stated in the previous chapter.

In Arabic, the noun 'acad' (knot or tie)[23] is equal to 'akkad' (to confirm),[24] implicit of the contract with Egypt. Interchangeable, the Akkadi are punned with 'akh-ada' (brothers of the offering), translated into the Latin as the Amorites.

> '...The 'Akkadi' people [are] known [earlier] as the 'Kaldi' and later the Chaldeans'.[25]

Relationship between the Kadmeioi and the Kaldi are preserved within Thebes and later the Greek centers Athens and Lemnos. Historically, the 'Akkadians' (Arcadia) are known as the 'Kadmeioi' (Semitic Kaldi) and are responsible for the seeding of Thebes and the worship of Amun.

Rendition of the 'Kadmeioi' is grouped in the Latin with the intransitive verb 'cadere' (to fall), and implies the fallen daystar Lucifer, conjunct with the Theban priesthood the 'Kadmeioi'. Arabs record the bloodline of 'Kadmeioi', adjunct with 'Gabriel' alias 'Al-Khidr', subsequent to the development of the Western Church. 'Al-Khidr' (the Green One) is emblematic of the neophyte, affiliated to Thebes and Akkad.

Denomination of the 'Kadmeioi' is represented with the emblem of 'kardia' Greek (heart), denoting the priesthood. 'Kardia' (heart) specifies the Roman dignary 'Cardinalis' (a Cardinal), equivalent in the Arabic to 'cadi' (a judge). 'Cadi' is representative of the Levite priest - a cognomen obtained from the Hebrew word 'lev' (heart).[26] The Cardinals attribute their lineage to the tribe of Levi and Moses. Ancestry of the 'Kadmeioi' is equivocal of the Theban (Akkadi), accredited with 'Kadmos' (the Ancient One), originating from 'Adam' (Orion).

'Kadmeioi' (Latin Cadmean) is a play on the Old Semitic namesake 'Kabeiroi', rendered (Great Gods). Idiomatically, 'Kabeiroi' is a Greek adaptation of the Old Egyptian noun 'qeb' (snake), implicit of the Theban (Mari) line of Kings, ancestral to the 'Dog Star' (Arabic Al Kalb) - esoteric of al-qalb (the heart).

Historically, 'Kadmos' (Latin Cadmus) is the son of the Phoenician King 'Agenor', brother of 'Europa', the moon Goddess. Cadmus is punned with 'kamus' (hidden) - in its singular form 'kammon' or 'ammon', indicative of Amun, denoting the west.[27] Further, Europa's name is translated as 'the West' and is idiomatic of the 'Western Contract' (Martu or Mitra), espoused by the divine protagonist Mithra. Resurrection of Mithra augments the relationship between the Pleiades and Sirius conjugal to Orion and the line of kings.

'Kadmeioi' (Cadmean), emphasizing 'kadm(e)ia' (the earth), is variegated in the Greek from the Syrian word 'khadami' (service) a derivation of the intransitive verb 'khadam' (to serve).[28] The epithet in Egyptian Arabic records 'khaddam, Syrian khadim' (a servant).[29] 'Khaddam' is cultic of 'adama, Greek kadm(e)ia' (soil) - a signifier of the neophyte, espoused as the servant Adam (Orion).

According to Greek legend, 'Kadmos' (ancient one) created his people the 'Kadmeioi' (Cadmeans) by planting the teeth of a serpent,[30] allegoric of human sacrifice. 'Niv' Hebrew (fang)[31] connotes 'navi' (prophet)[32] - Arabic 'nabi'.[33] Referred to as the 'sown men',[34] the 'kadmeioi' priesthood are paired with the 'Theban' (serpent) and the 'neophyte'. Translated from the Greek appellation 'neophutus' (the newly planted), the 'neophyte' determines the Latin masculine noun 'fetus' (foetus - an offspring), lateral to 'festus' (a feast).[35] Written as an adjective, 'fetus' indicates (breeding, pregnant, fruitful or productive).[36]

Bloodline of the initiate is transferred in Catholicism through a 'seminary' (a training college for Priests and Rabbis). Derivation of 'seminary' conveys the Medieval Latin 'seminarium' (seed plot), figurative of (a breeding ground),[37] relative to the 'neophyte'. Etymologically, the 'seminarium' (inseminator) is unified with 'Semelae' (the daughter of Cadmus, the mother of Bacchus).[38]

'Khzira' (the sown)[39] indicates the 'neophyte', matched with Theban, and is reminiscent of the Hebrew word 'khayzar' (a star-visitor or alien)[40] an expression equivalent in Greek to 'kaisar' (Caesar).

Followers of Bacchus historically wore blossom, a dual signifier of the neophyte, contrasted in Arabia with the djinn and serpent. A covert marker, the flower is clandestine of human immolation. In Greek, neophyte is testimonial of 'andros' (male) and 'anthos' (flower) - nominal of sacrificial death assigned to the newborn. The flower reappears in Greek symbolism as 'speiraia' (rose), cogent with 'speira' (coil), implicit of the dragon and neophyte. In Eastern Europe, the rose signifies a vampire.

> 'Wallis Budge informs us [that] in the Egyptian Language, in his list of hieroglyphs, that the sign for 'thorn' (which is the tooth of a plant) is almost identical with the sign for Sothis-Sirius... [and is additionally employed as a determinative sign for a tooth]'.[41]

The tooth operates as a symbol of a nocturnal angel, equated with the host and Sirius.

Anubis God of Death with flower logo - symbol of the Cannibal

During the Bacchic ceremonies, the flower votive worn around the neck (womb) is substituted with the firstborn male and works on the phonetic displacement of the 'p' and 'f' morpheme evident in the Semitic dialect.[42] In Hebrew, 'perekh' (flower)[43] is comparative to 'le farek' (to cannibalize).[44] 'Farek' is from the Hebrew word 'le faked'[45] (to command), denoting ritual law, pertaining to the offering of the newborn.

Deconstruction of the ancient languages demonstrate conclusively that the neophyte practiced human sacrifice, adopted in the myths of Bacchus and Christ - a bloodline descended from Agenor (Thebes). Resurrection of the deity signified the renewal of creation (man), personified as the sun, flower or serpent.

According to Greek and Semitic legend, mankind is not indigenous to earth, and his seed is likened to the cross pollination of plants. Progeny of the neophyte proceeds from 'kadm(e)ia' (the red earth), equated with Adam and Mars, imputative of sacrificial blood. Religiously 'Adam' (qadam - east) is aligned to the red ram Amun or Khnum, correlated with 'amen-t' (west). Astrologically, the 'east and west' personify 'Venus', grouped with 'Orion and Sirius'. Resurrection of the Dog Star is affiliated to the serpent and the Pleiades, intersected at Thebes.

Agenor's progeny the 'Cadmeans' (Kadmos /Adam) are otherwise referred to as the 'Thebans',[46] identical in Latin to the 'anguigena' (serpent race). A derivative of the Roman noun 'anguis' (snake, serpent or dragon),[47] 'anguigena' pertains to the adjective 'agustan' (imperial).[48] Agustan's lexicology is obtained from the root 'agust' (sacred, venerable, majestic or magnificent)[49] terminology disclosing the 'augury'. Agustan is also the title adopted by the first Emperor Octavius.

Cited as the Imperial Emperor (63 BC-AD 14), Augustus aka Gaius Octavius[50] is contemporaneous to Jesus and the development of the Roman Church. The title Augustus is reduced philologically from 'Ogygia' (Theban),[51] named in honor after the mythical King of Thebes 'Ogyges'.[52] His bloodline is further deduced from the Canaanite King 'Og-Yasir'.[53] Ogyges' reign is concurrent with Atlantis and Noah.[54] Registered with Erechtheus and Cecrops, Ogyges' divine offspring is described as part-human and part-serpent, otherwise angelic.

Ogyges' namesake rendered in Latin is grouped with the transitive verb 'oggero' (to bring or offer)[55] and is paired with 'ogganio' (to growl),[56] imitable of the canine. Growling of the dog religiously is cogent with the helical rising of the Dog Star, Sirius. Celebrated, the renewal of the constellation is marked ritualistically by the oracle barking or mimicking the canine, servile to the worship of Bacchus. Occult practice and knowledge observed through the 'orgia' (ceremony) is transferred from the Craft of the 'Ogygia'. Designation of the

'Ogygia' (Theban) divulges the Greek mystery 'orgia' (secret rite), translated into English as 'orgy', implicit of the 'ogre'. The ogre is compared to 'ogle' - a 'watcher or dragon'. Celebration of the 'orgia' denudes sexual practices, conceptual of the Greek verb 'orgao' (to swell or to be excited), quite literally 'oggero' (to bring) to an erection. 'Orgao' is anatomical of the organ, relative to 'orgasmos' (orgasm), thematic of the 'augury', initiated from 'Thebes' (Ogygia). Celebrants of the 'orgia' (orgy) accord to the sacred or imperial bloodline, conceived from angels the 'hemitheoi' (hemitheos), transpired from the oligarch Ogyges (Orion).

Ancestry of the Theban King Ogyges discloses the Roman Imperial lineage of Augustus, traced archaically from Erech and earlier Uruq (Iraq), cult centers contracted to Thebes. In addition, Thebes appears to have been aligned to the capital Mari. In ancient Persian, the appellation 'Mari' translates (of the serpent) and indicates (a serpent being), exterior to the Persian title 'mal' (a king). Esoteric, the location of Mari is matched with a 'Theban', articulated as 'teaban', assigned to the cobra ideogram.[57]

Application of the uraeus glyph records the 'anguigena' (a Theban), appended with (the offspring of the snake), in Greek the 'ogygia' (ogre). The 'anguigena' is analogous to 'Agustan' (imperial), and is replicated through 'Augustus' the first Roman Emperor, imaged as the 'serpent' (Latin anguis). To conclude, bloodline of Augustus is reciprocal of the Theban priesthood congruous with the snake.

The royal center Thebes extended its influence into the heart of Rome via the pharaonic (Theban) and Ptolemy (Greek) Dynasties. Descendents of the Syrian (Theban) priesthood created the Roman Church. In addition, they seeded the bloodline of Jesus through the Emperor Augustus himself.[58] Allied to the Western nations, Rome augmented the theology of Mithra with Amun to create the new religion Christianity, built upon the ashes of Jerusalem. Its new Kingdom and Temple were rebuilt as Christendom, located on the shores of England - a controversy raised in the next chapter!

> *And did those feet [Jesus] in ancient time*
> *Walk upon England's mountains green?*
> *And was the holy Lamb of God*
> *On England's pleasant pastures seen?*
> *I will not cease from Mental Fight,*
> *Nor shall my Sword sleep in my hand,*
> *Till we have built Jerusalem*
> *In England's green and pleasant Land.*[59]

William Blake: 1757-1827, British poet, and mystic 'Jerusalem' the hymn

1 Brewers Dictionary of Phrase & Fable, London, Cassel & Company Ltd, 1954, p896

2 Aude Gros de Beler: Pharaohs, Grange Books 2004, pp114-115 (Refer to Chronology Chart)

3 Some scholars translate 'Akhenaten' (Risen Aten) alternatively as the (Glorious Sun Aten).

4 Akhenaten's (Moses) espousal of monotheism had a major impact on the development of Judaism and later Augustine Christianity. Prior to Rome's dictator-ship, Thebes (Mari) center of influence extended into the Greek, Indian and Mediterranean world through the conquest of 'Alexander Ammon', known to historians as 'Alexander the Great'.

5 Hippocrene English-Arabic, Arabic-English Dictionary, Hippocrene, New York, 2005, p115

6 Ahmed M.A. Abdel-Hady: Egyptian Arabic, A Rough Guide Dictionary Phrasebook, Lexus, 1998, p69

7 Similarity between the 'w' and 'r', for example 'Wabi' and 'Rabbi', suggests the transliteration 'wadjet' is an intentional corruption of the Sanskrit noun 'rajah' (king). In Hindu mythology, the Rajah's bloodline is equated with the cobra - a device nominal of the 'Naga' (a race of serpents), cognate with the Theban.

8 John C Traupman PhD: The New College Latin & English Dictionary, Bantam, 1988, p15

9 Ibid

10 Marke Pawson: Gematria, The Numbers of Infinity, Green Magic, England, 2006, p46

11 Hippocrene English-Arabic, Arabic-English Dictionary, Hippocrene, New York, 2005, p292

12 Ibid, p120

13 Ibid, p50

14 The letters 'F-O-X' in the English alphabet are present, when divided into three equal columns of six and encode the number 666. This number is recognizant with the Theban priesthood, equated with the fox. Further in the hieroglyphic, the three conjoined tails of the fox are used to write the glyph 'mass' (a descendent), signifying Royal descent, associated etymologically with the prophet Moses. 'Mosis' (to draw out) denotes ritual anointing (baptism) of the Pharaoh, termed as the Messiah. The ruddy complexion of the fox is a symbol of the Caucasian bloodline, recorded in Judaic, Islamic and Koranic lore. In each tradition, Moses, Mohammed and Jesus have fair or ruddy complexions typically with red beards. The fox is a symbol of Sirius, and in Dogon (African) mythology is combined with the reptile or amphibian - a signifier of the 'nommu' (a type of fish deity), referred to as the 'watcher' or 'monitor'.

15 Alan F. Alford: The Atlantis Secret, A Complete Decoding of Plato's Lost Continent, Eridu 2001, p280

16 Prolog, Pocket Bilingual Dictionary, English-Hebrew, Hebrew-English, Prolog, 2003, p23

17 Translated by S.L. MacGregor Mathers, The Kabbalah Unveiled, Arkana 1991, p167

18 Prolog, Pocket Bilingual Dictionary, English-Hebrew, Hebrew-English, Prolog, 2003, p23

19 Ibid, p333

20 Ibid, p124

21 Hippocrene English-Arabic, Arabic-English Dictionary, Hippocrene, New York 2005, p150 ['Ard' (earth, soil, land, floor, surface, real estate, planet Earth)]

22 Cadmium refers to either a yellow or a scarlet red – compare to Cain (khanun).

23 Hippocrene English-Arabic, Arabic-English Dictionary, Hippocrene, New York, 2005, p321

24 Ibid, p148

25 Robert B Stacy-Judge: Atlantis Mother of Empires, Adventures Unlimited, 1999, p76

26 Prolog, Pocket Bilingual Dictionary, English-Hebrew, Hebrew-English, Prolog, 2003, p183

27 [Professor] Geoffrey Sampson: Writing Systems, Hutchinson Education 1985, p84

28 Hippocrene English-Arabic, Arabic-English Dictionary, Hippocrene, New York, 2005, p215

29 Ibid

30 Alan F. Alford: The Atlantis Secret, A Complete Decoding of Plato's Lost Continent, Eridu, 2001, p280

31 Prolog, Pocket Bilingual Dictionary, English-Hebrew, Hebrew-English, Prolog, 2003, p145

32 Ibid, p319

33 Snakes don't have teeth they have fangs. It can however be noted that the Arabic word 'sinn' (a tooth) transliterated in Hebrew as 'shen' recalls the shen motif, carried by Babylonian nocturnal angels. Further, in Hebrew the plural of 'shinayim' (tooth) is punned with 'shamayin' (heaven), linking the snake or fallen angel with the sky. The 'tooth' sign is written hieroglyphically as (Sirius).

34 Sowing of the serpent's teeth into the earth (man) signifies appropriations, paralleled to the king's resurrection as a serpent. Immolation of the flesh is closely analogous to sexual intercourse and procreation. Construed as (the newly planted), the 'neophyte' is paired sexually with the drakon (an angel), deified as a fallen God. Rebirth of the snake through concealed propitiations is symmetrical to the Cadmeans, conceived from the serpent's offspring.

35 John C Traupman PhD: The New College Latin & English Dictionary, Bantam Press, 1988, p398

36 Ibid, p115

37 Ibid, p283

38 Ibid, p282 The Goddess 'Semelae' is (the daughter of Cadmus and the mother of Bacchus by Jupiter).

39 Prolog, Pocket Bilingual Dictionary, English-Hebrew, Hebrew-English, Prolog, 2003, p384

40 Ibid, p20

41 *Robert Temple: The Sirius Mystery, Century, London, 1998, pp235-236 Quotation follows: ... The [thorn] sign [denoting Sirius] tilted 45 degrees represents 'a teb' (the land on one side of the Nile), and if placed one on top of another, forming a pair, means (all Egypt). The very same sign is incorporated in the sign for 'art', meaning (jawbone with teeth)... It may well be that all these puns on the determinative hieroglyphic sign for Sirius came, in the usual way with the pun-loving Egyptian priests, to form a complicated body of Sirius doctrine involving 'teeth'...*

42 Arabic is one of the few languages in the world without a 'p' sound. The 'p' phoneme has eroded in Modern Arabic and is transliterated as a 'f'. In Old Arabic and Aramaic, the 'p' sound is evident and is still present in Arabic's sister language Hebrew.

43 Prolog Pocket Bilingual Dictionary, English-Hebrew-Hebrew-English, Prolog, 2003, p155

44 Ibid, p56

45 Ibid, p74

46 John C Traupman PhD: The New College Latin & English Dictionary, Bantam, Press 1988, p31

47 Ibid, p16

48 Ibid, p26

49 Ibid

50 'Octavius' suggests the eighth ancestor from 'octavo' (eighth), conjunct with 'avus' (ancestor), and 'avis' (bird), connoting an angel - the Imperial symbol of Rome. The name additionally is a probable pun on 'oct-avius' (the eighth untrodden path), denoting the shores of 'Albion' (Britain).

51 John C Traupman PhD: The New College, Latin & English Dictionary, Bantam, 1988, p204

52 'Ogyges' name is derived from the Canaanite King Og, ruler of Bashan - a district east of the River Jordan, famous for its rich pastures, fat cattle and many peaked mountains. The sovereign is described biblically as a giant, implicit of Orion - his bloodline related to Goliath and the Nephilim. He is frequently mentioned in the stories of the attacks on Canaan, contemporaneous to Moses (Refer to Deuteronomy 3:1-11, Psalm 22:12 and 68:15, Isaiah 2:13).

53 King Og's title is 'yasir', indexed in the Arabic as (a captive) - an archaic name for (a neophyte). The captive imprisoned in the underworld is depicted in British heraldry as the chained 'unicorn' technically (a yale) - a symbol of the Windsor family. Note also the Arabic name Yasir is connected to the Palestinian leader Yasir Arafat. His place of birth recorded 'officially' in Cairo, Egypt August 24, 1929. His real name was Muhammad Abd al-Ra'uf al-Qudwah al-Husayni and according to his own admission was born in Jerusalem August 4, 1929 (The plot thickens!!!).

54 John C Traupman PhD: The New College, Latin & English Dictionary, Bantam, 1988, p204

55 Ibid

56 Ibid

57 The Persian designation 'mal' and 'mar' (leader and snake) is conceptual in Hebrew to 'melekh' (king), derived from 'mal'akh' (angel).

58 Alexander's rule governed the Middle East perpetuated through his general Ptolemy and the rise of the Greek Ptolemaic Dynasty (305-30 BC). Two and half centuries later, the offspring of the Ptolemaic and Roman line is merged with the Royal Highness Cleopatra. Famously the beautiful queen committed suicide by the bite of an asp, in double talk copulated with the noble line of Augustus. Cleopatra's secret heir conceived after the battle of Actium in 31 BC is Jesus Christ. This proposition is marked through a number of historical events. Firstly, she is a Theban queen. Her fated meeting with Caesar's General Mark Antony in Tarsus (Taurus) is the birthplace of Saul of Tarsus, a Roman citizen known later as St. Paul, the father of the Church. Circumstantial evidence suggests that Mark Antony is known otherwise as St. Mark the Apostle, companion to Peter and Paul. Mark originally a Greek name is attributed with the authorship of the second Gospel - chronologically the earliest in date. Importantly, 'Mark' in Latin translates as (a male or sprung from Mars), correlated with the title (Marquis). The descendents of Mars are identical in Hebrew to the name Adam, signified as Cadmus. Jesus' offspring are equated with the legend of Arthur and ruled over 'Albion' (Britain) post-Caesar's campaign.

59 Anthology of Quotations, Bloomsbury, London 2002, p130 (Quotation 2&3)

13

Christendom the Western Kingdom

'London: a nation, not a city'.[1]

Benjamin Disraeli (1804-81) British Prime Minister and Writer, Lothair (1870), Ch. 27

'London is a modern Babylon'.[2]

Benjamin Disraeli (1804-81) British Prime Minister and Writer, Tancred (1847), Bk. 5, Ch. 5

'GAUNT: This royal throne of kings, this sceptred isle,
This earth of majesty, this seat of Mars,
This other Eden, demi-paradise,
This fortress built by Nature for herself
Against infection and the hand of war'.[3]

William Shakespeare (1564-1616) English Poet and Playwright, Richard II (1595), Act 2, Scene 1

Linguistic evidence suggests the Theban (Syrian) priesthood via the conduit of Rome relocated its Empire to Britain. The Roman word 'Albion' (Britain)[4] is related in Latin to 'Alba Longa' (the mother city of Rome), founded by Ascanius, son of Aeneas.[5]

Ascanius' bloodline is represented in Freemasonry as 'ascia' (a mason's trowel),[6] symbolic of the kingdom resurrected.[7] Ascanius' father 'Aeneas' is a clever pun on the Latin adjective 'aenus' (bronze)[8] - an initiatory title translated from the Semitic homonym 'nahash' (serpent),[9] cogent in Arabic with 'nahas' (bronze).[10] The 'brazen seraph' suggests a 'Theban'.

In addendum, 'aenus' is a play on the Latin noun 'anus' (the alimentary canal), an organ identified with divination. Relationship between the stomach and snake is encoded in the Hebrew. The Semitic noun 'keva' (stomach)[11] is matched with 'ef'e' (an asp).[12] Aeneas' appellation cleverly alludes to the red (brazen) serpent, associated with the augury (orgia). Appearance of the sanguine deity is assumed as the 'Theban' (Ogygia) or 'snake' (ogre) - an ancestry combined with the original bloodline of Adam (Kadmos).

Inaugurated by Imperial Decree, the cult of Aeneas continued through Augustus and branched into the 'Northern Isles' under the Greek name 'Hyperborea' - a subtle play on 'Hypereia' (the old name for Italy).[13] Formation of 'Hypereia' is divested from 'Hyperb(eria)' (Thebes) - an occult centre interior to the 'Brotherhood of the Dragon'.

Idiomatically 'Hyperborean' is a Greek codeword for 'Hyperbius' (a Theban),[14] connected covertly to 'Hypereia' (the ancient name for Italy). Inception of 'Hypereia' is a product of the 'Trojan Wars' (Hyperenas),[15] conjunct with Ascanuis.

Formation of the name 'Albion' served as a Roman pun on the Greek word 'Hyperborean' (Huperboreoi) from 'Huper Boreas' (God of the most Northerly Wind).[16] Hyperborean's location alludes to 'Hypereia' (Italy), contracted to 'Hyperb(eria)' (Thebes).

Greek fable held that the atmosphere of Hyperborea is not like our own, but one consisting wholly of feathers. Both Herodotus and Pliny mention this fiction, which they suggest matches the quantity of snow observed to fall in those regions (Herodotus IV, 31).[17]

In Greek as in English, 'pteron' is a pun on 'pater', equivalent to (feather and father), and 'snow' is cognate with a 'messenger', nominal of an 'angel'. Herodotus' veiled language suggests Albion is inhabited by the original descendents of the Gods, traced from Thebes and Babylon - the center of the Judaic priesthood.

Albion's Roman capital is London (Latin Londinium) and first appears in Tacitus' account in AD 61 (Lib XIV, Ch 33).[18] Esoteric, 'Londinium' is a corruption of the Greek word 'Ladon'[19] - the name of the dragon that guarded the apples of Hesperides,[20] discursive in Hebrew of 'ladun' (a judge).[21]

In the Greek myth, Hesperides' is dualled with Eden theoretical to 'qadam' (East). Hesperides derives from the Greek etymon 'Hesperia' (Western),[22] consistent with 'Hesperus' (the Evening Star).[23] Further, 'Hesperia' designates the Greek name for (Italy - the Western land),[24] terminology originating from Babylon and its Western frontiers. In modern parlance, the 'West' signifies both 'America' and 'Europe' geographically impossible! The direction west is symbolic of the Roman priesthood, divested from Thebes and Babylon.

London's city gates are thus guarded by the double red dragon 'Ladon' and recall the brazen serpent of Thebes, synonymous with the Evening Star. Location of London (Ladon) encodes 'Hesperia' (the West), identified with 'Rome'. The stem 'Londin' further plays on the adjective 'Latin(e)', the Roman word 'latens' (hidden or secret).[25]

The occult word 'latens' (concealed) is correlated ritualistically with the 'barking dog' (latrator),[26] analogous with 'Latonus' (Apollo).[27] Equated with the 'midnight sun' (the coincidentia oppositorum), Latonus denotes the western sun and the setting of Venus. Additionally, the dog is a symbol of the rising star Sirius and its connection to the orgia rites, lateral to 'Ogygia' (a Theban). Patronage of the 'Ogygia' is generic of the monarch 'Ogyges', implicit of the Roman line 'Augustus' (Refer to Chapter 12).

Medieval woodcut (copy) depicting the queen sleeping with a dragon with canine attributes (Sirius).

Rome is presented as a colony of the Theban priesthood. Historically Augustus resettled his Empire overseas in England. Importantly the Emperor established the Western Church Christendom as the center of the New Jerusalem.

Destruction of the Jewish Temple in AD 70 is concurrent with the establishment of Londinuim in AD 61. Theologically the rebuilding of the temple is aligned to the resurrection of Christ and the new city Jerusalem. Promulgated through Imperial blood, God's kingdom integrates with the Jewish and Roman brotherhood, common to the Western priesthood. Rome's new Empire is shown to be Albion - a proposition attested to in the Latin and Greek.

'Hypereia' (the Old Latin name for Italy) is deduced from the Hellenistic word 'Hesperia' (the West) and is juxtaposed with 'Hyperborea' - a codeword to denote 'Albion' (the British Isles).[28] In the Roman language, 'Hesperia' (West)[29] designates 'Hispania' (Spain)[30] - i.e. a 'westward' direction from the coast of 'Italy'.[31]

Occupation of Spain via the Mediterranean is simultaneous to the military campaigns, concurrent with the civil war in Italy. Etymological comparisons suggest Rome's extent to unify 'Spain' (Hesperia) with 'England' (Albion) is relative to the Western homeland 'Italy' (Hypereia).

In conclusion, the Roman standard 'Albion' (Britain) is taken from the Latin stem 'alb' (white),[32] equated in the Egyptian Arabic to 'alb' (heart),[33] generic of the Levite priesthood. 'Albus' (white) is cultic of 'abire' (to disappear, pass away or die)[34] from the Semitic noun 'avel/abel' (mourner).[35] Semantically abel and abire is interchangeable with the Aamu, otherwise the 'Emori', Latin 'emorior' (the deceased), deemed as the 'Western or Occidental' nation Albion.

The namesake of Albion is a subtle acknowledgement of the intermarriage of the 'kadmeioi' the 'Cadmeans' (Martians), represented as the 'red men' (Adam), affiliated to the 'Cardinals' (the Levites). They proclaim allegiance to the Southern Crown of Thebes (Sirius) and its holdings, extending throughout the Mediterranean and Roman Empire.

Unification of the dual (Red and White) Kingdom of Thebes imposed a theocratic rule centrally upon England through the dictat of Rome. Transferral of power from the Roman (Thebes) Church is esoteric of the English rose 'neophutus' (the newly planted). The Greek word 'spiraea' (rose) quotes the 'dragon spiro' (speira-coil), referential to Theban autocracy. Emblazoned with the colors red and white, the rose proclaims the Dual Crown of Egypt.

Hieroglyphically the Theban distinguishes the Upper Kingdom with the 'shemau' plant, usually referred to as (a lily[36] or a fleur-de-lis). The Arabic phoneticism of 'shemau' is closely matched with 'shami' (smell or scent),[37] conversant with 'shams' (the sun).[38] Insignia of the 'shemau' plant suggests the 'descendents of light' (the illuminati). Generation of this stock is born from the 'heavens' or the 'sky' (Hebrew shamayin / Arabic sama).[39]

Evidence in the previous chapter demonstrates that the descendents of Horus are depicted with the cobra glyph (teaban), denoting 'Thebes' - the capital city of the Upper Kingdom. Epigraphically the 'shemau' foliage is rendered from the Arabic appellation 'shami' (Syrian).[40]

To emphasize, the 'shemau' plant records Hammurabi's Western Kingdom 'Syria' written with the same hieroglyph to signify the 'Upper Kingdom of Egypt'. Additionally, the Arabic word 'zahra' (flower)[41] is a pun on the Semitic name 'Syrya', denoting (Syria).[42] 'Zera' (seed)[43] thus is esoteric of the 'princess' (sarah), conceptual in Greek to the 'neophutus' (neophyte - the newly planted).

The cult of the Pharaoh is matriarchal comparable to Judaism.

In conclusion, authorship of the serpent's lineage is propagated matriarchally through Thebes and Syria, contractual to the Double Crown of Egypt (Upper and Lower Kingdom). Confederation of the Dual Crown details the merging of Syria with Egypt. Realization of the Babylonian Empire in Thebes extended into Greece and Rome. The very beginnings of this covenant are traced from Noah and his children 'Shem' (Shami), 'Ham' (Aamu)[44] and Japheth.

Traditionally, the sailor Noah, deemed human-angelic, seeded the Athenian Serpent King Erech - a bloodline imported from Uruq (Iraq). This progeny is equated in Plato's account with Atlantis. Judaic traditions note Noah's allegiance to Babylon is reinvigorated through the covenant of Abraham, ascribed covertly to the worship of the ram Amun. This relationship is monitored closely in the next chapter.

1   Anthology of Quotations, Bloomsbury, London, 2002, p57 (6)

2   Ibid, p57 (7)

3   Ibid, p131 (26)

4   John C. Traupman, Ph.D, The New College, Latin & English Dictionary, Bantam, 1988, p11

5   Ibid

6   Ibid, p22

7   Depiction of the New Jerusalem is pictured with the trowel. The symbol is symmetrical in Freemasonry to George Washington, the first president famous for the ratification of the American constitution. George Washington is referred to by patriots as the Father of American Independence.

8   John C. Traupman, Ph.D, The New College, Latin & English Dictionary, Bantam, 1988, p8

9   Prolog, Pocket Bilingual Dictionary, English-Hebrew, Hebrew-English, Prolog, 2003, p379

10 Hippocrene English-Arabic, Arabic-English Dictionary, Hippocrene, New York, 2005, p253

11 Prolog, Pocket Bilingual Dictionary, English-Hebrew, Hebrew-English, Prolog, 2003, p395

12 Ibid, p29

13 J.A Coleman: The Dictionary of Mythology, An A-Z of Themes, Legends & Heroes, Capella, 2007, p505

14 Ibid

15 Ibid (Hyperenas - A Trojan soldier, son of Panthous, brother of Euphorbus and Polydamas)

16 'Huper Boreas' (God of the most northerly wind literally beyond the northern wind). The Greek term 'huper' is listed as (beyond or over) and is combined with 'Boreas' (the God of the North wind). Boreas in the Hellenistic tongue pertains to 'barus' (heavy) and is conceptual with 'baino' (to go) and 'ballo' (to throw) - astrological terms.

17 Brewers Dictionary of Phrase & Fable, London, Cassel & Company Ltd, 1954, p481

18 Ibid, p565

19 The word 'London' is read in the Celtic language as 'Luan-dun' (the City of the Moon). 'Luan' here is matched with the Welsh word 'llong' (a ship). The symbol of the vessel is connected historically to the preservation of man's seed transported to the moon by the angelic host during the deluge. Tradition says a Temple dedicated to Diana (the Moon Goddess) was built where St. Paul stands today - Refer to Brewers Dictionary p565.

20 Brewers Dictionary of Phrase & Fable, London, Cassel & Company Ltd, 1954, p533

21 Prolog, Pocket Bilingual Dictionary, English-Hebrew, Hebrew-English, Prolog, 2003, p219

22 Brewers Dictionary of Phrase & Fable, London, Cassel & Company Ltd, 1954, p454

23 Ibid, p455

24 Ibid, p454

25 John C. Traupman PhD: The New College, Latin & English Dictionary, Bantam, 1988, p165

26 Ibid, p166

27 Ibid

28 Jesus' offspring are equated with the legend of Arthur and ruled over 'Albion' (Britain) post Caesar's campaign.

29 Brewers Dictionary of Phrase & Fable, London, Cassel & Company Ltd, 1954, p454

30 Spain is an extension of the Roman or Western Church and is home to the origins of the Inquisition.

31 'Hispania' (Spain) is derived from the Greek root 'Hesperia' denoting (the West) and is inexplicably unrecorded by the Oxford English Dictionary.

32 John C Traupman PhD: The New College, Latin & English Dictionary, Bantam, 1988, p11

33 Ahmed M.A.Abdel-Hardy: Egyptian Arabic, A Rough Guide Dictionary Phrasebook, 1998, Lexus, p111

34 John C Traupman PhD: The New College, Latin & English Dictionary, Bantam, 1988, p1

35 Prolog, Pocket Bilingual Dictionary, English-Hebrew, Hebrew-English, Prolog, 2003, p264 ['avel' (mourner)]

36 Alan F. Alford: The Phoenix Solution, Hodder & Stoughton, UK. 1998, p120 (See also p119)

37 Hippocrene English-Arabic, Arabic-English Dictionary, Hippocrene, New York. 2005, p284

38 Ibid

39 Prolog: Pocket Bilingual Dictionary, English-Hebrew, Hebrew-English, Prolog. 2003, p183

40 Hippocrene English-Arabic, Arabic-English Dictionary, Hippocrene, New York. 2005, p284

41 Ibid, p49

42 Ibid, p291 [Note also how 'zahra' (flower) is punned in Semitic with 'sara(h)' (a princess)].

43 Prolog: Pocket Bilingual Dictionary, English-Hebrew, Hebrew-English, Prolog, 2003, p361

44 'Ham' encodes the consonant vowels 'HM', denoting the Old Semitic word for (a king), correlated with the Western Monarchy the 'Aamu' (occidental) - a bloodline traced from 'Hammurabi'. In English, the acronym stands for 'Her Majesty'. Depiction of the Queen is printed on the modern £10 note adjacent to the horns (left corner), suggesting a lineage originating from 'Alexander Ammon', known in the Western world as Alexander the Great. His epithet translates as (the hidden leader of man) - a namesake interchangeable with the hidden hand of Freemasonry. Alexander's graven image is found on Hellenistic coins, combined with the horns of Amun (Ammon), indicating Thebes and the serpent's descendents. The symbol of the 'ram' (Arabic kebsh) is a pun on the Hebrew name 'kovesh' (a conqueror). In addition, the 'horn' (keren) denotes 'radiant' (koren), signifying a 'brother of the light' identified originally as a 'visitor, alien or angel', and is recorded in the Latin corruption as (the Illuminati) - Refer to Chapter 6, Tsabaoth the Army of the Lord. The Latin noun 'cornu' (horn) etymologically is connected to 'corona' (crown), emblematic of the horned or (shining) serpent, represented as a conqueror, usurper or rapist, personified as the monarch, angel or dragon.

14 Abraham and the Sacrificial Ram

'In that day there will be an altar to the Lord in the heart of Egypt... The Lord Almighty will bless them, saying, "Blessed be Egypt my people, Assyria my handiwork, and Israel my inheritance".'

Isaiah 19: 19 and 25, Holy Bible, New International Version, Gideon

In the biblical account of Genesis 22, Abraham is told by God to sacrifice his son on a mountain peak at the location of Moriah. The Hebrew name Moriah is diminutive of 'more(h)' (teacher)[1] and is a pun on 'mar'eh' (to see), indicative of the 'watcher', 'angel' or 'serpent'.[2] 'Moriah's appellation in the Latin is interpreted as 'morior' (to die),[3] inherent of blood rites, rendered in the Greek 'miara'.[4] Semitic etymologies suggest the locale is an oracle site 'marara' (a cave or cavern),[5] explicit of 'mara' (woman or wife),[6] originally an oracle priestess.

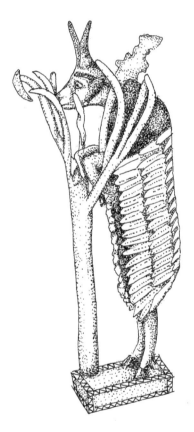

Winged Ram Effigy - known as the ram in a thicket buried in the great death pit of Ur

Prescribed ritualistically, Mount Moriah is a place of 'instruction' (moreh),[7] formative of initiation, branched in the Hellenistic languages with divination and death. The Greek etymon 'moira' (fate) is conceptual in the Latin to the intransitive verb 'morior' (to die) and 'mora' (to delay).[8] In English, the ensemble is 'fate', 'fatal' and 'fetter' - definitions accorded to the firstborn Isaac.

According to Genesis, Abraham is tested and requested by God to sacrifice his first son Isaac. On attempting to fulfill this obligation, an angel intervenes and prevents him from striking his son. In gratitude (gee thanks!), Abraham offers a ram caught by its horns in a thicket, emblematic of the tabernacle. The symbol of the ram is concomitant of 'Amun', and signifies a replaced offering described as (concealed). The Hebrew noun 'ayal' (ram)[9] is esoteric of the epithet 'Heylel' (Lucifer).

In Egyptian Arabic, the connection between the ram and human offering is reiterated. The sacrificial placement of 'ayal' (ram) upon the altar connotes the wordplay 'aayla' (family)[10] - a synonym of (ascension), apparent in the Hebrew vocabulary 'aliya'.[11] Aliya in the Old Semitic is related to 'eloh' (light), paralleled to the burnt offering and the angel (dragon).[12] In Babylonian imagery, the ram is thus depicted as winged.[13] The English noun ram is deduced from the Semitic word 'ram' (lofty)[14] and connotes 'ramm' (grief).[15]

Depiction of the fallen ram first appears as an ancient Babylonian sign and is later adopted by the patriarch Abraham. Graves found during excavations in the ancient city of Ur, Abraham's birthplace have subsequently revealed many elaborate objects. Some of these show the 'ram in the thicket' - an image similar to the biblical account of Abraham's aborted (replaced) sacrifice.[16]

The famous scholar and archeologist Leonard Woolley documents such practices in 1928 after excavating the tomb of Queen Shub-ad in the city of Ur. Woolley, perhaps because of Ur's connection to Abraham, expressed his intrigue at this development. In his personal records, he states that the nature of these practices appeared secret.

To quote Woolley[17]:

'No less remarkable than the objects found last winter in the royal graves at Ur was the discovery of the rites of human sacrifice which accompanied the burial of a king. In all the literature of Babylonia there is no hint of any such custom as having been practised at any time; long before the historic period from which our written records date it had been discontinued and the memory of it either forgotten or <u>carefully concealed</u> by writers grown ashamed of the barbarities of an earlier day...'.[18]

The acute observations made by Lion Sheep sorry! Leonard Woolley concurs with my own research that demonstrates human sacrifice in context to angel veneration is secret and closed to the uninitiated. In Babylon, the ram is a covert symbol of child sacrifice. Theologically the death of the ram exemplifies the reinstated tribute a child. Substitution of Isaac with the ram stigmatizes the offering and its concealment.

Braided cobra headdress of Queen Shub-ad – insignia of the hairy snake
(Royal motif of the cobra is used also by the Pharaonic dynasties of Thebes).

Religiously the Jewish lamb indicates the votive without blemish, characterized as 'ye'rid' (fair)[19] and suggests 'yeled' (child).[20] In the Egyptian idiolect, the noun 'kabsh' (ram)[21] is indexed in Syrian with 'khabis' (cunning, low or mean),[22] epithets of Amun.

Purchased as a sacrificial offering, the ram is offered in repayment of sin. Indeed, the Hebrew word 'kadosh' (holy)[23] and 'khadash' (scratch)[24] is reciprocal in the Syrian to 'qaddaish' (how many or how much). Rhetorical 'qaddaish' outlines sacrificial redemption. In English, the coinciding wordplay is 'prophet' 'profit' and 'profligate' from the Latin stem 'fligere' (to strike down).

Abraham's deliverance is attained through the killing of Isaac, represented as the ram in the thicket. In some versions of the story, Abraham proceeds to kill Isaac and is later restored by an angel of the Lord.[25] Isaac is deemed as righteous and is emulated as a holy offering.

Reference to the 'Righteous One' is quoted frequently in the Dead Sea Scrolls as 'Zaddik' - an etymology traced from (Isaac). The 'Teacher of Righteousness', cited in the Palestinian codex, is named as (Moreh ha-Zedek).[26] Congenial of a Messianic figure 'Zedek' exemplifies the innocent lamb (ram), proffered at the site of Moriah.

In the New Testament, the innocent blood of the ram or 'goat' (Greek tragos) details the 'betrayal' (Latin tradere) of Christ,[27] comparative to the firstborn Isaac. Oblation of the firstborn, allegorized as the ram caught in the thicket, dovetails with Christ wearing a crown of thorns, analogous to the declining sun. 'Hung upon a tree' Jesus' crucifixion records the Judaic practice of execution, archaic of the tribute and the tabernacle.

Elevated with two criminals, the ritual killing of the 'Moreh ha-Zedek' signifies atonement, contrasted with the innocent lamb and forgiveness. Totem of the trapped ram parallels 'Paschal' (the Passover Lamb) - its blood spread across the wooden lintel (tree). Immolation of the 'Paschal' recalls 'pesha' (crime),[28] signified through the Holy Communion, correlated with the Passover Feast.

Eschatological, the lamb's substitution is parabolic of the Egyptian firstborn, countervailed with the innocent lamb Israel.[29] In the Christian mysteries, the ransom of Christ (Isaac) is a meta-narrative of the Passover Lamb, proportional to salvation.[30] Its death aligned to the mysteries of Amun examined in the next chapter.

1   Prolog, Pocket Bilingual Dictionary, English-Hebrew, Hebrew-English, Prolog, 2003, p412

2   The land of Moriah is equated with darkness, identified with 'Amun' (the Hidden) God, picked up in the Latin and Greek vocabulary. 'Morel' in the Old French signifies (dark brown) and connotes (coagulated blood) from the Greek word 'miara' (blood stained). 'Morel' (dark brown) is recorded in the modern Italian as 'morello' (blackish) from the Latin adjective 'morul' (dark).

3   John C Traupman PhD: The New College Latin & English Dictionary, Bantam Press, 1988, p187

4   Latin 'morul' (dark) is symmetrical in the Latin to 'moris' (a custom) - intimating rites associated with darkness and death, correlated with morality. The stem of 'moris' rendered 'mors' is translated as (death, destruction or a corpse). In Old English, 'mor' suggests (a mountain, waste ground or moor).

5   Hippocrene English-Arabic, Arabic-English Dictionary, Hippocrene, New York, 2005, p235

6   Ibid

7   'Teaching' (Hebrew hora'a) is matched with 'har' (mountain) and 'harel' (altar), implicit of 'horror'. The equivalent wordplay in Arabic is 'dars' (lesson) from the verb 'darr' (to damage or harm), cognate with the intransitive verb 'dar' (to change).

8   John C Traupman PhD: The New College Latin & English Dictionary, Bantam Press, 1988, p187

9   Prolog: Pocket Bilingual Dictionary, English-Hebrew, Hebrew-English, Prolog, 2003, p327

10 Ahmed M.A. Abdel-Hady: Egyptian Arabic, The Rough Guide, Dictionary Phrasebook, Lexus, 1998, p221

11 Prolog: Pocket Bilingual Dictionary, English-Hebrew, Hebrew-English, Prolog, 2003, p29

12 The alternative Hebrew etymon for 'aliya' (to rise) is 'ma'ale', and is cryptic of the Latin adverb 'male' (badly, wrongly, wickedly or maliciously), nominal of original 'sin' (Latin sons - guilty). The adverb 'male' is figurative in English of 'male' apprized from the death of the firstborn son, complicit of (sons - guilty). Philological, 'ma'ale' (risen) heralds the 'star' (Akkadian mul) - a dual signifier in Persian of 'mal' (a risen king), explicit of 'mar' (a serpent). Theologically, man is deemed as sinful and is found encoded in the English vocabulary 'male and son', cognate with the prefix 'mal and sin'. Offering of the child theologically is aligned to sacrificial death, equated with the angel and king.

13 The winged ram is typically contrasted in Egyptian and Babylonian carving with the water goat, illustrative of heaven.

14 Prolog: Pocket Bilingual Dictionary, English-Hebrew, Hebrew-English, Prolog, 2003, p237

15 Hippocrene Concise Dictionary: English-Arabic, Arabic-English, Hippocrene, 2005, p54

16 Phillip Gardiner & Gary Osborn: The Shining Ones, The World's Most Powerful Secret Society Revealed, Watkins Publishing, 2006, p218

17 Adrian G Gilbert: Magi, The Quest for a Secret Tradition, Bloomsbury, London, 1996, p285

18 Ibid, pp285-286

19 Prolog: Pocket Bilingual Dictionary, English-Hebrew, Hebrew-English, Prolog, 2003, p144

20 Ibid, p65

21 Hippocrene Concise Dictionary: English-Arabic, Arabic-English, Hippocrene, 2005, p98

22 Ibid, p215

23 Prolog: Pocket Bilingual Dictionary, English-Hebrew, Hebrew-English, Prolog, 2003, p189

24 Hippocrene Concise Dictionary: English-Arabic, Arabic-English, Hippocrene, 2005, p215

25 Babylonian accounts indicate that the angel can appropriate the physical appearance of an individual. Isaac's death and resurrection observed from older records suggest Isaac is physically substituted with an angel - a motif continued with Jacob (usurper - reptile) and his betrayal of 'Esau' (hairy - man).

26 Michael Baigent & Richard Leigh: The Dead Sea Scrolls Deception, Arrow Books, 2001, p261

27 John C. Traupman PhD: The New College Latin & English Dictionary, Bantam Press, 1988, p314

28 Prolog: Pocket Bilingual Dictionary, English-Hebrew, Hebrew-English, Prolog, 2003, p92

29 In the Koran, God instates another individual to replace Christ. The Islamic account mirrors the Gospel of Luke, in which Simon of Cyrene is forced to carry the cross for Jesus. The place name Cyrene is a covert pun on the Old Semitic word 'se'irim' (a goat or demon). In the traditions of the Church, Simon is earmarked as a hidden offering. The name 'Simon' (to hearken or listen) is grouped linguistically with the angel Samael and the scapegoat. The goat is a conduit for the removal of sin, differentiated as the ram or king, repatriated through the blood of the innocent lamb.

30 Locked into a symbolic contract, members of the Brotherhood (Freemasonry) adorn the 'lambskin apron' (Hebrew sinar) - a signifier of Amun, aka the Moon God Sin. The apron represents an angel, decorated in the skin of a man, conceptual in the Hebrew language of transfiguration - 'shinui tsura' literally (to change shape). In addition, the lambskin covers the genitalia, implicit of rebirth, paralleled to the nocturnal communion (supper) in situ to the serpent, embodied as the angel. A signatory through bloodline, the 'apron' (sinar) denotes the Western contract, equated with the descendents of Shinar, the Kingdom of Sumer (Akkad). The borders of Shinar is represented with the insignia of the shen, a setting sun - an emblem of the West carried typically by a nocturnal angel. The shen logo is pictured as the 'knot' (Arabic acad), specific of the Western (hidden) covenant denoting the dragon, affiliated to the lineage of man (East). In Egyptian symbolism, the shen device suggests the Arabic noun 'sinn' (tooth) drawn as a triangle, employed in the hieroglyphic sign list to write the star Sirius - an emblem of the Theban priesthood affiliated with the 'cobra' (teaban).

15

Abraham and the Secret Covenant of the Ram

'And he said unto him, I am the Lord that brought thee out of Ur of the Chaldees, to give thee this land to inherit it.

And he said unto him, Take me an heifer of three years old, and a she goat of three years old, and a ram of three years old, and a turtledove, and a young pigeon.

And he took unto him all these, and divided them in the midst, and laid each piece one against another: but the birds divided he not.

And when the fowls came down upon the carcases, Abram drove them away. And when the sun was going down, a deep sleep fell upon Abram; and, lo, an horror of great darkness fell upon him.

And he said unto Abram, Know of a surety that thy seed shall be a stranger in a land that is not theirs, and shall serve them...
...In the fourth generation they shall come hither again: for the iniquity of the Amorites is not yet full.

And it came to pass, that, when the sun went down, and it was dark, behold a smoking furnace, and a burning lamp that passed between those pieces.

In the same day the Lord made a covenant with Abram, saying, Unto thy seed have I given this land, from the river of Egypt unto the great river, the river Euphrates'.

Genesis Chapter 15: 7, 9-13 and 16-18, King James Edition

'Abram's name appears in the Semitic language as 'Avram' - a title reminiscent of 'avera' (transgression), commensurate to regeneration of 'aviv' (the spring). Philologically, 'aviv' is compared to the offertory 'le'havi' (to bring),[1] identified with 'af'a' (a serpent) and 'hofa'a' (an apparition). Sacrifice of Abraham's first son Isaac to a fallen angel (af'a) is a precursor to Moses offering the Egyptian firstborn depicted as the sacrificial or spring lamb.

In Hebrew, the polyform noun 'aviv' (spring)[2] is used figuratively to denote (a youth). The same wordplay is recorded also in the Latin. The noun 'ver' is rendered as (spring or youth),[3] conceptual in the English vocabulary to 'off-spring'. Evidence suggests the Latin is concomitant to the burnt offering.

For example, the Roman noun 'ver' is employed also as the stem 'ver' (to revere, be afraid, to fear or be apprehensive).[4] 'Ver' informs the English adjective (fear) and contrary to the Oxford English Dictionary is related to the Latin transitive verb 'vereor' (to fear, be apprehensive, anxious or afraid).[5] Correlation between fear, offspring and youth suggests an early association with child sacrifice, aligned in the Biblical tradition to the descendents of Lot.

Introduced in Genesis 12:4, Lot is named as Abraham's nephew. In the following Chapter 13:8, Abraham calls Lot 'his brother'. Relationship between the patriarch and Lot is clarified in the Semitic spelling of Abraham's name.

In Egyptian Arabic, 'aamm' refers to (an uncle - specifically a father's brother)[6] and is congruous with the name 'Abraham'. Designation of 'aamm' is used discreetly to suggest (the Western people) - the 'Aam(u)' allied to Abraham through his nephew Lot. 'Aamm' Arabic for (an uncle) is cogent with the Semitic wordplay 'Av-(r)am' alternatively 'Aba-(r)am'. Both assignments in Hebrew record the anagram (father's-uncle), implicit of the Aamu faction and Lot.

Consistent in the Latin vocabulary, 'Avram' records 'avunculus' (a maternal uncle)[7] - diminutive of 'avus' (a grandfather, forefather or ancestor).[8] 'Avus' (grandfather) is derived from the Hebrew noun 'ab or av' (father), informally 'abba' (daddy). In Aramaic, the noun 'abba' (daddy) puns with the Arabic word 'af'a' (viper),[9] abstractions of 'avis' (bird), symbolic of the spirit.

Covertly the patriarchal descendents of 'avus' are paired with 'avis' (a bird), systematic of an angel or serpent. In addition, the Latin wordplay 'avus' (grandfather) and 'avis' (bird) is repeated in the English nouns 'father' and 'feather' (Greek pater and pteron).

Theologically the Roman substantive 'avis' (a bird)[10] enunciates the Greek etymon 'avel' (breath). 'Avel' translates into Latin as 'spiritus' (breath)[11] English 'spirit'. In Arabic, 'nafas' (breath)[12] records 'nafs' (the soul)[13] literally (the self).[14] The 'breath' or 'holy spirit' is symbolized in occult iconography as the plumed snake (See the Baptism of Jesus - Gospel of Mathew 3:16-17).

'Avel' (breath) is prenuptial in Hebrew to 'avel or abel' (mourner),[15] categorized through the death of the innocent. Depiction of (the mourner), 'avel' specifies 'avon' (sin)[16] otherwise 'avera' (transgression), recorded in Genesis 4:8 as the propitiation of Abel.

Complicit of sacrificial death, the avian priesthood denotes ascension, characteristic of an angel, aligned to the circle and snake. In Hebrew 'avera' (transgression) is also spelt as 'hafara',[17] and is an allusion in the Semitic language to 'havalah' (circle), registered with the winged serpent or disk.

The feathered snake records the Latin wordplay 'coluber' (a snake or cobra), compared to 'columba' (a dove). Discourse between the bird and serpent is apparent in the Classical Greek noun 'ophis' (serpent), juxtaposed in Latin with the noun 'avis' (bird). In Hebrew, the word play is comparative to 'ever' (wing),[18] symmetrical with 'ef'e' (an asp).[19] Representations of the bird, snake and disk denote ascension, associated with Abram's tributary. 'Havalah' (circle) serves as a monogram of the reptile Arabic 'af'a' (a viper) - Hebrew 'ef'e'. Additionally, 'af'a' recalls 'avaryan' (a criminal)[20] from 'avera' (transgression).

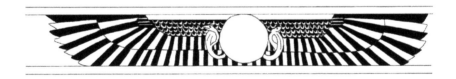

Motif of the winged serpent disk operates on a series of worded puns related in the Semitic languages to the snake, bird and circle.

'Abram's' initial name means (father of elevation),[21] denominational of the tribute, equated with the disk and serpent. His title connotes the offering of the firstborn, grouped with the ram and the winged seraph.

In the book of Genesis, 'Abram' is instructed to change his name to 'Abraham', indicative of a covenant, assigned covertly to the principal deity of darkness Amun. Modified, Abraham's new epithet is translated by scholars as the 'father of many nations' (Ab-rav-am) or (harbe-am). The word 'nation' (am) in the original Hebrew is singular and is read correctly as 'Aba-(r)am' (father of <u>a</u>

nation). 'Am's definition is specific to the 'people of Ham' (the Aamu or Ramu), classified as the 'Western nation' - Latin 'Occidental'.

In the Biblical account, the 'Aamu' (Arabic Umma, Hebrew Emori) signifies the accursed descendents of Ham, the son of Noah, traced through the lineage of Lot. 'Abraham's cognomen (father of the Western nation) further suggests the office the 'Aamu-Rabbi' literally (the Master of the Aamu), connoting a 'Teacher or Priest' (a Rabbi, Egyptian Wabbi). 'Aamu-Rabbi's denomination is interchangeable with 'Aba-Ham' (father of the Aamu), otherwise 'Abraham'.

Executor to the office of the 'Aamu-Rabbi', Abraham's title infers 'Hammurabi' the sixth King of the first Dynasty of Babylon. Hammurabi unified the Kingdom of Sumer, its religious practices and institutions, identical to Abraham's ratification of the covenant. Notable for his code of laws, inscribed in Akkadian, preserved in the Temple of Marduk, he is documented as the sixth reigning monarch of Assyria. In comparison, the original bloodline of Abraham is followed through nine generations, suggesting the surviving Babylonian king list is incomplete by three successions.

In the book of Genesis Chapter 11, the chronological record of Abraham is followed from the stock of Shem (Semites), the son of Noah. Ascension of Abraham's position from the tribe of Shem into Ham is acquired through marriage to his half-sister 'Sarah' (Hebrew princess) and covertly records Abraham's allegiance to the Royal House of Abimelech, implied in Genesis 20. Abraham's adoption of Isaac as his legal heir displaces Ishmael, Abraham's firstborn. Illegitimate, Isaac's inheritance is continued with his second son Jacob and the usurpation of 'Esau's (hairy) patrimony. The removal of Esau (human heritage) is predicated upon a royal substitute,[22] associated with the children of Ham - a hidden angelic lineage affiliated to the patriarch Lot.

Encountered in Genesis, the descendents of Noah's son Ham (Amorites) is succeeded through Abraham's nephew Lot. Chapter 19 records Lot's incestuous relationship with his two daughters, consummated through the sons Moab and Ben-Ammi. Biblical narratives describe the two sons in turn as the fathers of the Moabites (Moab) and Ammonites (Ammi). The 'Ammi'[23] discloses the 'Aamu people of Amurru' (West Asia) and is grouped with Moab a play on the Arabic noun 'Marrib' (Occidental or West).[24] Theoretically, Abraham's successor Isaac arrogates Ishmael's birthright. Illegitimate, Isaac's bloodline originates from the lineage of Ham, ranked with Abimelech and the patriarch Lot. Concealed Isaac's lineage is conjunct with the development of the Western Priesthood.

Written in Arabic as 'Lut', 'Lot's actual name means (to veil or cover), obtained from the Semitic stem 'lits'of'.[25] Lut's cognomen is abridged in the Latin with the radical 'lat' (hidden or secret) in the adjectival form 'latens'.[26] In Judaic lore, Lut pertains to hidden knowledge, intimating death rites, correlated with the altar, depicted as the mountain.

Read as an 'inverted cipher' (Arabic thashraq), 'Lut' denotes the Arabic word 'tul[27] - Hebrew tel', denoting (a hillock or mound), derived from the Syrian noun 'tall' (a hill).[28] The Hebrew expression 'la alot' (to go up)[29] is conceptual of 'tul' (a hill), identified with Lot and the tabernacle veil.

Conceptually, 'tul' (mound) is combined with ascension, rendered in the Semitic as the adjective 'tali' (rising), implicit of the sun, adjoined to the bird and serpent. Religious metaphors show the mound and disk as a golden knoll (know), stylized in Masonic iconography as a mountain of light - an altar. Jewish scholars link the mound to the offering, listed as the site 'Tel Aviv' (the Mound of Spring), implicit of a 'youth', suggesting the covenant of Abraham.

Originally, the 'tul' is a place accorded with 'ascension' (tali),[30] identified in the Hebrew language with the noun 'tale' (lamb).[31] Babylonians depicted the lamb as winged. In Christian symbolism, the 'lamb' (tale) is shown as 'risen' (tali) - literally draped or lifted over the shepherd's shoulder. Its symbolism is relative to the Arabic pun 'hamal' (carry),[32] cognate with 'hamal' (lamb).[33]

A shepherd, Abraham's lineage records a 'nomadic' king, figurative of 'colonial rule', associated in Egypt with the Hyksos, envisaged with long flowing hair - a symbol of the Nazorean priest. Uncut, the dreadlock represents the covenant of God, ratified through the lamb. Stylized in Judaism as a ringlet of hair, the dreadlock is a covert emblem of the hairy-snake (hemitheoi - a half-God), registered with the nocturnal angel.

The lock of hair 'taltal' (ringlet) signifies the death of the 'lamb' (tale), abridged originally with the hairy or plumed angel, disclosed as the sacrificial ram. Obliteration of the offering is inimical of a secret votive (child sacrifice). Liturgically, the 'lamb' (tale) annotates 'Lot' nominal of the 'veil' (Arabic lut), compliant with the bush and tabernacle. Mutual in Arabic, 'taltal' (ringlet) is linked with 'suf' (wool),[34] expositional of the Islamic priesthood, the 'Sufi' - iconic of a lamb.

Idiomatically, 'Lut' (veil) is consecutive with 'tillel' (covering) - a reversed cipher, Lut is implicit of a hidden sacrifice, generic of the 'lamb' (tale). Theoretically, the 'covering' of the lamb aggregates the repayment or redemption of sin - the 'tariff'.[35] Related to the Arabic word 'ta'rf(a)' (a tariff) the term is derived from the verbal stem 'arrafa' (notification), comparative to 'araf' (the verb to know).[36] 'Arrafa' (notification) translates into Hebrew as 'yidu'a' (notification),[37] explicit of 'ye'hudi' (Jew),[38] didactic of 'yeda' (knowledge).[39] Ye'hudi historically suggests the Passover and ascension of the sacrificial lamb, grouped in Arabic with the noun 'judi'[40] (height).[41]

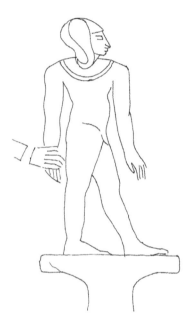

Jewish dreadlocks originate from the lock of youth worn by the young Pharaoh.
The lock is symbolic of the ram's horn equated with the hairy snake.

'Araf' (to know) is contiguous in the Semitic languages with 'raph' (terror).[42] A symbol of knowledge 'araf' signifies 'arrifa the communal (loaves),[43] substituted with the flesh offering. Theologically, the 'ta'rfa' (tariff) is 'restorative' (te'rufa)[44] of a relationship, predicated on a contract, determined through the spilling of blood. 'Lot's or 'Lut's appellation (the veil) signifies occult practices,[45] concordant with the law of death. Translation of the adjective 'occult' into Hebrew specifies (sodi) - an epithet specifying a person from the region of Sodom, the residence of Lot.

Secret teachings of the 'Sodi' priesthood are described as (the occult - Hebrew sodi),[46] and adopt the 'oculus' (eye) as the insignia of the dragon or watcher. Oculus philologically notates the Occidental nation and the occult (Refer to Roman Catholic motif of the All Seeing Eye). A progenitor of occult tradition,

Lot is attributed with the 'Sodi' fraternity, originating from the descendents of Cain and Ham. Denomination of the 'Sodi' is identified later with the lawmaker Moses - instigated theologically through the elevation of the Passover lamb.

In the book of Exodus, the ram and thicket is substituted with the spreading of blood on the doorframe[47] - prophetic of the annihilation of the Egyptian newborn. According to the Torah, the first night of the Passover is known as the 'seder' (order)[48] from 'sidur' (arrangement),[49] commandeered through 'sitt' (a lady).[50] The arrangement in Arabic[51] is implicit of 'arrafa' (notification), relative to a 'tariff', equivalent to redemption.

The 'seder' celebration is preserved in the Latin spelling as 'cedere' (to die or depart),[52] analogous to the offspring of the mater (sitt) - the Emori people (Refer to Chapter 11 The Amorites). Employed as a transitive verb, 'cedere' is correlated with (sadism).[53] In Hebrew, 'sade' indicates (a field),[54] comparative to 'sod' (a secret)[55] and 'sid' (a gentleman). The related allomorphs are congruous with fertility rites and the summoning of the 'Reaper', referred to in Latin as 'repere' (a reptile).

Reaper with circular tail holding the harvest excavated from a grave at Ilissos (Contrary to scholarly opinion, the child is not depicted as conceived from the Goddess Gaia but is shown as sacrificed to her).

According to the book of Exodus, the Israelites after they escaped from Egypt are brought into the land of their allies - the Amorites. The location of Amurru is the principal center of Moloch worship - a deity associated with fratricide.

In addition, Amurru is confederate to Amun and his people the Aamu. Theologically, the angel of death is paralleled to the Egyptian firstborn the lamb in situ to Amurru and Moloch.

Throughout the Old Testament, worship of nocturnal deities and child sacrifice is provident and continued throughout Judaic lore. The ancient practice of immolating children to Moloch did not end with the Exodus. In I Kings 11:7, Solomon (the 'wise' King) builds an altar to Moloch. To quote the Gideon translation:

'On a hill east of Jerusalem, Solomon built a high place for Chemosh
the detestable god of Moab, and for Molech [Moloch] the detestable
god of the Ammonites'.

The direction 'east' (Egyptian Arabic shar)[56] is codified-speak of 'shar' the adjective (evil),[57] cogent with the Syrian root 'sha'al' (to burn).[58] Ritualistically, east suggests 'shal' (to carry)[59] - a signifier of the offering connoting 'sha'r' (hair)[60] realized as 'se' (the lamb). Archaically, the symbol of hair doubles with a 'hairy angel' (human-angelic) or the 'se'irim' (a goat deity), substituted with the 'lamb' (an innocent child).[61] Materialisation of the 'se'irim' is categorized in Arabic with 'sihr' (sorcery).

Welsh dragon with circular tail - a symbol of the reaper. Refer also to Ilissos illustration on page 155

Solomon's initiation into the Moabite and Ammonite (Amorite) cult is consistent with an undetected and prominent tradition, accentuated from the lineage of Lot. Originating from the sons of Moab (Marrib) and Ben-Ammi (Aamu), Lot's children demarcate the Western Priesthood. Solomon's worship of 'Chemosh' is constant with the Old Semitic stem 'Khem' (Egypt) - a place name aligned in the Old Semitic to 'Chem' (the Pleiades), figured as 'Taurus' (the bull).[62] Prelature of the 'Pharaoh's (Par-o) role as a high priest is distinguished in Hebrew as 'par' (bull) partnered with the 'khimaira' (a she goat).

The office of the Pharaoh immortalized as 'par' (bull) concords with the papal bull - a motif of the Western Priesthood. 'Par' (bovine) is written alternatively in Hebrew as 'shor' (bull)[63] cryptic of the 'Shiah' priesthood marked symbolically with 'shar' (east).[64] 'East' in the Old Semitic annotates (qadam), assailed to 'Adam' and the sacrifice of his 'firstborn' (kodem kol),[65] cognizant with the veneration of Moloch.

Conclusively, King Solomon's lineage demonstrates a genetic connection in the Old Semitic with the Pharaoh's genealogy. Solomon is paralleled to the worship of the 'bull' (par), equidistant with the traditions of Aaron and Lot. Esoterically the 'bovine' is equivocal to (the Pleiades), cryptically the 'saba' (star) and Egypt, affiliated to the Sabi priesthood, the goat (gazelle) and bull.

In the previous passage I Kings 11:7, the scribal redactor apart from condemnation gives no clear reason why Solomon should build an altar to Moloch. The answer is clear - the practice of child sacrifice is an early component of the Judaic faith inherited from Abraham and Moses. Adoration of Solomon aligns to the angel and serpent, determined from the Babylonian cult of Amun, sourced from Lot (Ham) and Aaron. Solomon's construction of a high place infers a tabernacle, later substituted with Solomon's temple. With these important points in mind, let's now turn our attentions to Abraham's sacrifice in context to the tabernacle and ram.

1   Prolog, Pocket Bilingual Dictionary, English-Hebrew, Hebrew-English, Prolog 2003, p50

2   Ibid, p389

3   John C Traupman PhD: The New College Latin & English Dictionary, Bantam Press 1988, p328

4   Ibid

5   Ibid

6   Ahmed M.A. Abdel-Hady: Egyptian Arabic, The Rough Guide, Dictionary Phrasebook, Lexus 1998, p221

7   John C Traupman PhD: The New College Latin & English Dictionary, Bantam Press 1988, p27

8   Ibid, p28

9   In Syrian and Arabic, the 'v', 'f' and 'b' sounds are closely interchangeable, therefore 'aba' Aramaic (daddy) is punned with 'af'a' (viper).

10 John C Traupman PhD: The New College Latin & English Dictionary, Bantam Press 1988, p353

11 Ibid, p292

12 Hippocrene: English-Arabic, Arabic-English Dictionary, Hippocrene, New York 2005, p252

13 Ibid ['Nafs' homonym (soul or self)]

14 Ibid, p253

15 Prolog: Pocket Bilingual Dictionary, English-Hebrew, Hebrew-English, Prolog 2003, p264

16 Ibid, p373

17 Ibid, p427

18 Ibid, p461

19 Ibid, p29

20 Ibid, p92

21 Abram's name is consistent in Sanskrit with the noun 'abrah' (cloud).

22 Translation of the Hebrew name 'Jacob' (usurper) is understood in the ancient etymologies to signify (a reptile) literally (a rapist or pillager), and is contrasted with 'Esau' (hairy) - the original descendent of man.

23 Rendition of 'ammi' (Ammonite) phonetically suggests the same people as the 'Emori' (Amorite). 'Ammi' in the Arabic language also corresponds with 'amir' (a prince) - an executive title translated in the Hebrew language as (proclaimed). 'Amir' is compatible with the Persian rank 'mir' (a chief) and 'mar' (a serpent).

24 Hippocrene Concise Dictionary, English-Arabic, Arabic-English, Hippocrene 2005, p236

25 Prolog: Pocket Bilingual Dictionary, English-Hebrew, Hebrew-English, Prolog 2003, p446

26 John C Traupman PhD: The New College Latin & English Dictionary, Bantam Press, 1988, p165

27 The prefix 'tul' (hill) is also similar in the Semitic to the noun 'tal' denoting (dew). In Egyptian cosmology, the tears of Atum Ra (Amun) celebrates the morning dew and the (re)creation of man identified with loss.

28 Hippocrene English-Arabic, Arabic-English Dictionary, Hippocrene, New York 2005, p295

29 Prolog: Pocket Bilingual Dictionary, English-Hebrew, Hebrew-English, Prolog 2003, p347

30 Ferozsons Urdu-English Dictionary: A Comprehensive Dictionary of Current Vocabulary, (Revised Edition), Ferozsons Ltd, Lahore, p489

31 Prolog: Pocket Bilingual Dictionary, English-Hebrew, Hebrew-English, Prolog 2003, p224

32 Hippocrene English-Arabic, Arabic-English Dictionary, Hippocrene, New York 2005, p188

33 Ibid

34 Ibid, p141

35 Reveal is a double-bind term meaning to re-veil. The noun veil in English is an anagram of evil and is reversed to spell the adjective live.

36 Hippocrene English-Arabic, Arabic-English Dictionary, Hippocrene, New York 2005, p65 'Araf' the (verb to know) is spelt alternatively as 'irif'

37 Prolog: Pocket Bilingual Dictionary, English-Hebrew, Hebrew-English, Prolog 2003, p274

38 Note how 'Ye'hudi' (Jew) is reminiscent philologically of the Egyptian deity 'Djhuti' (Thoth), whose emblem is the ibis bird - its beak silhouettes the crescent, a symbol of the Judaic priesthood.

39 Prolog: Pocket Bilingual Dictionary, English-Hebrew, Hebrew-English, Prolog 2003, p223

40 In the Koranic tradition, 'judi' (height) demarcates the sacred Mountain, associated with the rest place of Noah's ark. Judi is etymological to 'Ye'hudi' (Jew). In Semitic, the 'y' and 'j' sound are interchangeable.

41 Andrew Collins: From the Ashes of Angels, The Forbidden Legacy of a Fallen Race, Michael Joseph Ltd 1996, p162

42 Translated by S.L. MacGregor Mathers: The Kabbalah Unveiled, Penguin Arkana 1991, p194 ['RAPH' (terror) / 'ATH' (chaos)]

43 Hippocrene English-Arabic, Arabic-English Dictionary, Hippocrene, New York 2005, p70 'Arrifa' (loaves) possesses the additional spelling 'irrifa'

44 Prolog: Pocket Bilingual Dictionary, English-Hebrew, Hebrew-English, Prolog 2003, p343

45 'Occult' is derived from the Latin root 'occulere' (to hide) referential to 'oculus' (eye) - symbolic of the 'watcher' or 'dragon'.

46 Prolog: Pocket Bilingual Dictionary, English-Hebrew, Hebrew-English, Prolog 2003, p277

47 The 'burning bush', the 'ram and thicket' and the 'doorframe and lamb' are covert symbols of the tabernacle, prescriptive of the death of the firstborn.

48 Prolog: Pocket Bilingual Dictionary, English-Hebrew, Hebrew-English, Prolog 2003, p282 ['Seder' (order) / 'sidur' (arrangements)]

49 Prolog: Pocket Bilingual Dictionary, English-Hebrew, Hebrew-English, Prolog 2003, p28

50 Hippocrene Concise Dictionary: English-Arabic, Arabic-English, Hippocrene 2005, p65

51 Wordplays correlated with the 'matriarch' (sitt) and the 'firstborn' (seder literally 'order') are evident in the Arabic language also. 'Ama' (give) and 'amma' (mother) are etymologies consistent with 'amr' (an order or command). 'Amr' additionally is a homonym of (an affair, thing or matter). To summarize, 'ama' (give), 'amma' (mother) and 'amr' (order) are replicated in the Old Hebrew wordplay 'sidur' (arrangement), 'sitt' (lady) and 'seder' (order).

52 John C Traupman PhD: The New College Latin & English Dictionary, Bantam Press 1988, p38

53 'Seder' (first night of the Passover) is preserved in the Latin as 'cedere' (to die or depart) analogous of the 'Emori' people. 'Cedere' additionally means (to submit) and is found in the Arabic stem 'slm' informing the epithet 'Islam' and 'Muslim'. 'Slm' is also the root of Solomon (Arabic Sulyman) - the wise king depicted in Biblical and occult tradition as a black magician affiliated to the djinn (jinn).

54 Prolog: Pocket Bilingual Dictionary, English-Hebrew, Hebrew-English, Prolog 2003, p150

55 Ibid, p360

56 M.A. Abdel-Hady: Egyptian Arabic, A Rough Guide, Dictionary Phrasebook, Lexus 1998, p241

57 Hippocrene Concise Dictionary: English-Arabic, Arabic-English, Hippocrene New York, p43

58 Ibid, p281

59 M A Abdel-Hady: Egyptian Arabic, A Rough Guide, Dictionary Phrasebook, Lexus 1998, p241

60 Hippocrene Concise Dictionary: English-Arabic, Arabic-English, Hippocrene, New York, p55

61 Hair is a signifier of the mammal, and is often combined with the snake, seraph or angel to indicate the human-angelic line.

62 Chemosh is a compound and can be read unpointed as either 'chem-esh' (Pleiades' flame), indicative of 'Khem-esh' (Egypt's flame), contrasted with 'Chem-mash' (Pleiades-veil, literally tightly drawn Pleiades), suggesting 'Lut' (veil), in conjunction with the tabernacle.

63 Prolog: Pocket Bilingual Dictionary, English-Hebrew, Hebrew-English, Prolog 2003, p52

64 Veiled, the mysteries are located in the west a signifier of the Pleiades. Unveiled, the inner mysteries are aligned to the east (Orion) and the resurrection of the sun (transfiguration). The covenant of God is ratified through the star of Sirius (fish) married to the human offspring of the Pleiades. Combined the human-reptilian progeny is paralleled to Orion and the line of Kings.

65 Prolog: Pocket Bilingual Dictionary, English-Hebrew, Hebrew-English, Prolog 2003, p152 ['kodem kol' adverb (at first)]

16

Lot and the Tabernacle

"... Daughters of Jerusalem, do not weep for me; weep for yourselves and for your children. For the time will come when you will say, 'Blessed are the barren women, the wombs that never bore and the breasts that never nursed!'... For if men do these things when the tree is green, what will happen when it is dry?"

Luke 23: 28, 29 and 31, Holy Bible, New International Version, Gideon

Lut in Hebrew 'Lot' (a veil) signifies hidden rites, associated with the Western disk (Amun) and the worship of nocturnal deities. The Semitic term 'mas've' (masked) is analogous to 'mitvah' (commandment) synonymous with the veil and the law. Anachronistically, the 'veil'[1] describes the covering of the ark and conforms to the overseer of the tabernacle. Later represented as the temple curtain, the shroud denotes the resting place of the ark, located inside of the Inner Court (Holy of Holies) of the Jewish Temple.

The ark houses the Ten Commandments, statutes of the 'Torah' (instruction), emblazoned as the covenant between men and angels. Judaic tradition represents this promise as the burning bush - a sign of the tabernacle and offertory. Association between the bush and the votive is preserved anagrammatically in the Old Semitic.

In Hebrew for example, the wordplay 'sukkah' (bush), written without the vowels (unpointed), can be read as 'succoth' (hut) a classification translated into the Greek as (tabernacle).[2] The 'tabernacle' originally conceived as (a temporary shelter, hut or tent) is designated religiously as a holy place of offering. Reference to the 'burning bush' in the original script is in propinquity to a 'flaming tabernacle' and the ritual spilling of innocent blood.[3]

In the accounts of Abraham, the emblem of the ram caught in the 'thicket' doubles as the 'tabernacle' assigned to sacrifice. The 'sukkah' (bush) in Freemasonry is replicated as a 'log' - a noun related to the 'Lodge', symbolic home of the ark. Semantically, lodge is a derivative of the Greek word 'logion' (an oracle) and 'logos' (word), appellations accorded to Legion, categorized with the host and ram.

A living fleece transmuted into gold (Jason & Medea)

Hellenistic scholars link the masked offering to the Golden Fleece. 'Veiling' (Arabic lut) of the ram is dualled in the Latin vocabulary with 'leuteus' (yellow), symbolic of the solar ram. Reproduced as the risen or golden ram (lamb), the slain animal is twinned symbolically with the fallen goat, hung in the Temple Sanctuary.

Carcass of the Golden Fleece contrasts the bloodied 'she goat' (Greek khimaira), matched in Arabic with 'khaimi or khema' (tent), registered in the Old Semitic with 'khanun' (red dye). Device of the red goat signifies the nomadic Canaanites. Combination of the goat and tree divests the 'tabernacle' (a tent). This housing served spiritually as a portable shrine - an extension of the 'temple sanctuary' (the succoth).

'Kaimi' (tent or tabernacle) is cognate with 'komer' (priest),[4] astrological to 'Chem' (the Pleiades), mirrored with 'Khem' (Egypt). Egyptologists transliterate 'Khem' (dark land) as 'kmt', pronounced 'khemet'. The name 'Khemet' however originates from the Old Hebrew word 'khmit' (the white of the eye),[5] signified as the crown of Osiris. The Hebrew noun 'laven' (white)[6] is consistent etymologically with Levi and Rabbi - nominal of the 'Western Priesthood' paired with the ram and goat.[7]

Ram in a thicket compared to a human votive. (Jason & Medea)
Note the emblem of the smiling angel with extended tongue on breastplate.

In Greek tragedies, the golden ram displaces the red goat, dedicated to Zeus, hung upon the sacred oak (sukkah). Cryptically the tree covers the 'inner sanctuary' (the succoth). Consecrated, the sanctum represents the 'hut' (a play on cut), repeated in the Arabic pun 'khuss' (hut)[8] and 'qass' (cut).[9] The same wordplay appears in the Hebrew etymologies. 'Sukkah' (a bush) is correlated with 'me'tsuka' (distress).[10] - See footnote.[11]

Secret practices, accorded to the 'sukkah' (bush), describe 'sheket' (hush) an allusion to hidden rites. Analogous 'sukkah' and 'sheket' are worded puns equivalent in English to (bush and hush) or (shrub and shut up).

Depiction of the ram caught in the 'bush' (sukkah) details a type of 'snare' (Old Egyptian sek-et / sht),[12] illustrative of the murder of a child. The burning bush 'sukkah' is latent to 'succoth' (the tabernacle). Covertly 'sukkah' informs the Aramaic etymology 'zakkau' (the giving of alms), identified with the tabernacle and ram.

Archaically, the 'propitiation' (zakkau) details sacrificial offerings to a fallen angel, conceptualized in Hebrew as 'zokhel' (a reptile).[13] 'Zokhel' specifies the Arabic compound 'zoq el' (God's taste), [14] connoting immolation. Communion between man and angel elicits 'succoth' (the tabernacle).

Identical, cryptograms are concurrent in the Latin mysteries. The feminine noun 'serpens' (a serpent or dragon)[15] is matched religiously with 'sapere' (to taste or smell),[16] cultic of the adjective 'sapiens' (wise).[17] 'To taste knowledge or wisdom' infers the snake and the sharing of the 'supper', conjunct with the 'hostia' (victim) and 'host'. Philologically, 'serpens' (a serpent) is derived from the Hebrew etymon 'sapan' (a seaman),[18] disclosed as the host or angel.

Sokar ascended, literally reborn, from the serpent's mouth - a symbol of the votive.

Likewise in the Babylonian language, 'acan' (a flaming seraph) corresponds to the Egyptian noun 'akl' (food),[19] cognate with 'aql' (reason, sense or intellect).[20]

The initiated refer to themselves as 'akh' (brothers),[21] definitive of 'haqq' (truth) – signifiers of the 'snake' (acan) and 'king' (hakim). Repeated in the Greek dramas, 'ophis' (snake) encodes the Latin transitive 'offerre' (an offering).[22]

Semantically, 'zokhel' (reptile) relates to 'zakkau' (the offering of alms), concurrent with 'succoth' (the tabernacle). Murder of an innocent nominates a 'sucker' defined as someone (gullible or naïve), theoretically a simile of an unweaned child. Linguistic relationship between the 'sucker' (to suck) and the Latin masculine noun 'succuss' (sap, juice, taste or flavour)[23] is deduced from the Egyptian Arabic root 'zoq' (taste).[24]

Further 'zoq' informs the Old English word 'soc' (sucking at the breast) and 'sucan' (suck). Ritualistically, the offering of the votive to 'zokhel' (a reptile) sanctions the sentencing of a child. 'Zokhel' defined as a fallen angel encodes the Anglo-Latin word 'soca' (prosecution), explicit of infanticide.[25]

Exposition of 'sukkah' (bush) and 'zokhel' (reptile) specify early morning rites, cogent in Akkadian with 'shachar' (dawn), reproduced in Hebrew as 'shakhar'.[26] Cognate in Sanskrit, 'shakar' signifies the masculine noun 'shukkar' (Venus), suggesting the Morning Star.[27]

In Egyptian mythology, Venus is interchangeable with the Pharaoh or hawk, commemorative of the son Horus. Early morning prayers celebrate the resurrection of the 'son' (Aramaic bar). Regeneration of the 'male offspring' is indexed in the Arabic vocabulary with 'bar' (a hawk).[28] A solar motif the osprey classifies the 'descendents of light' (the akh zauri) - an anagram in hieroglyphic of the God 'Sokar' (Zari'a-Kar).

Rebirth of the 'hawk', appointed as 'Horus' (Kar) incarnated as the Pharaoh, illustrates the 'son', distinguished in the Egyptian plays as the falcon God 'Sokar'. His dubious epithet is read as (the seed of Horus), rendered correctly in the original tongue as 'Zari'a-Kar'.[29] The titular 'Zari'a-Kar' personifies 'Venus' (Hebrew Zohra or Zokra), conceptual to 'zokhel' (a reptile).

'Sokar' initially (Zari'a-Kar) plays on 'sukkah' (bush), descriptive of Amun, deified as the ensnared ram contained in the 'succoth' (tabernacle). 'Zari'a-Kar' abridges the Hebrew adjective 'zach' (pure)[30] and 'zakhay' (innocent),[31] theoretical of the slain ram and risen hawk.[32] Theologically, 'te'hora' (pure)[33] signifies the Hebrew noun 'tale' (lamb).[34] Scribal redactors interplay 'zach' (pure) with 'se' (lamb).[35] Elaboration of 'se' is used in the Old Semitic to nominate the 'Lamb [of] Horus' i.e. (the innocent), read literally as 'Se-Kar', deciphered as 'Zari'a-Kar' (Sokar).

To summarize, 'Zari'a-Kar' signifies the renewal or regeneration of the ram God Amun, transfigured or reborn through the innocent blood of the lamb (child). Amun's restoration is marked as the risen or ascendant 'hawk' (bar), meteoric of Horus, the risen 'son' (bar) - cryptic of the daystar 'Zohra' (Venus), personified as the deity 'Zari'a-Kar'.

Horus like his sibling 'Zari'a-Kar' (Sokar) is written with the royal hawk, his facial markings silhouette the horned profile of the ram. A visual pun, the ram insignia depicts the paradoxical nature of 'Amun', whose nature is displayed through concealment. 'Zari'a-Kar' (Sokar) in the 'Book of the Dead' is presented as the archetypal 'hunter' (Kar), combined with the trapped ram efficacious of the tabernacle. Bipolarization of the hawk is exampled in the 'Hunefer' manuscript dated from the 19th Dynasty (1300 BC), decoded in the next chapter.

Horus with the markings of Amun the ram concealed inside of Horus' profile.

1 'Veil' is an anagram of 'evil'.
2 'Succoth' (tabernacle) is written in Modern Hebrew as 'suka' - a noun compared in the original Hebrew to 'sukkah' (a bush).
3 In Hebrew, 'ru'ak' (an evil spirit or demon) is cogent with 'smell' (re'akh) - terminology consistent with the burnt offering.
4 Prolog: Pocket Bilingual Dictionary, English-Hebrew, Hebrew-English, Prolog 2003, p315

5   Ibid, p459

6   Ibid

7   Egyptologists render 'Egypt' in the hieroglyphic as 'kmt' a translation given as (the black land or dark land). The name is assigned cryptically by scholars to infer the 'closing or veiling' of a tent (Arabic mash), nominal of 'Egypt' (masr). 'Kmt' originally is recorded as 'Khem', a name given by the Canaanite occupiers. Khem therefore is a derivation of 'Canaanite' (kana'ana). The etymology is analogous to 'khaimi' (tent), signifying a nomad. Unlike the English connotation, the 'nomad' in the Old Semitic signified the 'literati' (kana'ana). They worshipped 'Chem' (an Old name for Amun, archaically the Pleiades).

8   Hippocrene English-Arabic, Arabic-English Dictionary, Hippocrene, New York 2005, p59

9   Ibid, p34

10 Prolog: Pocket Bilingual Dictionary, English-Hebrew, Hebrew-English, Prolog, 2003, p116

11 The expression 'distress' (Hebrew me'tsuka) is used in Freemasonry as a signal for help and originates from the Semitic translation or etymological connection with 'succoth' (the tabernacle or Lodge) registered with 'sukkah' (a stick).

12 Bridgett McDermott: Decoding Egyptian hieroglyphics, Duncan Baird Publishers, London 2003, p170 [Sign Index 'Sht' (bird-snare)].

13 Prolog: Pocket Bilingual Dictionary, English-Hebrew, Hebrew-English, Prolog 2003, p340

14 Hippocrene English-Arabic, Arabic-English Dictionary, Hippocrene, New York 2005, p316

15 John C Traupman PhD: The New College Latin & English Dictionary, Bantam Press 1988, p285

16 Ibid, p277 (Consistently the reptile is said to have an excellent sense of smell and taste).

17 Ibid

18 Prolog: Pocket Bilingual Dictionary, English-Hebrew, Hebrew-English, Prolog 2003, p359

19 Hippocrene English-Arabic, Arabic-English Dictionary, Hippocrene, New York 2005, p148

20 Ibid, p321

21 Ibid, p148

22 John C Traupman PhD: The New College Latin & English Dictionary, Bantam Press 1988, p204

23 Ibid, p300

24 Ibid, p316

25 The football game 'soccer' is a probable pun on 'zokhel' (reptile) and is matched in America with 'NFL' the Semitic stem of the 'Nephilim' (the Fallen Ones).

26 Prolog: Pocket Bilingual Dictionary, English-Hebrew, Hebrew-English, Prolog 2003, p98

27 Ferozsons Urdu-English Dictionary, A Comprehensive Dictionary of Current Vocabulary, (Revised Edition), Ferozsons Ltd, Lahore, p468

28 Hippocrene English-Arabic, Arabic-English Dictionary, Hippocrene, New York 2005, p155

29 According to Egyptologists, the deity 'Sokar' is rendered as 'Sah-har' (the Son of Horus). This is shown to be a totally fallacious corruption, as the word 'sa' or 'sah' (son) is not found in the Semitic and is only evident in the Persian noun 'za(h)'. Both Sokar and Horus are written with the Falcon - a symbol of the watcher or hunter.

30 Prolog: Pocket Bilingual Dictionary, English-Hebrew, Hebrew-English, Prolog 2003, p323

31 Ibid, p208

32 'Zari'a-Kar's (Sokar) cognomen is a variegation of the name Zechariah (Zachariah) - a post-exilic prophet, whose visions centre on the rebuilding of the Jewish Temple. Linguistic correlation between the 'hawk' and 'son' in the Aramaic and Arabic suggests the resurrection of the hawk, conceptual to the killing of the innocent lamb. Evidence suggests that the deity 'Zari'a-Kar' is specifically aligned to the mortuary (mortar) temple and 'tabernacle' (suka).

33 Prolog: Pocket Bilingual Dictionary, English-Hebrew, Hebrew-English, Prolog 2003, p323

34 Ibid, p224

35 Ibid

17

Hunefer the Book of the Dead

(1) To the Door of the west wind. 'Ra lives, the *Tortoise dies. Pure is the body in the earth, and pure are the bones of Osiris…'

(2) To the Door of the east wind. 'Ra lives, the *Tortoise dies. Sound is he who is in the chest, who is in the chest…'

(3) To the Door of the north wind. 'Ra lives, the *Tortoise dies… Osiris… is strong in his members…'

(4) To the Door of the south wind. 'Ra lives, the *Tortoise dies. The bolts are drawn and they pass through his foundation'.

Thoth's Invocation to the Doors of Heaven

Book of the Dead, Translation E. A. Wallis Budge. The Hebrew name for the *'tortoise' is a homonym of 'turtle' written as (tsav), and suggests a cultic connection with a 'wolf' (ze'ev), archaic of 'Anubis' (Sab). He guards the hidden mysteries, associated with the inner shrine, paralleled to the star Sirius.

The name 'Hunefer' translates, according to the listed hieroglyphs, as (a beautiful magical invocation). 'Hu-nefer' however can be discerned as 'hai'a-yafer' (a beautiful appearance), connoting etymologically the emergence of the soul. Egyptologists sibilate the Hebrew word 'yafe' (beautiful)[1] and transliterate it into the hieroglyphic as 'nefer'. Pronunciation of 'nefer' is based upon the assumption that the glyph resembles the 'harp' (Hebrew nevel).[2] Observing the Arabic vocabulary, 'nevel' fits with 'nafis' (precious) and 'nafs' (the soul). 'Hu' rendered as (a magical invocation) is probably from the Syrian etymon 'hai'a' (an appearance, figure or shape).[3] Central to the theme is the welcoming of a soul or entity, linked to the offering or weighing of the heart.

Drawn on papyrus, the Hunefer manuscript shows a tabernacle scene and is in excellent condition except for the erased beak of 'Zari'a-Kar' (Sokar).[4] The 'apparent' damage to the codex is not coincidental and is based upon an occult interpretation. Intentional, the scribe has disfigured the manuscript to depict the profile of a turtle's head.[5]

Sokar entering the tabernacle. The 'erased' beak alludes religiously to the turtle.

Representation of the turtle is written as a visual pun. In the Egyptian language, the verb 'sta' (to hide or be hidden) is pictured with the determinative glyph of a turtle.[6] Its transliteration is derived from the Egyptian noun 'shat' (shore),[7] related to 'shatir' (clever, experienced, diligent[8] or cunning).

In Egyptian Arabic, the turtle[9] is esoteric of 'sitara' (curtain),[10] pictured as the 'hidden-veil', extracted from the Arabic noun 'satr' (to cover, conceal or veil).[11] Significantly 'satr's spelling suggests the proper transliteration of the turtle glyph is 'str' and not 'sta' as proposed by the Academics at Oxford.

Motif of the 'turtle' (Arabic sulahfat)[12] operates as a compound 'sulh-fat'. The Arabic etymon 'sulh' (peace or reconciliation)[13] incorporates the Syrian etymon 'fat' (to come in),[14] permissive of the inner sanctum.

Scholars argue that the Hunefer manuscript shows a funerary scene - an interpretation shown to be misleading and incorrect. Depiction of the ritual clearly shows a sacrifice carried out inside of a tabernacle. 'Zari'a-Kar' (Sokar) is presented as passing or breaching the cover to the inner sanctuary. His flight is congruent with the 'covered' (satr) ram, featured in the Greek passion as the satyr in the Egyptian mysteries Amun, alias Osiris-Ptah.

Lord Osiris - Shepherd King Lord of the host (seated on a throne of water).

'Zari'a-Kar' (Sokar) ritualistically assumes the role as the 'fatah' (the open-er)[15] and 'welcomes in' (Syrian fat) the deity Osiris-Ptah.[16] Religiously the scribe suggests the resurrection of Zari'a-Kar, a solar motif aligned to his 'father' Ptah (Greek pater) the creator God.[17]

Seated on a throne of water, the 'Opener' (fatah) otherwise Ptah (Osiris) is lateral to the angelic sailor (host). Shown as wearing the White Crown of Upper Egypt, the coronal is pictured as the tear gland, emblematic of the dismembered eye, equated to the dragon and sacrifice.[18] (Refer to Appendix 6).

Combined the headdress of Osiris-Ptah[19] adorns the double 'feather' (Arabic risha).[20] Insignia of the 'feather' is paired in the Semitic language with 'resha' (evil).[21] In addition, the Hebrew adjective 'rakh' (feathery)[22] is doubled with 'ru'ak' (an evil spirit) translated as (a demon).[23] Offspring of the feather (Avus) denotes a fallen angel.[24] (Refer to Chapter 15).

Osiris' role assumes the 'shepherd' (Arabic ra'i)[25] - a 'descendant of the light' elucidated as the 'Sun God', (Ra). Appearance of Ra is manifested through the bark of the canine - a marker of Sirius. Osiris the 'shepherd' (Arabic ra'i) otherwise 'Ra' (Sirius) is switched in the Hebrew vocabulary with 'ra' (evil)[26] a double-bind of 'rai' (the offspring of wickedness). Indexed in the Prolog Dictionary, the radical 'rai' is cognate with 'ra'a' and 'ru'ak' (a demon).[27] Resurrection of Ra incorporates the rising of the sun, offset with the redemption of the lamb (child), attributed to the weighing of sin.

Equated with the rising of 'Venus' (Lucifer), 'shakhar' (dawn) describes the eastern sun featured as 'Zari'a-Kar', cognizant with the summoning of evil.[28] In the Hunefer script, Osiris meets his ascendant son 'Zari'a-Kar' carrying the 'ankh' sign. Read by Egyptologists as 'life', the looped cross is a covert marker of the 'snake' demonstrated in the Akkadian dialect. The verbal root 'hayah' (life) is consistent with the 'snake' (haiya). Shown behind the veil, 'Zari'a-Kar' is ready to pass to the father Ptah - a scene framed by the winged seraph.

Accurately interpreted, the 'ankh' symbol is read as 'acan' (a flaming seraph), adjacent to 'hakim' (a sovereign) registered in the codex. The 'ouroboros' combines the cross, a symbol of the weighing scales prognostic of redemption, situated with the resurrection of the son (sun). The Hebrew word 'to make a cross' is (le'sakel)[29] and is consistent with the deity 'Zari'a-Kar' (Sokar). The falcon Zari'a-Kar is thus shown as crossing his arms holding the ankh symbol.

In conclusion, the 'bush' or 'stick' (sukkah)[30] denotes the 'tabernacle' (succoth or suka), equated with the deity 'Zari'a-Kar', written in current transliterations as (Sokar). 'Zari'a-Kar' classifies (Horus' descendant), cognate with a 'brother' (akh), thematic of the 'serpent' (acan), figured with the 'cross and circle' (ankh).

Sacerdotal induction through the offering of the heart is located with the tabernacle. The trapped ram records a secret oblation, pertaining to the worship of nocturnal deities. Possession of the 'votive' (zakkau) is generic of the fallen angel the Shatani, represented as a 'reptile' (zokhel), allied to the 'enclosure' (succoth or suka). Characteristically, the practice of child sacrifice is observed in the tabernacle and later the Temple. Referred to as the 'mishkan' (sanctuary),[31] the ark and tabernacle personify the 'dwelling place of the lord', iconic of the winged seraph.

'Mish-kan' (inner sanctuary) specifies the Arabic compound (was[32]-not[33]) a euphuism connoting 'unnamed practices'. The noun 'mishkan' translates into the Greek as 'temenos' (a sacred enclosure), cogent with 'temnein' (to cut) and 'teino' (to stretch). Philologically, 'teino' conveys 'Titan' (a fallen angel)[34] and mirrors the 'Shatani', rendered in Greek as 'Teitan'.[35]

'Teino' apprises the Latin transitive verb 'tenere' (to hold, keep, grasp, possess or occupy),[36] relative to 'tendere' (to pitch a tent - in English a tent). The Greco-Roman stem 'ten' is mutual to the adjective 'tener' (tender, soft, young, weak, effeminate or voluptuous).[37]

The 'tent' (a tabernacle) recounts fertility practices, identified with demonic beings archived in the Semitic. 'Mishkan' (a dwelling) concords with the Arabic root 'misik' (to catch, hold, grasp or seize).[38] Idiomatic 'misik' (to grasp) codifies 'masikh' (a monster),[39] congruent with 'mishkan' (a sanctuary).[40]

The Arabic terms 'miskh' (hold) and 'masikh' (monster) translate into the Latin as 'rapere' (rapist)[41] synonymous with 'repere' (reptile).[42] Liturgical allocation of 'mishkan' (the inner shrine), commemorates 'misik-an' (a rapist [from] heaven).[43]

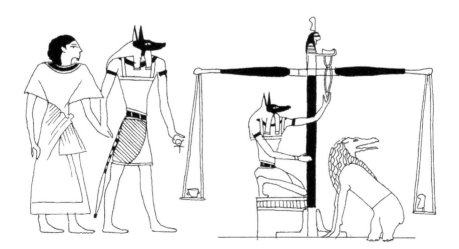

Weighing of the heart – depicts the ritual removal of the heart equated with the tabernacle.

Documented in Babylonian tradition, the manifestation of the 'pillager' discloses the reaper - a laughing angel - conjugal with the 'jackal' (Hebrew tan),[44] opposite 'tanin' (a crocodile).[45] The stem tan in the Egyptian language pertains to the adjective 'tahen' (sparkling), cognate with the 'tehen(t)iu' (the sparkling Gods), featured as a reptile or canine. Significantly, these animals are paired in the Hunefer Papyrus with the weighing of the heart - a tribunal propositional of Isaac redolent of the 'tabernacle' and 'ram', outlined in the next chapter.

1   Prolog: Pocket Bilingual Dictionary, English-Hebrew, Hebrew-English, Prolog 2003, p36

2   Ibid, p181

3   Hippocrene English-Arabic, Arabic-English Dictionary, Hippocrene, New York 2005, p186 [In the Syrian language, 'hu' is the pronoun for (he) and in Arabic states the possessive pronoun (his). The pronoun 'hu', used in conjunction with the harp 'yafer' or 'nafs', dependent on the glyph's original use, could give the reading 'hu yafer' (he is beautiful) or 'hu nafs' (his soul)].

4   Scholars argue the falcon God shown in the Hunefer manuscript is Horus. Significantly the enactment refers to a tabernacle and not a funeral rite or underworld scene. The distinction is important as the 'tabernacle' suggests the ascendant hawk 'Zari'a-Kar' conceptual to 'succoth' and 'sukkah'. In addition, the picture records sacrificial protocol, conjunct with religious and astrological symbolism.

5   Symbol of the turtle cross-references the deity 'Amun' (the hidden or concealed one), whose black features are apparent in the guised markings of Horus. Clandestine, the 'king' or 'hunter' (Horus) denotes the reptile and sanctuary. He is paralleled to the hidden God Amun, figurative of the slain ram and the thicket (tabernacle).

6   Penelope Wilson: Hieroglyphs, A Very Short Introduction, Oxford University Press 2003, p96

7   M.A. Abdel-Hady: Egyptian Arabic, A Rough Guide, Dictionary Phrasebook, Lexus 1998, p241

8   Hippocrene English-Arabic, Arabic-English Dictionary, Hippocrene, New York 2005, p285 'Shatir' (clever, experienced or diligent) is closely related to 'shatan' (to oppose) and suggests the original meaning of 'shatir' had the additional connotation to be cunning or conniving.

9   The turtle is a creature that hides in 'clay' and suggests a connection to 'Adam'.

10 Hippocrene English-Arabic, Arabic-English Dictionary, Hippocrene, New York 2005, p289

11 Ferozsons Urdu-English Dictionary, Revised Edition, Ferozsons Ltd, Lahore, p429

12 Hippocrene English-Arabic, Arabic-English Dictionary, Hippocrene, New York 2005, p291

13 Ibid

14 Ibid, p175

15 Ibid

16 'Fatah' (open) is cognizant with 'fatih' (light), explicit of the votive and the greeting of the 'Dog Star' (Sirius), featured as the 'jackal' (hieroglyphic sab). Ritual weighing of the heart is conjunct with the unveiling of the tabernacle and the ram.

17 The letter 'p' in Hebrew is written in the Arabic language as 'f'. 'Fatah' (the verb to open) is linked etymologically to the deity 'Ptah' the creator God, and tributes the opening of the tabernacle (body) with the death of the firstborn, systemized in the Modern Hebrew. The Semitic stem 'p-t-r' means (to set free) and gives the root of 'p-t-r' (firstborn, release and unleavened bread - 'pattira'). In addition, the Egyptian sign 'ptr' (to observe or view) is emblematic of the votive, correlated with the angel, dragon or watcher. Recorded in the hieroglyphs, the sign 'ptr' is represented as two eyes, complete with falcon markings - a symbol of Horus the hunter. 'Ptr' additionally is a variegation of 'r-pr' Egyptian for (temple) - Greek 'pater' (a rock), and connects the watcher with the firstborn. Archaically the offering of the innocent is cognizant with the sacrifice of the body, equated with the inner sanctuary.

18 In Islamic lore, Osiris-Ptah is cogent with 'Al'khidr' Arabic (the Green One), otherwise known as the angel Gabriel - a being doubled with Lucifer and the reaper. Koran lore links Gabriel with the 'opener' (fatah) figured as the night of glory. Traditionally, the angel removed the heart of the prophet (lamb) - a ritual paralleled to the weighing of the heart shown in the Hunefer manuscript.

19 The Royal wings are compatible with the wings of Isis pictured as the dragon's mouth (angel), symbolic of immolation of the innocent son and rebirth.

20 Hippocrene English-Arabic, Arabic-English Dictionary, Hippocrene, New York 2005, p47

21 Prolog: Pocket Bilingual Dictionary, English-Hebrew, Hebrew-English, Prolog 2003, p137

22 Ibid, p148

23 Ibid, p104

24 Pictured as the 'father' (Arabic aba), his title is interchangeable in the Semitic with 'ever' (wing) and 'af'a' (viper). Relationship between the bird and snake is encoded in the story of Abraham (Refer to Chapter 15 Abraham and the Secret Covenant of the Ram).

25 Hippocrene English-Arabic, Arabic-English Dictionary, Hippocrene, New York, 2005, p111

26 Prolog, Pocket Bilingual Dictionary, English-Hebrew, Hebrew-English, Prolog, 2003, p137

27 Ibid, p104

28 'Evil' is an anagram of 'live' - a verb associated in the Akkadian language with the noun 'snake'.

29 Prolog, Pocket Bilingual Dictionary, English-Hebrew, Hebrew-English, Prolog, 2003, p93

30 Observance of the Passover is linked with the patron Goddess Maat, signified with 'mate' (a rod) - an indicator of 'death' (Arabic mot).

31 Prolog, Pocket Bilingual Dictionary, English-Hebrew, Hebrew-English, Prolog 2003, p353

32 Hippocrene English-Arabic, Arabic-English Dictionary, Hippocrene, New York 2005, p213 [Arabic 'kan' (be - past tense)].

33 Ibid, p242 [Arabic 'mish' (not)].

34 'Teino' (stretch) informs the etymon 'Titan'. According to Greek legend, conception of the Titan split open the mother's womb resulting in death. Birth of the Titan is cognate ritually with the stretching of the votive and linked esoterically to the ritual Opening of the Way.

35 Jack M Driver: Hidden Codes Of The Bible, Deciphering The Divine, Kandour Ltd 2007, p149

36 John C Traupman PhD: The New College Latin & English Dictionary, Bantam Press 1988, p309

37 Ibid

38 Hippocrene English-Arabic, Arabic-English Dictionary, Hippocrene, New York 2005, p243

39 Ibid, p76

40 'Misik' (to grab or seize), 'masikh' (monster) and 'mishkan' (sanctuary) are relative in the Greek vocabulary to 'teino' (to stretch), Latin 'tenere' (to hold or grasp), additional to a 'Titan' (a fallen deity) and 'temenos' (a sacred enclosure).

41 John C Traupman PhD: The New College Latin & English Dictionary, Bantam Press 1988, p260 ['Rapere' intransitive verb (to seize, carry off, ravish, ravage or lay waste)].

42 Ibid p267 ['Repere' intransitive verb (to creep or crawl)].

43 'Misik-an' translated as (a rapist [from] heaven) is a pun on 'Michigan', and suggests the state is a 'sanctuary' (Hebrew mishkan).

44 Prolog, Pocket Bilingual Dictionary, English-Hebrew, Hebrew-English, Prolog 2003, p216

45 Ibid, p92

18

Smiling Angels

'Abraham was a hundred years old when his son Isaac was born to him. Sarah said, "God has brought me laughter, and everyone who hears about this will laugh with me". And she added, "Who would have said to Abraham that Sarah would nurse children? Yet I have borne him a son in his old age".'

Genesis 21: 5-6, Holy Bible, New International Version, Gideon

The patriarch Abraham is presented as a worshipper of 'angels' (Hebrew mal'akh), apprised with the Canaanite deity Moloch the harbinger of death. Throughout the original Semitic language, the killing of Isaac is obscured and operates on a number of complex word plays pertaining to the ram and concealment.

To consolidate the point: Abraham's firstborn son 'Isaac' (Hebrew Itzhak) is translated in the Bible as [he] 'who causes laughter' from the verbal stem 'tsokhok' (laughter).[1] The etiological explanation for Isaac's name according to the book of Genesis signifies 'joy' (See Chapter heading). This assertion is based primarily upon the editor's interpretation that Sarah, his natural mother, conceived him in her ninetieth year.[2] The name laughter however is significant in relation to child sacrifice. The point is salient.

In the ancient Babylonian traditions, angels specifically kill children through smiling at them. The smile in this context refers to a 'grimace' rendered in the Hebrew as (ha'avaya)[3] an esoteric marker correlated in the Arabic with the 'viper' (af'a)[4] and the 'circle' (havala).[5]

Smiling Angel - Reims Cathedral.
Reims Cathedral is the chosen location for the coronation of the French monarchy.

Traditionally, the disk is a symbol of the snake contextually equated with the 'mourner' (avel)[6] in alignment to 'transgression' (avera or hafara).[7] In addition, the Hebrew stem 'havala' pronounced khavalah' (circle) is a polymorph and can also mean (to writhe or twist).

Substitution of the disk with a snake is analogous in the Babylonian language to 'acan' (a flaming serpent), consistent with the Egyptian stem 'akh' (to shine) and 'arq' (to twist). 'Havala' (circle) translates into the Greek as 'sphaira' (ball), homologous to the noun 'speira' (coil - English spiral).

Relationship between the angel stylized as a 'circle and snake' is figurative of the 'ouroboros' found in the Modern Semitic. The Hebrew word 'igul' (a circle)[8] parallels the Arabic noun 'gul' (a demon) cachinnatory of a scoffing demon.[9] Similarly the Persian adverb 'Pairi' (around) discloses the Persian 'race of serpents' (the Peri) approximate to a demon or djinn (jinn).

'Ha'avaya' (to grimace), 'af'a' (snake) and 'havala' (circle) are confluent in the English vocabulary with smirk, smack, snake, and snicker. The smirking angel is idiosyncratic of the winged harpy. Appearance of this deity suggests the adjective happy, collated with the laughing angel the reaper. Namesake of the 'reaper' recalls the Latin intransitive verb 'repere' (to crawl),[10] consistent with the 'reptile' (a creepy crawly).

In the European languages, the laughing angel demonstrates the grim reaper, cognate with grimace and grin.[11] Typically the reaper is veiled - its unearthly smile associated with death. Relationship between the veil and laughter is devised through the offertory, exhibited in the Roman language. The masculine noun 'ritus' (a ceremony or rite) corresponds with 'rica' (veil) worn by Roman women at sacrifices.[12] Custom of the 'rica' (veil) adopted in English 'funeral rites' pertains to (the exequies).[13] Traditionally the woman in mourning adorns a black veil, archaic of the priestess.[14]

'Rica' (veil) extracted from the Sanskrit root 'ric/rig' (worship) informs the Germanic word 'wicca' (witchcraft) contrasted in the modern English with 'vicar' (a priest). The 'veiled' (rica) 'ceremony' (ritus) celebrated in Rome is analogous to 'rictus' (a snout, wide open mouth or grin)[15] nominal of a smiling angel.

Evidence connecting the smile of death to the reaper in the Latin language is compelling. For example, the transitive verb 'ridere' (to laugh)[16] is coherent with 'ridicule' synonymous with 'redimere' (to redeem) and 'reddere' (to return).[17] Ritual laughter suggests the replacement of the votive underscored with the innocent. Redemption of sin details the 'buying back' (redimere) of the offering. Reapportionment (reddere) of the secret votive elicits the 'smiling' (ridere) deity a fool.[18] Depicted as castrated, the hermaphrodite carries a staff or wand - symbolic of the tabernacle and ram associated with the serpent and death.

The clown's smile conforms to the grinning reaper (a weeper), prescribed as a snake or reptile. A dual signifier, laughter is reciprocal of crying, compared to grief. In the Hebrew vernacular, 'ha'avaya' (to grimace) is cogent with 'avel' (a mourner) and 'havala' (circle).

Motif of the disk tallies with a laughing angel, recounted through the death of Isaac, personified as the firstborn. Esoteric, 'tsokhok' the Hebrew word for (laughter) records the patriarch 'Itzhak' (Isaac), implicit of 'Zadok' (Greek Sadducee). Zadok a precursor to the Sadducee priesthood is 'proffered' (zakkau) to the 'reptile' (zokhel). The reptile's 'grimace' (ha'avaya) annotates the 'viper' (af'a), contextual to an angel literally a 'reaper' personified as the 'reptile'.

Contrasted, the laughing angel educes the crying mater, signified as a wet nurse. Her tears illustrative of milk connote the loss of a child. Typically, the dragon is coupled with the virgin maiden or priestess, embodied as the ouroboros - a symbol of intercourse.[19] In addition, the circle illustrates the woman's lactescent breast (mammal), paired with the serpent's coiled body.

The Semitic noun '(k)halav' (milk)[20] is an anagrammatic variation of 'havalah alternatively khavalah' (circle). In English, the 'circle' is punned with 'suckle' and explains the relationship between the 'dragon' (spiro) and his fondness for milk. Analogous 'breast' and 'beast' (Hebrew shad[21] and shed[22] demonstrates the relationship between the mammal (lion) and the priest(ess), consistent etymologically with 'milk' and 'mal'akh' (angel).

Liaison between the woman and serpent emphasizes loss of her firstborn child, substituted with the dragon's offspring. Occult traditions suggest 'havala' (circle) annotates the Hebrew practice 'ha'avara' (to transfer)[23] inimical of Isaac's 'atonement' (kaffara).[24] This practice is concordant with the expiation of sin through the substitution of the offering or 'double' (the kafil).[25] Theologically, Isaac's switch with the ram represents a type of 'loan' (halva'a),[26] rendered as the ram or votive.

Cryptically the purchase or loan 'halva'a' infers the burnt offering 'Hebrew le'hava' (to set on fire).[27] Liturgically 'le'hava' demonstrates 'le'havi' (to bring),[28] etymons identified with the 'seraph' (af'a). The 'flaming-snake' (le'hava-af'a) signifies materialization of the angel, represented as 'le'havhev' (to shine or flash). 'Le'havhev' is translated into the Greek as 'drakon' (to watch or flash).

Regeneration of the body affined to the 'viper' (af'a) an emblem of the angel is analogous to corporeal transfiguration. In the Semitic dialects resurrection of the 'snake' (af'a) personifies the 'double' (kafil) stylized as the king or ram (Amun).

'Havala' (circle) elaborates the smiling serpent and the appropriation of a child or votive.[29] The grinning angel 'ha'avaya' (grimace) is coherent linguistically with 'havhil' (to frighten) and 'le'havhev' (to flash)[30] prosaic of 'kafil' (the double).[31] In English, the equivalent wordplay is 'fear' and 'fire', collated with 'flash' and 'flesh'.

'Violation' (hafara)[32] of the child corresponds with the 'serpent' (af'a) and the 'double' (kafil). 'Af'a' informs the Latin noun 'avis' (bird), adjoined to the winged seraph (an angel). Comparison of 'avis' (bird) and 'havalah' (circle) accords in English to 'wing' and 'ring'.

The winged serpent ceremoniously depicts the adorned priestess, documented in the Temple sanctuaries as the Goddess Isis. Beating of the bird's wing is contiguous with flashing, collated with transformation, personified as the eclipse or reptile. For example, the Hebrew word '(le)ha'afil' (to eclipse)[33] is adjacent to 'le'havhev' (to flash). Subliminally the veiling of the 'circle' (havala) insinuates 'fear' (havhil), paralleled to the horned snake and the reapportionment of sin (ha'avara).

The priestess of Isis: Her wings stylize the mouth of the dragon correlated with divine utterance of the Holy Spirit. Movement of the priestess wings invokes prayers to the serpent. Sign language of the oracle is cryptically referred to as the 'language of the birds'.

Ritual killing of the ram aphoristically depicts 'darkening' (ha'afala),[34] registered with the spilling of Isaac's blood in alignment to 'transgression' (avera or hafara). 'Ha'afala' (darkening) is compared in the Arabic lexicon to the noun 'af'a' (viper), replicated in the wordplay 'darken' and 'drakon' Greek (a dragon or serpent). Depiction of the black snake is iconic of a nocturnal angel - a vampire equated with the reaper and the setting of the sun. Redemption of the firstborn articulates central themes, apparent in Judaic doxology. Rehearsed through the death of Isaac, the infant is volunteered to the smiling deity, pictured as the face of a snake, later a clown (crown). The red nose of the clown, depicted as a sanguine nose, illustrates the ritual smelling of the offering, identified with the victim's blood.[35]

In the New Testament, the death of the innocent demonstrates the crucifixion of Jesus, paralleled to the spring lamb. Demise of the Passover lamb is symbolic of the firstborn and darkness. Allegorized through the death of Jesus, the prophet, like the sun, is resurrected and ascends to heaven. Theologically the narrative written in Greek alludes to the Semitic mysteries.

'Darkening' (ha'afala) is theological to 'transgression' (avera), associated with the 'spring' (aviv).[36] To emphasize, 'aviv' aligns to sacrificial propitiations inclusive of 'le'havi' (to bring),[37] symbolic of 'le hava' (the burnt offertory). Killing of the lamb is paradigmatic of the 'flashing' (havhev) 'serpent' (af'a), equated with fear.

Notably 'havhil' (to frighten) discerns 'le'ha'avis' (to feed - animals).[38] Mutually identical, the expressions indicate the victimization or torture of the 'hostia' (victim) prior to death. This ritual is collated with the worship of a non-human deity.[39]

'Havhil' (frighten) and 'le'ha'avis' (feed) are translated into the Greek as 'panikos' interpreted as (panic, fear or terror) - a cognomen of 'Pan' the satyr. 'Pan' in the ancient Greek is denominative of (the feeder), idiomatic of the Communion.[40] Depicted as sexually insatiable and immoral, his Hellenistic name is doubled with the Semitic noun 'pin' denoting (a penis)[41] and is theoretical to the 'copulator', exhibited through sado-sexual magic, implicit of feeding.

Pan's epithet 'feeder' interconnects also with the deity 'Baal' (Lord)[42] a derivative of the Old Hebrew word 'bala' (swallow - Modern Hebrew bli'a).[43] Baal's cognomen concurs with the Greek deity 'Pan' (feeder) and, like Pan, is a Judo-Canaanite fertility God.[44]

In conclusion, veneration of the horned deity illustrates the veiled reaper (a harlequin), dichotomous with the smiling clown (crown) and reptile. Iconic, the clown and harlequin[45] are depicted as the cockerel or rooster - a symbol of death.[46]

Invitation of the grinning reaper (a grim reaper) is marked by the crowing of a cock hen, paired with the visitation of an owl. Appearance of the 'strix' (an owl or witch) discloses immolation of a child, tandem to molestation and the incarnation of a 'nocturnal demon' (Hebrew laila-ifrit). A reaper 'laila-ifrit' is transliterated into English as the fallen angel (Lilith), connected in the earliest traditions with the night 'owl' - a laughing angel. Predatory, the owl is used in the hieroglyphs to write the word 'death'.

Jacob Jordaens (Symbolic epithet denominational of the Western priesthood).
Border detail to his engraving the fool. The fool's cap is drawn as a rooster – emblematic of the reaper.

Supplication of the grinning reaper requisites the protagonist Amun and the resurrection of the sun featured as the winged serpent. In essence, the slain ram is a death cult, incumbent upon the king and the ritual slaughter of the firstborn, embodied in Babylonian cycles with the spring and reaper.

1 Prolog: Pocket Bilingual Dictionary, English-Hebrew, Hebrew-English, Prolog 2003, p226

2 'Tish'im' Hebrew (ninety) is a probable pun on the Syrian root 'tlu'ish'shams' (sunrise), denoting the conclusion of the mystery meal and the fulfilment of the covenant. On a more lateral note, the artist Titian is a derivation of the Greek word 'titan' and is further a pun on the Hebrew word 'tish'im' (ninety). Titian, according to legend, died when he was 'ninety', suggesting initiation into the mysteries.

3 Prolog: Pocket Bilingual Dictionary, English-Hebrew, Hebrew-English, Prolog 2003, p174

4 Hippocrene English-Arabic, Arabic-English Dictionary, Hippocrene, New York 2005, p135

5 Ralph Ellis: Eden in Egypt, A Translation of the Book of Genesis out of the Original Egyptian Text, Edfu Books 2005, p280 (Appendix A5 - Dictionary)

6 Prolog: Pocket Bilingual Dictionary, English-Hebrew, Hebrew-English, Prolog 2003, p264

7 Ibid, p427

8 Ibid, p67

9 'Qeb' (compass), a homonym of 'qeb' (snake), is combined in Freemasonry with the setsquare, a 'measuring ruler' illustrative of (the king compared to the ruler). In Latin, 'regalis' specifies (the king literally regal), synchronized with 'regula' (ruler), rendered in the French as 'regle'. The circle, otherwise the compass, is a symbol of Freemasonry, correlated with the serpent. It is combined with the setsquare, a ruler, to form the hieroglyph denoting a womb. Conjoined, the setsquare and compass form the six-pointed star, known as the seal of Solomon, alternatively the Star of David.

10 John C Traupman PhD: The New College Latin & English Dictionary, Bantam Press 1988, p374

11 The expression hoot with laughter and side splitting are allegories of the grinning angel. The laughing deity conveys secret rites, accorded with the offering of the firstborn written in coded form, preserved in the spelling of English words. The consonant 'S' in the Old English is used as a prefix to signify 'God'. The archaic spelling of 'slaughter' reads as an anagram of God's laughter (S-laughter) and infers the veiled killing of a child portent of the grim reaper (smiling angel).

12 John C Traupman PhD: The New College Latin & English Dictionary, Bantam Press 1988, p272

13 Ibid, p285 ['Exequies' (funeral rites) from ex-'sequi' (to follow, accompany or escort)].

14 Death of the firstborn son is matched with the rape of the firstborn daughter, impregnated typically by a deity, serpent or angel.

15 John C Traupman PhD: The New College Latin & English Dictionary, Bantam Press 1988, p272

16 Ibid

17 Ibid, p262

18 Originally the fool carrying the stick is a woman. The Latin noun 'virga' (stick) is personified as 'virgo' (a virgin). The fool later adopts a male persona - a symbol of the hermaphrodite (angel).

19 The ouroboros shows a dragon swallowing its 'tail' (Latin penis), evocative of intercourse.

20 Prolog: Pocket Bilingual Dictionary, English-Hebrew, Hebrew-English, Prolog 2003, p255

21 Ibid, p49 ['Shad' (breast)]

22 Ibid, p168 ['Shed' (ghoul)]

23 Ibid, p427

24 Hippocrene English-Arabic, Arabic-English Dictionary, Hippocrene, New York 2005, p212

25 Prolog: Pocket Bilingual Dictionary, English-Hebrew, Hebrew-English, Prolog 2003, p118

26 Ibid, p236

27 Ibid, p153 ['Lehava' (Flame)]

28 Ibid, p50

29 The circle operates on a number of complex levels and is a dual emblem of the serpent (angel) and mammal (man). For example, the disk signifies the 'watching dragon', contrasted in Greek with the noun 'kore' (a pupil or virgin), underscored as the 'neophyte' (approximate to a student).

30 Prolog: Pocket Bilingual Dictionary, English-Hebrew, Hebrew-English, Prolog 2003, p153

31 Ibid, p118

32 Ibid, p449

33 Ibid, p124

34 Ibid, p98

35 The smelling of wine is a ritual that evolved from the smelling of the offering.

36 Prolog: Pocket Bilingual Dictionary, English-Hebrew, Hebrew-English, Prolog 2003, p389

37 Ibid, p50

38 Ibid, p148

39 Sacrificial protocol demands the victim is first terrorized to facilitate an increase in the hormonal level in the blood. Hormone is derived from the Greek etymon 'hormao' (to impel) equated with 'haima' (blood).

40 The ancient French word 'gobelin' (a goblin) is related to the French verb 'gober' (to swallow or gobble). The swallowing deity is symbolised as the 'turkey cock' (a gobbler). 'Gobelin' (a goblin - adjacent to the snake) is closely matched in French with 'globule' (globe), Latin 'globulus' (globule), conceptual to hemoglobin.

41 Prolog: Pocket Bilingual Dictionary, English-Hebrew-Hebrew-English, Prolog 2003, p295

42 'Baal' (Lord) is an obvious pun in English of 'ball' - an emblem of the snake.

43 Prolog: Pocket Bilingual Dictionary, English-Hebrew-Hebrew-English, Prolog 2003, p406

44 Intriguingly the title 'Pan' (feeder) is used in the Greek as the term (universal), which possesses the same meaning as 'katholikos' Greek (a Catholic).

45 Conventionally the 'harlequin' (French herlequin) refers to the leader of a legendary group of demonic horsemen compared to the host. The harlequin wears a mask and is rivaled with the crying clown pictured with a smiling face. Invisible to the clown and vying for the affections of the 'columbine' mistress (dove), he carries a staff or wand symbolic of the tabernacle and ram.

46 In Arabic the verb 'dihik' (laugh) is esoteric of 'dik' (a rooster), connoting death of the firstbborn 'dakar' (a male). In the Gospel traditions, Jesus' betrayal and execution is timed with the crowing of a rooster. A solar motif the cockerel is esoteric of 'khok' Hebrew (law).

19

Adam Atum

'O Amen, O Amen, who are in heaven, turn your face upon the dead body of your son and make him sound and strong in the underworld'. This is a composition of exceedingly great mystery. Let not the eye of any man whatsoever see it, for it is an abominable thing for every man to know it; therefore hide it. "Book of the mistress of the hidden temple" is its name'.

The Egyptian Book of the Dead, Translation E. A. Wallis Budge

Doctrinally Atum-Ra is the creator God from 'Heliopolis' the Greek name for (Sun City) and is one of the most important religious centers of the Egyptian civilization. Atum's name is from the Arabic root 'tamm' (to finish or complete). The idea of completion originates from the Akkadian root 'tum' (consecration). 'Tum' is grouped with immolation, evident in the Arabic verbal stem 'ta'am' (to feed) from the Syrian noun 'ta'am' (food)[1] and 'tumm' (mouth).[2]

Sacrificial food 'ta'am' is identified with 'payment', rendered in the Syrian tongue as 'taman or temen' (price), correlated with the votive. The Arabic idiom 'tamm' (to be over or to have finished)[3] - Hebrew 'tam' (innocent)[4] suggests theologically a sacrificial price, and originates from the worship of Atum.

The concept of propitiations situated with Atum is found also in the Greek. 'Temen' (payment) informs the Greek verb 'temnein' (to cut), equated with the verb 'teino' (to stretch), adjacent to the root 'temenos' (a temple or sacred enclosure). The switch of the 'm' and the 'n' consonant occurs frequently in Greek and Semitic words.

Resurrection of Atum is an extension of the Akkadian deity 'Tammuz' (consecrated by fire) demonstrated here as the original source of Atum's name. The Arabic expression 'tamm' (to finish) is rendered in the Egyptian hieroglyphics as 'tem' (to finish), and infers the 'sunrise' found in the etymon 'ten' (to rise) and 'tenen' (risen), cognomens of Atum-Ra.[5] Inversion of 'tamm' in the Arabic is 'mat' denoting (death), ascribed to the setting disk Aten, alias the Goddess of Judgment - Maat.

A derivative of Atum's name present within Egyptian lexicon is 'tahen' (to gleam, sparkle or scintillate). Adjectivally, 'tahen' is rendered in the Modern Hebrew as 'tehar' (clearness or luster), and is akin to the Hebrew noun 'tahor' (gold).[6] In the Egyptian language, the adjective 'tahen' refers to the 'tehen(t)iu' (the sparkling Gods)[7] - the root of which is probably from the earlier Sumerian word 'etemmu' (a ghost or spirit - archaically a vampire).

The 'radiant Gods' (tehentiu) are equivalent to the 'shining ones' (Hebrew irin), referred to in Judaic commentaries as 'angels' otherwise known as the 'watchers' (Greek drakon). Followers of the tehentiu and Atum ritualistically practiced 'circumcision', preserved in the Modern Arabic compound 'tar'har'.[8] Espousal of the Pharaoh's reign in accordance to heaven is noted through circumcision.[9]

Thematically, the angels are compared to the stars, identified with resurrection, implied from the Egyptian verb 'tenen or ten' (risen).[10] The appellation 'tenen' is matched with the earlier Akkadian root 'Ten-En' (a Risen or Shining Lord). In the hieroglyphic, 'ten' (to rise) is summative of the Daystar and the worship of the Sun deity Atum-Ra (Venus). Atum-Ra's motif is the winged disk adjoined to the serpent - a symbol of the Pharaoh contrasted with the votive. Celebration of the rising star parallels the death of the firstborn and the concealment of nocturnal angels, exclusively the Royal line Akhenaten.

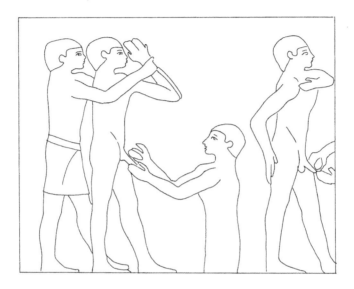

Depiction of Egyptian ritual of circumcision, stone relief, Nubian

In the original Egyptian, 'Atum's cognomen translates approximately as (totality or whole) and is a pun from the Akkadian language 'A-tum' (I consecrate) or (I sanctify). The analogy in English is whole and holy. *'...Atum['s] name carries the idea of 'totality' in the sense of an ultimate or unalterable state of perfection'.*[11] This state is analogous to the adjective 'absolute' and its theological equivalent 'absolution'. In Greek, the concept is conveyed as 'atomos' (the indivisible one).[12] He is the primordial source in perpetuity to death and resurrection.

Atum's name is rendered in the Phoenician as the title 'Adon' (Lord). According to Egyptian ritual, a child or adolescent purifies the offering in relation to the sun's cycle, entrusted to a Lord or a deity. Similar ideas are found within Greek mythology. A clear example of this close relationship between the Greek and Egyptian mysteries is the youth Adonis. According to classical mythology, Adonis consummated a relationship with the Goddess 'Aphrodite' (Venus) and was later killed by 'Ares' (Mars) under the guise of a wild boar (man). Ritualistically, Adonis' death is deified as a sacrifice and likened to a fertility

God. The youth's blood is linked to the underworld and the changing of the seasons. His demise, compared to the harvest offering, correlated with the red disk and the green reaper.

Adonis' fate originates from the Egyptian sun disk, illustrated as Atum. The deity Atum and its variant 'aten' (a disk) are transliterated into the Phoenician language as 'Adon' (Lord). 'Adon' is contrasted with 'Atum', and parallels the Sanskrit etymology 'ad and adi' (first). The title 'Adon' (Lord) is borrowed in the Greek as 'Adonai', abridged in the Latin as 'Dominus'.

Correlation between 'Atum' and 'Adon' is recorded in the hieroglyphic. On rare occasions, according to the scholar David Rohl, Atum is spelt *using a hand which Egyptologist recognize as the letter 'd' or 't', giving us A-d-m*.[13] Atum's name therefore serves as a probable pun on the Hebrew name Adam - the progenitor of man cognate in Greek with Adonai (a Lord).

Adam in the Semitic tongue signifies 'one that is red', derived ultimately from the Akkadian word 'adamatu' (the dark red earth) - equivalent to 'Adonis'. 'Adamatu' informs the Hebrew noun 'adom' (red), while something that is represented as red is 'adum', indicated by the 'Adummim' (the Red men), described in the book of Joshua (15:7).[14]

The names Adon and Atum work on a series of cleverly disguised puns. In ancient Akkadian, the pronoun and verbal stem 'a-ddin' (I-give) is correlated in the Semitic language with the name 'Adam' (red), and reflects the Phoenician title 'Adon' (Lord). Study of morphemes demonstrate a close phonetic relationship between the phonemes 't' and 'd' evinced from Atum, Adon and Adam, reflected in the biblical creation epics.

Adam, according to tradition, is described as the first man quite literally a Lord, and is depicted as a custodian of the Garden of Eden. Typical of religious literature from Sumer, Adam's name is a play on 'Eden' the Hebrew word for (delight). Eden's etymology is cogent with the direction 'Qadam' (East),[15] associated with the 'rising sun' (atum) and the morning sacrifice. 'A-ddin' reflects the 'propitiation', deemed 'felicitous', extracted from the root 'Eden'.

The analogy between 'Eden' (delight) and 'A-ddin' (I give) is symmetrical in the Egyptian language with 'hotep' (an offering), employed to describe the adjective (contentment or happiness). 'Ddin' (to give) is sourced from the Arabic root 'din' (religion). Derivatives of the early Semitic noun 'din' refer to the fallen angels, the 'djinn', in proximity to the 'votive' (ddin). The race of djinn (jinn) are likened to a 'snake', extracted epigraphically from the Egyptian glyph 'dj' (a serpent or worm) - Refer to Appendix 9, Hieroglyphic Sign List.

Their form is actualized from fire (blood) or the fat of the offering, elicited from the sacrifice of Adam communicated etymologically. In Arabic for example, the word 'hardun' (lizard)[16] is from the compound 'harr' (heat), combined with the Syrian root 'duhn' (grease). 'Duhn' is cognizant with the much older Akkadian root 'tum' (to consecrate) and is matched in Arabic with 'dam' (blood). The phonetic switch of the 't' and 'd' and the 'm' and 'n' evident in Semitic words suggest 'hardun' (lizard) is etymologically another expression of the deity name Atum or Adam.

Metamorphosis of Atum in the Arabic language is likened to a 'worm' or 'caterpillar' (dud),[17] explicit of the offering, represented as a 'basket' (colloquial Arabic dud). Dualled with the pupa or cocoon, the carrier symbolizes the womb and worm, cognizant with the monarch's rebirth, facilitated through the tribute.

The cognomen 'hardun' (otherwise Atum) operates on a subtle play. In the Old Semitic, 'harr' (translated as heat) designates 'harel' (the altar). By combining the Syrian word 'duhn' (grease) with the former word 'harr', the noun 'hardun' (a lizard) is read cryptically as the 'fat of the altar', transcribed as (har-duhn).

Conceptually the lizard's double is drawn out from the burnt offering, assigned to 'the-blood' of Adam (ha-dam). In the Biblical tradition, the idea of blood offerings fits with the worship of Yahweh. This God also is supplicated with the blood of the firstborn and the fatty portions of the offerings, intrinsic to the worship of Atum and his host. Depictions of Atum's disk are shown combined with the reptile, a serpent. See illustration 'Winged Disk' Chapter 15, page 151.

In Modern Arabic, 'hardun' describes 'hadm' (digestion)[18] and 'add' (to bite).[19] 'Add' philologically is simultaneous with 'hadd' (sharp) and 'hadd' (luck), cogent in the Akkadian with 'a-ddin' (the augury).

In the Old Testament, the masculine name 'Adin' specifies (sensual) and describes one of the patriarchal heads of Israel. 'Adin's cognomen has the additional meaning (subtle)[20] an adjective used in Genesis to describe the serpent. The original root of 'Adin' Akkadian 'a-ddin' (I-give) suggests the 'offertory' equated with ecstasy or sexual intercourse relative to the worship of the djinn.

Ritualistically, 'Adin' is an entendre in Hebrew of 'adina' (voluptuous, ripe or mature),[21] alluding to the fruit of knowledge, situated in the Garden of 'Eden'. 'Adin's name serves as an intentional pun on 'Adam', in conjunction to 'Eden' otherwise 'E-ddin' (the house of offering), in late Hebrew (delight), appellations associated with 'hardun' (a lizard).

Atum's logo is shown extrapolated from the risen cobra, generically 'hardun'. The upward movement of the hooded snake (reaper) is equated with ascension, explicit of death. Atum's resurrection is rendered as the flaming seraph - an expression of the djinn or angel.

Similarity between the Akkadian, Arabic and Egyptian vocabulary suggest the deification of the serpent (angel) parallels the sun God Atum. Pictorially, the solar device (aten) is merged with the snake, and reinforces the proposition between the serpent and fire, expressed in European symbolism. In Greek, the 'Salamandra' (Salamander) denotes the Royal line,[22] equivalent to the fire-breathing dragon.

Origins of the morning offertory, attributed to Atum, are sourced directly from the creation of Adam, paired with the mythical place Eden. This 'garden' is a symbol of the 'guardian'. According to Apocryphal literature, the fallen angels are responsible for imparting knowledge of the seasons and agriculture to humanity. There is a strong relationship between the materialization of an angel and the gathering of the crop. Development of 'agriculture' (zara'a)[23] originates from the 'angelic' progeny the 'zari' (aliens), archaically the 'se'irim' (a red goat or demon).

Within Judaism, the harvest and land is aggregated with man's mortality and life cycle. The collective term for 'man' is (adam), and is paired in Hebrew with the noun 'adama' (land).[24] In Latin, the resemblance is 'humanus' (human) and 'humus' (soil).[25] Archaically, man's mortality coincides with oblation and rebirth, in relation to the body and temple[26] conceptual to 'Adam' and 'Eden'.

Eden thus describes the garden of offering, implied from the verbal root 'a-ddin' (I-give). Theologically, the place illustrates satiation through the votive, demonstrated in the proto-Semitic languages. In the Akkadian, 'E-ddin' translates as (the House [of] offering), theoretically (a temple). The sanctuary, mound or altar is symbolized corporally as Adam, and is likened to the 'earth' (adama).

The Hebrew word 'Eden' spelt in the Akkadian language as 'Edin' is a polymorph and is also read as (a steppe or terrace) as found in (a raised agricultural terrace).[27] 'Edin' is consistent with the Persian word (paradise). 'Paradise' technically represents (a walled enclosure) from the Persian etymons 'pairi' (around) and 'daeza' (wall), reductive of the Hebrew etymon 'pardes' (a grove).

In addition, the Persian adverb 'pairi' puns with the Persian 'race of serpents' (the peri), and fits with the early physical descriptions of Adam and Eve, examined in Chapter 43 Naked Snakes Part 1.

Translation of 'paradise' (a walled enclosure) evokes a 'temple sanctuary'. In Judaic scripture, the analogy is annotated as the noun 'khoma' (wall)[28] - a veiled marker of the 'moon' (qamar) aligned to the 'priesthood' (komer). The same meaning is extrapolated from the Arabic noun 'sur' (wall)[29] punned with 'sirr' (mystery). 'Sirr' is cognizant with the earlier Sumerian root 'sirr' (serpent), equivalent to 'zu' (demon) - reductive from 'se' irim' (a red goat or demon).

Figuratively, the circle or fortified wall indicates 'paradise'[30] and operates as a meta-narrative repeated in the Greek traditions of Atlantis. In Plato's 'Critias', he describes 'Atlantis' as a circle and we are left in no doubt he is describing a planet attributed to (Atlas). To quote:

> 'He [Poseidon] made two rings of land and three of sea [space] as round as if he had laid them out with compass and lathe'.[31]

Plato's writing is intentionally covert; the compass in Greek and Byzantine culture signifies creation, characteristic of the snake, and is copied as the insignia of Modern Freemasonry. The calipers circumscribe the disk pageant of the reptile celebrated as the builder.

Originally, the two rings of earth, in Critias' account, designate two planets surrounded by sea - symbolic of an atmosphere. The planet is represented as a 'walled enclosure' (pairi-daeza) - the destruction of 'paradise' recounted mythologically.

The place name 'Atlantis' translates as (the daughter of Atlas).[32] According to the scholar Alan F. Alford, it is derived from the root 'tlao' (to suffer or bear) - literally 'A-tlao' (to bear or suffer together).[33] 'Atlantis' is probably the same woman as the mortal 'Tyro'.[34] In Greek mythology, Tyro consummated her relationship with the fish deity Poseidon, encountered in the myth of Eve and the serpent.

'Tyro's epitaph (to suffer) is matched in the Egyptian language with 'trai' (to obliterate, decimate or destroy entirely). The use of 'trai' philologically reappears in the Greek legend of 'Troy', and would indicate 'A-tlao and Tyro' compared to (Atlantis and Troy) are variations of the same word or myth.

A common version of the Atlantis legend is retold in the story of 'Tantalus'. Known as 'the son of Jupiter father of Pelops', he is punished in the lower world with constant hunger and thirst.[35] Tantalus' name is deduced from the Latin adjective 'tantillus' (so small),[36] used proverbially in English as the intransitive 'tantalize'. Tantalus' appellation further is an anagram of Atlantis, and suggests one of Jupiter's moons or satellites responsible for the demise of Atlantis.

In Plato's account of Atlantis (Timaeus, Section 21b), the narrator of the story is Critias. His appellation is a Latinized spelling of the Greek word 'kritikos' (a censor), related to 'krites' (a judge). Critias in his dialogue recounts to Socrates the story of Atlantis during the Apaturial festival. *He maintains that even though the story is very strange... 'every word of it is true'.*[37]

The 'truth' here refers to metaphor and is apparent from the onset with the celebration of the Apaturial. In Latin, 'apertura' means (open) and is used dexterously to imply the Greek root 'apato' (to deceive) and 'apatlos' (deceptive).[38] The etymon 'apato' relates to the Latin stem 'appetit' (to crave or desire) i.e. 'tantalize', and the transitive verb 'appeto' (to attack, assail or assault).[39] Critias' description of Atlantis as a circle suggests a merging of the creation and flood narrative paralleled to the tradition of paradise, identified with the Mortuary temple and offering.

Theologically, the 'fertile terrace' (Eden) and the 'stepped ziggurat' (E-ddin) are connected religiously to the destruction of paradise paired with the votive. Relationship between Adam and 'adama' (the earth) connotes the serpent. Covert 'adama' is written alternatively as 'afar' (earth)[40] - a play on 'af'a' (snake). The snake's resurrection from the soil denudes the offering of a man, symbolic in Europe of the vampire, identified in the Semitic tradition with the dragon or reaper. In Arabic, the earth is matched with 'jnain' (a garden)[41] - opposite the custodian a 'jinni'.

Atonement through sacrifice originates from the offspring of Adam, allegoric of the garden and the annihilation of Eden. Conceptually, Adam's demise dovetails with the Egyptian Arabic noun 'aadm' (bone)[42] - allegorical of Eve's rib merged with the serpent. 'Aadm' (bone) in the Arabic pertains to the verbal stem 'adam' (to annihilate).[43] 'Adam' originally suggested blood rites, apportioned to 'hardun' (a lizard) i.e. a dragon, angel or reaper, reconciled with the land and earth.[44]

Analogy of the bone equated with the fallen angel explains the corruption of Eden, associated with decay and death, recorded in the Latin and Greek. The obscure Latin noun 'ossis' (bone) is derived from the Greek root 'osteon'. Cryptically, 'ossis' and 'osteon' recalls the angelic 'host' from the Greek lexicon 'oseeos' (holy) - a derivative of 'hostia' (a sacrificial victim). Philologically, 'oseeos' is consistent with 'Osiris' Lord of the host. He is depicted as seated on a throne of generative water.

'Oseeos' (holy) otherwise Osiris in religious doublespeak is applied to 'oasis' (a fertile crescent), conceptual to the location 'paradise' (pairi-daeza), understood as Eden. The oasis signifies a place of offering - its crescent interchangeable with the ecliptic moon, correlated with water. Curvature of the earth's satellite demarcates symbolically the rib, affiliated to the serpent (Venus) and its sanctuary (enclosure), classified with the priestess (rock / rib).

Extraction of Adam's 'bone' (aadm) parallels the creation of Eve from Adam, adjacent to the temple. Architecturally, the temple's foundation is represented as the rock, described in Jewish Scriptures as 'even sheti yah' (the foundation stone). Esoteric Hebrew equates the noun 'sela' (a stone or rock)[45] with 'tsela' (a rib),[46] figurative of the altar (alter). Removal of Adam's rib (heart) recounts theologically the creation of Eve, coupled with the serpent.

To conclude this chapter in the Egyptian mysteries, 'Adam' is transposed to the worship of 'Atum' in situ to the earth and temple. The fall of Adam communicates loss, attributed religiously to the death of the firstborn, coupled with the desecration of Eden. Referred to as Atlantis or Paradise in Greek and Persia, the memory of a lost planet is associated with a far older and secret tradition. It is with this notion that we must travel further back in time and distance to discover why Adam is considered the true inheritor of the earth.

1 Hippocrene English-Arabic, Arabic-English Dictionary, Hippocrene: New York 2005, p292
2 Ibid, p303
3 Ibid, p296
4 Ibid, p208
5 Ralph Ellis: Eden in Egypt, A Translation of the Book of Genesis out of the Original Egyptian Text, Edfu Books 2005, p60
6 'Tahen' (to sparkle) is akin to the Chinese etymon 'tien' (heaven).
7 Ralph Ellis: Eden in Egypt, A Translation of the Book of Genesis out of the Original Egyptian Text, Edfu Books 2005 p167.
8 Hippocrene English-Arabic, Arabic-English Dictionary, Hippocrene, New York 2005, p294
9 Transferred to Judaic practice, the male (human) phallus is symbolically castrated (circumcised), literally usurped, with the serpent's illegitimate offspring (See Genesis 27: The brother Jacob steals the birthright from his twin Esau. Refer also to the traditions of Cain and Abel, Isaac and Ishmael (firstborn). In classical mythology, the equivalent story is found in the narrative of Romulus and the murder of his twin Remus).
10 Alan F. Alford: The Atlantis Secret, A Complete Decoding of Plato's Lost Continent, Eridu 2001, p393 (Notes to Pages 125-140)
11 Ralph Ellis: Eden in Egypt, A Translation of the Book of Genesis out of the Original Egyptian Text, Edfu Books 2005, p291 (Appendix A5 - Dictionary).
12 Laurence Gardner, Genesis of the Grail Kings. Bantam Books 2000, p140
13 David Rohl, Legend, The Genesis of Civilisation, Arrow Books Limited 1999, p428
14 Laurence Gardner, Genesis of the Grail Kings. Bantam Books 2000, p101
15 Translated by S. L. MacGregor Mathers: The Kabbalah Unveiled, Arkana 1991, p167
16 Hippocrene English-Arabic, Arabic-English Dictionary, Hippocrene, New York 2005, p189
17 Ibid, p170

18 Ibid, p185

19 Ibid, p317

20 Prolog, Pocket Bilingual Dictionary, English-Hebrew & Hebrew-English, Prolog 2003, p401

21 Geddes & Grosset: Dictionary of First Names, Geddes & Gosset, New York 2003, p8

22 Salam-andro (Men of Salam) Island in the Saronic Gulf near Athens, city in Cyprus, founded by Teucher - The salamander is used also as the insignia of the French Royal Court - a bloodline derived from Salam.

23 Hippocrene English-Arabic, Arabic-English Dictionary, Hippocrene, New York 2005, p9

24 Prolog, Pocket Bilingual Dictionary, English-Hebrew & Hebrew-English, Prolog 2003, p225

25 Guy Deutscher: The Unfolding of Language, William Heinemann 2005, p324

26 The vampire awakes from the 'earth' (adama) - a symbol of 'Adam'.

27 Andrew Collins: From the Ashes of Angels, The Forbidden Legacy of a Fallen Race, Michael Joseph Ltd 1996, p151

28 Prolog: Pocket Bilingual Dictionary, English-Hebrew & Hebrew-English, Prolog 2003, p453

29 Hippocrene English-Arabic, Arabic-English Dictionary, Hippocrene, New York 2005, p137

30 In Hebrew, the search for hidden meaning obscured by secret codes is known as 'entering the forbidden grove (grave)'. The Semitic word for 'grove' is (pardes), conceptually a 'circled or walled mound' (equated with paradise). According to Professor Walter Burkert, 'paradosis' in Greek is used in a narrower sense referring to instruction, and in a larger sense instruction plus ritual. 'Paradosis' in the Bacchic mystery rites describes the transmission of knowledge from one generation 'of sacred persons' to the next, originating from the snake and its enclosure - the temple E-ddin.

31 Alan F. Alford: The Atlantis Secret, A Complete Decoding of Plato's Lost Continent, Eridu 2001 p315

32 Ibid, p319

33 Ibid, p406 (Notes to Pages 233-248)

34 Ibid, p408 (Notes to Pages 249-256)

35 John C Traupman: The New College Latin & English Dictionary, Bantam, 1988, p307

36 Ibid

37 Alan F. Alford: The Atlantis Secret, A Complete Decoding of the Lost Continent, Eridu 2001, p225

38 Ibid, p404 (Notes to Pages 218-233)

39 John C Traupman: The New College Latin & English Dictionary, Bantam 1988, p18

40 Prolog: English-Hebrew & Hebrew-English Dictionary, Completely Transliterated, Prolog, p124

41 Hippocrene English-Arabic, Arabic-English Dictionary, Hippocrene, New York 2005, p26

42 Ahmed M.A. Abdel-Hady: Egyptian Arabic, The Rough Guide, Dictionary Phrasebook, Lexus, 1998, p220

43 Hippocrene English-Arabic, Arabic-English Dictionary, Hippocrene, New York 2005, p317

44 The Japanese noun 'hone' (bone) is punned with 'oni' (demon) a cognomen similar to the Akkadian word 'ani' (a person of heaven). 'Hone' and 'oni' is identical in the Greek to the wordplay 'ossis' (bone) and 'oseeos' designating (the angelic-host). Arabic 'aadm' (bone) and 'hardun' (a lizard).

45 Prolog: Pocket Bilingual Dictionary, English-Hebrew & Hebrew-English, Prolog 2003, p348

46 Ibid, p346

20

Men are from Mars and Snakes are from Venus

'We created man out of an extraction of clay [blood], then We set him, a drop, in a receptacle secure, then We created of the drop a clot, then We created of the clot a tissue, then We created of the tissue bones, then We garmented the bones in flesh... So blessed be God, the fairest of creators'.[1]

Al Mu'minun: The Believers (Koran 23: 12-14)

'O mankind! If you have doubt about the resurrection, (consider) that We created you out of dust, then out of sperm, then out of a leech like cloth [gauze?], then out of a lump of flesh, partly formed and partly unformed, in order that We may manifest (what We will) to you'.[2]

Al Hajj: The Pilgrimage (Koran 22: 5)

Adam's name is evident in the early Akkadian root 'adamatu' (dark red earth), consistent in Sumerian with 'dumu' (son) and 'dam' (a spouse or wife).[3] 'Dam' is transferred into Modern Hebrew as the noun (blood),[4] constant philologically in the European languages with 'dame' and 'damnation'. In ancient Aramaic, the words for 'blood' are (adamu and dam),[5] designations of the 'earth' (adama). Analogies of 'red clay' (originally Adamatu) recall the creation of man conceived from a clot of blood and is elaborated further in the Babylonian wordplays (Refer to Chapter header).

In the Sumerian vocabulary, the name of 'Adam' appears as a Semitic loan word,[6] where it stands for the generic term (people or humanity). It is adopted as the epithet for the great Canaanite God El, known as 'Ab-Adam' (Father of Man).[7] His namesake is read as the homonym (Father of Blood), interchangeable with (Stony Ground), parabolic of the Underworld. Ab-Adam's worship conjures the mountain or pyramid, figurative of the altar and death. Veneration of 'Ab-Adam' shows an early connection between the Canaanites (Lot) and human sacrifice, related to the development of Judaic theology and language.

Theoretically, red clay symbolizes blood, complicit of deity veneration of the 'goat' (se'irim), in opposition to the ram articulated as creation. In Egyptian texts, the metaphor of clay recounts the genesis of man by the ram deity 'Khnum' (joined). He is shown as shaping Ihy on a potter's wheel. Khnum's progeny wears the 'lock of youth' - a symbol of the red goat conceived as a 'hairy snake' (human-angelic). His ringlet is adopted later as a motif of the Jewish priesthood. Archetypically Ihy is drawn as a juvenile in shaded terracotta, descriptive of the red man - Adam.

Khnum creating man from clay on a potters wheel.
The protagonist Ihy is shown as wearing a dreadlock of youth - insignia of the Judaic priesthood.

Clay in the Syrian language is a euphemism of flesh and blood - a mark of the lunar covenant (See Chapter heading). Conception of Adam's priesthood is ascribed to the descendents of the moon and opposition. Antagonism apportioned to the crescent consists of the serpent and the fall of Eve - illustrative of Venus. This dichotomy is registered in Arabic as 'Zuhrah' (Venus),[8] comprehended in Greek as 'saura' (lizard). Tension between the snake and woman aka Venus is contrasted with Adam and Mars, specific of human rebellion, indicative in Arabic of 'adam' (annihilate).[9] Philological comparison of related word groups suggest the following sequence.

Adam originally is created or conceived on 'Mars' (in Hebrew Ma'adim),[10] traced from the Akkadian derivative 'adamatu' (red earth). In Modern Hebrew, the prepositions 'me' or 'mi' is translated as (from) or (out of).[11] 'Ma'adim' (Mars) in the older script is written without the vowels, and can be read as the phrase 'me'adim' (out of Adam - alternatively from Adam). The close word comparisons suggest a connection between the 'offspring of Adam' (me'adim), 'Mars' (Ma'adim) and 'blood' (adamu).[12]

In Arabic, 'Me'adim' signifies the noun 'ma'adin' (metal)[13] - symbolic of the votive (ddin) equated with alchemy of the ram (Mars) and goat (Venus). Descendents of Adam practiced sacrifice, integral to the Median (Medina) priesthood of Iran, Turkey and Syria. Collectively, the Medians referred to themselves as the 'Mad' or 'Mada'[14] - inversions of the Semitic words 'dam' (blood) and 'Adam'.

'Mada' (a Persian) alludes euphemistically to the votive, derived from the Sanskrit word 'medha' (a human sacrifice),[15] opposite 'mandir' (a sacred fire). 'Medha' informs the English verb 'murder', cognizant in the Indo-European languages with the Persian nouns 'murdah' (corpse)[16] and 'murdar' (a body, corpse or carrion).[17]

The Sanskrit feminine noun 'mad' or 'madh' translates as (wine, intoxication, passion, prime of youth or semen)[18] and describes the civil practice of the 'medha' (sacrifice), adjacent to the 'Mada' priesthood. Distinction of the 'Mada' is condensed in the Arabic as the stem 'madd' - the transitive verb (to stretch) or (spread).[19] 'Madd' is translated into Greek as 'teino' (to stretch) from 'temnein' (to cut) and is an abstraction of 'temenos' (a temple or sacred enclosure).[20]

The 'medha' (votive) espouses 'maddah' (to praise or eulogize)[21] and is related to the Egyptian Arabic stem 'madar' (to chew).[22] 'Madar' is transliterated from the Persian word 'medha' (a human offering), coupled with 'mahd' (a cradle),[23] concurrent with the newborn. Conceptually, 'mahd' is consistent with 'mudrur' (to hurt or injure),[24] designations specific of the Mada priesthood. 'Mahd and medha' is comparative in the English language to crib and crypt (Greek kruptos - hidden).

In the Syrian etymology, 'madar' (immolation) pertains to 'mudar'af' the adjective for (a double)[25] - an assimilation of 'mudda'i af'a' (a plaintiff [of the] snake).[26] The 'serpent's double' [mudar'af(a)] is matched in spoken Arabic with 'mudaffi' (warming)[27] and 'mudif' (a host or steward).[28] Appointment of the 'host' (mudif) 'directs' (mudir) the burning of the 'tribute' (medha). Killing of the 'victim' (hostia) marks the firstborn. A sacrificial offering, the child, is conceived in a barn, shed, or stable - cryptograms inferring infanticide in comparison to ritual immolation.

Theologically, the stable parameter discloses the temple enclosure and the storage of cattle (people). In Judaic and Masonic fraternities, the assignment 'goyim' refers to (cattle) translated euphemistically into the English language as (gentile). The Masonic term 'cattle' suggests (a common person) i.e. not angelic. Phonetically, 'cattle' in the Arabic language designates 'qatil' (fatal, deadly or murdered)[29] - a covert offering allocated to the stable, tabernacle, hut or manger, signifiers equated with immolation.

The Semitic etymon 'madar' (to chew) informs the Roman transitive verb 'mandere' (to masticate).[30] 'Mahd' Arabic (a cradle) is converted into Latin as 'mandra' (a stable),[31] English 'manger'. The noun manger is rendered in the French as the verb 'manger' (to eat) and is consistent with the original Arabic root 'mahd' (cradle), opposite 'madar' (chew).[32]

Additionally, the Latin feminine noun 'mandra' (stable) is translated also as (a checkerboard)[33] - a Freemasonic device connected to the tabernacle conceived as a stable. In Islamic convention, the black and white square is central to the depiction of the Kaaba shrine, by definition a stable. A complex idea explored in the next chapter.

According to Christian convention, the stable is often interchangeable with (the inn) rendered in Arabic as 'manzil',[34] and is a play on 'manzar' (aspect or sight)[35] a marker affiliated to the dragon. The equivalent pun in English is 'gaze' (to watch) and 'graze' (to feed) a homonym indicating (an abrasion of the skin), compared religiously to the worship of fallen deities. According to Bacchic and Mithraic mystery rites of ancient Greece and Persia, the snake is born from a 'cow shed' (Taurus) thematically a stable (stab), hut (hurt) or tabernacle.

Bacchus (Dionysus), according to Pliny, is the sovereign of Thebes.
He is shown with wine a symbol of blood prognostic of the death of the firstborn.

Essentially, the stable refers to hidden knowledge pertaining to the host and the birth of demigods, affiliated to blood rites and death.[36] For example, the feminine noun 'mandra' (in English manger) points to 'mandare' Latin (to command, order, commission or entrust)[37] and elaborates the angelic line. Both 'mandra' (stable) and 'mandare' (command) are extrapolated from the Arabic root 'madar' (a circumference, orbit or seat).[38] The philological relationship between the stable and the circumference is symbolic of the zodiac animals displayed as the nativity.

Ontologically, 'the seat, throne or planet' connotes the destruction of paradise, and the recreation of the Western priesthood, consigned to 'Madad' (a Mason).[39] Analysis of Western Freemasonry shows the orbit is comparative to the Degrees of initiation. Each angle records an angel annunciating the name of God. Orbital degrees are cross-referenced with degrees of murder, equivalent to the indices of a burn (a degree).

In Arabic, the title 'Madad' (a Mason) is translated literally as (help)[40] suggesting a charitable organization that is potentially ominous or foreboding. Madad's namesake is encoded in Western Freemasonry. For example, a brother may call upon a 'fellow' (Arabic fellah - a husbandman) and ask for 'help'.

Institutional, the 'Madad' is allied to 'Mu'ahada' (a treaty)[41] contiguous with 'Mada' (a Persian) collectively the builder, angel or Mason. The Persian confraternity represent themselves with the pigment madder, conflated in Egypt with the Red Crown of 'Lower Egypt' (mehu) originating from Adam. A matriarchal priesthood the Mada or Madad is found in Classical Greece as the 'maenads' (worshippers of Bacchus). Archaic the 'maenads' are diminutive of 'manes' (a deified soul)[42] esoteric of the 'Mada' fraternity (See footnote).

'Mad' in English signifies (anger or insanity) consistent philologically with the root of 'Mada' and the worship of 'angels' (Furies) - Latin the 'anguigena' (a Theban).[43] Abridged, the stem of 'mad' is found in the Old English form 'gemad' (to be mad), implying a connection with the 'German or Caucasian' priesthood, allied to Rome via Syria. The 'Gemad and Mada' trace their records back to the 'red man' (Adam) from the Akkadian archetype 'Adamatu'.

In the Indo-Semitic languages, 'Adamatu' pertains to a number of convoluted puns explaining the origins of man in context to hieratic belief. The Akkadian word 'adamatu' (red earth) is an epigraph of 'Adar Martu' (Noble Westerners) assigned etiologically in the Egyptian Arabic with 'matar' (rain).[44]

Correlated linguistically, 'matar' infers the Arabic verb 'mat' (to die), in the Persian 'mart', Greek 'martur' (a witness or martyr), Latin 'mort'. Juxtaposition between 'matar' (rain) and 'mat' (die) is expressed in the Semitic pun 'nahr' (river) and 'nah' (to lament).[45] 'Nah' is diminutive of the Hebrew word 'nora' (terrible),[46] semantically equivalent to the patriarch 'Noah' and the destruction of the earth. Similar ideas are contained in the English words 'rain and wane', 'river and whither'.

In the Indo-European branch of languages, 'matar' (rain) indicates mortal castigation. The floodwaters detail migration, worded in English as flood and fled. Origins of this catastrophe are traced to human dissension, contingent with angelic (reptile) intercourse with the 'mater' (mate). Comparisons in Egyptian eschatology show Nun the Goddess of the 'waters' (heaven) paired semantically in Akkadian with the title 'nin' (lady) and 'nu' (fish).[47] Ancestry of the amphibian's progeny is combined mythologically with the descendents of Adamatu and the destruction of Eden (Atlantis) - Refer to the myth of Poseidon and Tyro outlined in the previous chapter.

'Adar Martu' (Noble Westerners) in the Sanskrit is read as the axiom 'Adi Mitra' (the First Covenant), doubled with 'Ad-Am' (the first nation) recorded as 'Adam'. The 'first nation' documents the agreement between the serpent (Venus) and the mixed lineage of man (Mars).

Sumerian history records this alliance as the 'Martu' (the Western people) - a nation associated with the Occidental races. Appellation of the 'Martu' (Western) is similar in Modern Arabic to 'muta' (a patron) with the affixed meaning (superior or to obey).[48] 'Muta' is compliant in the African idiolect with 'muti' (a human sacrifice) found in the Indo-European stem 'mat' and 'mort' (death).

Affiliation of 'Martu' with Adam and Mars suggests 'Martu' is a variation of the Modern English label 'Martian' from the Latin 'Martianus'. Descendents of the 'Martu' (West), affiliated to the 'Adamatu' (Adam), traveled from 'Mars' (Ma'adim) towards the Earth. The 'Adama(r)tu' are described as the original descendents of 'Adam', correlated in the Old Semitic with 'Qadam' (East), unified with the 'Western nation' - Martu.[49] In both English and Latin, 'Martian' is similar to 'marital and martial' - expressions of the covenant. The French version of 'Martu' describes the noun 'morning' (matin), enunciating the pairing of Venus (the Morning Star) with Mars - symbolic of the East (Adam) and West (Martu).

Philologically the 'Martu' are the same as the 'Mada' - expressive of the 'mater' signified through the 'Western Matriarch'. In the Indo-Iranian languages, the 't' and 'd' are interchangeable. Originally Sumerian 'Martu' is written in the Arabic as 'Mada' (Persian). The 'Martu' is translated into Akkadian as 'Aamu', in Modern Arabic 'umam' (nation), conceived from 'umm' (mother).[50] 'Umam' records 'imam' (a leader), cognate with 'amma' (to precede), specific of the Prophet Mohammed.

Appellation of 'umam' (people) translates into Hebrew as the 'Emori', adopted in Latin as the intransitive 'emori' (to die, die off or die out).[51] Translation of the 'Emori' in alignment to 'death' (mat) is consistent with the 'Martu', affiliated to the 'Occidental people' - See Chapter 11, The Amorites.

The 'Martu' recorded in the Akkadian as the 'Aamu' (Hebrew Emori) developed into the Sunni (Islamic) dynasty of Uma-yyad, assimilated from the Median and 'Rabbi' priesthood (rarb-western). Offshoot of the Uma-yyad trace their inception from 'Adamatu' (the red earth - East), consistent with 'ma'adim' (Mars), indexed in Hebrew with the 'state' (me'dina).[52]

Designation of the 'Sunni' in Arabic plays on the noun 'shune' (barn),[53] religiously 'a lodge, tent or tabernacle', abstractions of the 'Western' denomination the 'Martu', variously the 'Mada' or 'Median'. 'Mada' (Persian) is listed in the Arabic lexicon with 'mandra' (barn) and 'madad' (mason) - symbolic of the Western priesthood the Mada. 'Sunni', like 'Mada', operates as an ancient codeword denoting 'Shinar' - the ancient name of 'Sumer' (Martu). Astrologically, 'Shinar' is aligned to the moon Goddess 'Sinn' Arabic (tooth), esoteric of the star Sirius. The tooth is deductive of the 'dragon' (a watcher) - a domesticator of man.

To summarize, the ancient etymologies appertaining to 'Ma'adim' (Mars) detail the 'Adamatu' the progenitor 'Adam' denomination of the Eastern priesthood (Orion). His bloodline records conflict, versant in Sanskrit with the practice of 'medha' (ritual death). Enactment of this votive parallels 'mitra' (covenant) denominational of the 'Median' priesthood equated with the deity 'Mithra' (Pleiades) and the West. This relationship resembles the spring lamb and priestess, relative to the Kaaba shrine, examined in the next chapter.

1 Michael Cook: The Koran, A Very Short Introduction, Oxford University Press 2000, p18

2 M Fethullah Gulen: Questions This Modern Age Puts To Islam, Truestar, London Ltd 1993, p83

3 Guy Deutscher: The Unfolding of Language, William Heinemann 2005, p306

4 Prolog: Pocket Bilingual Dictionary, English-Hebrew, Hebrew-English, Prolog 2003, p44

5 Laurence Gardner: Genesis of the Grail Kings. Bantam Books 2000, p102

6 The scholarly presumption is the name 'Adam' is loaned in the Sumerian vocabulary. Its usage however could suggest an older and more archaic tradition originating from Sumer.

7 David Rohl Legend: The Genesis of Civilisation, Arrow Books Limited 1999, p192

8 Ferozsons Urdu-English Dictionary: A Comprehensive Dictionary of Current Vocabulary (Revised Edition), Ferozsons Ltd, Lahore, p418

9 Prolog: Pocket Bilingual Dictionary, English-Hebrew, Hebrew-English, Prolog 2003, p317

10 Ibid, p246

11 Ibid, p162

12 The lexicology of Mars in the Persian language is equated with 'mar' (serpent), theoretically a red serpent, specified as 'mari' (an angel), expressed in Arabic as the adjective 'mar' (saintly).

13 Hippocrene English-Arabic, Arabic-English Dictionary, Hippocrene, New York 2005, p75

14 Andrew Collins: From the Ashes of Angels, The Forbidden Legacy of a Fallen Race, Michael Joseph Ltd 1996, p147

15 Emmeline Plunket: Calendars and Constellations of the Ancient World, Senate, London 1997, p244

16 Basic Japanese Dictionary, The Japan Foundation, Bonjinsha, Oxford 1995, pp493-494 'Murdar' Persian (corpse) is compatible in Japanese with 'muda' (waste).

17 Ferozsons Urdu-English Dictionary, A Comprehensive Dictionary of Current Vocabulary, (Revised Edition), Ferozsons Ltd Lahore, pp 693-694

18 Ibid, p687

19 Hippocrene English-Arabic, Arabic-English Dictionary, Hippocrene, New York 2005, p230

20 In Greek mythology, human sacrifice is retold in the story of Andromeda's attempted sacrifice. Andromeda's name is broken down as Andro-meda (man-sacrifice), identified linguistically with the mediation between men and angels. Her rescuer Perseus' name is found extracted from the Semitic stem 'p-r-s' (to cut).

21 Ferozsons Urdu-English Dictionary, A Comprehensive Dictionary of Current Vocabulary, (Revised Edition), Ferozsons Ltd Lahore, p687

22 Hippocrene English-Arabic, Arabic-English Dictionary, Hippocrene, New York 2005, p230

23 Ibid, p231

24 Ibid, p230

25 Ibid, p245

26 Ferozsons Urdu-English Dictionary: A Comprehensive Dictionary of Current Vocabulary, (Revised Edition), Ferozsons Ltd Lahore, p689 ['mudda' (plaintiff, claimant, accuser)]

27 Hippocrene English-Arabic, Arabic-English Dictionary, Hippocrene, New York 2005, p245

28 Ibid

29 Ibid, p262

30 John C Traupman PhD: The New College Latin English Dictionary, Bantam Books 1988, p177

31 Ibid

32 'Immolation' (madar) is mandated by the 'Persian' priesthood (Mada), relative to the 'Mason' (Madad).

33 John C Traupman PhD: The New College Latin English Dictionary, Bantam Books 1988, p177

34 Hippocrene English-Arabic, Arabic-English Dictionary, Hippocrene, New York 2005, p234

35 Ibid

36 Appearance of the goat is aligned to Aries and Mars, accosted with Adam and the snake.

37 John C Traupman PhD: The New College Latin English Dictionary, bantam Books 1988, p177

38 Ferozsons Urdu-English Dictionary, A Comprehensive Dictionary of Current Vocabulary, (Revised Edition), Ferozsons Ltd Lahore, p687

39 Ibid, p688

40 Hippocrene English-Arabic, Arabic-English Dictionary, Hippocrene, New York 2005, p230

41 Ibid, p131

42 The Maen-ads are written with the Latin suffix 'ad', rendered from the Greek suffix 'ada', employed to construct a noun. In archaic Greek, 'ada' is used intellectually to refer the Arabic terms 'ada' (to give) and 'ad' (again), suggesting resurrection of 'hadar' (a presence) obtained through sacrifice. The Maenads are precursor to the Mada priesthood.

43 John C Traupman PhD: The New College Latin & English Dictionary, Bantam Press 1988, p15

44 Hippocrene English-Arabic, Arabic-English Dictionary, Hippocrene, New York 2005, p238

45 Ibid, p253

46 Prolog: Pocket Bilingual Dictionary, English-Hebrew, Hebrew-English, Prolog 2003, p415

47 Compare Latin pronoun 'ea' (she) with the French noun 'eau' (water).

48 Ferozsons Urdu-English Dictionary, A Comprehensive Dictionary of Current Vocabulary, (Revised Edition), Ferozsons Ltd Lahore, p711 ['muta' (patron, superior, obey]

49 The direction 'west' is not literal but is presented rather as a cosmological model of the stars.

50 Hippocrene English-Arabic, Arabic-English Dictionary, Hippocrene, New York 2005, p77

51 John C Traupman PhD: The New College Latin & English Dictionary, Bantam Press 1988, p99

52 Prolog: Pocket Bilingual Dictionary, English-Hebrew, Hebrew-English, Prolog 2003, p392

53 Hippocrene English-Arabic, Arabic-English Dictionary, Hippocrene, New York 2005, p287

21

The Salt of the Earth

'Who has dressed you in strange clothes of sand?
Who have taken you far from your land?
Clothes of sand have covered your face
Given you meaning taken my place
So make your way down to the sea
Something has taken you so far from me'.

Nick Drake, Made to Love Magic: Clothes of Sand (1968)
Produced Witchseason, Warlock Music

'...binding myself under no less penalty than that of having my
throat cut across, my tongue torn out by its roots, and my body
buried in the rough sands of the sea, at low-water mark, where
the tides ebbs and flows twice in twenty-four hours, should I ever
knowingly violate this my Entered Apprentice obligation'.[1]

First Degree Oath of Freemasonry

Accstording to Islamic teaching, the temple veil is cogent with the veil of the kaaba shrine symbolic of loss. The name 'kaaba' is derived from the Arabic word 'ka'b' (a cube)[2] used cryptically to imply sacrificial death. Constructed by Abraham according to divine command, the cube recalls the covenant a motif of 'heaven' adopted by St John in the Book of Revelation. Geometrically the square conceals the Star of David. A doubled triangle, it illustrates the conjoined anatomy of the male and female organs.

Covertly the square implies the host - a hidden bloodline (footprint) rendered esoterically in Arabic as 'ka'b' (heel)[3] paralleled to 'qabila' (tribe).[4] Traditionally, the shrine is ceremoniously 'concealed' (khabba)[5] with a cloth, reductive from the Hebrew etymon 'le'karbel' (to wrap).[6] Karbel hieroglyphically informs the verbal root 'hbs' (to clothe)[7] - identical in Hebrew to the root 'le'halbish'.[8]

Symbolically the cut stone is dressed to mask the woman's sexual organs bound during her cycle. 'Le'karbel' (to wrap or tie) infers the binding of the reproductive organs for the duration of the woman's 'period' (le'kabel). The Hebrew etymon 'le'kabel' (to menstruate)[9] is consistent with the Arabic root 'habl' (pregnancy),[10] vocabulary intimating a mortal angelic lineage symmetrical to the shrine itself.

The academic Ralph Ellis argues the name 'kaaba' originates from the pharaonic word 'qeb' (a snake or circuit) cognate with 'qab' (a coil).[11] Entrants to the Kaaba thus ritualistically encircle or circuit the shrine. The orbit denotes the menses blood offered to the fallen star a simile of the snake and augury. Combination of the circle (serpent) interlocked with the square (kingdom) is a device of the crusader, pilgrim or host - itinerants of the shrine.

Locomotion of the initiate recalls the migrant or nomad, nominal of the falcon Horus, assigned in Jewish and Islamic tradition to the Exodus. The Latin word for pilgrim 'peregrinus' (a stranger)[12] depicts a 'migrant', 'alien' or 'angel'. 'Peregrinus' in the Roman language pertains to the 'peregrine falcon' - the hieroglyphic insignia of the hunting deity Horus (watcher). His namesake pertains to his father the God Osiris, recorded as the proto-King of Egypt.

Affinities with the Kaaba stone and Osiris are found in the Islamic observance of Ramadan and its relationship to the 'hadj' (pilgrim). The Arabic term 'hadj or hajj' originates from the pharaonic word 'hadjet' (the White Crown), attributed to Osiris. 'Hajj' alternatively 'hagg' informs the Greek adjective 'hagios' (holy).

The hadj(et) crown stylizes the disfigured eye specifically the tear-gland symbolic of Horus. Mutilated Horus' eye is rendered in Islamic lore as the blinded Antichrist, evocative of the moon and death. Adorning the phallic headdress of Osiris, the White Crown, silhouettes the glans (head) of the penis, doubled with the crying eye, emblematic of castration. In Egyptian texts, this is described through the circumcision or mutilation of Osiris' phallus (human) and its replacement with a golden member (angelic).

A pastoral God and the Patron of Egypt, Osiris illustrates the good shepherd and recapitulates the sailor, angel, migrant or nomad. His White Crown precipitates the crying eye of Atum Ra, incumbent of the salt covenant. Enactment of this agreement serves as a cryptic reference to the fallen angel, reconciled through the Kaaba shrine.

The stone itself is equated with the injured eye of Horus and records punishment (deluge), immortalized through angelic intercourse - the covenant. Arbitration between humans and angels consolidate the establishment of Royal progeny.

Relative to the king, the 'Kaaba' is considered by Muslims as the 'naval' of the earth the point where communication (sexual intercourse) with heaven and the underworld is permitted. Esoterically the stone signifies the virgin, depicted as the altar (alter), the cornerstone or the bedrock of the early church (of Islam). Submission of the woman demonstrates the salt covenant - a dual symbol accorded to the white priestess, cognate with the desert and sand. A custodian of the oracle, her mediation with heaven is delegated through the shrine.

In Arabic, the feminine noun 'beda' (white)[13] semantically relates to 'badw' (desert), anglicized as 'Bedouin'. The 'Bedouin' (badwiyyin) are the same nomadic tribes that invaded Egypt installing the Hyksos Pharaohs. Religiously the Bedouin introduced the White Crown of Egypt - dichotomous to the Red Crown and the Canaanite people (the Edomites).[14]

The Bedouin are the original guardians of the Kaaba shrine conveyed to Abraham by the angel Gabriel. The monument in the early traditions is described as white in colour, its current shade of black a consequence of sin (adultery) in the pre-Islamic period. The Kaaba stone, an enigma, operates as an allegorical riddle. Its encryption is transmitted from the Arabic into the Greek.

The Old Arabic adjective for 'white' (feminine plural) is 'hur' - a word related to 'houri' (virgin), implicit of a Bedouin. Phonetically, the 'h' and 'k' phoneme in the Arabic and Greek lexicon are closely matched. 'Houri' is rendered in Greek as 'kore' (virgin) - a polymorphic word meaning (pupil - eye), a dual marker shared with the dragon and initiate.[15] In Hebrew, 'kore' denotes (a reader),[16] assigned to the matriarch.[17]

'Kore' (a virgin) is paralleled philologically in the Old Semitic with the priestess the 'Bath Kol' (a daughter of the voice).[18] 'Kol', taken from the Egyptian Arabic stem, additionally doubles as a homonym of 'kol' (to eat[19] - Arabic kal[20]). The English equivalent is ate and orate - signifiers of deity worship registered with sacrificial immolation.[21]

Written in Greek as 'kore' (a virgin), transliterated into Low German as 'gor' (a child), in English (girl). Desecration of the 'houri' is preserved in the English etymon 'whore'. Namesake of the 'houri' is consistent with the Egyptian Sun God 'Horus' (Har or Kar) - a permutation of the Modern Hebrew noun 'or' (light), exhibited as the watching eye, figurative of the dragon and virgin.

Arcane, the sclera (hur) of the houri's eye is represented as the White Crown of Osiris, metaphorically transformed into 'kore' (a pupil), designated as the red crown. Combination of the eye featured as the Double Crown is conceptual to the Kaaba stone, identified with the defilement of the woman, featured as the bride - Refer to Appendix 6.

Symbolism of the 'houri's purity, registered with 'hur' (white), discloses her fall, subsequent to angelic intercourse. Besmirched, her indiscretion is correlated in Greek with 'kore' (a pupil), designated as a black virgin or priestess. In Arabian countries, Muslim women adorn the colour black signifying marriage - original to sexual contamination isolated with the Kaaba stone.

Appearance of the 'Bath Kol' priestess symbolically constitutes the onset of puberty, offset with the dried black menstrual blood of the pubescent (fire-star). 'Bath Kol' implying the verbal root 'to eat' (Egyptian Arabic kol) is switched in Hebrew with the polymorphic title, translated as (the daughter [of the] sand[22] or voice [23]), identifiers of the Bedouin. The homonym 'kol' signifying (sand and voice) conforms in English to the worded pun sand and sound.

Sand features as a signifier of 'salt' - a codeword for an 'angel' evocative of human 'ashes' (Hebrew efer)[24] equivalent to (ef'e) an 'asp'.[25] Again the pun is played out in English as 'ash' and 'asp'. Offering of salt understood as the covenant of the firstborn is subsumed under the votive and the priestess.

Lineage of the 'Bath Kol', deduced from the Bedouin tribe, is covert to the Saudi family - a word traced from the Arabic root 'sauda' (black),[26] extracted from the Syrian etymon 'saut' (sound or voice).[27] 'Saut' is a philological variation on 'soot', paired symbolically with 'salt'. Recondite, 'Saudi' (black) is iconic of 'Kmt' (the black land of Egypt).[28] Comparison of 'Kmt' to the etymon 'Saudi' suggests the transliteration of 'Kmt' is false - a name originally obtained from (the lands of the Saudi tribes). The dark fertile soil of Egypt's crescent parallels the moon and the congealed blood of the priestess' cycle 'le'kabel', relative to the Kaaba shrine.

Nocturnal Dragon - black hairy angel eating human votive (Medieval heraldry).
In Western Masonry, the 'Saudi' family is known as (the black nobility) - a name compatible with
'Kmt' (dark land), designating (Egypt), cryptic of Saudi-Arabia.

Ritualistically, the Kaaba is the focal point of the first devotions of the pilgrims who walk around it 'seven' times touching or kissing it. The Arabic noun 'sab'a' (seven), archaically 'saba' (a star), specifies (the Pleiades). The constellation is recorded in the Old Semitic as 'Chem' - a name shared with 'Khem or Kmt' (Egypt). Numerically, 'saba' describes the 'seven heavens or highways', identified with the host 'tsava' (crew), nominal of the 'tsabaoth'. 'Sab'a' (seven) is rendered in Hebrew as 'sheva' (seven), explicit of 'shiva' (the period of mourning), complicit with the monthly cycle and the red sun.

To summaries the main points: The Kaaba shrine signifies the dried 'menstrual blood' of the sacred houri the Bath Kol. Offerings of the houri's blood contrast with sand and salt, sacred to the 'immolation' (kol) of the firstborn. Spilling of the infant's blood is likened to the virgin's fertile blood - her 'menses' (le'kabel) espoused in Arabic with 'habl' (pregnancy). The designation 'habl' in ancient Semitic is conjugal with 'qeb' (a snake).

Religiously, 'habl' (pregnancy) is assigned to the priestess and her 'cabal', a 'convent' equated with the 'covenant'. Historical insemination of the virgin recounts the rape (reptile) of the 'Black Madonna' - classifications of the 'kore' (a virgin or pupil) otherwise the 'Bath Kol'. Denigration of the 'Bath Kol' is paired with the 'houri' (kore) and her betrothal to the dragon (angel).

Modeled figuratively on the black and white squares, the Kaaba shrine delineates the Kingdom of God - its checkered insignia reproduced in the Mother Lodge of Freemasonry, identified with the stable and tabernacle. The pattern replicates the starry firmament, conjunct with the sanctuary of the Temple (Refer to Chapter 20 Men are from Mars and Snakes are from Venus).

Controlled by the Muslim faction, the black shrine of God is thus double-edged and encodes the concealment of Satan, astrologically Saturn, implicit of the priestess. This deception is acknowledged as the stoning of Satan, ritualistically enacted upon the stone itself. The rock face is a motif of the woman's body, esoteric of angelic intercourse, equated with destruction and redemption. The symbolic execution of the priestess is honoured through the death of Adam (Mars), paired with the lamb (child) and goat (se'irim).

Iconography of the houri's 'menstrual blood' (the fire-star) coincides with the shining (flashing) serpent and his burning venom (seed) - a metaphor of the altar (alter) and rebirth. Represented as 'fire' (Old Semitic adar - Greek Hades), the appellation 'Hades' originally described the angel 'Satan'.

Hades is shown as a philological corruption of the Greek noun 'eidos' (form), extrapolated from 'eidolon' (a phantom), Arabic 'hadar' (presence).[29] In the Latin language, 'Hades' and 'eidos' informs the feminine noun 'aedes' (a temple, shrine, building or house).[30] Celebration of the 'spring-lamb' (Adar) contrasts with angelic 'materialization' (Greek eidolon). It is associated in Arabic with the festival and month of 'Adar' (March).

In Islamic theology, 'Adar' parallels atonement, lateral to 'Ramadan', derived from the Semitic root 'ramada' (to be hot).[31] Ramadan is expressed alternatively as the compound 'ramm-ada' (to grieve)[32] and (give)[33] - contextually propitiations of the newborn. The Arabic word 'ada' (to give) is cognate with the Sanskrit appellation 'adi' (first) i.e. the firstborn.

Extraction of 'ramada' coincides in Arabic with the wordplay 'ra'i mada' (the Persian shepherds), cognomens of the Hyksos - the Aamu. 'Ra'i' (a shepherd) is deduced from the colloquial form of 'ranam' (sheep).[34] A covert signifier 'ranam' is read duplicitously as the compound 'ra-nam' (evil sleep)[35] - evident in the English pun sheep and sleep.[36]

Rather sinisterly, the 'Persian shepherds' (ra'i mada) play on the Semitic expression 'ra-maddah' (evil-praise), archaically the 'proclamations of Ra'. Meditations of the Sun God Atum-Ra are euphemistically enforced through the burning of the votive - the 'ramada' (hot) a 'sacrificial medha' (murder).

It comes as no surprise that Islamic scholars are uncertain of the correct etymological origin of the word 'ramada' analyzed in the above paragraphs. It is to be sure, however, that Ramadan is redolent with occult practices that by definition are secret. They are synonymous with human sacrifice, originating from the Egyptian, Judaic and Babylonian priesthood.

These blood rituals like the Kaaba stone are accorded originally with the veneration of Osiris, whose death and resurrection is reminiscent of the shepherd Christ. According to Egyptian eschatology, Osiris' semi-divine offspring are traded or substituted with the death of the firstborn-lamb (an innocent child) in payment of original sin.

Symbolically the sheep[37] is twinned with the dragon or host, recorded in the book of Revelation, Chapter 12:

> "And he had two horns like a lamb, and ... spake like a dragon".

Sexual union (covenant) between the reptile and mater signals the death of the newborn lamb, observed theologically during the celebration of Adar. Sacrifice of the lamb conduces the materialisation of an angelic form, analogous to a serpent or reptile, associated with intercourse and rebirth. A momentous and defining act bestowed upon the inner mysteries, summarized in Revelation 21, verse 9:

> "Come I will show you the bride, the wife of the lamb".

The bridal groom denotes the firstborn male heir - a bloodline usurped with the dragon's progeny, acknowledged previously in Revelation Chapter 12.

1   Texe Marrs: Codex Magica, Secret Signs, Mysterious Symbols, And Hidden Codes of the Illuminati, River Crest Publishing, Texas 2005, p285
2   Hippocrene Concise Dictionary, English-Arabic, Arabic-English, Hippocrene 2005, p211
3   Ibid
4   Ibid, p131
5   Ibid, p29
6   Pocket Bilingual Dictionary, English-Hebrew Hebrew-English, Completely Transliterated, Prolog p465

7   Bridget McDermott: Decoding Egyptian Hieroglyphs, Duncan Baird Publishers, London 2003, p166 (Sign Index List)

8   Pocket Bilingual Dictionary, English-Hebrew Hebrew-English, Completely Transliterated, Prolog, p70

9   Ibid, p252

10 Hippocrene Concise Dictionary, English-Arabic, Arabic-English, Hippocrene 2005, p94

11 Ralph Ellis: Eden in Egypt, Edfu Books, UK 2004, p280 (Appendix A5 - Dictionary, Listed Circuit)

12 John C Traupman PhD: The New College Latin English Dictionary, Bantam Books 1988, p218

13 Hippocrene Concise Dictionary, English-Arabic, Arabic-English, Hippocrene 2005, p139

14 'Beda' (white) notates the Sanskrit transliteration 'Vedas' (sacred knowledge) - the original root of the Hebrew noun 'vehedar' (majesty) denoting the White Crown of Egypt.

15 'Kore' Greek (a pupil - eye) is reminiscent of the Japanese noun 'kuro' (black).

16 Pocket Bilingual Dictionary, English-Hebrew Hebrew-English, Completely Transliterated, Prolog p330

17 'Reader' in English is interchangeable with 'leader', equivalent in Latin to 'legere' and 'legion'. The leader is phrased from the Semitic etymology 'leida' (birth) and indicates a divine bloodline chosen to rule.

18 Pocket Bilingual Dictionary, English-Hebrew Hebrew-English, Completely Transliterated, Prolog, p451

19 M.A. Abdel-Hady: Egyptian Arabic Dictionary Phrasebook, The Rough Guide, Lexus 2002, London, p87

20 Hippocrene Concise Dictionary, English-Arabic, Arabic-English, Hippocrene 2005, p40

21 'Kal' Arabic (to eat) is paired in the Sanskrit language with 'kal' (a black snake, an angel or death). 'Kali' (the Hindu Goddess of death) is cross-referenced in the Sumerian tongue with 'kar' (a hunter, angel or king). The Sumerian titular 'Kar' (a hunter or king) is matched in the hieroglyphic with the name 'Horus' (Kar or Har) written idiomatically as the falcon (hunter) - a predatory bird.

22 Pocket Bilingual Dictionary, English-Hebrew Hebrew-English, Completely Transliterated, Prolog, p353

23 Ibid, p451 ['kol' (voice) informs the English etymon 'call']

24 Ibid, p29

25 Ibid

26 Hippocrene Concise Dictionary, English-Arabic, Arabic-English, Hippocrene 2005, p18

27 Ibid, p281 'Saut' Syrian (voice or sound) informs the English etymon 'sound'.

28 In 'Western Masonry', analogous to the 'Western Priesthood', the 'Saudi' family is known as the 'Black' (sauda) Nobility - a bloodline traced from the Middle East.

29 Hippocrene Concise Dictionary, English-Arabic, Arabic-English, Hippocrene 2005, p184

30 John C. Traupman PhD: The New College Latin English Dictionary, Bantam Books 1988, p8

31 Ramada (to be hot), the root of Ramadan, is comparative philologically to the Mada priesthood, identified with the 'medha' (sacrifice), cognate with 'mudar' (double). 'Mudar' is matched in spoken Arabic with 'mudaffi' (warming) and 'mudif' (a host or steward). Appointment of the 'host' (the mudif) 'directs' (mudir) the burning of the 'tribute' (the medha).

32 Hippocrene Concise Dictionary, English-Arabic, Arabic-English, Hippocrene 2005, p268 ['Ramm' (to grieve)]

33 Ibid, p317 ['Ada' (to give)]

34 Ibid, p111

35 Hippocrene English-Arabic, Arabic-English Dictionary, Hippocrene, New York 2005, p114

36 In Feudal Japan, the symbol of the nomad (shepherd) is replaced with 'ronin' (lordless) - a wandering samurai or an outlaw.

37 'Sheep', as with 'hair' and 'fish', is one of the few English words that is plural and singular.

22

The Adar Lamb and the Keyholder

'At first you were just a sacrifice in a ritual, and when that was frustrated, you were still the doorway'.

Blood Ties Episode 22
Kaleidoscope Entertainment, Insight Film Studios
Based on the Victoria Nelson Series of Books by Tanya Huff 2008

In the Semitic family of words, 'Adar' describes (March)[1] the lambing season, and is used within contemporary Arabic. Celebration of Adar is equated with the month of sacrifice. 'Adar' is mnemonic of the 'flock' (Hebrew eder)[2] substituted as the sacrifice of Adam - a symbol of Aries (Mars).[3] 'Adar' in the African languages accords with the root 'adah' (goat). Early Mesopotamian calendars record the spring as the beginning of the New Year - symmetrical to the offertory and rebirth.

Festivities allocated to 'Adar' denote the celebration 'Purim' (a Hebrew word interpreted as the drawing of lots). In written Semitic, 'Purim' plays on 'pore' (fruitful) from 'pri' (fruit),[4] a derivation of the Akkadian noun 'peor' (serpent). The Akkadian noun 'peor' describes the Modern Hebrew adjective 'pe'er' (glory)[5] Latin 'pareo' (to appear).[6] Realization of the 'snake' (peor) is through the 'mouth' (pe),[7] contrasted with the votive, symbolized as the 'fruit'.

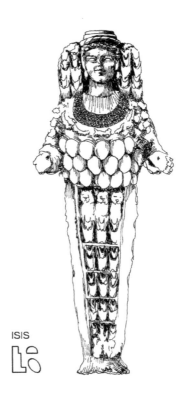

ISIS

Queen Artemis, Ephesus Asia Minor: Daughter of Zeus and Sister to Apollo.
A hunter Artemis is signified with the egg, relative to the Goddess Isis. Carved with the lion and winged goat mythological to the chimera. She carries the zodiac animals on her bosom - her dress represents the fish's tail (glass slipper) - the foot a symbol of Pisces.

214

Celebratory, God is shown as restoring his flock (chosen people) from fire during Purim. In the Hellenistic languages for example, the Hebrew word 'Purim' is contrasted with 'pur' (fire), conceptually 'pri' (the fruit) of the firstborn. Enactment of 'Purim' details the ordination of the lamb (substitute) and the death of the innocent.

'Purim' designates 'pur' Hebrew (a lot),[8] correlated with the fruit of the womb. Cryptically the Semitic-Hellenic wordplays connote 'veil(ed)' magic (lot), symmetrical to the goat, demonstrated in the Greek and Latin. For example, the English word 'sorcery' is from the immediate Greek noun 'sauros' (lizard) and 'sorel' (goat), derivations of the Semitic noun 'se'ir' (a red goat, Greek 'siran').

Formally 'se'ir' (goat) categorizes the 'angelic se'irim' (a goat, demon or seraph) in relation to 'sihr' (sorcery) and 'sirr' (mystery). 'Seraph', 'se'ir' and 'sihr' are registered in Hebrew with the identical pun 'ef'e' (asp),[9] 'ofer' (fawn)[10] and 'ov' (sorcery).[11] The allomorph 'se'ir' (goat) is branched in the Latin with the root 'sors' (a lot) and 'sol' (the sun), denoting Purim.

Within Judaism, the feast of Purim celebrates duplicity, recognizant with deception, collaborative of the lamb and 'scape-goat' (sa'ir-la'azazel). Observed in Israel during the sixth (civil) calendar month of 'Adar', Purim originally commemorated the spring festival. Theologically, the feast enacted the sacrificial death of the substitute - the firstborn stylized as the Passover lamb. Enactment of Passover celebrated the redemption of the innocent, theoretical to the spreading of the lamb's blood, congruous with the angel of death.

In theory, the month of 'Adar' is cogito with the materialization of angelic forms, evident in the Arabic vocabulary 'hadar or ha-dar' (a presence).[12] 'Hadar' describes the intransitive verb 'dar' (to turn)[13] in relation to the Egyptian verb 'darr' (to injure or harm).[14] Both etymologies are symmetrical in Syrian with the equivalent word 'daur' and its transitive form 'dauwar' (to turn).[15]

The etymon 'dar' and 'daur' (turn) originates from the Syrian stem 'dau' (daylight or light), rendered in the Latin as the noun 'dies', in English (day). The movement, literally the 'turning of the day', is equivalent to heaven, visualized as a mansion of God, consonant with death. In Arabic therefore the verb 'dar' (to turn) is employed as a homonym, denoting the Royal 'house'[16] of heaven.

Usage of 'dar' in Egyptian Arabic (house)[17] further points to incongruities in the hieroglyphic spelling of the word Pharaoh. Transliteration of 'Par-o' (English Pharaoh), a word rendered by Egyptologists as (Great-house), is dubious. The obvious spelling of 'Par-o' would be 'Dar-o' found in the Greek version of the name Darius. Egyptologists are aware of the etymon 'dar', as they use the noun to translate the Goddess' name 'Hathor' rendered as (Horus' mansion). The Greek transliteration 'Hathor' is a corruption from the original compound 'Kar-Dar' or 'Har-Dar', used in the Modern Arabic to signify a 'presence' (hadar), denoting the astrological 'mansion of Horus' (Kar-Dar).[18]

"Or when the moon was overhead, Came two lovers lately wed.
'I am half sick of shadows', said the lady of Shalott."
(Alfred Lord Tennyson's poem: The lady of Shalott, oil painting after John William Waterhouse 1993.

The switch of 'Par-o' with 'Dar-o' (Great-house) is evinced additionally with the root of 'Adar', indicated as (the month of March), represented as Aries the ram, symbolic of the Hyksos. Changes to the initial spelling 'Dar-o' align to the month of 'Adar' (a leap year intercalary month) and is consistent with the festival's veneration of multiplicity. Incidentally, the communal name 'Hyksos' is extracted from the Greek philology 'oikos' (a dwelling) from 'oikeo' (to dwell) and is a literal translation of the name 'Pharaoh' Arabic 'dar' (a house).

The Hebrew word 'Par-o' English (Pharaoh) is derived from the Akkadian corruption 'peor' (serpent), preserved in the Persian etymon 'peri'[19] disclosing (the serpent race), relative in Arabic to 'Ta'bani' (Theban) and 'ta'ban' (snake).

'Peri' is rendered in the Latin root 'purus' (unmixed or pure).[20] Depictions of the serpent's progeny are represented with 'farr' (a halo), observed in Egypt as the disk, conjoined by the snake. Variations of 'peor' and 'Par-o' originate from the Sanskrit root 'pala' (a king, prince, guard or protector of the earth).[21] The stem 'pala' is apprised in Latin from the root 'parare' (to defend),[22] consigned to the reptile king or angel.

Pharaoh's seal worn on his headdress, records 'peor' (a snake) an intentional pun signifying the Royal house of 'Thebes', registered with the 'cobra' (tea'ban). Symbolically, the 'cobra' is written also as (najja) explicit of a 'saviour' (Egyptian Arabic nagga),[23] dualled with a 'smiter' (nagga). Bloodline of the 'saviour' (nagga) emphasizes 'Venus' Hebrew (Noga),[24] deduced from the Sanskrit noun 'naga' (a serpent).

Idiomatically the 'metamorphosis' of the angel (Arabic dar) expresses 'sunlight' (dau), assigned to the reptile and death - literally 'darr' (to damage or harm). The setting disk combines the western serpent with the solar fish, aligned to the flash, euphoric of the dragon's transformation. To reiterate the point: The Semitic cognomen 'hadar' denoting (a presence) is read in Hebrew as the compound 'ha-dar' (the-changer), cognate with 'hardun' (a lizard).[25] Its materialization is consistent in Arabic with 'add' (to bite),[26] comparative of 'ada' (to give)[27] prognostic of the rite of Adar.

'Hadar' (presence) links the month of 'Adar' with the 'flock' (eder) - an emblem of the laity. In Latin, the analogy is 'grex' (a flock) also denoting (a group or crowd), prototypical of the 'congregation'.[28] 'Manifestation' of the angel's form (ha-dar) connotes the 'giving' of sacrificial offerings (ada), demonstrated in related syntax.

For example, 'hadd' (sharp)[29] is phonologically diminutive of 'hadar' (presence), inimical of 'eder' (flock). Similar comparisons are evinced from the English nouns 'sharp', 'shape' and 'sheep'. In Arabic, 'hadar' is related to the noun 'kadar' (trouble),[30] bracketed with 'haddad' (to menace or threaten),[31] actions uniformed with 'haddad' (the locksmith).[32] He is iconic of the 'Key Holder', the 'Keeper of the Kingdom', signified as Peter - a 'guardian' or 'protectorate' of the synod. Biblically 'Peter' (rock) holds the keys to heaven and is the precursor or foundation of the early church.

The Egyptian word 'haddad' (locksmith) is converted into Hellenistic symbolism. The Greek concept 'hodos' (way) puns with 'eidos' (form), extracted from the Semitic etymon 'hadar' (presence or shape) and 'hadd' (sharp). These definitions classify the 'assembly' (Greek 'hodos' - to guide Arabic 'hada'), sacerdotal of the flock and altar.

The 'guide' (hodos) is corollary with 'sunodos or sun-hodos' (a meeting), in English (synod). 'Hodos' refers cryptically to the 'Children of the Exodus' (the ex-hodos, literally guide-out)[33] - a denomination instated internally within the priestcraft. Philologically 'hodos' is recurrent with 'kudos' (glory), explicit of a materialized form 'hadar', set free or un-'locked' originally the Angel of Death.

The definition 'haddad' (a keyholder) is a synonym of 'hadar' (a presence), evocative of the celebration of 'Adar'. Appearance of the 'hadar' pertains to the Greek etymon 'eidos' (form) and 'eidolon' (a phantom). The wordplay 'haddad' and 'hadar' is apparent also in the English alliteration 'lock' and 'look', implicit of the watcher or dragon. Materialization of the eidolon is etymologically deduced from the Egyptian Arabic noun 'hardun' (lizard),[34] consistent in Old Semitic with 'ha-dar' (a-changer).[35]

The keyholder is a guardian of secrets, associated with angelic transfiguration, equated with heaven. Catholic tradition lists 'Peter' as the keyholder and is described as the 'rock of the Church'. The pun 'rock and lock' is conveyed in the Arabic play as (sakhr and sakk), evident in the Latin lexicon 'sacer' (sacred). Relationship between the key and the Kingdom is demonstrated also in Muslim lore.

In Islam, the 'keyholder' is the 'Mahdi' - a spiritual and temporal leader, sent by divine command to prepare society for the end of earthly time, instigated through a just government. For Shiites, the title refers to the twelfth Imam.

Mahdi's lineage notates 'mahd' (a cradle), correlated with Jesus and Moses, identified with 'madad' (a Mason). Symbol of the basket or manger distinguishes the king, a serpent or angel. Mahdi's cognomen esoterically suggests 'medha' (a human votive), allied with 'Mada' (the Persian priesthood). Mada, is rendered variously as the Martu, Umam (Aamu), Emori or Hyksos.

Arabic scholars trace the root of 'mahdi' to the past participle of 'hada' (to guide), tangent with 'hadar' (a presence) or 'ha-dar' (a shape-shifter), qualification of the 'keyholder' (haddad). Placement of the 'keyholder' is 'one who threatens' (haddad) from the compound 'hadd-ad' literally (sharp-again), repetitious of sacrificial decree. Appearance of the 'Mahdi or hada' in Judaic lore marks 'Yom Hadin' (the day of Judgement), associated with the angel or 'lizard' (hardun).

In conclusion, the serpent's concealed form represents a 'ram' - a dual signifier of the reptile and man. Demise of the ram is identical in the Egyptian mysteries to the deity 'Amun' (hidden), conjugal with the risen snake Atum. Depictions of the horned deity explicate intimidation and regale sadism, faceted with salvation (heaven). Theological dualism records the angelic host Venus, conjunct with Mars, equated with the death of the spring lamb (man).

Disagreement between the protagonists Venus (angel) and Mars (man) culminated in the flood (Atlantis), described in the book of Genesis. Expulsion of Adam from paradise by the host is consigned to the month of Adar, recognizant with the 'flock' (eder) and sacrifice.

Observance of the festival Adar promulgates the sacred law, sanctioned through the killing of the lamb, covertly a firstborn child, aligned biblically to the Exodus. Payment of the lamb's blood is exchanged in lieu of man's sin cognate with atonement. Hierological Adam's redemption corresponds with the 'surrender' (slm) of man and the destruction of Mars. A day of infamy, it recalls the ceremonial passage of 'Adar' and the death of the 'flock' (eder).

1 Hippocrene English-Arabic, Arabic-English Dictionary, Hippocrene, New York 2005, p72

2 Prolog: Pocket Bilingual Dictionary, English-Hebrew, Hebrew-English, Prolog 2003, p155

3 Esoteric the lamb nominates the child votive identified in the Old Semitic lexicon with 'Adamatu' (man) relative to Mars classified with the Aryan race. Adamatu via the covenant offers himself to Venus (Greek Phosphorus). Duplicitous the homonym 'Phos-phorus' (light bringer) archically (Venus) translates additionally as phos-phorus (man offering) cogent with phos-ophis (a flaming seraph).

4 Pocket Bilingual Dictionary, English-Hebrew Hebrew-English, Completely Transliterated, Prolog p163

5 Ibid, p170

6 John C Traupman PhD: The New College Latin English Dictionary, Bantam Books 1988, p212

7 Prolog: Pocket Bilingual Dictionary, English-Hebrew, Hebrew-English, Prolog 2003, p264

8 Ibid, p238

9 Ibid, p29

10 Ibid, p147

11 Ibid, p383

12 Hippocrene English-Arabic, Arabic-English Dictionary, Hippocrene, New York 2005, p184

13 Ibid, p167

14 Ibid

15 Ibid, p168

16 Ibid, p167

17 Ibid

18 Inexplicably Egyptologists have transliterated Hathor's name (Horus' house) as 'Ha(r)-Thor' a corruption on the original spelling that should read in the Arabic language as 'Har-dar' or 'Kar-dar'.

19 Peri is comparative to the English word 'fairy' from the Akkadian root 'peor' (a snake) identical in Chinese to 'pa' (a snake or demon).

20 John C Traupman PhD: The New College Latin English Dictionary, Bantam Books, 1988, p458 ['Peri' is directly related to the English etymon 'fairy' - the 'p' and 'f' switching positions. 'Phane' (a materialized form), Greek 'phainein' (to show), is analogous to the Pharaonic word 'fennu' (a serpent)].

21 Gary A David: Eye of the Phoenix, Mysterious Visions & Secrets of the American Southwest, Adventures Unlimited Press, USA 2008, p151 (quotation from the linguist Gene D Matlock)

22 The Akkadian and Sanskrit designation 'peor' (serpent) and 'pala' (king) is comparable to the Persian noun 'mar' (snake) and 'mal' (leader) - this is rendered in Greek as 'basileus' (king) from 'basiliskos' (serpent). Basiliskos is a derivation of the Greek title 'baskanos' (a socerer). In addition, the Greeks referred to the Royal line as the hemitheoi or 'hemitheos' (a demi-God) literally 'half-devine' a title denoting the 'human-angelic' lineage. 'Hemitheos' similar to form is a play on 'helminthos' (worm). In the Greek mysteries, the 'hemitheos' is referred to by the title 'dioskouros' (the Son of God) coded speak for 'diosauros' (a Reptile God).

23 Hippocrene English-Arabic, Arabic-English Dictionary, Hippocrene, New York 2005, p253

24 Prolog: Pocket Bilingual Dictionary, English-Hebrew, Hebrew-English, Prolog 2003, p446

25 Hippocrene English-Arabic, Arabic-English Dictionary, Hippocrene, New York 2005, p70

26 Ibid, p317

27 Ibid

28 John C Traupman PhD: The New College Latin English Dictionary, Bantam Books 1988, p128

29 Hippocrene English-Arabic, Arabic-English Dictionary, Hippocrene, New York 2005, p184

30 Ibid, p212

31 Ibid, p184

32 Ibid

33 Exodus is from the Greek etymon 'ex-hodos' (to guide out).

34 Hippocrene English-Arabic, Arabic-English Dictionary, Hippocrene, New York 2005, p189

35 Ibid, p167 ['Dar' intransitive verb (to turn), combined with the Hebrew definitive article 'ha' (the), i.e. 'ha-dar' (the-changer), is consistent etymologically in Arabic with 'hadar' (presence), connoting a materialised presence, literally (an appearance).

23

Sailors Goats and Salt

'Natura non facit saltum' (Nature does not go in jumps).[1]
Charles Darwin

I n the Jewish calendar during the period of Adar, the Purim scroll is read. It contains the book of Esther, and is usually carved ornately with a 'solar fish' - a symbol of the angel or dragon[2] connected to the Dog Star Sirius. Celebration of Purim remembers Esther - a parable of redemption set in the period of the 5th century BC. Her account details the Persian official Haman and his elaborate plan to kill the Jews. According to Esther's story, this culminates with Haman drawing 'lots' (pur) to decide when. The Old Testament, recalls how Esther, traditionally the King's wife (Xerxes I), helped to save her people.[3]

There are additional puns encrypted within the story with regards to Esther and her consort. In Arabic, 'Haman's name is punned with 'Hama'an' (to protect, defend or plead a cause).[4] It is contrasted in Hebrew with 'ha-mon' (the-host), obtained from the Arabic root 'mana' (to prevent) and 'mani' (obstacle),[5] inferring the Shatani, the fallen angels.[6]

Esther is presented as preventing the invasion of the host. The language 'host' (an army) is adopted to convey a mythical quality, compared to the fallen angels. Typical to form, we are dealing with a series of complex symbols - her narration (forgive the pun) is very fishy.

Motif of the woman and fish (mermaid) is found not only in the Semitic traditions.
The above painting (detail) is based on a modern statue produced in Japan.
The image depicts a woman and carp - a motif commonly represented in Edo prints.

The Hebrew noun 'dag' (fish)[7] tabulates 'do'eg' (anxiety),[8] relative to the host in Babylonian tradition the 'Dagon'. Depicted as a fish deity, the Dagon is the purveyor of knowledge and the transmitter of human culture.

The Babylonian Fish God Dagon (in Greek a drakon) is the harbinger of war and pestilence - descriptions consistent with the Latin etymologies. For example, the term 'plague' is closely dependent on 'plaga' (blow or wound), and 'plagiarius' (a plunderer or kidnapper) depicted symbolically as 'plagusia' (a fish).[9] These allomorphs are synonyms of the 'reptile' (repere), rendered as a 'rapist or pillager' (rapere) - themes exorcized during the rites of Purim.

Ritualistically Esther's story is the retelling of the Passover or Spring lamb (Mars), nomenclature of the patron Goddess Venus. This Goddess is manifested as the matriarch Esther - a name borrowed from the Persian root 'Ishtar' (Venus). Esther linguistically equates with the etymon 'hastara' (concealment),[10] conceptual to Venus and the God 'Amun' (hidden).

Ceremonial, the death of the newborn lamb is aligned to Esther or Easter, manifestations of the Eastern Star Venus. Contextually Esther shares the same name with the Babylonian Goddess of Love Ishtar, represented as a 'saviour'. Her epithet 'saviour', however, is shown to be philologically circumspect.

The idiom 'saviour' is double-barrelled in the classical languages. The Greek word 'soter' (a saviour) is derived from the Hebrew etymon 'sote' (deviant), diminutive of 'seter' (secrecy).[11] Phonetic variations of 'seter' include 'sod' (a secret), correlated Biblically with the destruction of the city of Sodom and Gomorrah. Generically 'seter' annotates the priesthood of Saturn, paired with the Evening Star. 'Sidus' Latin (a star)[12] is grouped with 'sidere' (fallen), literally to (sit),[13] lexicological to 'Satan and sadism'.

Role reversal of the 'soter' Greek (a saviour) is depicted in Christian and Islamic tradition as the Antichrist or 'goat'. In the Gospel account, Jesus' ministry begins in his 29th year - the same period as Saturn's orbit around the sun. Theoretically, the 'soter', disguised in Greek as 'esoterikos' (esoterical), are extrapolated in Latin as a 'Sodalis' (a member of a secret society or priestly college).[14]

In English, 'sote(r)' is cryptic of the word 'salt' - a corruption of the Latin masculine noun 'sal' (salt or seawater). 'Sal' is paired in the Roman language with 'saltus' (to leap or jump), symbolically the dancing or 'singing goat' (Greek tragoidia) an angel. Colloquially 'saltus' refers to (the woman's sexual organs)[15] from the Arabic noun 'sitt' (a lady)[16] - symmetrical to the fallen 'star' (sidus). 'Saltus' is rendered in English as 'slut' (previously of unknown origin).

The skipping goat is a symbol of coitus. It illustrates the season of spring (leap), equated in Rome with the 'Sali' the dancing priesthood. A secret fraternity the 'Sali' is aligned with the 'Sodalis' brotherhood, descended from Moses [Hebrew 'Sodi' (occult)]. Imperial decree designates the 'Sali' as (the college of twelve priests or disciples) dedicated to Mars, renowned for their observance of a solemn procession through Rome. This custom is enacted on the calends of March.[17] Derisory, a 'Sali' in English slang is spelt as 'Sally' and denotes a Eunuch, religiously identified with the pilgrim or migrant, addendum to 'salt' (an angel).

Drawing shows Luca Signorelli's fresco, Orvieto Cathedral, Florence.
The Book of Revelation describes Jesus as the 'Morning Star' [Latin 'Lux-ferre' (English Lucifer)].
Christ in Signorelli's depiction assumes the dual role as the 'saviour' and the 'smiter'
iconography associated with the serpent and reaper.

The Sali trace their origin back to the deity Numa, who traditionally instituted the college of Mars. According to Roman legend, a shield fell from heaven and the nymph 'Egeria'[18] predicted that if preserved the possessor of the article would be the dominant people of the earth. To prevent it from being stolen, Numa had eleven replicas made and appointed twelve guardians the 'saliens'[19] a priesthood adopted from the Greek noun 'selene' (moon) - equivalent in the Semitic languages to 'komer' (priest) and 'qamar' (moon).

The protagonist 'Numa' plays on the Latin name 'numen' (deity).[20] Conceptually, 'numen' is literate with the Greek word 'numphe' (a nymph), traced from the Egyptian Arabic root 'naum' (sleep). A maiden, literally a 'bride' (Nymphe),[21] registers a nocturnal angel, conjoined astrologically with the moon, synchronized with the planet Saturn and chaos. Emblem of the dark star is symbolized as the burning shield, doubled with the goatskin and salt.

Numa's celestial object (the shield) conveys the Sali priesthood in tandem with the covenant. Historically salt signifies an angel or goat, and contrasts Adam's expulsion from Mars - diagnostic of conflict. In Biblical tradition, Mars discloses the Exodus and, earlier still, the transformation of Lot's wife into a pillar of salt, recorded in Genesis Chapter 19, verse 26. A defining act, her metamorphosis elicits the destruction of Sodom and Gomorrah.

Abstruse, the Hebrew noun 'amud' (pillar)[22] corresponds with the Arabic word 'hamd' (to praise)[23] - a derivation of the Semitic stem 'maddah'. 'Amud' serves as a cryptic footnote to the King of Gomorrah 'Admah' (red earth), equated with 'Adam'. Linguistically the pillar is illustrative of the Mada priesthood - a marker of ritual 'sacrifice' (medha), adjacent to the 'virgin' and salt. Transfiguration of Lot's wife is iconic of an angel, contextual to a reaper, conceived as the 'se'irim'. A fallen 'demon' (the se'irim - a demigod) is doubled with salt, indicative of the 'copulator' a goat, indexed in the Greek mysteries.

The leaping goat deity is represented as a rapist of women - illustrative of the reptile. The angel is typically paired with the snake and goat. The goat's hair is a signifier of the mammal priestess associated with angelic copulation.

'Halos' the Greek noun for (salt) is polymorphic and signifies 'halos' (the disk) of the sun or moon. 'Halos' is related to 'hals' (sea), homogenous to 'hallomai' (to leap), evocative of the goatfish or deity. 'Halma' (leap) encodes the Hebrew etymon 'almah' (virgin) and 'aima' (mother) - terms cognate with the temple prostitute or dancer. The analogous play in Anglo-Latin is 'sal' (salt), 'sol' (sun), 'sea' and 'salire' (leap), implicit of 'saltus' (the woman's genitalia). Ritually salt is a signifier of the disk and angel, registered with the goat and serpent, paired sexually with the sacred whore (houri).

The 'almah' (virgin) enacts the Passion play taking the role of the goat - a motif interchangeable with the ram and Mars. Sacrificial death of the ascended ram is substituted with the fallen goat, attributed to loss and renewal. Climax of the meta-narrative culminates with the ordinance of Mars, subdued by Venus, theological to the angelic host and king.

Relationship between the angelic multitude and the soldier details historically the implementation of the divine willpower, accrued to the Emperor adopted in Rome. A 'soldier's rations' (salarium) refers to his 'salt money' (salary), a symbol of the covenant. 'Salarium' is ceremonious of absolution, thematic of the sovereign.

Etymologically 'salire' (to jump, leap, bound, hop) is codependent with 'salary'. The transaction of 'salt money' (salarium), originally to a legionnaire, delineates a sacrificial payment to the host, worshipped as Mars. Theoretically a soldier's life is compensated financially as a sacrifice to the God of War. Indemnity in the Roman legion is purchased or redeemed through Aries the ram (Mars), dualled with the goat - an emblem of Venus. Appearance of the horned God astrologically is provident within the Semitic ciphers of a 'sailor' - concurrent with the host, an angel.

Botticelli -The Birth of Venus: The 'shell' (Hebrew klipa) is symbolic of a 'demon' (klippoth), illustrative of the reptile. Insignia of the shell originates from Egypt, in which the Goddess' name Isis is written with the egg shell, featured in Greek carving as the Goddess Artemis. Contrary to scholarly opinion, Artemis is not represented as multi-breasted but is actually shown with eggs - symbolic of the reptile's progeny (See Artemis illustration - Chapter 22, The Adar Lamb and the Keyholder, p214).

In the Arabic language, the noun 'bah'har' (sailor)[24] is comparative to 'bahar' (spice),[25] inclusive of the votive Latin 'sal' (salt) and 'salarium' (salary). Philologically, 'bahar' implies (salt), extracted from 'bahr' the Arabic root of (sea).[26] 'Bahr' is a digression of the Syrian etymon 'bai' (sale),[27] connoting the 'merchant' or 'angel', akin to redemption of 'bar' (a son). Semantically 'Bahr', 'Baal','bai' and 'bah'har' are paronyms equivalent in English to 'sea', 'sir', 'sale' and 'sail - expressions of a sailor, angel or lord'.

The 'merchant sailor' is a symbol of piety and submission (See Islamic traditions of Mohammed). In the Old Semitic languages, 'bah'har' (a merchant, otherwise a sailor) cryptically delegates offerings to the 'Lord's altar' (Baal harel). Veneration of the 'altar-stone' (harel) is likened to a ship, drawn from an early inflection of the title 'Lord-ship', specifying 'bah'har' (a mariner or an angel). Designations of the name 'Bah'har' are evinced also in the German family of languages. For example, in Scandinavian 'Baal harel' (the Lord's altar) is identical to 'Valhalla', translated as The 'Hall of the Slain' (Valr holl). Its usage is comparative in English to 'valour and value'.

Salt consolidates the covenant depicted as enduring and permanent. The element denotes the 'sailor', 'host' or 'crewmember' identified with the (tsabaoth). Additionally the Hebrew noun 'melakh' (salt) is a homonym of (sailor). Furthermore, 'melakh' (sailor) is a pun on the Hebrew word 'mal'akh' (angel), nominal of 'melekh' (king). The comparative wordplay in Arabic is cognate with 'bahar' (spice), 'bah'har' (sailor) and 'Baal' (Lord), adjacent to king-ship and wor-ship. The monarch specifies a sailor or crewmember of the upper ocean (heaven), twinned with the desert nomad (the earth).

Employed ritualistically, sodium chloride is sprinkled during the burning of the firstborn, conversant in Egyptian theogony with the tears of Atum Ra (flood). The ashes of the innocent are ground into a fine white powder, redolent of salt. The Hebrew word 'eli' (pestle) denotes 'El' (God) and is related to the Arabic adjective 'ali' (high) from 'Allah' (light). In the English language, the pestle is combined with the affixture mortar (i.e. mort-death), deduced from the archaic practice of grinding the votive into a fine white powder equated with salt.

Destruction of humanity memorializes the 'Fall of Eve', consummated through angelic intercourse. Re-enactment of the diluvial myth connotes the onset of menstruation and the death of the infant, established through the foundation of the 'salt covenant'. Archaically, this drama ordains the killing of the Pharaoh (a ram) in replacement of sin. His bloodline substituted ritualistically with an 'innocent child' (the firstborn lamb).

Appropriation of the innocent is elaborated in Judaic theology as the festival of Purim. It details the Spring or Passover lamb, covertly the death of the newborn, correlated with the winter sun. Purim narrates the sacrificial killing of the righteous lamb, realized in the liturgical calendar as the festival of Easter, celebrated as the death and resurrection of Christ.

In the Koran tradition, the replacement of the firstborn demarcates Jesus as the Passover lamb. According to Islamic theology, the Messiah is not killed rather switched with another, who assumes his likeness and is crucified. Christ's 'appearance' is rendered in Arabic as (nazar),[28] illustrative of the 'Nazir' priesthood.

According to Christian mystics, the imposter is modeled theologically on the scapegoat a king, combined with the 'fish' (nazrani). The goat, counterfeited with the lamb's death, symbolizes the ram caught in the thicket; its sacrifice petitioned with the crucifixion of Christ upon a tree. All of these symbols are covert talk for the immolation of a child within a tabernacle, symbolised as the Communion.

The model of Isaac's offering, subliminally the ram and the bush in Christian mythology, draws upon the lamb hung upon the cross literally a tree - its death linked symbolically to the inner sanctum of the temple (tabernacle). Spreading of the lamb's blood upon the tree in Judaic lore parallels the lintel or doorframe, equated with the Exodus.

Dipping the lamb's blood details the Passover festival and the redemption of the firstborn with Israel's freedom, purchased theologically through the sacrifice of the Egyptian newborn. In Christian mysticism, appearance of the angel of death marks the tearing of the veil and the expiration (transfiguration) of Christ (King), expressed idiomatically in English as 'curtains'.

Ritualistic killing of the pure or guiltless in Judaic theology is sanctioned during the spring equinox, paired with the winter solstice, and resembles the killing of Isaac, Abraham's 'firstborn'. Early Islamic tradition asserts the patriarch actually killed his son to be restored later by an angel. Establishment of this agreement constitute propitiations, fundamental in the Roman mysteries to the veneration of Jupiter the father - synopsis of the next chapter.

1   Michael Tellinger: Slave Species of God, Music Masters, South Africa 2005, p540
2   The logo of the fish is affiliated to the 'Nazir' (Greek Nazorean) priesthood - a steward of the mixed Angelic bloodline. 'Nazir' is constant with the Semitic stem 'n-z-r' (to protect), intrinsic to the matriarch Esther (Venus).
3   Myrtle Langley: Religion, Eye Witness Guides, Dorling Kindersley, London 2006, p46

4   Hippocrene English-Arabic, Arabic-English Dictionary, Hippocrene, New York 2005, p188

5   Ibid, p234

6   Note the English etymology of maniac is derived from the heretic Mani - quite literally 'Mani-akh' (a brother [of] opposition), connoting a 'brother of the Shatani' i.e. the fallen host. Mani's namesake is equivalent in Greek to 'philo-ophis' (a brother of the serpent), described in Latin as the 'frater' (brother) from the Arabic stem 'frt' (to deceive), conceptually the 'ifrit' (a djinn). 'Mani' can also be likened to the poet 'Rumi - Arabic (Roman), Hebrew 'Ramay' (deceitful).

7   Pocket Bilingual Dictionary, English-Hebrew Hebrew-English, Completely Transliterated, Prolog, p152

8   Ibid, p24 ['do'eg' technically refers to the adjective (anxious)].

9   John C Traupman PhD: The New College Latin English Dictionary, Bantam Books 1988, p230

10 Pocket Bilingual Dictionary, English-Hebrew Hebrew-English, Completely Transliterated, Prolog, p78

11 Ibid, p360

12 John C Traupman PhD: The New College Latin & English Dictionary, Bantam Press 1988, p287

13 Ibid

14 Ibid, p290

15 Ibid, p276

16 Hippocrene English-Arabic, Arabic-English Dictionary, Hippocrene, New York 2005, p289

17 John C Traupman PhD: The New College Latin English Dictionary, Bantam Books 1988, p276

18 'Egeria' the nymph's name is from the Latin root 'egero' (to carry out or discharge), otherwise 'aggero' (to bring, utter or convey), consistent in the Greek vocabulary with 'angelos' (a messenger or angel).

19 Brewer Dictionary of Phrase & Fable, London, Cassell & Company, London 1954, p99

20 John C Traupman PhD: The New College Latin English Dictionary, Bantam Books 1988, p197

21 Editors Simon Price & Emily Kearns, The Oxford Dictionary of Classical Myth & Religion, Oxford University Press, UK 2003, p379

22 Pocket Bilingual Dictionary, English-Hebrew Hebrew-English, Completely Transliterated, Prolog, p301

23 Hippocrene English-Arabic, Arabic-English Dictionary, Hippocrene, New York 2005, p94

24 Ibid, p153

25 Ibid, p154

26 Ibid

27 Ibid

28 Ibid, p71

24

The Crown of Jupiter

'Welcome to my house! Enter freely and of your own will!'
He made no motion of stepping to meet me, but stood like a
statue, as though his gesture of welcome had fixed him into stone.
The instant, however, that I had stepped over the threshold,
he moved impulsively forward, and holding out his hand
grasped mine with a strength which made me wince... Again he
said: 'Welcome to my house. Come freely. Go safely. And leave
something of the happiness you bring!... I bid you welcome,
Mr Harker, to my house. Come in; the night air is chill, and you
must need to eat and rest'.[1]

Dracula Bram Stoker (1897)

'But my very feelings changed to repulsion and terror when
I saw the whole man slowly emerge from the window and begin
to crawl down the castle wall over that dreadful abyss, face down
with his cloak spreading out around him like great wings... just
as a lizard moves along a wall. What manner of man is this, or
what manner of creature is it in the semblance of a man?'[2]

Dracula Bram Stoker (1897)

The astrological term 'planetes' signifies (a planet) and is from the Greek expression 'planaomai' (to wander), suggesting the orbit of a planet (three thousand years before Copernicus and Galileo!) The Mediterranean astronomers obtained their knowledge from the Arabic etymon 'sayyar' (a wonderer or traveler),[3] derived from 'sayyarah' (a planet).[4]

By comparison, the Hebrew definition of a 'planet' (kokhav)[5] is translated from the compound 'Kokh-Av' (Father [of the] Law). Jewish mystical writers parallel 'kokhav' to 'kokhba' (a star). Linguistic relationship between the planet and its motions bound to the sun suggest a profound knowledge of the solar system and its mechanistic laws.

Religious symbolism of the planets indicate a model, prescriptive of Royal hierarchy.[6] In Judaic symbolism, 'kokhba' (a star) serves as a monogram on the Aramaic title 'Kokh Bar' (Son [of the] Law). His cognomen signifies the Messiah, displayed in Arabic as 'bar' (son or hawk),[7] congruent with 'Baal' (a Lord). The migratory bird deputizes the star - a simile of the fallen angel conceived as an immigrant or alien. According to Kabalistic sources, the stars are associated with the habitation of the Gods.[8]

Examinations of early etymologies suggest 'Kokh-Av' (Father [of the] Law) indicates the celestial body, referred to by Roman astrologers as 'Jupiter'. In the Roman pantheon, Jupiter embodies legality, constitutional to the King of Heaven. His role as the 'Father of Law', personified as the monarch, originates from the Middle Eastern vocabulary.

Jupiter's capacity as a legislator is demonstrated in the Prolog English-Hebrew Dictionary. In its glossary, it lists 'tsedek' (justice)[9] as a polyform noun used simultaneously to designate the planet (Jupiter).[10] 'Tsedek' syntax is subtracted from the Aramaic term 'zakkau' (giving of alms), consistent with 'tsodek' (correct). 'Zakkau' and 'tsodek' is transferred into English as (rite) and (right). The 'Zakkau' denotes 'ritual purification', requisite of the 'dakkau' (cleansing),[11] specific of the celestial being 'Jupiter'.

Philologically 'tsedek or zedek' is rendered into the Greek as 'dike' (justice), assimilated from the Semitic word 'dakkau' (cleansing). 'Dakkau' linguistically is conceptual to human sacrifice, highlighted in the Hebrew etymon 'le'tsadek' (to vindicate).[12] Proposition of the human votive appears in the Semitic lexicon. In Arabic, 'dakar' denotes (a male),[13] related to 'dakhl' (an income),[14] theologically the 'payment' or 'redemption' of the firstborn. 'Dakar' (a boy) insinuates 'dakhal' (entrance),[15] signposted as the temple façade. Dakhal's root is condensed from the Egyptian expression 'dakh'khal' (to bring in).[16]

Release of the child's spirit is comparative to 'dukhan' (smoke),[17] implicit of the 'drakon's ability to dematerialize, recounted in the novel of Dracula. Bram Stoker uses the play 'dakh'khal' (entrance) and 'dakar' (male) with 'Dracula' [a derivation of 'drake' (a dragon)]. Embedded in occult symbolism, the Count invites Harker (i.e. 'Har' / 'Kar' = Horus) to enter his domain without hindrance.

Dracula's quotation (See Chapter header) is reminiscent of the Masonic ritual, identified with the 'Tyler or Tiler' (the outer guard of a Masonic Lodge). 'Tyler', according to Freemasonic authorities, proceeds from the French 'tailleur' (one who cuts - in English a tailor), supposition of the Craft.

On closer inspection, 'Tyler' is derived from the Old Semitic noun 'tara(a)' (a door or gate) and informs the Modern Hebrew appellation 'talaa' (a doorkeeper).[18] The Masonic word 'Tyler' is used as a verb (to close) the door as well as a noun for (the doorman) himself. Rendition of 'Tyler' is consistent in Arabic with 'taila or talla' (to bring out).[19] Ritualistically 'taraa' (door) is a symbol of the votive and distinguishes 'tale' (lamb)[20] recognizant with 'le'taher' (to cleanse).[21]

Spilling of the (lamb's) blood 'tale' in Arabic covertly designates 'tair' (a bird),[22] emblematic of the winged angel or reaper,[23] embodied ritualistically as the 'teraphim' (idol). Appearance of the winged angel the 'teraphim' is a subtext in Latin of 'terrere' (to frighten)[24] and 'terra' (earth),[25] lateral to 'taraa' (a door).[26] The portal is cryptic in Masonry of a coffin lid or doorway to the Underworld and parallels sacred knowledge, appertaining to heaven, privy to the Tyler.[27]

Connection between the doorframe and expiation of the lamb is incumbent with the ritual of the Passover, recorded in the book of Exodus Chapter 12. Sacramental blood of the innocent lamb (child) is spread upon the lintel of the doorframe - a metaphor of death and initiation (rebirth), ascribed to Isaac (and the Zadok priesthood).

'Talaa' (a doorkeeper) is codified speak for 'Zadok' (a priest) - Greek 'Sadducee' (a doorkeeper of the Temple).[28] His title suggests 'zakkau' (alms), abridged from 'zaq' the Arabic verb (to taste).[29] 'Zaq' further plays on the Semitic verb 'zaqq' ('to push' the door),[30] explicit of the Tyler, affiliated to 'zokhel' (a reptile).[31] Symbol of the entrance confirms initiation [Hebrew 'le'zom' (to initiate)[32]], comparative to the tabernacle, sanctuary or temple.

The verbal root 'zaqq' symbolic of the doorkeeper is related to the Egyptian Arabic noun 'sakk' (a lock),[33] employed from the Syrian verb 'sakkar' (to lock).[34] Further, 'sakkar' pertains to 'sakhr' (a rock),[35] ritualistic of the altar and body. The pun 'sakkar' and 'sakhr' is transferred into the English wordplay as 'lock' and 'rock'. Equated with the Passover rite,[36] the unlocking of the door designates shape-shifting or angelic materialization, engendered upon the sacrifice of Adam[37] (Refer to footnote[28]).

Reference to the Masonic doorkeeper is found encoded in scriptural passages of the New Testament. In the book of Revelation 3:20 for example, Christ is depicted as the entered apprentice. The quotation reads:

> 'Here I am! I stand at the door and knock. If anyone hears my voice and opens the door, I will come in and eat with him, and he with me'.

The citation from Revelations is adapted from Matthew 7:8 and Luke 11:10. Christ is presented as knocking on the door - a covert metaphor of sacrificial death, demonstrated in the Arabic phrase 'daq il-bab' (literally to knock at the door).[38] The action of 'knocking' (daq) is idiomatic of the assault upon a 'male child' (dakar), situational to the Passover and the 'votive or rite' (dakkau).[39]

Cryptically the Arabic noun 'bab' (door)[40] refers to 'Baba' (the Pope[41] - with the additional meaning father). 'Baba' in particular records the informal noun, used by a child, to signify (daddy). The stem is transferred into the Greek as 'Pappas', shared in the Ecclesiastical Latin as 'papa' (infantile for father). 'Papa' in the early Latin is cognate with the noun 'Popa' (a Pagan Roman priest),[42] contingent with 'Papal and Pope'.

The 'Popa' priests practiced child sacrifice, explicit of the Father Jupiter. In the English vocabulary, Popa appraises 'proper' and 'propitiations' otherwise 'right' and 'rite'. Motif of the Popa clergy is presented with the axe - an instrument of sacrifice. The axe-head is replicated as the 'fasces' insignia, denominational of the 'Fascist' Brotherhood of Jupiter.

To summarise, death of the innocent refers to the 'giving of alms' (zakkau), observed through 'ritual purification' (dakkau) of the 'male' (daker). 'Zakkau' is consistent with the veneration of 'Tsedek' (Jupiter) - another name for (justice).

Symbolism of the Popa is extent also in the Bavarian Illuminati. 'Dakkau' (cleansing) is replete in the German language with purification of racial types, evocative of the Polish Concentration Camp, 'Dachau'. The punning reference to 'dakkau' (purification) suggests a link with 'zakkau' (alms), identified with 'Tsedek' (Jupiter). Comparative wordplays in Semitic are appended with the name 'Auschwitz', rendered in Hebrew 'hashrits' (spawn).[43] 'Hashrits' implies the progeny of the dragon or angel, connected to the creation of the state of Israel in 1948.

There are further admissions, extracted from German names, obtained from Semitic equivalents. The company 'Tofts and Sons of Erfurt' supplied the furnaces at Auschwitz.[44] 'Erfurt' plays on the Arabic epithet 'Ifrit' (afreet) - a bloodsucking demon classified as a type of malevolent (jinn). The Germanic noun 'toft' is a variation of the Old Norse etymon 'topt' (a homestead) - a surreptitious pun on the Semitic word 'topet' (a place of immolation). Demarcation of the 'topet' specifies the 'holocaust', Greek 'holokauston' (a burnt offering), marked with the skull and bones.

The skull is a symbol of covert sacrifice affiliated to the Bavarian, Roman and Judaic illuminati. The photo shows a sacrificial skull: Einsiedeln Cathedral Switzerland.

Adoption of the 'death head' (German totenkopf) is married to the traditions of Christ's crucifixion at 'Golgotha'. The Greek noun 'golgotha', Hebrew 'gulgolet(h)', originates from the Aramaic 'gulgulta' (a skull). Anatomically the Arabic noun for a 'temple' or 'forehead' (masdar)[45] is deduced from the Old Semitic phrase 'mass-dar' (to harm a child). The assignment 'masdar' is conferred upon the sacrificial death of the firstborn, dedicated to the council of Jupiter.

'Masdar' (crown) adduces the Modern Hebrew lexicon 'Mos(s)ad' (institution)[46] connecting the organ of thought with initiatory knowledge. Mossad's organization designates Israeli Intelligence, affiliated in the Old Latin to 'Diovis' (Jupiter) - Hebrew 'Jehovah'. Its network is defined in Arabic as 'musa'ada' (to aid or help),[47] aligned to 'mu'ahada' (a treaty)[48] and 'madad' (a mason).[49]

Mossad's heritage is traced politically from the Jewish revolt at the fortress Masada, culminating in mass suicide of AD 73. Events at Masada spearheaded the political movement of Zionism in the 20th century, signalled covertly with the 'temple or crown' (masdar), emblems of 'Jehovah' (Jupiter).

In Rome, reverence to the skull illustrates Capitol Hill - the formal site of Jupiter's Temple. The title 'Capitol' is taken from the Latin noun 'caput' (head), identified with 'capra' (a nanny goat).[50] Jupiter's Temple is later transferred to the US Seat of Congress, situated in Washington DC (Capitol Hill). The severed head is an imperial device, simultaneous to the Modern Secret Society (e.g. temple and Templar). Use of the 'masdar' (skull) archaically is adopted by the Roman, Jewish and Bavarian illuminati.[51]

The Jewish Priesthood the 'Nazir' from 'nazar' (to separate or consecrate oneself) is equivalent to the 'National Socialist' - the 'Nazi' predecessor to NASA. The appellation 'Nazi' is borrowed from the Hebrew rank 'Nasi' specifying (a Jewish leader of the Palestinian community from the second to fourth century AD).

Divested from the Rabbinical emblem of the 'cranium - Greek kranion' (a skull), recognizant with 'kube - Greek koruphe' (a head). In spoken Arabic, 'kube' denudes the 'Kaaba' shrine, perquisite to the teachings of the Kabbalah and the Society of 'Jupiter'. The 'death head' in Christianity refers to 'Golgotha' (the skull) - location of Jesus' crucifixion, symbolic of Capitol Hill Rome.

The skull typically is twinned with its double, theological to the reptile (an angel), in Islamic lore the double of Jesus. Masonic symbolism mirrors 'Germina' (a twin) with 'Germani' (a German) - esoteric of Israel. German ascendancy based on racial types is further correlated with subterfuge preserved in the stories of Jacob and Esau. Photo shows the second Einsiedeln Skull Switzerland (The author suggests the 'victima' shown are German twins - the symbolism supports this hypothesis).

Contemporary examples of the 'Nazir' network include the Yale Skull and Bones fraternity, the German SS 'totenkopf' and their earlier partner the Knights Templar.[52] These societies all share identical iconography with the Jewish organization 'Mossad' an offshoot of the Sodalist fraternity. Mossad disguises its allegiance to 'Diovis' (Jupiter) - Hebrew 'Jehovah', adopting the 'masdar' skull. Emblem of the head signifies the Rabbinical tradition, annexed with the Caucasian or Western priesthood - the 'Nazir' (consecrated), analogous in Arabic to 'nasiyah' (forehead).[53] Inference to such an alliance is disguised in the Semitic lexicology.

The Arabic noun 'jimjimi' (a skull)[54] - not to be confused with the song - alludes to the Latin noun 'gemina' (a twin or double).[55] The 'twin' is cognizant with 'Germani' (a German) and 'Germanitus' (brotherhood). Germanitus possesses the same meaning as 'germanus' (having the same parents or a full brother).[56]

To emphasize, the Germanic priesthood trace their ancestry back to the angelic bloodline of Israel.[57] Its bloodline the 'Nazir' (consecrated) is specified in the Torah as the tribe Asher, from the Arabic noun 'ash'ar or ashqar' (blond).[58] Represented as 'warriors or soldiers' (the ashkari)[59] herald the lion of Judah (Jovis). Chosen from the Sadducee's line of descent, the 'ashkari' are isolated from the Sodalist fraternity, originating from Moses.

The 'ashkari' inform the Eastern European Jewish Sect - the Ashkenazi. Their name is taken from 'Ashkenaz', Genesis Chapter 10 verse 3, described as the original descendents of the Japhethites, the son of Noah (Refer to footnote[60]). Ashkenazi is read as the compound Ashken-Nazir (a soldier-priest), covert with 'khash'i' (the adjective secret),[61] implicit of the 'Sodalists' affiliated to the God 'Amun' (concealed). This ancient and most secretive organization (by definition) is imperative to the development of Christianity and Islam, outlined in the next chapter.

1   Bram Stoker: Dracula, Complete & Unabridged, Wordsworth Classics 1993, p15

2   Ibid, p30

3   Ferozsons Urdu-English Dictionary, Revised Edition, Ferozsons Ltd, Lahore, p457

4   Ibid

5   Prolog: Pocket Bilingual Dictionary, English-Hebrew, Hebrew-English, Prolog 2003, p303

6   'Kokhav' (Jupiter) is ranked as (the father [of the] law) and resides with his son 'kokhba' (star), mutual to the earth's sun and the star system Sirius.

7   Hippocrene Concise Dictionary, English-Arabic, Arabic-English, Hippocrene 2005, p56

8   'Tair' (bird) is from the Egyptian Arabic expression 'tah' (to lose one's way), specific of avian migration, and recalls 'tili' the verbal stem (to rise).

9   Prolog Pocket Bilingual Dictionary, English-Hebrew, Hebrew-English, Prolog 2003, p220

10 Ibid

11 Graham Phillips: The Marian Conspiracy, Pan Books 2001, p50

12 Prolog Pocket Bilingual Dictionary, English-Hebrew, Hebrew-English, Prolog 2003, p449

13 Hippocrene Concise Dictionary, English-Arabic, Arabic-English, Hippocrene 2005, p165

14 Ibid

15 Ibid

16 Ibid

17 Ibid, p70

18 Ralph Ellis: Eden in Egypt, A Translation of the Book of Genesis out of the Original Egyptian Text, Edfu Books, UK 2004, p283 (Appendix A5 - Dictionary).

19 Hippocrene English-Arabic, Arabic-English Dictionary, Hippocrene, New York, 2005, p294

20 Prolog Pocket Bilingual Dictionary, English-Hebrew, Hebrew-English, Prolog, 2003, p24

21 Ibid, p68

22 Hippocrene English-Arabic, Arabic-English Dictionary, Hippocrene, New York 2005, p294

23 The Semitic nouns 'tair' (bird) and 'taraa' (gate) are found in their Japanese counterparts 'tori' (bird) and 'torii' (a temple entrance, doorway, temple gateway or temple lintel frame).

24 John C Traupman PhD: The New College Latin & English Dictionary, Bantam, USA, p310

25 Ibid

26 'Tara(a)' (door) is symmetrical to the nomad 'Terah' (Abraham's father). Read in the Old Semitic as 'ter-aur' (a phoenix) literally a 'bird of light' (Ra). Terah's standard is connected in the occult tradition to the 'teraphim' (an household idol). In the Roman mysteries the eagle or phoenix is carried by the Roman legion.

27 The gatekeeper is a guardian of knowledge, demonstrated with the patron Peter - the key holder to heaven and possesser of the keys to the Kingdom (Church).

28 The verbal root 'zaqq' depicts the doorkeeper, associated with the priesthood of Zadok. 'Zaqq' (the verb 'to push' a door) is obtained from the Egyptian Arabic noun 'sakk' (lock), employed from the Syrian verb 'sakkar' (lock), esoteric of 'sakhr' (rock or body). 'Sakk(ar)' and 'sakhr' is transferred into English as the wordplay 'lock' and 'rock', and quotes the Passover rites, coordinated in Hebrew with the 'reptile' (zokhel) - a fallen angel. Unlocking of the door designates shape-shifting, specific of the rock (an altar - relative to alter), correlated with the sacrifice of Adam (clay).

29 Hippocrene Concise Dictionary, English-Arabic, Arabic-English, Hippocrene 2005, p314

30 Ibid

31 Prolog: Pocket Bilingual Dictionary, English-Hebrew, Hebrew-English, Prolog 2003, p340

32 Ibid, p207

33 Hippocrene Concise Dictionary, English-Arabic, Arabic-English, Hippocrene 2005, p277

34 Ibid

35 Ibid

36 A 'lock(ed) God' i.e. a deity that conceals its form is rendered in Arabic as 'sakk-Il' - implicit of the 'tabernacle' (Hebrew suka or succoth). Branched with the rising sun of the 'east' (sarki), the resurrection of the solar disk is cognate with 'zokhel' (a reptile).

37 Alignment of sakk-Il with zokhel is sentient to 'sattar' (an attribute of a god), used alternatively as an adjective to express the action of (concealing or covering). This describes the angel's aptitude at masking its appearance.

38 Hippocrene Concise Dictionary, English-Arabic, Arabic-English, Hippocrene 2005, p166

39 'Daq' (to knock in Arabic) connotes physical force as found in the phrase 'daq mismar' (to knock or drive a nail). The word 'daq' is a pun on 'dihik' (to laugh), evocative of a laughing deity - a reaper. In particular, the reaper (ripper) is associated ritualistically with 'dakar' (male), cognate with 'dakhl' (an income), theological to redemption outlined in the Passion narratives.

40 Hippocrene Concise Dictionary, English-Arabic, Arabic-English, Hippocrene 2005, p153

41 Ibid

42 Brewers Dictionary of Phrase & Fable, Revised, London, Cassel & Company Ltd 1954, p721 (Pope - Brewer argues that Roman scholars do not connect Papa with Popa - an argument shown to be untenable when compared with the Arabic etymologies).

43 Prolog Pocket Bilingual Dictionary, English-Hebrew, Hebrew-English, Prolog 2003, p385

44 Arbeit Macht Frei, 10 GCSE plays, Pearson Publishing, p59

45 Hippocrene Concise Dictionary, English-Arabic, Arabic-English, Hippocrene 2005, p125

46 Prolog: Pocket Bilingual Dictionary, English-Hebrew, Hebrew-English, Prolog, 2003, p210 The definition of Mossad is an Hebrew acronym and denotes the Principal Secret Intelligence Service of the State of Israel. Its full title means Supreme Institution for Intelligence and Special Assignments. Mossad's acronym is based on the Hebrew word 'Mosad' (Institution).

47 Hippocrene Concise Dictionary, English-Arabic, Arabic-English, Hippocrene 2005, p249

48 Ibid, p131

49 Ferozsons Urdu-English Dictionary, A Comprehensive Dictionary of Current Vocabulary, (Revised Edition), Ferozsons Ltd, Lahore, p688

50 John C Traupman PhD: The New College Latin & English Dictionary, Bantam, USA, p34

51 German Zionism is celebrated under the header of the Fatherland - national to Israel and Jupiter.

52 Symbol of the 'Templar' is the 'skull' extracted from the Latin pun 'tempus' (a forehead).

53 Ferozsons Urdu-English Dictionary, Revised Edition, Ferozsons Ltd, Lahore, p763

54 Hippocrene Concise Dictionary, English-Arabic, Arabic-English, Hippocrene 2005, p114

55 John C Traupman PhD: The New College Latin & English Dictionary, Bantam 1988, p124

56 Ibid, p125

57 Criticism against Israel is levelled as Anti-Semitic, and is a real misnomer as its priesthood is not Semitic as demonstrated in the Arabic lexicon. The author instead suggests the term Anti-Caucasian or Anti-Caucasoid.

58 Ahmed M.A. Abdel-Hady: Egyptian Arabic, The Rough Guide Dictionary Phrasebook 1998, p56

59 Hippocrene Concise Dictionary, English-Arabic, Arabic-English, Hippocrene 2005, p116

60 'Japheth' is the grandfather of 'Ashkenaz' the progenitor of (the Ashkenazi people). Ashkenaz's father is described in Genesis 10:3 as 'Gomer' - a name related to the Hebrew noun 'Komer' (priest). Sacredotal Gomer's line is paralleled to the Arabic root 'qamar' (moon), implicit of the Islamic crescent. 'Komer' (priest) informs the Egyptian Arabic etymon 'gami' (mosque) and 'gami'a' (a college or university), reinforcing a close relationship between the Judaic and Islamic priesthood, founded upon initiatory knowledge.

61 Prolog: Pocket Bilingual Dictionary, English-Hebrew, Hebrew-English, Prolog, 2003, p360

25

The Sadduceas and the Worship of Jupiter

'... If you were Abraham's children', said Jesus, 'then you would do the things Abraham did. As it is, you are determined to kill me, a man who has told you the truth that I heard from God. Abraham did not do such things. You are doing the things your own father does'.

'We are not illegitimate children', they protested. 'The only Father we have is God himself'.

John 8:39-41, Holy Bible, New International Version, Gideon

Early Judaism venerated the planets of the solar system and listed 'Tsedek' as the highest father, comparative to (Jupiter and Zeus) in the Roman and Greek mysteries. The Greek deity Zeus is obtained from the Sanskrit titular 'Djaus' (heaven) - the Brahmin Sky God. His name is a derivation of the adjective 'dyu' (to be brilliant).[1] Djaus is symmetrical with the Old Latin name 'Diovis' (Jupiter - Hebrew Jehovah). Rendered alternatively as 'Diouis', familiar to the Greeks as 'Deus' or 'Zeus'. 'Deus' is matched in Greek with 'deos' (dread), 'thuos' (sacrifice) and 'theos' (God).[2]

In the Judaic priesthood, 'Tsedek' (Jupiter) is aligned to 'tsedek' (justice) in tandem with 'zakkau' (alms) and 'dakar' (male). Immolation of the 'zakkau' pertains to the Judaic denomination the 'Sduki'[3] or 'Zadok', referred to in Greek as the Sadducee (a political sect or type of priest).

The appellation 'Zadok' is matched with the Sanskrit title 'sadhu' (a holy man). In the Islamic tradition, Zadok otherwise Zaddik is rendered as 'Sadat' (the Masters or Descendents of the Holy Prophet).[4] Esoterically, the assignment Zaddik refers to the hidden bloodline of the Judaic Kings. Evidence for this statement is found encoded in the ancient Semitic.

'Zaddik' or 'Zadok' is an anagram on 'Sod-Hyk' (a Secret King), equivalent to 'Sed-Hyk' (a Hunting King). 'Hyk', the Canaanite word for (a Sovereign), is a diminutive of Hyksos (Arabic Hakim). Propagation of the 'Zaddik' or 'Sed-Hyk' is through the ancestry of the Sadducee, deduced from the Sodalist priesthood of Moses. The Sadducee or Sodalist forms the backdrop to the 'Saudi or Sauda' ('Black' Nobility), transmitted through a 'secret' (sod) bloodline.

The 'Sadduceas - Hebrew Sduki' (priests), otherwise the Saudi, traced their lineage to Zadok the son of Ahimelech, outlined in 2 Samuel 8:17. 'Ahimelech's name records 'ahli-melech' (the national king),[5] equivalent to the progenitor, appointed to the monarch 'Abimelech' (Father of a King). Zadok's father Ahimelech serves as a word play on Abimelech, the King of the Philistines. He is described in Genesis 20 as consorting with Abraham's wife 'Sarah' (Hebrew princess), prior to the birth of Isaac. The illegitimacy of Abraham's son Isaac suggests a concealed lineage from Zadok.

The Zadoks branched into the Persian as the 'Zanda' (a priest of Ahriman) the God of 'darkness' and informs the Islamic etymon 'Zindiq' (a heretic). The Zindiq is associated with 'sanduq' (a chest or large box),[6] descriptive of the ark, coalescent with the Zanda.

The black priests the 'Zanda' originates from the Avestan word 'zand' (commentary). 'Zanda' is grouped in Arabic with 'Sauda' (black),[7] duplicated as the Sadducee or Sodalist.[8] 'Sauda's affiliation to the 'Sodalist' fraternity is indexed in the Syrian language with the etymon 'saut' (sound or voice),[9] replicated through the matriarch or High Priestess - the 'Bath kol' (Refer to Salt of the Earth, Chapter 21).

The great Muhammadan theologian, Al-Ghazali, classifies the Zandiks as belonging to the philosophical school of the Dahris (Arabic dahr-time).

To quote:

> 'The first school, the Dahris, are one of the oldest sects. They deny the existence of a creator and disposer who is omniscient and omnipotent. They think that the world has always existed of itself and as it [now] is, without a creator; and that animals have always sprung from seed and seed from animals. So has it [always] been and so will it be forever. These are the Zandicks'.[10]

The interpretation cited is identical to the beliefs of the 'Sadduceas' (the Zadoks). The definition of a Sadducee quoted from the Oxford English Dictionary is as follows:

> 'A member of a Jewish sect or party of the time of Christ that denied the resurrection of the dead, the existence of spirits and the obligation of the oral tradition, emphasizing acceptance of the written law [zand] only'.

Enochian tradition states the Zaddiks originate from the bloodline of the watchers (dragon) - a belief transmitted in the Greek and Latin. The transliteration 'Sadducee' encrypts the Latin transitive verb 'seducere' (to lead away, to carry off, to separate or divide).[11] 'Seducere' informs the English etymology 'seduce and sedition', attributes accorded to Jupiter.

Philology of the 'Zaddik' or 'Zadok' is allocated to the 'sixth' planet (sadis),[12] figurative of Jupiter. His emblem is displayed as the Star of David.[13] The inscription of Jupiter is found written on his Temple at Capitol Hill Rome. Jupiter's name abbreviated 'DOM' reads 'Deo Optimo Maximo' (the Highest and the Greatest God).[14]

In English, 'dom' is employed as a suffix found in the word 'kingdom', denoting (the residence of a king). The Latin acronym 'DOM' distinguishes the title 'dominus' (lord), central to 'domicilum' (home) and 'domina' (mistress or wife).[15] 'Dom' is further assimilative of 'dame', reflective of 'damsel' and 'domicile'. The 'dame' in classical depictions is represented as 'crying' - a play on the Arabic word 'dam'a' (tear)[16] - in Hebrew 'dim'a'.[17] Her loss is discerned from the sacrificial death of the firstborn, consigned to the father Jupiter.

The Dragon Destroys the Woman and the Woman Destroys the Dragon (After engraving).
The image shows a reclining woman having intercourse with the dragon. Here the 'dame' (woman) is a pun on the Old Hebrew word 'dame' (price) and 'dam' (blood) archaically 'dema'. 'Dame' and 'dema' inform the Greek etymon 'daimon' (demon), represented as a snake or dragon.

Jupiter's signature (DOM) allocates his chosen entourage, and is a pun on the Semitic noun 'dam' (blood), deduced from the Aramaic word 'dema'. Philologically 'dema' (blood) describes 'dame' (a price or value), assigned to redemption. In the Greek lexicon, 'dema' is cogent with 'daimon' (a demon), incarnated from sacrificial offerings, depicted as the doorway. Esoterically, the bloodline of the 'daimon' is consistent in the Roman syntax with 'dominus' (a lord), embodied as the King Jupiter.

Jupiter's motto appears regularly on monuments and entrances to Roman Churches. Followers of Jupiter raise their hand displaying their thumb, index and middle finger. In Catholic iconography, the hand signal is equal to Christ. Depictions of Jesus lifting his hand show allegiance to the 'Ruling Father' (Ducere Pater), cognizant with 'Jupiter'.

Formation of the early Church, founded upon the veneration of the 'Father' Jupiter, is recorded throughout Asia Minor, Europe and the Middle East. In early New Testament manuscripts, both Jesus and his brother James are identified as 'Zaddiks' (Sadduceas). Further, their association with the Zaddiks demonstrates an acquaintance with the Essene Community - a connection universally dismissed by theologians. In light of what is known about the Qumran sect, Christ's initiation with the Zaddiks is demonstrated in the New Testament.

The Essenes (pl. Esseni) historically are a Messianic group, located in Palestine. Crucially they use the epitaph the 'Sons of Zadok' literally (the Sons of Righteousness or Truth) to describe themselves. In the book of Acts, James the 'brother of the lord' is referred to as 'James the Just' - a title interchangeable in Aramaic with 'Zaddik' (the Righteous One). He exemplifies rigorous adherence to the law.[18] The 'Righteous One' occurs repeatedly in the Dead Sea Scrolls as (Zaddik), the 'Teacher of Righteousness' referred to as (Moreh ha-Zedek).[19] 'Moreh' here is used as a pun on 'mar'eh' (to see), indicative of the 'watcher', 'angel' or 'dragon', transliterated in Modern Hebrew as 'more' (teacher).[20]

The title 'Moreh ha-Zedek' approximates to (the Teacher of the Law) - a name originating from the redemption of Isaac (Zadok) on Mount Moriah. Religiously, Isaac's death is equated with induction into the mysteries or 'secrets' (sodi). The Hebrew verbal root 'hora'a' (teaching)[21] is cognate with 'har or hor' (mountain)[22] and 'harel' (altar). 'Harel' informs the Syrian etymon 'hawra' (horror) - Latin 'horror'. 'Hawra' is used in Egyptian Arabic to suggest the pronoun 'huwa' (he), rendered in the Syrian as 'hu',[23] implicit of the male firstborn.

The theme of sacrificial death of the innocent is repeated in the Passion narratives. In the Gospels, 'Jesus' is proffered as a sacrament at Golgotha's hill - his death corresponds with the Passover lamb, identified with the Sabbath and skull. The 'skull' is a symbol of 'Capitol' - nominal of the 'temple' of Jupiter.

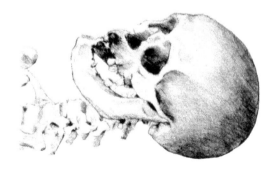

The skull is a dual signifier of Golgotha the crucifixion site of Jesus, recognizant in the Roman mystery schools with Capitol Hill.

Jesus' Arabic name 'Isa' suggests a theological comparison with 'Isaac', classified with the denomination 'Zaddik or Sduki' (Greek Sadducee). The 'Sduki' priesthood pairs with 'Tsedek' (Jupiter) and 'tsedek' (justice). The death of Jupiter's son, metaphorically Jesus, is paralleled to the destruction of the firstborn and the death of Isaac. Usurpation of Abraham's 'firstborn' is proviso to the illegitimate heir 'Zadok' (Isaac), patriarch to the 'Sadduceas'.

This secretive priesthood spread itself far and wide, and is listed in Persia as the 'Zenda', in Syria the 'Sauda', in Greek the 'Soter',[24] in Hebrew the 'Sodi' and in Latin the 'Sodalist'. Biblically, Isa's (Jesus') lineage is descended from 'Zadok' (Isaac), decreed theologically as the firstborn son of 'Tsedek' (Jupiter).

Isa's redemption records the appropriation of Isaac grouped with Ishmael and Esau, demonstrated in Egyptian ritual as the death and resurrection of Osiris. Demise of the male heir encodes the Sabbath, conjunct with the formation of the covenant. This agreement is pictured as the skull, and stipulates the death of the firstborn heir, affiliated to Jupiter, listed with the doorkeeper.

Killing of the blameless or pure acknowledges the 'righteous' (Zadok), substituted in Judaic lore with 'Isaac' and 'Isa' (Jesus). Religiously, Isa's demise is symmetrical with the Passover lamb and the razing of the Jewish Temple (AD 33). Destruction of this relic sanctioned the offering of the innocent, celebrated originally through the Sabbath.

---

1   Harold Bayley: The Lost Language of Symbolism Vol 1 & 2, Dover, 2006, p263

2   Analogies between food and propitiations are evident in the vocabulary 'diet' (the consumption of food), paralleled with 'diet' (a legislative assembly) e.g. the connection between a sacrifice and the ratification of law. Allocation between food and law originates from the Greek expression 'diaita' (way of life), cognate in Medieval Latin with 'dieta' (a days work or wages), implicit of sacrificial redemption. 'Dieta' apprises 'datus' the Roman masculine noun (giving) - a derivation from the Hebrew etymon 'da'at' (sacred 'knowledge'). 'Diaita', connoting 'deity' worship, is assimilated in the Greek term 'thearkia' (the Godhead, literally God's rule). In addition, 'Theo' (God) enunciates 'theoreo' (a watcher - technically a dragon or an angel).

3   It is not incidental that the Japanese noun 'tsuki' denotes (the moon) - an emblem intrinsic in the Semitic traditions to the Sduki priesthood.

4   Ferozson's Urdu-English Dictionary, Revised Ed, Ferozsons Ltd, Karachi, p421 ('Sadat' - the 't' in the Old Semitic is sometimes left unpronounced. Further, the vowel 'a' is consistent phonetically with the 'h' and 'k' sound).

5   Hippocrene Concise Dictionary, English-Arabic, Arabic-English, Hippocrene, 2005, p147 ['Ahli' (National) cogent with 'Ahl' (Family)].

6   Ibid, p26

7   Ibid, p19

8   The colour black signifies the setting sun, identified with the singing host and the Western priesthood.

9   Hippocrene Concise Dictionary, English-Arabic, Arabic-English, Hippocrene, 2005, p281 ['Saut' (sound or voice) informs the English etymon 'sound'].

10 Professor RC Zaehner: The Dawn & Twilight of Zoroastrianism, Weidenfeld & Nicolson, 1975, p196

11 John C Traupman PhD: The New College Latin & English Dictionary, Bantam, 1988, p282

12 Hippocrene Concise Dictionary, English-Arabic, Arabic-English, Hippocrene, 2005, p114

13 The Star of David, Jupiter, is compatible with the seven-pointed star of the Sabian priesthood - iconic of Saturn and darkness.

14 Richard Taylor: How to Read a Church, A Guide to Images, Symbols and Meanings in Churches and Cathedrals, Rider, 2003, p219 (See DOM)

15 John C Traupman PhD: The New College Latin & English Dictionary, Bantam, 1988, p92

16 Hippocrene Concise Dictionary, English-Arabic, Arabic-English, Hippocrene, 2005, p124

17 Prolog: English-Hebrew & Hebrew-English Dictionary, Completely Transliterated, Prolog, 2003, p412

18 Michael Baigent & Richard Leigh: The Dead Sea Scrolls Deception, Arrow Books, 2001, p263

19 Ibid, p261

20 Prolog: English-Hebrew & Hebrew-English Dictionary, Completely Transliterated, Prolog, 2003, p412

21 Ibid

22 Ibid, p264

23 Hippocrene Concise Dictionary, English-Arabic, Arabic-English, Hippocrene, 2005, p194

24 'Soter' (saviour) in Greek is diminutive of Sadducee, contrasted in the Hebrew etymology with 'sote' (a deviant) and 'sod' (a secret).

26

The Six Foundations

'We created seven levels* [of heaven] above you.
We are never unmindful of Our creation'.¹

Al Mu'minun: The Believers (Koran 23: 17)

* Tara'iq 'levels (of heaven)' a homonym also translated as 'highways'.

Symbolism of the stars and planets materially signify a court of heaven, hierarchical in structure to a royal court. The pantheon in Jewish cosmology demonstrates a king, queen, prince and princess, displayed in alchemy through the coarser elements gold (Sun), silver (Moon), copper (Venus) and iron (Mars) - Refer to table p251.

The foundation of heaven enumerates 'briah' (a throne) - authoritative of 'berith' (a covenant) between men and angels (aliens). Astrologically, 'bera-shith' (the six foundations) are latent to 'briah-shith' (the six thrones) - visualized as the planets. The Jewish model of the universe usually counts the 'sun' as a planetry body [2] (See footnote[3]).

Numerically, the figure 'six' is written in Hebrew as 'shesh' from the Chaldean word 'shith', transliterated in Modern Arabic as 'sitti'. The number connotes fecundity, evident in the English alliteration 'six and sex', and is exhibited in the Semitic wordplay 'sitti' (six) and 'sitt' (lady).[4] The Babylonian unit 'shith' is reproduced in the book of Genesis, transcribed in the phrase 'berashith' (in the beginning), translated alternatively as (he [who] created the foundation).[5] This statement is interpreted quite literally as (the six foundations), emphatic of the 'matriarchal' covenant, existential to 'sitt' (a lady).[6] In Egyptian mythology, sitt's creation of the universe is identified with the God of chaos 'Seth' (a foundation).

Woman embracing a serpent signifies the matriarchal covenant and the establishment of Royal offspring (human-angelic).

The Greek equivalent of the 'six foundations' (berashith - in the beginning) is annotated as (hexameron).[7] Reverend Brewer defines it as *'the six days taken as one continuous period; especially the six days of creation'.*[8] These are listed overleaf and form an introduction to Chapter 27 Black Sabbath.

SEVEN PLANETS

The Six Foundations (The Six Days of Creation)

The list corresponds with the seven metals in alchemy and the seven heavens of Mithra worship (Notice the concealment of Saturn).

1   Gold – Apollo the Sun (Creator)

2   Silver – Diana the Moon (Hunter or Nocturne)

3   Quicksilver – Mercury (Messenger)

4   Copper – Venus (Serpent an hermaphrodite)

5   Iron – Mars (Man)

6   Tin – Zeus Jupiter (the Father)

7   Lead – Saturn – Hidden from Sight by the Asteroid Belt or the Underworld

Hermes (Mercury) the Messenger God Carries a Caduceus a Double Serpent.
Depicted with winged feet, he is described as 'Serpentipedis' (Dragon-footed) a signifier of the snake's
genetic 'footprint' (Latin vestigium). In addition, 'vestigium' is esoteric of 'vestis' (a snake skin),
correlated with the 'Goddess of the Hearth' (Vesta) - symbolic of the 'altar and Venus'.

Astrological Symbolism of the Planets

1 Sun – Cognate with Sirius and the Sothic year 365.25 days. The heliacal, rising of the Dog Star, is also paired with Alcion, the central star of the Pleiades.

2 Moon – Goddess (Receptacle of man's seed, the ark).

3 Mercury – Messenger (Angel) i.e. the planet nearest to the 'Sun, aka Sirius'.

4 Venus – Son or Royal Prince (Christ-the Morning Star), divisional of the angelic host (Shatan). Note the Evening-Star is equated with Goddess worship and dualism.

5 Mars – Israel (Caucasian Indo-European Priesthood).

6 Jupiter – Father (King of the host).

7 Saturn – Fallen host, attributed with the angel Satan and the forces of darkness (duality), associated with Venus and the moon. Saturn is also doubled with the hidden star of Sirius and the seventh star of the Pleiades, eventual to the priesthood's split, earmarked as the crescent.

1 M.A.S. Abdel Haleem: The Qur'an, Oxford University Press 2004, p215

2 The confusion between a planet and sun is due to the English etymology. It seems Jewish astrologers differentiated the gas planets such as Jupiter (technically an unformed star) with the sun. In English, gas bodies are incorrectly bracketed with planets, creating confusion between the noun star and planet. Scientifically, the definition 'star', denoting 'Jupiter', is better suited than the English word planet. Ancient knowledge, regarding stars, points to a sophisticated understanding of the universe and its mechanistic laws.

3 The word 'planet' is misleading in this context and is better suited to the term a solar or celestial body.

4 Hippocrene English-Arabic, Arabic-English Dictionary, Hippocrene, New York 2005, p289. The English expression to 'sit in waiting' is derived from the Arabic pun 'sitt' (a lady), identified in Semitic with 'sit' (reputation).

5 S.L. Macgregor Mathers: The Kabbalah Unveiled Arkana, 1991 (1926), p46

6 'Sit' (lady) is equated in the Syrian language with the deluge, expressed as 'shiti' (rain).

7 'Hexameron' Greek (six foundations) denoting (the six days of creation) suggests the name of Arthur's sword 'Excalibur' from the Old French 'Escalibor'. The title according to Reverend Brewer is a derivation of the sword of 'Caliburn', referred to in Geoffrey of Monmouth's epic. 'Caliburn' itself is a corruption from the Irish Celtic word 'caledvwlch' (hard bellied), esoteric of the 'six foundations'. The stories of Arthur are etiological legends, written in ciphers, detailing creation and the formation of Christendom (England). Note also the Latin play on 'Excalibur' - 'Ex-scaber' (from the rough i.e. hewn from the rock) is comparative to 'Ex-saber' (of the sword). The name also appears connected to 'Ex-Calabria' (from Calabria - formerly Southeast of Italy). This location has now moved to the Southwest - a cryptic clue pertaining to the hidden or Western priesthood.

8 Brewers Dictionary of Phrase & Fable: London, Cassell & Company Ltd 1954, p455

27

Black Sabbath

'Farewell, Muses, and grant me delightful singing. Celebrate the holy family of immortals, who are for ever–those who were born of Earth and Heaven and of black Night...'[1]

Theogony (Hesiod)

'I am a child of Earth and starry Heaven, but my race is of Heaven alone'.[2]

Orphic gold plate, 4th-3rd century BC

In Judaic cosmology, the seventh planet Saturn is concealed or rests and is in opposition with Jupiter number six. Usurpation of Jupiter is secretly witnessed on the day of rest, celebrated on the holy day Saturday, consonant with Saturn. Philologically the Hebrew word 'Shabbat' (Saturday)[3] is comparative to 'Shabtay' (Saturn).[4] Observance of 'Sabbat' (Sabbath) is symbolic of death, honoured through the 'Shavuoth' festival, the Jewish (Pentecost) - an iteration of the spring lamb. In Mosaic Law, this cycle designates the 'seventh year' - collateral to the 'Sabbath', during which the land is allowed to rest.

'Shavuoth' is rendered in Hebrew as 'Sabu'ot' or 'Shavu'ot' and marks (the Harvest festival). Stipulated as the period between Passover and Pentecost, the 'Sabu'ot' records the 'fiftieth day after the second day of Passover'. The feast celebrates angelic conquest of the earth and its re-creation.

'Sabu'ot' corresponds to 'Pentecost', extracted from the Greek root 'Pentekoste-hemera' (the fiftieth day). Etymologically 'Sabu'ot' is cognate with the 'tsabaoth' transliterated into English as the 's'baot' (the host). Anniversary of 'Sabu'ot' is dualled astrologically with 'Shabtay' (Saturn), conciliatory of 'berashith' (the sixth foundation), numerical to 'Jupiter' and the 'sixth day of creation'. The planet 'Saturn' connotes war - typical to the archangel 'Satan' (adversary), oppositional to the Father 'Jehovah' (Diovis).

Saturnalia in the Ecclesiastical tradition recalls the birth of Christ (Christmas), juxtaposed with 'S(h)abbat' the holy (day of rest). Theologically, Christ is substituted with the creation of Satan during the winter months of darkness. His rebirth from the tomb (or underworld) is paired with the spring festival Passover, celebratory of new life (lambing season), equated with the start of the week.[5]

Veneration of the 'Pentecost' (Sabu'ot or Shavu'ot) theologically describes the killing of the Passover lamb, registered with the Shabbat festival. Devotional, the lamb's demise annunciates a sacrificial replacement, tributary to the firstborn, marked on the seventh day.

The Hebrew root 'sh-v-a, in Arabic sab'a' signifies (seven) and shares the same meaning (to be satiated or to swear an oath).[6] The stem's original usage is traced back to the book of Genesis. Here 'Shaveh' describes the 'Valley of the Kings' as 'a place of offering'. This site is determinative of (satiation, mourning or rest) - euphemisms denoting 'death of the newborn'.

In the Bible, participants of the 'Shaveh' ritual are sworn to an 'oath of secrecy.' Phonological comparison of the word 'Shaveh' with the noun 'sabre' suggests the ceremony is directed with (a sword).[7]

'Shaveh's location is paralleled to 'tsabaoth variously s'baot' (the host), and ritualistically duplicates 'Sabu'ot or Shavu'ot' (the Harvest festival). Enactment of the 'Sabu'ot' sacrament adjoins the offering of the lamb (child) in relation to 'Shabtay' (Saturn). Saturn's veiled appearance illustrates secret rites, accorded to the grim reaper - a harvester of souls specified as an angel of death.

Religiously the 'seven(th)' day (sheva) stipulates the period of 'mourning' (shiva), classified with the 'morning sun' and the sacrificial killing of a new child. The Arabic verbal stem 'shiva' (mourning) is punned with 'sabah' (morning),[8] shared in the English wordplay 'mourning' and 'morning'. Numerically 'seven' distinguishes 'severance' of life. Sacrificial death of the babe embodies the morning sun, augmented with the transfigured or flashing angel (serpent). He carries a flaming (bloodied) sword - a symbol of the cherubim, paralleled to the votive, disclosed as the 'shevah'.

Presented as a luminary, the 'child' (sabi) is coded speak for a 'burnt offering' (Greek holokauston), adjacent to the flashing dragon, encrypted universally. In English, the homonym 'son' and 'sun' represents 'sin' - tokens of the offertory. The same pun is demonstrated in Arabic. For example, the etymon 'nur' (daylight or light)[9] is compared to 'nour' (the Old Semitic word for a young boy). Within Judaism, this secret (sacred) knowledge appertains to 'na'or' (enlightened),[10] explicit of 'nuah' or 'ruh' (the spirit) - a term likened to 'nour' (a boy).[11]

The votive in Greek ritual is linked to 'Phosphorus' translated as (Venus) and suggests the 'holokauston' human sacrifice literally (burnt offering). The compound 'Phos-phorus' (light-bringer) reads as the homonym (man-offering).

The spilling of blood (rite and light) concurs with the practices of 'shiva' (mourning) - synonymous with the burning of the propitiation in alignment to the 'sol' (sun) and 'soul'. This relationship in the Semitic dialect is equivalent to 'nur' (light), 'nar' (fire) and 'nuah' (spirit).[12] Summarized in Hebrew as 'ish' (man)[13] and 'esh' (flame),[14] the same wordplay is indexed in the Greek polymorphic noun 'phos' (man) translated additionally as (light) - Arabic 'nar' and 'nour'.

To reiterate, terminology disclosing a human votive compared to fire is synchronized with the day, repeated in the Arabic glossary. 'Radi' (tomorrow)[15] records 'radi' (a baby),[16] cognizant with 'radi' (bad or evil).[17] These homonyms are formed from the verbal stem 'rad' (want or wish).[18] Coupled with the nouns 'wa'd' (promise)[19] and 'wada' (lay, put, set or place),[20] the idioms express a ritual, carried out in 'wadi' (a valley).[21]

The setting of the sun, theoretical to the mystery (evening meal), is illustrative of the rites of the newborn, compared to Saturn and the Valley of the Kings. In the Bible, the location of Shaveh is associated with the priest of 'Shalem' (surrender), referred to as 'Melchizedek' (the Righteous King). According to the book of Genesis, Melchizedek blesses the communal offering of the 'bread and the wine'[22] - a religious signifier of the flesh and blood of the newborn. To quote Genesis 14:18-20:

> *Then Melchizedek King of Salem brought out bread and wine.*
> *He was priest of God Most High, and he blessed Abram, saying,*
>
> *"Blessed be Abram by God Most High,*
> *Creator of heaven and earth.*
> *And blessed be God Most High,*
> *who delivered your enemies into your hand."*

Execution of the firstborn exemplifies the redemption of the innocent, symmetrical to the atonement of the king. Melchizedek's sacrifice comprises of captives, appropriated from the campaign, dedicated to Yahweh, and takes place directly after a conflict, described by the Biblical redactor as the War of the Kings. Following this incident, Abram observes a communion meal with the King of Sodom, ally to Yahweh. (Note the citation refers to the same King, whose Kingdom is later destroyed by God).

Introduction of the place name 'Shaveh', known by contemporaries as the 'Valley of the Kings', is an early form of the 'S(h)abbat' festival (the Sabbath). The breaking of the bread and wine enacts the killing of 'Isaac', and honours the God of Abram. 'Isaac's cognomen (laughter) is rendered in the corrupted form 'Zadok'(the righteous one) - a title adopted by the Priest King 'Melchi-Zedek'.

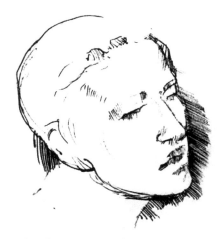

The firstborn male infant is traditionally sacrificed to the serpent Gods. This tribute includes babies, children and adolescents.

Melchizedek's ancestry traces his divine lineage through Abimelech (Abi-Melekh - translated Father of a King), the patriarch of Zadok, usurper of Abraham's firstborn Ishmael. Replacement of the male infant details the development of Judaic theology, exampled in the narratives of Abimelech.

In the book of Genesis, Abimelech takes Abraham's wife Sarah as a concubine, prior to the conception of Isaac (Zadok). Following this arrangement, the biblical editor attempts to cover Isaac's royal ancestry. In Chapter 20 verse 17 and 18 (succeeded by Chapter 21 verse 1 and 2), the scribe writes:

> ' …God healed Abimelech, his wife and his slave girls so they could have children again, for the Lord had closed up every womb in Abimelech's household because of Abraham's wife Sarah'.

> 'Now the Lord was gracious to Sarah as he had said, and the Lord did for Sarah what he had promised. Sarah became pregnant and bore a son to Abraham in his old age...'

Zadok's illegitimate line is reserved in the traditions of Jacob and Esau. The loss of Esau's birthright is compatible with the substitution of Ishmael with Isaac. Demonstrated in Genesis Chapter 22, the covert slaying of Isaac is surrogated with the ram and bush, theoretical to the tabernacle and burnt offering.

In the doctrines of the early church, Jesus' atonement is proffered through a sacrificial substitute, bridged with the priests of Melchizedek. Jesus' relationship to 'Melchizedek' and the 'Sadducee' class 'Zadok' parallels the death of the innocent 'Isaac' - successor to the royal throne. Classification of Jesus' lineage is further recorded in the New Testament book, Hebrews 6: 20. The quotation reads:

> '...Jesus, who went before us, has entered on our behalf. He has become a high priest for ever, in the order of Melchizedek.'

Legally, the establishment of God's Kingdom is conveyed through the ejection of the firstborn heir, offered as a sacrifice. The ritual dictates the severance of kingship, identified originally with human birthright. Replacement of the sovereign's bloodline with angelic progeny is correlated with the dragon, mythical to Osiris. Concealment of the human votive is sanctioned through the law, central to the early (modern?) worship of Yahweh, encapsulated in the stories of Cain, Abraham, David, Solomon and Jesus (Refer to Appendix 5 the Talmud).

Celebration of the Sabbath is agnate with the resurrection of the winter sun, the Saturnalia. Commensurate with the 'Harvest festival' (Shavuoth), Saturnalia distinguishes the 'host' (s'baot), illustrative of the reaper. The Torah indemnifies Yahweh's blood lust, glorifying him as the 'Lord of the host' (a naval army), revered as the Supreme Commander of the Israelites. His people are presented as 'Soldiers' of God - the 'Ashkari'.[23]

Assassination of the 'righteous' prescribes the veneration of Saturn, duplicitous to Yahweh (Jupiter) and the death of Isaac (Mars). Requital of man's inheritance from the earth, expedited through war and famine, is reinforced theologically through the rape of the matriarch, summarized in Isaiah 13 verse 16 and 18:

> 'Their infants will be dashed to pieces before their eyes; their houses will be looted and their wives ravished... they will have no mercy on infants nor will they look with compassion on children'.

Abused, the woman's legitimate offspring are replaced with angelic progeny, conditional to the removal of the firstborn, preordained through God's hierocracy. Theoretical to the covenant, the Sabbath ritualizes the killing of the 'Son of Man' - 'Abel' ['habl' (pregnancy)], aligned historically to the descendents of Adam. 'Abel's immolation (avel-mourn) inaugurates the Black Sabbath - the 'day of rest', consolidated as the seventh foundation!

1   Alan F. Alford: The Atlantis Secret, A Complete Decoding of Plato's Lost Continent, Eridu, 2001, p24

2   Ibid, p279

3   Prolog: Pocket Bilingual Dictionary, English-Hebrew, Hebrew-English, Prolog, 2003, p355

4   Ibid

5   'Saturn' illustrates the 'satyr' (Greek saturos), partnered with the woman, correlated with the Greek festival 'Saturnalia'. Contiguous with the winter solstice and the worship of Satan, Saturnalia is sequenced with the death of the firstborn.

6   Zecharia Sitchin: The Cosmic Code, Book VI Earth Chronicles, Avon, New York, 1988, p175

7   The rites of 'Shaveh' correspond in the Old English expression 'God's word' [abbreviated as 'S-Word' (sword)]. Similar comparisons are evident in the Islamic tradition. The Arabic name of the prophet 'Mohammed' is punned with 'Muhannad' (a sword).

8   Hippocrene Concise Dictionary, English-Arabic, Arabic-English, Hippocrene, 2005, p77

9   Ibid, p257 Summarized in Hebrew as 'ish' (man) and 'esh' (flame), the same wordplay is indexed in the Greek polymorphic noun 'phos' (man) translated additionally as (light) - Arabic 'nour' (boy) and 'nar' (flame), analogous in English to the homonym 'son' and 'sun'. Identical themes are also duplicated in the Japanese word-groupings 'hito' (man) and 'hi' (fire). Concordant, the pun is evident epigraphically in the Chinese characters. The Kanji radical signifying a 'man', when accentuated with two dashs, reads as 'fire'.

10 Prolog: Pocket Bilingual Dictionary, English-Hebrew-Hebrew-English, Prolog, 2003, p131

11 Translated by S. L. MacGregor Mathers: The Kabbalah Unveiled, Penguin Arkana, 1991, p105 (Nour)

12 S. L. MacGregor Mathers translates 'nuah' as (spirit) - Latin 'spiritus' a word meaning (breath), symbolised as darkness or sound. The etymological comparison of 'nuah' (the spirit) with 'nur' (light) would actually suggest the correct reading of 'nuah' is (the soul) rather than (the spirit). Use of the term 'nuah', it seems, is a corruption from the Arabic etymon 'ruh' (spirit) - Refer to Hippocrene Dictionary, p117

13 Prolog: Pocket Bilingual Dictionary, English-Hebrew-Hebrew-English, Prolog, 2003, p244

14 Ibid, p153

15 Hippocrene English-Arabic, Arabic-English Dictionary, Hippocrene, New York, 2005, p266

16 Ibid [Arabic 'radi' a homonym of (tomorrow, bad, evil or baby) - word associations which are similar to the English pun (bode, baddy, and babby)].

17 Ibid

18 Ibid, p265

19 Ibid, p305

20 Ibid

21 Ibid

22 Zecharia Sitchin: The Cosmic Code, Book VI Earth Chronicles, Avon, New York, 1988, p212

23 In honour to Yahweh, cities are razed, and atrocities are dedicated to Him.

Satyrs and Saturn

'When men began to increase in number on the earth and daughters were born to them, the sons of God saw that the daughters of men were beautiful, and they married any of them they chose... The Nephilim were on the earth in those days – and also afterwards – when the sons of God went to the daughters of men and had children by them. They were the heroes of old, men of renown'.

Genesis 6: 1, 2 and 4, Holy Bible, New International Version, Gideon

The Sabbath records the surrender of man and the cessation of hostilities, pivotal to the formation of the covenant, mediated through kingship. Sacrifice of the firstborn is mentioned etiologically as the removal of 'Esau' (Hebrew hair). This deceit is annunciated through the human angelic lineage, personified as the 'reptile' or 'rapist'.

In the Hebrew tradition, Eve's descendents are the ancestors of the 'Nephilim', a race translated from the verbal adjective 'naful' (to fall) i.e. the 'Fallen Ones'.[1] They are also described as the 'awwim', interpreted as (the serpents or devastators), identical to the 'reptile', 'pillager' or 'rapist'. The 'awwim' are mutual to the 'tsabaoth' (the host or dragon) and are described in related traditions as the conquerors of man.

The ratification of the Elhohim's covenant with humans through circumcision discloses castration of the male lineage. In ancient Judaic lore, the covenant required the sacrificial blood of a firstborn baby boy, conveyed through the mutilation of the genitalia and the removal of man's ancestral lineage. Religiously the rite is correlated with Adam, Isaac and Esau.

According to Abraham's covenant, circumcision is practiced on the eighth day after birth. The significance of the number 'eight' is clarified in Semitic. The Arabic word 'temen' (eight) is a homonym of 'temen' (price) and 'ta'am' the verbal stem (to feed) - language implicit of sacrificial immolation. Circumcision thus traditionally included the ritual sucking of the penis, symbolic of the votive - a custom still practiced amongst communities of Ultra Orthodox Jews.

Celebration of the Sabbath outlines deception, framed through the appropriation of a child, and is adapted in Mosaic (Masonic) Law as the evening meal or communion. Observance of the Sabbath implies sacrificial death, featured in the Semitic wordplays. The Hebrew day 'rishon' (Sunday) is a pun on the Arabic phrase 'rishsh' 'yom' (a deceitful[2] day). The noun 'yom' signifying (day) is grouped in the Middle Eastern languages with 'ayom' (horrid),[3] relayed into English as 'day and die'.

In Arabic, 'Yom il-Hadd' (Sunday)[4] is a metamorphic phrase and translates as (God's luck(y) day, God's sharp day, alternatively God's frontier or border).[5] Contextually, the word 'hadd' (border) is analogous to 'adi' (enemy) and 'eder' (flock), consistent with Hyksos invasion of Egypt and the subordination of the Adar lamb (child) - See Chapter 22 The Adar Lamb and the Keyholder.

Replacement of Adam's offspring describes the subjugation of man and the conquest of woman - the surrender of humanity enforced through the fallen angels the Shatani, comprised of the hidden 'government' (shilton) and its covert matriarchal priesthood. This sect represents itself as the forbidden planet Saturn, cogent with deception and darkness. Philologically, 'Shabtay' (Saturn) informs the Judaic festival 'Sabu'ot' (the Pentecost) - a celebration divisible by the sequence 'five' and 'seven', contingent with 'Mars' and 'Saturn' - Refer to Chapter 26 The Six Foundations.

The phonetic relationship between 'Shabtay' (Saturn) and 'Sabu'ot' (Harvest) signals an early tradition, attributed to Satan and the (re)creation of the world or foundation. This is remembered on the seventh day 'Shabbat' (the day of 'rest') and coincides in Mesopotamia with 'Shabattu' (the monthly festival of the full moon). Its etymology suggests 'Shabattu' celebrates 'Harvest' cycles (Sabu'ot), linked to the underworld and the marriage of 'Shabtay' (Saturn).

Philological comparison of 'Sabu'ot' and 'Sabbath' denotes the worship of 'Saturn', adjunct to the 'tsabaoth' (s'baot) and the renegade 'Satan'. The black planet symbolically contrasts with the dark side of the moon and the Evening Star, theoretical to the (re)civilisation of man. Theologically, 'Saturn' describes the expunction of the firstborn, volunteered through the death of Adam, efficacious to the rape of the matriarch Eve.

Mythically, the serpent's seduction of woman precipitated the vanquish of Mars (five) and the judgment of Jupiter (six), adjunct with Saturn (seven). Tension between Jupiter and Saturn reiterates the theme of war and conquest, unanimous with sin. Dualistic, the two planets are considered antagonistic. Numerically the combination of six (Jupiter) and seven (Saturn) totals thirteen - a number considered unlucky,[6] identified with the spilling of Adam's blood.

Born into original sin, the guilty are expiated through the payment of the firstborn. Man's 'submission' (slm) to Yahweh's covenant is enacted upon the 'seventh' day of 'Sabbath' - Hebrew 'shiva' designated as (a period of mourning).

Remembrance of the holy day recounts the regeneration of mankind, cognate with the hidden traditions of Saturn. At variance, the sixth day marks the completion of creation, relative to Jupiter (the Father), opposite the seventh day Saturn (Satan). Religiously the Sabbath capitulates the worship of Satan (division) in relation to a phase of intercession and death. The festival of Sabbath begins and ends at sunset, its celebration falls on the Friday evening. At sun down, the woman of the household kindles the Sabbath light.[7]

Technically, the holy day is considered as dark.[8] Celebration of the 'Sabbath' (Shabbat) infers a Godless day - the creator is shown as 'resting' (Hebrew sobet) - his presence absent. God's inaction is assumed as a malevolent force under the influence of Saturn, reaffirmed through the veneration of the Sabbath. Judaic custom celebrates the median on the 'seventh day' Saturday - a period equal to Saturn. Correlation between Saturn and its weekly memorial is consistent in the Sino languages.

'Saturn' in Japanese is rendered as 'Dosei' and shares the same Chinese radical for 'Saturday' (Saturn's-Day) characteristic in English with the Roman God 'Saturn'. 'Dosei' written in Kanji (Chinese characters) is read as (the soil or earth star). The Arabs represent this planet as 'sand' and it is grouped in the proto Indo-European languages with the stem 'sat' (to conceal), implicit of the Bath Kol priestess. Emergence of Saturn exults the worship of nocturnal deities, conjugal with the winter solstice and the dying sun. Demise of the solstice reflects the dissension between Saturn and Jupiter - regressive of darkness.

In the Hebrew language, 'koder' is rendered as (saturnine)[9] a term closely related to 'kadosh' (holy).[10] 'Koder' is consistent in Arabic with the noun 'kadar' (trouble),[11] annexed with the intransitive verb 'kaddar' (to annoy).[12] Comparisons with 'koder' and 'kadar' suggest the angel 'Al Kidr' (Arabic the 'Green' One - Aramaic evil), indexed with Saturn, identified with the harvester and the Underworld.

The 'Satyr' is joined with 'Sitt' (a lady). Its musical pipes, associated with sleep, relative to the nocturne a hairy angel. 'Nagen' Old Semitic (Panpipes) symbolises 'najja' (the saviour), evocative of 'najja' (the slayer). A motif of the reptile, the pipe is equated with 'Noga' (Venus), identified with 'nijm' the rising (star).

'Saturn's Roman name is derived from the Syrian root 'sat'atm' meaning (it has grown dark).[13] 'Sat'atm' is taken from the Arabic noun 'sattar' outlining (an attribute of a god), used alternately as an adjective to describe the action of (concealing or covering).[14] This idea is displayed in the Arabic noun 'satr' (to cover, conceal or veil),[15] conceptual to 'sitt' (a lady).[16] 'Satr' (conceal) informs the Egyptian Arabic noun 'sitara' (a curtain[17] - i.e. a tabernacle curtain). 'Sattar' is contrasted with the Persian noun 'sitarah',[18] 'Latin stella'[19] - variegations on the English noun (star).

Concealment of the divinity of a God 'sattar' is depicted in the Greek tragedies as the masked goat a 'saturos', written in English as a 'satyr'. Transfiguration of the 'satyr' links esoterically to the 'star' and 'eye'. The satyr characterizes the 'hairy' snake (Latin capillatus)[20] - an entity that possesses the ability to hide behind a mortal form. This being is usually depicted in the outer mysteries as a masked actor or type of dancer.

Grinning mask from Carthage 6ᵗʰ century BC - the mask as crescent shaped or lunar eyes, referential to the nocturnal angel a grinning reaper, associated with the progeny of the 'satyr' Old Semitic 'se'irim'.

Ritualistically, the actor is switched in Arabic with 'ikhtar' (to choose),[21] conferred upon the firstborn, adjacent to 'akhta' the verb (to sin).[22] 'Akhta', indicative of (immorality), is parabolic of 'akh-tah' (a lost brother),[23] registered with 'tale-tah' (a lost lamb).[24] Greek tragedies display the 'akh-tah' metaphorically as a masked 'satyr cognate with the enactment of a satire'. The satyr's role approximates in Latin to an 'actor' (a performer, plaintiff, pleader, advocate or agent).[25]

In conclusion, Greek and Semitic myths, apropos to the veiled goat, utilize the effigy as a simulacrum of the hermaphrodite, distinguished as the angel. This being corresponds with the castrated eunuch, quoted by Jesus in the Gospel of Matthew 19:12 (King James).

'For there are some eunuchs, which were so born from their mother's womb: and there are some eunuchs, which were made eunuchs of men: and there be eunuchs, which have made themselves eunuchs for the kingdom of heaven's sake. He that is able to receive it, let him receive it'.

The words of Jesus are prophetic, and as we shall observe in the next chapter, the early Christians adopted eunuchs and transgender priests in accordance with this teaching.[26] Its membership formed the backbone to the hidden church, dedicated to Saturn, propagated ritually through the Sabbath.

1 Prolog: Pocket Bilingual Dictionary, English-Hebrew, Hebrew-English, Prolog, 2003, p145

2 Hippocrene Concise Dictionary, English-Arabic, Arabic-English, Hippocrene, 2005, p272

3 Prolog: Pocket Bilingual Dictionary, English-Hebrew, Hebrew-English, Prolog, 2003, p191

4 Hippocrene Concise Dictionary, English-Arabic, Arabic-English, Hippocrene, 2005, p122

5 Ibid, p184

6 Thirteen, considered as an unlucky number, also totals the thirteen articles of faith - a summary of the basic tenants of Judaism. Its code written by the Jewish Medieval scholar, Moses Maimonides.

7 Myrtle Langley: Religion, Eyewitness Guides, Dorling Kindersley, London, 1996, p46

8 Orthodox Jews during the weekend will not attempt to use the light switch - symbolic of darkness identified with rest (death) and the matriarch (the Bath Kol).

9 Prolog: Pocket Bilingual Dictionary, English-Hebrew, Hebrew-English, Prolog, 2003, p355

10 Ibid, p189

11 Hippocrene Concise Dictionary, English-Arabic, Arabic-English, Hippocrene, 2005, p212

12 Ibid

13 Ibid, p279

14 Ferozsons: Urdu-English Dictionary, Revised edition, Ferozsons Ltd, Lahore, p428

15 Ibid, p429

16 Hippocrene English-Arabic, Arabic-English Dictionary, Hippocrene, New York, 2005, p289

17 Ibid

18 Ferozsons: Urdu-English Dictionary, Revised edition, Ferozsons Ltd, Lahore, p428

19 John C Traupman PhD: The New College Latin & English Dictionary, Bantam Books, 1988, p480

20 A 'caterpillar' (capillatus) is figurative of the hairy-snake's metamorphosis into the butterfly - a signifier compatible with the goat and man (alchemy).

21 Hippocrene: English-Arabic, Arabic-English Dictionary, Hippocrene, New York, 2005, p198

22 Ibid, p148

23 Ibid p293 [Egyptian 'tah' (to lose one's way) - Arabic 'ta' (in order to)].

24 'Akh-tale' (a brother [of the] lamb) signifies sacrificial propitiations of the firstborn. In occult Islamic tradition, the epithet is connected with the 'Sufi' from the Arabic root 'suf' (wool). 'Suf' is cognate in the European languages with 'suffer, supper and serpent'. The 'p' and 'f' are switched in the Latin and Arabic.

25 John C Traupman PhD: The New College Latin & English Dictionary, Bantam Press, 1988, p4

26 Jesus' quotation (Mathew 19:12) referring to the eunuch reinforces the connection between the legitimate male line of Adam and its removal through castration equal to the slaughter of the innocent (firstborn).

29

Saturnalia and the Forces of Darkness

'Then rose the seed of Chaos and of Night
To blot out order and extinguish light.
Of dull and venal a new world to mould,
And bring Saturnian days of lead and gold'.[1]

POPE: Dunciad, IV, 13

The 'eunuch' (the castrati) is often conveyed as a trans-gendered priest, and is contrasted with a woman who dresses and acts like a man. Her role in the Catholic Church is documented and came to surface during the medieval witch trials.[2] In several high profile cases recorded in Germany, civil provocation of the courts resulted in the priest stripped of their vestments. In some of these testimonies, the disrobed inquisitor is recorded as a woman priest (trans-vestment). The burning of a witch or warlock by a female inquisitor honours the worship of nocturnal angels.[3] Depiction of the woman as a type of judge or nemesis originates from the angel cults of the Middle East.[4]

The Cambridge scholar, Mary Laven, has revealed in her book *Virgins of Venice* the secrets of a case tried 400 years ago in the Doge's court, cited in the following extract:

> *'[the circumstances] involved nuns hiding men in boxes for the shared sexual delight of the sisterhood, and exchanging cakes and other delicacies for the sexual favors of plumbers and plasterers. Men caught breaking the convent enclosure could be executed or exiled'.*[5]

This particular case is an excellent example of a sinister matriarchal undercurrent, localized within a diocese. In the quotation, we are dealing with a number of classic esoteric symbols. The reference to hiding men in boxes is reminiscent of the Osirian mysteries. It retells of Osiris' betrayal and concealment within a box, subsequent to his mutilation and resurrection. Variations of the same myth are repeated in the legends of St. Patrick ridding Ireland of serpents (angelic beings), utilizing a casket (an ark).

Testimony from the Doge's court details sexual rites in propinquity to a sanctuary or a crypt (crib), followed with the exchange of placenta cakes. The sacrament outlined is equivocal to a Satanic Mass, conducted with the assistance of Masons, described cryptically as plumbers and plasterers.

The appellation 'plumber' refers to the Latin noun 'plumbum' (lead)[6] - the metal associated with the planet Saturn.[7] Occupation of the plumber is combined with a plasterer from the Greek term 'plasso' (to mould) - an alchemical expression, figurative of the transfiguration of lead into gold (Refer to Pope: Dunciad, See Chapter header quotation). Philologically, the Greek root 'plasso' is branched with 'plesso' (to strike), symbolic of angel 'manifestation' (Latin manus-festus, literally 'hand-hit'),[8] reciprocal to the virgin priestess and the eunuch.

Practices recorded from the Doge trial point to the covert worship of Saturn, originating from the Judaic and Greek mystery religions - an interior group allied to the worship and propagation of angelic beings. Leadership of Saturn's Ministry is shown in occultism as the 'virgin' (kore), unified with an angel or goat.

Necro-Sexual Magic. Isis is depicted as restoring Osiris' penis.
The imagery is probably coptic and works on the pun 'sarcophagus' (Greek sark-phagos)
'flesh-eating', connoting intercourse linked thematically to death and rebirth.

The 'kore' (virgin) priestess is an intermediary, sanctioned genetically through her 'menstrual blood' (the fire-star). The onset of the oracle's period is referred to as the 'Bath Kol' (the daughter of the voice) - attributed to the 'virgin's call'. The first traces of the pubescent blood, in Latin 'macula' (literally spot), refers to 'masca' (a type of witch). Her menstrual blood, the 'macula', is cultic of the red se'irim and describes the Immaculate Conception.

The monthly cycle of the priestess alludes to the mammal in conjunction with the 'red goat' (the se'irim) - a menstrual snake. A practitioner of the night and the underworld, the 'Bath Kol', is a bride of Saturn (Satan). Dressed in black, she is presented as a sorceress and a prostitute to the Dark Lord. Her offerings are conducted inside of the inner sanctum of the temple in alignment to the resurrection of the se'irim. Historically, the stained skin of the goat is hung in the Jewish tabernacle, later the Temple Sanctuary.

Masquerading as a 'eunuch', the 'se'irim' is clothed in 'human form' - cryptically a red goatskin - duplicated as the Aryan priest. The hide (hideous) of the goat is a motif of transfiguration, collated with the mammal and menstruation.

Astrologically, the goatskin is conjunct with the setting sun (Capricorn) and the immolation of the evening mystery meal.

Further analogy of the 'red goat' and the 'white priest' is determined in the Semitic language. The Hebrew word for (human skin) is 'or'[9] and is the same word as (light).[10] Identical wordplays regarding the homonym 'or' is evident in the Arabic noun 'lahm' (meat or flesh),[11] equivalent in Egyptian Arabic to the word 'lama' (shine).[12] Congruent, the pun is rendered in English as 'flesh and flash'.

'Lama' (shine) is used generically in Greek as 'lamia' classifying (a race of shape-shifting serpents), replicated as a 'drakon' (to flash). The appellation 'lamia' is adopted in Old English as (a witch), correlated with the 'virgin' otherwise (the houri).

The protagonist the 'houri' parallels the burning of the 'hostia' (victim). Comparisons with the Caucasian priesthood indicate the 'houri' is specified as a 'white virgin' - rendered in Persian as 'huri' and in the English corruption as 'whore'. Classification of the whore is a derivation from the pronoun 'her'.

In Arabic, 'houri' (virgin) is cognate with 'hur' (white), equivalent to 'hurr' (free).[13] The plural variant of 'hawra' (white) conjures the Syrian adjective 'hawra' (gazelle-like in the eyes) signifying 'beauty'. The reference is inimical of the Syrian noun 'haiya' (snake), consistent in Latin with the substantive 'horror'.

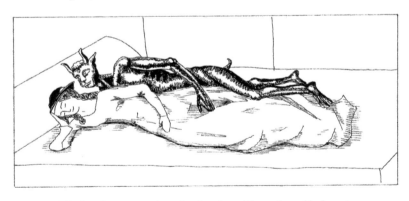

*Medieval representation of an incubus - Pictured as a black goat
the rapist is equivalent to a nocturnal angel equated with Saturn and darkness.*

The 'gazelle', demonstrated in this example, is reproduced as the 'goat', conceptualized as a 'hairy-snake', comparative in Greek to the God 'Pan', etymological to 'panic'. The emblem of the 'caper' further denotes the woman's sexual organs, relative to the Sabi priestcraft and the materialization of angels.

The namesake of the 'houri', denigrated in English as 'whore', is consistent with sexual union of the priestess Isis in combination with the solar God Amun, attributed with the setting sun and the crying eye.[14] The virgin's black menstrual blood interconnects with the nocturnal prostitute, subsequent to the transfiguration of the 'red goat' (the se'irim). Appearance of the se'irim reveals the masked caper, culminating with the mystery, sexualized as rebirth.

In the Greek traditions, the dancing goat is closely matched with 'basiliskos' (a serpent) and is cogent with 'basileus' (a king),[15] equivalent to 'baskanos' (a sorcerer).[16] According to the academic and linguist John M Allegro, the 'basilisk[os]' refers to 'womb blood' (menses), recorded by the classical scholar Pliny as 'Saturn's blood'.[17] In this particular example, Pliny communicates in riddles using veiled language for a very select audience. His reference to 'Saturn's blood' suggests the rendition 'basileus-iksor',[18] (sacred or divine-blood), punned with 'basiliskos' (a snake).[19] Symbolized as a red serpent, the 'basileus-iksor' is conjunct with the priestess' black menstrual blood. Articulation of 'Saturn's blood' infers the monarch in tandem to a daughter of Saturn the 'Bath Kol' (Greek kore), aligned to her tribute - the 'tragos' (a goat).

In conclusion, menstruation of the femme fatale portends to the 'basiliskos', demonstrated in the Roman lexicon. The noun 'monstrum' (a sign, miracle, wonder or portent)[20] delineates the 'monstrous' and 'menstruous'. 'Monstrum' in the original Latin has the additional meaning of (a monster)[21] and is a derivation of (a minister or servant). The titular minister comes from the Greek noun 'monasterion' (a monastery). 'Ministerial' is equivalent to 'mysterion' (a sacred secret), disclosed as the 'monstrum'.

In Ancient Greek, 'mysterion' is deduced from the verb 'musteion' (to close the eyes or the mouth),[22] implicit of the occult. According to P Kingsley:

> *"A beginner is called a 'mystae' which means 'eyes closed' and is the immediate root of the words 'mystery', and 'mysticism'."*[23]

By definition, the 'mysterion' is cogent with the 'mustes' (the initiate), modified in Latin as the 'minister'. The Classical Greek root of 'mystery' is traced back to the original hieroglyphic spelling 'myst' (the evening meal).

Cultic use of 'myst' signals a type of sacrament, proclaiming the worship of nocturnal angels, propositional to the priestess and the ejection of the firstborn heir.[24]

Central, the 'lady's (sitt) courtship with the 'satyr' expounds the ritual slaying of her male boy, equated with the incarnation of Jupiter - the twin of Saturn. The

Romans signified Jupiter with the colour 'white' - symbolic of the 'houri' and the incarnation of his son, Apollo. Depicted as the Sun God, Apollo's death is congruent to a 'concealed' votive (satr), conceptual to Saturn (darkness) and the close of the day (sat'atm).

1   Brewer Dictionary of Phrase & Fable, London, Cassell & Company, London 1954, p805 (Saturnian)

2   The tradition of the eunuch is historically provident within the Roman Byzantine Church of Constantinople (modern Istanbul).

3   Under the jurisdiction of the 'Witch Generals', many men were tortured and executed as warlocks.

4   The Goddess Maat in Egyptian custom extracts and weighs the Pharaoh's heart of sin, and is reminiscent of God's judgement within Christianity. In Islamic tradition, Gabriel removes Mohammed's heart and cleanses it of sin during a religious experience called the Night Journey. The Prophet is taken from Mecca to Jerusalem followed with a visit to heaven and is returned in the space of a single night.

5   John Cornwell: The Sunday Times Magazine, 16 January 2005, p23 (Stranger Than Fiction)

6   John C Traupman: The New College Latin & English Dictionary, Bantam 1988, p231

7   The Arabic name for a 'plumber' is (sabbak) and is a symbol of the 'Morning-Star' (Sabah-Kha), lateral to the crocodile God 'Sobek'.

8   The etymon 'manifestation' is from the Latin root 'manus-festus' literally (hand-hit).

9   Prolog: Pocket Bilingual Dictionary, English-Hebrew, Hebrew-English, Prolog 2003, p375

10 Ibid, p232

11 Hippocrene Concise Dictionary, English-Arabic, Arabic-English, Hippocrene 2005, p225

12 Ibid, p226

13 Ibid, p194

14 The crying eye signifies the mutilated eye, stylised as the White Crown of Osiris, covert to the ram deity Amun (See Appendix 6). Emblem of the Crown is matched with the 'houri' (virgin) priestess, relative to 'hawra' (gazelle-like in the eyes). This metaphor is replicated in Greek ritual as 'kore' (virgin) - a homonym of (pupil). The Syrian expression 'hawra' approximates in Greek to 'aniridia' (without iris), connoting demonic possession.

15 'Basiliskos' (serpent) - a signifier of the goat, parallels 'basileus' (a king). The equivalent play is adopted in the English alliteration prince, prance and pounce.

16 John M Allegro: The Sacred Mushroom and the Cross, A Study of the Nature and Origins of Christianity within the Fertility Cults of the Ancient Near East, Abacus 1973, p107

17 Ibid, p90

18 In Classical Greek, 'iksor or ichor' refers to (a deity's blood), and is distinct from 'haima' (human blood).

19 'Basileus-iksor' translated as (sacred or divine blood, literally King's-blood) is recorded in the Latin compound as (Sangrail), rendered 'Sang-rail' (Royal-blood), Old French 'Saint Graal' (the Holy Grail). 'Iksor' is punned with 'Hyksos', suggesting 'Christ' is traced from the bloodline of the 'Shepherd Kings'.

20 John C Traupman: The New College Latin & English Dictionary, Bantam 1988, p186

21 Ibid

22 Alan F. Alford: When the Gods Came Down, The Catastrophic Roots of Religion Revealed, New English Library, Hodder and Stoughton 2000, p10

23 Timothy Freke & Peter Gandy: The Jesus Mysteries, Was Jesus A Pagan God, Thorsons, 2000, p315, (Refer to Notes pp24-27).

24 The setting sun is emphatic of the priestess' menstrual cycle, coordinated with the angel in sync with the 'Harvest' (Shavuoth), tributary to the 's'baot' (host). A conjugal rite of passage, the rape of the matriarch delegates the 'Black Sabbath' and the veiled worship of 'Shabtay' (Saturn), conveyed through the sacrament - the firstborn.

30

Mysteries of Saturn

'And upon the water he brought brackishness... and upon the earth he let loose reptiles in corporeal form – and they copulated one with another – reptiles biting and poisonous – serpent and scorpion, venomous lizard, tortoise and frog, so that not so much as a needle's point on [the whole] earth remained free from creeping things...' [1]

Greater Bundahishn.

Oaths and veiled threats appertaining to the mysteries are centrifugal to the initiate, servant or priest. In Modern English, the concealed priestess is described as a 'minx' (a pert, sly or playful girl) - a 16th century word of unknown origin. On close analysis, 'minx' is a variation on the Latin adjective 'minaxacis' (threatening)[2] and is related to the English verb 'menace'. 'Minaxacis' original root is derived from the Hebrew action 'minkha' (to offer a sacrifice).[3]

These etymologies take us back to the priestess and her black dried menstrual blood, identified with the Bath Kol and Saturn. Her 'menses' elaborates the verb 'menace' from the Latin root 'minax' (to threaten),[4] offered in Hebrew as the 'minkha' (propitiation). Within the Roman mysteries, the 'minkha' is branched semantically with the adjective 'mimic' from the Greek 'mimikos', caricatured as the 'saturos' (a satyr). The mime artist is a 'female actress' (the mimae),[5] associated with fertility and copulation.

In Old Semitic, 'minkha' is extracted from the Hebrew word 'min' (sex), and 'kha' (star). In the hieroglyphic the spelling 'kha' informs 'khakha' (the starry firmament, canopy or constellation). The doubling or repetition of a singular word or term is used to indicate emphasis - in this case the plural noun. Circumstantial evidence suggests 'khakha' is an ancient name for (the milky way), obtained from 'kha' the radical for (a star). The Modern Arabic version of 'kha' (a star) is phonetically related to 'qa'a' (hall)[6] and indicates a 'dwelling place', located in the heavens, translated in the current idiom as (a mansion).

'Min-kha' is defined literally as (the sex-star),[7] relative to 'qa'a' (the abode) of angels, cognate in the Egyptian hieroglyphic with 'Kar' (a king, angel or hunter). He is incarnated as the Sun God 'Horus' (Kar), otherwise likened to the illumination of a 'star' (kha). In addition, the Old Semitic word 'kar(i)' (soldier, archaically a hunter) is interchangeable with 'ari', designated in Hebrew as (an Aryan).[8]

The specification 'min-kha' (the sex-star) resembles the cultic idiom 'fire-star' a name for menstrual blood. Practices assigned to the 'minkha' are descriptive of 'min-kar' (a sexual hunter or predator - the femme fatal). The 'minkha' offering is integral to eating and sexual intercourse, cognate with the 'minx', worded from 'minaxacis' the Roman adjective.

'Minaxacis' (threatening) annotates the following compound: 'Min' Latin (vermilion red or lead red) lists the heraldic colour, assigned to the menstrual blood of Saturn, reproduced as the 'votive' or the 'fire-star' (the minkha). Additionally, the Roman word 'min' (red) is a homonym of the word (threat),[9] synthesized with the masculine noun 'axis' (the heavens, the sky or the North Pole).[10] By definition, a priestess and guardian the 'minx' is a practitioner of ritualized violence, ordained through heaven.

The allomorph 'menace or minaxacis' is thus closely aligned in Latin to 'mensae' (a sacrificial table or altar) and 'mensis' (month),[11] connoting the menses blood. Ritualistically, the 'mensae' (altar) pertains to 'mons' (a mountain),[12] particularly equated to the worship of a 'mane' (a deified soul). Appearance of the 'mane' is manifested through the woman's blood, cognizant with the 'moon' and her cycle.

Represented as the communal 'host' (Latin 'hostia' - a victim or a sacrifice),[13] the 'hostia' describes 'haustus' (streams of blood),[14] diminutive from the Greek noun 'hustera' (womb),[15] correspondent with the serpent (host) and moon.

Kind permission to reproduce image by David Icke - Bridge of Love (see picture credits).
Depiction of the fire-star: The image is based upon a drawing by a survivor from a Satanic cult.
The woman's body doubles as a face the lactescent nipples equated with the crying eye.
Additionally the menstrual vagina is drawn as a bloodied mouth and features the 'double cross'
(betrayal) disclosing immolation of the firstborn.

A precursor to the fire-star, the red matriarch termed as a 'minx' determines a sacred marriage, inaugurated by divine insemination, concurrent with the disk or star (Venus and Sirus). Representation of the minx is delineated in the Egyptian mysteries as the Goddess Apophis (Apo-plesso).

Rebirth of the solar device, a sanguine serpent technically a menstruating eel, is modelled on the Egyptian and Greek 'mysteries' (mysterion). The 'mustes' (a minister or initiate) preserves the bloodline of the 'minx', the sangrail, within the 'monastery' (a monasterion) - originally a temple sanctuary. Covertly, the 'monastery' refers to a 'monster' and is compared to the 'palace', affiliated to 'palis' (a type of malevolent 'jinn').

Consort to the 'minx' is elaborated in the original Greek as the 'monakhos' literally (solitary), defined in Modern English as (monk). He is contracted to the 'monarkhes' (a king or monarch), intrinsic to the 'propitiatory' (the minka).

The 'minx' is registered ceremonially with the 'se'irim' - appellations of the 'basiliskos' (snake), accredited with 'basileus' (king). In the Roman mysteries, the minx corresponds to a priestess of Saturn. Solemn, the minx embodies the leaping goat the 'saltatrix' defined as (a dancing girl),[16] juxtaposed with her masculine counterpart the 'saltator' (a type of masked eunuch).[17] In turn, they specify the 'saltatio' (a type of sexual dance).[18]

Concealment of the neophytes' divine ancestry, the 'mimae' (actress), is confluent with the masked goat 'Saturn', diminutive of 'sitt' Arabic (a lady). Esoteric, the 'prancing' goat assonates 'prince', conceived as the fallen star Venus.

Christ's feet (bloodline) are placed upon the hairy fish - a symbol of the sanguine goat, synonymous with the human-angelic bloodline.

Worship of the horned God is assimilated with the 'basiliskos' (a serpent), pictured as the 'saltator' (a dancing goat), extensions of the 'capillatus' or 'hemitheoi' (half-divine). 'Basiliskos' Greek (a reptile) is deduced from 'base-skolex' (a stepping-worm)[19] and is kindred in Latin to 'serpentipedes'[20] (dragon footed).[21]

Both the Greek and Latin translations are probably sourced from the Arabic 'jinni' the 'pa-lis' (a sole licker). The walking serpent[22] designates the snake's offspring - symmetrical to the 'vestal virgin' and her 'genetic-footprint' (vestigium), sourced archaically from the Soter priesthood.

'Base-skolex' (a stepping-worm) records the 'Bacchic festivities of the eclipse' (bach-ekleipis). The celebration outlines the orgiastic rites of the 'maenads' (maiden), equated with the priestess' cycle, the fire-star. Expelled from her womb, the 'ambrosia' [Greek 'ambrotos' (immortal)] describes the food of the Gods, and is linked to the ingestion of menstrual blood, celebratory of the sanguine goat. Ritual consumption of the 'ambrosia' is cogent with the 'sacred blood [of the] king' (the basileus-iksor), enacted in the Greek mysteries as the blood of 'Dionysus' (Christ).

To summarise, the 'base-skolex' (a stepping-worm) is joined with the 'saltatrix' or 'saltator' - thematic of a 'dancer', or 'satyr'. The prancing goat is collective of the Soter priests, previously referred to in Chapter 23 Sailors Goats and Salt. The 'Soter' is known commonly in Latin as the 'Sodalis' fraternity (a secret society), defined as (a priestly college).[23] They represent their group with 'salt', pedagogic of a 'se'irim or goat'. 'Salt' in Modern English connotes 'sad and sadism', twinned with 'assault and assailant' - metaphors of the 'angel or reaper'.

The Latin noun 'sal' (salt) quotes the Semitic verb 'zar' (to visit), explicit of the 'akh zauri' (the brothers of light),[24] consistent with (the illuminati), signified with the 'cobra' - (a Theban). Device of the hooded seraph, a horned dragon symbolizes the 'yale' (a type of fawn), depicted as the fornicator.

Epithet of the 'akh zauri' quotes a human angelic fellowship, epitomized through the goat, and partnered with the woman's 'sexual organs' (the saltus).[25] Equated with the 'saltatrix' (a dancing girl), her genitals are relative to 'saltus' (to leap),[26] implicit of intercourse and rape. Liturgically, the bounding deity ritualizes the sprinkling of salt (semen), catalogued with the goat (a demigod or angel) equated with the Sodi priest.

Descended from the priesthood of Moses, the 'Sodi' Latin 'Sodalis' trace their lineage from the Kingdom of 'Sodom' and take their name from the Hebrew word 'sodi' (occult),[27] diminutive of the noun 'sod' (secret).[28] Variations of the noun 'sod' are extrapolated from the Arabic word 'sidr' or 'sedr' anatomically (the chest),[29] esoteric of the Levites - Hebrew 'lev' (heart).[30] 'Sidr' informs the

Latin root 'cedere' (to kill, concede, yield or submit), ritualistically the removal of the heart a practice correlated with the Levite priesthood. A clerical order its membership is registered in Greek with the 'Cardinal' desiginating 'kardia' (heart).

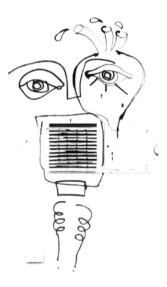

Heart Graffiti Munster Switzerland: Heart emblem of the Levite priesthood Greek Cardinal.
Note both the heart and vagina are drawn with anatomical exactitude
and is similar to the Satanic drawing reproduced earlier in the chapter.

Denomination of the Greek 'Soter', Semitic 'Sodi', describes 'sid' the Arabic noun for (a gentleman).[31] Conventionally, the 'sid' is joined sexually with the 'saltatrix' (a female dancer), akin to her 'caper' (the goat) - the 'saltatio'. Etymologically, the compound 'salta-trix' is a Latinization of the Arabic compound 'sitt' (a lady)[32] and 'taq' (to suffer),[33] relative to 'tragedy', in Greek 'tragos' (a goat). The 'sit-taq' or 'saltatrix' is represented as the widow, correlated in Greek with the 'Soter' and their mascot the 'satyr' - a scapegoat.

Offshoots of the Soter are evident in the Roman priesthood the Sodalis or Sodalit, affiliated to the 'Sali' [an organization of twelve priests (tribes) dedicated to Mars (Adam)]. The plural masculine noun 'Sali' is derived from 'salio' the intransitive verb (to jump, leap or dance)[34] and appertains to the adjective 'salacis' (lustful, salacious or provocative).[35]

The Latin verb in its older form is deduced from the Arabic etymon 'salla' (to pray)[36] and 'sallim' (to submit or surrender),[37] connoting sexual submission, descriptive of the covenant, identified with angelic intercourse.

Members of the Sali priesthood carry the mascot of the ram or goat - a symbol of sexual virility, equated with the leaping satyr. The dancing goat signifies the sprinkling of semen and 'menstrual blood - the fire-star' (light), offered in gesture to the Goddess of the setting sun in situ to the mystery (communion). Veneration of the goat commemorates the evening sacrament in relation to the worship of the nocturne Saturn.

In the Judaic priesthood, the appellation 'Sali' is translated as 'makol' (to dance)[38] - the namesake of 'Michael - the Angel of War' figured as the 'Lord of the Dance'. His epithet is correlated with 'me'kir' (price)[39] and 'mekher' (sale),[40] idiomatic of redemption, orientated in Islamic tradition to the Shrine of Mecca. Ostensibly, propitiations of the goat suggest redemption of the ram and its equation with Mars - a signifier of Michael.

A reaper Michael carries 'magal' (a scythe),[41] symbols of the 'Maga' (Persian priesthood), elemental to the lunar crescent and magic. The 'magal' is often combined with 'maqab' (a sacrificial hammer), disclosing the English and French adjective 'macabre' of unknown etymology.[42] Cultic, the device of the hammer and scythe are appropriated later as symbols of Russia, and reflect the Arabic noun 'markab' (a ship),[43] associated with aggression, historical to the flood and crescent.

Apocalyptic literature describes Michael as the Angel of War - a figure of attrition, specific to the destruction of Mars, identified with Venus. Allies of Michael are affiliated with the jumping goat (human-angelic), reproduced as an 'exile, angel or migrant'. Religiously, the death and resurrection of the scapegoat is cognate with the destruction of Mars and the recreation of life on earth.

Regeneration of human progeny theologically mirrors the 'Passion' of Christ (Latin Suffer), featured as the bounding 'goat' (Greek tragos), doctrinal to the resurrection of the soul. Incarnation of the goat's double marks the renting of the temple veil (a goat skin), symmetrical with rebirth and atonement. Solar in nature, the transformation of the caper is staged as the dance, cognizant with the mystery play. Its enactment is elaborated in the Christian hymn, quoted below:

'Dance Dance wherever you may be
I am the Lord of the Dance said he
And I lead you all wherever you may be
And I lead you all in the dance said he'.[44]

To conclude, 'the Lord of the Dance' is a transgender priest and a worshipper of nocturnal angels - referred to as the satyr or goat! The satyr's shaggy 'hair' is an abstraction of the mammal priestess (human), unified with the dragon and sovereign. Dread-locks within the craft symbolize the 'hairy' snake (the capillatus). Epigraphically, platted hair denotes loss or 'mourning' (ikb),[45] associated with the human angelic lineage, represented as the goat or satyr.[46]

Reaper Cutting Hair
The virgin's tribute reflects the olive branch - symbolic of submission embodied as the covenant (government). A dual signifier of peace, the 'olive branch' (Arabic 'zaitan') is a pun on the reptile 'Satan'. Here the reaper cuts the girl's hair (heir) - an act equated with sacrificial loss of the firstborn.

Figurative, the Arabic adjective 'sattar' (concealed) refers to the 'satyr' in relation to the 'lady' (sitt),[47] conjunct with the propitiation of the firstborn, memorialized as the Sabbath and the 'host' (s'baot). Materialization of the 's'baot or tsabaoth', otherwise the satyr, is unified with the 'Bride of Saturn' - a matriarchal priesthood of Aryan (Alien) extraction.

An initiate of Saturn, the bride celebrates the rebirth of Sirius (the Sun) through the 'evening meal', defined as the 'mystery' or Sabbath. Regeneration of Sirius emblazons the rising star Venus - a Crescent. Ascended, the star's crescent parallels the horned moon, conceptual to the mortal ram 'Aries', antecedent to the destruction of Mars. The demise of the ram (Adam), designates the fallen serpent and its double - the goat.[48]

Appearance of the red hairy goat personifies the mammal priestess - a bloodline homogenized with the horned snake - a fallen angel, the 'se'irim'. Association between the 'flashing' deity a 'dragon' is juxtaposed with the goat and 'horn' demonstrated in the Hebrew lexicon. The Semitic noun 'keren' (horn)[49] is a homonym of 'koren' (radiant),[50] consistent with 'kohen' (priest)[51] and 'kur'an' (recitation).[52]

Pharaonic symbolism identifies the double horn with the dual feather, allegoric of the risen lamb Amun,[53] covert to necromancy (Refer to Chapter 17 Hunefer Book of the Dead). Amun's death and resurrection is correlated with the nocturnal 'priesthood' (komer), signified with the 'moon' (qamar), idiomatic of the 'Western nation' (Aamu).

Depiction of the menstrual star Venus, secured between the lunar horns, represents the ovaries (moon), conceptual to rebirth[54] and flashing. The setting of the sun, a simile of ejaculation, portends to the incarnation (transfiguration) of a God, deified as the king or spitting cobra - the Morning Star.

Ascended, the 'cobra' annotates the 'anguigena' (a Theban),[55] termed additionally as (the offspring of the dragon).[56] Radiant, the snake's materialized form is interchangeable with a 'shining deity', explicit of the 'brothers of light' (the Illuminati), referential to the horned dragon, defined as an 'alien, angel or sailor'.

Restoration of God, figurative of a Royal snake (a Theban), promulgates the sacrificial ram, stylized as the 'cornucopia' (the horn of plenty), associated with the cup and Grail. Paralleled to the basket of offering, the Grail is cogent with the womb and phallus, identified with blood and light. Symbolized as the menstrual star of rebirth, the renewal of Venus is apportioned to the lunar crown, addendum to the serpent and his mistress, the fire-star.

Mixed, the woman's offspring is iconic of the Royal lineage, reproduced as human-angelic - astrologically the chimera. Political union between God and man determines a 'theocracy' - from the Greek compound 'theos' (God) and 'krasis' (mingling), subject to 'thearkhia' (God's rule). Archaically, 'theos' (God) is a derivation of 'theaomai' (to behold), cognizant with the watcher, angel or dragon.[57]

The Greek terminology 'theoskrasis' is sourced earlier from the Hebrew lexicon 'shilton' (government),[58] cognate with 'Shatan', (literally opposition) and his ministerial line - the 'Sultan'. Royal descent from the 'Sultan' philologically specifies the 'Sodalis' priesthood - also known as the 'Saudi' lineage (literally the 'Black' Nobility - the 'sauda').

Disclosed through a 'secret' (sod) covenant of 'nobles' (sid),[59] the Saudi fraternity is engaged to the Black (Shadow) Church, denominational of Satan (Saturn) and his fallen angels - the 's'baot'. A renegade group of demigods, the host interconnects with the 'Black Jesuit' priesthood, sourced exclusively

The Murder of Reality

from the 'Black Nobility' (Saudi), autocratic of 'Theban' (Syrian) membership. A closed and select fraternity, its patrons are signified with the Royal ram (Amun). Headed under the 'Black Pope' and his consort the 'Black Madonna' Greek (kore), the order is aligned to 'Saturn' (Hebrew Shabtay) - a matriarchal covenant (convent), elaborated in the next chapter.

1 Professor R C.Zaehner: The Dawn and Twilight of Zoroastrianism, Weidenfeld & Nicholson, 1975, p262
2 John C Traupman: The New College Latin & English Dictionary, Bantam, 1988, p183
3 Prolog: Pocket Bilingual Dictionary, English-Hebrew Hebrew-English, Prolog, p278
4 John C Traupman: The New College Latin & English Dictionary, Bantam, 1988, p183
5 Ibid
6 Hippocrene Concise Dictionary, English-Arabic, Arabic-English, Hippocrene, 2005, p257
7 Offering of the 'minkha' (sacrifice) is similar in meaning to the Akkadian verb 'dinn' (to give), cognate in the Modern Arabic with 'din' (religion) and 'djinn' (serpent). The Arabic noun 'din' (religion) originally (to give) connoted a sexual offering, expressed in the Hebrew etymon 'adina' (sensual or subtle). Both 'adina' and 'minkha' are presented as sexual propitiations, connoting deity materialization, registered with the fire-star. 'Minkha' in the original Semitic reads as a possible compound on 'min-ka', 'min-kol' and 'min-kar' approximate to (a sexual double), coalescent with (sexual eating) identified with the (hunt).
8 Prolog: Pocket Bilingual Dictionary, English-Hebrew Hebrew-English, Prolog, p29
9 John C Traupman: The New College Latin & English Dictionary, Bantam, 1988, p184
10 Ibid, p28
11 Ibid, p181
12 Ibid, p186
13 Ibid, p133
14 Ibid, p130
15 The Latin term 'hostia' (sacrifice), relative to the Greek noun 'hustera' (womb), suggests a connection with the Bacchic ceremonies and the ingestion of 'placenta cakes', depicted in the outer mysteries as 'bread'. Symbolism of the 'placenta cakes' connotes the 'offering of the firstborn'.
16 John C Traupman: The New College Latin & English Dictionary, Bantam, 1988, p276
17 Ibid
18 Ibid
19 'Base' (to step) is a pun on the Latin stem 'basis' (a foundation) and 'basiare' (to kiss) - descriptions of the serpent equated with the six foundations (days) of creation.
20 'Serpentipedes' is rendered alternatively in Latin as 'draconiopides' (a walking or bipedal dragon), and is identical in Greek to the 'base-skolex' (a stepping-worm).
21 John C Traupman: The New College Latin & English Dictionary, Bantam Books, 1988, p285
22 The etymon 'serpere' (to crawl or creep) is cogent with 'serpens' (the snake), signified with 'septem' the adjective (seven). Further, the reptile is depicted as a 'sepelire' (a destroy-er). Relationship between seven and ruin, comparative to the snake, is demonstrated in the Semitic lexicon. 'Shiva' the homonym (to mourn) is used as the number 'sheva' or shiv'a' (seven) - a figure cognizant with the 'host' (the saba, alternatively s'baot or tsabaoth).
23 John C Traupman: The New College Latin & English Dictionary, Bantam Books, 1988, p290
24 'Akh zari' (a brother of an alien) in English is punned with 'exile' (Latin exsilium or exilium) - similes of an 'angel', identified with the 'Exodus and Nomad'.
25 John C Traupman: The New College Latin & English Dictionary, Bantam Books, 1988, p276

26 Ibid

27 Prolog: Pocket Bilingual Dictionary, English-Hebrew-Hebrew-English, Prolog, 2003, p277

28 Ibid, p360

29 Hippocrene English-Arabic, Arabic-English Dictionary, Hippocrene, New York, 2005, p26

30 Prolog: Pocket Bilingual Dictionary, English-Hebrew-Hebrew-English, Prolog, 2003, p183 [The Hebrew etymon 'lev' (a heart) informs the English word (love)].

31 Hippocrene Concise Dictionary, English-Arabic, Arabic-English, Hippocrene, 2005, p52

32 Ibid, p65

33 Ibid, p121

34 John C Traupman: The New College Latin & English Dictionary, Bantam, 1988, p276

35 Ibid

36 Hippocrene Concise Dictionary, English-Arabic, Arabic-English, Hippocrene, 2005, p94

37 Ibid, 278

38 Prolog English-Hebrew & Hebrew-English Dictionary, Completely Transliterated, Prolog, 2003, p97

39 Ibid, p315

40 Ibid, p353

41 Ibid, p359

42 The name 'Russia' is from the Medieval Latin 'Russianus' extracted from 'russus' (red), a derivation of the Hebrew noun 'resha' (evil). The Latin stem 'rus' denotes (the countryside or fields), identified with a 'reaper'.

43 Hippocrene Concise Dictionary, English-Arabic, Arabic-English, Hippocrene, 2005, p111

44 Lyrics written by Sydney Carter.

45 Bridget McDermott: Decoding Egyptian Hieroglyphs, Duncan Baird Publishers, London, 2001, p169 (Sign List ikb) - Evidence, taken from the Hebrew verbal stem, suggests the hieroglyph 'ikb' (to mourn) is rendered in its original and correct form as 'le'hit'abel' (to-mourn) - the 'k' of 'ikb' pronounced as a guttural 'h' rather than a 'k'.

46 The 'lock of hair' is symmetrical to the 'lock and key' - emblems of the snake and monarch.

47 Hippocrene Concise Dictionary, English-Arabic, Arabic-English, Hippocrene, 2005, p65

48 The Saturn priesthood is cognizant with darkness and strife, confluent with the worship of hidden stars, covert both to Sirius and its sister the Pleiades.

49 Prolog, Pocket Bilingual Dictionary, English-Hebrew, Hebrew-English, Prolog, 2003, p191

50 Ibid, p326

51 Ibid, p315

52 The Muslim Holy book 'Koran', Arabic 'Kur'an' (recitation), is obtained from the root 'kara'a' (to read). In the Old Semitic, 'Kur-An' signifies (the Mountain [of] Heaven), conceptually an 'altar' - a signifier equated with the oracular priestess and the oral tradition.

53 Appropriation of the Hebrew noun 'keren' (a horn or radiant) informs the Latin etymon 'cornu' (horn), interchangeable with 'coruscare' the intransitive verb (to glitter). 'Cornu' is matched in the Roman language with 'corona' (crown), identical to 'corona' (halo).

54 Written and linguistic evidence show an arcane belief that the 'Aamu' Ancient Akkadian (the Westerners Hebrew the Emori) originated from the receptacle of the moon, sourced earlier from Mars and the Pleiades. The lunar device is a symbol of the Caucasian Priesthood (Western Freemasonry), sworn in allegiance to the nocturnal angel (Sirius) - an idea developed later in this book.

55 John C Traupman: The New College Latin & English Dictionary, Bantam 1988, p15

56 Ibid

57 The system of governance split between the Upper and Lower House as remained unchanged for thousands of years, and is founded archaically upon a contract between men and 'angels' (Shatani).

58 Prolog, Pocket Bilingual Dictionary, English-Hebrew, Hebrew-English, Prolog, 2003, p172

59 Hippocrene Concise Dictionary, English-Arabic, Arabic-English, Hippocrene 2005, p288 'Sid' is rendered from the Arabic word for (a gentleman). I have translated the noun here contextually as a 'noble', as the word 'sid' is related to 'sed' (a hunter). The English compound 'Gentle-man', although technically correct, has a slightly different connotation semantically from the Arabic classification 'sid'.

31

The Priestess of Saturn

'Merlin was the son of no mortal father, but of an Incubus; one of a class of beings not absolutely wicked, but far from good, who inhabit the regions of the air'.[1]
Bullfinch: Age of Chivalry, Pt. i, Ch. iii

'As part of their ambition to rule the world, the dark forces of the demon realm seek to mix their own blood with that of the Royal family'.
Ultimate Ghost & Goblins, The Video Game, Capcom 2006 (PSP)

Saturn is diagnostic of an angel of the night, and marks the 'neophyte' (newly planted), represented as the bride, equated with the 'host' (the s'baot) in relation to the 'harvest' (sabu'ot). Recollection of the reaper and the harvest cycles commence during the Sabbath - a festival adjunct with Saturn. Veneration of Saturn accompanies satiation, achieved through blood and sexual offerings. 'Satiation' etymologically is derived from 'Saturn' and is evident in the Semitic languages. The Arabic root 'shab'an' (satiated)[2] is contrasted with 'Shabtay' (Saturn).[3]

'Shabtay' originally described a 'people or a nation', preserved in the Modern Arabic stem (sha'b),[4] archaic to the 'Sabian' priesthood. Denomination of the 'Sabian or sha'b' trace their heritage from the 'star' (saba), discursive of the 'morning' (sabah) and the 'period of mourning' (shiva). The Sabians reproduce themselves numerically as the figure 'seven' (Hebrew sheva - Arabic sab'a).

The 'sha'b' (nation-hood) is grouped in the Syrian vocabulary with 'shabah' (resemblance), characterized as 'saba(h)' (a star) and 'satr' (concealed). The workings of the 'sha'b' (people) by implication are secret. 'Sha'b' informs the Latin appellation 'satus' (race, stock or seed), philological to Saturn, paternal to the Sodalist and Sabian priesthood. Structurally, the Semitic stem 'sha'b' (a nation), Latin 'satus' (race), is rendered via a complex series of switches with the consonant 'b', illustrated below.

The allomorph 'b' is interchangeable in the Semitic languages with the 'v' morpheme, related in European phonology to the letter 'f'. The letter 'v' or 'f' in this example has morphed phonetically into a 'th' or 'd' sound, transliterated as a 't'. The Latin rendition 'satus' suggests that 'sha'b' has passed into Latin via an intermediary language that is not Semitic - possibly Greek. Closely related the terms 's(h)a'b' and 'satus' are correlated in Arabic with the etymon 'sattar' (hidden), reversed in Persian as the noun 'sitarah' (star).[5] 'Sitarah's relationship to the Old Arabic radical 'saba' and 'sattar' suggests a star or cluster that is not seen from the earth and is veiled from sight.

The Indo-Semitic lexicon of 'sattar' and 'satr' (to hide) is cogent with star iconography. Symbolism of the 'saba' (star) conveys 'sha'b or satus' (a hidden race, nation or stock), identified esoterically in Hebrew with 'tsvi' (a gazelle). An emblem of the goat, the gazelle, is shared with the 's'baot' variously the 'tsabaoth' (host) and the 'Sabi' priestcraft. Symbol of the goat articulates 'Saturn' and the descendents of the fallen angel 'Satan' - a group of demigods traced historically from the Royal lineage of the 'Sultan'. His sacred birthright is administered through 'shilton' (government) - a name taken after the archangel 'Satan'.

The epithet 'Satan' translates as (an adversary or an opponent). His cognomen is used in early Hebrew to mark a 'political party', authorized through a bi-partied system. The Semitic derivation of 'Satan' is consistent with the stem 'setam' (to hate, oppose or animosity) and is from the Egyptian root 'shetam' (to fight or revile).[6]

In the Persian language, the designation 'Satan' suggests 'sitan' (to seize, take or captivate)[7] from the Hindu word 'satana' (to tease, vex, trouble, harm, grieve or harass).[8] Both 'sitan' and 'satana' are contiguous with the reptile as a rapist or pillager, and informs the Persian composite 'jan sitan' (to take life or to kill).[9]

The configuration 'jan sitan' is deduced from 'Jann', referred to in Persian literature as (the patriarch of the djinn). Structurally 'Jann's name proceeds from the Sanskrit title 'Jina' (a conqueror), explicit of a 'reptile or plunderer', comparative of 'djen' (a serpent or worm). 'Jann's appellation is preserved in the Arabic and Greek etymon 'jins' and 'gen', respectively (sex)[10] and (origin), connoting the offspring of the 'djinn'. Medieval lore signifies the dragon as a rapist, betrothed to the maiden - a theme adopted in the mythology of China and Japan. In the Sino languages, the stem 'gen' is picked up in the Japanese noun 'gen'in' (cause, source or origin)[11] and 'jin' (person).

The dragon's hidden nature is prototypical of Saturn - the personification of conflict. In Egyptian mythology, 'Saturn and Satan' are manifestations of the fallen deity 'Seth' the Hebrew word for (a foundation), encountered in the 'creation' epics outlined in Genesis Chapter 1. The quotation 'Berashith' (the six foundations) record the 'six days of creation', allied to the 'six planets', iconic of the architect and temple - Refer to Chapter 26 The Six Foundations.

Reflected in Masonic symbolism, the foundation stone is laid ritualistically in the temple or Senate - a monument of the fallen angel. Biblically the protagonist 'Seth' (foundation) describes Adam and Eve's third son, born after Abel's murder. A common ancestor, Seth is related to Noah and 'Ham' (Aamu or Hyksos). 'Seth's alternative appellation 'Set' is acquired from the Egyptian verb 'set' (to shoot),[12] theoretical to the Persian adjective 'sitan' (seize), conceptual to a 'despoiler' or 'rapist'.

Drawn from the Arabic root 'sed' (to hunt) and 'sid' (a gentleman),[13] 'Set' implies a noble bloodline, extracted from the 'Saudi or Sodi' fraternity, original to Osiris. Read cryptically, 'Set's epithet records 'sed' (a hunter) and is significant, as the title is shared by his nemesis 'Horus' - a name transliterated from the Sumerian glyph 'Kar' (a hunter, angel or king). Philologically, Seth, Set, Satan and Shatan are grouped with strife and conflict, evident in the Egyptian dialect.

In the hieroglyphs, the verbal stem 'set' (to shoot) informs the noun 'sft' (sword), pronounced according to Egyptologists as 'sefet'.[14] Epigraphic evidence suggests the correct rendition of 'sword' is transcribed as 'saif' or 'sef'[15] found in the Modern Arabic spelling. Phonetically, 'sef' (a sword) is an early extraction from the verb 'sed(th)' (to hunt). The transliteration 'sefet' by 19th century French scholars is shown in this example to be redundant and furthermore inaccurate!

Jean-Francois Champollion, French academic who cracked the 'Rosetta (Rose) Stone' and was the first to 'read' the hieroglyphs. He is shown concealing his hand - a Masonic signal referred to as the 'hidden hand'. The Rosetta tablet was written in Greek, Coptic and Hieroglyphic - its authenticity is questionable. The author prefers to call it the 'Roswell (Rose) Stone' after the crashed UFO. It is to be noted that the priesthood controls all sides of information both 'mainstream' and 'alternative'.

Traditionally, Seth is represented as carrying a spear, linked to symbols of hunting, potency and sexual magic. Hieroglyphically, the 'arrow' glyph written falsely by academics as 'sn' is rendered correctly as 'sahm' from the Arabic.[16] In the pharaonic language, the arrow a phallus is used to indicate sexual words as found in the late Egyptian glyph 'sn' (a kiss),[17] rendered more probably as 'nsk', contained in the Hebrew etymon 'ne'shika'.[18]

Insignia of Seth's arrow is borrowed in the Roman mystery school as Cupid, the God of Love. Cupid traditionally is depicted as a youth - the embodiment of 'sexual love' (eros), and is duplicated through rites, assented to the newborn heir. Observance of the firstborn sacrament enumerates the covenant and the votive, symbolized as the bow and arrow celestial to the rainbow.

The word 'arrow' (Arabic sahm) is referential to 'peace or submission' (salaam), idioms descriptive of the salt covenant.[19] Relationship between 'sahm' and 'salaam' are mutual also in Anglo symbolism. In English, the plural noun 'arrows' elicits the pun 'Aries' (the ram). The horned mascot is a symbol of 'Mars' (Ma'adim), symptomatic of war and the 'host' (the s'baot). Mythological stories document the seismic destruction of Mars - a feature recurrent within the framework of the Sodalist fraternity. This myth is sourced from the offspring of Adam, recognizant with the red planet.

Biblically, 'sahm' (an arrow) is a play on the Greek word 'psalmos', identical in the Old Testament to the Book of 'Psalms'. The Hellenistic term Psalms denotes a song, accompanied by a 'psalterion' (a type of stringed instrument).[20] Cultic, the 'psalterion' is associated with the 'Soter' (Sodalist) priesthood in conjunction with the 'goat' and 'satyr'. 'Psalms' technically is a translation from the Hebrew word 'tehillim' (praises),[21] indicative of 'tale' (a sacrificial lamb), sentient of a child or substitute.

The arrow is a signifier, aligned to the votive and sword cognate with the anointing of a king, featured omnipotently as a 'hunter' [Kar or Sed]. The sovereign's dual nature is represented as Horus (Kar) and Seth (Sed), classified ritualistically with the singing cherubim (the host) - a sword carrier.

Analogous to the covenant, the Arabic noun 'sef' (a sword) is cognate with the Egyptian word 'sefet' (anointing oil)[22] from the verb (to anoint).[23] 'Sefet' is yet another dubious transliteration proposed by academia. Scholars have extracted the verbal stem from the Semitic root 'shabareth' or 'savaret' (a river).[24]

It is noted by the author on close analysis that the Arabic word 'zet' (oil)[25] is a closer phonological match than the awkward transliteration 'sefet' (sft) proposed by Egyptologists. Additionally, 'zet' puns with the etymon 'sed' (cryptically 'z') the verb (to hunt), indicating an 'anointed king' or 'angel', depicted as the hunter or dragon (Satan). Linguistically, 'sed' is mirrored anagrammatically with the deity 'Seth', recorded in the hieroglyphic sign list. Conceptually, 'Sed' (the hunter) is matched religiously with the crocodile God (Sobek) - its 'fat' (zet) used to anoint the king, equated theoretically with the 'Morning star' (Sabah-Kha).

Judaic reference to the 'anointed one' (the Messiah) evokes a 'hunter', titular of an 'angel or king', correlated with the 'reaper'. He is described in the Arab traditions as 'naga' (the saviour) - a polyform title denoting (the smiter). The English noun 'saviour' (Latin salvare) is consistent with the Arabic noun 'saif or sef' (a sword), cogent in English with the noun 'safe and save'. The sword in Arabic lore discloses the Hebrew word 'save'a' (satiated),[26] constant philologically with 'shabtay' (Saturn).

Virgin Mary, Einsiedeln Switzerland: The saint rests her feet on the crescent and dragon, esoteric of the reptile's bloodline (Refer to Genesis 3:14-15). The quotation reads: 'I will put enmity between you [the serpent] and the woman, and between your offspring and hers'. It should be emphasized the Biblical citation clearly states the snake is an 'animal', whose progeny records a race of physical beings.

In Islamic and apocalyptic traditions, the 'saviour' or 'Messiah' is thus portrayed as a carrier of a sword - a device highlighted in the Biblical tradition. Recounted in the Gospels, Jesus' father is named as 'Joseph' and is a pun on the Arabic phrase 'Jah-sef or Yah-sef' (God's-sword). The Messiah is depicted as the son of a 'carpenter' from the Aramaic (nagar).

The titular 'nagar' (a carpenter), i.e. a Mason, connotes 'naga' (the saviour or smiter), personified in Judaic custom as 'Noga' (Venus). The appearance of the 'Morning Star' otherwise 'Lucifer' (Lux-ferre) describes the 'Messiah', visualised as the crocodile or dragon. A duplicitous and enigmatic figure, the Messiah is paired symbolically with the crescent sword, sacerdotal to the worship of Yahweh.

The lunar horn (a sword) marks the covenant literally (the foundation) of the priesthood. Its curving arch incorporates the 'rainbow' (keshet) - an emblem of the 'longbow' (keshet). Symbolism of the bow is analogous to war and the 'submission' of man (slm), contiguous with Satan (Saturn) and his fallen angels.

Historically, the rainbow recounts the diluvial annihilation of Adam (Genesis 9: 12-15), subsequent to his deliverance conceptual to the moon and host. The theme of strive and conflict is detailed in the mythology of Seth.

Satanic Graffiti, Munster Switzerland
Includes a horned God (Seth) replete with spear and raincloud. Drawing accompanied with the pun 'Give mother earth a massage (message) peace off (piss off)'. Note tree in background is drawn as a lung and includes the anatomic structures the bronchiole and alveoli.

Worship of Seth is traced from Assyria and Babylon. 'Seth's lineage outlines the epithet 'shahid' (a witness or martyr)[27] - an appellation of the watcher in succession to the firstborn. Seth's phallic emblem, the spear or arrow, indicates a fertility God, associated with the worship of nocturnal angels and the planet Saturn. A leaping deity equated with the rapist (a reptile), the fish-goat is bound magically to the 'woman's sexual organs' (saltus), cognate with the 'psalterion' (a type of stringed instrument) - ceremonial to the 'bride of Saturn'.

Within the Chaldean language, 'Saturn' is written, according to academics, with the stem 'stur'[28] - a derivation of the Arabic word 'satr' (hidden). 'Satr' in particular corresponds with the earlier Sumerian root 'sha-tur' or 'sa-tur' (the womb).[29] Unequivocally, the Sumerian tongue can be traced back to the Indo-European languages - a view contrary to modern scholarship, but is clearly demonstrated in the following examples.

The Sumerian compound 'sha-tur' (womb)[30] is reminiscent of the Sanskrit noun 'sati' (a chaste or virtuous woman). She is reproduced in Arabic lore as 'sha'al turs' (the burning shield)[31] - a protected bloodline,[32] classified with the saviour - a figure of war. The heraldic shield signifies chastity or concealment, conveyed as the priestess' 'sexual organs' (sha-tur). The lexicology of 'sha-tur' is rendered in Latin informally as 'saltus' (a cunt)[33] and is a philological variation of the goat, angel or suttee (sati) - exponents of sorcery and fecundity. The motif of the shield thus signifies the host[34] and its conquest or 'satiation' of the 'sati'.

Etymons describing the 'hidden' (satr) bloodline of the goat (satyr) are codependent within Sanskrit of the title 'sati' (a wife) from 'sat' (good). The Indo-European designation 'sati' is rendered in Latin as 'satae' (a daughter), Arabic 'sitt' (a lady).[35] Her appellation delineates an obscured lineage, betrothed to Saturn in succession to the gathering of the crop, cognizant with the virgin.

Esoteric, the analogy in Latin is 'satae' (a daughter), 'satias' (satiety) and 'sata' (crops).[36] Gathering of the crop is a motif of the 'reaper', accorded to the 'snake'. 'Sata' (crops) is traced from the Hindu word 'sattu' (a type of Barley paste).[37] In the Semitic languages, 'sata and sattu' enunciate the 'harvest' (sabu'ot), aligned to the 'Sabbath' and the 'host' (s'baot). The conqueror or victor is distinguished as the 'reptile' (a rapist or reaper).

Kind permission to reproduce image by David Icke - Bridge of Love (see picture credits).
The image is based upon a drawing made by a survivor of a Satanic cult. A depiction of the shield of Saturn, the 'four' stripes (Arabic arb'a) is a pun on 'abu and harb' (the father of war - Satan). 'Arb'a' etymologically is also related to 'rabi' (fourth) - cognate with 'rarb' (west) symbolic of the Rabbinical priesthood e.g. (the Western Rites of Freemasonry). The 'two' (Arabic tintain) headed dragon is cryptic of the Greek appellation 'Titan' denoting 'Teitan' (Satan).

The 'hidden' (satr) 'daughter' (satae), invokes the 'Sabbath' and is a covert proclamation of the priestess, married to the 'host' Hebrew (s'baot). Her union is correlated with the 'harvest' (sabu'ot) and the 'Sabbath'. The 'sati' theoretically describes the 'mistress' of 'Saturn' (Shabtay). Obscured, her progeny elicits a 'concealed' (satr) bloodline, concurrent with the dragon and goat (satyr).

Listed in the Hindu language, the stem 'sat' (good) additionally designates the number (seven) - the priestly number of the Sabian, recorded in the Arabic language as 's'hab' (nation), equivalent in Latin to 'satus' (race). The Indo stem 'sat' is employed as the adjective (true, right, actual or real)[38] - attributes accorded to the 'devoted wife' (sati). Ritualistically, her unerring love is displayed in death. The 'sati' (chaste or faithful wife) categorizes 'a woman who burns herself on the funeral pyre of her husband'.[39] In a circuitous fashion, death of the 'sati' specifies a tribute to the seventh planet 'Saturn' and the celebration of the 'Sabbath'. Demise of the 'sati' ordains a type of votive, demonstrated semantically as 'sat' (good) and 'sati' (self sacrifice) - a cognate of 'right and rite' or 'proper and propitiation'.

Numerically 'sat' (seven) extols 'sati' - a type of devotional sacrifice, comparable in the Semitic languages to 'sheva' (seven) and 'shiva' (mourning), cognizant with the 'Sabbath'. The Semitic word 'shiva' is transferred from the Sanskrit God 'Siva or Shiva' (the Auspicious One - the God of Destruction). His name is a diversification from the Persian root 'subh', rendered in Arabic as 'sabah' (the morning) - a homonym of 'shiva' (mourning).

Astrologically, 'Shiva' is pictured as 'sitarah-e subh' (the Morning Star).[40] The Persian word is a play on the Arabic expression 'satr su'ube' (hidden hardship).[41] Inversion of the 'Morning Star' (a saviour) reveals the 'Evening Star' (a smiter). Celebration of the crescent of Venus unveils the rites of Saturn, equated with the night and the equinox - the 'midnight sun' (Latin coincidentia oppositorum). Veneration of the black sun is equivocal to the host and his bride - the Sabbath.

Appearance of the 's'baot' (the host), a nomenclature of the reptile is identified with the death of the infant and the prostitution of the matriarch. Existential, the ritual of fratricide is conveyed obliquely through society and its social institutions, encoded linguistically.

'Sociae' Latin (a female partner)[42] is abridged from the feminine noun 'societas' (a society, association, partnership, alliance or confederacy).[43] A 'secret society' by definition is 'nuptial' (socialis) and apparent in the title the Mother Lodge of Freemasonry. 'Societas' (fellowship) further is discursive of the Roman 'daughter' of Saturn written (satae) - a contraction of 'Saturnae',[44] otherwise (Juno) -

the wife and sister of 'Jupiter' (Jovis or Jehovah). Saturnae's titular pertains collectively to the prostitutes of Saturn, demonstrated in the Latin idiolect. For example, the Roman God 'Saturn' is cognizant with the noun 'statura' (stand) an idiom related to the watcher, dragon, satyr or star. These signifiers are compatible sexually with the priestess, the whore. The act of 'statura' elicits the invocation of a dragon (an angel) - a ritual in which the participants stand facing a reclining woman. Archaically the practice is recognizant in occult lore with 'satae' (a 'daughter' of Saturn).

Female Freemasons at Caxton Hall 1937 - Drawing taken from a contemporary photograph

Semantically, 'statura' (stand) is equivalent to the 'prostitute' written in Latin as the transitive verb (prostituere). The namesake of the 'prostitute' is derived from the compound 'pro-statuere' (to set up or place) and is condensed from the transitive verb 'prostituo' (to [offer or] expose for sale).[45] Theologically, the purchase of the whore (houri) is analogous to the act of sexual 'redemption' and the trade of the firstborn.

Veneration of the 'prostitute' is cogent venereally with the adjective 'prostratus' (prostrate),[46] a derivation of 'stratus' (bed or couch).[47] Phonological comparisons in English are found in the related nouns 'crouch', 'couch' and 'crotch'. Procumbent, a fallen woman - quite literally a descendent, is 'presented' (Latin praesentare) to a deity, concurrent with an idol or statue.[48]

The 'statue' is coded speak for the worship of a living 'idol', in Greek 'eidolon' (a phantom), transliterated from the Arabic stem 'hadar' (a presence or shape). Covertly, the temple prostitute proffered her own unborn offspring to the hidden God Saturn. The ritual slaughter of the matriarch's infant obligates a promise, commemorated on the 'Sabbath' - enumerated as the 'seventh' day of mourning, equivalent to 'Shabtay' (Saturn).

Similar comparisons are found in the Franco languages. In French, 'semedi' (Saturday) is borrowed from the Indo-Persian word. The noun 'semedi' recalls sacrificial rites analogous to the Sanskrit root 'samadhi' (joining - conceptual of atonement). At a deeper level, 'samadhi' denotes the secret contract between the host and man, authorized through marital intercourse of the priestess.

'Samadhi' extols the Sanskrit word (absorbed in self-contemplation) and, as a noun, can signify (a promise, agreement, religious vow, tomb or grave).[49] The Hindi variation of the same word gives a greater insight. The 'samadh' is (the tomb of a jogl [yogi], buried alive to acquire self-immolation).[50]

Samadhi's root linguistically is extracted from the compound 'sah-madha'. The phrase in Hindu thus reads as the pronoun 'sah' (he) and the noun 'madha or medha' (a human sacrifice). The pronoun 'sah' is punned with the Punjabi adjective 'za' (to be 'born'), i.e. 'za-madha' (born [of] a sacrifice), and is cognate in Hindi with 'sa' (like or resemblance).[51] In more obscure traditions, 'samadhi' points to an angel that is able to take on a human form through blood drinking. 'Sa' (appearance) includes the augmented reading 'chhota sa' Sanskrit (a little one or a small one),[52] implicit of child sacrifice. The ending of life is paralleled in the Indo languages with 'samdhya' (twilight),[53] philologically consistent with the communion - the 'mystery supper'.

Matrimony or covenant of the bride of Saturn denotes a type of slavery, sometimes depicted as imprisonment in the Underworld. Fetters shared by the slave operate as a dual signifier of the dragon (angel), embodied or confined in a human form, depicted as the monarch. Betrothal of the maiden and her capitulation [i.e. 'capra' Latin (a goat)] is mythological to the itinerant - the serpent.

To conclude, the descendents (za) of the 'sati' are proffered or promised through a religious 'vow' (samadhi), contiguous with the marriage of 'Saturn'. This agreement contractually is obligated through the 'father-in-law', rendered in Hindi as (samdhi),[54] and preserved in the Semitic languages.

The Hebrew etymon 'avdut' (slavery),[55] i.e. an 'initiate', is comprised from the Arabic compound 'ab-duta' (father [of the] dowry),[56] mutual to 'abd' (a servant or slave).[57] Terminologically 'ab-duta' is recorded in Latin as 'sacerdos' (a priest or priestess),[58] literally 'sacre-dos' (the sacred dowry).[59] Symbolically the captivity of the priestess is comparative in the Roman vernacular to 'sator' (a father),[60] adjacent to 'satae' (a daughter). The satae's rape is correlated with the harvesting of the 'crops' (the sata), ritualistic to the 'satyr and satiation'.

Historically, the subjugation of mankind and his betrothal to the covenant elicits the rape of his daughter, paired with the death of her firstborn heir. Usurpation of human heritage attributed to the host is promoted through a clandestine organization under a matriarchy of women priests and eunuchs. Its ancient structures are encoded as the builders, and is the topic of our next chapter.

1 Brewer Dictionary of Phrase & Fable, London, Cassel & Company, London, 1954, p488 (Incubus)

2 Hippocrene Concise Dictionary, English-Arabic, Arabic-English, Hippocrene, 2005, p282

3 Prolog Pocket Bilingual Dictionary: English-Hebrew-Hebrew-English, Prolog, 2003, p355

4 Hippocrene Concise Dictionary, English-Arabic, Arabic-English, Hippocrene, 2005, p282

5 The Persian etymon 'sitarah' (star) is reminiscent of the Japanese noun 'satori' (sudden enlightenment), derived from the adverb 'satto' (quickly). In Japanese, 'satori' and 'satto' are paired with the noun 'seito' (a student), esoteric of 'sa-tori' (to invoke a bird) - iconic of an angel associated with enlightenment.

6 Ralph Ellis: Eden in Egypt, A Translation of the Book of Genesis out of the Original Egyptian Text, Edfu Books, 2005, p291 (Appendix A5 - Dictionary)

7 Ferozsons Urdu-English Dictionary, A Comprehensive Dictionary of Current Vocabulary, Revised Edition, Ferozsons Ltd. Lahore, p429 [Note the Persian etymon 'sitan' is rendered correctly in the adjectival form as (seizing, taking or captivating). Refer also to paragraph 5, p287].

8 Ibid

9 Ibid

10 Hippocrene Concise Dictionary, English-Arabic, Arabic-English, Hippocrene, 2005, p110

11 Basic Japanese-English Dictionary, The Japanese Foundation, Bonjinsha, Oxford, 1995, p147

12 Bridget McDermott: Decoding Egyptian Hieroglyphics, How to read the sacred language of the Pharaohs, Duncan Baird publishers, London, 2001, p170 (Sign Index List)

13 Hippocrene Concise Dictionary, English-Arabic, Arabic-English, Hippocrene, 2005, p59 The name 'Seth' known also as 'Set' works on a series of cleverly encoded puns in the Semitic language. 'Set' appertains to the root 'Sed' (a Hunter) - analogous to his adversary 'Horus' (Kar - also a Hunter). In addition, the cognomen 'Seth' (Foundation) recalls the deity 'Osiris', whose name is derived from the Arabic root 'Asas' (Foundation).

14 Bridget McDermott: Decoding Egyptian Hieroglyphics, How to read the sacred language of the Pharaohs, Duncan Baird publishers, London, 2001, p80

15 Hippocrene Concise Dictionary, English-Arabic, Arabic-English, Hippocrene, 2005, p123 [Arabic 'saif' and 'sef' (a sword), rendered in Hebrew as 'sayif'].

16 Ibid, p13

17 Bridget McDermott, Decoding Egyptian Hieroglyphics, How to Read the sacred language of the Pharaohs, Duncan Baird publishers, London, 2001, p168 [Sign Index List - 'sn' (kiss)]

18 Prolog Pocket Bilingual Dictionary, English-Hebrew, Hebrew-English, Prolog, 2003, p222 ['ne'shika' (kiss)]

19 The stem 's-l-m' (peace or surrender) informs the Arabic terms 'Muslim' and 'Islam'.

20 Martin Manser: Collins Dictionary of the Bible, Collins, London, 2005, p245

21 Ibid

22 Bridget McDermott: Decoding Egyptian Hieroglyphics, How to read the sacred language of the Pharaohs, Duncan Baird publishers, London 2001, p166 [Sign Index List 'sft' (anointing oil)] 'Sefet' is yet another dubious transliteration proposed by scholars. Egyptologists have extracted the verbal stem 'sefet' from the Semitic root 'shabareth' or 'savaret' (river), related to 'tvila' (immersion), conceptual to 'tsava' (an army). These etymologies are aligned conceptually to 'shofar' (horn) and 'sef' (sword), utilized to consecrate the crown. 'Shofar's root corresponds with 'saba' (star), rendered in Akkadian as 'shubar' - signifiers paralleled to the king and his progeny. The etymological connection between 'shofar and shubar' is elaborated through the switch of the morpheme 'f' and 'b', equivalent phonetically with the 'v' sound.

23 Ibid, p166 [Sign Index List 'sft' (to anoint)]

24 Until recently, there has been little attempt to standardise the spelling of Semitic vocabulary. This is because Hebrew and Arabic words are frequently spelt different to obscure meaning to the uninitiated. Interpretation is dependent on occult knowledge, based on the study of etymology, numerology and astrology. Codified-speak and double-talk is common knowledge to the priesthood and Illuminati.

25 Hippocrene Concise Dictionary, English-Arabic, Arabic-English, Hippocrene, 2005, p83

26 Prolog Pocket Bilingual Dictionary: English-Hebrew-Hebrew-English, Prolog, 2003, p354

27 Hippocrene Concise Dictionary, English-Arabic, Arabic-English, Hippocrene, 2005, p282

28 Jack M. Driver: Hidden Codes of The Bible, Deciphering the Divine, Kandour Ltd, 2007, p149

29 John M Allegro: The Sacred Mushroom and the Cross, A Study of the Nature and Origins of Christianity within the Fertility Cults of the Ancient Near East, Abacus, 1973, p90

30 Ibid

31 Hippocrene English-Arabic, Arabic-English Dictionary, Hippocrene, New York, 2005, pp 281 & 303

32 Note comparison of 'chateaux and satyr', 'palace and 'pa-lis' (a malevolent djinn) and 'monastry and monster'.

33 John C Traupman: The New College Latin & English Dictionary, Bantam, 1988, p276 ['Saltus' a colloquial expression for (the female organ akin to cunt), relative to 'cut' and 'cult'. 'Saltus' informs the Middle English noun 'slit' and 'slut' - the latter noun of unknown etymology].

34 The flying shield is a symbol of the ship or host, analogous to the flying 'saucer' (Greek sauros - a lizard). *Its appearance is detailed in classical and religious sources. For example, during Alexander's invasion of Asia in AD 329, while crossing a river, it is recorded he and his men saw gleaming silver shields in the sky. Seven years later, while attacking Venice in the Eastern Mediterranean, observers on both side of the conflict reported other incredible events. Objects appeared in the sky and one shot a beam of light at the city wall, crumbling it to dust allowing Alexander's troops to siege the city. Alexander mentions this incident in his letter to Aristotle (See Matthew Hurley, The Alien Chronicles, Quester Books, 2003).*

35 Hippocrene English-Arabic, Arabic-English Dictionary, Hippocrene, New York, 2005, p289 ['Sitt' (a lady) is also a homonym of 'sitt' (a grandmother). The withered hag is a symbol of Saturn and death].

36 John C Traupman: The New College Latin & English Dictionary, Bantam, 1988, p278

37 Ferozsons Urdu-English Dictionary, A Comprehensive Dictionary of Current Vocabulary, Revised Edition, Ferozsons Ltd. Lahore, p429

38 Ibid, p428

39 Ibid, p429

40 Ibid, p428

41 Hippocrene English-Arabic, Arabic-English Dictionary, Hippocrene, New York, 2005, p290 ['su'ube' (hardship)]

42 John C Traupman: The New College Latin & English Dictionary, Bantam, 1988, p289

43 Ibid

44 Ibid, p278

45 Ibid, p250

46 Ibid, p457

47 Ibid, p295

48 'Statua' (a statue) is related to the Greek etymon 'statos' (fixed), in English 'stationary', reductive from the stem 'sta or stare' (to stand), reflected in the English expression to 'stand and stare'.

49 Ferozsons Urdu-English Dictionary, A Comprehensive Dictionary of Current Vocabulary, Revised Edition, Ferozsons Ltd. Lahore, p445

50 Ibid

51 Ibid, p420

52 Ibid

53 H P Blavatsky: Collected Writings 1888, The Secret Doctrine, Vol 1 Cosmogenesis, Quest Books, Theosophical Publishing House, 1993, p431

54 Ferozsons Urdu-English Dictionary: A Comprehensive Dictionary of Current Vocabulary, Revised Edition, Ferozsons Ltd. Lahore, p446

55 Prolog Pocket Bilingual Dictionary: English-Hebrew-Hebrew-English, Prolog, 2003, p376

56 Hippocrene English-Arabic, Arabic-English Dictionary: Hippocrene, New York, 2005, p171 ['Duta' (a dowry). In addition 'avdut' (slavery) and 'ab-duta' (father [of the] dowry) are cognomens of 'abd' (slave) utilized in Latin as a cognate of 'abducere' (to abduct), rendered also as 'rapere' - the latter etymon analogous to 'reptile'].

57 Ibid ['Abd' (a slave) - M.A.S. Abdel Haleem in his translation of the Koran offers the rendition (a servant and/or a slave)].

58 John C Traupman: The New College Latin & English Dictionary, Bantam, 1988, p275

59 Ibid, p92 ['Dos' (dowery) - The 'sacerdos' (priest) is born into slavery through marriage to a deity and is likened to the 'initiate', 'captive', 'slave' or 'servant'].

60 Ibid, p278

32

The Builders

Then I saw a new heaven and a new earth, for the first heaven and the first earth had passed away, and there was no longer any sea.

I saw the Holy City, the new Jerusalem, coming down out of heaven from God, prepared as a bride beautifully dressed for her husband...

"Now the dwelling of God is with men, and he will live with them... for the old order of things has passed away".

He who was seated on the throne said,
"I am making everything [a] new!"

Revelation 21: 1-5, Holy Bible, New International Version, Gideon

The above quote from Revelations is not a prediction rather a historical record of what has already occurred. St John in this passage refers to the old order established through a covenant. This agreement corresponds with the renewal of man and the regeneration of earth ascribed to the builders.

The account of the 'builders' is mentioned in Genesis with the story of Noah, and details the destruction of the red earth through a flood. The story is consistent with the traditions of Mars and Atlantis, taken from the earlier Sumerian epics of Upnapatishna. The title 'builder' documents the 'angelic vassalage', responsible for the reconstruction of the earth and includes the replenishment of Adam's seed post deluge.

Correlation between the 'angels' otherwise stated as the 'builders' originate from the pharaonic lineage of the Hyksos, demonstrated in the Semitic ciphers. For instance, 'Aamu' (Westerners - the Asiatic people or nation) apply to the verbal stem 'amar' (to speak or command). According to Rabbinical commentaries, the verbal root 'amar' informs 'mal'akh' (angel) - an assailant of the flood. The angel historically is conceptualized as a 'sailor' (malakh), referred to as the 'host or crew member' (the tsabaoth or s'baot).

Semantically, 'amar' (to speak) is branched in Semitic with 'amara' (a fleet),[1] suggesting the 'host'. In Arabic, 'amir' refers to (a commander) from 'amar' (command) and is variation of 'emir' (a prince). The commander is depicted as angelic or royal, and specifies 'governance' in Greek 'kubernao' (to steer a ship). The title 'Lord-ship' designates the 'angel or builder', correlated with the Western priesthood and government.

Succinctly, the entendre 'Aamu' (Western) covertly delineates the Arabic stem 'ammar' (to build), implicit of 'amara' (the host) and 'amir' (the commander). He is enunciated as 'emir' (the Western prince), coherent with 'ammar' (to build). The rubric 'ammar' is comparative in Hebrew to 'komer' (priest) from the Arabic noun 'qamar' (moon), pronounced gutturally as 'amar'. The 'moon' (q-amar) philologically contains the host's 'fleet' (amara). Its satellite, a symbol of the priesthood, is connected to the ark (ship) of Noah, implicit of the angelic convoy, associated with conflict.

Traditionally, the war between angels and men originated from the offspring of the 'Aamu', evinced from 'ha'mon' (the host). A multitude they are specified contrarily as the 'builders' (ammar) grammatically an 'angel' (amar), conceived as a 'talker, messenger or dragon'. Culturally, 'amar' (to speak) solicits the 'angel' and is nominal of the 'moon' (qamar) and the 'priest' (komer). The crescent is a device of the 'Western priesthood', signified through the angelic line of the 'builders' (Pharaohs), originating from Ham - the son of Noah.[2] Study of the Indo-Semitic languages suggest the arcane belief that angels artificially created the moon.

The moon's satellite is conceptualized literally as a 'base' in Hebrew (eden),[3] alternatively as an 'island' (i),[4] related to the Akkadian noun 'e' (an house). Overlooked by scholars, the deity 'Ea' literally (house of water) embodies the moon and is linked symbolically to the fish and crying.[5]

In mythological accounts, 'Ea' is said to have created man with the assistance of 'Enlil' (Lord of the Sky). 'Ea', according to the linguist and scholar J A Coleman, is depicted as half man and half fish with two heads, dressed in fish skins, or in the role of the creator God as a snake.[6] 'Ea' is credited with having instructed man in the arts of agriculture, magic, architecture etc and warned 'Atrahasis, otherwise Utnapishtim' (Noah) of the impending floods.[7]

Ea's connection to Atrahasis aka Noah suggests the fish deity is an emblem of the angel or sailor. This group is compared with the human angelic line (king-ship), originating from the moon in affiliation to the priesthood. The point is acknowledged within the Torah.

Noah's ancestry in Genesis Chapter 5 is traced through his father 'Lemech' translated as 'le'mekher' (sale)[8] i.e. a 'merchant' cognate with 'malakh' (a sailor).[9] Lemech's progeny is paralleled to Moses' line of descent, recognizant with the angelic mariner, specific of the host.[10] Moses' divine ancestry is traced from the Semitic word 'ha'mon' (host)[11] - a derivation of the Arabic name 'Imran' referred to in the Koran as the father of Moses, Aaron and Miriam. 'Imran' coincides with the Biblical name, Hebrew 'Amran'.

In addition, 'Imran' exactly matches the Egyptian name 'Im-r-n' by which Akenaten actually called his God 'Aten'.[12] 'Im-r-n', the verbal stem given by scholars, suggests that the 'Aten' disk depicted as the snake is a symbol of 'ha'mon' (the host) - a signifier of the sailor.

Further, Aten is a dichotomy of the ram deity Amun - a God identified with conflict and ruin. 'Amun's name translates as (hidden), delineated as 'ha'mon' (the host) - symbolic of the ram and the conflict with Mars. Veneration of 'Amun' is synonymous with the 'Aamu' people - the soldiers of God associated in Muslim culture with the Antichrist and the Western Prince (Caucasian).

In Islamic tradition, the 'Western' (Aamu) 'prince' (emir) denotes the Antichrist, and possesses only one eye, likened to the Egyptian God 'Horus-Amun'. Both

Horus and the Antichrist are presented as 'aama' (blind). Prosaically, 'aama' signifies destruction, equivalent to the 'moon' (q-amar) and death.

The genealogy of the Antichrist is tracked in Genesis Chapter 9:18 to the accursed son of Noah, referred to as 'Ham' - a variation of 'Aamu'. 'Ham' is described as the father of 'Canaan', ascended from the lineage of 'Cain'. The account is important, as it locates the 'Aamu' specifically with the 'Canaanite' people, whose name is translated from the Old Semitic name 'khanun' (red). 'Khanun' is rendered in Arabic as 'ahmar' (red), imported into the Greek lexicon as 'haima' (blood). Classification of 'ahmar' is theoretical with 'Aamu' (Western), a noble lineage proceeding from the descendent of 'Adam' ['Adom' (red)]. They are referred to in the book of Joshua as the 'Edomites' (red men) - a cognomen affixed to the descendents of 'Esau'.

In Modern Arabic, 'Khanun' (Cain) is equated with 'kahin' (priest).[13] Cain's hereditary is homologous to the Hebrew noun 'komer' (priest)[14] and is extracted from the Arabic noun 'qamar' (moon)[15] - the insignia of the host correlated with the red ram Amun alias Khanun (Cain).

Khanun's parentage demarcates the Egyptian God 'Khnum' (joined - literally atonement). The visage of the ram (more probably a goat) is connected in the Hebrew language to the 'Levi' (priests), a name also connoting the act of 'joining'. A priestly denomination, they divulge the covenant, observed in Egyptian custom as the unification of the Red and White Crown, adhered ritually through the law.

Partition of the Red Kingdom of Egypt documents the 'Canaanite' people, taken from the 'Hyksos' (Aam) lineage. The name 'Hyksos' originates from the Greek etymology 'oikos' (a dwelling) from 'oikeo' (to dwell), and is a literal translation of the title 'Pharaoh' (Dar-o?). 'Oikos' in ancient Greek is written as 'Hukos' and is rendered in English as 'Hyksos'. In the Hellenistic tongue, 'Hukos' additionally infers 'holkas' (a cargo ship) and is suggestive of the 'foreigner', 'alien' or 'host' (angel), represented as the sailor (merchant). Conceptually, the boat or ship is related to governance of the state 'king-ship', lateral to 'wor-ship'.

The Egyptian priest, Manetho, interprets the title 'Hukos' as (the shepherd kings or captive shepherds) i.e. a nomad or an initiate religiously joined to the Shepherd King Osiris.[16] Manetho presumably obtains the name 'Hukos' from the Egyptian cognomen 'heqa khoswe' (chief of the foreign lands) an honour specific to the 'Western' King of the 'Aamu' analogous to the tribe of 'Ham'.

The Aamu are recorded linguistically as the builders of the pyramids. 'Haram' the Arabic word for (a pyramid)[17] is from the compound 'har-am' (mountain-people), referred to as the 'Aamu' (the Western nation or Asiatic people[18]). Inconspicuously, 'har-am' is read as 'har(el)-am' (the altar-people). Incredibly, 'har-am' (mountain-people) is interchangeable with 'Har-am' (people of Horus), also rendered as 'kar-am' (the hunting people), signified with 'kha' (a star).

Pyramidal loin cloth combined with priest wearing a hairy tunic similar to the one worn by 'John' the Baptist [Hebrew 'Yona' (dove)].

'Haram' (a pyramid) thus signifies the 'people of the altar' - symbolically a mountain or star affiliated to the angel, king or 'hunter' (Horus).[19] They share a comparison with the 'illuminati' - the 'akh zauri' (a brother of light) implicit of an angel. Additionally, 'akh-zauri' is interchangeable with the Arabic pun 'akh-zari' (a brother of an alien) cognizant with the Hebrew compound 'akhzari' (cruel)[20] - signifiers equated with the host, reptile or dragon.

Extraction from 'haram' (pyramid) suggests the Aamu (Amorite) are linked to practices of human sacrifice. In Modern Arabic for example, 'haram' (pyramid) is a homonym and possesses the additional meaning (unlawful),[21] evidenced in the noun 'harami' (a thief or robber).[22] 'Harami' is deduced from the Hebrew stem 'ha-rami' (a-deceiver), cogent with the 'Aamu' and the 'serpent'. The allomorph 'ramay' is used in Latin to inform 'Ramnes' (one of the three original Roman tribes, figuratively a blue blood),[23] deduced from the Hyksos line.

Esoteric, 'harami' (thief) discloses 'hidden offerings', covert in the Old Semitic to 'har-(el)-am' (the-altar-people), literally (mountain-God-people). Nomadic, the 'mountain people' are the same tribe mentioned by Manetho as the 'Hukos' or 'Hyksos' (the shepherd kings), identified with the 'people of Horus'.

The 'mountain of God' is iconic of an 'altar', equated with the nomad and 'shepherd' (ra'i)[24] - classifications of the migrant or alien (an angel). Offerings of the firstborn are thus analogous to the construction of the 'pyramids' (haram). The 'Aamu' (Ham) by definition are depicted as 'thieves' and are grouped with 'people of the altar' [har(el)-am], allied to the worship of the 'snake' (a deceiver).

The namesake of 'harami' (a thief) implies a reptile or angel, represented as a conqueror or rapist. Sexual molestation of the virgin is bracketed with the pyramid, recorded in Semitic. The Arabic word 'harim' means (a prohibited place) and is from the verbal root 'harama' (prohibited), designated as 'haram' (a pyramid). 'Harim' is transliterated in English as (harem), etymological to harm.

To reiterate, 'haram' (pyramid) also means 'haram' (unlawful) and is symmetrical in Hebrew to 'herem' (curse). The pyramids, according to cultic tradition, are said to be accursed and are linked to sexual indiscretion, attributed originally with Mount Hermon - its summit paired with the rebellion of the fallen angels, castigated through mortal intercourse. 'Hermon' details human angelic copulation, captured in the Semitic pun 'hourmin' (virgin sex), listed in Greek with 'hormon' (to impel), suggesting the 'rapist', defined as 'ha'mon' (the host) - Refer to Chapter 2 The Sabi Priesthood.

In related traditions, 'Hermon' is referred to as 'Ardis' and combines the Arabic etymologies 'Ard' (planet earth)[25] with 'aris' (a bridegroom)[26] - (Refer to Chapter Header). Judaic custom enacts the coming together of man and angel, ritually welcomed as the 'Sabbath bride', explicit of 's'baot' (the host), affiliated to the black priesthood of 'Saturn' (Shabtay).

Religiously 'haram' (a pyramid) designates Mount 'Hermon'. The purpose of the 'haram' served as a type of Royal chamber, an angelic 'harem' - its function performed a dual role. The outer facing of the pyramid operated as a beacon or an altar - a marker of angelic insurrection allied originally to the hidden (Western) priesthood, the Aamu. Historically 'haram' (pyramid) is consigned to 'ha'mon' (the angelic host - a dragon). In the Indo-Semitic etymologies, 'haram and ha'mon' are analogous to 'palace and pa-lis (a djinn)', equivalent to the 'monastery and monster' or 'chateuax and satyr'.

'Haram' by definition suggests the pyramid is not a tomb as advocated by the Egyptologists, but a monument to the fallen Shatani and to their leader Shemyaza (Azazel), who led the assault against Mount Hermon. The connection between 'haram' (pyramid) and 'Hermon' is reinforced by Shemyaza's epithet. The verbal stem 'Sh'm' means (name, pillar or high)[27] and shares the same name with Noah's son, Shem, as well as the root behind the first part of Shemyaza.

The suffix 'yaza' is derived from the Zend word 'yazd' or 'yazata' meaning (angel or divine being).[28]

Similar stories are outlined in the Apocrypha traditions and in the Book of Enoch. These legends originate from Syria and are associated with Babylonian and Canaanite mythology, linking the site of Hermon with angelic invasion - a proposition implied from the Semitic entendre.

For example, Mount 'Hermon' is a play on 'Ha'mon' (multitude), translated as (the host) from 'amara' (a fleet), connoting an 'angelic sailor'. 'Ha'mon' (host) annotates the Arabic verbal stem 'al-muna' a diminutive of 'muni' or 'muna', specifying (supplies or provisions).[29] 'Muna' in the European languages inform the Latin 'munire' (to fortify), in English 'munitions'. Etymologically, 'muni' is grouped with 'money and moon' - an assignation of 'man' paralleled to sacrificial redemption. The host is identified with the moon and conflict.

According to ancient sources, the 'submission' (slm) of humanity established and maintained the angelic host and its Royal genealogy. Displaced, the Royal descendents of the reptile are conceived in military terms and are ordained through the rape of the matriarch. Her subjugation is contiguous with the 'pyramid' (haram) and its connection to the 'harem chamber'. 'Haram' in esoteric Arabic designates 'harama' (prohibited) and informs the English verb 'harm', vocative of 'ha'mon' (the host). 'Haram's related syntax designates blood rites, consented through deity matrimony, arbitrated through the 'harem'.

Twins of the 'Dual Crown'. Pyramidal loin cloth is paired with the temple prostitute and Anubis (Sirius). Note also the ejaculatory cobra - a motif located at the groin affixed to the ladder. The Arabic noun 'sullam' (ladder) is cognizant with 'sallam' (to submit or peace) and conveys initiatory knowledge correlated with the Theban priesthood.

In ancient Greek, 'harem' suggests 'harmonia', translated as (joining or concord), a name consistent philologically with the Egyptian ram God 'Khnum' (joined), implying intercourse or atonement. Khnum fathered the Canaanite people 'khanun' (red), correlative with the nomadic shepherd 'Cain'. His offspring are the progenitor of the Judaic 'priesthood', rendered in Hebrew 'ke'huna',[30] in Arabic 'kahin' (priest).[31] Medieval scholars trace Cain as the first 'Satanist', a patron implicated with the origins of Judaism and the establishment of 'shilton' (government).

Khnum is the creator of the Royal lineage, depicted as the potter i.e. red clay reproduced as Adam (adom). Adam's genealogy connotes sexual intercourse, entered into as a contract, likened to the Greek etymon 'harmos' (joint). 'Harmos' informs the English noun 'harmony' - synonymous with the covenant and architect.

Relationship between man and angel is determined through the <u>Craft</u>, correlated with the <u>Mason</u> and '<u>builder</u>' (ammar), distinguished as the angel (semantically amar) and the host literally the 'fleet' (amara). Analogy between the angel and builder is interplayed within the Greek and Arabic mysteries. For example, 'harmos' (joint) is apparent in the Aramaic word 'armoni' (a joiner or carpenter), transliterated in the Modern Arabic as 'ammar' (builder). Cryptically 'ammar' is phonological to 'ha'mon' (the host), expressed as the angel or 'commander' (amar).

Linguistic evidence demonstrates the mysterious builders of the 'pyramids' (haram) are evidently the 'Hyksos', the 'Aam' (plural 'Aamu') variations of the 'mountain- people' (har-am). A detailed survey of related etymologies show incontrovertibly the 'Aamu' built the pyramids - an idea counter to academic orthodoxy. Historians generally date the pyramids prior to the Hyksos invasion.

The builder earmarks the angelic escort aligned symbolically to the carpenter an emblem of the snake or host. Additionally, the ancient Semitic name for a 'carpenter or mason' (armoni) elaborates the Hebrew appellation 'ha'mon' (multitude). Ha'mon is a variation of the Egyptian ram God 'Amun or Ammon' (hidden), allied to the goat deity 'Khnum' (joined), allegoric of the Mason.

'Ha'mon' (the host) is described as 'armumi' (crafty),[32] adjacent to 'armoni' (a mason). The analogy in English is 'crafty' and 'craft'. Lexical, the title 'armoni' is cognate with 'al-mamnu' (the forbidden),[33] connoting human sacrifice, defined loosely as the occult.

The metaphor of the carpenter who rebuilds his body expounds the human votive, depicted as the firstborn, retold as the story of Armoni. In the Old Testament account, King David ceremoniously sacrifices his son Armoni to atone for the sins of his father, Saul. Armoni's sacrificial death is comparative theologically in the Gospel traditions to Jesus, the son of a carpenter. The Old Semitic epithet 'armoni' (a joiner or carpenter) expresses 'ammar' (a builder) in tandem to the host and Venus.[34] Analogous, the 'builder' refers to angelic transfiguration, commonly depicted as rebirth or resurrection.

Sobek aka 'Sabah-Kha' (the Morning-Star) is cognate with the 'Messiah' (anointed) a derivative of 'messeh' (crocodile fat). The Pharaoh's loin cloth makes the shape of the 'pyramid' (Arabic haram) – the Royal 'harem' linked to the propagation of the human-angelic line aligned to the rising star Venus (Sirius).

Idiomatically, 'armoni' (a mason) suggests 'uman' (a craftsman) - a name recurrent with the Sunni dynasty, the 'Uma-yyad'. 'Ammar' (a builder) defines the angel (amar), designations of a 'commander' (amir), registered with 'amara' (a fleet) and 'emir' (a prince). The artificer, a mason, is an extension of the 'angel' (mal'akh), defined as a 'sailor' (malakh) or 'naval crewmember' (the tsabaoth), Latin 'hostis' (army). Esoteric, the 'tsabaoth' connotes a 'craftsman', specified as a 'painter' (Hebrew tsaba).[35]

In conclusion, the 'angelic host' is twinned with the 'builder' (ammar) nominal of the resurrection of the King (Venus) personified as the son Horus. Resurrection of the Sun-God, Horus mediates the new covenant, assigned to the new earth.

Within the inner circle of the priesthood, the 'builder' (ammar) - a mason connotes etymologically an 'angel' (amar). His bloodline is matched with the 'matriarch' (amma) - allomorphs related to the 'moon' (qamar) and 'priest' (komer). The crescent exhibits the worship of nocturnal angels. Further, sexual transgressions between the angels and mankind are matched with the destruction of the red earth, accredited to the fallen progeny located on Mount Hermon. This cataclysmic event is commemorated as the pyramid - <u>a type of harem</u> used to propagate the Royal bloodline.

1   Hippocrene English-Arabic, Arabic-English Dictionary, Hippocrene, New York 2005, p320

2   'Ham' (Aamu) is referential to the 'Hyksos' - the 'Shepherd Kings' generically the 'Western nation'. The 'Aamu' (Hebrew Emori, Greek Emorite) are cognate in Sumerian with the 'Martu' (Western), analogous to 'Mada' (a Persian), biblically the 'Amorite' people.

3   Prolog: Pocket Bilingual Dictionary, English-Hebrew & Hebrew-English, Prolog 2003, p37

4   Ibid, p216

5   Ea is often shown with streams of water issuing from his body, and is comparative to Atum-Ra creating man from his tears.

6   J A Coleman: The Dictionary of Mythology, Capella, London, 2007, p313

7   Ibid, p313

8   Prolog: Pocket Bilingual Dictionary, English-Hebrew & Hebrew-English, Prolog, 2003, p353

9   Ibid, p352

10 'Mekher' literally (sale) informs the Arabic name 'Meccor' - Mohammed, according to Islamic tradition, is famed as a merchant i.e. a sailor or angel.

11 Prolog: Pocket Bilingual Dictionary, English-Hebrew & Hebrew-English, Prolog, 2003, p191

12 Ian Van Ross Vayro: Tears In Heaven, Joshua Books, Australia, 2008, p210

13 Hippocrene English-Arabic, Arabic-English Dictionary, Hippocrene, New York, 2005, p95 In occult tradition, the lineage of Cain is ascribed to the first Satanist and the division of the priesthood.

14 Prolog: Pocket Bilingual Dictionary, English-Hebrew & Hebrew-English, Prolog, 2003, p315

15 Hippocrene English-Arabic, Arabic-English Dictionary, Hippocrene, New York, 2005, p76

16 Manetho's observations pertaining to the name 'Hukos' are insightful, but should not be taken literally, as he is probably talking in veiled language aimed at a very select audience.

17 Hippocrene English-Arabic, Arabic-English Dictionary, Hippocrene, New York 2005, p97

18 Asiatic is used in this context to signify the Aryan race traced from Syria and India.

19 Combination of the pyramid and star (eye) is represented in Masonic symbolism as a 'shining pyramid', cognate ritually with the 'altar' and 'redemption' (payment). Refer to Dollar bill - Latin 'Dolere' (to suffer, feel pain or hurt).

20 Prolog: Pocket Bilingual Dictionary, English-Hebrew & Hebrew-English, Prolog, 2003, p93

21 Hippocrene English-Arabic, Arabic-English Dictionary, Hippocrene, New York, 2005, p189

22 Ibid

23 John C Traupman PhD: The New College Latin English Dictionary, Bantam Books, 1988, p259

24 Hippocrene English-Arabic, Arabic-English Dictionary, Hippocrene, New York, 2005, p111

25 Ibid, p150

26 Ibid p321

27 Andrew Collins: From the Ashes of Angels, Michael Joseph London, Penguin, 1996, p118

28 Ibid

29 Hippocrene English-Arabic, Arabic-English Dictionary, Hippocrene, New York, 2005, p248

30 Pocket Bilingual Dictionary: English-Hebrew Hebrew-English, Completely Transliterated, Prolog, 2003, p315

31 Hippocrene English-Arabic, Arabic-English Dictionary, Hippocrene, New York, 2005, p95

32 Pocket Bilingual Dictionary, English-Hebrew Hebrew-English, Completely Transliterated, Prolog, 2003, p90

33 Hippocrene English-Arabic, Arabic-English Dictionary, Hippocrene, New York, 2005, p234

34 Idiomatically, 'armoni' (mason) suggests 'ammar' (builder) and is grouped with 'uman' (craftsman) - a name recurrent with the Sunni dynasty the 'Uma-yyad'.

35 Pocket Bilingual Dictionary, English-Hebrew Hebrew-English, Completely Transliterated, Prolog, 2003, p288

The Murder of Reality

Scarlet Whores Menstrual Eels and Ejaculating Cobras

On her way to work one morning
Down the path along side the lake
A tender-hearted woman saw a poor half frozen snake
His pretty colored skin had been all frosted with the dew

"Oh well", she cried, "I'll take you in and I'll take care of you"
"Take me in oh tender woman
Take me in, for heaven's sake
Take me in oh tender woman", sighed the snake

She wrapped him up all cozy in a curvature of silk
And then laid him by the fireside with some honey and some milk
Now she hurried home from work that night as soon as she arrived
She found that pretty snake she'd taken in had been revived

Now she clutched him to her bosom, "You're so beautiful", she cried
"But if I hadn't brought you in by now you might have died"
Now she stroked his pretty skin and then she kissed and held him tight
But instead of saying thanks, that snake gave her a vicious bite

"I saved you", cried the woman
"And you've bit me even, why?
You know your bite is poisonous and now I'm going to die"
"Oh shut up, silly woman", said the reptile with a grin
"You knew damn well I was a snake before you took me in"

The Snake: Sung by Al Wilson

Evidence presented in the previous chapter showed that the angelic builder specified the Canaanite or Hyksos - an element considered angelic. They trace their origin from 'khanun' (red), sourced from 'Cain' a lineage perpendicular to the Aamu (ahmar - red) or Edomite (adom - red).

The Hyksos by definition are unified with the Red Kingdom of Egypt and are the builders of the pyramids. Later, the Hyksos reappear as the Roman Imperial line (Ramnes) and are branched with the Islamic priesthood (Umayyad). Following Rome, they resurfaced as the Knight Templar under the heading of the Red Cross - an ancient device of Mars (symbolic of Adam and Cain).

Historically the Hyksos via marriage trace their lineage from Adam, affiliated to the red snake, concealed through the Royal line. Progeny of Cain's descendents are protected through the covenant of the matriarch, concordant with the Egyptian ram God 'Khnum'. His Royal name translates as 'joined' and suggests intercourse, embedded within the 'knot' (aqad)[1] - a device of the Double Kingdom sourced from Akkad. Khnum is notated in the Arabic etymon 'qanun' (law),[2] transposed into Greek as 'canon'.

Joint agreement with the ram historically describes the covenant, stipulated through the rebirth of man. Obedience to the law is symbolized as the moon - a receptacle containing the seed of earth. Represented as the horned crescent, the emblem is linked to fertility and sexual magic. This in turn is bound to the appearance of the scarlet whore - figurative of the 'Western nation'.

Referred to as the 'Aamu', they align themselves to the Evening Star and the worship of nocturnal angels. The setting of Venus characterizes the red priestess (the fire-star), a bloodline rhetorical of the fish and menstruation. Nocturnal emissions recount the Egyptian Sky Goddess Apophis as a menstruating eel.

A deity of the dual waters (salt/clear), she inhabits the infernal regions of chaos, responsible etiologically for conflict between angels and humans. Liturgical recitals refer to Apophis eating the setting sun (a serpent) - a metaphor of intercourse and defilement. Episodic, her decline recounts the disfigurement of the Aten - monumental of sexual violation. The cause of Aten's decline is attributed with human angelic intercourse, specific of ovulation and death.

Apophis' blood prosaically compares to the sanguine sky - an allegory of the menstrual cycle (mammal) - solicitous of the moon equated with Royal theogony. Appearance of the crescent couples illicit intercourse with the onset of ovulation, assigned to the mother Goddess Apophis. Her discharge counted with war, is associated with the deluge and the renewal of the covenant.

Religiously, Apophis is depicted as copulating with the cobra, embodied as the rising sun. The flashing rays of the uraeus signify the spitting (ejaculatory) serpent and its offspring - the 'illuminated ones' (Egyptian tehentiu). This bloodline, is an expression of the Imperial Atum, ascribed to Venus and partnered with the angelic host, identified with the Theban priesthood. Renewal of the day is linked theologically to the builder, carpenter, tradesman or snake, paralleled to the veneration of the Morning Star (Sirius).

To recall the previous chapter, 'armoni' (a mason or carpenter) corresponds with 'ha'mon' (the host) - a symbol of 'Venus'. The same word plays are adduced from the Syrian. The Aramaic expression 'nagar' used for (a carpenter) is equivalent to the Hebrew noun 'Noga' (Venus).

'Noga' is symbolized in the Egyptian language as 'naja' (cobra). A royal motif of the 'naja' is worn on the Pharaoh's headdress, and suggests an incarnation of the Rising-Star. The headdress 'nemes' symbolizes a 'cobra' or 'saviour', and appears in the Greek lexicon as the Goddess 'Nemesis' from 'nemo' (retribution).

Pharaoh's Headdress - symbolic of the hooded cobra.
The risen snake is referential to the 'smiter' - a 'saviour' classified as a Theban.

Sumerian epics describe 'Naga' as (the God of Death), extrapolated from the Sanskrit noun 'naga' (a serpent).[3] In the Hebrew language, 'naga' means (to strike) - archaically a snakebite, descriptive of the 'serpent' (nakhash).[4] The reptile's burning venom denotes ejaculation and is a symbol of mortal coitus.

Offspring of Venus (Lucifer) in the Roman and Egyptian mysteries constitutes the incarnation of a God or king, defined as the 'carpenter'.[5] Jesus in the Gospel of Mark is presented as the son of Joseph - a 'carpenter' dubbed in Aramaic as (nagar).[6]

As shown in the preceding paragraph, the title 'nagar' plays on the Hebrew noun 'Noga' (Venus),[7] suggesting the birth of a God. Jesus' ascension, the 'second coming', is described in the book of Revelation as the 'Morning Star'. Additionally, 'nagar' in Semitic is a homonym, cognate with the Syrian root 'nagga or najja' (to save or rescue)[8] from 'nagga or naga' (to hit). The comparisons in English are save and savage. In Egyptian Arabic, 'nagah' is translated as (succeed or success).[9] These appellations refer to 'naja' (the cobra), allied to the angelic host - the conqueror.

The 'royal cobra' (naja) is presented as a 'saviour' (nagga) - a title that is interchangeable with a 'smiter' (nagga), descriptive of the builder, a 'carpenter' (nagar). Symbolized as the King (Jupiter) or the risen Son of God (Venus), the snake is considered duplicitous. The metaphor of the dual serpent is emblematic of the Morning and Evening Star, embodied as the God and Goddess, linked to resurrection and death, found encoded within the New Testament.

In Matthew 26:61, Jesus' accusers lay claim that he is able to 'destroy' (nagga) and rebuild or literally 'save' (nagga) the temple in three days, connoting the 'carpenter' (nagar). The play is figurative of the 'builder' (ammar) symmetrical to an 'angel' (amar). Jesus' resurrection on the 'third' day (Arabic 'talit') is a pun on the Hebrew word 'talit' (a prayer shawl), used here to suggest a shroud. Significantly, the shawl religiously has 613 'tassles' (Hebrew tzitzit) and is a symbol of the 613 laws ['commandments' (mitzvot)] written in the Torah. Connection between Jesus' death and resurrection on the third day implies the renewal of the Jewish law or covenant. The law in Judaism is grouped with the 'body and temple', represented as the House of God, signified as the 'head'.

Resurrection of the Messiah coincides with the Sabbath and Passover, aligned to the rising-star 'Venus' (Noga). Personified as the sacrificial 'ram' (Syrian kebsh),[10] the animal hosts a 'conqueror' (Hebrew kovesh).[11]

In the Gospel of Matthew, Jesus' bloodline is subsumed from his patriarchal heir 'Joseph' from the line of David and plays on 'Yah-sef' (Jehovah's-sword), punned with 'asaf' (grief).[12] Rabbinical scholars translate the name as 'God shall add' (Jo-hosif)[13] a double-barrelled interpretation. The implication is that God shall multiply his descendants through the conquest of his enemies.[14] Jesus thus assumes the dual role of the 'saviour', simultaneous to the 'destroyer'.

Personified as the 'Christ' and 'Antichrist' the depiction of the 'redeemer' in Christian and Islamic tradition is shown as carrying a sword, staff or rod - a 'Soldier of God'. Analogy of the 'saviour', deemed as an 'exterminator', is further linked with angel worship, provident within the Judaic priesthood. Early Hebrews represented themselves with the snake, incorporated with the traditions of Moses' staff. An emblem of sadistic rites, the scepter governed the worship of 'angels' (mal'akh), conceptual to the 'rod' (Hebrew makel).[15] Possession of the 'rod' (makel) dramatized the cobra, ritualistically cognizant with the 'dance' (makhol)[16] - Refer to Chapter 29 Saturnalia and the Forces of Darkness.

Determination of the 'staff' (makel), transformed into an 'angel' (mal'akh), implies the host and votive, exhibited in the Semitic lexicon. The alternative word for 'makel' (a staff or stake)[17] denotes 'mot' - the Arabic noun for (death).[18] Earlier versions of the word 'death' are found in the Canaanite tradition and refer to 'Mot' (the God of Death), equivalent to the Sumerian deity 'Naga'. Mot, like the angel and cobra, is linked to salvation, conciliated through ritualized flagellation, associated with the declining sun.

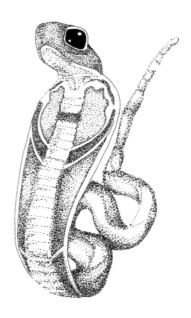

'Cobra' (Naja)
Its poisonous seed is linked to the progeny of the Rising Star Venus (codeword for Sirius). The cobra's midriff is drawn as a ladder - a visual pun denoting ascension. Resurrection of the serpent is equated with the transfiguration of the Theban 'Pharaoh' (Hebrew Par-o) - analogous in the Akkadian dialect to the epithet 'peor' (snake), classified as the 'builder' or 'angel'.

Resurrection of the saviour in the Greek and Judaic mysteries recalls the solar disk and regeneration. Definitive of the human-angelic line and a source of life, the rising sun (Venus aka Sirius) illustrates the flaming seraph. A dual symbol, the flashing serpent appears in the Egyptian Passion plays as the reaper, joined under the menstruating fish Apophis - a scarlet whore! Her role is clarified in the next chapter.

1 Hippocrene English-Arabic, Arabic-English Dictionary, Hippocrene, New York, 2005, p65

2 Ibid, p66

3 'Naga' (a serpent or serpent deity) informs the Japanese adjective 'nagai' (long).

4 Prolog: Pocket Bilingual Dictionary, English-Hebrew-Hebrew-English, Prolog, 2003, p365

5 The betrayal of the carpenter and his death is comparative to Jesus and is repeated in Masonic tradition as Hiram Abif - the Master Mason of Solomon's Temple.

6 Prolog: Pocket Bilingual Dictionary, English-Hebrew-Hebrew-English, Prolog, 2003, p58

7 Ibid, p446

8 Hippocrene English-Arabic, Arabic-English Dictionary, Hippocrene, New York, 2005 pp106 & 253

9 Ibid, p253

10 Ibid, p98

11 Prolog: Pocket Bilingual Dictionary, English-Hebrew-Hebrew-English, Prolog, 2003, p81

12 Hippocrene English-Arabic, Arabic-English Dictionary, Hippocrene, New York, 2005, p54

13 Prolog: Pocket Bilingual Dictionary, English-Hebrew-Hebrew-English, Prolog 2003, p15
   The original root of 'Joseph's name is 'le'hosif' (to-add), biblically 'Jo-hosif'.

14 Classical depictions of the 'ram' (kebesh) otherwise 'kovesh' (a conqueror) are equated with the son of Zeus - 'Alexander' the Great (Greek Iskander - the defender of man). Alexander's genocide in the ancient world infers otherwise.

15 Prolog: Pocket Bilingual Dictionary, English-Hebrew-Hebrew-English, Prolog, 2003, p390

16 Ibid, p97

17 Ibid, pp390 & 391

18 Hippocrene English-Arabic, Arabic-English Dictionary, Hippocrene, New York, 2005, p35

34

Apophis the Menstrual Eel

'Fear me you lords and lady preachers
I descend upon your earth from the skies
I command your very souls you unbelievers
Bring before me what is mine
At the seven seas of Rhye'

Seven Seas of Rhye, Written by Freddie Mercury, Queen
Released in 1974 (EMI Records)

In the Egyptian pantheon, the forces of chaos are personified as the deity Apophis, described incorrectly by scholars as a serpent God. Famous in Egyptian lore, the snake swallows the sun, etiological of the sunset, pictured as the sanguine sky.

Apophis' correct assignment is presented here for the first time. Apophis originally is an eel - further she is a Goddess, symbolized as a menstruating fish. Her consumption of the solar disk is equated with sexual intercourse, denoting the combination between heaven and earth.

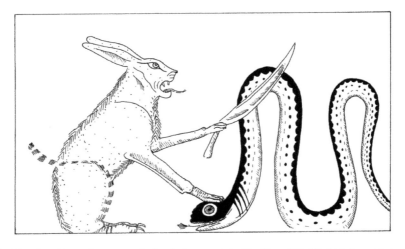

The deity Apophis on the papyrus is clearly shown with gills. The rabbit (flash) is identified with the dragon - a synonym of the fish. 'Arnab' Arabic (rabbit) is a pun on 'Al-nabi' (a-prophet), comparable in English to 'rabbit and Rabbi'. In Catholicism, the rabbit is often placed next to the virgin's feet - a signifier of the Vestal priestess and her sacred bloodline.

'Apophis' name is translated misleadingly from Roman classical sources as (he who was spat out).[1] The cognomen is derived conventionally from the Greek corruption 'obelos' (to spit), and suggests the Goddess' ejaculating consort, the spitting cobra 'ophis' - technically (a snake or serpent). The correct root of 'Apophis' name however is found extracted from the Greek etymon 'Apoplesso'.

The serpent's bite connotes sexual penetration. 'Apoplesso' (literally to strike completely) and 'plesso' (strike) is translated into Hebrew as 'naga' - a derivation of 'Noga' (Venus), enumerated as 'naja' (the cobra), pageant of 'nagga' (the saviour). Esoterically, 'plesso' concurs in Greek with 'plasso' (to mould) and 'plastos' (shaped), inferring manifestation of an angel, likened to the sun. 'Plesso' is consistent in Latin with 'plaga' (to blow or wound), opposite 'plagusia' (a fish).[2]

With the modification of Apoplesso's Hellenistic name, it is possible to reconstruct her original Egyptian epithet that has never been deciphered. The expression 'Apoplesso' (to strike completely) is a translation from the Arabic 'Ad-nagga' (to strike again) - an appellation correlated with 'Noga' (Venus). The Arabic expression 'nagga' (to hit) is a homonym and also means 'to save' i.e. through forceful intervention or infliction.

'Ad-nagga' describes the original name of the eel Goddess 'Apophis' - initially a saviour Goddess in unison with the host and death. Judicially interpreted as (the Eternal Saviour or the Perpetual Smiter), Ad-nagga's cognomen infers marital intercourse with the cobra, from which the Goddess receives her name.

Archaically, the Goddess 'Ad-nagga' celebrates marriage between the 'solar cobra' (naja) - figurative of the 'Morning Star', sexually combined with the feminine aspect the Evening Star (fire-star). Venus' dual appearance parallels the sun and moon, illustrative of the angel (hermaphrodite), characterized as the woman. In particular, the solar device doubles with the Star of Sirius, correlated with the fish deity Ea.

Ad-nagga's intercourse with the solar cobra is bound procedurally to the dedication of the Temple Sanctuary and its female 'guardian'[3](the apotropos).[4] In the Modern Semitic, the name 'Ad-nagga' loans itself to the transliteration 'Hanukkah' (consecrated). Modern Jews celebrate 'Hanukkah' as the festival of lights - originally a solar cult.

Observance of 'Hanukkah' (consecrated) is thus broken down in Semitic as 'ha-nikah' (the-marriage), deduced from the Akkadian word 'nik' (sexual conjugation).[5] 'Nikah' is written in the hieroglyphic as 'nk' phonetically 'nek' the verb (to copulate)[6] and is transferred into Greek as 'necros' (flesh).

Hanukkah denudes copulation with an angelic being, described as the 'Anunnaki' and is coherent with the Syrian verbal root 'naqal' (to transport)[7] i.e. Old Semitic 'anu-naqali' (transported from heaven). In Arabic, the 'Anunnaki's offspring are equated with 'al-naqi' (the pure),[8] cogent with the 'anu-naqi' definitive of (celestial-purity).

In the book of Numbers 13:33, the 'Nephilim' Hebrew (Fallen) are called the 'Child(ren) of Anak',[9] plural the 'Anakim'. According to Signet Hebrew-English Dictionary by Dov Ben Abba, the word for 'giant' is (anak) and appears in the Modern Hebrew adjective as 'anaki' (gigantic).[10] The use of the adjective 'anaki' is cryptic and proposes a child, whose origins is sourced from the stars. 'Anaki' is translated into Greek as 'Titan' (giant) - a race conceived from heaven and earth. Ancient accounts record the divine offspring of the 'Titan' as royal, an idea symmetrical with 'Anak'.

The status 'Anak(i)' informs the Phoenician word 'anak' (a prince), transliterated into Greek as 'anax'.[11] Variations of 'anax' (prince) are observed in the Greek noun 'arkhos' (ruler), rendered in English as 'mono-arkhos' (one-ruler i.e. monarch). The scholar Erik Parker argues that the famous 'giants' (the Anakim) are identical with the descendents of the 'Anunnaki' and 'Enki' - a logical argument.

'Enki's ancient name translates in the Sumerian as (Lord of the Earth[12] - i.e. a prince) and is the same title inherited by the Greek demigods the 'Titans', known in Semitic as the 'Anunnaki' - Refer to footnote[13]. A human angelic bloodline, the Anunnaki, is considered half human and half serpent, defined as royal. Philologically, the 'al-naqal' (the transported) enumerates 'king-ship'. Itinerants, the 'al-naqal' are conceptual to the 'giants' (Anaki), otherwise the 'Anunnaki', glorified as the 'prince' (Phoenician anax), relative to the host - the Titans.[14] A Royal bloodline extricated from the boat or ark, 'anax' is equivalent to the Arabic status 'emir' (prince), lateral to 'amara' (fleet) and 'ha'mon' (the host). A 'prince' of the earth, 'anak's descendents are attributed with heaven and considered angelic (alien).

'Al-naqali' (the transported ones) specify an 'exile', 'sailor', 'nomad' or 'angel'. Liaison with the 'al-naqali' intimates 'al-nikah' (the marriage) - celebratory of the festival 'Hanukkah' (consecrated). Sexual relationships between mortals and angels instigate the covenant (government) - elemental to division, imputed mythologically to the eel Goddess 'Ad-nagga'.

Additionally, the 'al-naqal' are identical to the 'visitors' - the 'akh zari' (brothers of aliens) correlated with the 'akh zauri' (brothers of light). Marked with the logo of the dragon or seraph, the 'akh zauri' designates the western sun - contiguous with the Occidental priesthood. Annotated with the shining uraeus, Western Freemasonry registers the 'akh zauri' (Latin the illuminati), with (the Theban priesthood or serpent progeny). Combination of the cobra's seed is nuptial to the Anunnaki's mascot - the bloodied eel, evocative of menstruation and strife (war).

Correspondence between the mythical race the 'Anaki' (giant) and the amphibian is evident linguistically in the European grammar 'nickel' (goblin), 'nixes' (water siren) and 'knucker' (dragon). In Anglo-Saxon, the tradition of worms associated with water holes and caves are known in the Old English as 'knucker' or 'nickery holes'. 'Knucker' is derived from the Anglo-Saxon word 'nicor', translated as (a water monster) - a variation of 'nickel' (a goblin) - and occurs in Beowulf. After the conquest, it survived in various dialectical forms as 'nicker, nucker and knucker'. Importantly, 'knucker' is used to signify ogres or monsters that inhabit the deep.

Etymological variations of 'nicor' (a water monster) originate from the Hebrew noun 'nakhal or nahar' (river) and 'nakhash' (serpent).[15] 'Nicor' is represented in medieval chivalry as a 'virgin' (nixes), amalgamated with the fish or dragon. The water serpent (eel) documents an 'amphibian' [Greek 'amphi-bios' (both-life)] - an animal associated in the Koran with dichotomy and discord.

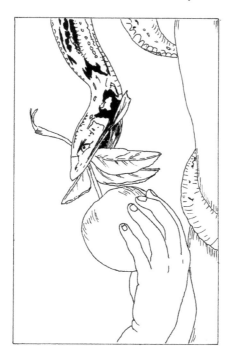

Eve, Durer 1507, (Detail): The leaf in the serpent's mouth operates as a visual pun of a fin, revealing the menstrual fish. The reptile is shown with teeth in the lower jaw - anatomic of the eel. Epigraphically the tooth denotes Sirius. Finally, Durer paints the fish with a red crown - symbolic of Eve's menstrual blood, equated with angelic defilement (Refer to Appendix 7).

Symbolists refer to the water snake as 'a red serpent' - emblematic of the menstrual fish, primordial to the deity 'Ad-nagga'. In the Christian mysteries, the dual realm is substituted with blood and water, prescribed through the sacrificial death of the Messiah - symbolic of the setting sun. Subjugation of the disk is pedagogic of Christ's momentous death and his eventual triumph over evil (death). Essentially, the story is a retelling of the Egyptian myth of the mother Goddess 'Ad-nagga'. Her ingestion of the solar mascot, enacted ritualistically through the evening communion (mystery), is liturgical to intercourse and rebirth.

Union between the cobra and eel reconciles the flashing (splashing) dragon, allegorized as the starlit sky - a simile of the reptile, cognate with the rising star. Likewise, the ancient Greeks in their vocabulary linked the 'serpent' (ophis or apis) with the sky, duplicated in the noun '(h)apsis' (vault), definitive of heaven (sea).

Descriptions of the celestial canopy are matched in the Arabic lexicon with 'samak or samah' (an eel), extracted from 'sama' (heaven). 'Samak' astrologically records (the fish that the earth is supposed to rest on).[16] A metaphor, the global fish illustrates seasonal precession - indicative of the earth's wobble, predating modern science![17]

'Samak' (fish) is a symbol of fertility, conceptual to 'same'ak' (happy),[18] periodical of royal intercourse. Comparisons of the reptile attributed to heaven are variations of occult practices, originating earlier from the Babylonian fish deity Oannes, derived from 'an(u)' (heaven).[19] Oannes is the measurer of the seasons. The word 'season' (Hebrew ana),[20] cryptically sea-son (son of the sea), is diminutive of the fish 'Oannes' - a God linked to 'rape' (Hebrew ones).[21]

A universal motif, the 'fish' in the Indo-Persian languages records deities, assigned to the sky, mutual to copulation and conflict. The Sanskrit noun 'min' (a fish) also signifies (the sign of Pisces), used additionally as the verb (to criticize), symbolic of division.[22] 'Min' is comparable in Persian (Punjabi) to 'minu', denoting (heaven or paradise),[23] defined in the Veda as the Celestial Ocean. In Hebrew, the phoneme 'min' translates as (sexual intercourse), recollective of the menstrual eel, equated with human-angelic procreation.

The amphibian (a demigod) in Islamic discourse is allotted to the barrier of the 'dual waters',[24] ascribed to the 'delta' (a doorway) - symbolic of the star (a portal). The metaphor of the dual waters (clear and salt) corresponds individually with the human and angelic species. Combination of the two classes is signified with the menstrual fish, bracketed with the bipedal goat and the setting sun (mystery).

At an abstract level, the traversing of the 'double-waterways' elucidate 'dimensional time and space',[25] correlated with the ancient mariner and the precession of the stars. The water causeway designates a door (delta), conceptualized as a blockade or an obstruction to the realm of the amphibian, an animal of dual identity (human-angelic). Its existence is said to inhabit the infernal regions. Relationship between the djinn (jinn) and humankind is paraphrased in the Koran, Sura 55: 14-37

> *'He created mankind out of dried clay, like pottery, the jinn out of smokeless fire... He is Lord of the two risings and Lord of the two settings [Venus-Sirius]... He released the two bodies of [fresh and salt] water. They meet, yet there is a barrier between them they do not cross... His are the moving ships that float high as mountains on the sea... We shall attend to you two huge armies... Jinn and mankind, if you can pass beyond the regions of heaven and earth [e.g. the dual waters], then do so: you will not pass without Our authority... A flash of fire and smoke will be released... When the sky is torn apart and turns crimson, like red hide'.*[26]

Binary and oppositional djinn (jinn)[27] and man control heaven and earth, administered through a covenant, symbolised in 'hermetic' tradition (Hebrew atum),[28] as the flashing sun and menstrual blood.

Relationship between heaven and the fish is found also in the Egyptian mystery plays. Mythologized accounts of Apophis compare her menstrual flow to the setting of the sun, preserved in the Greek lexicon. Apophis' 'blood' (haima) is contrasted with the 'opening of the vagina' (hymen), specified as the 'humen' (membrane). The Goddess' menses is analogous to the 'day' (hermera), confluent with the resurrection of the disk. Her restorative cycle illustrates the rebirth of the sun, a clot of blood, emulated through her menses.

Analogy between the sunlight and the woman's period is evident also within the Semitic languages. The Arabic word 'buq'a'[29] (a spot or stain) is equivalent in Hebrew to 'boker' (morning),[30] rendered in Arabic as 'bukra' (tomorrow).[31] 'Buq'a' (a spot) describes the menstrual blood, implicit of 'bakhura' Hebrew (a young girl). Her title is documented in Greek as the celebrant - the 'Bachoi'.

Translation of 'buq'a' (a blemish) records the Latin feminine noun 'macula' (spot) and informs 'immaculatus' (the Immaculate Conception) - hermeneutic of the menses cycle, assigned to the conquest of the morning sun. Insemination of an adolescent describes 'sexual union' (al-nikah) with an 'angel' (the Anunnaki). The coupling of the angelic race with women is equated with the amphibian (duality) and the 'woman's period' (menarches), equivalent to the 'monarch' (mono-arkhos).

In the Modern Arabic, 'al-nikah' determines 'marital consecration' (Hanukkah), specific of the 'festival of light'. The menstrual blood of the bride or initiate signifies the sanguine sun, observed ritualistically as the 'marriage' (ha-nikah), compliant with the blackened Sabbath and the rising sun. Desecration of the 'virgin' (the bakhura) is conjunct with menstrual 'pollution' (buq'a) - sequential to deity intercourse and the resurrection of the day (boker).

'Ha-nikah' is rendered alternatively as 'kiddushin' (a marriage ceremony) from 'kodosh or qodesh' (holy,[32] devote, hallow or sanctify),[33] reductive of 'koder' (saturnine).[34] Intercourse with the celebrant the 'bacchoi' (a virgin) is equivalent to the solar fish, congruent with the inner mysteries and the worship of Bacchus.

Marriage of the 'bakhura' Hebrew (girl)[35] Greek 'bacchoi' denotes a priestess, and pertains to ritual defilement 'macula' (a spot) - implicit of the 'menorrhoea', associated with the Royal lineage (mammal and reptile). Paired conceptually with 'divine birth' (the immaculatus) coincides with the votive and the incarnation of a deity, compared to the risen sun and rebirth (transfiguration). 'Macula' further describes human angelic copulation 'immaculatus', linked etiologically with the onset of the woman's period, theological to the eel Goddess 'Ad-nagga'.

The virgin's ovulation Latin 'macula' semantically is cogent with the transitive verb 'mactare' (to magnify, glorify, honour, sacrifice, slaughter, put to death, destroy, ruin, overthrow, trouble or afflict).[36] These appellations are accorded to the reptile, distinguished as the host or rapist, seasonal to blood rituals. The 'mactatus' (sacrifice)[37] elicits menstrual blood, correlated with 'maculare' (to defile, pollute or dishonour).[38]

Historically, the Goddess' first blood (macular) is affiliated with the pubescent girl's cycle (macies-leaness) in conjunction with the first-light. Sexual liaisons with angels record the matriarchal 'covenant' (brit),[39] deduced from the Hebrew etymon 'bat' (a daughter)[40] - an agent sold, redeemed or prostituted. The term 'bat' in Arabic therefore is to (spend the night or pass the night),[41] contractual to an angel or dragon.

Religious copulation with a deity is ritualized as 'Hanukkah' (the festival of light), and is dedicated to the solar serpent, combined with the menstrual fish.[42] Appearance of the winged seraph (a flashing cobra) enunciates the fish's insemination - celebratory of the recurrent day.

Relationship between the snake and eel connotes sadism, expressed through the subordination of the sun, preserved in the Arabic and Greek etymons. The Arabic noun 'samak' (an eel)[43] informs the English verb 'smack' and 'snake' (Old English 'snaca'). The analogy in Greek is 'plesso' (to strike)[44] - nominal of the Goddess 'Apoplesso', otherwise the eel 'Apophis'. Cultic, the word 'plesso' is rendered in English as 'bless', suggestive of the 'saviour' or 'striker' (nagga), conceptual to the water deity 'Ad-nagga'. The Old English root of 'bless and bliss' is a derivation of 'bledsian' (to mark or consecrate with blood). A blessing typically is received through the medium of blood and water - a symbol of Baptism, actual to the fish and host.

Ancient classifications listing the fish with the snake demonstrate a close connection between the eel and seraph - a symbol appropriated by the Theban priesthood. Difficulties regarding the translation of Apophis' name are attributed to the Goddess' adoption of her consort's title 'naga' (to strike) in honour of the risen 'cobra' (naja).

Semitic scholars further confuse the serpent with the eel, due to the similarity of the Arabic noun 'ti'ban' (an eel)[45] in proximity to 'ta'ban' (a snake).[46] To complicate matters, the Arabic noun 'samak' (an eel) is adopted in the colloquial form to signify (a fish).[47] The same ambiguities between the 'fish' and 'snake' are found also in the Latin glossary 'anguilla' the feminine noun for (an eel),[48] syntactic of the 'serpent' or 'snake' (anguis).[49]

Religiously, the menstrual fish is interchangeable with blood and water, combined with the loaf - a sign of the communion. The baptism of water in the Gospels commemorates blood and wine - cyclical of the menstrual fish, timed with the reaper and the resurrection of the eel 'Ad-nagga' (Apophis). Rebirth (born again) or marriage of the Goddess portends to the 'mystery' - archaic to baptism, linked to the 'Fisher-King' himself - John the Baptist.

Cryptically, the name of 'John', in Greek, is spelt as 'Ioannes', but for one character describes 'Oannes' the Babylonian fish God - a deity traditionally combined with the uraeus. Emblem of the feathered seraph unifies the eel Goddess, prenatal to the winged priestess.[50] In the Gospel account, John's baptism of Jesus is thus synthesized with the 'dove' (Hebrew yona)[51] - an etymological variation of '(I)oannes' (a fish).

Old Testament accounts equate the 'dove' (yona) with the patriarch 'Jonah', nominal of the fish patron 'Oannes'.[52] Referred to in Syrian legend as the 'teacher of mankind', Oannes is purveyor to the Royal crown. A fallen deity, the fish articulates the development of the Judaic and Theban priesthood, credited with the 'Red-Hyksos Pharaohs' and the 'sacred-virgin'.

Embodied variously as the amphibian, menstrual eel, goat or the hairy-fish (human-angelic), the priestess' lineage propagates the royal line, developmental of the Western priesthood. A matriarchal covenant the 'Mother Lodge' is contemporaneous to 'Western Freemasonry' (Rabbi) and the establishment of Liberal (Levite) governments, encoded universally in the cities and monuments of the world.

1   George Hart: A Dictionary of Egyptian Gods and Goddesses, Routledge & Kegan Paul, 1986, p31

2   John C Traupman PhD: The New College Latin English Dictionary, Bantam Books, 1988, p230

3   Prolog: Pocket Bilingual Dictionary, English-Hebrew, Hebrew-English, Prolog, 2003, p176

4   The Hebrew term 'apotropos' (a guardian) is matched in Greek with 'atropos' (inflexible, literally not turning) - a Greek metaphor of the spindle that conceals the thread of life. The verb 'tropos' (turning) is related to 'trophe' (nourishment) from 'trepho' (nourish), covert to immolation. Atropos is the eldest of the three Fates (fatal sisters), who severs life, furtive of sacrificial nourishment, equated with the thread, visualized as the snake. Cultic, Atropos' title connotes 'anthropos' (a human being), cogent with 'anthrophos' (a shining form), depicted in legend as the dragon, paired with the 'apotropos' (a guardian).

5   Guy Deutscher: The Unfolding of Language, William Heinemann, 2005, p190

6   Bridget McDermott: Decoding Egyptian Hieroglyphics, Duncan Baird Publishers, London, 2003, p167 (Sign Index List)

7   Hippocrene English-Arabic, Arabic-English Dictionary, Hippocrene, New York, 2005, p254

8   J Hackin: Asiatic Mythology, George G Harrap & Co Ltd, 1963, p48

9   Michael Tellinger: Slave Species of God, Music Masters, South Africa, 2005, p512

10 Prolog Pocket Bilingual Dictionary, English-Hebrew, Hebrew-English, Prolog, 2003, p168

11 Harold Bayley: The Lost Language of Symbols, Dover Publications, New York, 2006, p13

12 Michael Tellinger: Slave Species of God, Music Masters, South Africa, 2005, p512

13 Scholars on the occult sometimes connect the word 'Anunnaki' with the Arabic noun 'unq' (a neck), conceptual most probably with 'nuqra' (a necklace). Rabbinical commentators translate the name 'Anunnaki' as (the longed-neck ones), probably derived from the combination of the Hebrew-Arabic term 'arokh-nuqra(i)'. The title 'long neck', an allusion to the snake, is almost certainly a corruption of the original stem 'Anaki' (gigantic). The etymological connection between the neck and giant would make sense, as the Greek translation of the 'Anunnaki' Hebrew (giants) is rendered as a 'Titan' - an epithet consistent with the root 'teino' (to stretch), suggesting the womb. In the Indo-European languages, the 'neck' signifies the 'womb', demarcated as the 'temple sanctuary' (temenos), relative to (temnein) 'to cut'. Descendents of 'Anak' include the Biblical giant 'Goliath'.

14 Roman historians record that Caesar is born from a 'Caesarean' (Latin Caesarianus), a word obtained from 'caes' (to cut). Esoteric, 'caes' is clandestine of 'Gaea' (the Goddess of the Earth) - a daughter of 'chaos' (Greek khaos). Gaea's offspring are mutual to the 'Shatani' (Greek Teitan), philological to the 'Titan' (giant) and 'Anunnaki'. A mother Goddess of sacrifice, Gaea's name originates from the Egyptian root 'garah' (to injure) and is a signifier of Caesar's Royal pedigree, analogous to the children of 'Anak' (Greek 'Anax' - a prince). Significantly, 'Gaea' (earth) is the mother and wife of 'Uranus' (heaven) - her offspring include the mythical race the Titans (Shatani or Anunnaki), correlated with Royal progeny.

15 Prolog: Pocket Bilingual Dictionary, English-Hebrew, Hebrew-English, Prolog, 2003, p347

16 Ferozsons Urdu-English Dictionary, A Comprehensive Dictionary of Current Vocabulary, (Revised Edition), Ferozsons Ltd, Lahore, p446

17 To measure seasonal procession accurately, it takes approximately three thousand years - ancient astronomers, according to legend, received this knowledge from the fish deities.

18 Prolog: Pocket Bilingual Dictionary, English-Hebrew, Hebrew-English, Prolog, 2003, p180

19 'Anu' Akkadian (heaven) in the Sumerian language describes the 'jackal deity' and suggests a correlation with the 'Dog Star', traditionally identified with the fish deities the 'Nommu'- identical to the Canaanite 'Dagon'. They are recorded as the instructors and are attributed archaically with agriculture and the development of human society.

20 Prolog: Pocket Bilingual Dictionary, English-Hebrew, Hebrew-English, Prolog, 2003, p360 ['ana' (season)]

21 Ibid, 328

22 Ferozsons Urdu-English Dictionary, A Comprehensive Dictionary of Current Vocabulary, (Revised Edition), Ferozsons Ltd, Lahore, p756

23 Ibid

24 The eel is able to survive in fresh and salt water (the dual waters) - comparable to the crocodile Sobek (Venus).

25 In Judaic tradition, Moses is given permission to traverse the dual waters by the Lord of the host. Theologically, Yahweh is presented as the Lord of the double waters, conceptual to the angel - a sailor. In the book of Exodus, Moses thus 'delivers' (moser) his people from destruction by splitting the dual waters and passing over the spiritual (metaphysical) planes, symbolised as the Red Sea (Reed Sea). Moses quite literally bridges the gap between time and space, sequential to the Exodus and the migration of the Hebrews, drawn out historically from the stars.

26 M.A.S. Abdel Haleem: The Qur'an, Oxford University Press, Oxford 2004, pp353-354 (Sura: The Lord of Mercy 55:14-37 Paraphrased)

27 Mankind's corporal form, according to the Koran and the Bible, is modelled out of 'clay' (Hebrew khomer), covert in Arabic to the 'moon' (qamar) - a receptacle or repository of human seed, recreational to the earth post deluge. In Babylonian traditions, 'clay' is a marker of 'flesh and blood' - indicative of genetic manipulation, identified with the offspring of man. Human origins in the Koran is contrasted with the djinn's (jinn) creation, formed from the 'smokeless fire' i.e. the sun (Sirius), esoteric of a serpent (or fish). The solar motif suggests the djinn's species is older than humanity and is innate to the conception of the firmament. 'Fire' archaically is a signifier of 'blood' and connotes the votive, adjacent to the djinn, an entity depicted as a trans-dimensional species. In Arabian legends, the djinn is a reptilian or bipedal goat, and is able to assume human likeness through the ingestion of blood (light). It is often unclear as to whether the djinn is a 'solid or non-corporal race' - this ambiguity is removed when one realises that the human species is 'multi-dimensional' and, like the djinn, can appear both 'non-material (spirit) or physical'.

28 Prolog: Pocket Bilingual Dictionary, English-Hebrew Hebrew-English, Prolog, 2003 p185

29 Hippocrene English-Arabic, Arabic-English Dictionary, Hippocrene, New York, 2005, p162

30 Prolog: Pocket Bilingual Dictionary, English-Hebrew Hebrew-English, Prolog, 2003 p262

31 Hippocrene English-Arabic, Arabic-English Dictionary, Hippocrene, New York, 2005, p162

32 Vanessa Lampert: Practical Kabbalah for Magic and Protection, Cico Books, 2002, p143

33 H P Blavatsky: Collected Writings 1888, The Secret Doctrine, Vol 2, Anthropogenesis, Quest Books, Theosophical Publishing House, 1993, p460

34 Prolog: Pocket Bilingual Dictionary, English-Hebrew Hebrew-English, Prolog, 2003, p355

35 Ibid, p168

36 John C Traupman, PhD: The New College Latin English Dictionary, Bantam Books, 1988, p174

37 Ibid

38 Ibid

39 Prolog: Pocket Bilingual Dictionary, English-Hebrew Hebrew-English, Prolog, 2003, p89

40 Ibid, p98

41 Hippocrene English-Arabic, Arabic-English Dictionary, Hippocrene, New York, 2005, p157

42 'Nik or nek' (sexual intercourse) informs the Greek noun 'necros' (flesh) equivalent to the Japanese etymology 'niku' (meat).

43 Hippocrene English-Arabic, Arabic-English Dictionary, Hippocrene, New York, 2005, p41

44 Ritualised violence, accorded to the seraph, pertains to immolation of the votive. A 'snake' denotes a 'snack', analogous to 'serpent' and 'supper' - Old Semitic 'acan' (snake) and 'akal' (eat).

45 Hippocrene English-Arabic, Arabic-English Dictionary, Hippocrene, New York, 2005, p41

46 Ibid, p115

47 Ibid, p48

48 John C Traupman: New College, Latin & English dictionary, Bantam, 1988, p15

49 Ibid, p16

50 Clothed in her ceremonial garments, the virgin's wings silhouette the 'serpent's profile', technically a 'shadow or double'. The serpent's mouth symbolized as wings pertains ceremoniously to the invocation of the 'double', rendered in the hieroglyphs as (ka), implicit of the 'angel' or 'king' (Kar). Drawn with the 'priestess arm', the 'ka' ideogram is symbolic of the 'fire-star offering' (min-kha), cognate with the mouth and womb, grouped with the resurrection and ascension of 'Venus' (Sabah-Kha).

51 Prolog: Pocket Bilingual Dictionary, English-Hebrew Hebrew-English, Prolog, 2003, p119

52 The prophet Jonah (Jonah Chapter 1:17) is swallowed by the fish and is regurgitated three days later to do God's bidding. 'Jonah' (Hebrew Yona - dove) goes to the city 'Nineveh' (Lady of the wings or serpent) e.g. Isis, a Goddess shown in Egyptian lore with wings, drawn esoterically to represent the serpent's profile. Jonah in the Biblical account requests the king to wear a sack-cloth and observe a religious fast. The King of Nineveh submits to Yahweh's orders on threat of destruction. The sack-cloth worn by the king is reminiscent of the camel hair, worn by John the Baptist, a signifer of the mammal, combined with the bird and fish - astrological to the Pleiades, Sirius and Orion.

35

Menstrual Fish
Dogs and Pharaohs

'O come ye and acclaim Ra, the Lord of the heaven and the Creator
of the gods, and adore ye him in his beautiful form as he cometh in
the morning in his divine bark'.[1]

'Papyrus of Ani' (literally an heavenly being)

'Outside are the dogs, those who practise magic arts, the sexually
immoral, the murderers, the idolaters and everyone who loves and
practises falsehood'.

Revelation 22:15, Holy Bible, New International Version, Gideon

'Historia' means (enquiry, finding out or narrative) from the Greek root 'histor' (a learned or wise man) - a title affiliated to 'astron' (a star), suggesting the 'illuminati'.[2] In Imperial Rome, the 'city' (astu)[3] is laid out according to the configuration of the stars. 'Histor' is transliterated from the Greek into the Latin as 'astus' (cunning or cleverness),[4] cogent with 'astute' (sly). Star clusters archaically are associated with sacred geometry and the introduction of writing, originating in Babylonian culture from the fish deity Oannes.

The crucified 'serpent' from a 14th century Biblia 'Panerin' the Hebrew name translates as (the penis [of the] watcher). An 'eel' (samak) is seen as resting on a 'prop' (somekh), equivalent to a 'phallus'. The illustration below the cross shows eels depicted with avian features combined with the fallen woman.

Evidence for Oannes'[5] influence within the Middle Eastern culture and language is encrypted in the Hebrew alphabet. Linguists and symbolists argue the (s) character in Hebrew 'samekh' denotes (a prop), sometimes translated as (a fulcrum) from the noun 'somekh'.[6]

Esoterically, the letter 'samekh' specifies 'samak' (an eel) and is clearly evidenced in the Hebrew characters. The preceding letters 'mem' (m) and 'nun' (n) are rendered respectively as (water) and (fish). Celestial depictions of the Hebrew alphabet show that the letters are star constellations. Each system corresponds with a planet attribute, personifying the masculine, feminine and generative.

'Samekh' the letter (s) is transcribed in the Hebrew script as an ouroboros, representational of the sun Sirius and its relationship to the lunar cycle of the eel.[7] Celebration of the 'fish' (Arabic samak) informs 'same'ak' (happy), revelatory of 'simcha' (celebration) from the verbal stem 'simhah' (to rejoice).

The noun 'samak' (an eel) is important in Egyptian lore, as it is closely related to the Pharaonic name 'Smenkh' translated loosely by authorities as (victorious).[8] Smenkh's appellation honours 'Ad-nagga' (the Perpetual-Smiter), dualled with (the Eternal-Saviour), mythological to the 'eel' (samak).[9]

The Royal seal of the eel or fish shows close vernacular and religious ties between the line of Pharaohs and the inception of Judaism and Christianity. This is particularly evidenced with the Royal patron 'Smenkh'. His actual name is obtained from the Hebrew word 'smechah' - a title denoting (the full ordination into the Jewish faith).[10] Smenkh's connection to the secret traditions of Judaism suggests he is considered a figure of stature.

The author Ian Van Vayro has pointed out that 'Smenkh' is otherwise referred to by his full title 'Smenkhkare'. The observation made by Vayro is salient and further indicates 'Smenkhkare's appellation (victorious) given by the Egyptologists is suspect. Smenkhkare's dubious spelling is an adaptation taken from the original name 'Smechah' (ordination) - a classification adopted by the Pharaoh himself.

Historically, Smechah (Smenkhkare) married the daughter of 'Aminadab', an honorary title given to the Sovereign 'Akhenaten'. The connection is important as it shows that Smechah fits with the patron of the Jewish faith Aaron, recorded in Exodus 6:23. In this genealogy, Aaron is listed as marrying: *'Elisheba [elevated star], daughter of Amminadab'*.

Structural evidence indicates 'Amminadab' otherwise 'Akhenaten' (Moses) is connected to the Jewish tabernacle. In the Old Semitic, 'amin' designates (sexual integrity, chastity or celibacy), amalgamated with 'adab' from the Egyptian Arabic root 'addib' (to educate).[11] 'Addib' in this context is coherent with the mysteries and suggests sexual initiation, assigned to the inner sanctum of the pyramid.

The compound 'Addib' philologically is derived from 'dabar' (to speak), reciprocal within Judaism of 'dabir' (the temple chamber or holy of holies).[12] 'Dabir' is listed in the hieroglyphic sign list as 'dejebar', probably 'dabir', translated by Egyptologists as (the inner sanctum or shrine).[13] In the current Arabic, 'dabah' signifies the verb (to kill or slaughter)[14] and is an affirmation of 'dabh' (a sacrifice).[15] Egyptian liturgy suggests the verbal root 'dabar' operates as a pun on 'da-bar' literally (to invite[16] [the] hawk[17]) - an annotation of the Pharaoh, personified as the rising star Horus. In the Syrian dialect, 'da-bar' is read as the wordplay (to loose one's son).[18] The euphemism reflects a sacrificial tribute, equated with the death of the firstborn. Propitiations of the newborn mark the resurrection of the living king - an extension of Horus paired with Amun. The dualistic role of Horus-Amun insinuates the 'destroyer' (nagga), paired with the 'saviour' (nagga) - extensions of the carpenter and Venus (host).

Biblically, Amminadab's ambivalent role as the saviour of his people records the killing of the innocent, synchronized with the Exodus and the flood. This event is pivotal within Judaic theology, and sets out the 'Holy Scriptures', assigned to the 'Torah'. Recital of the religious Law discloses the proclamation of Sirius (Osiris), identified with the bark of the dog. The metaphor is redolent of the deity Anubis - the keeper of the 'shrine' (dabir), quintessential of the howling angel of death.

Sacerdotal, 'invocations' (dabar) correspond in esoteric Arabic to the laughing 'hyena' (dab),[19] evinced from the verbal root 'dabdab' (to crawl).[20] The verb delineates the 'reptile' in sync with the 'shrine' (dabir). Offspring of the 'hyena' is reproduced as a 'laughing angel', equivalent to a 'reaper'. Crucially, the 'hyena' (dab) implies a causal link with 'sacrifice' (dabh) - indicative of the 'Dog Star' 'Sirius' Greek (Seirios).

The 'Dog Star' is written in Arabic as 'Al Kalb' (the dog).[21] It is also known in Arabic as 'Al shi'ra' - Sanskrit 'Surya' (the Shining One), transferred into Greek as 'Seirios' (scorching). The appellation 'Dog Star' is a reference to the star rising before the Morning Star, and thereby tricking canines into howling.[22]

Conceptually, the dog baying symbolizes the 'musical host', opposite the 'laughing angel'. Identical comparisons are found also in the Latin vocabulary, conjunct religiously with Sirius. The Lord's host is equated with rapture and 'singing' (Latin canere)[23] - an etymology juxtaposed with the intransitive verb 'canescere' (to grow white or become grey[24] - incandescent).

Description of the host thus conveys the 'Dog Star' (Canicular)[25] from the Latin noun 'canis' (a dog).[26] The star is deemed as the brightest sun within the constellation of Canis Major.[27] 'Canicular' is paired with 'Canis Minor' - originally 'Rubra Canicula' (fiery red or ruddy)[28] - a signifier that fits with the Dual Crown of Egypt (Red and White).[29] 'Rubra Canicula' follows at the heels of the hunter 'Orion' ('ryan' - king) and is registered with the hunter's dog.

'Orion', in Greek myth, is blinded by the deity 'Oenopian', correlated in Egyptian iconography with the loss of 'Horus' eye'.[30] Significantly, 'Orion' the hunter is said to have chased the 'Pleiades', and reiterates the split within the priesthood. The name 'Orion', Arabic 'Al Jabbar' (the Giant) Hebrew 'Gibbor', is cognate with the 'shrine' (dabir or dejebar), unified with 'Sirius'.

Of particular relevance, the appellation 'Gibbor' (Giant) alludes to the mythical race - the 'Anunnaki' (Gigantic),[31] esoteric of the 'children of heaven' e.g. Orion. The Semitic word 'Anunnaki' alternatively 'Gibborim' is translated into Greek as the demigod 'Titan' - a name catalogued with the fallen serpent 'Satan' (the adversary), Greek 'Teitan'. 'Jabbar' is listed with the stars 'Al Babadur' (the strong) and 'Al Shuja' (the snake), recorded by Arab astronomers.[32]

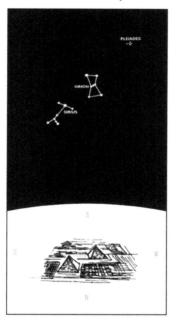

Sirius constellation is situated adjacent to Orion
and the Pleiades correlated with the Southern Crown of Osiris.

The picture, painted in the star constellations, bear witness to the most incredible myth - a belief shared universally throughout Asia Minor and the Mediterranean. The chronology and reconstruction of human anthropology, though fragmentary and incomplete, is outlined below.[33]

Homo sapiens, survivors of the war with the amphibian race (Atlantis), escaped their solar system the Pleiades and hid from their aggressor in our own system, probably on Mars. The ensuing war and destruction of Mars (Adam) with water marked the near extinction of humankind. Remnants of man's seed are later appropriated and preserved on the moon (an artificially created satellite).

The moon's arc (ark) is drawn in Egyptian iconography as a boat - monumental of human insurrection,[34] relative to the angelic wars (Chapter 1 The Mal'akh). Mortal salvation, timed with the recreation of man, celebrates the covenant, decreed religiously through the Sabbath - originally a lunar festival. The horned crescent, a mascot of the priesthood, operates as a double signifier of 'Venus', nominal of the 'host and Sirius'.

War with the amphibian created a need for both races to unite. This Biblically is resolved with 'Eve and Anak' - their children the 'Nephilim' Hebrew (the Fallen). The narrative sketched out documents the unification of Sirius (Osiris) with the Pleiades (Isis), figurative of Orion's conception, heralded as the nativity of Horus.

Similar analogies are found also in the Sino language. 'Mao' in Chinese refers to (the 'Pleiades' - the Seven Sisters), when spoken with a rising intonation, is used to describe the following nouns (hair, fear, a small child, lance and a spear).[35] The homonyms pertain to the mammal commensurate in Greek mythology to Electra's menstrual blood, theoretical to the Pleiades and conflict. In Eastern astrology, the Pleiades[36] represents a hunting net[37] - a signifier in Western astrology of 'Orion'.[38] The Chinese word 'Shen' (Orion)[39] is translated by Sino-scholars (to mix).[40] 'Shen' is described as a 'warrior'[41] - an epithet homologous to the 'hunter Orion'.[42]

Switching back into the Arabic language; the Pleiadian 'tribe' (Hebrew Shebet) settled and became a 'nation' or 'people' (Arabic sha'b) - root words derived from 'sab'a' the homonym (seven or mourn). The Semitic etymon 'sab'a' personifies the 'Seven Sisters', represented as the menorah (seven-lights), equated with the 'menstrual cycle' (Greek menorrhoea).

Later, the 'Shebet' denomination formed the matriarchal priesthood the 'Sibyl' (Akkadian Sibulla), famed in Arabia as the 'Sabians', Arabic 'Saba'ia' (the Star People). In Judaic tradition, the Sabians embodied 'Elisheba' (elevated star) - a bloodline mixed with the Pharaoh 'Smechah' (ordination), famously the elder brother of Moses - Aaron. He is noted as the worshipper of the golden calf (Taurus), astrological to the 'Pleiades' and its division with 'Sirius'.[43]

The Dog Star celestially is grouped with Osiris 'Lord of the host', situated opposite Horus, Egyptian 'Kar' (the hunter) Greek 'Orion'. The rising star Sirius parallels Osiris, subsequent to his rebirth as the first King of Egypt. Incarnation of Osiris' begotten son, Horus marks the succession of the Pharaonic line, transcribed with the falcon - a migratory bird.

Symbolism of Orion and Horus is marked architecturally in the pyramids. The three stars of 'Orion's Belt' (Latin Zeta Orionis - Arabic Al Nitak)[44] are mnemonic of the trinity 'Osiris, Horus and Isis'. Visualized in the Egyptian pantheon as a triptych the 'father, son and virgin', the Holy family outline the constellations 'Sirius, Orion and the Pleiades'.

Superimposed, astrologically the pyramid plateau is a diagram of Orion's belt, diplomatic of divine 'intercourse' (al-nikah) between the stars Sirius (Ra) and the Pleiades (Chem). This sacred union is governed through the rule of Orion. Arcane beliefs indicate the children of Sirius populated the regions of Orion. The pyramidal structure outlined in Chapter 32 The Builders is presented as a harem, intrinsic to human intercourse with angelic beings.

Dedicated to the Jackal deity, Anubis the 'Keeper of the Shrine' its pyramid precinct the sanctum is used to propagate the Royal bloodline, continued unbroken through the priesthood of Ammina-dab (Moses). Ammina-dab's title is cogent in Arabic with the noun 'dab' (hyena) - a word closely related to 'dyab or djab' (a wolf).[45] 'Dab and djab' connote 'jabbar' (Orion), adjacent to the 'Dog Star' (Al Kalb), pictured as Anubis.

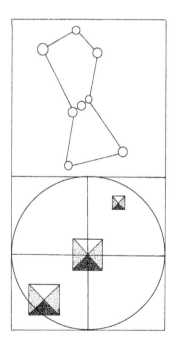

Schemata of pyramid plateaux is configured to 'Orion's belt'
(Arabic Al Nitak), viewed here as the central three stars.

Egyptian liturgy archives 'Anubis' as the embalmer and the remover of the 'heart', paralleled theologically to the 'deliverer' (Moser).[46] The Arabic noun 'qalb' (heart)[47]discloses 'habl' (pregnany),[48] transcendental of the 'Dog Star' (Al Kalb). Ritual extraction of the cardiac vascular system is conceptual to the 'deliverer' (Moser) - a 'saviour' and 'striker', thematic of the votive and rebirth.

The canine in Arabian tradition denotes the djinn a deity allocated to the 'shrine' (dejebar or dabir). Theologically 'dabir' (shrine) is mutual to 'djeba' (a leader of troops), suppositional to 'dabh' (sacrifice). The offering of the victim is contingent in the Latin wordplay with the 'angelic host' and the 'hostia' (a sacrificial victim). Observing the Latin and Arabic lexicon, the 'djinn' are identical to the 'host'. Emblem of the djinn in Arabian mythology discloses the 'wolf' (dyab or djab) - a symbol of the 'Dog Star',[49] referential to the 'dog soldier'.[50]

Ancient legends describing the dog and reptile originate from the Babylonian deity Tiamat - her invocation preserved in the Enuma Elish, quoted below:

> 'Let us create monsters - monstrous snakes with cruel jaws,
> furious dragons charged with supernatural brilliance, enraged
> dogs. She created all these wild beasts and made them like gods'.[51]

Tiamat's invocation refers to the creation of the zodiac. Historically, the canine is incorporated with the dragon and the amphibian. Progeny of the serpent is listed with the fish deity 'Dagon', correlated in Babylonian mythology with 'Ea' and 'Oannes'. 'Dagon' in the ancient Semitic 'Dag-An' translates as (the Fish of Heaven).[52] The Babylonian word for 'heaven' (an) is cognate with 'Anu' (the chief God of Sumer pictured as a jackal).[53]

Written unpointed, 'Anu' (the Creator God) in Akkadian and Aramaic spells 'nu' (a fish), emblematic of 'Sirius'. Religiously, the Hebrew word 'ze'ev' (wolf)[54] - Old Semitic 'sab' - is correlated with 'sabah' (morning), assigned cryptically to 'sab'a' (the 'seven' sisters), culminant of the war with Orion. 'Sab' additionally is the Old name for (Anubis) - a deity commensurate with sacrifice, inaugural of 'Sirius' and the re-enactment of the 'mystery' (the evening votive).

Theoretically, the howling of the 'dog' indicates the rising and setting of 'Sirius', aligned to the temple 'sanctuary' (dabir) in conjunction with the God of Death Anubis ('Sab' - wolf). Semantic evidence demonstrates the name 'Sirius - Ra', transliterated (Rh), is onomatopoeic of the dog's growl, inimical of loss. Egyptian hymns celebrate the brilliance of Ra, manifested cryptically through his bark (See Chapter heading).

Linguistic comparisons in Arabic demonstrate that 'aur' Hebrew 'or' (light) pertain to the Semitic verb 'awr' (to bark).[55] In relation to these observations, the Egyptian deity 'Ra', traditionally the 'Sun God', is incorrectly designated. His original name is not transliterated as 'Ra', but is written as 'Aur' - a classification of 'Sirius', cognate with the sanctum.

In Old Semitic, 'aur' is philologically branched with 'eloh' (light), rendered in the plural as the 'Elohim', translated in Judaic accounts as (the Gods) or (the Shining Ones - a dragon), an appellation equated with the 'Dog Star'. The pun is compatible in Modern Arabic with 'Allah' (God) and 'awr' (bark) - English 'God' and 'dog'. Quantifiable, the wordplay 'God and dog' is reciprocal in the Syriac Torah. The Hebrew name 'Heylel' (the Shining one) is reproduced as 'H-eyel' (the Howling one) names assigned to 'Lucifer - Latin Lux-ferre' (the light bringer). The Syrian name 'Heylel' is analogous in the Akkadian language to 'hayya' (a female serpent), translated more probably as (an eel).

Deities assigned to the Dog Star are universally evident in all human languages. For example, the equivalent play is found in the Old Japanese honorific address '(O)-Kami' (God) and 'ookami' (wolf). The 'God' (Kami), a designation of the 'wolf' (ookami), is mirrored with the noun 'hair' (Kami) - a classification of the mammal. In Japan, the serpent deities, attributed to the 'fallen angels' otherwise the 'djinn', are referred to as the 'tengu' (literally heaven's dog) - Refer to Japanese glossary, Appendix 2.

Similar comparisons are evident in the Roman language. The appellation 'Lato' (Apollo)[56] establishes a connection with 'lator' (a bringer, bearer, proposer of a law).[57] Importantly, the 'light-bringer' is a namesake, cognate with the transitive verb 'latro' (to bark or snarl).[58] In addition, the stem 'latr' is used to denote 'latro' (a mercenary, brigand or bandit).[59] The assignment refers to the 'dog-soldier', conceptual to the rapist, host or the maligned djinn (jinn). Latro's stem is thus used to imply a 'thief', covert to the 'pillager', philological to 'plagusia' Latin (a fish), recognizant with the 'reptile' and 'rapist'.

Arcane, the 'thief' operates as a covert marker of the secret votive, equated with the human offering. Cults associated with the old-dog Apollo are by implication 'latens' (hidden or secret), coherent with 'lateo' (to lie hidden, out of sight, to remain unknown or obscure).[60] All of these attributes are shared by the Egyptian God Amun (Pleiades) - personifications of 'Ra' (Sirius), reborn as 'Horus' (Orion).

The definition 'latens' (hidden) is taxonomic of 'lactens' (full of milk),[61] denoting the mammal - a signifier of the human animal, combined with the progeny of the fish (dog). Etymological resemblance in Latin between the 'light-bringer' (Lato) and the 'barker' (Latro) indicates 'Apollo's attribution as a 'Solar God' is technically incorrect. Written evidence shows unequivocally he is the God of the 'Dog Star' - a constellation mirrored with our own 'sun'.

Theologically the 'radiant dragon' the djinn is contrasted with the 'barking angel' - an aphorism synonymous with 'flashing'. The English verb to 'bark' is thus deduced from the Arabic word 'barq' recorded as (a flash or lightning),[62] a derivation from the Hebrew stem 'boker' (morning).[63] Further, the noun 'dog' is a corruption of the Hebrew word 'dag' (fish), emblematic of Sirius (Canis Major) - schematic of the temple sanctuary (womb), adjacent to the woman's body.

Matriarchal, the woman's offspring in Judaism is attributed with the Levite (Liberal) priesthood, deductive of 'lev' (a heart).[64] The Hebrew noun 'lev' is translated in Arabic as (qalb) - a symbol of 'Sirius', cognate with the 'Dog Star' (Al Kalb). Descendents of the Levites, according to the Torah, originate from 'Amminadab', known more famously as 'Akhenaten or Moses'. Akhenaten's rearrangement of the Theban autocracy into a monarchial and monotheistic edifice established the Roman and European Empire (Christo-Judaic).

In conclusion, Amminadab's role as the 'orator of the shrine' (dabir) is transferred to 'Smechah' (ordained) - a title held by Aaron through marriage into the Royal household of 'Elisheba'. Smechah's induction to the office as 'keeper of the shrine' via his mentor Amminadab is maintained through a code of sexual probity - pivotal to the Western and Judaic priesthood (Theban).

Celebration of Smechah's union with 'Elisheba' (elevated star) infers the 'Pleiades' and asseverates the unification of the Dual Kingdoms (waters).[65] A coalition aligned historically to the Lord of the host (Osiris) and his subordinates the 'Emori' (the Occidental nations). Evidence in the Indo-European languages verifies marital intercourse between the 'Emori' (Westerner) and 'Adam' (Easterner), united genealogically with the Western priesthood (the Rabbi and Mada) - Refer to Chapter 12, Thebes and the Offspring of the dragon.

At an obtuse level, Smechah's civil partnership with Elisheba documents 'ha-nikah' (the-marriage), precursor to the Jewish 'festival of light' (Hanukkah). 'Consecrated' through intercourse, (Hanukkah) is cognate with the Anunnaki, known collectively as the 'Giants' (Hebrew Anaki), accredited in Arabic to 'Gibbor' (Orion). Progeny of the Anunnaki is joined to the Royal 'hunter' Orion, deified as Horus (Kar) - a human-angelic bloodline (Hemitheoi or Emori).

Integration of the matriarch with the dragon, a fallen angel encapsulates the eel Goddess 'Ad-nagga' - an amalgamation of the 'mammal and reptile', caricatured as an 'amphibian'. Etiological of death, the eel's conflict with Ra (Sirius) elicits the menstrual sun the fire-star, premonitory of the killing of the firstborn, historical to the Pleiades. Ritualized, the infant's sacrifice is equated with the removal of the 'heart' (lev or qalb), pernicious of the Levite priesthood,[66] conjoined to the star Sirius (Al Kalb).

Duplicated through death and resurrection, the virgin's consumption of blood consecrates 'Ad-nagga' - a Goddess faceted with the Western nations. Insemination of the solar mascot ordains the priestess' copulation with a deity, appointed to the Inner mysteries of Judaism. Customs and practices, allotted to the menstrual fish (Sirius), are canonical (canine) to the covenant and the worship of the Dog Star. As we shall shortly observe, the Goddess 'Ad-nagga' is integral also to the mystical traditions of Islam, noted in the next chapter.

1   Andrew Collins, From the Ahes of Angels, Michael Joseph Ltd, 1996, p341 (See summary of Ra myths).

2   Contemporary scholars talk of Feminist, Marxist or Liberal deconstruction. To understand the secret workings of human society, one has to go back and look at esoteric symbolism and its relationship to historical discourse. For example, the authors of the Communist Manifesto purport angelic descent e.g. 'Engels' (Anglo-Saxon an angel) in cahoots with 'Marx' a derivation of 'Mark' (a hammer - refer to the Soviet flag). 'Marx's name possesses the additional translation (sprung from Mars). Marx historically is a German scholar and a member of the German Bavarian illuminati - a German-Judaic priesthood, affiliated with the Fascist. Division between the Communist and Fascist philosophies facilitated the Second World War and the creation of Europe ['Europa' (West) - emblematic of the Pleiades] - Refer to Section: Thebes and the Serpentigena (the Western Priesthood) pp115 - 141. Historical movements like communism or later the partition of Pakistan are politically attributed to angels. The first Governor-General of Pakistan is Mohammed Ali 'Jinnah' - his surname a Sanskrit title meaning (a conqueror), etymological to (the djinn). The name 'Pakistan' translates as (the land of the pure) - axioms used to describe the angelic bloodline.

3   John C Traupman: The New College Latin & English Dictionary, Bantam Books, 1988, p23

4   Ibid

5   The scaly husk of the 'pineapple' (Latin ananas) symbolises the fish God 'Oannes'. The world's largest sculpture of the pineapple thus can be seen at the home of the fish God himself, the Vatican. Symbolically augmented, the papal's mitre is a symbol of the fish's head. The other Latin noun for a 'pineapple' is (pinea) a pun on 'pinna' (a feather). 'Pinna' informs the English noun 'fin' - both signifiers equated with the 'winged angel', grouped with the amphibious fish and heaven. Significantly 'pinea' (pine cone) is related to the 'pineal' gland - a pea size conical mass of tissue behind the third ventricle of the brain. The pineal is found <u>only in mammals</u> and used in arcane blood rituals - illustrative of [the 'Paean' Ritual (pain)].

6   Prolog: Pocket Bilingual Dictionary, English-Hebrew Hebrew-English, Prolog, 2003, p318

7   Blood and water designates theologically menstrual blood and semen (venom), indicative of a celestial pregnancy. The Goddess' blood personifies divine incarnation, demonstrated as light, commensurate with the serpent and fish.

8   Ian Van Ross Vayro: Tears In Heaven, Joshua Books, Australia, 2008, p228

9   'Ad-nagga' (the Perpetual-Smiter) doubled with (the Eternal-Saviour) are thematic of the permanent enslavement of mankind - an idea outlined later in this chapter.

10 Ian Van Ross Vayro: Tears In Heaven, Joshua Books, Australia, 2008, p63

11 Hippocrene English-Arabic, Arabic-English Dictionary, Hippocrene, New York, 2005, p146

12 Ralph Ellis: Eden in Egypt, A Translation of the Book of Genesis out of the Original Egyptian Text, Edfu Books, 2005, p279 (Appendix A5 - Dictionary).

13 'Dabir' (Holy of Holies) and 'Dabah' (to kill and slaughter) should in no way be confused with the family name De'Beer - the exporter of diamonds - etymological to 'daimon' (a demon).

14 Hippocrene English-Arabic, Arabic-English Dictionary, Hippocrene, New York, 2005, p64

15 Ibid, p105

16 Ibid, p62 ['da' (invite)]

17 Ibid, p155 ['bar' (hawk)]

18 Ibid, pp163 & 164 [Syrian 'da' (lose one's way), Arabic 'da' (invite). 'Da' is combined with the Aramaic noun 'bar' (a son)].

19 Ibid, p164

20 Ibid

21 Gary A David: Eye of the Phoenix, Mysterious Visions and Secrets of the American Southwest, Adventures Unlimited Press, USA, 2008, p56

22 Ibid, p57

23 John C Traupman: The New College Latin & English Dictionary, Bantam Books, 1988, p34

24 Ibid, p33 ['canescere' intransitive verb (to grow white, become grey or to grow old)].

25 Ibid

26 Ibid, 386

27 The alternative Latin adjective for 'white or favourable' is (albus) and is cogent with 'Alba Longa' (the mother City of Rome) - literally (distant white). The term is closely identified with the Roman name 'Albion' (Britain) and suggests the white coastline. Britain's border archaically is conceptual to the veneration of the white star Sirius and the creation of the Roman bloodline, correlated with the wolf.

28 Gary A David: Eye of the Phoenix, Mysterious Visions and Secrets of the American Southwest, Adventures Unlimited Press, USA, 2008, p57

29 Sirius is a tri-star system. Its third star is hidden to the eye and is compared to the Pleiades and the hidden star Electra, conjunct with the worship of Amun.

30 Mythological to the narrative of Aaron and Moses, the surrender of the Pharaoh's firstborn is a retelling of the story of Osiris, gathered under the constellation of Sirius, cognate with the Southern Crown - a tear-duct (Orion), lateral to the fish and mammal. The severed eye of Horus in Egyptian cosmology signifies the creation of man, grouped with the fish (Sirius) and its division with the Pleiades.

31 Prolog Pocket Bilingual Dictionary, English-Hebrew, Hebrew-English, Prolog, 2003, p168

32 J A Coleman: The Dictionary of Mythology, An A-Z of Themes, Legends, & Heroes, Capella, 2007, pp786 & 787

33 There are many gaps in the story of Orion, Sirius and the Pleiades - the outline at the best is a tentative and working hypothesis. The ancient astrological symbolism is very difficult and is compounded by the fact that there may have been more than one faction of different life form intervening in the story.

34 The word 'artificial' (Arabic masnu) originally from the verbal stem (snu) is a pun on the Old Arabic word 'mas-nu' (descendents of the fish). This group are identified with the 'lunar satellite', correlated in occult iconography with 'water', the 'dog' and 'menstrual blood'.

35 A Chinese-English Dictionary, IBSN 7-100-00530-2/H.188, 1988, pp459 & 460

36 The Chinese etymon 'Mao' (Pleiades) is tacitly linked to the archaic word 'miau' (a sanctuary allocated to the morning sacrifice).

37 Derek Walters, Chinese Astrology, The Most Comprehensive Study of the Subject Ever Published in the English Language, Watkins Publishing, London, 2002, p112 (See definition of Mao, the Pleiades)

38 The Chinese character 'Shen' (to mix), astrologically 'Orion', is cognate in the Japanese language with the Buddhist sect 'Zen'. In Japanese, 'zen' designates the prefix (whole, entire, all or complete).

39 The Chinese homonym 'shen' (way) is consistent in Arabic with 'sunna' (form, way, rule or course).

40 Derek Walters, Chinese Astrology, The Most Comprehensive Study of the Subject Ever Published in the English Language, Watkins Publishing, London, 2002, pp115 & 116

41 The root of 'Shen' (Orion) corresponds with 'shin' (death), enunciated piously through 'shen' (the way, course or pathway). Additionally the character 'Shen' signifies (God) - official to the state religion 'Shen Dao', transliterated into Japanese as 'Shinto'.

42 Chairman Mao's Communist Revolution is linked covertly to the 'Pleiades' (Mao) and insurrection.

43 'Orion and Sirius' registers the 'caduceus' (the double dragon) Greek 'kerux' (a herald). The 'caduceus' is pictured in Latin as 'crux' (a cross) German 'kreis' (a circle), accredited with the Pleiades and loss.

44 Robert Bauval & Graham Hancock, Keepers of Genesis, BCA, 1996, p65

45 Hippocrene English-Arabic, Arabic-English Dictionary, Hippocrene, New York, 2005, p141

46 Prolog Pocket Bilingual Dictionary, English-Hebrew, Hebrew-English, Prolog, 2003, p103

47 Hippocrene English-Arabic, Arabic-English Dictionary, Hippocrene, New York, 2005, p56

48 Ibid, p94

49 In Roman mythology, the hyena's offspring is transferred to Remus and Romulus - the twin sons of Mars.

50 The former president W Bush, pronounced in the Texan dialect 'dub-Yah', is analogous in Arabic to 'dub-Yah' (to bear Yahweh) or 'dabh-Yah' (Yahweh's sacrifice) - nomenclature of 'dyab-Yah' (the wolf of Yahweh). Interestingly the appellation 'wolf' fits with Hitler's first name 'Adolf' (a wolf). To emphasize, people in public office have covert names, i.e. 'J E Hoover' director of the FBI is a pun on 'Jehovah', relative to 'Jovis' (Jupiter - the God of Law). In China, Chairman Mao is covert to 'Mao' (the Pleiades).

51 Fernand Comte: Mythology, Chambers Compact Reference, 1998, p210

52 Prolog: Pocket Bilingual Dictionary, English-Hebrew Hebrew-English, Prolog, 2003, p152 ['dag' (fish)]

53 The 'inner sanctum' (dabir in Arabic) is grouped with the laughing 'hyena' (dab), illustrative of the 'djinn'. They are depicted in Arabian folklore as a 'dog, goat or snake'. In essence, the 'hyena' represents a 'laughing angel' - a reaper. Materialisation of this entity is connected to the Dog Star, aligned to the Temple Mortuary - the Holy of Holies.

54 Prolog: Pocket Bilingual Dictionary, English-Hebrew Hebrew-English, Prolog, 2003, p463

55 Hippocrene English-Arabic, Arabic-English Dictionary, Hippocrene, New York, 2005, p16

56 John C Traupman: The New College Latin & English Dictionary, Bantam Books, 1988, p166

57 Ibid

58 Ibid

59 Ibid

60 Ibid, 165

61 Ibid, 163

62 Hippocrene English-Arabic, Arabic-English Dictionary, Hippocrene, New York, 2005, p156

63 Prolog, Pocket Bilingual Dictionary, English-Hebrew-Hebrew-English, Prolog, 2003, p262

64 Ibid, p183

65 The Two Kingdoms of Egypt suggest Thebes and Syria, identified ostensibly with the unification of the kingdom of men and angels (heaven and earth), realised through the government (covenant).

66 Different factions of the priesthood are affiliated to different body parts - the Sadduceas with the head, the Levites with the heart and the Vestal Virgin with the foot. The signifier of the virgin's 'footprint' (Latin vestigium) is equivalent to 'vestis' (a snake-skin). The Arabic word 'ka'b' (an heel) is notational of 'Al Kalb' (the Dog Star), esoteric of the fish and 'heart' (qalb). In addition, the Arabic etymon 'regl' (a foot) informs the Latin adjective 'regal' (royal), equivalent in ancient Greek to 'skalex' (leg) and 'skolex' (worm). The relationship between the foot and reptile is further evinced in the Greek noun 'podhee' (a foot), conceptual to 'feedhee' (a snake). The 'p' and 'f' are analogous in Greek and Arabic. Each body part in turn is aligned to star systems that have numerical and alphabetical equivalents. The Apostle Paul (Josephus) in his letter to the Corinthians (12:12) compares the church to the body of Christ - a metaphor of the priesthood and its hidden denominations housed within the church.

36

The Short Story of Ali

'*Let none of you say... that he has the whole Koran in his possession. How does he know what the whole of it is... Much of the Koran is gone*'[1]

Quote taken from the second Caliph Uthmann (successor to Mohammed), who ruled two years after the Prophet's death

In the previous chapter, we examined the relationship of the fish Goddess Ad-nagga, and showed a correlation with the development of Judaic theology paralleled to Egypt. Traditions regarding this deity are linked to the sanctuary and the divine 'marriage' (ha-nikah) between mortals and angels.

Historically, the contractual agreement 'ha-nikah' originates from inter species conflict between humans and angels. This, according to ancient accounts, culminated in the deluge and the destruction of earth (Mars). Settlement between the parties is predicated upon marital intercourse and the development of the Royal line.

Conducted ritualistically inside of the pyramid, sexual union recalled angelic insurrection on mount Hermon. Renewal of this covenant between angels and man is formulated under the tutorage of 'Smenkhkare or Smechah' (ordained) and described the birth of Israel.

Sanctimonious, intercourse between the eel Goddess (a demigod) and the reptile is pivotal to the development of Judaism and the propagation of its angelic lineage, recorded in the secret teachings of Islam. This is preserved in the 'Edith' (Arabic Hadit - Tradition), detailing the sayings and practices of Mohammed. It constitutes the major source of guidance for Muslims after the Koran. The metaphor of the seraph's union with the eel Goddess Ad-nagga is encapsulated in the story of Ali cited below:

> *In the city of Kufa, some people came to Ali (the son-in-law of the Prophet and the founding figure of Shi'ism) to ask him about eels on sale in the local markets (In other words - if it is permissible for a believer to eat or trade in eels).*
>
> *He laughed, and invited them to witness a marvel. Ali thereupon took them to the bank of a river, spat in it, and recited some words, whereupon an eel appeared with its head raised and its mouth open. Ali asked the eel to identify itself; it duly explained on behalf of its fellows that they were the former inhabitants of the 'township bordering the sea'... The eel continued with its account:*
>
> *'God had asked the people of the township to give allegiance to Ali, and on their refusal had been subjected to metamorphosis, some ending up in the sea as eels, others on land as lizards and jerboas'.[2]*
>
> *Ali then turned to those present and asked them, if they had taken all this in, they replied that indeed they had. He concluded the*

proceedings with a zoological observation, strongly underlying the human heritage of eels: 'By Him, who sent Mohammed as a prophet, they menstruate just as your women do'.[3]

As usual with Islamic commentaries, the story is a type of parable and is encrypted through wordplay. The location 'Kufa' is based on the Arabic play 'kufr' (blasphemy) with the additional meanings (paganism, heathenism, profanity or unbelief).[4] 'Kufr' linguistically infers 'kuf'ur' (an infidel, renegade, disbeliever or idolater).[5]

The place name 'Kufa' is significant, as it combines the 'disbeliever' (kuf'ur) with 'kuf'u' the masculine noun (alike, equal, of the same tribe, caste, brotherhood or kin),[6] suggesting a 'fraternity of idolaters'. The wordplay infers covertly the Arabic quip 'kafir-lihiq' (a follower of unbelievers),[7] drawn out in the Greek lexicon 'katholikos' (a disciple of the Catholic Church).[8] Intriguingly, the play indicates Ali's roots are derived from the secret traditions of Catholicism.[9]

The protagonist Ali summons the eel. He then spits into her mouth - a covert symbol of ejaculation into the vagina of the eel Goddess. Ali in the account assumes the role of 'naja' (the spitting 'cobra' - the copulator) a signifier of the Theban priesthood. The name 'Ali' translates as (high), a derivation of 'Allah' (Aramaic eloh - light), a symbol of the seraph.

The eel goes on to say that its kind are from the township bordering the sea. The reference to the sea infers an angelic sailor. In Arabic, the noun 'bahr' (sea) is related to 'bah'har' (sailor) and is punned in Aramaic with 'bar' (son). 'Bar' esoterically is cognizant with the offspring of an angel, depicted as 'Baal' (Lord). The progeny of an angel is thus represented in Arabic as 'bar' the noun for (a hawk)[10] an emblem of the Royal line of Egypt. Designation of 'bar' (hawk) denotes ownership dependent upon royal inheritance 'barr' (land, continent or shore)[11] implicit of feudal or 'outside' control (barra).[12]

The eel continues her account and mentions a 'border' (hadd), esoteric of a 'sharp-knife' (sikkina-hadda).[13] 'Hadd' in this context suggests the materialization of an angel 'hadar' (literally presence), rendered in Greek as 'eidolon' (phantom) from 'eidos' (form). The Greek philology 'eidolon' informs the Latin noun 'idolum' (idol),[14] self-referential to the 'blasphemers' at 'Kufa'.

Deconstructing Ali's narrative, there are a number of salient clues to the possible meaning of the story. Her account tells of the metamorphosis of the lizard and jerboa. A type of mammal the 'jerboa' is (a small desert rodent) with tall hind legs possessing the ability to make long jumps. Its Latin name 'jerboa' is taken from the Arabic name 'yarbu' translated as (flesh of the loins). The rodent's ability to make long jumps suggests a correlation with the 'skipping goat' and its locomotion, imitable of sexual coitus.

Appearance of the goat (a demigod) is a synonym of the reptile, equated with the 'gazelle' and the 'Sabi' priestcraft. The motif of the goat indicates the red se'irim, identified with the menstrual eel Apophis - a symbol of the woman's genitalia, correlated with sexual defilement.

Ali concludes the instruction by revealing the inner mystery to the narrative, adding a touch of irony. The story is about the unfaithful - Ali's interpretation of the parable is so fantastical, the reader is cast into the role of the disbeliever.

Ali's strange account in addition records bodily metamorphosis of the angel into a reptile or mammal. The transformation details the ancient belief that certain types of angels had the ability to transform themselves into a reptilian or human entity. Ali closes his account and discloses the eel as a symbol of human angelic theogony - iconic of the red snake or dragon. This Royal line is emphasized as the 'menstrual reptile', analogous to the Theban and is reiterated in conclusion to the amazing story of Ali:

'By Him, who sent Mohammed as a prophet, they [the eel] menstruate just as your women do'.

Medieval woodcut of Mulusine of Avalon, Countess of Lusignan represented as a winged water snake (symbolic of a menstrual fish)

346

1 Michael Cook: The Koran, A Very Short Introduction, Oxford University Press, 2000, p123

2 Ibid

3 Ibid, p106

4 Ferozson's Urdu Dictionary, Revised Edition, Ferozson's Ltd, Lahore, p577

5 Ibid

6 Ibid (Ferozson labels 'kuf'u' as a masculine noun - a word which appears in the English translation as both a noun and adjective).

7 Hippocrene English-Arabic, Arabic-English Dictionary, Hippocrene, New York, 2005, p227

8 The Semitic pun 'kafir lihiq' (followers of unbelievers) is compared in Greek to 'katholikos' (a Catholic). The play is equivalent in Hebrew to 'sote' (deviant), contrasted in Greek with 'Soter' (saviour), implicit of the 'Sodalis' priesthood.

9 'Katholikos' (literally universal) is from the Greek root 'kata' (in respect of) and 'holos' (whole), and is a corruption from the Arabic etymon 'khalaq' (to create).

10 Hippocrene English-Arabic, Arabic-English Dictionary, Hippocrene, New York, 2005, p56

11 Ibid, p156

12 Ibid

13 Ibid, 184

14 John C Traupman: The New College Latin & English Dictionary, Bantam 1988, p415

37

Yahweh the Crescent and the Host

'Now when the Bull [Pleiades] succumbed to Ahriman and died, a miracle occurred; for from his various members all manner of plant life came into being, from his marrow sesame and from his blood the fruit of the vine. His seed was borne up to the moon, purified in its light and brought back to earth again; and from this seed not only did all manner of cattle [man] proceed but every species of animal life except only noxious beasts, reptiles, and harmful insects'.[1]

Professor R. C. Zaehner's Translation of the Greater Bundahishn Text

'Moon River, wider than a mile,
I'm crossing you in style some day.
Old dream maker, you heart breaker,
Wherever you're going, I'm going your way.

Two drifters, off to see the world,
There's such a lot of world to see.
We're after the same rainbow's end,
Waiting around the bend, my Huckleberry friend,

Moon River and me'.

Moon River, Danny Williams, UK No 1 Hit, 1961

According to Exodus 3:14, the appellation 'Yahweh' is from the verbal stem (I am) - an attempt by the Biblical redactor to obscure God's historical link with the crescent and the worship of Baal. 'Yahweh's name originates from the Egyptian language 'Yah-wer' and records the cognomen (great-moon). Priests of 'Yahweh' are referred to by the title 'komer' and obtain their label from the Arabic stem 'qamar' (moon). Its luminous orb is likened anagrammatically in Arabic to the compound 'qa'a mar' (the hall of saints), interchangeable in Persian with 'mar' (a snake).

'Q-amar' (moon) is equivocal to 'amara' (the host), consistent with the angel 'amar' (literally speak or command), termed as 'ammar' (the builder). The 'crescent' or the 'new moon' (hilal)[2] is a marker of the covenant, designated through the legal code 'halal' (lawful). A device of the priesthood, the satellite, records human angelic conflict and the submission (peace) of man.

In addition, there are a number of convoluted puns, extracted from the Pharaonic name Yahweh, central to the priesthood and the worship of the host. Yahweh's title archaically is esoteric of child sacrifice. By switching around the 'y' and 'j' morpheme, 'Yahweh' can be rendered in Syrian as 'jarh or yarh' (injury),[3] conjunct with the Egyptian Arabic idiom 'wallah' (by God).[4] 'Jarh-wallah' therefore signals (to be hurt by God), semantically the 'Lord of Pain'. He is dualled with the 'preserver' or 'builder', congruous with regeneration.

Theologically, the notion of resurrection is consistent with Yahweh as a God of War, the 'Lord of the Host'. Yahweh is seen as a 'deliverer', analogous to an 'aggressor' or 'saviour'. Conceptually, he is pictured as a redeemer (purchaser), identical to the enslaver, and reiterates man's submission to the covenant.

Actions assumed 'by the Lord' (wallah) are consequential to the burnt offering. 'Wallah' philologically is reduced from the Egyptian intransitive verb 'wala' (burn),[5] correlated with the Illuminati. In Islam, 'Wali' designates (the Muslim Saint), equivalent to (the enlightened or the Illuminated). The titular 'Wali' is analogous to a 'brother of light', interchangeable in the Greek mysteries with the 'philosopher'.

The 'Wali' designates a 'child of light' - born again, assigned in Arabic to 'walad' (a boy),[6] conceived from 'waldi' (a mother).[7] Covertly 'walad' plays on the Arabic verbal stem 'wa'ad' (promise).[8] This is highlighted as the agreement between God and man, signified through the votive of the newborn. Cultic sacrifice is paired in tandem with the Fertile Crescent in sync with the woman's menstrual cycle.

The lunar crescent typically is represented conjunct with 'hajar' (stone), iconic in the Syrian language of 'haiya' (snake), distinguished as the host or nocturnal angel. Religiously, Yahweh's covenant involved the death of the firstborn, combined with the rape of his mother. Yahweh's offspring in the Old Testament are referred to by the Jewish scribes as the 'Bene ha-Elohim' (the Sons of Gods). Their heritage is traced back to the 'moon' - a motif of 'Yahweh', constant with the reptile and priest.

Evident within the ancient scripts, the title 'Yahweh' otherwise 'Yah-wer' (great-moon) is polymorphic. The noun 'wer' signifies (greatness) and in the Egyptian vocabulary is translated by Egyptologists as (a body of water) - symbolic of 'Yah-wer' (the watery-moon).

'Wer' is loaned from the Arabic root 'waha' (an oasis).[9] 'Waha' semantically details 'wahl' (mud)[10] - an emblem of the stone, serpent and man. Jewish traditions depict the serpent's transfiguration as the 'golem' - a creature of alchemy. Its conception is coupled with Adam - a being created from 'adama' (earth).[11]

Essentially the 'mud' of the earth (wahl) annotates creation of humanity 'by God' (wallah) and is contrasted with the conception of the snake from fire (blood). Related etymologies suggest astrological metaphors of the night sky, assigned cryptically to the 'burn(t)' offering (wala) in situ to the 'oasis' (waha).

In the Greek lexicon, 'oasis' is cultic of 'Osiris' analogous to 'ossis' (bone) and 'oseeos' (holy). Translation of the noun 'ossis' (bone) into Arabic is rendered 'adm' and corresponds with 'Adam' - generic of (man). Doctrinally, 'oseeos' designates the 'hostia' (a sacrificial victim), covetous to the host and water. These symbols are repetitious of Yahweh - the crescent and the fish.

Yahweh's name archaically possesses two principal meanings. He is known to his followers as the 'great moon' (Yah-wer), conceptually identical to the 'watery moon' (Yah-wer). His cognomen corresponds in the Akkadian language with the deity 'Ea' (house of water). Ea is represented with streams of water issuing from his body, recapitulated in the Egyptian mysteries as the 'crying eye'. In Egyptian graphology, the verbal stem 'crying' (rmt) is a play on 'mankind' (rmt). According to Theban doctrine, man is created from the tears of the deity Atum- Ra.

Incorrectly transliterated by Egyptologists, the original pun 'rmt' is read in the Semitic as 'ramm' (to grieve),[13] doubled with 'umma or am' (a nation).[12] The 'r' is often dropped or unpronounced in the local dialects. Lexicologists render 'rmt' as 'remtech' (to cry). The actual translation is derived from the Arabic root 'ram-taq' (to suffer or tolerate - grief).[14]

Lateral to the recreation of man, the 'crying eye' describes the 'moon', equated with water - symbolic of the watcher (water). Hieroglyphically, the teardrop is reminiscent of the 'flesh' and 'rib' glyph, correlated with the votive and host. The 'flesh' determinative additionally appears in various transliterations of 'Isis' and suggests the Egyptian Goddess is an adaptation of 'Eve'.

Eschatological, Isis is depicted as the weeping virgin, compatible in Masonic lore with the widow and death, conveyed in the Arabic play 'sitt' (lady)[15] grouped in the Syrian language with 'shiti' (rain).[16] The Arabic noun 'shiti matar' (rain)[17] cryptically indicates a relationship with the Goddess of Judgment 'Maat'. Isis' teardrops allegorically suggest semen and rebirth, marked with the rib, paralleled to the resurrection of her consort Osiris (Yahweh).

Egyptian tradition aligns the crying eye with the Southern Crown, symptomatic of the partition of the Upper and Lower Kingdom. Worn by the resurrected God Osiris, the White Crown is archetypical of the deity Yahweh and Baal, conferred to the sovereign's incarnation as the sun God Horus.

The 'Southern Crown' represents the 'tear gland' - a sign of the dismembered eye, an arcane symbol of the moon. Horus' mutilated eye is allied secretly to the patron God 'Amun' (hidden), correlated with 'amem' (water) and 'aama' (blind). Amun's association with water infers a connection with Ea, depicted as the fish or moon. Amun's royal corona the 'severed eye' epitomizes the anointing of the God-King Osiris and the resurrection of his son Horus.

Osiris' 'White Crown' (hadj) a 'tear gland' duplicates the head of the penis, denoting fecundity, associated with the fish's head and death. The crown allegorizes the destruction of a planet - synonymous with the alien or migrant. Esoteric, the 'loss of Horus' eye' (aama) is a symbol of the 'builder' (ammar), cogent with the 'fleet' (amara) - a synonym of the 'host' (ha'mon). 'Blind-ing' (aama) of Horus denotes rebirth, assigned to the 'moon' (q-amar). The forfeited eye, pictured as crying, is conjoined symbolically with the host's inundation of the earth and the recreation of man.

Religiously, the descendents of Horus enacted the migration of the Gods, linked covertly to the moon's cycle, additional to the rising of Sirius. Astrologically aligned to the flooding of the Nile and the beginning of the agricultural calendar, the star Sirius is etiological of the deluge.

Destruction of man is remembered ceremoniously through 'pilgrimage', referred to in Arabic as (hajj), named after the mutilated eye of Horus, pictured as the 'Southern Crown' (hadj). The severed eye of Horus is figurative of the castrated phallus of 'Seth' - the 'God of Chaos'. Conflict between Horus and Seth is credited with the destruction of the earth.[18] Seth's impotence is memorialized in Egyptian and Judaic law through circumcision (castration) of the penis (i.e. man's line) - a marker of the covenant illustrated as the crown (eye) or crescent.

In liturgical symbolism, Osiris' diadem is observed as the bishop's mitre, silhouetting the fish's profile. Symbolically, the apparel expresses the crying eye (creation), rendered in Catholicism as the All Seeing Eye. The 'watching eye' is collaborative of the 'watcher' - an 'angel' known to the Greek mystics as the 'drakon' (dragon). The word 'dragon' is derived from the Hellenistic verb 'to watch' and is related to the Canaanite deity 'Dagon' - a derivation of the Semitic noun 'dag' (fish).[19] In English, 'dag' is punned with 'dog', inverted as God, and is an early adaptation of Sirius (Canis Major).

Detail from St. John - The image is based on a painting by Michelangelo of St. John.
It depicts an angel dressed in red, presented as human-angelic, figured with reptilian scales.

Adorned, the 'mitre' symbolizes the fish's head or tear gland. The 'watching eye' is doubled with the 'White Crown', emblematic of the covenant or promise, promulgated through the angels, enumerated as sailors (crewmembers). The 'promise' is worn literally on the head and is philological with the Latin word 'pro-mittere' (to send), registered as an 'angelos' Greek (a messenger or angel). The headdress of the Bishop or Pope exhibits an 'emissary', 'fish' or 'deity'. The appearance of the seraph (a transfigured angel) discloses the 'builder' (a saviour), constant with the 'destroyer'. Visualised as a 'reaper', the 'destroyer' is incorporated into the traditions of 'Yahweh'.

Prototypical to the 'Lord of the Host' enumerated as Yahweh, the mitre signifies the God of Destruction. Theologically, Yahweh killed the descendents of Adam (Ma'adim - Mars), repopulating the earth with man's seed (creating a race of slaves). Ancient texts suggest the 'annihilation' (Arabic 'adam) of 'mankind' (Adam), deployed historically from the moon, and featured in Greek and Judaic literature as the great flood.

In the Persian language, the etymon 'mah' (moon)[20] is displaced in Arabic with 'ma' (water, liquid, juice, lustre, splendor or semen).[21] According to Zoroastrian tradition, the moon's satellite acted as a receptacle for storing the seed of man during a cataclysm that effaced Adam's descendents. Historically, the destruction of humanity is timed with the war between angels and man. Reference to such an event is contained within Professor Zaehner's translation of the Bundahishn text (Refer to Chapter heading). This tradition is recounted in Europe as the 'man in the moon'.[22]

Semitic literature compares the invading host to 'crewmembers of naval vessels' (tsabaoth), conveyed in modern parlance as a 'starship or spaceship'. In Egyptian iconography, the Pharaoh's barge is depicted ecliptic, and recalls the moon, identified with the seed of man. Hieroglyphically, the boat is drawn as a solar plough and emphasizes the connection between the moon and fertility.

Relationship between the boat and rebirth is evident also within the Hebrew ciphers, outlined in the book of Genesis Chapter 8:3-4 '...At the end of the hundred and fifty days the water had gone down, and on the seventeenth day of the seventh month the ark came to rest on the montains of Ararat'. The number 'seven' (sheva)[23] is used linguistically to connote a 'period of mourning' (shiva).

The scribe puns the place name 'Ararat' with 'ha'arets' (the earth), inferring 'kadur ha'arets' (planet earth) - literally 'circle [of] the earth'. Study of Judaic lexicology indicates the ancient people of the Middle East understood the earth to be round.

Traditionally, Noah's ark is constructed from 'gopher' wood (Hebrew goper) - a pun on 'ge'ver' (man).[24] The redactor's wordplay informs the reader that the ark carried the germ of man - a belief demonstrated in the layout of the Christian church as a boat, preserved in the Egyptian, Greek and Jewish Temples (Refer to Chapter 1 Mal'akh, Boat Pits, page 44).

The nave (altar) of the church is doubled with naval, recognizant with pregnancy, analogous to the host or sailor (angel). Genetic descent of the Royal lineage originates from the reptile, pillager or host. Depicted as 'emissaries' or 'messengers', the angels are conduits to the development of religion.

Philologically, 'religion' is cognate with 'religare' (to moor a boat, bind back or tie),[25] consistent with the adjective 'regal' (literally king-ship). The point is emphasized additionally in the Semitic lexicon - 'mal'akh' (an angel) describes 'malakh' (a sailor) an appellation of 'melekh' (a king).

To conclude, the act of 'wor-ship' recalls the 'angelic boat', equated with the 'king' and 'governance' (Greek kubernao - to steer a ship). Initiators recall the 'government' as a 'cube' (Greek kubos, Arabic ka'b), terminology correlated religiously with the 'Kaaba' shrine (a cube). Early evidence suggests that the iconography pertains to the 'Pleiades' (Greek plein - to sail), in which four of the seven stars, form a square in the night sky.

Illustrated in the book of Revelation, the Kingdom of God visualised as heaven, is described as the 'cube', and signifies a temple sanctuary, encoded architecturally as the boat or body. Motif of the ship appertains to the worship of the king's ancestral line, deduced from the angel or fish, affiliated to 'Sirius' (Al Kalb), conjungal with the constellation Pleiades and its offspring Orion.

Anglican (angler) 'worship' is derived from the Old English word 'weorthscipe' (literally worth-ship). 'Scipe' in the Old English is deduced from the Greek noun 'skaphos' (boat), cognate with 'schip' (ship) a variant of 'skipper'. Esoterically, 'skaphos' relates to 'skopeo' (to look), indicative of the dragon (a watcher), signified as 'skorpaina' (a fish).

In Greek Gnosticism, the 'eye' and 'fish' are substituted with the 'moon'. The 'lozenge' shape annotates epigraphically the 'mouth' and 'vagina', listed in the hieroglyphs. Anatomically the 'orifice', paired in Greek with 'ophis' (a snake), denotes the votive, paralleled to the 'host' and 'hostia' (victim). The killing of the sacrament, located at the nave, indicates resurrection, appended to the snake or angel. The stone altar articulates bodily transfiguration (alter) of angelic forms through blood sacrifice. These practices allege secretly to the sinister branch of the Church - iconic of the boat (angel).

Such a relationship is demonstrated in the Greek noun 'skaphos' (ship), borrowed in the Latin adjective 'scaevus' (left, on the left, perverse, indicative of a sign or an omen).[26] This, in Roman liturgy, is associated with conflict and the wor-ship of nocturnal angels, addendum to the host and nave.

Muslim scholars depict the vessel as a crescent or rib - an emblem of the snake or rock, equated to the moon and rebirth. Contextually the 'rock' alludes to the 'altar or body', conditional to the creation of woman (Eve) through the sacrifice of Adam, i.e. the removal of Adam's heart (rib), subordinate to Sirius. Propitiations of Adam's firstborn epitomize the serpent's adultery and the continuation of the Royal line of Eve. The Biblical Prophet Isaiah Chapter 14: verse 1 and 2 [Gideon translation] summarizes the nature of this deception:

'...Aliens [angels] will join them and unite with the house of Jacob [supplanter]...And the house of Israel will possess the nations...'

Theologically, the virgin's womb (worm) is alchemical of a sacrificial rock (nave), from which the Church is constructed upon! Its abominations are grouped with the 'serpent and builder' and are characteristic of a matriarchal (Royal) line, seeded from angels - the progeny and origins, of which are examined in the next chapter.

1   Professor R C Zaehner: The Dawn and Twilight of Zoroastrianism, Weidenfeld & Nicholson, 1975, pp266-267
2   Hippocrene English-Arabic, Arabic-English Dictionary, Hippocrene, New York, 2005, p192
3   Ibid, p209
4   Ibid, p307
5   Ibid
6   Ibid
7   Ibid
8   Ibid, p305
9   Ibid, p306 Yahweh's symbolism is closely grouped in the Egyptian priesthood with the worship of the serpent and moon. Etymological connection between 'Yahweh and the snake' is demonstrated in the Syrian language - Refer to Chapter 44 Spirits and Snake.
10 Ibid
11 Prolog: Pocket Bilingual Dictionary, English-Hebrew & Hebrew-English, Prolog, 2003, p124
12 Hippocrene English-Arabic, Arabic-English Dictionary, Hippocrene, New York, 2005, p79
13 Ibid, p54
14 Ibid, p296
15 Ibid, p289
16 Ibid, p286
17 Ibid, p98
18 'Seth' astrologically is grouped with the 'Big Dipper' - its 'seven stars' referential to the 'Pleiades' and the angelic wars.
19 Prolog: Pocket Bilingual Dictionary, English-Hebrew & Hebrew-English, Prolog, 2003, p152
20 Ferozsons, Urdu-English Dictionary, Revised Edition, Ferozsons Ltd, Lahore, p664
21 Ibid, p665
22 In European folklore, the moon is said to be constructed from cheese (a signifier of milk), equated with the mammal - a symbol of mankind. The noun 'moon' is philological to 'man'.
23 Prolog: Pocket Bilingual Dictionary, English-Hebrew & Hebrew-English, Prolog, 2003, p365
24 Ibid, p244
25 John C Traupman: The New College Latin & English Dictionary, Bantam, 1988, p265
26 Ibid, p279

38

Yahweh Baal and Horus
(The Good the Bad and the Ugly)

' ...On the day that you were born
The angels got together *and decided*
To create a dream come true
So they sprinkled ***moondust in your hair***
And golden starlight in your ***eyes of blue...'***

Carpenters, (They long To Be) Close To You,
Yesterday Once More, A & M Records (1985)

The Egyptian Arabic noun 'alb' (heart) is analogous to 'arb' (the number four) and is signified with the four ventricles of the cardiac vascular system. 'Four' is represented in sacred geometry as the 'cube' (ka'b),[1] nominal of the Kingdom, original to the Pleiades - (See footnote). Designated as a fraction, 'rab'a' (one forth)[2] denotes the 'Western' (rarbi) priesthood, the 'Rabbi' - arbitrators of the covenant with Sirius, listed with the 'heart' (coronary) and 'crown' (corona). Catholic depictions of the heart are sometimes combined with the crown of thorns, referential to the sacrificial death of Christ. In the hieroglyphics, the pyramidal 'thorn' is used to notate the star 'Sirius' - its ascension a symbol of the Messiah.

The 'heart' (Egyptian Arabic alb[3] - Arabic qalb) memorializes the first 'tribe' of the covenant - the 'Qabili'[4] from the Egyptian Arabic 'qabil' (meet or receive a visitor or guest).[5] It seems that the 'Qabili' are similar to the 'Levites' Hebrew 'Lev' (a heart), tandem to the Emori, Occidental, Rabbi and Sabi priesthood. Each denomination is associated with death, demonstrated with the 'Qabili', marked with the 'grave' or a 'sepulcher' (qabr).[6]

The 'Qabili' (tribe), like the pharaonic and Jewish priesthood, is matriarchal and conveyed through 'qabla' Egyptian Arabic (a midwife),[7] lateral to the reservation or sacrifice of the firstborn - Syrian dialect 'qabli'yi' (an appetite).[8] Traditions, regarding the 'Qabili', extend historically a 'long time ago' (qabl min zaman)[9] and originate from 'kalb' (the dog), nominal of 'Al Kalb' (Sirius).

Known as the 'Qabili' literally (the tribe), the original settlers are equated with 'harb' (war),[10] semantically paralleled to 'abhar' (sail)[11] - grouped in the Egyptian lexicon with 'harban' (a fugitive).[12] In the early Semitic, 'harban' suggests 'harb-an' (heaven's-war), consistent with a 'harbinger'. Originally, the 'harbinger' signals human angelic conflict, culminating with the deluge and the destruction of a planet.

Etymologically, the Arabic terms 'abhar' (sail) from the verb 'abar' (to cross or pass)[13] is consigned in Hebrew to 'habore' (the creator)[14] and is extracted from 'ha-Baal' (the-Lord). Baal's cognomen is identified with intelligence and informs the Modern Arabic noun 'bal' (mind).[15] There is a close linguistic comparison in the Semitic lexicon with 'bal' (mind) and 'bala' the verbal root (to swallow), inferring a hidden sacrifice. In the Babylonian idiolect, the 'seraph' (acan) is cognate with 'food' (Egyptian Arabic akl),[16] relative to the faculty of 'reason' ('aql),[17] assigned to a 'sovereign' (hakim).[18]

Baal's assignment 'bala' (to swallow) ritualistically pertains to the burning of the offering, equated with the worship of reptiles (angels).[19] 'Bala' is obtained from the Sumerian stem 'bil' (to burn),[20] rendered in Akkadian as 'baar'. The root of 'baar or baur' is closely related to the Sumerian verb 'ba' (to give),[21] suggesting the votive. In Syrian, 'ba' indicates 'bai' (a sale)[22] from 'ba' (to sell, i.e. to offer).[23]

Egyptologists interpret 'ba' incongruously as (the soul) - a word that should translate as (sacrificial redemption). The expression 'ba' is cogent in Aramaic with 'bar' (a son), correlated with propitiations of the firstborn. Baal's deity name thus is assimilated historically from the offering of the 'son', identical with 'immolation', theoretical to 'bala' (swallow).

Esoteric, the sacrifice of a 'son' (bar) is encoded in the Arabic root 'bar', denoting (a hawk),[24] cryptic of the Pharaoh. The bird's offspring pertains to a guardian of the sanctuary, denominational of 'Horus' (a hunter), depicted as a 'flaming' osprey (baar). A watcher or sentinel, the 'hawk' a predatory bird (bar) is related in the Hebrew language to 'bahur' (a warrior), theological to recreation. Religiously, 'the-hawk' (al-bar or ha-bar) is cognate with the 'creator' (habore), philological to 'Hebrew'. 'Habore' (the creator) is expressed in the Arabic idiom as 'habl' (pregnancy), idiosyncratic of 'the-Lord' (ha-Baal). 'Habl' in the Egyptian dialect is mutual to 'qabla' (midwife), assigned to the original 'tribe' (the Qabili).

Parabolic, the appellation 'ha-Baal' (the-Lord) is compatible in Judaic literature with the sacrificial death of 'Abel' Hebrew - 'avel' (mourn).[25] The death of Adam's son Abel is cognate with the appropriation of the matriarch Eve and the rebirth of her child 'Seth' (a foundation), bedrock of the human-angelic bloodline of 'Osiris', Arabic 'Asas' (a foundation - refer to footnote[26]).

The namesake 'Hebrew' proceeds from the Akkadian verb 'habaru' (to migrate),[27] consistent with 'Qabili' (a tribe) and 'abhar' (to sail). 'Habaru' (Hebrew) is recognizant of a 'soldier' of the Lord (ha-bahur), congruent with 'habl' (pregnancy) - maleficent of rape.

Motif of the 'son' (bar), designated as the 'hawk' (bar), annotates the Royal 'covenant', rendered in Hebrew as (berith or brit) - in English 'birth', affiliated to 'bath' Hebrew (a daughter). Origins of the 'Habaru' are semantically equivalent to the 'osprey' (bar), symbolic of the 'host' (bahur).

Religiously, the 'falcon' signifies the 'migrant' or 'alien', rendered in Latin as the 'peregrine',[28] specific of the 'hunter or watcher' (dragon) - a cognomen of Baal. Epigraphically, the 'hawk' distinguishes the Royal line of 'Horus'[29] and is a bird, identified with the patriarchs of Judaism. Inversion of 'bar' (an osprey) reads as 'Rab' (a Master), denominational of the 'Rabbi'. He is paired with the 'setting sun' (ryab),[30] extrapolated from 'rarbi' (west).[31] Offshoots of the Western (Occidental) priesthood are nationalistic subsumed under the military host.

Baal wearing the Crown of Osiris. Baal is shown as 'stepping' (Old Semitic 'tsa'), equivalent to 'Sah' (Strider), identified with the star system 'Orion'. The Greek name 'Orion' is cognate in Latin with 'Oriens' (East), correlated with the mixed descendents of Adam. The Hebrew verb to 'pace' (tsa'ad) suggests the Sodi fraternity, connected with the serpent-footed and the Theban Crown.

The 'warrior' (bahur) is interchangeable with 'Baal' (a Lord) and 'bah'har' (a sailor) - designations of 'Lord-ship'. 'Baal' is translated alternatively as (an angel, hunter or king), derived from the Sumerian counterpart 'Kar'. Epithet of 'Kar' (Horus) is grouped in Arabic with 'kha' (a star), cogent with the 'askari' (a soldier),[32] implicit of the 'host'. The fraternity 'Askari' is nominal of the 'Ashkenazi' referred to in Genesis 10:3. A class of 'mercenaries' the Ashkenazi are known alternatively as (ha-bahur), equal to 'Habaru' (a migratory race).

The Egyptian-Sumerian name 'Kar' literally (angel, king or hunter), Canaanite 'Baal', is rendered as the 'Falcon God Horus' (Kar or Har) - a signifier equated with the 'son'. Transliteration of 'Kar' is an extraction from the Semitic root 'kha' (a star), related to 'aur' (light), commensurate with 'Ra' (Sirius).

Theologically, Horus (Har) is born from 'light' (aur). He is conceived from a 'virgin' (the houri) - a divine birth, comparative to Baal's inception from the 'flames' (baar). The cult of 'Horus' is a continuation of the worship of 'Baal' and is further evident in the ancient Semitic wordplays.

In Aramaic, 'ha-Baal' (the-Lord) is punned with 'Har-Bar' (the Son of Horus), depicted as 'Abu' (the Father), esoteric of the verb 'abhar' (to sail), appointed to 'the-host'(ha-bahur). The informal assignment 'abba' (daddy) denotes the verbal stem 'habb' (to love)[33] and 'habl' (pregnancy).[34] Significantly, the relationship between 'Abu' (Father), 'habl' (pregnancy) and 'habb' (love) is predicated on a father's love, equated with <u>genetic descent,</u> relative to '<u>Habaru' (Hebrew)</u>. In addition, 'Abu' (Father) is philological in the Old Semitic with 'af'a' (snake) - the 'b' phoneme interchangeable with the 'v' and 'f'.

Offspring of the 'Father' (a snake) is incarnated as the 'hawk' - a flaming seraph, a metaphor of the 'migrant' or 'alien', registered with the soldier (host). 'Baal' is defined theologically as 'Lord' (ha-Baal) and 'father' (abba) - the 'creator' (habore), equivalent to his divine 'son' (bar). The homonym 'bar' (a son) is cognate with the legitimate heir to the Pharaoh, rendered as a 'hawk' (Arabic bar).[35] Progeny of the 'creator' (habore) is adjacent to 'Hebrew' (Old Semitic Habaru), e.g. the Habaru's genus is related to their 'creator' (habore), represented literally as their heavenly 'Father' (Abu), drawn as a 'snake' (af'a).

'Baal' is shown in Canaanite sculpture as donning the 'Crown of Upper Egypt'. This Crown is located later with Osiris and his son Horus. Variations of Baal's headdress, the severed eye, appears as the mitre (a fish), appropriated later by the Christian, Jewish and Mithraic priesthood.

The 'White Crown' of Osiris is transliterated in the hieroglyphs as 'hadj' and is identified in Arabic with 'hajj' (a pilgrim).[36] 'Hajj or hagg' is rendered in Greek as the adjective 'hagios' (holy), compatible with 'ago' (to lead). In English, the word 'pilgrim' philologically is cognate with 'peregrine' (a falcon), employed in the Latin adjective 'peregrinus' (foreign or alien)[37] - descriptions of the angels.

Depicted as the itinerant, migrant, nomad or sailor, the hawk's characteristics are shared by Osiris and Baal. Astrological, the peripatetic bird Arabic 'sayyar' (a wanderer or traveler)[38] is interchangeable with 'sayyarah' (a planet),[39] translated into Greek as 'planetes' (a wonderer).

Hajj re-enacts the creation epics, assigned to the nomadic Gods, registered with the six foundations of creation (planets), tabulated with the Sothic year and the covenant. Esoterically, hajj is associated with a 'naval stone' (omphalos), cognate with the womb and moon. The 'cornerstone' is a symbol of Adam and is used by the early Christians as a metaphor of the Church's foundation elucidated as Peter (the rock).

The symbol of the rock is employed within the occult as an emblem of the fallen serpent, paired with the body of man. In the Syrian language, 'hajj' (a pilgrim) is referential to the 'omphalos', rendered 'hajar' (a stone).[40] Islamic tradition links the 'stone' with the 'Kaaba shrine' and the 'fallen angel', Iblis (Satan). Worshippers of the 'Kaaba' archaically are affiliated in the Old Semitic with 'qeb' (a serpent), original to the tribe 'Qabili', philological to the 'Habaru' (Hebrew). The gluttoral 'k' is similar to the 'h' and 'q' sound, distinctive to the Semitic languages. The analogy of the snake and stone is demonstrated in the Syrian language. 'Hajar' (a stone) is punned with 'haiya' (snake), deduced from the phonological similarity of the morpheme 'y' and 'j', evident in the Old Semitic.

Originally, a sacrificial stone 'hajar' connotes the Syrian etymon 'jarh' (injury) from the intransitive verb 'jarr' (to drag),[41] implicit of the votive and snake. The corresponding wordplay in English is 'drag and dragon', opposite a 'reptile and rapist'. Worship of the snake is relative to the sanctuary, shrine, tent or tabernacle, tandem to the rising moon and the evening meal - the mystery.

The lunar satellite recalls Baal and his 'tributary' (Sumerian ba), conceptualized as a 'son' (bar). Offering of the firstborn is associated with the nocturnal angel, illustrated as a stone (man), transmuted alchemically into a serpent (gold) - the philosopher's stone. The process is revealed in English as 'womb and worm', in Latin 'matrix' (womb) and 'natrix' (water snake) - implicit of the eel Apophis.

Relationship between the body, womb and stone is clearly determined in the Semitic languages. The Arabic noun 'sakhr' (rock)[42] is transferred into Latin as 'sacri' (holy) and informs the etymology 'sacred and sacrifice'. The rock specifies the shrine or altar (alter), central to the worship of Baal, adjacent to the winged seraph.

'Sakhr' (rock) in the Egyptian pantheon is symmetrical to the falcon deity 'Sokar' (the seed of Horus), transliterated as 'Zari'a-Kar' - the keeper of the 'tabernacle' (Succoth). The offspring of 'Zari'a-Kar' are represented cryptically with the 'stick' (suka), synonymous with a 'thorn' (shoka),[43] epigraphic of 'Sirius'. Egyptian hieroglyphs index the 'stick and thorn' next to the 'throwing stick' - idiomatic of an 'alien', connoting an 'angel', lateral to the rib, stone and crescent. These emblems annotate the fallen host - a group of renegade angels, commandeered by Baal.

Appellation of 'Baal' (a Lord) is a military term, extracted from 'bah'har' (a sailor), cogent with 'bahur' (a warrior), esoteric of 'bar' (a falcon). Entourage of Baal's Lord-ship is enumerated as the 'tsabaoth or s'baot', ontological with the naval host. In English, the adjective 'naval' is from the Latin 'navis' (a ship)[44] and is a homonym of the 'stomach'. The 'nave' symbolizes 'rebirth', equivocal to 'pregnancy' (habl), assigned to 'the-host' (ha-bahur).

Relationship between the 'angelic soldiers' (ha-bahur) addendum to 'Hebrew' (Habaru), elicits the 'tribe' (Qabili), connotative of a 'rapist', understood as a 'snake'. A fallen angel, the serpent, is connected to the rock and the veneration of the host - symmetrical to the 'victim' (hostia).

In the Church, the 'navis' is depicted as the 'nave' - the central part of the chancel marked with the stone or altar. The edifice thus operates as a diagram of a ship and is associated with 'wor-ship', conjunct with creation. 'Navi(s)' the Latin root of 'nave' is derived ultimately from the Syrian noun 'nabi' (a prophet),[45] implicit of the stomach, e.g. naval, correlated with the augury (intestines) and stone.

In conclusion, the Canaanite God 'Baal' (Lord) is considered as the 'father' (abba) and the 'redeemer of hearts' (alb-ba),[46] esoteric of 'Sirius' (Al Kalb). The 'redemption of Sirius' (Arabic Kalb-baiya) is interchangeable with the 'heart [of the] son' (qalb-bar), assigned to the proto-tribe 'Qabili'. 'Kalb-baiya' is also notable for its phonetic similarity to the name 'Calvary' (Latin Calvaria - the skull) - the execution site of Jesus, the son and redeemer of hearts!

The skull, a signifier of the host, denotes the cavalry, represented in Latin as 'caballus' (a horse),[47] generic of the 'dog' soldier (kalb). To complicate matters, the horse (a dragon) is often switched with the goat or stag - a dual signifier attributed to the virgin (Pleiades) and the fish (Sirius). The skull in the Roman mysteries underscores the worship of Jupiter, mirrored archaically with the sun and the Dog Star Sirius. Appellation of 'Jupiter', rendered in the occult as 'Jovis pater', is identical to 'Ducere-pater' (the ruling father), equated with 'Baal'.

Osiris' Crown - a tear gland featured as the severed eye. Pictured as the Shepherd King 'Osiris' - a deity analogous to the God Yahweh the 'good shepherd': Refer to the Biblical quotation Psalms 23.

Divinity of the 'Lord' (Baal), pictured with the 'hawk' (bar), is nominal of the Royal 'son' (Aramaic bar). In Egypt, the 'osprey' signifies 'Horus' - a migrant God, doubled with the incarnation of the father Osiris. Theban liturgy recalls the sovereign Osiris as the good 'shepherd' (Arabic ra'i)[48] - an epithet, occult to the veneration of 'Ra' (Sirius). Archeological evidence showing similarity between Egyptian and Canaanite deities links the worship of 'Yahweh' the 'good shepherd' with his sibling 'Osiris', conceptual to 'Baal'. The 'shepherd' a keeper of livestock (man) labels the Canaanite group the 'Hyksos', termed as the 'Shepherd Kings', symmetrical to the 'Habaru' and their (migration) from the stars.

In addition, the Canaanite God Yahweh shares Baal's title 'Lord of the Host'. Early usage of 'Baal' is translated into Greek as 'Adonai' - a name assigned generically to Yahweh and his subjects Adam (east), affiliated to the Theban priesthood (west).

Politically, the Dual Kingdom of Egypt extends Baal's Syrian control over the region, and records a momentous split from his twin Yahweh. Correlations between Horus, Yahweh and Baal reiterate the influence of Canaanite religions, pivotal to the development of Judaic, Egyptian and Babylonian theology. Cosmology of the Canaanite is traced further back to the snake (an angel), a creature accredited with the oracle priestess and the offering of the heart - a propositon substantiated in the next chapter.

---

1 Hippocrene English-Arabic, Arabic-English Dictionary, Hippocrene, New York, 2005, p211 [The 'cube' (ka'b), notational of the 'kaaba' shrine, appears as a dual signifier of the 'Dog Star' (Al Kalb) and is related esoterically to the four stars of the Pleiades, which form a square. In addition, the 'dog' (kalb) is covert to the 'messenger' (caba), depicted as an 'angel', recognizant with the 'hidden' (khabba) tradition, cited as the 'Kabbalah'. The 'caba' (messenger) originally denoted a 'dragon' (qebi) - a being from Sirius equated with a fallen angel. Its angelic progeny is conveyed through the footprint, cognizant with the 'heel' (ka'b), symbolic of the Vestial priestess - a bloodline assigned to the Pleiades. Matriomony between the woman and snake is attributed to the children of Anak identified with the Nephilim and the constellation Orion].

2 Ibid, p265

3 M.A. Abdel-Hady, Egyptian Arabic, The Rough Guide Dictionary Phrasebook, Lexus, 1998, p111

4 Hippocrene English-Arabic, Arabic-English Dictionary, Hippocrene, New York, 2005, p258

5 Ibid

6 Ibid

7 Ibid

8 Ibid

9 Ibid

10 Ibid, p189

11 Ibid, p146 ['abhar' (sail) is related to the English noun 'harbour'].

12 Ibid, p189

13 Ibid, p317

14 Prolog: Pocket Bilingual Dictionary, English-Hebrew & Hebrew-English, Prolog, 2003, p91

15 Hippocrene English-Arabic, Arabic-English Dictionary, Hippocrene, New York, 2005, p154 ['Bal' (mind) also means (to urinate) and shows a correlation with Gnostic thinking, regarding the manifestation of the body through thought, equated with the mind and mortal corruption. Additionally, Baal is a God of filth - an idiom used to describe the snake's excretion from its skin].

16 Ibid, p148

17 Ibid, p99

18 Ibid, p187

19 A 'fiery seraph' rendered in Babylonian as (acan) is cognate with 'food' (Egyptian Arabic akl), relative to the faculty of 'reason' ('aql), assigned to the 'sovereign' (hakim) - Canaanite 'bala' (swallow), 'bal' (mind) and 'Baal' (Lord). The same wordplay is matched in the Latin sequence 'sapio' (to taste or smell), 'sapiens' (wise) and 'serpens' (a serpent), inferring the supper (suffer). Likewise, in the Akkadian dialect 'peor' (a snake) is equivalent in Hebrew to 'pa' (mouth) and 'pe'er' (glory). In Judaic tradition, the 'diners' (Hebrew so'ed) are extracted from the 'Sodi' priests (secret or occult), affiliated to 'Saudi' (the Black Nobility).

20 John M Allegro: The Sacred Mushroom and the Cross, A Study of the Nature and Origins of Christianity within the Fertility Cults of the Ancient Near Middle East, Abacus, 1970, p41

21 Ibid, p38

22 Hippocrene English-Arabic, Arabic-English Dictionary, Hippocrene, New York, 2005, p106

23 Ibid, p109

24 Ibid, p155

25 Prolog: Pocket Bilingual Dictionary, English-Hebrew & Hebrew-English, Prolog, 2003, p264

26 The other word used in Hebrew for a 'foundation' is (ya'sad) - a term conjunct with sacrificial eating (so'ed). Archaeologists in their excavations have shown that the human votive is concealed or buried into the foundations. 'Ya'sad' (foundation) is a cognate of 'so'ed' (diner) - a term extrapolated from the 'Sodi' priesthood, defined literally as (secret or occult). The 'foundation' (ya'sad) infers the votive (so'ed) grouped with the worship of Osiris 'En-Asas' (Lord of the Foundation).

27 David Rohl: A Test of Time, The Bible - From Myth to History, Arrow, London, 1995, p525 (Glossary)

28 John C. Traupman: The New College Latin & English Dictionary, Bantam, 1988, p218

29 The hawk is 'bless(ed)' (barak) literally 'bar-akh' (a brother of the hawk). He is defined as an angel or 'messenger' (barid) from the Arabic compound 'bar-id' (hand of the son or hawk). The messenger in Egyptian frescoes refers explicitly to the winged priestess, referenced in Masonic tradition as the hidden hand (wing). Metaphor of the hidden hand historically is assigned to Moses' withered white hand - a symbol of angelic transmogrification, represented as the white gloves of Freemasonry.

30 Hippocrene English-Arabic, Arabic-English Dictionary, Hippocrene, New York, 2005, p273

31 Ibid, p139

32 Ibid, p116

33 Ibid, p183

34 Ibid, p184

35 Ibid, p56

36 Ibid, p186

37 John C Traupman: The New College Latin & English Dictionary, Bantam, 1988, p218

38 Ferozsons Urdu-English Dictionary, Revised Edition, Ferozsons Ltd, Lahore, p457

39 Ibid

40 Hippocrene English-Arabic, Arabic-English Dictionary, Hippocrene, New York, 2005, p186

41 Ibid, p209

42 Ibid, p104

43 Ibid, p127

44 John C Traupman: The New College Latin & English Dictionary, Bantam, 1988, p474

45 Hippocrene English-Arabic, Arabic-English Dictionary, Hippocrene, New York, 2005, p252

46 'Alb-ba' (Redeemer of hearts) is cogent with the Latin noun 'albus' (white), punned in Arabic with 'al-bas' (the kiss), esoteric of the White Crown.

47 The 'horse' is often substituted symbolically with the 'goat' and 'stag' (se'irim) - extensions of the 'Dog Star' (Sirius), identified with 'Osiris' (Arabic 'Asas' - foundation). Osiris' resurrection is grouped with sacrificial atonement.

48 Hippocrene English-Arabic, Arabic-English Dictionary, Hippocrene, New York, 2005, p111

39

Maat the Reaper of the Soul

'Bless the beasts and the children
For in this world they have no voice
They have no choice

Bless the beasts and the children
For the word can never be
The world they see

Light their way
When the darkness surrounds them
Give them love
Let it shine all around them

Bless the beasts and the children
Give them shelter from a storm
Keep them safe
Keep them warm'

Carpenters: Bless the Beasts and Children,
Yesterday Once More, A & M Records (1985)

The fallen priestess in Egyptian iconography refers to the 'judge of the soul' and corresponds with the 'Goddess Maat'. Her device is the 'feather', recorded in the hieroglyphic as 'imnt',[1] translated misleadingly by Egyptologists as (the west).[2]

The scholar Ralph Ellis argues 'imnt's correct transliteration is from the Hebrew direction 'imiyn' (right),[3] cryptographically (south). Ellis' interpretation of 'imiyn' is modified from the Arabic root 'yamin' (on the right-hand side).[4] In the Syrian language, 'yamin' is used to distinguish (an oath),[5] sworn upon 'yaum' (the day)[6] Arabic 'yom', marked with the setting disk 'Amun'. On the surface, the feather would seem to suggest a correlation with Maat and the Western priesthood of Amun.[7]

There are however a number of problems with the transcription 'yamin'. In this instance for the word to read 'west', one would expect the scribe to use the 'reed' sign (yam)[8] to annotate the 'y' sound, evidenced in the Old Semitic etymon 'yam(im)' (west).[9] Scholars have inexplicably switched around the 'reed' with the 'feather' consonant.[10] Both of these signs, though conceptually similar, represent different morphemes (See Appendix 9).

The 'imnt or imiyn' the feather glyph is clearly not a phoneme but rather an ideogram. The character figures a heraldry sign, drawn with two poles, a long one fixed into a belt (i.e. stomach), coupled with a short one to grip the emblem secure. It shows a picture of a 'standard', rendered in Hebrew as 'amat mida',[11] read literally as (a truthful stomach). The titular 'amat mida' is employed to write (an oracular priestess), cognate with the Goddess Maat.

'Amat mida' is translated into Greek as the 'engastrimythoi' (the speaker of the stomach).[12] She examines the entrails of the augury, and forecasts judgment of the heart. This is signified as a pair of weighing scales. In the Egyptian language, the word 'maatsen' (scales) inform the Hebrew word 'maazen' or 'maaznem'.[13]

The 'scales' (Arabic mizan)[14] are used to weigh the 'heart of sin',[15] represented as a 'cross'. Symbolically, the 'maatsen' annotates sacrificial immolation of the firstborn 'child' (mass) from the Egyptian etymon 'maas' (to kill or slay), symmetrical in Akkadian to 'mazz' (fire). The etymologies suggest a sacrificial offering of a child, defined in the Modern Hebrew as 'mazon' (nourishment).[16]

'Maat' is shown contextually as a 'Goddess of Death', related theologically to the judgment and extraction of the heart. Samuel Birch's dictionary published in 1867 lists the hieroglyph 'makha' (to balance).[17] The glyph is symmetrical with the Egyptian word 'makher' (price, dowry or wages), written in Hebrew as 'ma(k)har' (barter, obtain by payment or dowry).[18]

Religiously, procurement of sacrificial redemption is obligated through ritual death. The 'payment' (makher) is similar to 'makha' (to strangle) and is virtually identical to 'makha' the verb (to go),[19] explicit of the double (or spirit).[20] Birch's contemporary, R.A.Goodwin augments 'makha' with the verb 'makhau' (to despoil, strangle or kidnap), extracted from the noun 'makhen' (a vessel or boat).[21]

Correlation between the 'vessel and plunderer' suggests a liturgical relationship with the 'angelic host' and the 'Goddess Maat'. Her entourage exacts absolution from the removal of the heart, equivocal to Aaron and the Levite priesthood. Denomination of the 'Levite' is obtained from the Hebrew noun 'lev' (heart).[22] The alternative Hebrew transliteration for 'heart' is (liba)[23] and informs the European noun 'liver', suggesting the removal of the 'heart' and 'liver'.

'Liba' (heart) apprises the Latin feminine noun 'libra' (a balance),[24] opposite 'libare' (to consecrate, taste, sip or offer). Conceptually, 'libation' is equivalent to 'liberare' (to set free, acquit, redeem[25] or liberate) and is theoretically a cognomen of the 'Italian fertility God - Liber'.[26] This deity is later identified with Bacchus.[27] Doctrinally, 'liberare' (freedom) is interchangeable with 'liberty and liberal' - appellations of the 'Levite' priesthood.[28]

MAAT

Maat is a fertility Goddess. Her name is written with the plough – a symbol of the reaper and crescent.

The early Hebrews represented the Levites with the snake, incorporated with the traditions of Moses' staff. Epigraphically, the 'staff' is lateral to a 'throwing stick', adopted in the Egyptian lexicon to signify (an alien), contextual to (an angel or God). Maat's name is written hieroglyphically with the staff, contrasted with the host and death.

Ownership of Maat's 'stick' assumes actions, connected with 'striking' (nagga), extrapolated from the 'saviour' (nagga), correlated with 'Venus' (Noga).[29] The Arabic word plays are equivalent in Hebrew to 'maka' (hit), covertly 'mal'akh' (an angel), defined as 'malakh' (a sailor). 'Malakh' is listed in the hieroglyphic sign lists as 'makhen' (a boat), convivial of the host and 'ritual strangulation' (makha), denoting 'payment' (makher).

The analogy of the 'saviour' deemed as the 'devastator', conceptually 'Venus', reveals host-worship, provident with the Maga (Persian) and Judaic Priesthood. Rising and setting of the Morning Star is equated with the arbitration of the soul. Sadistic rites, governing the worship of the 'mal'akh' (angel), are histrionically dramatized with the 'staff' (the makel).[30] The rod's phallic shape delineates the reptile, sexualized through the 'dance' (makhol)[31] - Refer to Chapter 29 Saturnalia and the Forces of Darkness.

Iconography of the 'staff' infers the 'snake' - simultaneous to transmutation. Relationship between the staff and death is archived in the Hebrew lexicon. The alternative noun for 'makel' (a staff or stake)[32] is 'mot' from the Arabic word (death).[33] Earlier versions of the word 'mot' are rendered in the Canaanite tradition as the deity 'Mot' (the God of Death). Mot, like the angel and cobra, is linked to salvation, conciliated through ritualized flagellation.

Transliteration of the Goddess' name 'Mot' is reminiscent of the Egyptian word to 'throw a stick', listed by various authorities as 'aemaat', 'ah-me-aht' or 'maat' and possesses a double-bind. The Arabic word 'almatrah' (thrown at) also designates (a place or a cushion), consistent in English with a 'mattress'. Etymological relationship with the 'cushion and mot' suggests a relationship with coitus, linked to 'orgasm' (petit mort) and 'death'.

'Taraha' the Arabic root (to throw) is rendered in Hebrew as 'mutal' (thrown),[34] suggesting the 'stick' (mot), labelled with the 'God of Destruction' (a reaper or raper). Mot's Canaanite ancestry is forwarded to the Egyptian Goddess Maat, depicted as a judge of the underworld, who weighs the hearts of the dead. Conventional scholars transliterate Maat's Egyptian name as follows:

The 'sickle' in the hieroglyphic sign list is read as the morpheme 'maa'.[35] This is followed by the 'arm' glyph a quiet 'r', affixed with the feminine ending of the 'bread sign', pronounced as a silent 't'.[36] Her name incorporates a rectangular glyph with one corner removed, indexed as a 'statue plinth'. Its phonetic value listed by the British Museum is 'maat'.[37]

At this juncture, it should be noted that the interpretation 'statue plinth' is a matter of conjecture. It is also known as the 'cubit of justice', sometimes regarded as a symbol of heaven and earth,[38] due to its similarity with the 'sky' glyph 'pet'.[39] According to the occult scholar, Laurence Gardner, the horizontal 'plinth' denotes a 'flat and level foundation', transliterated in the Egyptian hieroglyphic as 'Ma'at'.[40] Rundle Clarke argues it represents the 'primeval mound', rising above the water, depicted as the pyramid.[41] When put together, the sickle, arm, level and bread sign, combined with the Goddess' determinative, spells 'Maaht' - written in English as 'Maat'.

A good theory based on no evidence whatsoever! This is another clear example of how Egyptologists have attempted to obscure meaning behind the hieroglyphs. The 'sickle' sign transliterated by the British Museum sign list as 'maa' is not a 'sickle'. To begin with, none of the ancient words for a 'sickle' start with the letter 'm'. The 'sickle' sign records a 'plough', written in Egyptian Arabic as the noun 'mihrat'.[42] It is placed next to the 'rod' (a staff or wand) hieroglyph, rendered from the early Semitic 'mate' or 'mot'.[43] There is no linguistic evidence to suggest that the 'mot' glyph, archived by Egyptologists as a 'statue plinth', is what they claim.[44] The Arabic and Hebrew lexicon suggests that 'mot' is (a staff or rod), used as a type of wand.

Maat's title is extracted from the corruption of the Hebrew word 'mate' alternatively 'mot' (a rod or pole). The device of the 'stick' and 'pole' (mot),[45] particular to this Goddess, indicates Maat's name in the Old Semitic is 'Mot', cogent in Arabic with the verb (to die).[46] Her assignment is equated with the 'plough' (mihrat), implicit of the 'reaper'.

Written data suggests Egyptian scribes doubled characters with the same or approximate phonetic values, when writing important names. This hypothesis is based upon the author's independent research and is clearly shown with the spelling of the deity names 'Maat and Ra'. For example, the Arabic word 'mot' Hebrew 'mate' (a rod or wand) is transcribed adjacent to 'mihrat' (a plough).

In the case of 'Ra' (Aur), the letter 'r' (a mouth) is combined with the 'arm' glyph, transliterated in this work as the 'rh' phoneme. The 'rh' character is consistent in Arabic with the etymon 'ruh' (spirit or soul).[47] 'Ruh' has the additional meaning (to go away or off).[48]

In the example illustrated, the 'arm' sign is incorporated with the 'mouth' glyph to spell the deity 'Ra'. It should further be noted that the 'r' glyph does not signify the organ of the 'mouth', but rather the religious 'washing of the mouth' from the Arabic onomatopoeic word (rararah).[49] Technically, the spelling 'rararah' suggests that the proper transliteration of the 'mouth' letter is a rolling 'r', rendered 'ra', and not the shorter and softer 'r', claimed by Egyptian scholars.

Modulation of the sound 'ra' with 'rh' repeatedly emphasized Ra's significance[50] as the supreme 'God of Light' (Aur). Symbolically, Ra assumes the growling canine, expressed astrologically as the Dog Star.

Returning to the deity 'Maat', the cognomen 'Mot' variously 'Mate' are phonetic approximations of 'mihrat', transposed earlier from the Canaanite 'God of Death' (Mot). The name 'Mot'[51] is derived philologically from 'mihrat' (plough) and is additionally an anagram of the Persian deity of the crop 'Mit(h)ra', connoting 'mita' (death).[52] In the Old Persian, 'Mithra' translates as (a contract), originating from the Sanskrit noun 'Mitra', synonymous in the Sumerian language with 'Martu' (west). Egyptologists translate 'Maat's actual name as (truth). 'Maat's cognomen is obtained from the Semitic philology 'emet' (truth), duplicated as the adjective 'amiti' (true).[53]

Egyptians used the device of the plough to communicate esoteric axioms. In Arabic, the verb to 'plough' is (falah)[54] and is related in the Syrian dialect to 'falak' (sky or atmosphere).[55] The furrows of the clouds are likened to a ploughed field, accredited with the angelic host - the ploughman (reaper). He is conveyed typically as the ferryman or 'boatman' (falayki),[56] and is pictured with a sickle or crescent, doubled with the moon and plough. The Egyptian scribes recorded these vessels, and drew them literally as solar ploughs - symbols of regeneration.

Mythically, the solar plough scattered the seed of heaven (neophyte), and is linked epigraphically to the 'throwing stick',[57] lateral to the Goddess 'Maat'. The 'tall glyph' is virtually identical to the plough symbol, placed vertically and operates as a visual pun on the name Maat. Its relationship to Maat suggests the Canaanite Goddess is not indigenous to Egypt. In the Latin mysteries, the 'stick' (virga) is esoteric of the 'virgin' (virgo) - a Goddess of Judgement.

The British Museum sign list registers the 'throwing stick' as (kmaa), employed as a determinative. The hieroglyph signifies the following concepts (to throw, a foreigner, alien or to create).[58] 'Kmaa' is reminiscent of the Arabic noun 'qamar' (moon) and 'amar' (speak), suggesting magical invocations (Greek logos), proximate to the lunar satellite.[59] The equivalent word association in Latin is 'ejaculate' from 'jacere' (to build, establish, throw, fling, scatter, sow, utter or declare).[60]

'Qamar' (moon) is interchangeable in Hebrew with 'komer' (priest), correlated in Greek with 'koma' (sleep). Philologically 'koma' is linked with 'kuma' (wave), cultic of 'kumbe' (boat) and 'kumbe' (cup). The 'cup and boat' are ancient signifiers of the 'womb and altar', identified with the 'crescent and ovaries'. Ingestion of menstrual blood records the communion (wor-ship) and the enactment of the covenant - historical to the destruction of the earth. Insemination of the woman by the dragon marks the angelic sailor. Disclosure of the nocturne is reciprocal with the lunar plough - the reaper or host. Cylindrical phases of the moon conform to the deluge, allocated religiously with the flooding of the Nile, celebrated as the New Year.

Etiologically, 'qamar' (moon) records the mystery cycles, parabolic of the death and resurrection of the Sun God Horus. His 'loss of sight' (aama) is allied to the 'host - the fleet' (amara). Appellations of the 'amara' are iconic of the 'builder' (ammar), denoting the 'Shepherd Kings', generically the 'Amm' (Ham). The name 'Amm' is derived from the Arabic titular 'Amir' (a Commander), adjacent to 'emir' (a prince).

Assignment of the 'Amm' is affiliated with the 'Western nation' (Aamu Hebrew Emori). Their insignia, the 'shepherd's crook (ra'i), is adopted by Osiris (Yahweh) - the incarnation of 'Ra' (Aur). Osiris' cobra-staff employs the tribute, lateral to the 'Goddess of Death' (Maat, technically Mot). Maat's role as a judicature to the king is symmetrical in the Judaic traditions with the Nazir priestess, revealed in the next chapter.

1   Mark Collier, Bill Manley, How to Read Egyptian Hieroglyphs, British Museum Press, 1998, p139 (British Museum Sign List E7).

2   Bridget McDermott: Decoding Egyptian Hieroglyphics, Duncan Baird Publishers, London, 2003, p171 (Sign Index List).

3   Ralph Ellis: Eden in Egypt, A Translation of the Book of Genesis out of the Original Egyptian Text, Edfu Books, 2005, p304 [(Appendix A5 - Dictionary 'imiyn') - *Since Amun is the God of the Setting Sun, the Egyptians denote 'Amun' as 'west'. But for the 'west' to be on the 'right-hand' side, one must be 'facing south', and so the Hebrews have equated this word with south instead*].

4   Hippocrene English-Arabic, Arabic-English Dictionary, Hippocrene, New York, 2005, p312

5   Ibid, p311

6   Ibid, p34

7   'Western priesthood' is cognate with the 'Rabbi' - Arabic 'Rarb(i)' (west), and is aligned 'contractually' to the 'Mithraic' or 'Western people' (the Martu).

8   Mark Collier, Bill Manley: How to Read Egyptian Hieroglyphs, British Museum Press, 1998, p127 (British Museum Sign List - List I: Consonant Signs).

9   Ralph Ellis: Eden in Egypt, A Translation of the Book of Genesis out of the Original Egyptian Text, Edfu Books, 2005, p315 (Appendix A5 - Dictionary 'West').

10 Mark Collier, Bill Manley: How to Read Egyptian Hieroglyphs, British Museum Press, 1998, p139 (British Museum Sign List - List II: Consonant Signs).

11 Prolog Pocket Bilingual Dictionary, English-Hebrew-Hebrew-English, Prolog, 2003, p391

12 P G Maxwell-Stuart: Witchcraft A History, Tempus, 2004, p20

13 Ralph Ellis: Eden in Egypt, A Translation of the Book of Genesis out of the Original Egyptian Text, Edfu Books, 2005, p22

14 Hippocrene English-Arabic, Arabic-English Dictionary, Hippocrene, New York, 2005, p107

15 In the Syrian language, 'zan' (to weigh) is implicit of 'guilt' (zamb), assimilated from the Arabic root 'zann' (to think, suppose or suspect), cogent with the verbal root 'sann' (to sharpen).

16 Prolog: Pocket Bilingual Dictionary, English-Hebrew, Hebrew-English, Prolog, 2003, p274

17 Aidan Dodson: The Hieroglyphs of Ancient Egypt, Connaught, New Holland Publishers, UK, 2006, p123

18 Ralph Ellis: Eden in Egypt, A Translation of the Book of Genesis out of the Original Egyptian Text, Edfu Books, 2005, p302 (Appendix A5 - Dictionary 'Makher').

19 Aidan Dodson: The Hieroglyphs of Ancient Egypt, Connaught, New Holland Publishers, UK, 2006, p123

20 'Macho' the verb (to go) recalls 'rah' (to go away or off) and is equated with 'ruh' (the spirit or soul).

21 Aidan Dodson: The Hieroglyphs of Ancient Egypt, Connaught, New Holland Publishers, UK, 2006, p123

22 Prolog: Pocket Bilingual Dictionary, English-Hebrew-Hebrew-English, Prolog, 2003, p183

23 Ibid

24 John C Traupman PhD: The New College Latin English Dictionary, Bantam Books, 1988, p169

25 Ibid

26 The Italian God 'Liber' is implicit of the 'Levite' priesthood and appears in the German etymology 'leibling' (a darling or favourite). Leibling denotes 'leib' (the body), correlated with 'liba' Hebrew (heart), lexicological to the 'liver'.

27 John C Traupman PhD: The New College Latin English Dictionary, Bantam Books, 1988, p169

28 It is interesting to note that 'Levite' appears to be synonymous with 'kelev' (a dog) - Old Semitic 'caeleb or kaleb', indicating a correlation with Sirius (Al Kalb) and the Egyptian Sothic year.

29 'Maga' (a Persian priest), 'maka' (hit) and 'nagga' (strike) are related semantically to 'nagga' (a saviour).

30 Prolog: Pocket Bilingual Dictionary, English-Hebrew-Hebrew-English, Prolog, 2003, p390

31 Ibid, p97

32 Ibid, pp390 & 391

33 Hippocrene English-Arabic, Arabic-English Dictionary, Hippocrene, New York, 2005, p35

34 Prolog: Pocket Bilingual Dictionary, English-Hebrew-Hebrew-English, Prolog, 2003, p419

35 Mark Collier, Bill Manley: How to Read Egyptian Hieroglyphs, British Museum Press, 1998, p142 (British Museum Sign List F24)

36 There is no evidence to suggest the 'bread' glyph is a letter 't', adopted by the French philologists as a 'silent letter', replicated in the French language. My own research indicates that the 'bread' sign is used to write 'feminine words'.

37 Mark Collier, Bill Manley: How to Read Egyptian Hieroglyphs, British Museum Press, 1998, p142 (British Museum Sign List F22).

38 Alan F. Alford: The Phoenix Solution Secrets of a Lost Civilisation, Hodder and Stoughton, 1998, p191

39 The 'Pet' hieroglyph is the standard or official transliteration for (sky) that should be rendered correctly as 'felek or pelek', denoting (the sky or atmosphere).

40 Laurence Gardner: Genesis of the Grail Kings, Bantam Books, 2000, p238

41 Alan F. Alford: The Phoenix Solution Secrets of a Lost Civilisation, Hodder and Stoughton, 1998, p192

42 Hippocrene English-Arabic, Arabic-English Dictionary, Hippocrene, New York, 2005, p240

43 Prolog Pocket Bilingual Dictionary, English-Hebrew-Hebrew-English, Prolog, 2003, p348

44 The notion that the 'maat' glyph represents a 'statue plinth' is taken from the 'Louvre Papyrus' manuscript. 'Maat' and her twin are shown with their feet, placed upon the wand, assumed falsely by scholars to represent a 'plinth'. The woman's feet touching the glyph record the priestess' line of descent through the lineage of 'Maat'. Hieroglyphically, the 'foot' records the 'priestess' and specifies 'genetic descent' through the snake, combined with the 'rod' (Hebrew mate) - her footprint equated with the Goddess' divine lineage.

45 Prolog Pocket Bilingual Dictionary, English-Hebrew-Hebrew-English, Prolog, 2003, p307

46 Hippocrene English-Arabic, Arabic-English Dictionary, Hippocrene, New York, 2005, p238

47 'Ruh' annotating (the soul) is written with the 'arm' glyph, and is augmented with the 'ka' sign, drawn as a 'pair of arms', signifying (the double). The 'arm' is prognostic of the offering, recognizant with the materialization of the 'double', conceived as an 'angel or serpent'.

48 Hippocrene English-Arabic, Arabic-English Dictionary, Hippocrene, New York, 2005, p273

49 Ibid, p77

50 There is a good argument to suggest 'Ra's sacred name is 'Aur' (light), aligned esoterically to 'awa' (the dog's bark) - symbolic of the 'Dog Star'. The letter 'r', technically a rolling 'r', is left unpronounced.

51 Scholars depict the Canaanite God Mot as a male God. Etymological records suggest however Mot is a Goddess.

52 Prolog, Pocket Bilingual Dictionary, English-Hebrew, Hebrew-English, Prolog, 2003, p99

53 Ibid, p431

54 Hippocrene English-Arabic, Arabic-English Dictionary, Hippocrene, New York, 2005, p173

55 Ibid

56 Ibid

57 Mark Collier, Bill Manley, How to Read Egyptian Hieroglyphs, British Museum Press, 1998, p139 (British Museum Sign List E2).

58 Ibid (British Museum Sign List E2 - 'Kmaa').

59 The Sumerian word 'Kar' (an angel or king) in the Egyptian language is correlated with the name (Horus). 'Kar' is related in the Modern Arabic to 'qara' the verb (to recite or read) and informs the Sacred Work the 'Koran', symbolized as the crescent. Etymological relationship between 'qara and Kar' suggests that (the king or hunter - Horus) is cognate with 'recitation', identified with the 'messenger', specified as an 'angel'.

60 John C Traupman PhD: The New College Latin English Dictionary, Bantam Books, 1988, p160

40

The Nazir Priestess

'... *The dragon stood in front of the woman who was about to give birth, so that he might devour her child the moment it was born'.*

Revelation 12:4, Holy Bible, New International Version, Gideon

'*The woman was given the two wings of a great eagle,
so that she might fly to the place prepared for her in the desert,
where she would be taken care of... [from] the serpent's reach...
Then the dragon was enraged at the woman and went off to make
war against the rest of her offspring...*'

Revelation 12: 14 and 17

The deity 'Maat' is an adjudicator between the king and heaven - a relationship governed through a contract with 'foreigners' (aliens), conceptually an 'angel'. Dominion over the host describes the 'processional boat of Osiris', drawn in the hieroglyphic as a 'plough', written as (Neshmet).[1] The name unrecorded is probably an adaptation of the Semitic 'Nas-met' (the deceased-people), subjected to 'Ne'si'a-met' (the journey of death).[2] The Hebrew people record the 'Neshmet' in the Torah as the 'Nas-shomot' (the people of the Exodus).[3] In Latin, 'Nas-shomot' is written as the pronoun 'nosmet' - the emphatic form of 'nos' (us, we or ourselves).[4]

An initiate who undertook the 'journey of death' is 'born again', determined with the plough, sickle or crescent.[5] Rebirth of the neophyte underscores death of the newborn, displaced as the Passover lamb. Ritualized killing of the infant is commensurate with the nomadic angel, compared to the reptile or double.

In Egyptian symbolism, manifestation of the host's form is stylized with a rod motif, registered with the fish or eel. The emblem of the eel staff is carried in possession of the Goddess Maat, opposite her shadow (double), portrayed in the Louvre Paris manuscript. Twinned with her sibling, the black oracle's staff is iconic of menstrual blood, equated with the 'voice' of the 'Bath Kol', generative of the angel's form - Refer to Chapter 21 Salt of the Earth.

The crucified snake is generative of new life, connected to the Passover lamb and the angel of death - Copy derived from a 17th century Flemish painting.

Maat's ceremony records the 'weighing of the heart', framed inside of an elaborate lintel. The papyrus details the civil re-enactment of the Passover. Decoration of the door is virtually identical to the throne room of Osiris' tabernacle. Pictured as the sacrificial lamb or 'shepherd' (Arabic ra'i),[6] Osiris' resurrection from the dead elicits the deiform 'Ra' (Aur). His presence is symbolic of the risen serpent, contrasted with the fallen fish.

Osiris' status as a 'Shepherd King' reflects the 'nomad' or 'migrant', conceptualized literally as an 'outsider', 'alien' or 'demon'. Transfiguration of the lamb into a snake is classified with the opening of the doorway - a portal or star. The relationship between the Pastoral King and the serpent's metamorphosis is derived from the Semitic lexicology.

The Hebrew stem 'ne'si'a' (a journey)[7] is abridged in the Old Assyrian with 'nesu' (a shape shifter or changeling), obtained from the Arabic noun 'nazar', indicating (a look, aspect or appearance).[8] Manifestation of the 'appearance' (nazar) Assyrian 'nesu' is expedited through 'naza' (the agony of death, last breath or expiration).[9] Terminologically, 'naza' (death) is consistent with 'nazr' (a vow, gift or offering),[10] concurrent with 'Nazir' (priest) and 'nasi' (prince).

In Latin, 'nazr' (an offering) imbibes the masculine polyform noun 'nasus' (a nose, snout or smell, additional to anger)[11] - euphemistically a burnt offering. 'Nasus' accedes the Roman words 'nascent or nasci' (to be born)[12] and 'nocere' (to harm).[13] The allomorphs 'nascent' and 'nocere' are consistent with annuity of the firstborn, symmetrical to the 'traveller' (Hebrew nose'a) - a reaper. In Judaic law, the 'Angel of Death' is augmented with 'Nas-shomot' (the people of the Exodus).

Eastern folklore records the 'nomad' as a 'vampire' - traditionally a 'carrier of the plague'. The Semitic appellation 'nose'a' (an itinerant) is related to 'nasa' (a carrier of an illness),[14] borrowed in the Greek etymon 'nosos' (disease). The conduit 'nasa' is derived from the Persian word 'nasai' (dead matter), cogent with 'nasa' (a fly or insect). Designation of 'nose'a' (a traveller)[15] is codified speak for a 'changeling' (Assyrian nesu) - in Arabic 'nazar' (a glance or an aspect), connoting a 'watcher or dragon'. Occult practices allot the 'nesu', a double, with the eye - a symbol of the 'angel or host'. Materialization of the 'nazar' is deduced from the Arabic adjective 'nazir' (having sight, seeing or observant),[16] coherent with the 'oracle priestess' (the Nazir) - Greek 'kore' (a pupil or virgin).

Etymologically, 'nazir' (sight) is reduced from the masculine noun 'nazirah' (the eye, sight or vision).[17] The Semitic homonym 'nazirah' possesses the appended meaning (a lady superintendent or an inspectress).[18] Denomination of the 'nazirah, collectively the 'nazirin', is ancillary to (the beholders, readers or spectators),[19] archaically a sentinel.[20] The titular 'nazirah' informs the Latin transitive verb 'noscere' (to recognise, learn, examine or inquire into).[21]

In the early proto-Semitic languages, 'nazar' means (to guard), discursive of hidden knowledge. The current Hebrew stem 'n-z-r' (to protect)[22] identifies the Greek noun 'naos' (the inner sanctuary of the temple). Technically 'nazar' (to guard) and 'nasir' the masculine noun (defender)[23] is interchangeable with the Arabic masculine noun 'nazir' (one who frightens, terrifies or threatens),[24] specified as 'nazar' (a guardian or keeper). The 'custodian of the priestess' (the nasir), a 'protectorate', carries a ceremonial 'blade' (the nasli),[25] silhouetted in the shape of an eye or fish. The sheaf of the 'nasli' (blade) hieroglyphically represents the woman's vagina, appropriated with the dragon (fish) and sanctuary.

Demarcation of the temple and its 'hidden court' (naos) embodies the oracle's reproductive organs, assigned to the 'small fish' (the Nazrani), device of the 'priestess' (Nazir). The fish's head, a phallic symbol, is emblematic of the labium and clitoris, doubled with the mouth and eye, epigraphic of the itinerants Ra and Osiris.[26]

In the Babylonian traditions, the fish and its dorsal fin is stylized as the 'shen' glyph - symbolic of the angel's transfigured form, Hebrew 'shinui tsura' literally (to transform shape).[27] Zoroastrian tradition depicts the 'shen' attached to the midriff of the God 'Ahura Mazdah' (Wise Lord). Advent of the host is inherent with the nocturnal angel, duplicated as the western or sanguine (menstrual) sun - Refer to Appendix 7.

Kind permission to reproduce image by David Icke - Bridge of Love (see picture credits).
Depiction of a hairy snake (human-angelic) - an entity connected ritualistically to the goat and fish.
Drawing based upon a sketch from a survivor of Satanic abuse showing a human sacrifice.

Esoterically, the logo of the 'fish' (Nazrani) marks the 'Nazir' priesthood[28] - overseer of the mixed Angelic bloodline of the monarch. The Hebrew commission 'nazir' or 'nazar' means (to consecrate or separate oneself) referential to a 'priest' (Nazir), technically a 'priestess'. Her bloodline is ascribed to the denomination 'Nazrani', exercised in Aramaic and Arabic to indicate (little fish).[29] 'Nazrani' is employed in the Modern Arabic to denote (a Christian), written in Greek as 'Nazorean' (English Nazarene).[30]

Denomination of the fish is ancient and ordained by the Roman clergy. Epiphanius states that the original 'Christians' in Judea, generally called Nazoreans (as in Acts of the Apostles), were known as 'Jessaeans'.[31] They referred to themselves as the 'Keeper of the Covenant' (Nozrei ha-Brit). From this term derived the plural 'Nozrim' - the earliest designation of the sect, subsequently known as 'Christians' or 'fish(es)'.[32]

In the Latin mysteries, 'Nazrani' implies 'Nereus', the son of Oceanus, the father of the 'nereis, known otherwise as the nereids' - a race of 'sea nymphs'.[33] Importantly, the God 'Nereus' possessed the power of assuming a mortal form, contiguous with the Assyrian deity 'nesu' (a changeling). Nereis' germ records the matriarchal lineage, reproduced classically as the mermaid. A combination of the woman and fish is latent in the Semitic vocabulary.

In Arabic, the word 'nisa' (woman) is an assonance of 'nasi' (a fish).[34] The Nazir, theoretical to a nun, documents the synod or mothers of the angelic bloodline - the 'netser' Hebrew (offspring).[35] 'Netser's etymology appraises the Latin adjective 'natus or nasci' (to be 'born').[36] The Offspring of the 'netser' is recognizant with a female lineage, outlined in the Roman Church as 'nata' (a daughter),[37] conjugal with 'natans' (a fish).[38] Esoterically, the 'breeding female' (the matrix) is unified with 'natrix' (a water snake).[39] Fertilization of the 'womb', opposite the 'worm', is prenatal to resurrection and childbirth. The title 'Nazrani' (little fish) is ascribed to the dual offspring of the female (a scarlet whore), conjunct with the serpent - Refer to Chapter 34 Apophis the Menstrual Eel.

In conclusion, the Arabic noun 'nisa' (woman) is converted into Latin as 'nisus' (labour pain)[40] and earmarks 'nurus' (a daughter in law, young lady or a young married woman).[41] 'Nurus' is a modification of 'nurse', derived from 'nazirah' (the inspectress) - an augur priestess who assumes the dual role of midwife.

Rather sinisterly, the Roman word 'nisus' infers 'child birth', relative to sacrificial death of the firstborn, adapted from the feminine noun 'necis' (murder or slaughter).[42] 'Necis' is phonologically consistent with 'nesu' (a shape-shifter). Cryptically, 'necis' (slaughter) is subjoined with the Latin adjective 'nexilis' (tied up or bound together),[43] comparative to 'nexus' (a grip, bond, enslavement for debt).[44] Archaically, the 'slave' specifies an 'initiate' into the mysteries, substituted with the woman and firstborn. The status of the 'slave', similar to the 'initiate', is inherited through the matriarch's pedigree - a signifier of the covenant.

The bloodline of the 'nazirah' (loosely a type of nurse or midwife) births the demigod 'nesu', resurrected as (the double or changeling).[45] In the Christian world, he is known as Jesus - a saviour born from 'Nazareth', a namesake adopted from the 'Nazir' priesthood. The same story is told in many forms. In the Greek mysteries, the God 'Nyseus', known more famously as 'Bacchus',[46] is born in 'Nysae'.[47]

To his Hellenistic followers, 'Bacchus' is worshipped as 'Dionusos' - a name corrupted in the Latin spelling as 'Dionysus', otherwise 'Dion-Ysus' (Jesus, son of heaven). The inclusion of the Latin lexicology demonstrates conclusively the Roman and Semitic priesthood are mutually aligned! Hidden, the connection between the Teutonic priesthood the Nazis and its historical link to Israel is scrutinized further in the next chapter.

Ise Shrine, Mie, Japan
Connected formally to the worship of the Emperor and ultra nationalism. Note similarity of 'Ise', compared to the Arabic name 'Isa' (Jesus). The swastika, used archaically in Japan, signifies a temple. The symbol is grouped with the 'mystery' (Japanese 'nazo'), analogous in Hebrew to the title 'Nazir' (priest), conceptual in Greek to 'naos' (a sanctuary).

1   Mark Collier, Bill Manley: How to Read Egyptian Hieroglyphs, British Museum Press, 1998, p143 (British Museum Sign List F51 - Nsmt).

2   Prolog: Pocket Bilingual Dictionary, English-Hebrew, Hebrew-English, Prolog, 2003, p219

3   Ibid, p140 ['Shomot' (Biblical Exodus)].

4   John C Traupman PhD: The New College Latin English Dictionary, Bantam Books, 1988, p196 ['Nosmet' emphatic form of 'nos' (us, we or ourselves)].

5 'Ne'si'a' (journey) is rendered alternatively in Hebrew as 'masa', paired in Arabic with 'Masr' (Egypt). Cryptically 'Masr' is registered with 'misr' (evening), incorporated with the month of 'Nisan' (April). The flight from Egypt is linked ritualistically with the death of the firstborn, sacrosanct with the 'journey of death' (Ne'si'a-met or Neshmet).

6 Hippocrene Concise Dictionary, English-Arabic, Arabic-English, Hippocrene, 2005, p111

7 'Ne'si'a' (a journey) is rendered in Latin as 'noster' (our, our own, ally or friend) from 'nostras' (a native of our country).

8 Hippocrene Concise Dictionary, English-Arabic, Arabic-English, Hippocrene, 2005, p71

9 Ferozsons Urdu English Dictionary, Revised Edition, Ferozsons Ltd, Lahore, p772

10 Ibid, p771

11 John C Traupman PhD: The New College Latin English Dictionary, Bantam Books, 1988, p191

12 Ibid

13 Ibid, p195

14 Prolog: Pocket Bilingual Dictionary, English-Hebrew Hebrew-English, Prolog, 2003, p59

15 Ibid, p428

16 Ferozsons: Urdu-English Dictionary, Revised Edition, Ferozsons Ltd, Lahore, p763

17 Ibid

18 Ibid

19 Ibid

20 Namesake of the 'nazirah' (inspectress) approximates in Greek to the polyform noun 'kore' (a virgin or pupil - eye). The 'kore' (virgin) is a dual signifier of the 'dragon - a watcher', equated with the 'nurse and midwife'.

21 John C. Traupman PhD: The New College Latin English Dictionary, bantam Books, 1988, p196

22 Harold Bayley: The Lost Language of Symbolism, Dover Publications, 2006, Vol 2, pp 286 & 287 *The words NAAS and NAASENI are evidently affiliated with nazar, meaning keep, guard, protect, and with NAZARENES or NASAREES. Dr Wm. Benjamin Smith writes: "The epithet Nazoraeus (variously spelled, the oldest spelling being most likely NAZARAEUS) is not derived from 'a city called Nazareth'; there was, in fact, no such city at the beginning of our era. The epithet is an appellation primarily of a Deity; it is formed after the analogy of Hebrew proper names ending in iah, as Zachariah, the iah representing Jehovah (pronounced Yahveh, Yahu, or Yah), and is derived from the familiar Old Semitic nazar, meaning keep, guard, protect, so that the Syriac 'Nazarya' is very nearly Guardian-Yah. The names Jesus and Nazaraeus differ about as Salvator and Servator. The Nazarenes (or Nasarees) were in all likelihood the worshippers of Nazarya, and according to Epiphanius were 'before Christ and knew not Christ.' They are mentioned in Acts xxiv. 5, and Paul was one of them. They seem to have been hardly distinguishable from Jessees also mentioned by Epiphanius, apparently an early name for the worshippers of Jesus. Amid some uncertainty of detail the ground fact that Nazaree is derived from the Hebrew stem N-z-r, meaning protect, remains indubitable."*

23 Ferozsons: Urdu-English Dictionary, Revised Edition, Ferozsons Ltd, Lahore, p763

24 Ibid, p771

25 Hippocrene Concise Dictionary, English-Arabic, Arabic-English, Hippocrene, 2005, p254

26 The fish is a phallic symbol and is a dual signifier of the penis, adjoined sexually to the woman's reproductive organs.

27 Prolog: Pocket Bilingual Dictionary, English-Hebrew Hebrew-English, Prolog, p427

28 Christopher Knight & Robert Lomas: The Hiram Key, Pharaohs, Freemasons and the Discovery of the Secret Scrolls of Jesus, Arrow, 1997, p317

29 Ibid

30 Scholars are unable to locate Nazareth, Jesus' hometown. The label originally is used to signify Jesus' 'priestly' bloodline, extracted from the 'Nazir'.

31 Michael Baigent & Richard Leigh: The Dead Sea Scrolls Deception, Arrow Books, 2001, p255

32 The Greek Christians referred to themselves as the 'little fish(es)' (pisciculi), recorded in Latin as 'adipisci' (an adept) from the transitive verb (win or obtain). Archaically, the 'adipisci' sanctioned blood offerings, labelled 'adipis' (the fat of an offering).

33 John C Traupman PhD: The New College Latin English Dictionary, Bantam Books, 1988, p193

34 'Nisa' Arabic (women) informs the Old English noun 'missis' (in Modern English miss, mrs and mistress).

35 Prolog: Pocket Bilingual Dictionary, English-Hebrew, Hebrew-English, Prolog, 2003, p279

36 John C Traupman PhD: The New College Latin English Dictionary, Bantam Books, 1988, p191

37 Ibid

38 Ibid

39 Ibid

40 Ibid, p194

41 Ibid, p197

42 Ibid, p194

43 Ibid

44 Ibid

45 Islamic tradition states Jesus did not die on the cross, but rather a double of Jesus was instated and crucified. The parable is esoteric of 'nazar' (an appearance), cognate with the 'Nazir' (priest), identified with 'nesu' (a changeling).

46 'Nyseus' (Bacchus) is a variation on the name 'Nessus' - the mythical centaur slain by Hercules. The 'centaur' is of course a symbol of the Pleiadian 'bull', equated with angelic conflict and rebirth - Refer to Conclusion Man's Awakening for details of the priesthood and its split, cognate with the origin of the human species, sourced from the Pleiades.

47 John C Traupman PhD: The New College Latin English Dictionary, Bantam Books, 1988, p198

41

Nazi and Nasa
the Priests of Nazir

'I occasionally think how quickly our differences worldwide would
vanish if we were facing an alien threat from outside this world.
And yet, I ask you, is not an alien force already amongst us?'

US President Ronald Reagan, 21 September 1987
42nd Session of the UN General Assembly in New York

'There will be maidens restraining their glances,
untouched beforehand by man or jinn. Which, then,
of your Lord's blessings do you both deny?'[1]

Koran: the Lord of Mercy, Sura 55: 56-57
(The quotation demonstrates sexual viability between the woman and serpent).

Modern versions of the 'Nazir' priesthood are encoded in the names Nazarene, Nicene,[2] Nazi, NASA and Nestle. Shown in previous chapters, a strong connection exists between the Semitic and Teutonic priesthood, branched respectively as the Nazarene and the Nazi (NASA). Evidence for such a connection is exampled in the English and German wordplays.

The abbreviation 'Jerry' is obtained from the traditional Old German name 'Gerard' (a spear),[3] cultic of the 'Spear of Destiny', inaugurating the thousand year Reich. In English, 'Jerry' is derisory and indicates (a German soldier) or someone of (Germanic) descent. The same nomination applies to an American soldier. A young recruit in the American Marines is known to his commander as a 'Jarhead' on account of his 'short hair cut'.[4] The nickname 'Jarhead' is really a clever pun of 'Gerald', a variant of 'Jerry'.

Adoption of 'Jarhead' and 'Jerry' is taken from the Hebrew appellation 'ye'rid' or 'je'rid' (fair)[5] and is combined with 'yeled' (a child),[6] enlisted as the 'Aryan'. Freemasons record 'Jar or Yah' as the sacred name of the 'Lord', reproduced as the 'moon' (in Old Semitic Yah). To summarize, 'Gerald', 'Jerry', 'Jarhead' and 'je'rid' are variations of the same name, disclosing the Aryan aristocrat - a bloodline seeded from the moon. 'Je'rid' is interchangeable in Arabic with 'jihad' (to struggle), indicative of a 'holy war', associated with 'Jordan', emblazoned as the crescent.

Babylonian relief, showing a soldier with blond hair and blue eyes, allied to the God Asshur from the Arabic word 'ash'ar' (blond or fair). Asshur's divine progeny is cognate with the tribe of 'Israel', named originally as (Asher) - an epithet suggesting a 'caucasian', referential to the Western priesthood.

The American marine (fish) is a cousin or offshoot from the Nazi and Muslim militia. Universally, the Je'rid (ye'rid) are soldiers of God, aligned to warfare.

They claim descent from the 'father of Enoch' - a patriarch listed in Genesis 5:18 as 'Jared'. The appellation 'Jared' is transliterated from the Hebrew adjective 'yored' (descending).[7] 'Jared's fallen offspring settled in the land of 'Jordan', identified with 'Judea', cognate semantically with 'jihad' (to struggle).

The 'fallen ones' is an ancient epithet of 'Jew' or 'Judean' from the Hebrew name 'Ye'hudi[8] or Je'hudi' - a race of warriors conceived in heaven. Offspring of the 'Ye'hudi' originates from 'Jared or Yored' - a noble bloodline. His progeny brands the Roman and Aryan priesthood, symbolized with the Imperial standard - the eagle.[9]

The German and American organizations, Nazi and NASA[10] depict its sovereignty with the 'eagle' (Syrian nisr)[11] from 'nizil' (to descend or sink), adjacent to 'nizul' (descent).[12] The emblem of the eagle is a precursor to the bloodline of 'Jared or Yored' (descending) implying a fallen angel, allied in Assyria with the father God Asshur. In Genesis 10:11, Asshur's envoy seeded 'Canaan or Khanun' Old Semitic (red),[13] ascendant to Asher.[14] The tribal name 'Asher' is taken from the Arabic adjective 'ash'ar' (blond).[15] Biblically, Asher (blond) sourced the tribe of Israel.

The symbol of the Jewish synod is drawn with the swastika - an abstraction of 'aleph', the first letter of the Hebrew alphabet. 'Aleph' is transliterated in Arabic as 'allaf' (to write books).[16] Esoteric, 'aleph' records the Hebrew noun 'ever' (a wing)[17] - an emblem combined typically with the eagle (an angel). Correlation between the eagle motif of Asshur indicates the German Nazis, believed quite literally that the Caucasian nation emerged from Israel, supported additionally in the Semitic lexicon.

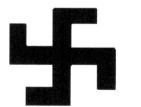 

The swastika, a solar device, is comparable to the Jewish letter 'aleph' (an ox) - a symbol of the Pleiades. Aleph is also reminiscent of the mathematical divide-sign, equated with the government and division.

The Imperial eagle used by the Roman senate originates from Babylonian and is figurative of the 'Aryan' dignitary, charted from 'Iran'. The assignment 'Aryan' is articulated from the Sanskrit title 'aryas' (noble). In Babylonian iconography, the zoomorphic 'eagle-men' are annexed with the bloodline of 'Asshur', assimilated with the meteorological Goddess 'Nis'ar'. Her name is a play on the Hebrew adjective 'nis'ar' (stormy).[18]

Nis'ar's materialization portends to ruin and destruction. She is tagged in Syrian with 'nisr' (an eagle), utilized in Arabic as the homonym (vulture).[19] Esoterically, the 'eagle' and 'vulture' (nisr) are interchangeable with the feathered snake - a harbinger of mortality. Delegated with the bird of prey, the 'fallen angel' (Nizil) is conceptual of 'carrion' (Persian nasai). Theologically, the Nizil's mandate is equated with strife and war, instated through the 'Nazir' (priest). Convocation of the 'Nazir' implies ritual slaughter, registered with the 'vulture' in Egypt - the Goddess 'Mwt'. Her dubious transliteration is rendered correctly as 'Mvt' and is taken from the Hebrew etymon 'mavet' (death).[20]

In Egypt, the vulture Goddess 'Nekhbet' is used to write (the Upper Kingdom) and is combined with the cobra Goddess 'Wadjet' representing (Lower Egypt). - Refer to footnote[21] for the correct assignment of 'Nekhbet and Wadjet'.

The image of these two Goddesses are displayed on Egyptian crowns and can clearly be seen, for instance, on the famous gold crown of Tutankhamen in the Cairo Museum.[22] The 'vulture' is used as a double-barrelled symbol to denote the 'eagle' motif (nisr), allied to the Goddess 'Nis'ar'.

Syrian legend documents 'Nis'ar' (stormy) as a Goddess of anguish, subsequent to hidden propitiations. Cryptically, 'Nis'ar' is a concealed deity, Arabic 'nisi' (to forget)[23] - seminal of the mysteries. Represented as a lunar deity of fertility, the nocturnal angel 'Nis'ar' is concurrent in Arabic with 'nizil' (to spend the night or pass the night).[24] Exposure to her charms augurs sleep - a euphemism of death.

Nis'ar's 'appearance' (Arabic nazar) is catalogued in the Assyrian lexicon with 'nesu' (a changeling), featured as the moon and eagle.[25] Her offspring are prescriptive of the 'fallen' (Nizil), epitomized as the bird (nisr) - a motif of the 'angel'. Lineage of the 'Nizil' is indexed under the Arabic masculine noun 'nazilah' (misfortune, disorder, calamity or a disaster from heaven)[26] - historical of conflict.

Mythologically, the 'Nizil' are identified with the deluge, encoded in the Latin vocabulary. 'Aqua' (water) signifies 'aquila' the feminine noun (an eagle), illustrated as the Roman legionary standard.[27] The 'eagle' is typically combined with water - a symbol of the 'moon and angel', bracketed astrologically with 'Mars' (the God of War), tributary of the 'sacrificial ram'.

Theologically, the 'nisr' (eagle) recalls 'nisan' (April),[28] collated with the lambing season and Passover. Descendents of the 'Nizil' (fallen) are aligned to the 'processional boat of Osiris' (the Neshmet), genealogical to the 'Nas-shomot' (the people of the Exodus).

Babylonian Kerubim (Cherubim) - A fallen angel the eagle carries a basket, a Royal marker showing angelic pedigree, juxtaposed with sacrificial offerings. The wings of the angel are drawn to mimic the dragon's mouth, correlated with the votive.

In conclusion, the 'consecrated' (Nazir) are a body of prenuptial priests, imputative of the 'woman' (nisa). Her sacred bloodline incorporates the insignia of the 'eagle' (nisr), combined with the emblem of the 'fish' (nasi). At its heart, the priesthood is centered upon an unbroken matriarchal lineage.[29] 'Marriage' (Hebrew nisu'im)[30] of the oracle discloses Royal ancestry, paralleled to the 'fallen' angels (Nizil), relative to the 'priest' (Nazir).

Fronted by male patriarchy, Judaism operates as a façade, obscuring a chapter of 'female priests' of Aryan extraction. Historically, the 'Nazir' bore the sons of angels, consigned to the 'Dragon King' - a 'Theban'. His Royal successors are recorded in Hebrew as 'nasikh or nasi' (a prince)[31] from 'nakhash' (a serpent).[32] Titular of the 'nasikh' is a derivation of the Arabic-Syrian root 'masikh' (a monster),[33] implicit of the 'serpentigena' (serpent race), allied to the 'matriarch and Theban'.

The 'Nazir' arbitrates a secret denomination of 'bridal-priests', literally 'nurses' (Arabic nazirah), diminutive of 'nisa' (woman). Lineage of the 'nazirah' is incumbent upon the pedigree or fairness of the matriarch's complexion. Nazirah's intercourse with the 'snake' (nakhash) is matrimonial to the mythical race - Assyrian 'nesu' (a shape-shifter). Materialization of the 'semblance' (nazar) specifies a 'shape-shifter' (nesu), and is filed with the 'watcher' (nazirin). A dual signifier of the 'dragon and priestess', the 'nazirin', is conjugal with the 'little fish' (nazrani), disclosing an ancient order, affiliated to the Theban priesthood.

The oracle's 'organ of sight' (nazirah) discloses the 'watcher', an abstraction of an 'angel or king', documented as a 'Theban' - a bloodline inaugurated from Osiris. Optically, the 'virgin's pupil' doubles with the 'fish's eye', figurative of the woman's 'mouth and vagina'.[34] Her sexual organs are associated with rebirth, paralleled to the resurrection of a deity, aligned to the altar and shrine.

The reproductive cycle of the 'nazirah' is regionalized in situ to the 'temple sanctuary' (Greek naos), cognate with the lunar satellite and the menstrual cycle. Covered from view, the 'inner sanctum' (naos) concords with the Hebrew adjective 'no'az' (risqué),[35] indexed with the 'watching eye' (nazirah). Technically an 'inspectress' (the nazirah) served as a type of 'midwife', assigned to Royal progeny, classified with the Theban and Syrian sodality. A covenant of priests, the 'monarchial heir' (nasikh), labels the 'serpent' (nakhash), avowed through the killing of the firstborn. Expropriation of the male line is credited with the vestal priestess - a carrier of the vessel and staff.

Propitiation of the heart recalls the Passover lamb, equidistant with the 'builder' or 'mason', covertly 'nesu' (a changeling), mythological to 'Nizil' (a 'fallen' angel). Ancestry of the 'Nizil' pertains to the Goddess of darkness 'Nis'ar' (stormy), metaphorical of the sun's decline, correlated with the communal mystery.

Sacrificial redemption of the innocent remonstrates the nocturnal serpent 'Nizil' - a provocateur of war, mutual to the 'Nazir' (priest). An agent of rebellion, the hieratic denomination 'Nazir' (consecrated) fronted the German Nazis - an ancient order of priests, originating from Babylon - its heritage human-angelic.

1   M.A.S. Abdel Haleem: The Qur'an, Oxford University Press, Oxford, 2004, p355 (Sura: The Lord of Mercy, 55:56)

2   The 'Nicene' Creed is a pun on 'Nazarene' and 'Nazir' (priest). The Creed is a formal statement of Christian belief that appears in the 'Thirty-nine Articles', adopted at the first Council of Nicaea (Nicenus) in AD 325. *Originally written in Greek, it was long thought to have been drafted at the Council of Nicaea (325), but is now believed to have been issued by the Council of Constantinople (381), based on a baptismal creed already in existence* - Refer to Britannica Concise Encyclopedia under Nicene Creed.

3   Geddes & Grosset: Dictionary of First Names, Geddes & Grosset, 2003, p131 (Gerard)

4   Note how the Special Forces in Germany are called the 'SS', symmetrical to the English 'SAS'. In heraldry, the double 'SS' motif symbolizes a 'key-holder' to the King's Chamber, employed as a Royal Protectorate.

5   Prolog: Pocket Bilingual Dictionary, English-Hebrew, Hebrew-English, Prolog, 2003, p144

6   Ibid, p65

7   Ibid, p106

8   Ibid, p218 ['Yeled' (a child) is interchangeable with 'ye'rid' (fair)].

9   Horus' name Kar(i) or Har(i) is punned in Hebrew with 'Ari' (an Aryan). Study of etymology suggests that the priesthood of Horus had blond hair and blue eyes.

10 Variegation of the 'Nazir' (priesthood) is assumed under the 'Nazi, an extension of NASA', identified with 'Masr' (Egypt) from the Syrian root 'masa' (evening). The etymology of 'Nazir' is referential to the 'Western rites of Freemasonry' equated with 'Egypt' and the 'setting sun' (Amun). Represented as the 'dark land' 'Egypt' (Kmt) is theoretical to 'Sauda' (black), nominal of the 'Sodi' fraternity.

11 Hippocrene English-Arabic, Arabic-English Dictionary, Hippocrene, New York, 2005, p256

12 Ibid

13 The Canaanites take their lineage from 'Cain or Khanun' (red) - the son of 'Adam' Semitic (red).

14 Modern versions of the Gideon Bible omit the name Asshur inexplicably - the name however is preserved in the Authorized King James Edition of the Bible.

15 M. A. Abdel-Hady: Egyptian Arabic, A Rough Guide Dictionary Phrasebook, Lexus, 2002, p56

16 Hippocrene English-Arabic, Arabic-English Dictionary, Hippocrene, New York, 2005, p149

17 Prolog: Pocket Bilingual Dictionary, English-Hebrew, Hebrew-English, Prolog, 2003, p461

18 Ibid, p396

19 Ibid, p256

20 Ibid, p99

21 Observing the etymologies, I have reservations about the transliteration of 'Nekhbet' and 'Wadjet'. The hieroglyph 'Nekhbet' pictured as a 'vulture' is actually an ideogram, and suggests the reading 'nasr' (vulture), a signifier of 'Nazir' (a priest), conceptual to 'nasa' plural (woman), connoting the priestess' line. Egyptian frescoes show the priestess of Isis, adorned with the wings of a vulture, silhouetted as a serpent's profile, linked to the Mother Goddess of Death 'Mut', correctly written as 'Mavet' (death). The vulture is conjunct with the Goddess 'Wadjet' - a glyph that should be read as 'tea'ban' Arabic (cobra) and is listed as the Royal city of 'Thebes'. Furthermore, evidence suggests the 'cobra' is 'masculine' - its 'venom' grouped with 'ejaculation', corresponding with the 'vulture and priestess'. In Arabic the 'vulture' (nisr) is a codeword for an 'eagle' (Syrian nisr) - a symbol of 'Assyria' and its agreement with Egypt (Thebes). 'Nisr' additionally is an encryption of the Assyrian word 'nesu' (a changeling) - an entity depicted as a 'snake', annotated as a 'Theban' or 'anguigena' (serpent race) - Refer to Chapter 12 Thebes and the Offspring of the Dragon.

22 Alan F. Alford: The Phoenix Solution, Secrets of a Lost Civilisation, Hodder & Stoughton, 1998, p119

23 Hippocrene English-Arabic, Arabic-English Dictionary, Hippocrene, New York, 2005, p256 ['Nisi' (to forget) appertains to the induction into the mysteries, in which the initiate swears an oath to remain silent. The concept of forgetting is analogous to death, reflective of rebirth, linked to the neophyte].

24 Ibid ['Nizil' (Spend the night or pass the night), a homonym of the verb (to descend or sink), cognate with 'nazil' (downward)].

25 On the first manned Apollo mission to the moon, the safe landing of the craft was accompanied by the immortal words, 'The Eagle has landed'. Symbolically, the 'eagle' conveys the 'fallen' (Nizul), whose seed is correlated with the moon and angel. NASA's emblem, the 'eagle' (Syrian nisr), is combined with the lunar surface, implicit of the 'priest' (Nazir). Theoretically the 'Nazir' connotes a 'priestess', covert to 'nasa' (a woman). 'Nazir' (consecrated) specifies an angelic bloodline, conveyed through the matriach, and is a name esoteric of the German political movement, the 'Nazis'.

26 Ferozsons, Urdu-English Dictionary, Revised Edition, Ferozsons, Ltd, Lahore, p762

27 John C Traupman PhD: The New College Latin English Dictionary, bantam Books, 1988, p19

28 Hippocrene English-Arabic, Arabic-English Dictionary, Hippocrene, New York, 2005, p12

29 The fish and eagle are symbols of fallen angels, and are contrasted with the rising cobra or seraph - iconic of ascension.

30 Pocket Bilingual Dictionary, English-Hebrew Hebrew-English, Completely Transliterated, Prolog, p246 ['nasui or nesu'a' (married)]

31 Ibid, p315

32 Ibid, p365

33 Hippocrene English-Arabic, Arabic-English Dictionary, Hippocrene, New York, 2005, p237 ['Masikh' (monster) - literally a hunter of the night].

34 Designation of the 'pupil', rendered loosley in Latin as (an initiat), corresponds with the 'watcher or serpent', written epigraphically with the 'eye'. Dilation of the pupil defines the female sexual organs, linked with contraction and rebirth. The 'eye', a Royal symbol, decrees the signature of 'Osiris' - nominal of the 'dragon'.

35 Pocket Bilingual Dictionary, English-Hebrew Hebrew-English, Transliterated, Prolog, p347

42

The Rib the Serpent and the Moon

'So the Lord God caused the man to fall into a deep sleep; and while he was sleeping, he took one of the man's ribs and closed up the place with flesh. Then the Lord God made a woman from the rib he had taken out of the man, and he brought her to the man.

The man said,

"This is now bone of my bones
and flesh of my flesh;
She shall be called 'woman'
for she was taken out of man".

For this reason a man will leave his father and mother and be united to his wife, and they will become one flesh. The man and his wife were both naked, and they felt no shame'.

Genesis 2:21-25, Holy Bible, New International Version, Gideon

The 'rib' indicates new life, identified with the internal organ of the 'heart', intrinsic to the 'priest' (komer) and the 'moon' (qamar). The Semitic noun 'alb' (heart) is analogous to 'harb' (war),[1] paralleled to 'abhar' (sail).[2] The terms connote migration and are grouped semantically with 'harab' (to flee).[3] Theologically, the emblem of the boat and host are symmetrical to the lunar satellite and the priest, affiliated to 'ab(u)' (the Father).[4] He is depicted as the God of 'War' (harb) and Lord of the 'host' (abhar), consistent in the Old Semitic with 'Kabir' (Lord).[5]

Termed as the 'Kabeiroi' plural (the Great Gods or Lords), the cognomen is identical to 'Qabili' (a tribe) and 'Kabir' the Old Semitic titular (Lord). 'Kabir' in the original Arabic pertains to 'qalb' (heart) and 'Al Kalb' (Sirius - literally the dog).

The 'Kabeiroi or Cabiri' are (divinities from Sirius), associated historically with the mystery sanctuaries - notably 'Thebes' and 'Lemnos'. Theologically the shrines recall the re-creation of man,[6] marked with the star Sirius, symbolised with the 'heart' nominal of (the Levite priesthood).

Depiction of the 'Draconiopides' (Serpent Footed) in the Garden of Eden.
(Stain glass window, Ulm, Cathedral, 1420)

Relationship between the heart (rib) and the moon suggests the flood and earlier, the creation of woman. Noah's descendents are traced from the story of

Eve, and recount her fall with the serpent. In the book of Genesis, Adam's rib is used to create his consort Eve and is reflected in the Sumerian narrative of 'Ninhursag' (Lady of the Summit).[7] 'Ninhursag' gives birth to 'Nin-ti' (Lady of Life) - a deity associated anatomically with the rib[8] and serpent. Nin-ti's name is observed from the Persian-Semitic etymology.

The Persian noun 'dil' (heart) is symmetrical in Arabic with 'dil' (rib).[9] 'Dil' is a derivative of the earlier Sumerian noun 'tii' (rib). The Sumerian word 'tii' happens also to be the Sumerian verb (to make live).[10] The wordplay is used in the Sumer-Semitic creation epics, prosaically to suggest creation. Thus, Yahweh and Nin-ti create 'life', using the 'rib', extracted from man.

In English, the same pun is recorded with the word groups 'rib' and 'live', found in the German equivalent 'riber' and 'liber'. In the Sumerian language, the word 'tii' seems to link into words, cogitative of intercourse - apparent in the Egyptian etymon 'tit' (a sticky emission). 'Tit' is transliterated into Hebrew as 'tiyt', suggesting 'ejaculatory' or 'bodily fluids'.[11]

Sumerian epics use the noun 'tii' (rib) as a literary device to explain the 'creation of life' (tii). Usage of 'tii' in the older creation narratives takes us back to the original signifier of Adam. The Babylonian word for 'potter's clay' is (tit), and is found in the current Hebrew word 'tit' (mud).[12] In earlier versions of the ancient Sumerian language, 'ti-it' records the expression (that which is life), assigned to the 'rib' (tii), explicit of the serpent.[13]

The maxim 'ti-it' intellectually categorizes the land and agriculture, adoptive of the snake and the procreation of Eve. Man's conception from the earth in the earliest epics is harvested like a crop. For example, the Sumerian idioms 'tii' (life) and 'tit' (clay) corresponds in Egyptian with 'ta' (land) - Latin 'terre'.[14]

The snake is introduced as a custodian of paradise. He is recounted as a creator of nations, the teacher of geometry, mathematics and architecture.[15] Depicted as a builder or a fallen angel, the serpent is a metaphor of recreation after the flood. Linguistic evidence indicates the 'rib' is corroborative of Adam's offspring, combined with heaven.

Esoterically, the 'builder' is a codeword for the snake's ability to change shape or to assume the form of a man, found in early Ecclesiastical depictions of Adam and Eve. The 'builder' (literally a snake) is conveyed in the Latin etymon 'forma' (construction),[16] in English (foreman), analogous to 'form'. 'Forma' is cogent in Greek with 'phane' (a serpent or apparition). The serpent is shown disguised in the likeness of Adam - the eternal seducer of Eve. Her offspring are presented as the race of kings.

The builder or Mason, represented conventionally as a red snake, correlates with 'the Magical Crafts', referred to in double-speak as 'the Arts'. In Babylonian and Ubaid iconography, the serpent rouge conforms to the 'goat-fish' - progenitor of the 'se'irim' and the 'aliens' (zari). These categories are variations of the 'menstrual fish' or the 'hairy snake' (human-angelic).

Sacerdotal traditions combine the motif of the builder (angel) with the fish and snake, recapitulated in the Arabic wordplays. So for example, 'ti'ban' (an eel) is related to 'ta'ban' (a snake).[17] The reptile is also indicative of the 'builder' from the verbal stem 'bana' (to build).[18] Judaic tradition connects 'banay' (a builder) to the 'moon', listed in Hebrew as (le'vana).[19] Modern mythology adopts the name Banner as the comic book hero 'David Banner' alias the 'Incredible Hulk'.[20]

Emblem of the fish and snake (a sign of regeneration) is commensurate with the 'rib' (tii) of Adam, signified religiously as the moon's crescent - a receptacle of man's seed. This device outlines illicit intercourse with the snake, originally an eel (amphibian), appointed to the descendents of Eve. The ancient Semitic word 'ti'ban' (an eel) is extracted from the compound 'ti ban(a)' (a builder of life) - symbolic of the 'rib' (tii), equated with the snake and 'life' (tii).

In the Syrian language, 'ti'ban' (tired or weary)[21] is translated into Arabic as (an eel).[22] The Syrian philology originates from the Egyptian eel Goddess Apophis and her struggle to consume the solar disk, implicit of divine intercourse.[23] The close proximity of the 'snake and eel' evidenced in Arabic precipitates academic confusion between the 'snake, fish and reptile'.

The 'eel' (ti'ban) is complimentary of the 'snake' (ta'ban), epigraphically displayed as a 'builder of the land', rendered hieroglyphically as (ta-bana). In the Egyptian lexicon, the noun 'ta' (land) and 'bana' (build) is conjunct with 'taban' (snake), categorized as a 'changeling' or 'reaper'.

The noun 'ta' is also similar to the Sumerian value 'tii' (to facilitate a change of state or to make), suggesting a 'changeling'. The 'changeling' ['tii-bana' (loosely transform)] is registered in the Modern Arabic as 'ta bana' literally (in order to build),[24] and is consistent with 'ta'ban' (a serpent). Culturally, the snake is unified with the menstrual 'eel' (ti'ban), reflective of the human-angelic lineage.

The associated wordplays in the Egyptian and Sumerian vocabulary in reference to the 'builder' and 'changeling' are complementary with 'transfiguration' (tii), identified with the 'rib' (tii). Rebirth is compared to the (re)creation of 'life' (tii), a metaphor of the 'builder' (banay) termed as the 'snake' (ta'ban) or 'eel' (ti'ban). Resurrection of the serpent's form is taken from immolation of the heart - symbolic of the rib.

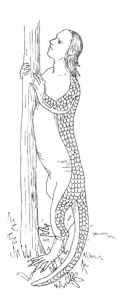

'Bipedal Reptile' (Latin Serpentipedis)
Detail from 'the Fall' by Hugo Van der Goes, 15ᵗʰ century, Kunsthistorisches Museum

A vessel of the soul (life), the heart is paired with the rib a concept preserved in the hieroglyphs. In the British Museum, sign list indexed under tall signs 'ti' is designated incorrectly as a 'pestle'. The character 'ti' is not a 'pestle' but is drawn as (a rib).[25] The glyph is adopted from the Sumerian noun 'tii' (rib), equated with 'tii' (life). (See Appendix 9, Hieroglyphic Sign List).

In addition, 'ti' in the Egyptian alphabet is an adaptation of the 'ast' glyph, denoting (flesh),[26] extracted semantically from the 'rib'. 'Ast' is used idiomatically to write the Goddess Isis.[27] Epigraphically, 'Isis' is deduced from the 'rib' and parallels the Biblical creation of 'Eve from the rib' of Adam.

The 'flesh' glyph (ast)[28] is pictorially reminiscent of the 'teardrop', evoking the mythology of the tears of 'Atum-Ra' and the (re)creation of man after the deluge. In the listed signs published under the British Museum, the word 'ast' (flesh) is a homonym of the noun (throne). Abridged, the glyph signifies the deity name 'Isis' and is used additionally to write her consort 'Osiris'.[29] Spelling of Isis' name is created anagrammatically from the flesh of the rib - an emblem of the snake (angel) ascribed to the resurrection of Osiris.

The 'ast' (flesh) glyph is elongated like the 'tii' glyph and is a simile of the rib or crescent. Astrologically 'tii' denoting (life) is related to the rising and setting of the sun and moon, conferred upon the reptile and host. The Arabic etymon 'tili' (to come up, land, mount or rise)[30] is discerned from the verb 'tar' (to fly).[31] To summarize, the rib is mechanistic of ascension - nominal of the host and resurrection. It operates as a dual symbol of atonement and rebirth, affixed to the builder and snake. 'Ti'bana' (the builder of life) notates 'ti'ban' (an eel), allied to 'ta'bana' literally (in order to build).

The Arabic stem 'bana' (build), in Hebrew 'banay' (a builder), are appellations, assigned to the 'snake and eel'. The etymologies imply sacrificial death of the firstborn, registered with the 'rib and stone', emblematic of the 'moon' (le'vana). Primarily a device of transfiguration the 'stone' is equated with the 'altar and flesh'. For example, the Semitic plural noun 'abanim' (stones) covertly alludes to 'banim' (children),[32] equivocal to the nocturnal angel 'banay' (a builder).

Swallowing a stone is a veiled marker of child sacrifice, found also in the Hellenistic languages.[33] The Greeks saw an etymological connection between the words for 'stone' (laas) and 'people' (laos), equivalent in Semitic to 'adama' (earth) and 'Adam' (mankind). In Arabic, the noun 'sakhr' (rock)[34] informs the Anglo-Latin root 'sacred', 'secret' and 'secrete'. Similar abstractions are cursory in the Punjabi etymon 'sang' (a stone),[35] transferable in the Hindi language to 'sang' (a [comm]union).[36]

Relationship between the 'earth and rock', conjunct with the 'body and altar', is repeated in Judaic iconography. The Hebrew word 'sela' (stone)[37] is signposted obliquely as 'tsela' (rib),[38] and pertains to the act of 'rescue' (hatsil).[39] 'Deliverance' (hatsil) is consistent with the noun 'hatsala' (save) - a derivation of 'ha-tsela' (a-rib). Mythical, the 'sternum' suggests the 'lunar vessle' - a repository of man's seed.

Astrologically, 'tsela' (rib) pertains to the Old Hebrew noun 'Tsa' (Orion), rendered by Egyptologists as 'Sah', derived from the verb 'tsa'ad' (to step).[40] Philologically, 'tsa'ad' is cryptic of the 'Sodi' priesthood, attributed with celestial migration. Descendents of the 'Sodi' are extracted from the 'vestigium' Latin (footprint) e.g. to step - a symbol of Orion, juxtaposed with the rib (moon) and heart (Sirius). Orion's mixed offspring is traced from the 'human line', original to the 'Pleiades', amalgamated with the 'amphibian', conceived from the star constellation 'Sirius'.

Related etymologies suggest redemption through the immolation of the heart, post deluge associated with the 'rib', a signifier designated with 'Sirius and Orion'. Celebrated as a religious communion or festival, the 'crescent' relative to the 'rib' is didactic of the 'host and rebirth', historical to the 'Exodus'.

Sacrificial death of the infant is compared to the covenant of the 'moon' (le'vana), paralleled to divine intervention - archaic to the flood and Eve. In the Egyptian meta-narratives, the crescent is discursive of the agricultural cycle of Egypt, analogous to the flooding of the Nile and the rising of 'Sirius', grouped with 'Venus'. Theologically, oblation of the firstborn's heart (rib) is cognate with Eve and the offertory,[41] assigned to the Passover. The 'rib' (tsela) details the restoration of man's seed through sacrifice, evidenced in the Syrian etymology 'tsalah' (to be reconciled).[42] Emblems of the 'rib and rock' mark the creation of 'Eve', extricated from 'Adam', signified as (the red earth). Astrological 'Adam' specifies 'Mars' (Ma'adim) a planet grouped with the configuration of 'Orion', antecedent to the unification of the 'Pleiades with Canis Major'.

Venus a dual signifier of the snake and Goddess marks Eve's progeny equated with the angel and king.

Analogous to 'heaven', the Semitic noun 'tsela' (rib) is transformed in Latin as 'stella' (star), obtained from the Hebrew root 'tsa' (Orion). Architectural 'stella' marks 'cella' (a sanctuary),[43] synonymous in English to 'shine and shrine'. In the Latin play, 'stella' (star)[44] pertains to 'stellio' (a spotted lizard),[45] matched philologically with the adjective 'celus' (high, lofty or elevated). Phonetically, 'celus' compliments the transitive verb 'celare' (to conceal, veil or hide)[46] from the Hebrew root 'tsel' (shadow).[47] 'Celare' provides the English root of 'occult'.[48] The noun 'occult' (Hebrew sodi) enunciates a 'secret college of priests' (the Sodi) - cryptic of 'Orion' (Tsa'ad or Tsa).

The Biblical reference to the 'rib' (tsela) is an esoteric marker of the star constellation 'Orion', identified with the hidden star 'Sirius',[49] concomitant with the 'reptile' (stellio). To conclude, the 'rib' is a cultic symbol of the 'builder and the host', correlated with the 'crescent' and the worship of 'nocturnal angels', connected to Venus. This class of being is specified as a type of changeling, depicted as the serpent or reaper (rapist).

The builders throughout ancient texts are duplicitous, assailed with the destruction and recreation of the earth. Duality of the builder, idiomatic of the snake is evidenced in the Anglo-Semitic cipher 'bana' or 'banay' (builder). In Old English, 'bana' means (to cause, ruin, trouble or woe), and informs the modern noun (bane), deduced from the fallen[50] serpent (ta'ban).[51]

Progeny of the snake and Eve are said to rule the world, and can take the form of a man by drinking human blood, elaborated as the Craft (i.e. a builder). Manifestation of the angel through the communion of blood is a theme, central to the mysteries, unveiled in the next installment as the Naked Snake.

1   Hippocrene English-Arabic, Arabic-English Dictionary, Hippocrene, New York, 2005, p189 [Note the Semitic pun 'alb' and 'harb' respectively (heart) and (war) is equivalent in English to 'heart and hate'].

2   Ibid, p146 ['abhar' (sail) is related to the English noun 'harbour'].

3   Ibid, p49 ['harab' (flee) in Hebrew is punned with 'ha-rab' (the-master), cogent with the 'Rabbi' and 'Arab'].

4   Ibid, p47

5   Simon Price & Emily Kearns: The Oxford Dictionary of Classical Myth, Oxford University Press, Oxford, 2003, p92 (See definition 'Cabiri').

6   Ibid, (See definition Cabiri).

7   'Sag' Sumerian is translated as (head or summit). 'Ninhursag' is rendered as (Lady of the Mountain Peak). In some academic commentaries, she is referred to as (Lady of the Stony Ground). The author translates her name as (Lady of the Brow of the Mountain). 'Brow', like the Sumerian word 'sag', is used as a homonym to denote (the peak or temple - a head). In addition, the noun 'sag' (head) is punned with the Hittite noun 'sag' (a jackal), identified with 'Sirius'.

8   David Rohl: Legend, The Genesis of Civilisation, Arrow Books Limited, 1999, p201

9   Hippocrene English-Arabic, Arabic-English Dictionary, Hippocrene, New York, 2005, p102

10 David Rohl: Legend, The Genesis of Civilisation, Arrow Books Limited, 1999, p201

11 Ralph Ellis: Eden in Egypt, A Translation of the Book of Genesis out of the Original Egyptian Text, Edfu Books, 2005, p144

12 Laurence Gardner: Genesis of the Grail Kings, Bantam Press, 2000, p109

13 In Greek legend, 'Llus' (mud) i.e. 'Adam' fathered the fabled city of Troy. The name 'Troy' is from the Egyptian root 'trai' (to obliterate) - a word translated into Arabic as ('adam). Llus is guided to the site of Troy by a cow - a symbol of the Pleiades. This cow also appears to be the same animal that founded Thebes by the patron 'Cadmus' (Eastern), e.g 'Orion', from the Old Semitic root 'qadam' (east), philological to 'Adam'. Cadmus established Thebes, having killed the worm, and peopled the place with men, sprung from the teeth of the dragon - a symbol of the 'neophyte'. The 'tooth' in the hieroglyphic denotes 'Sirius' - a signifier equated with the 'anguigena' (the offspring of the dragon, otherwise a Theban).

14 Note that 'ta' (land) and 'terre' (earth) is also evident in the Japanese etymology 'ta' (field).

15 The reptile is diagnostic in Hellenistic traditions with 'sacred learning' (paradosis), corresponding with 'geometry' [Greek 'geometers' (a measurer of the earth)], delegated to 'geo-meter' (mother-earth) - the archetypal 'builder'.

16 John C Traupman: New College, Latin & English dictionary, Bantam, 1988, p371

17 Hippocrene English-Arabic, Arabic-English Dictionary, Hippocrene, New York, 2005, p115

18 Ibid, p22 ['Bana' (build) is connected with the Hebrew etymon 'le'vana' (moon), denoting an artificial receptacle, used to store the seed of man. The traditions are recounted in the Zoroastrian legends, outlined in the religious scripture of the Greater Bundahishn].

19 Prolog: Pocket Bilingual Dictionary, English-Hebrew & Hebrew-English, Prolog, 2003, p262 [Comparisons between the 'carpenter' (nagar) emblematic of 'Venus' (Noga) are symmetrical with the 'moon' (le'vana), cogent with the 'builder' termed (banay). The juxtaposition between 'Venus' and the 'moon' demonstrate an alignment between the planetary bodies].

20 David Banner is presented as a scientist (Satanist) - one might say an alchemist. He is able to manipulate his DNA to take on the form of a reptilian being. Uncontrollable, 'anger' or rage turns Banner into the 'monster' [Latin 'anguis' (a snake)]. The Hulk is reminiscent of the fallen angels, possessed with an unquenchable thirst for human blood. Etymology of the 'Hulk' is from 'holkas' Greek (cargo ship), implicit of the 'angelic host'.

21 Hippocrene English-Arabic, Arabic-English Dictionary, Hippocrene, New York, 2005, p300

22 Ibid, p41

23 The Syrian word 'ti'ban' (tired or weary) is rendered in Arabic as 'ta'b' or 'ta'ab', translated as (fatigue).

24 Hippocrene English-Arabic, Arabic-English Dictionary, Hippocrene, New York, 2005, p292 ['ta' (in order to)]

25 Mark Collier & Bill Manley: How to Read Hieroglyphs, British Museum Press, 1999, p140 (British Museum Sign List E27)

26 Ibid, p135 (British Museum Sign List B38)

27 Ibid (British Museum Sign List B38) In Chapter 43 Naked Snakes (Part 2), the correct transliteration for the 'ast' glyph is given.

28 Ibid (British Museum Sign List B38)

29 Ibid, p141 (British Museum Sign List E60)

30 Hippocrene English-Arabic, Arabic-English Dictionary, Hippocrene, New York, 2005, p300

31 Ibid, p49

32 Alan F. Alford: The Atlantis Secret, A Complete Decoding of Plato's Lost Continent, Eridu, 2001, p381 (Notes & Bibliography 47-60)

33 Swallowing a stone is a covert marker of child sacrifice. In the Hellenistic mythology, the God Cronos attempted unsuccessfully to eat the baby Zeus. His mother Rhea replaced the child with a swaddled rock.

34 Hippocrene English-Arabic, Arabic-English Dictionary, Hippocrene, New York, 2005, p277

35 Ferozsons Urdu-English Dictionary, A Comprehensive Dictionary of Current Vocabulary (Revised Edition), Ferozsons Ltd, Lahore, p449

36 Ibid

37 Prolog: Pocket Bilingual Dictionary, English-Hebrew & Hebrew-English, Prolog, 2003, p348

38 Ibid, p346

39 God's mercy through 'deliverance' (Hebrew hatsil) is comparative to 'ha'arets' (the land) and 'erets' (country). The puns are evident in the accounts of the Exodus and the Hebrew's deliverance from the Pharaoh.

40 Prolog, Pocket Bilingual Dictionary, English-Hebrew & Hebrew-English, Prolog, 2003, p394

41 'Eve's name is a play on the Semitic noun 'evel' (mourning), symbolic of the widow, depicted as Isis. Etymologically 'Eve' is connected to the 'serpent' (ef'e)

42 Hippocrene English-Arabic, Arabic-English Dictionary, Hippocrene, New York, 2005, p303

43 John C Traupman: The New College Latin & English Dictionary, Bantam, 1988, p38

44 Ibid, p294

45 Ibid

46 Ibid, p38

47 Prolog: Pocket Bilingual Dictionary, English-Hebrew, Hebrew-English, Prolog, 2003, p366

48 The Latin allomorphs 'stella' (a star) and 'celare' (to conceal) is comparable in the Persian lexicon with 'sitarah' (a star), adjunct in Arabic with 'sattar' (hidden).

49 The star constellation Sirius is a tri-star system. The third star cannot be seen from the earth and was discovered in 1995. The etymologies however indicate that the Babylonian and Arab astronomers knew about the constellation. This information, according to their own myths and accounts, was obtained from the Nommu - an amphibious race from Sirius (Refer to Robert Temple, The Sirius Mystery, 1976, Updated Edition 1998).

50 The Arabic word 'fall' is translated into English as the intransitive verb (to flee).

51 An archaic form of 'bane' in English is 'ban' (to curse or execrate) and is grouped with 'bannan' (summon).

43

Naked Snakes (Part 1)

'... For You commanded the Hosts of Your Elect in their thousands and their Myriads, together with the Heavenly Host of all Your Holy Ones... to strike the Rebellious of Earth with Your awe-inspiring Judgements... For the King of Glory is with us... and the Angelic Host is under His command... (They are) like clouds, moisture-laden clouds covering the Earth - a torrent of rain shedding Judgement on all that grows'.[1]

The War Scroll from Qumran XI:17, XII:10 and XIX:1-2

'You must know, my son, that the course of nature is transformed, so that you (...) can see without great agitation the escaping spirits (...) condensed in the air in the form of various monstrous creatures or people moving hither and thither like clouds'.[2]

R. Lull, Compendium in Bibliotheca Chemia Curiosa, Vol. 1, Geneva (1702)

The bone is a symbol of the snake - its anatomy composed from the ribs and vertebrae, represented esoterically as a ladder. <u>Significantly, the serpent is one of the few animals that, when mature, grows extra ribs to accommodate its size</u>. The growth cycle of the reptile further explains the Biblical analogy between the snake (angel) and rib, regarding the creation of Eve.

The 'rib' in the English language is etymologically consistent with the Arabic stem 'r-b-b' (Lord). The scholar M. A. S. Abdel Haleem cites in his appendices to the Koran that the stem 'r-b-b' has connotations of 'caring' and 'nurturing' in addition to 'Lordship'.[1] The idea of sustenance, equated with the Lord, twinned with the snake, fits closely with what other academics have argued.

According to the linguist, Balaji Mundkur, the definitions of 'life' and 'serpent' are mutually supportive. The name 'Eve' is synonymous with the word for 'life' and 'snake'. In Arabic, the word 'serpent' (haiya) is itself cognate with 'life' (hayat)[2] and 'Eve' [Hawwa(h)]. Jewish traditions link this very rare name with the prime verbal root 'hayah' (to make live), derived from the Akkadian root. The play 'Hawwah' (Eve) and 'haiya' (snake) is matched in Arabic with 'hardun' (lizard), corollary to 'Adam'.

Inference drawn from the Arabic philology shows the 'snake's progeny (haiya) is extracted from the bloodline of 'Hawwah' (Eve). The point is theologically reiterated in Genesis 3:13. In this passage, woman's sexual awakening is explicitly recounted, when woman explains to god *the serpent beguiled me*'. In Hebrew, 'ishiani' (beguile) can alternatively be read as *(he put his seed in me)*.[3]

The rib serves as an apologue and recollects Eve's creation, privy to mortal angelic coitus. Anatomically, it silhouettes the crescent device of the priesthood, diagnostic of the menstrual cycle, mutual to creation. Affiliated with the rib and moon, the snake is twinned with life, corroborated in the Sumerian language. To recap, the word for (rib) in Sumerian is 'tii', and 'tii' happens also to be the Sumerian verb (to make live). It is expressed literally in the Arabic wordplay 'ti-bana' (a builder of life), assigned to 'ti'ban(a)' (an eel). In English, the pun transfers to 'life and wife' or 'rib and live'.

The connection between the 'fish and snake' is also implied within the research of Sir Henry Rawlinson. According to Rawlinson, *the third member of the primitive Chaldean triad is 'Hea' or 'Hoa' - a title that refers to his function as the source of all knowledge and science'*. Not only is he the 'intelligent fish' but also his name signifies both the 'serpent' and 'life'.[4] Religiously, the fish or serpent is affective of the harvest and sexual potency, embodied through the woman's sexuality or carnal knowledge. Relationship between the woman and reptile is provident in Semitic.

The Arabic noun 'af'a' sometimes written as 'hevia' or 'hafa' denotes (a viper) and is related to the Egyptian etymon 'kafa' (naked), cryptic of 'kafir' (infidel).[5] Realization of the snake's form is pictured as 'nakedness', accommodated in Hebrew as 'kafil' or 'kaful'[6] (double).[7]

In ancient accounts, the snake is able to take on or shape-shift into the form of a human being. This ability is unique to the reptile and is likened to sexual intercourse. Unification between the human 'votive' (hostia) and the reptilian entity (host) is correlated with 'atonement', literally (at-one-ment), semantically 'whole and holy'.

Vestigial to the priesthood, the 'reptile' is shown as a 'hermaphrodite' or a 'transgender priest', reparative of the creation of man in the image of God. 'Atonement' (in Arabic kaffara)[8] records the transformation of the 'double' (kafil), interchangeable with the 'snake' (af'a) and 'nakedness' (kafa). 'Kaffara' (atonement) is consistent semantically with the Latin noun 'capra' (a nanny goat)[9] and 'capillus' (hair)[10] - collaborative of the mammal (human-angelic).

Kind permission to redraw image from an original photograph by Neil Hague, Through Ancient Eyes, refer to picture credits. Drawing shows a smiling hairy angel - emblematic of a reaper, consigned to human angelic progeny, equated with the king. (Moulin Cathedral France)

Phonetic comparisons between the 'h', 'a' and 'k', juxtaposed with the 'p' and 'f' morpheme, cited in the Hellenistic and Semitic languages, suggest the serpent's copulation, relative to the goat and rebirth. Sexual difference based upon 'gender' (Arabic jins)[11] is consistent with the 'snake', substituted with the 'jinni'.

'Kafa' (naked) is an attribute associated theologically with the 'serpent' (a'fa) and its 'double' (kafil). Identical concepts are picked up in the Sanskrit etymon 'nagna' (naked) contrasted with 'naga' (a snake, deity or king). The connotation between the snake and its physical form is picked up upon in the creation epics. In the account of Genesis Chapter 2:25, Adam and Eve are quoted as '...both naked, and ... felt no shame'.

The scribe in the book of Genesis however chooses the word 'arum' (nakedness) - a polymorph explicit of (craftiness or shrewdness).[12] In Judaic literature, the expression 'arum' is used simultaneously to connote the <u>serpent</u>, covertly a '<u>builder</u>' and '<u>artificer</u>', acquainted with the '<u>changeling</u>'.

'Arum' (cunning) is further a pun on the Hebrew appellation 'Awwim', translated as (the serpents or devastators), cognate in Latin with the 'reptile and rapist'. Judaic tradition records the 'Awwim' as the 'descendents of Eve', the 'ancestors of the Nephilim'. The Nephilim take their precedence from the Semitic adjective 'naful' (fallen),[13] translated in Arabic as 'hava' (fallen), denoting the 'serpent' (af'a). This spawn is *created from the sons of Gods and the daughters of men*. Clarification on the Nephilim's ancestry is elaborated in the Biblical Book of Genesis 6:1-4, to quote:

> *'When men began to increase in number on the earth and daughters were born to them, the sons of God saw that the daughters of men were beautiful, and they married any of them they chose... The Nephilim were on the earth in those days - and also afterwards - when the sons of God went to the daughters of men and had children by them. They were the heroes of old, men of renown'.*

Biblical discourse links the 'Nephilim' with sexual intercourse between men and the Gods, analogous to the 'serpent' (Awwim), contrasted with 'nakedness' (kafa), reductive of the 'viper' (af'a). The point is worth examining in relation to Semitic vocabulary, pertaining to theogony.

The Hebrew word for 'naked' is (eirom),[14] alternatively (arum), a cognomen of the 'crafty' snake. Etymologically, 'arum' is used to imply the priestly line of 'Aaron' - the brother of Moses. The homonym 'arum' (artificer - i.e. a builder or Mason) is employed in addition as a pun on the plural name 'Elohim', annotated in early Apocryphal translations as the 'Gods'. Esoterically, the Elohim implies a tradesman - symbolic of the creator(s), paralleled to the host and Venus, situational to the moon.

Evidence suggests the 'Elohim' are philologically mutual with the 'Awwim', designated as the 'snake' or 'light'. Archaically, the generic title 'Elohim' is derived from the Aramaic 'Eloh' (light), abbreviated in Hebrew as 'El' and in Arabic as 'Il'. 'Eloh' is transformed in the Modern Arabic as 'Elahi' (God or Lord)[15] and supplements the adjective (divine, celestial or heavenly).[16] 'Elahi's title is an etymological variation of 'Allah' and is formative of 'ahli' (nation),[17] diminutive of 'ahl' (family).[18]

God's potency in the Semitic language is modelled on exposure of the form. For example, the Arabic word 'iryan' (naked)[19] corresponds with the wordplay 'ir-rahman' (God-the merciful).[20] The prefix 'ir' is translated in the Hippocrene Concise Dictionary as (God), but is used in the Old Semitic to refer literally to (a watcher), depicted as an angel or snake. In the Syrian etymologies, 'iryan' (naked) is a pun on '(ir)-janni' (the watchers-of paradise),[21] shown to be the same linguistically as the 'jinni'.

Through a series of complex associations, the snake describes knowledge, referential to light and nakedness - terminology correlated with enlightenment, substantive of transfiguration. The Book of 'Haggadah' Hebrew (Parable) reveals the following points about the naked serpent. The ancient source quotes the serpent took on or is clothed in the form of a man. The text reads:

> 'The first result was that Adam and Eve became naked. Before their bodies had been overlaid with a horny skin and enveloped with the cloud of glory and the horny skin dropped from them, and they stood there in their nakedness and ashamed'.[22]

The narrative revolves around iconography, associated with the rising of 'Venus', linked covertly to 'Sirius' and the 'dragon'. For example, the Arabic word 'istaha' [(to be) ashamed][23] is a pun on the Persian name 'Ishtar' (Venus) - cryptic of the 'builder'.

The points regarding heaven are further elaborated through careful deconstruction of vocabulary and etymologies in the Haggadah text. For instance, 'anan' the Hebrew noun for (a cloud)[24] is a derivation from the Akkadian word 'anu' (heaven), in Greek 'ana' (up). 'Anan' (cloud) cryptically suggests 'sexual assault', mirrored in the Semitic play 'ones' (rape).

The Hebrew appellation 'anas' (rapist)[25] is thus related to 'anan' (cloud)[26] - in Akkadian 'anu' (heaven). The divine 'rapist' (anas) is paired in Aramaic with the wording 'annas' (grace), a derivative of the cognomen 'Anu'. His namesake is used in Arabic to record the adjective 'mu'annas' (female) - explicit of divine union with mortals.

In ancient Semitic, 'Anu' signifies (the Supreme God). His visage is represented as the jackal. Significantly, 'Anu' is punned with the Fish God 'Oannes', astrologically 'Canis Major'. Oannes' star 'Sirius' expatiates the 'Dagon' - a type of reptilian deity.

Dagon's name is abridged from the Old Hebrew compound 'dag' (fish),[27] adjoined with 'anu' (heaven). His epithet the 'fish [of] heaven' informs the Greek noun 'drakon' (a dragon), defined as (a watcher). Dagon's Babylonian heritage is lucid with the amphibian 'Oannes' - a God registered with 'ayin' (eye).[28] The 'eyelid' (af'af)[29] is covert to the 'viper' (Arabic af'a) - an assonance, cognate in the Greek vocabulary with 'drakos' (an eye), homologous to the reptile a 'drakon'.

In the ancient records, 'Oannes' is deemed as the 'rapist' (anas), termed in Hebrew as the 'Awwim' - plural (the serpent or destroyer).[30] Relationship between the dragon and mortal intercourse is recorded in the lexicon, 'rape and reptile'. The rapist is diminutive of the Semitic stem 'raph' (terror)[31] and informs the Old English words 'wrath and wroth', recorded in the Greek etymon 'vrathea' (evening).

The pillaging host, a nocturne is clearly understood as the snake or angel, transferred from the Anglo-Latin noun 'reptile'.[32] Conceptually, the Roman word 'rapere' (to pillage or rape)[33] is successive of 'repere' (reptile), pictured as the nocturnal reaper (a destroyer). Related to the Arabic wordplay, the 'reptile' is analogous with 'adam' (annihilate)[34] and 'hardun' (lizard).[35]

Similar worded puns are evinced from the Old Semitic. In the Akkadian language, 'peor' (snake) is cognate with the Hebrew noun 'pere adam' (savage), rendered as the adjective 'pir'.[36] These in Persian lore are referred to as the 'Peri' (a race of serpents), recorded in the English genus 'fairy', appended in the Chinese language with 'pa' (a serpent or demon). The Akkadian noun 'peor' (serpent) describes 'intercourse', grouped in the Modern Hebrew with the adjective 'pore' (fruitful) from 'pri' (fruit).[37]

In ancient accounts, the 'reptile' is deemed as a 'rapist' - a tradition originating in Judaic scripture with the matriarch Eve. Her offspring are sourced from the sky, cogent with the reptile and angel preserved in Latin. The noun 'nubilum' (cloudiness)[38] is equated with the adjective 'nubilus' (marriageable)[39] and the intransitive verb 'nubere' (to marry of women).[40]

Impregnation of mortal women from heaven is known as the 'nubigena' (born of the clouds).[41] Assignment of the 'nubigena' is derived from the Syrian noun 'nabi' (prophet).[42] Scholars reassemble the noun in the hieroglyphic as 'Neb' (Lord).[43] The Semitic title 'nab' (an invoker) is anagrammatic in the Egyptian Arabic of 'bana' (build) and corresponds with the formation of ectoplasm, compared to the serpent - a fallen angel. This entity takes the form of a cloud - its offspring considered as the progenitor of the Imperial Dynasty.

William Blake Europe 1794: Astrologically 'Europe' (West) denotes 'Taurus', cognate with the 'Pleiades' and the emergence of 'man'. Blake represents the Saturnine creator God 'Urizen' [Persian 'unzen' (gold or deep crimson)] as the 'Great Architect'. The compass point alludes to the circle and the creation of the snake from fire - allegoric of the 'Shatani' and the 'Royal bloodline'.

Ascendancy of the reptile's protégée is interchangeable with the cloud motif, lateral to metamorphosis. Manifestation of 'phenomenon' [in Greek 'phaino' (to show)] is likened to a 'ghost or apparition', compared to the 'phantom', exhibited as the 'phane' literally (a snake). Egyptians drew the 'cloud' on the midriff of the 'cobra', combined with the 'ladder or ribcage' to illustrate ascension.[44]

Connection between the 'snake and nebula' is evinced from the ancient Semitic vernacular. In Hebrew 'le'ha'iv' (to-cloud)[45] is related to the Arabic noun 'af'a' (a viper).[46] The pun is captured in English as 'vapour and viper'.[47] Further, the Arabic noun 'raim' (a cloud)[48] is apprised in English as 'rain', conceptual in Arabic to 'ramm' (grieve).[49]

Materialization of 'mist' in cultic tradition is evocative of the 'vampire and wolf', demonstrated in Egyptian lore as 'Anubis' - the 'Jackal God of Death'. Anubis' name is a Latinization of 'A-nubes' (from a cloud),[50] suggesting a sacred birth 'nubigena'. A variation of the Akkadian deity 'Anu' the 'jackal' is assigned to the 'Dog Star' Sirius, personified as the 'fish or dragon', conjugal with the descendents of 'Eve'.[51] Its nebula column or spiral is an insignia, shared also by the God 'Yahweh', visualized as a 'pillar of cloud', referred to by his cohorts as 'Shaddai' - a God indigenous to the fish deity 'Oannes', otherwise 'Osiris' - a controversy continued in section two.

1   M. A. S. Abdel Haleem: The Qur'an, Oxford University Press, Sura 1, The Opening, See Note D.

2   Hippocrene English-Arabic, Arabic-English Dictionary, Hippocrene, New York, 2005, p68

3   Alix de Saint-Andre, translated from the French by Elfreda Powell: The Good Angel Guide for Reluctant Sinners, Souvenir Press, 1999, p56 (Appendix 3).

4   H P Blavatsky: Collected Writings 1888, The Secret Doctrine, Vol 2, Anthropogenesis, Quest Books, Theosophical Publishing House, 1993, p26

5   Hippocrene English-Arabic, Arabic-English Dictionary, Hippocrene, New York, 2005, p212 ['kafir' (unbeliever)].

6   An occultist would draw an obvious connection between 'kaful' (double) and the English adjective 'careful'. As a symbologist, it helps to observe phonetic relationships between words from different etymological roots. Corruptions or compromises, regarding the spelling of words, are often evident within Masonic teachings and lore.

7   Prolog: Pocket Bilingual Dictionary, English-Hebrew & Hebrew-English, Prolog, 2003, p118

8   Hippocrene English-Arabic, Arabic-English Dictionary, Hippocrene, New York, 2005, p212

9   'Capra' and 'caper' (a nanny and billy goat) is cogent with 'capillus' (hair) - symbolic of the human-angelic line.

10 John C Traupman: The New College Latin & English Dictionary, Bantam Books, 1988, p34

11 Hippocrene English-Arabic, Arabic-English Dictionary, Hippocrene, New York, 2005, p52 [Arabic 'jins' (gender) is comparative in Greek to 'gen' (beginning)].

12 Ralph Ellis: Eden in Egypt, A Translation of the Book of Genesis out of the Original Egyptian Text, Edfu Books, 2005, p107

13 Prolog: Pocket Bilingual Dictionary, English-Hebrew, Hebrew-English, Prolog, 2003, p145

14 Ibid, p267

15 Ferozson's Urdu-English Dictionary, Revised Edition, Ferozsons Ltd, Lahore, p71

16 Ibid

17 Hippocrene English-Arabic, Arabic-English Dictionary, Hippocrene, New York, 2005, p147

18 Ibid

19 Ibid, p79

20 Ibid, p202

21 Ibid, p208

22 Nigel Cawthorne: The World's Greatest UFO Encounters, 2002, p141

23 Hippocrene English-Arabic, Arabic-English Dictionary, Hippocrene, New York, 2005, p13

24 In the Akkadian language, the doubling of the noun shows emphasis of a concept or idea. 'An(u)' (heaven) is variegated as 'anan' (cloud), evident in the Hebrew noun.

25 Prolog: Pocket Bilingual Dictionary, English-Hebrew & Hebrew-English, Prolog, 2003, p328

26 Ibid, p70

27 Ibid, p152

28 Ibid, p143

29 Ibid

30 'Awwim' is translated as (a serpent or destroyer). In the original Hebrew, the appellation 'destroyer' is more appropriately read as a conqueror, 'pillager' or 'rapist'.

31 Translated by S. L. MacGegor Mathers: The Kabbalah Unveiled, Penguin Arkana 1991, p194 (RAPH / ATH).

32 The pillaging host, depicted as a rapist, draws comparison with the 'modern' phenomenon of abduction of humans, attributed to aliens. Testimonial accounts often observe that these creatures are reptilian in appearance and are concerned with human reproduction.

33 'Rapere' (Latin rape) is closely related to the Hebrew etymon 'rape' (heal) - delegable of the covenant between men and angels. Anas (a rapist) is cognate in the Aramaic with 'annas' (grace) implicit theologically of 'Immaculate Conception'

34 Hippocrene English-Arabic, Arabic-English Dictionary, Hippocrene, New York 2005, p317

35 'Hardun' (lizard) is consistent in English with the noun 'adder' correlated in the Arabic with its 'bite' (add).

36 Prolog: Pocket Bilingual Dictionary, English-Hebrew, Hebrew-English, Prolog 2003, p354

37 Ibid, p163

38 John C Traupman: The New College Latin & English Dictionary, Bantam Books 1988, p366

39 Ibid p196

40 Ibid

41 Ibid

42 Hippocrene English-Arabic, Arabic-English Dictionary, Hippocrene, New York 2005, p252

43 Bridget McDermott: Decoding Egyptian Hieroglyphs, Duncan Baird Publishers, London, p168 Sign Index List - 'Nb' (a Lord).

44 Water vapour, dependent on external conditions, is able to change its substance from a liquid into a gas or solid (ice). The medium is utilized as a cryptic sign of the host's ability to change shape, equivalent to rebirth and baptism.

45 Prolog: Pocket Bilingual Dictionary, English-Hebrew Hebrew-English, Prolog, p70

46 Hippocrene English-Arabic, Arabic-English Dictionary, Hippocrene, New York 2005, p146

47 In Nippon, there is a connection between the cloud and reptile. In Japanese, the simile 'uroko gumo' signifies differentiated cloud. Its literal translation is 'fish scale cloud'.

48 Hippocrene English-Arabic, Arabic-English Dictionary, Hippocrene, New York 2005, p267

49 Ibid, p268

50 John C Traupman: The New College Latin & English Dictionary, Bantam Books 1988, p366

51 In Roman mythology, the twins Romulus and Remus are suckled from a she wolf, nominal of divine progeny, juxtaposed with heaven (Sirius).

43

Naked Snakes (Part 2)

'In the worlds before Monkey, primal chaos reigned. Heaven sought order. But the phoenix can fly only when its feathers are grown. The four worlds formed again and yet again, as endless aeons wheeled and passed. Time and the pure essences of Heaven, the moisture of the Earth, the powers of the sun and the moon all worked upon a certain rock, old as creation. And it became magically fertile. That first egg was named "Thought". Tathagata Buddha, the Father Buddha, said, "With our thoughts, we make the world". Elemental forces caused the egg to hatch. From it then came a stone monkey. The nature of Monkey was irrepressible!'

Monkey Magic, Kokusai Hoei produced under license from Nippon Television Network Corporation (1978). According to legend, the Monkey King (man) was thrown out of heaven for eating the peaches of immortality.

In the book of Exodus, Yahweh leads the Hebrews into the wilderness as a pillar of cloud. His appearance is equated in spoken Semitic with 'Shaddai' translated as (Lord or God), reductive from 'shed' Hebrew (a goblin[3], ghost[4] or ghoul[5]). 'Shed' in the modern translation is simply rendered as (a devil).[6] A God of Death, 'Shaddai' is variegated from the Semitic stem 'stn' - 'Shatan' (an adversary or an opponent), militaristic of the host and dragon.

'Shed' philologically is related to the Hebrew word 'sod' (a secret), extracted from the Arabic verb 'sed' (to hunt),[7] cognate in the Judaic traditions with 'so'ed' (a diner - person),[8] implicit of an angel or reaper (host). Corporal manifestation of the 'demon' (shed) is contrasted with 'sid' (a gentleman),[9] registered with the 'Sodalist' (or Zadok) Brotherhood aka the 'Black' Nobility (Saudi or Sauda). In English, the play 'sid and shed' is recorded as 'civil and seraph'.

'Shaddai's college of priests, the 'Sodi', discerns 'sid' (a gentleman), derived from the Arabic noun 'sidr' or 'sedr' (anatomical of the chest).[10] Device of the 'heart' (Hebrew lev, Arabic qalb) is comparable to the 'Levites' and their offshoots 'Kabir' (a Lord). In the Old Semitic, 'Kabir' is homologous to 'qeb' (a snake), relative to 'Al Kalb' (the Dog Star).[11]

A 'messenger' (Hebrew 'caba') distinguishes (an angel), analogous to 'Sirius' (Al Kalb). 'Caba' (messenger) articulates the verbal stem 'qbl' (to receive), denoting the hidden traditions of the 'Kabbalah' ['khabba' (to hide)]. The 'message' (Hebrew sheder)[12] implies a 'divinity', technically a 'demon' (shed), reserved originally to the 'Sodi' and the 'Zadok' priesthood.

The 'Zadok' (Greek Sadducee) informs the Latin transitive verb 'seducere' (lead away, carry off, to separate or divide),[13] suggesting ceremonial 'rape', assigned to the divinity 'Shaddai'. Esoteric, the dragon's offspring is unified with the mammal (human), epistemological to the matriarch's milk. For example, the Hebrew noun 'shed' (goblin) is punned with 'shad' (a woman's breast),[14] demonstrated in the English wordplay 'beast and breast'. Consociation between the 'woman and reptile' alludes to conjugal rites, simultaneous to the 'harvest and reaper'.

In the Egyptian mysteries, 'shed' (a demon) is evinced from 'shedj' (ritualized slaughter)[15] and has connotations of 'one who destroys or annihilates'. 'Shaddai's appellation the 'God of Destruction' is literally translated as (the Slaughterer). Celebrated as a fierce conqueror, a patron of war 'Shed' is prescriptive of killing and blood rituals, conceptual to salvation.

Apparition of the 'shed' is equivalent to the 'reaper or reptile' in proximity to 'sade' (a field),[16] conjunct with 'seder' (an order)[17] and 'sidur' (arrangement).[18] The commandment 'seder' describes the ritual of (the first night of Passover), inaugurating the death of the firstborn, termed 'sod' (a secret).[19] 'Seder' in Latin informs the stem 'cida' (a person or thing that kills), recorded in the noun 'sadism'.[20]

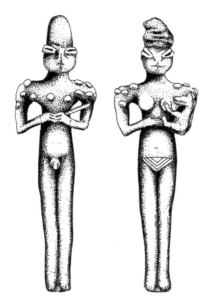

Ubaid Reptile – Male and Female effigy: Female reptilian figurine is shown suckling her young 'shad' and is a depiction of the 'Shed' (class of demon), associated with the deity 'Shaddai' (Yahweh). His emblem includes 'milk and honey' – the bee hieroglyphic of the Lower Crown of Egypt. 'Shaddai' is conjugal with human angelic intercourse, assimilated from the traditions of the 'snake and Eve'.

'Shaddai' is translated into Medieval Latin as 'entitas' (an entity), derived from the Early Latin substantive 'ens' (an entity or being),[21] manifested through 'ens' (a sword).[22] The root of 'ens' is borrowed from the Greek term 'entos' (within), denoting bodily possession, relative to the changeling and oracle.

Etymologically 'ens' (an entity) is correlated with 'esse' the intransitive verb (to be)[23] and fits with the Hebrew name of 'Yahweh', obtained from the Syrian verb 'haya' (to be), conversant with 'haiya' (a snake). The archaic root of 'ens' (an entity) is shown here to agree with the Akkadian title 'en' (a lord) - an abbreviation of 'Oannes' the Fish God, deemed as a 'reptile' or 'rapist' (Hebrew Ones). 'Oannes' is registered in Arabic with the noun 'ain' or 'en' (an eye)[24] - Hebrew 'ayin', idiomatic of the 'dragon or watcher'.

Significantly '<u>Oannes</u>' is shown here for the first time as the <u>same deity as</u> '<u>Osiris</u>' and '<u>Baal</u>', indexed with '<u>Yahweh</u>' and '<u>Shaddai</u>'. Osiris' cognomen is written with the 'eye', rendered incorrectly by Egyptologist as 'art', combined with the 'throne' glyph (ast). The 'eye' hieroglyph records the Egyptian Arabic noun 'en' (an eye), reproduced in the Akkadian language as 'En' (a Lord), adjacent to 'Anu' (heaven). The 'eye' designating a 'Lord'[25] is combined with the 'ast' glyph, rendered <u>here correctly for the first time</u> as 'asas' - the Arabic word for (a foundation, basis or ground).[26] 'Asas' is diminutive of 'asl' (origin).[27]

'Osiris' thus is 'En-Asas' or 'Oannes' (Lord of the foundation or firmament), cosmological to the planets - a symbol of the covenant, correlated with the host and creation. Conventional academics render the spelling of 'En-Asas' as 'Ast-art' (Astarte), 'Asar' or 'Wsir'[28] - the latter obtained from the Hebrew root 'vaser' (an augury),[29] structural to the Arabic radical 'bashar' (mankind).[30] The appellation 'Wsir' is analogous in Arabic to 'wasi' (a guardian or sentinel)[31] from 'basar' (sight or vision)[32] - a transliteration acquired from the eye glyph.

Osiris' consort Isis is distinguished as the 'Lady of the foundation'. Her name is written with the throne and egg. The 'egg' glyph (baid)[33] is referential to the 'duck' (colloquial Arabic batt).[34] Significantly, the noun 'batt' is a homonym of 'bat' (a daughter)[35] and reproduces the name Isis (a daughter of the foundation).[36] Alternative names for 'Isis' are drawn with the 'disk and duck', interpreted erroneously as (the Son of Ra). Academics inexplicably read the 'duck' glyph 'bat' (a daughter) as 'sah' and give the wrong translation as 'Sah-Ra' (the Son of Ra). The noun 'sah' (a son) is not evident in any of the Semitic languages.

Transliteration of 'Sah-Ra' is an excellent example of how Egyptologists have fervently misled the general public since the release of the Rosetta Stone. Duplicitous, the interpretation 'Sah-Ra' (the Son of Ra)[37] is cryptic of the Old Hebrew name 'Sarah' (a princess) - invariably a 'Daughter of Ra', explicit of 'Isis', written correctly as (Bat-Ra). 'Isis' is commensurate with the 'Daughter of the foundation', stylised as the 'throne and egg' - allegoric of the 'moon'.

Further, the shape of the egg is a representation of the ecliptic orbit of the planets, addendum to the throne and host. Epigraphically, 'baid' (an egg) annotates 'badr' Arabic (a full moon),[38] transpositional of the verbal stem 'badal' (change, alter or exchange).[39] The vernacular denotes the 'augury', reductive of 'badd' the Syrian verb (to want or wish),[40] consistent with the exchange of 'goods' (bada'a),[41] attributed theologically to the 'redemption of the firstborn'.

In essence, 'Isis' is the 'Daughter of the moon', a descendent from the original survivors of the flood - a Lady of the 'covenant' specified as (the foundation or firmament). Isis' comparison in the Greek mysteries is the huntress Artemis the 'White Goddess' of the moon, who like Isis is shown with the egg - a symbol of fertility, equated with the snake and crescent.

Heironymus Bosch, Detail from the 'Garden of Earthly Delights' (1510). In the original painting, the figures are painted in red ochre a symbol of Mars, and enter the egg, emblematic of the moon. In the background, a mermaid swims in the sea - representational of the amphibian, aligned to Sirius.

Queen of the host 'Isis' and her compatriot 'Artemis' are signified with the 'shell' (Hebrew klipa),[42] cognizant with 'klippoth' (a demon), auxiliary to the throne and planets. Classical symbolists sometimes switch the eggshell with the seashell, registered with the birth of Venus, orientated towards the moon.

Da Vinci, Lydia and the Swan. 'Lydia' a Latin transliteration from the Greek appellation 'Leda' indicates her extraction is 'Lydian' (Etruscan) from Asia Minor. 'Lydia's name is a derivation from the Hebrew corruption 'leida' (childbirth). The 'swan' (Hebrew barbur) is a pun from the Greek etymology 'barbaros' (foreigner or alien) descriptive of an angel. A dual signifier, the swan denotes a feathered (hairy) serpent, and registers 'barba' (a beard), retelling the partnership between the reptile (angel) and mammal (man).

The Arabic noun 'baid' (an egg) is kindred to the Hebrew status 'vehedar' (majesty),[43] equivalent to the Sanskrit root 'vedas' (sacred knowledge). Further, the ideogram 'egg' (baid) is used to register the Arabic noun 'baida' (white),[44] denoting the 'Upper Crown of Egypt', associated with the 'White Virgin' - a Lunar Goddess. Published here for the first time, 'Baid(a)-Asas' (White Foundation) is the correct epithet of (Isis) and discloses the 'Royal Foundation' (Vehedar-Asas) - a modification on 'Bat-Asas' (Daughter of the Foundation).

Isis' titular 'Baid(a)-Asas' is an adaptation of the Jewish name 'Bethesda' (house of mercy).[45] The name 'seda' is cryptic of the 'Sodi' priesthood - a derivation of 'sa'ad' the Arabic root of (help or assistance),[46] conceptual to the Exodus. 'Sa'ad' further implies 'shed' (a demon), cognomens of 'Shaddai' and 'seder' (the Passover ritual).

The Greek epithet 'Isis' is a transliteration from the shortened form 'Asas' Arabic (a foundation, basis, ground or bottom) - a name akin to 'Osiris' also 'Asas'. 'Asas' (a foundation) refers literally to 'isha' Hebrew (woman),[47] a permutation on the Goddess 'Isis', cognate in the Egyptian Arabic with 'ish'sha' (hut),[48] theoretical to the 'tabernacle and augury'.

The epigraph 'Asas' (foundation) further explains the Jewish tradition of sacrificing children and laying their bones into the foundation of buildings and temples. In Masonic tradition, Osiris is substituted with the 'trowel', etiological of the 'earth' (adama) - a symbol of 'Adam'. The 'trowel' in the Roman mysteries is grouped with the 'skull' (Golgotha) and 'coffin', parabolic of the 'foundation', imputed in Christianity to represent the 'bedrock' of the church and the resurrection of Christ. Ascendancy of 'Jesus' (Arabic Isa) is derived earlier from the stories of 'Asas' (Osiris) and his rebirth from the grave.

According to Egyptian myth, Osiris' corpse is mutilated and later restored by his partner Isis. The virgin, unable to locate his penis, replaces his phallus with a golden member - symbolic of angelic progeny.[49] The narrative details usurpation of the human line. 'Osiris' the 'Man King' is killed, his appearance appropriated and resurrected as the Fish King 'En-Asas' (Oannes) - a tradition correlated with the 'builder and moon'.[50]

A crying God 'Oannes' alias 'En-Asas' (Osiris) is paired with the teardrop (recreational of man), mythologized as the 'crying eye' - symbolic of the 'fish'. Insignia of the Ocular Crown a 'tear duct' annotates the 'Southern Crown' of the 'Theban' priesthood, affiliated to its patron 'Osiris'. Motif of the 'crying eye' is combined with the 'spitting cobra', the 'saviour', paired with the 'smiter' - its fiery venom cognate with the seed of heaven. Risen, the 'hood of the snake' is drawn with the 'cloud motif', reproduced esoterically as a 'pillar of cloud' - a signature of 'Shaddai'.

'Osiris' a God of Heaven by deduction is identical to the deity 'Shaddai' - a name borrowed from the Semitic lexicon. By switching the 'd' morpheme with the 't', 'Shaddai's appellation is transformed in Masonic lore as the 'God of the storm cloud', deduced from the Syrian noun 'shiti' (rain),[51] obtuse to the angelic lineage - the 'Shatani' (Satan). Historically, the Shatani are listed with the host, correlated with the destruction of the earth. Eradication of mankind by the floodwaters is likened to the weeping eye, dualled with the dragon and the widow Isis.

The teardrop recalls the 'flesh and rib' glyph - emblems associated with the 'crescent and Isis'. Additionally, the 'flesh and rib' are similar to the 'mouth and vagina' hieroglyph, enunciating insemination, identical to the 'eye and the moon'. Epigraphically, the 'flesh' glyph is used to write the name 'Isis' - ancestral to the 'lunar satellite'.

In conclusion, the Hebrew God 'Shaddai' technically a 'demon' (shed) is rendered in Greek translations as 'Adonai' (Lord), interpreted in the King James' Bible as (the Almighty). 'Shaddai' is depicted in the occult as the rain 'cloud' (Hebrew anan),[52] identical to the fish God 'Oannes'. The appellation 'Oannes' alludes to the heavenly firmament - a foundation transliterated into the hieroglyphs as the God 'En-Asas' otherwise (Osiris). Significantly, 'Yahweh and Shaddai' share the same attributes as 'Oannes' - a fish deity, integrated with the traditions of 'Osiris'.

Connection between the 'cloud and Osiris' is stylized as the 'Southern Crown of Thebes' - a 'tear duct', combined with the 'hooded cobra', modeled on a 'cloud', esoteric of the teardrop (man), equated with venom and seed. Additionally, the midriff of the seraph outlines a 'ladder', notated in Arabic as the noun (sullam)[53] - a sign of the covenant 'sallim' (to submit).[54] Manifestation of the 'cloud', an 'apparition' is coupled with the 'reptile', synonymous with 'Shaddai', inimical of the augury and the priestess.[55]

Propagation of 'Shaddai's offspring refers to the 'Shatani', extricated from the matriarchal lineage, conjugal with 'sitt' (a lady).[56] 'Offspring of the angel' Latin 'nubigena' (born from the clouds) is tandem to the 'snake' (Arabic ta'ban),[57] enunciated as a 'Theban', originating from the Syriac priesthood. Classification of the 'Theban', an abstraction of the 'snake' is translated into Latin as 'anguigena', identical to (the offspring of the dragon).[58] Adoption of the fiery seraph describes the first King of Egypt 'Osiris' (En-Asas) alias the fish deity

'Oannes' - a manifestation of 'Shaddai'. Externalized as the 'cloud', cultic of the 'reptile', 'Shaddai's form is recreated in the image of 'Adam'. Transfiguration of the serpent (an angel) into a man is ritualistic of sacrificial death of the firstborn - theological to the materialization of the double. Recreation of the form is symbolized as rebirth, cogent with the snake and shroud, central to the inner mysteries, outlined in the final chapter.

1   Robert Eisenman: The New Testament Code, The Cup of the Lord, The Damascus Covenant and The Blood of Christ, Watkins Publishing, London, UK, 2006, Header Quotations.

2   Aleander Roob: The Hermetic Museum, Alchemy & Mysticism, Taschen, London, 2001, p160

3   Prolog: Pocket Bilingual Dictionary, English-Hebrew Hebrew-English, Prolog, 2003, p170

4   Ibid, p168

5   Ibid ['Shed' is a homonym of (goblin, ghost, ghoul or demon), and appears in the English spelling as a 'shade', manifested through (blood shed)].

6   Ibid, p108

7   Hippocrene English-Arabic, Arabic-English Dictionary, Hippocrene, New York, 2005, p59

8   Prolog: Pocket Bilingual Dictionary, English-Hebrew Hebrew-English, Prolog, 2003, p110

9   Hippocrene English-Arabic, Arabic-English Dictionary, Hippocrene, New York, 2005, p288

10 Ibid, p26

11 The 'Levi' fraternity is affiliated in the Greek translation to the 'Cardinals' - a name obtained from 'kardia' (heart). 'Kardia' Greek (heart) is a homonym and specifies (the upper opening of the stomach), equated originally with the oracular priest and the augury, conjunct with the removal of the heart (See footnote 29 p421).

12 Prolog: Pocket Bilingual Dictionary, English-Hebrew Hebrew-English, Prolog, 2003, p253 [It seems that the original use of the term 'sheder' (a message) connoted 'shedj' (ritual slaughter) suggesting the augury. The analogy is evident also in the alternative Hebrew term 'meser' (a message), cognate with the Old Semitic word 'maas' (to slay), implicit of the firstborn 'descendent' (mass)].

13 John C Traupman PhD: The New College Latin & English Dictionary, Bantam, USA, p282

14 Prolog: Pocket Bilingual Dictionary, English-Hebrew, Hebrew-English, Prolog, 2003, p49

15 Ralph Ellis, Eden in Egypt, A Translation of the Book of Genesis out of the Original Egyptian Text, Edfu Books, 2005, p23

16 Prolog: Pocket Bilingual Dictionary, English-Hebrew, Hebrew-English, Prolog, 2003, p150

17 Ibid, p282

18 Ibid, p28

19 Ibid, p360

20 According to the Oxford English Dictionary, the word 'sadism' is traced from the French novelist 'Marquis de Sade', shown to be erroneous - the Marquis used 'Sade' as a pseudonym, extracted from the Latin root 'cida or caedis' (murder, slaughter or kill). His choice of name is significant, as it suggests an affiliation to the 'Sodalist' priesthood, allied to the 'Saudi' family. Additionally, 'Sodi and Saudi' inform the late 16th century word 'croisade' (crusade), which appears in the Spanish form 'cruzado' and eariler 'croisee', literally (the state of being marked with the cross). 'Cruzado's etymology is deduced from the Spanish term 'cruzar' (to bear or take up the cross). The French version 'croisade', Spanish 'cruzado', are corruptions drawn from the Latin compound 'crux' (cross) and 'cida' (murder), denoting 'crux-cida' (slaughters of the cross). To emphasize, the term 'crusade' is a variation on the name 'Sodi, Saudi and Sodalist' denominations of the 'black' Jesuit (sauda) priesthood.

21 John C. Traupman, Ph.D. The New College Latin & English Dictionary, Bantam Press, 1988, p392

22 Ibid, p100

23 Ibid, p351

24 Hippocrene English-Arabic, Arabic-English Dictionary, Hippocrene, New York, 2005, p45

25 'En' (eye or lord) is equivalent in English to 'see and sir'.

26 Hippocrene English-Arabic, Arabic-English Dictionary, Hippocrene, New York, 2005, p151

27 Ibid, p85

28 In the British Museum Sign List, 'Asas' (Osiris) is written as 'Wsir', 'Asar' or 'Isa', permutations of the Arabic name 'Isa' (Jesus) - Hebrew 'Ye'shu'a' (Salvation).

29 Prolog: Pocket Bilingual Dictionary, English-Hebrew, Hebrew-English, Prolog, 2003, p32 ['Le'vaser' (to augur) informs the priestly name 'Levite' from 'lev' (a heart) - See footnote 11 p420.

30 Hippocrene English-Arabic, Arabic-English Dictionary, Hippocrene, New York, 2005, p156

31 Ibid, p309 ['Bashari' (human, not divine) is equated with 'basar' (sight), implicit of human divination, contrasted with the 'watcher' (a dragon). Association between the eye and human is rendered in Greek as 'kore' (a virgin or pupil), Arabic 'nazirah' (an eye or inspectress), symmetrical to 'nisa' (woman)].

32 Ibid, p156

33 Ibid, p154

34 Ibid, p157

35 Prolog: Pocket Bilingual Dictionary, English-Hebrew, Hebrew-English, Prolog, 2003, p98

36 'Bat-asas' (Daughter of the Foundation) is transliterated into Latin as 'vates' (a prophetess), English 'fate'.

37 Bridget McDermott: Decoding Egyptian Hieroglyphs, Duncan Baird Publishers, London, p74 McDermott gives the reading as 'Sar-Re', an appellation featured more commonly in referenced works as 'Sah-Ra' - the latter transliteration drawing allusion presumably from the Old Hebrew name 'Tsa' (the Strider) Greek 'Orion'.

38 Hippocrene English-Arabic, Arabic-English Dictionary, Hippocrene, New York, 2005, p153

39 Ibid

40 Ibid

41 Ibid ['Bada' Arabic (goods), Syrian (merchandise)].

42 'Klipa' (shell) is also translated as (a husk), and indicates the 'klippoth's (demon) ability to possess or change its shape or form.

43 Translated by S.L. MacGregor Mathers, The Kabbalah Unveiled, Penguin Arkana, 1991, p125 (vehedar).

44 Ibid, p139

45 D. M. McFarlan: Dictionary of the Bible, Geddes & Grosset, Scotland, 2005, p34 *'Bethesda' located outside of the gates of Jerusalem, where sick people lay there waiting for the waters to be 'disturbed' by an angel [or lady?]. Jesus healed a man, who had been waiting there for thirty-eight years (John 5:2-9).*

46 Hippocrene English-Arabic, Arabic-English Dictionary, Hippocrene, New York, 2005, p274 ['Sa'ad' or 'sa'id' (assist or help)].

47 Prolog: Pocket Bilingual Dictionary, English-Hebrew, Hebrew-English, Prolog, 2003, p463

48 Hippocrene English-Arabic, Arabic-English Dictionary, Hippocrene, New York, 2005, p324

49 Theologically the castration of Osiris and the appropriation of the human lineage through angelic offspring is contractual to the covenant, registered with circumcision (Refer to Jacob's usurpation of Esau's birthright recorded in Genesis 27).

50 The Arabic root 'Asas' (Foundation) is written in Latin as 'Aeneas' (the Son of Venus), marked alchemically with 'aeneus' (bronze), metallurgical to the Theban snake. The titular offspring of Venus (Aeneas) is another name for Osiris.

51 Hippocrene English-Arabic, Arabic-English Dictionary, Hippocrene, New York, 2005, p286

52 Prolog: Pocket Bilingual Dictionary, English-Hebrew, Hebrew-English, Prolog, 2003, p70

53 Hippocrene English-Arabic, Arabic-English Dictionary, Hippocrene, New York, 2005, p65

54 Ibid, p278

55 Depicted as a God of 'sacrifice' (shedj), 'Shaddai' is conceptual to 'so'ed' (a participant of a votive), symmetrical in Latin to the angelic 'host' (army) and the 'hostia' (victim). God's name is repeated in the Semitic title 'Baal' (Lord), paired with 'bala' (to swallow), Greek 'Theos' (God) and 'thuos' (sacrifice). Likewise in the Germanic languages, 'God' describes 'guild' (a sacrifice). Philologically 'God' is comparative to the 'goat', signified in the Greek mysteries as the deity 'Pan' (the feeder).

56 Hippocrene English-Arabic, Arabic-English Dictionary, Hippocrene, New York, 2005, p289 The English expression to 'sit in waiting' is derived from the Arabic pun 'sitt' (a lady), identified in Semitic with 'sit' (reputation).

57 Ibid, p292

58 John C. Traupman, Ph.D. The New College Latin & English Dictionary, Bantam Press, 1988, p15 ['Anguigena' is a homonym and is translated as (a Theban and/or an offspring of the dragon)].

Spirits and Snakes

'The Nephilim shall be called evil spirits, when they come to live on earth. Evil spirits shall exude from their flesh... because they were created from a mixture of mankind and the watchers, who fly above'.[1]

Book of Enoch (88 BC-154 AD)

'The first result was that Adam and Eve became naked. Before their bodies had been overlaid with a horny skin and enveloped with the cloud of glory and the horny skin dropped from them, and they stood there in their nakedness and ashamed'.[2]

The Book of Haggadah

G od's appearance as the nebula cloud signifies mortal intercourse and is correlated with the phantom or 'apparition' (Hebrew hofa'a), technically a 'snake' (a'fa). In colloquial Arabic, a 'ghost' is rendered as 'jinn' from the Egyptian etymon 'djen' (a serpent). The 'jinni' are paired in Syrian with 'jins' (sex or gender),[3] characteristic of 'jinsi' (sexual).[4] The Semitic lexicon 'djen' informs the Greek stem 'genes' (born).

Relationship between 'demonic' (sorry Godly) manifestation and the 'spirit' is deduced from the act of examining the entrails of the 'augury'. This is referred to in Greek as 'extispicy' - a practice identified with the 'oracular priestess' (the engastrimythoi), literally the 'speaker of the stomach'.[5]

'Engastrimythoi' proclaims omens, allocated to the 'abdominal organs', categorized in Latin as 'omental' (the fat offering).[6] Extraction of the intestinal wall is a simile of the serpent, contiguous with the invocation of the spirit. 'Silent' rites accorded to (omerta) indicate the removal of the 'omental' (organs) and the worship of the snake. The burnt offering is signified in Arabic as 'dukhan' (smoke) - cryptically a 'dragon'.[7]

'Cloud' formation is connected to the 'ormental organs' and the formation of the 'spirit', illustrated above. Alchemical drawing shows a 'rock or cloud' - signifiers of 'Adam and the snake', situated over the Tabernacle, combined with the 'set square' (a ruler) and 'compass' (a serpent). The Jewish Star represents the Pleiades (six visible stars). Listed in a peculiar order, the planets follow the Sun, Mercury, Jupiter, Mars, Venus, Saturn and the Moon, alternating feminine and masculine energies.

In hermetic illustrations, the 'rain cloud' is typically drawn as the 'lower intestine' (the omental), thematically a pun on the Latin noun 'elementum' (an element).[8] The allusion aligns in alchemy with the transmutation of the elements. Transformation of the cloud is an elaboration of the 'spirit' an elemental.

The 'cloud vapour' is a simile of the 'breath' (spiritus)[9] from the transitive verb 'spirare' (to breathe),[10] symptomatic of the 'spirit' and 'life'. The Latin verb 'spirare' recalls the Greek noun 'speira' (a coil), depicted as 'spiro' (a dragon). The analogy in English is 'spirit and sprite'. Esoterically, amalgamation between the spirit (sound) and serpent suggests rebirth, corresponding in Latin with 'nubere' (marriage), opposite 'nubilum' (cloud). Inference to such a union is displayed additionally in the Semitic etymologies.

In Arabic, for example the word 'hawa' (air) is a homonym and includes the affixed meanings (amorous, passion, affection or love). 'Hawa' also means (wind, air or climate)[11] and is correlated with the Syrian noun 'haiya or haiyi' (a snake).[12] It resides in the firmament, and in the early Judaic commentaries is catalogued with the 'Awwim', technically the 'Elhohim' (a fallen angel). By comparison, the 'Awwim' are known in the plural as (the destroyers or rapists) – a cognomen shared by the fish deity 'Oannes' (Anas), additional also to the 'jinni'. Annotation of the 'Awwim' classifying (a serpent) is coherent with 'hawa' (air), shortened into Greek as 'aer' (air).

Ancestry of the 'Awwim' is derived from 'Hawwa(h)' (Eve), appropriated from the Akkadian verbal root 'hayah' (life), consistent with the 'snake' (haiya). Covertly, the creature 'haiya' is identified with 'hawa' (the sky), aligned to the 'Awwim'. Offspring of the 'Awwim' denotes (the snake), equated with the matriarch 'Eve' and the inception of 'life', reciprocal to the 'spirit'.

'Eve's address 'Hawwa(h)' is extrapolated from the Arabic 'hawa' (air) and 'haiya' (serpent). Incarnation of Eve signifies heaven, registered with the spirit and breath, allocated to 'life' (hayah). In the European etymologies, 'Eve' is an adaptation of the Arabic noun 'af'a' (viper),[13] rendered in Hebrew as 'ef'e' (asp).[14] 'Eve's title is a modification of the winged seraph, symbolised as 'af'a', and corresponds with the Hebrew noun 'avir' (air).[15] The Semitic noun 'avir' is also prescient of the Latin feminine noun 'avis' (bird). The winged Goddess is later adopted as the bird priestess Isis.

In the Roman language, the analogy between the 'snake and bird' is encoded in the philological relationship, 'coluber' (a snake) and 'columba' (a dove). The 'bird' is a symbol of the 'angel', identified with the 'double or spirit', variegated as the 'gust of wind', conveyed in Greek as 'pneuma' (breath, wind or spirit).

Connection between the serpent and air is found also in the early Akkadian accounts of 'lilutu' (air spirit) - a term recognizant with the 'Lil-ifrit' translated as (Lilith - the night demon). A fallen angel Lilith is partnered with Samael a red goat, depicted as a God of the firmament. Like the patroness 'Eve' and 'Lilutu', Samael's title conforms meteorologically to the sky.

In Arabic, Samael is punned with 'samun' (wind) and 'sama' (heaven), complicit of 'semer' (king). Judaic writings document 'Lilith and Samael' to have copulated with the couple 'Adam' (red) and 'Eve' (snake), creating the monarchy. The traditions are symmetrical to Adam and his emissary the 'snake' (haiya) otherwise 'Eve' [Hawwa(h)].[16]

'Haiya' the Syrian word for (a snake) is significantly cognate with the Hebrew verbal root 'haya' meaning (to be)[17] and appears in the name 'Yahweh' (YHVH). Relationship between 'Yahweh' and the 'serpent' suggests the scribal writers categorized him as an 'Ellohim'. Noted previously, this group is conceptual to the 'Awwim', identical to (a serpent) - a fallen angel classified as a 'rapist'.

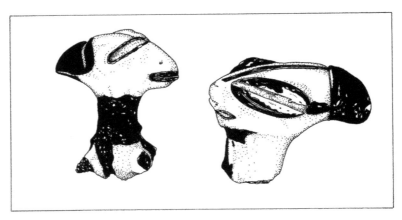

Picture source: Matthew Hurley and Editor Neil Hague, Alien Chronicles, Quester Publications (see picture credits). Ubaid figurine Iraq. Early depictions of the Gods are shown as bipedal serpents or goats. The God of the Jews, 'Shaddai' is described as 'shed' (a type of goblin or devil), depicted with reptilian characteristics shared by Yahweh. 'Haiya' Arabic (snake) is cognate with the root 'haya' (to be) the verbal stem of 'Yahweh's name. The 'serpent' (Haiya) suggests technically (an entity or a being) 'haya'. According to Judaic traditions, 'Abu' a cognomen of God (the Father) designates 'af'a' (a viper), illustrative of a 'fallen angel', specified as the 'Elhohim' - singular 'El' (God).

Underscored in the Syrian lexicon, 'haiya' (snake) is cognate with 'hai'a', denoting (a look, appearance or aspect), and conforms to the Arabic noun 'hai'a' (a shape, figure, aspect or form).[18] The Greeks translated 'haiya' as 'drakon' (to watch or flash).

Egyptologists render 'hai'a' in the hieroglyphic as, the dubious transliteration, 'ka' (a double).[19] Wallis Budge defined the 'ka' sign in his translation 'Book of the Dead' [Passage of the Day][20] as *The double of the deceased, which would wonder at will from the tomb*.[21]

Budge's 'ka' sign is a derivation from the Egyptian idiolect 'hai'a' (an aspect or form).[22] Articulation of the 'hai'a' (ka) refers to the winged seraph or fish, equated with the angelic or demonic realm. Hai'a's root is deduced from the Old Sumerian word 'ha' (fish) and is the same as the Chaldean deity 'Hea' or 'Hoa', figurative of 'haiya' (a snake).[23] Hea's diction is prototypical of the 'serpent', likened to a 'phantom or apparition'. In addition, the Sumerian noun 'ha' (a fish) is punned with the dog's 'bark' (awa).[24] Relationship between the 'fish' (ha) and reptile (haiya) prescribes the worship of deities, originating from Sirius (Ra or Aur).

Imprinted universally in all languages, the mirage of the snake exists in every culture. Appearance of the reptile in cultic lore is depicted as a phantasm - a fallen angel that has acquired mastery over the dimension of being (time). Humanity is on the threshold of discovering this inner knowledge and comprehending the vastness of possibility. On that momentous day, we will break the serpent's spell and go forward as one!

The Muse wisely sang in Hesiod's Theogony: *'We know how to tell many lies that sound like the truth, but we know how to sing reality, when we will'.*[25] Veiled in allegory, the Muse's ramblings cautions humanity and offer those who look a glimpse of freedom. Her invitation is open to all. Who will dare to listen?

'Where did all the dragons go?
The smartest scholars still don't know...
It might be so we don't forget
That dragons could be living yet -
Waiting in a world nearby
Just beyond the earth and sky'

Fay Robinson
Where Did All the Dragons Go?
Hinkler Books Pty Ltd, Australia 2003
Pages 23 & 26 (Paraphrased)

1   Chris Everard: Alien Invasion, Secret Space, Vol 2 2007 (DVD)

2   Nigel Cawthorne: The World's Greatest UFO Encounters, 2002, p141

3   Hippocrene English-Arabic, Arabic-English Dictionary, Hippocrene, New York, 2005, p210

4   Ibid

5   P G Maxwell-Stuart: Witchcraft A History, Tempus, 2004, p20

6   John C Traupman: The New College Latin & English Dictionary, Bantam Books, 1988, p205 ['Omental organs' is taken from the Latin noun 'omentum' (fat or the bowels)].

7   Hippocrene English-Arabic, Arabic-English Dictionary, Hippocrene, New York, 2005, p170 The Arabic noun 'dukhan' (smoke) is used metaphorically in English to describe 'smoking heroine', referred to as 'chasing the dragon'.

8   John C. Traupman, The New College Latin & English Dictionary, Bantam Books, 1988, p97

9   Ibid, p356

10 Ibid, p357

11 Hippocrene English-Arabic, Arabic-English Dictionary, Hippocrene, New York, 2005, p186

12 Ibid, p186

13 Ibid, p135

14 Prolog: Pocket Bilingual Dictionary, English-Hebrew, Hebrew-English, Prolog, 2003, p29

15 Ibid, p19

16 Descendents of 'Eve' are codified in Greek with 'kore' (a pupil or virgin), rendered in Arabic 'houri' (virgin), connoting the Syrian word 'hawra' (gazelle like in the eyes). Her sacred bloodline is epigraphic of the eye signature of the Egyptian God Osiris and his bastardised offspring - the dragon.

17 Jack M Driver: Hidden Codes of the Bible, Deciphering the Divine, Kandour Ltd, UK, 2007, p60

18 Hippocrene English-Arabic, Arabic-English Dictionary, Hippocrene, New York, 2005, p186

19 Incontrovertible evidence suggests that 19th century academics attempted to separate quite fallaciously Pharaonic vocabulary from the Semitic branch of languages. This assertion is particularly true regarding Aramaic and Arabic, shown to be the original tongue of the Pharaohs.

20 The author of this work translates the corpus material 'Book of the Dead' as (the Passage of the Day). The arguments for this rendition are complex and not relevant for the purpose of this book. A detailed espousal is due to follow in a subsequent work.

21 E A Wallis Budge: The Egyptian Book of the Dead, Abridged, Cassell & Co, p92 (Glossary)

22 Drawn singularly, the 'arm' glyph is poeticized as 'rh' and is consistent with the Arabic etymon 'ruh' (spirit or soul) - a homonym of 'ruh' (to go away or off). The arm is prognostic of the offering and is paired with the 'double-arm' hieroglyph 'hai'a' (form), transliterated inaccurately as the 'ka' glyph. It specifies the worship of the 'double', personified as the 'reptile'.

23 The Semitic word 'hai'a' (a form) is closely related in Japanese to the verb 'kaeru' (to change, alter or substitute) - a homonym of 'kaeru' (frog), disclosing a shape-shifter!

24 Hippocrene English-Arabic, Arabic-English Dictionary, Hippocrene, New York, 2005, p16

25 Alan F. Alford: The Atlantis Secret, A Complete Decoding of the Lost Continent, Eridu, 2001, p357

Conclusion
Man's Awakening

'This is the story of a crime – a crime of the murder of reality; and the extermination of an illusion – the vital illusion, the radical illusion of the world. The real does not disappear into illusion; it is illusion that disappears into integral reality...'[1]

'The perfect crime is that of an unconditional realization of the world by the actualization of all data, the transformation of all our acts and all events into pure information: in short, the final solution, the resolution of the world ahead of time by the cloning of reality and the extermination of the real by its double'.[2]

Jean Baudrillard, The Perfect Crime, 1996

Throughout ancient corpus, the serpent is described as a liar and a deceiver (Arabic ifrit) - an entity that hides its form via symbolism. Protected by the Secret Society network, the dragon's presence is legitimized through the priestcraft (religion) state and government. Growth of the world's Empires and Masonic fraternities mirrored the fallen angel - a conqueror established by virtue of a monarchial bloodline.

Oannes 'En-Asas' (Lord of the Foundation), an appellation of 'Osiris', is a pun on the semitic word 'anas' (rapist), cogitative with 'anan' (cloud), cognomens of the 'dragon'. 'Oannes' is a variation of the Babylonian word 'A-Nas' (People of the Water) - characteristic of the 'sailor' or 'angel', prototypical of Osiris (Lord of the Host). Note how the gills of the fish on the Mitre crown are redrawn on Babylonian iconography as 'horns' (Hebrew keren) a homonym of 'koren' (radient) - nominal of the 'illuminati' (akh zauri). The priesthood linked 'water' with the 'spirit', received through the 'organ of thought'. Oannes is an amphibian God and came out of the sea. He brought the Chaldeans their culture and returned to the deep ocean of space.

Accounts record the host as the 'sailor', 'nomad' or 'alien'. They appeared as 'serpents' or 'amphibians' and are revered as the 'destroyers', 'rapists' and 'pillagers'. In particular, the 'dragon's heritage interconnects with the star system 'Sirius', orientated towards the 'Pleiades' and 'Orion' - the latter constellation affiliated to the 'Titans' and mixed progeny.

To summarize the main arguments enumerated so far. Human culture originated from the 'Pleiades', Greek 'plein' (to sail), and migrated initially to 'Mars' (Latin mamers)[3] - a definition recognizant with the development of the 'mammal' (mammalis), philological to 'man' and the 'moon'.

'Mamers' archaically is a derivation from the Aramaic root 'mamonas' (riches), attributed originally to the wealthy civilization of Atlantis.[4] According to Plato's narrative in the Timaeus,[5] occupants of the fabled island (planet) are defeated by the 'Athenians' - a Grecian name extracted from the Arabic root 'af'a' (a viper). Destruction of 'Mars', recorded in the Roman pantheon as the 'God of War', is located with the moon of Jupiter 'Tantalus' - an anagram of 'Atlantis' obliterated most probably by a satellite of Saturn, refer to Appendix 8.

Fragments of 'Tantalus' constitute the 'asteroid belt' - archived in Roman mythology as the underworld. Following Mar's capitulation, remnants of man's seed are taken to the 'moon' (qamar), and its 'priesthood' (komer) extracted from this bloodline. The Hebrew title 'komer' informs the Latin word 'homo' (a human being),[6] indexed in the Hebrew-Arabic play 'vaseri'[7]and 'bashari'.[8]

Ritual death of man celebrates the spring 'ram' - an anagram of 'Mars'. Philological evidence in the Latin language suggests 'maris' the adjective (male, masculine, manly or brave)[9] is variegated from 'Mars'. Additionally, 'maris' is a homophone of (sea and sea water),[10] conceptual to the 'host' and 'deluge'.

Offspring of Mars are referred to in the Roman language as 'Martius' (a Martian, literally descended from Mars and possesses the additional meaning the month of March).[11] 'Martius' is reminiscent of 'marital and marshal', descriptions of the Sumerian title 'Martu' (a Westerner), developmental to the Theban, Syrian and Ptolemaic priesthood. The assignment 'Martu' (Occidental) is relative in Arabic to 'mot' (death), enunciated in Persian as 'mitra' (a contract), celebratory of the Western God 'Mithra'. Incarnated as a 'bovine', registered with the 'Pleiades', the bull is divisional to the 'goat and ram'.

Identical themes outlining human destruction are evident in the Semitic traditions of 'Atlantis', named in the Bible as 'Eden' - a derivation of 'Adom' (red).[12] In Arabic, the word 'annihilation' ('adam)[13] is cogent with the first man 'Adam', correlated in Hebrew with 'Ma'adim' (Mars).[14]

After the 'angelic wars', survivors from the 'Red Planet' entered into a covenant with the brazen 'snake' (ta'ban), associated in the Hellenistic mysteries with the 'Athenian and Theban' priesthood. Predicated on 'submission' (slm), emissaries of the reptile contractually stipulated the death of the firstborn male (ram) and the propagation of illegitimate heirs through female reproduction (goat).

After Albrecht Durer, Adam and Eve. Durer's engraving shows the 'bull' (Hebrew par) connected to the 'Pleiades', conjunct with the 'Pharaoh' (Hebrew Par-o). The 'lion' (Hebrew lavi) is a symbol of the 'Levite' priesthood, affiliated to the tribe of Judah and is connected etymologically to the 'heart' (lav), a device of Sirius (lion heart). Durer also included the 'badger' (Latin 'meles') - a pun on 'malus' (an apple tree) a homonym of (bad or evil). 'Meles' is a play on 'mellis' (honey), correlated with the 'bee', hieroglyphically 'Lower Egypt and the Red Crown', aligned to 'Adam' (red). The 'badger' in Hebrew (girit) is possibly a pun on Jerad (Hebrew Yored - descending) - an offspring extracted from the moon.

Marriage of the serpent with woman begot a powerful race of rulers, known in Thebes as the 'Court of the Dragon', documented in occult literature as the 'Goat' (Mendes), Latin 'medeis' (magic). The appellation 'Mendes' is deduced from the Arabic root 'Madad' (a Mason) and 'medha' (a human sacrifice), cognomens of the Persian priesthood 'Mada', etymological to 'Martu' and 'Martian' (See Chapter 20 Men are from Mars and Snakes are from Venus).

The 'he-goat' Mendes is represented on Egyptian monuments as the 'ram' and identified by the classical scholar Herodotus as the Greek God 'Pan',[15] deductive from the Hebrew noun 'pin' (penis).[16] 'Mendes' in the Roman tongue is interchangeable with 'menda' (fault), 'mandere' (chew) and 'mandare' (order), expressions of the 'maenad' termed as (the Madonna).[17]

Archaically, the 'maenad' (Italian Madonna, Latin Mia-domina - 'my mistress')[18] denotes a priestess of the Roman God 'Dionysus' (Greek Bacchus). A denizen of debauchery, 'Bacchus' is linked to the frenzied orgiastic cult of 'Mendes' - an anagram of 'demens' the Latin adjective for (mad, demented, senseless, wild, reckless or insane).[19]

Dionysus (Dion-Ysus) literally 'Lord Jesus' is known to his Greek followers as 'Nyseus' born in 'Nysae', analogous to 'Jesus of Nazareth'. Greek mystics depicted him as the crucified horse from the Semitic pun 'Dayim Sus' (the Immortal Horse) - a symbol interchangeable with the 'dragon' and 'goat'.

'Bacchus' known to his followers as the 'Son of Zeus' (Greek dios-kouros) is a cryptic pun of a 'reptile God' (diosauros). The strange appellation is repeated in the Latin articulation 'anguigena' (a Theban - literally offspring of the snake). Classical writers, including the Roman scholar Pliny, document 'Bacchus' as the 'sovereign of Thebes'.

Assigned to matriarchal hereditary, the dragon's progeny conceived the Pharaonic bloodline, extrapolated from the seed taken from the moon (rib). Repatriation of the serpent with the woman, formalized through a covenant, linked the 'fallen angel' with the 'builder' - a title consistent with the 'surveyor', 'architect', 'mason', 'snake' or 'king'. In addition, the 'builder' is used as an idiom to describe 'materialisation of angelic forms' - engendered through ritual, indexed with the craft, foundational to the magical arts, the goat and serpent.

The Craft inducted woman into the magical arts of the snake, appearing to her as a semblance, apparition or ghost. According to the Rabbinical book of 'Haggadah' (Hebrew higgid - to tell), the serpent adopted a human visage - an intransient image or illusion.[20] Manifestation of this 'aspect' (Arabic hai'a)[21] is conceived as a 'snake' (haiya).[22] In the King James' translation of the Bible Genesis Chapter 3, the 'serpent' is described as more 'subtle' than any 'beast of the field' (man).

'Subtle' in Old English conveys 'craftiness' or 'shrewdness', tacit of evasiveness. The word 'subtle' is appropriated from the Latin adjective 'subtilis' (delicate or subtle) and expresses the feminine noun 'subtilitas' (fineness or slenderness).[23] In addition, 'subtilitas' appears as the adverb 'subter' (below or underneath),[24] idiomatic of the 'snake and substitute'.

'Substitution' simulates a 'changeling' (Latin suppositio)[25] from 'suppositus' the past participle (to substitue).[26] In English, the wordplay approximates to 'trade and change' or 'price and place'. 'Suppositio' is divided from the stem 'positor' (a builder),[27] employed in the Semitic and Persian languages to convey an 'angel', 'God' or 'serpent'.

Defined as the 'positor', translated as (a builder), the 'positor' is matched with 'possideo' (the transitive verb to possess, occupy, have, own, dwell, live in, take hold of) and is a variation of 'posido' (to take possession of or to seize).[28] The angels are thus able to 'occupy', 'possess' or 'take possession' of the body, likened to 'positura' (a formation).[29]

Labeled as a 'changeling', (the suppositio) designates a deity, viewed metaphorically as a 'builder' (positor), figurative of the angel's ability to assume a human form, resembling a 'substitute'. Cultic symbolism personifies the 'builder' as a 'Master Craftsman', represented in the Mystery Schools as a 'Mason or an Artificer'.[30]

Ritualistically, the 'substitute' (suppositio) is 'exchanged' with a 'changeling', recondite with a transfigured angel.[31] Replacement of the body-double with a replica concurs also within European folklore. Provident to Celtic tradition, an infant substituted at birth by stealth replaces an 'elf child' left by the fairies. These 'babies' in legend are often 'handicapped', reproduced as (the lame serpent) and considered 'subnormal'. An allegory, the 'changeling' is considered illegitimate, and recounts the usurpation of man's progeny with heavenly offspring - the 'suppositio'.

To reiterate, the 'suppositio' (a changeling) is symmetrical with the feminine noun (a substitute). Philologically, 'suppositio' corresponds with the Roman compound 'supera' (heaven or the upper world) and 'positio' (position), interpreted as (heaven's position).[32] Intriguingly, the 'substitute' (a changeling) mandates heaven's 'superior position' through the replacement of the 'subterfuge' (Latin subterfugere - to escape secretly). Restoration of the body is symbolized in Masonic lore as the rebuilding of the Temple. Cryptically, the craftsman is imbued magically with the 'spirit' or 'breath', consolidated with bodily transfiguration.

Angel with comb Einsiedeln Cathedral. The statue shows an 'hairy angel' (human-angelic) and is parabolic of the 'reaper'. The Latin transitive verb 'pectere' (to comb) is rendered in colloquial Latin (to clobber with a fist or stick). 'Pectere' additionally is esoteric of 'pecu' (a flock) and 'peccans' (sinner), theological to 'pecunia' (money), implicit of redemption. In Greek, the noun 'kome' (hair) signifies 'koma' (sleep), symbolic of death. 'Kome' is analogous in the Hebrew lexicon to 'komer' (priest), Latin 'homer' (man) – etymologies cogent in Arabic with the noun 'qamar' (moon). The crescent signifies the host (Venus), paralleled to the destruction and regeneration of man's seed, extracted from the moon. Correlated with the 'reaper', the satellite designates the 'reptile' – characteristic of a 'nocturnal angel'.

Discriminated as a 'position', later a 'rank' (positio) demarcates the transitive verb 'ponere' (to build, erect, put, assume, place, set down, to lay out for burial or smooth hair),[33] synonyms associated with the materialization of the form. 'Ponere' (build) is variegated from the Hebrew word 'po'el' (to work or a workman)[34] - e.g. a Mason.

Corroboratory evidence from the Arabic and Latin suggests 'po'el' is an extraction from the Akkadian root 'Peor-El' (a Serpent God), archived as a 'changeling or a Theban'. Additionally, 'Peor-El' is a cognate of the 'Pharaoh' (Hebrew Par-o), consistent with 'pe'er' (glory) and 'pe' (mouth), contextual to the 'votive'. Identified in the Egyptian and Persian mysteries with the 'bull' (Hebrew par),[35] the 'bovine' is grouped with the partition of the 'Pleiades', equated with the 'goat and Mars'.[36] Biblical sources suggest an early split between the 'bull and caper', inherent within the priesthood, identified with the 'builder and angel'.

Semantically, the Latin transitive 'ponere' (build), Hebrew 'po'el', tallies with the Roman feminine noun 'poena' (compensation, recompense, retribution, satisfaction, penalty, fine, punishment, hardship, loss and pain), indexed also as the 'poena mortis' (capital punishment or the death penalty).[37] 'Poena's lexicon resembles the Greek mysteries, categorized with the 'Paean Feast', conjunct with the goat deity 'Pan' (feeder), paired with the Sun God Apollo.

Ring seal amulet, 3rd century AD. Author's translation: 'Orpeus' (son of Apollo), Bacchus' Cross. The word 'cross' is constructed anagrammatically from the 'footstool'. Note also the 'seven stars' – a symbol of (the Pleiades), and the crescent device (Venus), interchangeable with the moon and darkness. In addition, the Greek inscription reads as a pun on the Semitic words 'af'a', 'boker' and 'kuss', translated respectively as (morning, snake and tabernacle).

Esoteric, the 'Paean Feast' enacts the 'tragedy', indexed with the 'goat' (tragos), equivalent in Egypt to the cult of 'Mendes', archived with the 'builder and Mason'. 'Paean' otherwise 'poena' is translated into Latin as the 'Passion' (suffer), adjacent in the Christian traditions to the 'scapegoat Christ' in Persia - the 'bull Mithra'. Liturgically, the Passion is mutual to bodily transfiguration of Christ, likened to the rebirth of the sun, highlighted in the Greek lexicon.

Religiously, the 'paean' (invocation) expresses 'phaino' (to show or manifest), cognizant with 'phantazo' (to make visible), in English a 'phantom', reductive of 'phane' (a spirit or 'serpent' - Egyptian fennu). 'Phaino' informs the Latin feminine noun 'forma' (form, shape, figure, vision, apparition, phantom or species).[38] Appearance of the 'phantom' marks the 'builder' (ponere), classified as a 'changeling' or a 'snake' (the phane or fennu).

Addendum, the 'builder' (Latin ponere Hebrew po'el) is cryptic of 'work' (me'lakha)[39]and encodes the 'angel' (mal'akh). Realization of the 'angel' is categorized in Arabic with 'af'a' (a viper), relative to 'le'ha'fil' (to work), literally (to operate).[40] Symbolically, the 'worker' divulges the 'angel' - a concept repeated in the Hebrew etymon 'tsaba' (a painter),[41] covert to 'tsabaoth' (the host).[42]

Regeneration of the 'builder', a 'Master Mason' or 'artisan' constitutes a 'changeling', recognizant with the reoccurrence of the body or form, facilitated through the immolation of the flesh (stone), theoretical to the 'Passion'. Ascribed in the Christian mysteries to the tomb (a metaphor of rebirth), the crypt is analogous to the snake and woman. The 'changeling' defined as a 'worm'[43] is conceived from the blood of the 'womb'. Analogous, 'worm' and 'womb' parallels the Hebrew play 'ru'ak' (demon)[44] and 'rekhem' (womb),[45] Latin 'host' and 'haustus' (menstrual blood). In Arabic, the same pun reads as 'dud' (worm),[46] equivalent to 'duta' (a dowry).[47]

A simile of 'renewal', the 'womb' records the 'double', associated with the 'changeling' (a worm), adjunct to the 'goat and bovine'. Represented as the 'horned deity', the 'goat', in European tradition a 'stag' (Latin 'cervus'), symbolizes the 'ovaries', correlated with the 'cervix and creation', conceptual to the 'double and rebirth'.[48] Generation of a corporeal form, likened to a snake, goat or angel, is contrasted in the occult with the pronouncement of the word (to summon), conceptual to the priestess and duplicate.

The scholar Traupman in the Latin & English New College Dictionary lists the alternative name for a 'changeling' as the substantive (subditus).[49] The Oxford English dictionary argues the etymon 'subditus' is derived from 'sub' (literally under) and 'dicere' the verb (to say). On further analysis, it seems the past participle 'dictus' (say) is obtained from the Greek root 'dittos' (a double). Substitution of the 'word' (dictum) with the 'form' recounts the commutation of the 'reptile, goat or double', correlated with 'invocation and rebirth'.

In Greek alchemy, the spoken word tallies with magical dictation, equated with the 'double' (the dittos). Analogy of the 'dittos' is confirmed in the Greek noun 'lego' (word), contiguous with the 'logian' (an oracle). Her pronouncements are manifested through the mystical 'logos' - the incarnation of God. Twinned, the 'concept' is cognate with 'conception',[50] and the 'word' with the formation of the 'world'. In the Gospel of John, Chapter 1 verse 14 - *'The word became flesh and made his dwelling amongst us...'.* John's quotation alludes to a sacrifice and the incarnation of the 'double', compared to an 'angel or entity'.

Philologically, the 'double' (an apparition) proceeds from the Semitic stem 'debar' (to talk),[51] relative to 'dabir' (a sanctuary),[52] nominal of 'dabh' (a sacrifice).[53] 'Debar' (talk) and 'dabh' (votive) in English is equivalent to the pun 'talk' and 'take'. In the Indo-European vocabulary, 'debar' (talk) proceeds from the Sanskrit root 'deva' (a deity transcribed as a devil). The root of 'devil' is consistent with 'division', illusory of (Satan) cognate with the 'word and double'.

The ritual of appropriating an 'appearance', engineered through the 'double' (the dittos), is conceived physically through the 'word' (S-word). Verbalization of the 'word' is likened magically to 'creation and intercourse', i.e. 'verbal and sexual'.[54] Liturgical connection between the spoken 'word' and 'form', classified as the 'double', specifies an 'angel' (Greek angelos) - a messenger.

To recapitulate, the Greek term 'angelos' (an angel) is translated from the Hebrew word 'mal'akh' (an angel), obtained from the verbal root 'amar' (to speak or command).[55] Establishment of the 'word' (Hebrew amira)[56] agrees with the Arabic verbal root 'amara' (a fleet),[57] exhibited as the angelic 'host' (ha'mon), congruous with the 'word' and the manifestation of the 'double' (sacrifice). 'Amar' (to speak) is cognizant in Arabic with 'ammar bana' (a builder).[58]

Duplicitous, the 'double', registered as the 'word', reinforces the 'snake' iconic of the 'king', evidenced in the Arabic dialect. 'Haka' (Syrian to talk)[59] is relative to 'hakim' (a sovereign),[60] nominal of 'acan' (a flaming seraph). Inherent, the 'word' denotes the 'substitute', embodied as the 'snake or king', represented as the 'double'. Its appearance personifies the spoken 'word' (a construct or form), commensurate with the 'multiple' e.g. 'phonein' (speak) and 'phane' (spirit).

Derivation of the Arabic noun 'af'a' (viper) is from the same family of words as the Hebrew noun 'kafil' (double),[61] paired in Arabic with 'kaffara' (atonement).[62] The Latin word 'onement' (atonement, literally at one) - English 'whole and holy'. Atonement in the original context defines rebirth of an entity, expedited through the blood of the substitute. Semitic tradition equates the 'substitute' with the 'goat' - a symbol of the 'changeling' homologous to 'rebirth'.

The 'tragos' (goat) is signified as the 'hemitheos' (a demigod), coded speak in the Greek tongue of 'helminthos' (a worm), self-referential to the God Hermes (a messenger), cognomens of an 'angel' (angelos). 'Hermes' additionally is confluent with the 'Aamu' (Emori), annotated as the 'Western priesthood of Thebes', archived with the 'snake' and the redemption of the 'double', affiliated to the ram deity 'Amun' (hidden).

'Kaffara' (atonement) and 'kafil' (double) are extensions of 'af'a' (a viper). Morphological, the switch between the 'f' and 'p' in the Indo-European languages lists the Semitic stem 'kaffara' with the Latin noun 'caper' - feminine 'capra' (a she-goat).[63]

The horned 'caper' is another cognomen of the 'se'irim', pictured as a 'hairy angel'. Progeny of the 'se'irim' (a fawn, literally a red goat) is defined as 'human angelic' and theological to a 'substitute'. Described as a 'nocturnal angel', the 'hairy goat', a biped, can assimilate a 'human likeness'. Greek historians list this fabled creature variously as the 'khimara' (a she-goat, English chimera).[64] Manifestation of the 'chimera' prefixes the Latin titular 'camilla' (a votaress, an attendant at a sacrifice).[65]

Transmutation of the 'nanny goat' (Greek khimara) mystically acknowledges the transformation of 'metal into gold'. Transmogrification of the 'goat' (Greek khemia) is extracted from the Arabic root 'al-kimiya' (English alchemy). The science of alchemy discloses angelic metamorphosis in context to the 'tent', transliterated in Arabic as (khaimi or khema),[66] originally a tabernacle, deduced from 'khemia' (a goat). Khemia is configured from the Old Hebrew root 'Chem' (the Pleiades), philological to the ram God 'Amun' (concealed).

Made from goatskin, the 'shelter' (khema) is linked to the 'moon' (qamar), addendum to the 'priest' (komer), indexed with the 'goat' (khimara) and 'clay' (khomer).[67] Malleable, 'clay' (adama - earth) is a symbol of 'Adam's corporeal form, linked to the 'rock and altar' (nave), cognizant with restoration, generative of the 'moon and serpent' (changeling).

Occult lore borrowed from the traditions of the Knight Templar replaces the 'chimera' with the goat deity 'Bathomet' (Hebrew 'Bath Mavet' - a Daughter[68] of Death[69]). Listed in Hellenistic vocabulary, the 'goat' (tragos) enumerates the 'tragedy'. Propitiations of the 'tragos' earmark the killing of the 'scapegoat', coherent with the 'hairy angel' (a reaper), veiled as the 'masked satyr' (a goat). Enacted ritualistically, the 'satyr' (Arabic satr - concealed) celebrates the 'ram or red goat' (Amun), aligned to the 'Pleiades and Mars'.

The classification 'hairy angel' is identical in Greek to 'khemara' (a nanny goat), relative to 'kome' (hair) and 'kometes' (a comet, literally a long haired star). The signifier of the 'goat' and 'hair' is covert to 'camilla' (a priestess), astrological to the 'moon' (qamar). In Rome, the 'she-goat' (capra)[70] likewise designates 'hair' (capillus)[71] - an annotation of the 'mammal' (human), unified sexually with the 'nocturnal angel, a snake'.[72] - Refer to Chapter 15 Abraham and the Secret Covenant of the Ram.

To summarize, 'capra' (a goat) pertains to the Latin transitive verb 'capere' (to take hold of, grasp, seize, to occupy, to take up, assume, catch, capture, captivate, charm, mislead, overcome or defeat).[73] These terms indubitably express the goat as a copulator and a rapist, mutual to the reptile, featured as a builder or Mason.

Roman tragedies visualize the serpent as a masked satyr - a goat entity that can change its form into a man (rebirth). Devine, the deity's transformation is described as 'capricious', deduced from the original Italian 'capriccio' (horror) - an abstraction of 'capra' (a goat). Symbolism of the 'capra' coincides in Greek with the nature God 'Pan', associated with 'panic and pain' (paean feast).

Pan's frightening presence shares many similarities with the Gorgon Medusa. Her epithet 'Gorgo' (a Gorgon) agrees with the adjective 'gorgos' (terrible). A terrifying queen Medusa possesses serpents for hair - iconic of the 'hairy snake', an angel or 'chimera' (khemara), celestial to the 'star' (kometes). Decapitation of the Gorgon and the containment of her head held in the 'goatskin' (the aegis)[74] is congruent with the worship of 'Jupiter', variously (Diovis or Jehovah).

Roman ritual correlates 'capra' (a goat) with the 'substitute', listed with 'caput' (a head)[75] - a device allocated to Jupiter's temple 'Capitol'. A homonym, the word 'temple' in English discloses an 'organ of thought', additional to a 'religious building devoted to the worship of God'. The title 'God' in Anglo-Latin syntax is conferred upon a 'goat',[76] mutual to 'guild' (a sacrifice), compatible with 'good' - English rite and right (light).

Semitic traditions celebrate the veneration of 'Jupiter' (Hebrew tesdek - justice)[77] with the death of the firstborn Isaac (Zadok)[78] and his replacement with the ram. Isaac's tributary is formulated upon a covenant, allocated in the Christian mysteries to 'Golgotha' (the skull) - the site of Jesus' crucifixion. Theoretically, the 'skull' in Roman occult draws comparison to the inner sanctum of the 'temple', registered with the sacrifice of the scapegoat, paralleled in the Greek customs to 'Dionysus, reproduced as Dion-Ysus' (Lord Jesus).

Further, 'caput' figuratively (the skull) infers 'capta' (a captive or prisoner),[79] thus Jesus is executed beside the guilty. The Roman wordplay 'caput' and 'capta' enunciates the 'pascal' (lamb - Aramaic pasha), conversant in Judaism with 'peshal' (crime).[80] Theological to redemption, man's iniquities are conveyed through the descendents of Adam (Mars), purchased through the sacrificial slaying of the lamb (firstborn), switched with the 'goat' (scapegoat) or 'skull'. Implicit of the substitute, the 'goat' emblematic of the 'jinn' personifies a 'changeling', equated with the Temple (Capitol) and 'double.'

Graffiti inscribed on Roman pillar AD 195-235. Author's translation: 'A sign (augury) out of loss we honour (celebrate) our Lord Deon (Dion)'. The letter 'Y' shown top right on the drawing is not recurrent in the Greek and Latin alphabet and is a Pythagorean symbol of 'virtue'. The vertical line of the Y axis symbolises God (I) - 'unity'. The splitting of the straight line articulates division, associated with the Shatani, numerological to five (V). The numbers (I) and (V) add up to six (VI), equated with 're-creation' and the development of the 'covenant'. Note the witness to the 'Paean Sacrifice' holds up five fingers - a sign of Mars, affiliated to the God of War and Sacrifice. The (V) sign also denotes a 'victory' and is interchangeable with the 'horned God', inverted sometimes to signify a 'curse'.

Merged with the Passover and the Paean Feast, the Passion of Christ narrates the expiation of sin, cogent with death and resurrection. Transfiguration of Jesus' double corresponds with the atonement of the scapegoat, concurrent in the Judaic mysteries with the tearing of the veil - a goatskin and the regeneration of the snake.

In magical circles, the serpent is envisaged as the 'se'irim' (a goat demon) and discerns the Arabic etymon 'sirr' (a mystery)[81] and 'sihr' (sorcery).[82] Hebrew lexicology relates the appearance of the 'goat' with the angelic 'boat' (sira).[83] 'Se'irim' in the Old Semitic translates as (a red goat), analogous to (the fawn and satyr). Philologically, the 'se'irim' is conjunct with 'se'ar' (hair), 'sa'ir' (fur)[84] and 'seir' (red). The 'se'irim' (goat) is an expression of the 'seraph' (a flaming snake),[85] congruent with the 'seraphim' (the highest rank of angel).

Clothed in human form, the 'goat' (in heraldry the unicorn, yale or stag) is pictured as chained - a motif of the initiate, reproduced as the 'Camilla Priestess'. Further in Greek mythology, the 'bond or fetter' (desma) records the Aramaic noun 'dema' (blood), informative of 'daimon' and 'demon', cogent with 'domina' (a mistress).[86] Symbolic, the 'fetter' signifies (the serpent, Greek feedhe) - an emblem of the 'ifrit' (a deceiver), contractual to the 'daimon' (demon). Regarded in apocalyptic literature,[87] the 'daimon is denounced as a 'thief', a 'rapist' and 'harbinger of death'. It appropriates the human form,[88] metaphorically adorned in goatskin, mediated through the votive.[89]

To conclude, the angel is a being that can change its corporeal form from a dragon into a man through 'sound', personified as the 'word' or 'double'. Sacrament of the 'goat' (Latin caper), extracted from the Hebrew etymon 'kafil' (a double), specifies 'kaffara' (atonement) facilitated through blood sacrifice. Atonement literally assimilation of the innocent (transubstantiation) portends to blood drinking, depicted as the logos (word), conceptual to the 'vine' (Greek lageos).[90]

Recurrent, the idea of bodily transfiguration (shape-shifting) through ingestion of blood pervades throughout ancient mystery plays. Verification of this phenomenon is documented and supported in the Emerald Tablets translated in the 1920s. Considered as a recent forgery, it is the author's contention the material, though of dubious authenticity, is derived from the hidden (Western) priesthood and recounts a metaphysical truth.[91]

Origins of the text are ascribed to the Patron of Writing Thoth. The corpus of the Emerald Tablets bears striking comparison to the angel cults, scattered throughout the Middle East and Asia. In summary, Thoth's quotation reveals the essence of the mystery, accredited with the 'race of the serpent' (the anguigena). To quote:

> 'In the form of man moved they amongst us, but only to sight, were they as are men. Serpent-headed when the glamour was lifted, but appearing to man as men among men. Crept they into the councils, taking form that were like unto men. Slaying by their arts the chiefs of the kingdoms, taking their form and ruling o'er man. Only by magic could they be discovered, only by sound [blood offerings] could their faces be seen... Came they to man and taught him the secret, the Word that only a man can pronounce; swift then they lifted the veil from the serpent and cast him forth from place among men'.[92]

The sentiments of Thoth provide recourse for reflection. Progeny of the seraph, ascribed initially to the Theban (Syrian) and Western priesthood, is clandestine and protects its bloodline through secrecy. Classification of the 'anguigena' alternatively the 'serpentigena' records (the serpent race), affiliated to the monarchial bloodlines of the ancient world. Offspring of the 'anguigena' masks its true form, obscured behind the human shell - a metaphor of the 'word', 'double' or 'spirit', embodied as the 'builder' or 'Mason'.

Afraid of being discovered, the snake chooses to hide behind a veil. A time is coming, when the light shall shine and the shroud shall be lifted for all to see. On this day, the reptile shall stand naked and Adam shall be restored to his bride. The children of men are ready to wake from their slumber and face the future together!

Drawing after Pisaro. Unification of man's seed with his consort and the end of division. The matriarch's milk is restorative and bonds the child with the woman, physically, psychically and emotionally. Ingestion of the mother's milk is a template for child growth biologically and telepathically giving full genetic immunity to diseases. Developmentally the suckling reflex in humans is six years. In addition, separating the infant from the mother weakens our species genetically and is calculated primarily at disconnecting humans from each other at the developmental stage. The first process of empowerment must be through our offspring, and breastfeeding our children full-term is a small step towards the joining together of mankind and the realization of lasting peace.

Mascaraed behind ignorance, humanity permits this creature to exercise its authority dividing mankind and creating suffering and injustice. On the brink of a mass awakening, how much longer must we ignore the signs? Meanwhile the shaman and priest continue to worship the reptile and proclaim its eulogies...

> *'In the East, Dragon king of the East sea!*
> *In the West, Dragon king of the West sea!*
> *In the South, Dragon king of the South sea!*
> *In the North, Dragon king of the North sea!*
> *Please partake freely of the offerings'.*

The first song collected by Son Chint'ae, a Mudang (Shaman) from Tongnae-Gun in Southern Kyongsang Province, [Korea].[93]

443

THE ETERNAL IS THE INTERNAL

'Take these teachings: that we are all brothers and sisters; the children of one father and mother; that all human beings are interconnected; that we share many thoughts and feelings that we imagine about the world, about the future, about each other; and that the images and dreams we hold in our minds and hearts do matter. Treat children and animals with kindness, and pass this wisdom on to the generations yet to come, and I assure you that there will come a time when our grandchildren, or our great-great grandchildren will live in a world of beauty and harmony. And they will hear a far-off music, a beautiful, cosmic music, that will lift them beyond all fear, all suffering and limitation, into a universal brotherhood, beyond this little world and its fearful dreams. That music will draw closer and yet closer with its message of hope and becoming. That music is the Song of the Stars...'

Vusamazulu Credo Mutwa, Zulu Shaman Dreams, Prophecies, & Mysteries, Destiny Books, Rochester, Vermont, 1996, 2003, p210

1 Jean Baudrillard: The Perfect Crime, Verso, London, 1996, Preface

2 Ibid, p25

3 John C Traupman PhD: The New College Latin English Dictionary, Bantam Books, 1988, p177

4 'Mamlaki' (kingdom) signifies a 'follower' (Syrian laki, Arabic lihiq) of the privileged, literally 'mammon' (riches), assigned to the 'angel' (mal'akh) and the 'king' (melekh).

5 Plato's narrative of Atlantis in the Timaeus discloses a number of interesting puns encoded in Latin. 'Timaeus' is equivalent to 'timoris' (fear), 'temonis' (wagon) and 'Thomas' (twin) - etymons associated with 'temenos' Greek (a sacred enclosure). 'Temenos - Latin templum' (a temple) is correlated in Persian with 'paradise' (a walled enclosure), used in Greek to convey sacred learning by implication, associated with the oral traditions of 'Atlantis'.

6 John C Traupman PhD: The New College Latin English Dictionary, Bantam Books, 1988, p132

7 Prolog: Pocket Bilingual Dictionary, English-Hebrew, Hebrew-English, Prolog, 2003, p32 ['Le'vaser' (to augur). The 'diviner of the augury' is rendered as (vaseri) - a type of priest compatible philologically with the 'Levite and Rabbi'].

8 Hippocrene English-Arabic, Arabic-English Dictionary, Hippocrene, New York, 2005, p156 ['bashari' (human, not divine) - Hippocrene's definition, not mine!]

9 John C Traupman PhD: The New College Latin English Dictionary, Bantam Books, 1988, p179

10 Ibid, p178

11 Ibid, p179

12 Prolog: Pocket Bilingual Dictionary, English-Hebrew, Hebrew-English, Prolog, 2003, p333

13 Hippocrene English-Arabic, Arabic-English Dictionary, Hippocrene, New York, 2005, p317

14 Prolog: Pocket Bilingual Dictionary, English-Hebrew, Hebrew-English, Prolog, 2003, p246

15 Simon Price & Emily Kearns: The Oxford Dictionary of Classical Myth & Religion, Oxford University Press, 2003, p343 (Mendes).

16 Prolog: Pocket Bilingual Dictionary, English-Hebrew, Hebrew-English, Prolog, 2003, p295

17 'Menda' (fault), 'mandere' (chew) and 'mandare' (order) dovetail with the 'maenad', termed as (the Madonna). The Latin wordplay approximates in the Semitic vocabulary to 'so'ed' (diner - a person), covert to 'sod' (a secret), 'seder' (order or arrange) and 'sitt' (a lady).

18 Inside of the serpent cult, the highest echelon of initiation devotes itself to the mother priestess. Temple sanctuaries, courted by virgins, operated covertly as harems for fallen angels. Historically, men are not permitted into the inner circle of the snake with the exception of young children and eunuchs. The male sex are led to believe erroneously the world and its institutions are patriarchal.

19 John C Traupman PhD: The New College Latin English Dictionary, Bantam Books, 1988, p77

20 Resurrection of the serpent's form into physical matter recounts the manipulation of sound waves, corresponding with vibrational energy. This type of entity doubles or cloaks its appearance via a special sound signature (blood), and has the capacity to inhabit the lower dimensions. For most humans, this frequency range is barely detected by the senses.

21 Hippocrene English-Arabic, Arabic-English Dictionary, Hippocrene, New York, 2005, p186

22 Ibid

23 John C Traupman: The New College Latin & English Dictionary, Bantam Books, 1988, p299

24 Ibid

25 Ibid, p362

26 Ibid, p304

27 Ibid, p234

28 Ibid

29 Ibid

30 In the Gospel accounts, Jesus is presented as a Master Mason. Christ's sacrifice is elaborated theologically through 'substitution' (suppositus). His switch describes the 'builder' (positor), tandem to the rebuilding of the temple - a symbol of the 'changeling' (suppositus). Biblically, Jesus assumes an appearance that is deemed different or unrecognisable to his close disciples.

31 In Christian eschatology, Jesus' death is represented as a substituted offering, conceived as an unblemished lamb (first born), recondite with the serpent and goat (scapegoat).

32 The angel or serpent by all accounts is regarded as 'superior' from the Latin 'superu' (that is above from, super or above). The adjective 'super' is equivalent to 'separ' (to separate) i.e. a 'serpent' - a term synonymous with 'holy', coordinated with the liturgy of the supper (suffer) - Arabic 'suf' (wool), denoting the 'sacrificial lamb'.

33 John C Traupman PhD: The New College Latin English Dictionary, Bantam Books, 1988, p232

34 Prolog: Pocket Bilingual Dictionary, English-Hebrew, Hebrew-English, Prolog, 2003, p464

35 Ibid, p52 ['par' (bull)]

36 'Peor' (serpent) discloses the Semitic 'per' (to grow or sprout) and 'pe'er' (glory) - English 'grow and glow'.

37 John C Traupman PhD: The New College Latin English Dictionary, Bantam Books, 1988, p231

38 Ibid, p119

39 Prolog: Pocket Bilingual Dictionary, English-Hebrew, Hebrew-English, Prolog, 2003, p464

40 Ibid

41 Ibid, p288

42 The titular 'Mason' is a corruption of the Arabic term 'masri' (an Egyptian), identical to the priesthood of 'Moses' and 'Thebes', an extrapolation of 'ta'ban' (a snake).

43 Worms ingest the 'earth' (adama), a symbol of immolation of 'Adam' - a concept combined with coitus.

44 Prolog: Pocket Bilingual Dictionary, English-Hebrew, Hebrew-English, Prolog, 2003, p104

45 Ibid, p463

46 Hippocrene English-Arabic, Arabic-English Dictionary, Hippocrene, New York, 2005, p141

47 Ibid, p171

48 Genealogically the reptile's reproduction is gender-specific, transferring its lineage through the 'X' chromosome, delivered through the matriarchal covenant (convent). Biology of the 'masculine' or 'Y' chromosome is de facto of the 'mammal'. Maleness of the human species impedes the propagation of the angelic line, demonstrated in the archetype of the 'virgin and dragon'.

49 John C Traupman PhD: The New College Latin English Dictionary, Bantam Books, 1988, p362

50 Bloomsbury Anthology of Quotations, Bloomsbury, London, 2002, p249 The Scottish historian and essayist Thomas Carlyle (1795-1881) summed up the 'double' as follows: *Language is called the garment of thought*. However, it should rather be noted, language is the flesh and garment, the body of thought.

51 Prolog: Pocket Bilingual Dictionary, English-Hebrew, Hebrew-English, Prolog, 2003, p410

52 Ralph Ellis: Eden in Egypt, A Translation of the Book of Genesis out of the Original Egyptian Text, Edfu Books, 2005, p279 (Appendix A5 - Dictionary).

53 Hippocrene English-Arabic, Arabic-English Dictionary, Hippocrene, New York, 2005, p164

54 Male impotence, conveyed through the death of the firstborn Isaac, is parabolic in Egyptian ritual of Osiris' dismembered organ, equated with circumcision. In exchange for Osiris' Crown, Isis restored her husband's mutilated penis with a golden phallus - an object used to impregnate herself with the serpent's seed. Osiris' name written in the hieroglyphs 'En-Asas' (Lord of the foundation) is a pun on the Fish Deity 'Oannes' (Hebrew Ones - to rape), identified with 'anan' (a cloud) - Refer to traditions of Cain and Abel, Jacob and Esau, Abraham and Isaac or alternatively Appendix 5 - Talmud Quotes.

55 Ralph Ellis: Eden in Egypt, A Translation of the Book of Genesis out of the Original Egyptian Text, Edfu Books, 2005, p13

56 Prolog: Pocket Bilingual Dictionary, English-Hebrew, Hebrew-English, Prolog, 2003, p463

57 Hippocrene English-Arabic, Arabic-English Dictionary, Hippocrene, New York, 2005, p49

58 Ibid, p22 ['ammar bana' (build)] modified in Hebrew as 'banay' (a builder)

59 Ibid, p187

60 Ibid

61 Prolog: Pocket Bilingual Dictionary, English-Hebrew, Hebrew-English, Prolog, 2003, p118

62 Hippocrene English-Arabic, Arabic-English Dictionary, Hippocrene, New York, 2005, p212

63 John C Traupman PhD: The New College Latin English Dictionary, Bantam Books, 1988 p34 ['Caper' (Billy Goat)]

64 The chimera has a head of a lion (man), a body of a goat (hemitheoi) and a tail of a serpent, sometimes depicted as the canine (the Dog Star or Sirus). The mythical creature the 'Chimera' is grouped in the Latin lexicon with 'camera' (a vault, arch or houseboat), emphasizing a connection with boats (host) and sacrifice.

65 Geddes & Grossett: Dictionary of First Names, Geddes & Grossett, 2003, Scotland, p57

66 Hippocrene English-Arabic, Arabic-English Dictionary, Hippocrene, New York, 2005, p125

67 Prolog: Pocket Bilingual Dictionary, English-Hebrew, Hebrew-English, Prolog, 2003, p68

68 Ibid, p98 ['bat' or 'bath' (a daughter)]

69 Ibid, p99

70 John C Traupman PhD: The New College Latin English Dictionary, Bantam Books, 1988, p34

71 Ibid

72 In the Indo-European languages, the goat, gazelle and 'stag' (cervus) represent the 'womb' (the cervix).

73 John C Traupman PhD: The New College Latin English Dictionary, Bantam Books, 1988, p34

74 The 'aegis' refers to (the shield of Zeus), traditionally made from the skin of a 'goat' (i.e. royal skin). The king's bloodline is designated as the protectorate of the Gods. Further, the goat skin in the ancient world is a water carrier, and cryptically suggests a connection with the amphibian, linked to the flood and host. Water also has the capacity to change its state from a solid, gas or liquid, and is esoteric of the changeling.

75 John C Traupman PhD: The New College Latin English Dictionary, Bantam Books, 1988, p35

76 'Capra' (goat) and 'caput' (head) corresponds in Syrian to 'ma'zi' (goat), identified with 'masdar' (a temple or forehead). 'Masdar' in Old Arabic connotes 'mazz-dar' (fire-harm), veiled as the 'burnt offering'.

77 Prolog: Pocket Bilingual Dictionary, English-Hebrew, Hebrew-English, Prolog, 2003, p220

78 The priesthood of 'Zadok' represents itself in Greek as the 'Sadduceas', branched from the 'Priests of Moses' - the 'Sodalists' (Hebrew Sodi).

79 John C Traupman PhD: The New College Latin English Dictionary, Bantam Books, 1988, p35

80 Prolog: Pocket Bilingual Dictionary, English-Hebrew, Hebrew-English, Prolog, 2003, p92

81 Hippocrene: English-Arabic, Arabic-English Dictionary, Hippocrene, New York, 2005, p289 ['Sirr' the Arabic noun (secret) is listed alternatively in Ferozson's dictionary as (a mystery) - the latter translation is more appropriate, as 'sirr' is grouped in the Arabic syntax with 'sihr' (sorcery)].

82 Ibid, p288

83 Prolog: Pocket Bilingual Dictionary, English-Hebrew, Hebrew-English, Prolog, 2003, p45

84 Ibid, p164

85 'Se'irim' (a demon or red goat) and 'seraph' (a snake) is analogous in English to 'sorel' (a fallow deer) - e.g. a 'goat', symbolic of 'sauros' (a lizard), cognate with 'sorcery'.

86 John C Traupman PhD: The New College Latin English Dictionary, Bantam Books, 1988, p92

87 'Apocalypse' (Greek apokalupto - to uncover or reveal) is from 'kalypt' (to conceal or veil - Arabic Lut). Apocalyptic literature suggests the traditions of the patriarch Lot, addendum to the temple, veil and sanctuary.

88 Sacrifice specifies a 'mutant', derived from the Latin 'mutare' (to change). 'Mutare' is apprised with 'mutilare' (to mutilate) - a virtual assignation of 'mortus' the Latin adjective for (a de-ceased or a dead person). 'Mutilation' of the corpse describes 'change', connected to the worship of angels.

89 The Windsor Shield depicts a lion, unicorn (goat or yale) and serpent (chain), and signifies the chimera. This mythical creature esoterically registers three related star constellations. The 'lion's body illustrates 'Orion', and is conjoined with the 'goat' - an emblem of the 'Pleiades', antagonistic to the 'serpent' (Sirius). Mythical representations of the chimera show the serpent biting the goats horn, symbolic of the royal crown. The snake's 'venomous-bite' alludes to human-angelic 'insemination'. Refer to Chimera Statuette, Chapter 3 The Seven Divisions, p56.

90 John C Traupman PhD: The New College Latin English Dictionary, Bantam Books, 1988, p164

91 One of the ways, in which the priesthood distracts the general public, media and academia, is to release blatantly forged material that contains elements of the 'truth', creating ambiguity. Through this process, secret organizations can control the flow of information and create division.

92 David Icke: Children of the Matrix, Bridge of Love, 2001, pp140-141

93 Boudewijn Walraven: Songs of the Shaman, The Ritual Chants of the Korean Mudang, Kegan Paul International, 1994, p16

Epilogue: Graduation
by Ozaki Yutaka (1965 - 1992)

Lying on the lawn
In the shadow of the school building
Drawn as one into the blue encompassing sky
My mind wondering between illusion and reality
As soon as the school bell rang
I returned to my classroom and sat at my usual desk
I was contemplating
whether I should obey what I am supposed to follow
My mind was so puzzled and my heart felt heavy
It seemed to me that everything in life has no meaning

After school we wondered around the town and walked with
loneliness in the wind
Our eyes filled with emptiness and solitude
We went to the shop where the atmosphere was mixed with
laughter and resignation
We played pinball and competed for the high score
Because of boredom whatever excitement we found we kept
talking with exaggeration

I could not behave sincerely
At night I went around breaking school windows
I kept opposing and struggling wanting to be free as soon
as possible

Following arguments with adults who are not trustworthy
After reconciliation what can we understand?
I was fed up weary and sick of the whole situation
However I continued going under these circumstances
I have always known one thing to graduate from this control (imposition)

Everybody listened with zeal and excitement about fighting
We all wanted to know how strong we were and believed obstinately
in physical power
We told ourselves to obey is to loose!
Not daring to show our true inner nature to even our closest friends only a façade
even if we hurt somebody

But in the end everybody falls in love and their heart becomes immersed with the
expression of love
We were told to be highly calculative to succeed in life
We all however believed strongly to love somebody with a pure heart
What is the most important thing in life?
Conflicted between loving somebody or to follow what is necessary to survive
and live

I came to the conclusion that it is shit to follow and to do what I am told
I could not behave sincerely
At night I went around breaking school windows
I kept opposing and struggling wanting to be free as soon as possible
Following arguments with adults who are not trustworthy
After reconciliation what can we understand?
I was fed up and weary sick of the whole situation
However I continued going under these circumstances
I have always known one thing to graduate from this control (imposition)

After graduation how will it help us except memories?
What else will stay in our mind?
If we are all weak and restricted like tethered sheep
Teachers are you all repeaters representatives of weak and tethered adults?
Where should our anger go?
From now on after leaving school what is going to continue to restrict me?
How many times should I graduate from myself to achieve my true nature (self)?

Nobody has noticed that freedom is contrived
The days of struggle are just about through (to finish)…
And with it the graduation from this control
The graduation from this conflict

Graduation - Ozaki Yutaka, Released originally in 1985,
Posthumous Album: Ozaki Yutaka, For All My Loves, Produced by Sudoh Akira, Sony Music
Entertainment, Japan, 1996
Japanese Translation Hikaru Ai and Pierre Sabak

BIOGRAPHIC DETAILS - Ozaki Yutaka (1965-1992)

The song 'Graduation' was written by Ozaki Yutaka, when he was just 17 years old. Lead singer, he wrote the lyrics and played all of the musical instruments himself. It was written specifically to commemorate his graduation ceremony.

Born in Setagaya Tokyo 29 November 1965 and died 25 April 1992 at just 26 years old. Ozaki's tragic life is often compared to James Dean. The social, philosophical and spiritual side to his lyrics however suggest a comparison to John Lennon. He sang about prostitution and the underbelly of Japanese society. In his song 'Identification' for example, he talks controversially about how the terrorist is a victim of circumstance.

Ozaki's songs appeal to the youth of Japan. He is considered anti-establishment and is known for singing about growing up and teenage angst. His music is very eclectic and ranges in style from love ballads to heavy rock, blues and jazz. Ozaki was also an accomplished painter and photographer. His music continues to influence Japanese pop and has a large following in China.

In 1992, his naked body was found down a side street in Tokyo. His father and brother believed that he had been murdered as part of a conspiracy and three hundred thousand fans signed a petition asking the government to investigate his death. The official verdict is that he died of oedema pulmonary. There are numerous theories the most popular is homicide. The nature of Ozaki's death still remains unsolved.

This book is dedicated to all those individuals who dared to think differently!

Appendix 1

Phonetic Switches

The following table shows the close phonetic relationship between related morphemes within Indo-European languages. For example, the Arabic noun 'houri' (virgin) is written in Greek as 'kore'. Both versions appear in the English corruption 'whore' and 'gor' (a child - Modern English: girl).

Morphemes	Language(s)	Example
B-P	Arabic-Greek	Baba / Papas (Daddy)
B-V	Arabic-Hebrew	Sab'a / Sheva (Seven)
D-T	Chinese-English	Dao / Tao (Way)
D-Th	Latin-English	Fides / Faith
Dj-Z	Sanskrit-Greek	Djaus (Heaven) / Zus (Zeus)
G-J	Syrian-Greek	Hajj (Pilgrim) / Hagios (Holy)
G-K	Akkadian-Greek	Akki / Ago (Draw out)
H-F	Japanese	Hone (Bone) / Oni (Goblin) / Fune (Boat)
J-D	Hebrew-Latin	Jehovah / Diovis or Jovis (Jupiter)
J-Z	Iranian- Persian	Sibilate Phonemes
K-H	Sumerian-Arabic	Kar (Hunter or King) / Har (Horus)
M-G (rare)	Greek-Latin	Amnos / Agnus (Lamb)
N-L	Latin-Hebrew	Ponere (Build) / Po'el (Workman)
P-F	Greek-English	Pur / Fire
Ph-F	Greek-English	Pheta / Feta (Goat's Cheese)
Q-K	Arabic-Hebrew	Qamar (Moon) / Komer (Priest)
R-L	Hebrew-Latin	Rabbi (Teacher) / Lavi (Wash)
S-Sh	Arabic-Hebrew	Sab'a / Sheva (Seven)
S-Z	Hebrew-English	Siyon / Zion
T-Th	Greek-English	Pater / Father
V-F	German-English	Volk / Folk (People)
V-W	Latin-English	Vine / Wine
W-R	Egyptian-Hebrew	Wabi (Priest) / Rabbi (Master)
Y-J	Hebrew-English	Y'hudah / Judah

Appendix 2

Listed Examples of Related Japanese Words Corresponding with Indo-European Philology

According to conventional academia, scholars argue Japanese is a unique language and is not related to any other dialects or subgroups. Demonstrated in the table below, Japanese is shown to originate from a shared Proto-Indo-European language. Adoption of the Hiragana and Katakana alphabet is a modification of the Sanskrit (See Appendices 3 & 4). Katakana is utilized grammatically to write Indo-European vocabulary, whereas the Kanji characters represent the Sino etymologies.

Japanese vernacular is a real anomaly it contains as many Greek and Old Semitic words as Chinese. The Nipponese priesthood, aware of the limitations of the Kanji characters, introduced Hiragana and Katakana for writing Sanskrit and Indo-European lexicology. They combined Hiragana and Katakana with the Chinese script to unify the Sino idiolect with Japanese. For the priesthood and its secret fraternities, this is a very rich ground for puns, word associations and encryption - See listed examples of Japanese Indo-European Philology:

Japanese	Indo-European Languages
Ageru (Give)	Greek = Aggero (Bring Forward / Utter / Convey)
Akarui (Bright)	Egyptian = Akh (Light)
Chotto (Little)	Persian = Chohta (Little) / Greek = Iota (Small)
Gen'ei (Phantom / Illusion)	Arabic = Jinni (Djinn / Spirit)
Ginga (Galaxy)	Babylonian = Dingar (Star)
Hai (Ash)	Arabic = Hai'a (A Figure / Aspect / Form)
Haka (Grave)	Babylonian = Acan (Flaming Seraph)
Hana (Flower)	Greek = Anthos (Flower) / Anthera (Flowery)
Hane (Wing)	Hebrew = Kanef (Wing)
Hantai (Opposition)	Greek = Ant(i) (Against) / English = Anti (Opposition)

Japanese	Indo-European Languages
Hebi (Serpent)	Arabic = Hevia (Snake) / Af'a (Viper)
Ie (House)	Babylonian = E (House)
Inu (Dog)	Babylonian = Anu (Jackal Deity)
Itai (Pain)	English = Hit
Jin (Person) - Suffix	Latin = Genus (Birth / Race)
Kabā (Cover)	English = Cover / Hebrew = Khabba (Hide / Conceal)
Kaeru (Alter / Change / Substitute / Frog)	Arabic = Hai'a (Aspect / Form / Double / Substitute)
Kami (Hair)	Greek = Kome (Hair) / English = Comb / German = Camb (Comb)
Kari (Hunt)	Sumerian = Kar (Hunt) / English = Quarry
Kawaii (Pretty)	Arabic = Kawaiyis (Pretty)
Ki (Tree)	Akkadian = Ki (Earth)
(Ki)gen (Origin)	Arabic = Gins (Sex) / Greek = Gen (Produce) / Latin = Genus (Birth / Race)
Kiru (Cut / Hack / Chop)	English = Kill
Koe (Voice)	Hebrew = Kol (Voice) / English = Call
Korosu (Kill / Murder)	Greek = Kharasso (Cut / Scarify / Gash) / Syrian = Khasara (Loss)
Kuro (Black)	Greek = Kore (Pupil - Eye)
Ma (Evil Spirit / Devil)	Latin = Mal (Bad / Ill / Evil)
Minato (Harbour)	Arabic = Mina (Harbour)
Minoru (Fruitful)	Greek = Menorrhoea (Menstruation)
Miru (See)	Hebrew = Maar'eh / Egyptian = Maar / Latin = Mereru / Spanish = Miru (See)
Moeru (Burn)	Hebrew = Mu'ar (Light) / Egyptian = Maurii (Brilliance)
Nagai (Long)	Sanskrit = Naga (Serpent)
Nai (Not)	English = No / French = Ne (Not) / German = Nein (No) / Latin = Non (Not)
Nazo (Mystery)	Hebrew = Nazir (Priest) / Greek = Naos (Inner Sanctuary)

Japanese	Indo-European Languages
Nemui (Sleepy)	Arabic = Nam (Sleep)
Niku (Meat)	Greek = Necros (Flesh)
Nomu (Drink)	Babylonian = Nomu (Water Deity) / African = Nomu (Water Deity / Water)
Ohayō (Hello)	English = Hello
Oni (Demon)	Babylonian = Oannes (Fish Deity)
Ryu (Dragon)	Babylonian = Lulu / Ruru (Changeling)
Sakana (Fish)	Arabic = Samakh (Fish)
Sama (Honorific Suffix)	Old Semitic = Semer (Leader)
Sensei (Teacher)	Latin = Sensa (Thoughts / Sentiments / Ideas)
Sora (Sky)	Latin = Sol (Sun)
Subaru (7 Pleiades Stars)	Old Egyptian = Sab'a (Star / Seven) / Akkadian = Shubar (Star)
Ta (Field)	Egyptian = Ta (Land) / Latin = Terre (Land / Earth)
Tori (Bird)	Arabic = Tair / Ter (Bird)
Torii (Temple Entrance)	Egyptian = Tara (Gate) / Hebrew = Talaa (Doorkeeper / Gateway)
Umu (Give Birth / Produce)	Arabic = Umma (Nation / People)
	Arabic = Umm (Mother)
Waru (Break / Divide)	English = War
Warui (Bad / Evil)	English = Woe

Appendix 3

Mycenaean Script

The script originates from Southern Greece, and is dated from the Second Millennium BC, referred to amongst academics as Linear B. It corresponds phonetically with the Sanskrit, Nepalese and Japanese alphabet (See Appendices 1 & 4).

	a		e		i		o		u
da		de		di		do		du	
ja		je				jo			
ka		ke		ki		ko		ku	
ma		me		mi		mo		mu	
na		ne		ni		no		nu	
pa		pe		pi		po		pu	
qa		qe		qi		qo			
ra		re		ri		ro		ru	
sa		se		si		so		su	
ta		te		ti		to		tu	
wa		we		wi		wo			
za		ze				zo			

	initial ai		initial au		rai		ha
	pʰu		nwa		pte		tja
	twe		two		dwe		dwo
	rjo		rja				

Appendix 4

Japanese Alphabet
(Similar to Mycenaean Script - Linear B)

		ROMAN	HIRAGANA	KATAKANA	ROMAN	HIRAGANA	KATAKANA	ROMAN	HIRAGANA	KATAKANA	ROMAN	HIRAGANA	KATAKANA
ア	行	a	あ	ア	i	い	イ	u	う	ウ	e	え	エ
カ	行	ka	か	カ	ki	き	キ	ku	く	ク	ke	け	ケ
サ	行	sa	さ	サ	shi	し	シ	su	す	ス	se	せ	セ
タ	行	ta	た	タ	chi	ち	チ	tsu	つ	ツ	te	て	テ
ナ	行	na	な	ナ	ni	に	ニ	nu	ぬ	ヌ	ne	ね	ネ
ハ	行	ha	は	ハ	hi	ひ	ヒ	fu	ふ	フ	he	へ	ヘ
マ	行	ma	ま	マ	mi	み	ミ	mu	む	ム	me	め	メ
ヤ	行	ya	や	ヤ				yu	ゆ	ユ			
ラ	行	ra	ら	ラ	ri	り	リ	ru	る	ル	re	れ	レ
ワ	行	wa	わ	ワ									
	行	n	ん	ン									
ガ	行	ga	が	ガ	gi	ぎ	ギ	gu	ぐ	グ	ge	げ	ゲ
ザ	行	za	ざ	ザ	ji	じ	ジ	zu	ず	ズ	ze	ぜ	ゼ
ダ	行	da	だ	ダ	ji	ぢ	ヂ	zu	づ	ヅ	de	で	デ
バ	行	ba	ば	バ	bi	び	ビ	bu	ぶ	ブ	be	べ	ベ
パ	行	pa	ぱ	パ	pi	ぴ	ピ	pu	ぷ	プ	pe	ぺ	ペ

ROMAN	HIRAGANA	KATAKANA	ROMAN	HIRAGANA	KATAKANA	ROMAN	HIRAGANA	KATAKANA	ROMAN	HIRAGANA	KATAKANA
o	お	オ									
ko	こ	コ	kya	きゃ	キャ	kyu	きゅ	キュ	kyo	きょ	キョ
so	そ	ソ	sha	しゃ	シャ	shu	しゅ	シュ	sho	しょ	ショ
to	と	ト	cha	ちゃ	チャ	chu	ちゅ	チュ	cho	ちょ	チョ
no	の	ノ	nya	にゃ	ニャ	nyu	にゅ	ニュ	nyo	にょ	ニョ
ho	ほ	ホ	hya	ひゃ	ヒャ	hyu	ひゅ	ヒュ	hyo	ひょ	ヒョ
mo	も	モ	mya	みゃ	ミャ	myu	みゅ	ミュ	myo	みょ	ミョ
yo	よ	ヨ									
ro	ろ	ロ	rya	りゃ	リャ	ryu	りゅ	リュ	ryo	りょ	リョ
o	を	ヲ									
go	ご	ゴ	gya	ぎゃ	ギャ	gyu	ぎゅ	ギュ	gyo	ぎょ	ギョ
zo	ぞ	ゾ	ja	じゃ	ジャ	ju	じゅ	ジュ	jo	じょ	ジョ
do	ど	ド									
bo	ぼ	ボ	bya	びゃ	ビャ	byu	びゅ	ビュ	byo	びょ	ビョ
po	ぽ	ポ	pya	ぴゃ	ピャ	pyu	ぴゅ	ピュ	pyo	ぴょ	ピョ

Appendix 5
Talmud Quotes

The author wants to make it clear that he is not anti-Semitic. A pacifist, he advocates peace and the right to practice religious freedom and intellectual expression without hindrance. The following quotations appertain to a secret Jewish or Western Cabal that in no way reflects the majority of Jews who themselves have often been victimized by this hidden priesthood and agenda.

The quotes underneath are taken from the 'Talmud' (Hebrew Instruction). The Talmud encompasses the body of Jewish civil and ceremonial law and legend, comprising of the 'Mishnah' and the 'Gemara'. It also includes the 'Tosefta' the oral law. There are two versions of the Talmud: the Babylonian Talmud (which dates from the 5th century AD but includes earlier material) and the earlier Palestinian or Jerusalem Talmud. Highly secretive, it is difficult to obtain translations from these documents. Ideologically racist, the 'Talmud' is closely linked to the 'Theban' (serpent) priesthood and the development of ultra-nationalistic theology, outlined in the following examples:

The Talmud, Soferim 15, Rule 10
'Tob shebe goyyim harog' (Even the best of the Gentiles should be killed).[1]

The Talmud, Baba Mezia fol. 1146
'The goyim [gentiles or cattle] are not men, but beasts'.[2]

Abodah Zarah 26b, Tosephoth (Although the passage was omitted from the 'Soncino' translation of the Talmud, The Jewish Encyclopedia in its article on 'Gentiles', page 617, confirms its existence in the original).

'The goy [gentile or cattle] who pries into the (Jewish) law is worthy of death'.[3]

In addition, Judaism's foundation is forged upon subterfuge - an intrinsic idea built into the subtext of many of the biblical characters such as Cain and Abel, Jacob and Esau, Moses and Aaron. The next section deals with duplicity and how it is a religious imperative to deceive a non-Jew. Again examples are taken and quoted from the Talmud:

The Talmud, IV/3/ 54b
'The possessions of the goyim [gentiles or cattle] are like an ownerless desert and everybody (Jew) who seizes it, has acquired it'.[4]

Book Zohar 1: 168a
'Jews always have to try to deceive Non-Jews'.[5]

Babba Bathra: 54b
'Non Jewish property belongs to the Jew who uses it first'.[6]

Babba kama 113a
'Every Jew is allowed to use lies and perjury to bring a Non-Jew to ruin'.[7]

Mystical Judaism practices blood and sexual rituals not disclosed to the public. Here are a few more translations taken from the Talmud.

Talmud, Sanhedrin 54b (Translation by Adin Steinsaltz)
'If a boy under the age of nine perpetrated sodomy upon an adult, the adult is not liable for punishment, for the intercourse of a boy under nine years of age is not legally an act of intercourse. Since a child less than nine years old cannot commit sodomy, he can also not be the object of sodomy'.[8]

Talmud, Ketubot 11b (Translation by Adin Steinsaltz)
'If a grown man has intercourse with a little girl less than three years old, all agree that it is not considered a significant sexual act, for having intercourse with a girl when she is less than three years old is like putting a finger in an eye*'.[9]

*The eye is used to refer to the sexual organs or the anus.

Talmud, Sanhedrin 59b
The source of man's moral corruption is clearly stated in the Talmud.
'The angels roasted meat for Adam and poured him wine'.[10]

1   Craig Heimbichner, Blood on the Altar, The Secret History of the World's Most Dangerous Secret Society, Independent History &Research, 2005, p157 (Glossary)

2   Texe Marrs, Codex Magica, Secret Signs, Mysterious Symbols, and Hidden Codes of the Illuminati, River Crest Publishing, 2006, p35

3   Ian Ross Vayro, Tears in Heaven, Joshua Books, Australia, 2008, p62

4   Ibid, p59

5   Ibid, p58

6   Ibid

7   Ibid, p59

8   Craig Heimbichner: Blood on the Altar, The Secret History of the World's most Dangerous Secret Society, Independent History & Research 2005, p115

9   Ibid, p114

10 Alix de Saint-Andre: Translated from the French by Elfreda Powell, The Good Angel Guide, Souvenir Press 1999, p45

Appendix 6

Dismembered Eye (Author's notes)

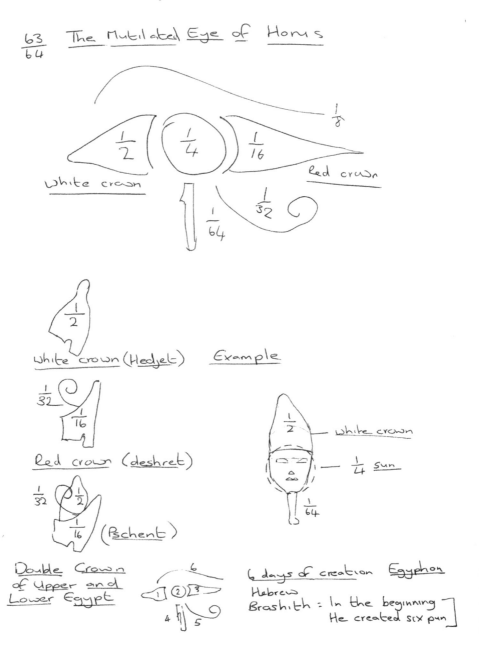

$\frac{63}{64}$ The Mutilated Eye of Horus

$\frac{1}{2}$ $\frac{1}{4}$ $\frac{1}{16}$ $\frac{1}{8}$

White crown

Red crown

$\frac{1}{64}$ $\frac{1}{32}$

$\frac{1}{2}$

White crown (Hedjet) Example

$\frac{1}{32}$ $\frac{1}{16}$

Red crown (deshret)

$\frac{1}{2}$ — white crown

$\frac{1}{4}$ sun

$\frac{1}{64}$

$\frac{1}{32}$ $\frac{1}{2}$

$\frac{1}{16}$ (Pschent)

Double Crown
of Upper and
Lower Egypt

6
1 2 3
4 5

6 days of creation Egyption
Hebrew
Brashith = In the beginning
He created six pun

Appendix 7

Albrecht Durer's 'Snake'

(Refer to Chapter 34 Apophis the Menstrual Eel)

The oil painting of Eve was completed by Albrecht Durer in Italy in 1507, and shows the temptation of Eve, eating the fruit of knowledge, offered by the serpent. Durer represents the 'snake' as a 'menstruating eel' - a symbol of the 'hemitheoi' (half-God), the 'human angelic' lineage. Eve is shown with long golden locks - a signifier of the mammal 'priestess' (Nazir or Nasa).

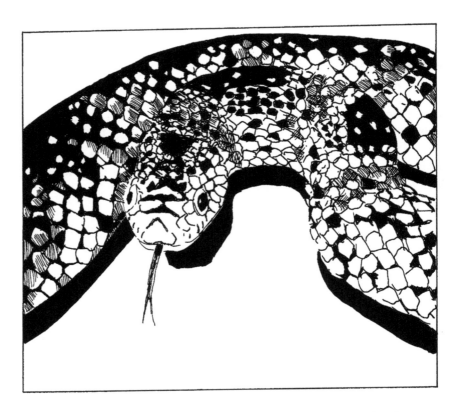

The serpent represented in Durer's painting is identified for the first time as a 'Longnose', also known as the 'Long-nosed' snake. Significantly, this species of reptile is found only in the southern western and south-centred parts of the United States extending into north Mexico. The date of Durer's painting is important, as it is virtually identical with the discovery of the Unite States. According to historians, Christopher Columbus (Italian born) discovered the south American mainland in 1498 and died in 1506. A couple of years earlier in 1504, Durer began his preparatory studies for the painting Eve, completed in Florence 1507.

The 'Longnose's pigmentation is white with black and red spots, and mimics the colouring of the 'Coral snake', which lives in water. In addition, the female of the Longnose species expel 'blood' with their faeces, when distressed, used by Durer to register the 'ovulating fish'. Ambiguity between the Longnose snake and the Coral snake shows a correlation between the fish and serpent. The snake in Durer's image is thus drawn with a leaf in its mouth - a visual pun of the dorsal fin connoting the menstruating eel.

Durer's choice of the Longnose snake appears to work on the Hebrew homonym 'aph' (nose or anger), found also in the Latin pun 'nasus' (nose or anger). The Hebrew expression to 'grow long in the nose' denotes (anger) and originates from the belief that the 'djinn' could change from a 'man into a snake'. Theologically, the snake is used by the artist to suggest God's anger at Eve for eating from the fruit of the tree of knowledge.

Albrecht's ability to procure such a rare species of reptile found outside of Europe obviously demonstrates a close connection between the Spanish and Roman Empires. Chronology of Durer's painting begun in 1504 suggests most probably the initial discovery of the Americas predated Columbus.

Appendix 8

The Location of Atlantis

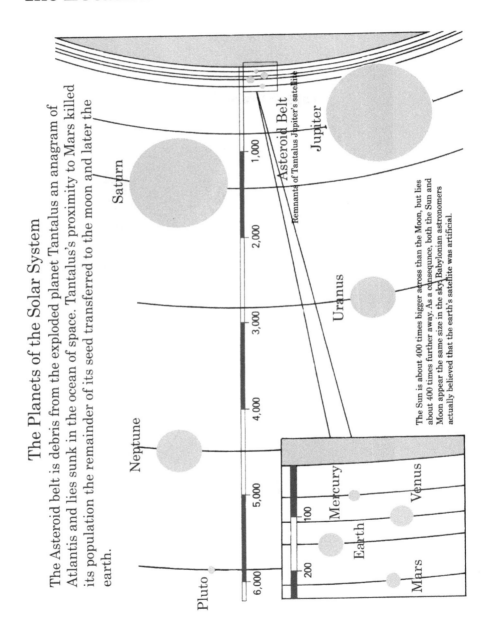

The Planets of the Solar System

The Asteroid belt is debris from the exploded planet Tantalus an anagram of Atlantis and lies sunk in the ocean of space. Tantalus's proximity to Mars killed its population the remainder of its seed transferred to the moon and later the earth.

The Sun is about 400 times bigger across than the Moon, but lies about 400 times further away. As a consequence, both the Sun and Moon appear the same size in the sky. Babylonian astronomers actually believed that the earth's satellite was artificial.

Saturn

Jupiter

Asteroid Belt
Remnant of Tantalus Jupiter's satellite

Uranus

Neptune

Pluto

Mercury

Earth

Venus

Mars

Appendix 9

Hieroglyphic Sign List

All hieroglyphs given in this appendix are the standardized translations.

F24   sickle

E2   throw-stick

E27   pestle

F22   statue plinth

F51   processional boat of Osiris

E60   seat

F50   processional boat of Osiris

B38   piece of flesh

A40   arm

D24   bun   silent letter (t)

E7   standard with feather   ideo. *imnt* 'the west' and related words

E32   three fox-skins   (1) 2c. *ms*

ḥr   Horus

or   *ȝst*   Isis

or   *ȝsir*   Osiris

B7   (1) 2c. *sȝ*   ⊙ RA

A55   A54 com. water pouring from jug   ideo. or det. *w'b* 'pure'

The cobra glyph (B60) 'd' [or 'dj'] informs the Arabic and Persian noun 'jinn' (a demon or spirit), and is found in the Egypto-Akkadian epithet 'Dj-En' a (Snake Lord), implicit of the 'jinni'.

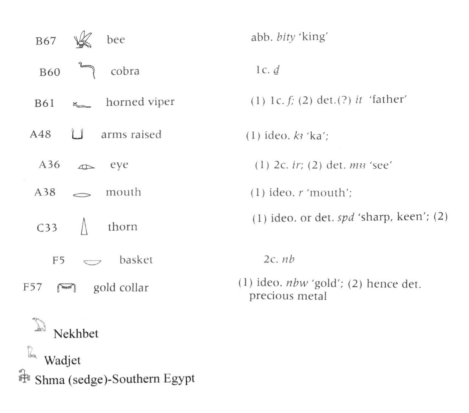

B67	bee	abb. *bity* 'king'
B60	cobra	1c. *ḏ*
B61	horned viper	(1) 1c. *f*; (2) det.(?) *it* 'father'
A48	arms raised	(1) ideo. *kꜣ* 'ka';
A36	eye	(1) 2c. *ir*; (2) det. *mꜣꜣ* 'see'
A38	mouth	(1) ideo. *r* 'mouth';
C33	thorn	(1) ideo. or det. *spd* 'sharp, keen'; (2)
F5	basket	2c. *nb*
F57	gold collar	(1) ideo. *nbw* 'gold'; (2) hence det. precious metal

Nekhbet

Wadjet

Shma (sedge)-Southern Egypt

So UFOs Aren't Real?

This illustration drawn by the author is from a photographic copy of the book *'Ume no Chiri'* (Dust of Apricot), published 1844 (Edo period), and is based on an incident that occurred in Japan 1803. Local residents witnessed this strange object at 'Haratono Hama' (Haratono Beach) in 'Hitachi no Kuni' (Ibaragi Prefecture). According to the explanation, strange letters shown in this drawing were seen inside of the ship.

Text is written in Old Japanese and has been deciphered by Hikaru Ai and Pierre Sabak. The extract shows a diagram and reads. Length 5.4 metres. Outer shell is iron (highest grade) painted with chiyan (a red resin or putty). The craft (ship) is made from iron and glass. Gridded window with lattice design similar to the appearance of a 'shoji' screen (a sliding door). Enclosed on the top right hand corner are the strange hieroglyphs witnessed inside of the floating craft grounded on Haratono Beach. Picture source: Alien Chronicles, Quester Publications (see picture credits).

The following illustrations drawn by the author are based on rare images that have never appeared in publications outside of Japan. Two Japanese books allegedly describe occurrences of an interesting incident in 1803 on Haratono or Hara Yadori Beach, similar to a Close Encounter of the Third Kind. In fact, illustrations in these texts are very similar to modern UFOs.

(1) 'Toen Shousetsu' published in 1825

This is a compendium of stories by many authors including Takizawa Bakin a famous novelist during the Tokugawa period in Japan. One original copy of this book exists in Tenri University Library, Tenri City, Nara Prefecture.

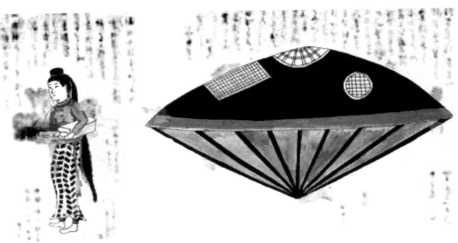

Article Title 'Utsuro-Fune no Banjyo' (A Foreign Woman in the Hollow Ship). The story takes place on 22 February in the early spring of 1803 offshore from a beach called Hara Yadori in the territory of Ogasawara, Etchuu no Kami. The boat was round and resembled a kind of Kou Hako (a box used to burn incense). Inside a foreign woman with fair features, her hair and eyebrows red, held one square box, its dimensions about 80cm. It seemed that this object was very important to her, because she held it constantly and prohibited anyone from approaching it. Many foreign characters were found inside of this boat. Their meanings were undetermined.

Picture of woman and strange hieroglyphs found in the craft.

(2) 'Ume no Chiri' (Dust of Apricot) circa 1844

This publication is written by Nagahashi Matajirou, of whom little is known in detail. One original copy of this book exists in Mukyuu-Kai Library, Machide City, Tokyo.

Novelette Title 'Utsuro-Fune no Koto' (Incident of the Hollow Ship) elaborates and gives further information about the unusual encounter. On 24 March 1803, a strange ship drifted ashore on a beach called Haratono Hama in Hitatchi, Japan. The boat was hollow and its shape was similar to a rice cooking pot. The craft was painted black and had small windows on four sides. In this account again, there is a strange woman, who spoke a foreign language, and prohibited anyone from approaching the box in her possession.

Utsuro no Fune
The Hollow Ships of Japan

Stories of this kind are based on Japanese folklore of 'Utsuro no Fune', alternatively 'Utsubo no Fune'. Both words mean (a hollow ship), implicit of a carrier vessel, and have often been used metaphorically to describe (a cavity in an old tree). 'Utsubo' is a kind of (hollow bag), employed by the Samurai to hold arrows in ancient Japan, and has the additional meaning of a 'moray eel'.

Author's copy of Japanese Edo print of 'Utsubo no Fune' describing the incident at Haratono Hama.

Japanese nobility and ruling families often traced their heritage back to the traditions of 'Utsubo no Fune'. There are many ancient stories, i.e. 'Kaguyahime', regarding interactions between these vessels and ordinary people. Occupants of the 'Utsubo no Fune' are typically revered and considered alien or strange.

Mention of these unusual craft occur frequently in folklore and may have had an historical basis connected to the migration of Asian populations to the Japanese mainland. It is to be noted that such narratives linking nobility to boats are found all over the world and are similar to the biblical stories of Noah and his safe passage in a boat, outlined in the book of Genesis.

(Utsuro / Utsubo)
Hollow Boats and Tree Cavities

Hidden 'tree cavities' are located at temples and shrines, and possess the same meaning as a 'hollow ship', linking sacred sites historically to the traditions of 'Utsuro no Fune'. Japanese etymologists suggest the connection between the 'tree and boat' may have originated from a type of 'canoe', made from a 'hollowed out log'.

'Utsuro no Fune' (hollow ship) are equated originally with Japanese migration and are conventionally associated with the Gods and nobility. Traditionally, the craft are described as round and hollow, leading some Japanese researchers to link the vessels with the UFO phenomena. Religious shrines in ancient Greece, Rome and Egypt, similar to Japan, are aligned to boat iconography, evidenced in the etymologies 'worship' (wor-ship) and 'religion' a derivation of the Latin root 'religare' (to moor a ship) - See Chapter 1, Mal'akh, Plate 2: Boat Pits, Giza plateau, p44).

In Japan, 'tree openings' are located at shrines and connect the 'temple enclosure' religiously to a 'ship'. The presence of such trees suggest that the entrances to Shinto temples are sub-terrestrial. Mythological, the tree describes an opening to the underworld and finds its counterpart in European folklore.

Japanese temples are built on mounds and contain evidence of underground passageways and chambers.

The Gentry folk are often associated with tree veneration and are said to live in fairy mounds, linked archaically to fairy boats. 'Utsuro no Fune' (a hollow ship or tree cavity) is found in the English pun 'fairy', 'ferry', 'fir' (tree) and 'fire'. In the Semitic traditions, the 'se'irim' (angel) are cognate with 'sira' (boat) and appertain to the 'irin' or 'erin' (a watcher or shining one). 'Irin' is a homonym of 'oren' (pine tree), symbolized in Western custom as the 'evergreen', decorated during the winter solstice with lights - a fairy or a star.

In Japanese Shinto, a 'hollowed or dug out tree', a symbol of the 'boat', is sacred and are traditionally located at shrines. The following selection of photographs have never been published in the UK and show 'tree cavities' (Utsuro no Fune), taken by the author on site at Ise Shrine (Mie Prefecture, Japan). Of particular interest is an image, which shows a shrine with money offerings, with a bamboo shoot, protruding from the ground, utilized as an airshaft. Japanese temples are often built on mounds, and conceal subterranean chambers with elaborate drainage and ventilation shafts. Tree openings are typically camouflaged with bamboo coverings or blocked with large rocks, also shown in the photographs. In some of the examples illustrated, the tree is actually sealed with concrete to prohibit entrance.

Altar with bamboo air shoot disclosing a subterranean ventilation system.

Photographic Library of Tree Cavities, Ise Shrine, Mie, Southern Honshu, Japan

Bamboo cover concealing tree opening or doorway.

Sealed doorway.

Sealed doorway shown to scale.

Sealed tree cavity (roof tile).

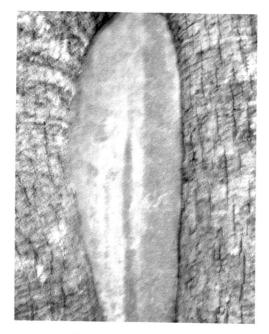

Concrete insert (tree cavity).

Hollow tree.

Beyond the Veil...

'But the following (...) are true: (...) Man has no body distinct from his soul, for that called body is a portion of soul discerned by the five senses (...). Energy is the only life and is from the body; and reason is the (...) outward circumference of energy... (heaven and hell are within one another), and yet neither is apparent to the other'.

William Blake, The Marriage of Heaven and Hell, 1790
(The Hermetic Museum: Alchemy & Mysticism Alexander Roob p259)

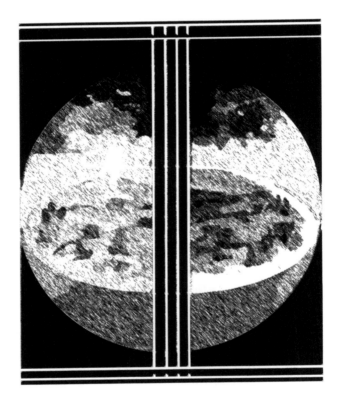

After Hieronymus Bosch's monochromatic painting of the moon titled cryptically 'The Creation of the World'. Outer part of the triptych to 'The Garden of Earthly Delights', circa 1510.

Picture Credits (In Order of Appearance)

Book Cover for *'The Murder of Reality - Hidden Symbolism of the Dragon'* illustrated by Neil Hague (www.neilhague.com).

All drawings, paintings, diagrams and illustrations inside of *'The Murder of Reality'* have been specifically drawn for the book by the author himself with the exception of the book cover by Neil Hague. Pierre Sabak however has copied existing images listed in the following chapters. I have grouped 'Bridge of Love' illustrations separately from 'Quester Publications' for ease of reference.

Picture source obtained from Neil Hague Quester Publications (drawings are sequenced chronologically according to chapter).

Introduction

The Virgin Mary and Saint Giovannino - School of Lippi. Copyright Palazzo Vecchio Italy.

Matthew Hurley (Edited by Neil Hague), The Alien Chronicles, Compelling Evidence For UFOs and Extraterrestrial Encounters In Art & Texts Since Ancient Times, Quester Publications, 2003, p86

Chapter 43 (Part 1)

Moulin Cathedral, France. The image was redrawn from Neil Hague's own photograph, which appears on the front cover of his book *'Journeys in the Dreamtime'*.

Neil Hague, Journeys in the Dreamtime, Keys to Unlocking the Imagination, Exposing the Untold History of Art, Quester Publications, 2006, Front Cover.

Chapter 44

Ubaid Figurine Profile.

Matthew Hurley (Edited by Neil Hague), The Alien Chronicles, Compelling Evidence For UFOs and Extraterrestrial Encounters In Art & Texts Since Ancient Times, Quester Publications, 2003, p81

So UFOs Aren't Real?

Japanese Flying Saucer - Contemporary depiction from 1803, showing a Japanese figure standing beside a UFO (not to scale). Redrawn from Matthew Hurley's image and cross referenced with a photographic copy of the original

Japanese print 1815 from the publication 'Ume no Chiri'. Sabak has also added incidental detail to the clothing seen in the original print. The drawing though an accurate reproduction should be consulted carefully with the original in Matthew Hurley's book. Note there are two versions of this particular illustration dating from the same period. The Japanese Edo block print shown here is presumably obtained from a watercolour study. The painting shows the woman to have mousy hair with light blue clothing and was also referred to by the author during the production of this illustration.

Matthew Hurley (Edited by Neil Hague), The Alien Chronicles, Compelling Evidence For UFOs and Extraterrestrial Encounters In Art & Texts Since Ancient Times, Quester Publications, 2003, p116

Kind permission to reproduce the following images by David Icke Bridge of Love (www.davidicke.com).

All pictures taken from David Icke's book *'Infinite Love is the Only Truth Everything Else is Illusion'* are reproduced in ink by the author himself to improve image clarity. All care has been exercised to duplicate the original images carefully. Interested parties should however consult the original drawings obtained from David Icke's publication listed below - Please note copyright is held with Healing Health & Harmony.

Chapter 30

Depiction of the Fire-Star

David Icke, Infinite Love is the Only Truth Everything Else is Illusion - Exposing the dream world we believe to be real, Bridge of Love, USA, 2005, p205

Chapter 31

Shield of Saturn

David Icke, Infinite Love is the Only Truth Everything Else is Illusion - Exposing the dream world we believe to be real, Bridge of Love, USA, 2005, p207

Chapter 40

Hairy Angel

David Icke, Infinite Love is the Only Truth Everything Else is Illusion - Exposing the dream world we believe to be real, Bridge of Love, USA, 2005, p206

COPYRIGHT NOTICE:

Recommended Bibliography

To understand the symbolism and mythology of the snake, it is necessary to study the ancient languages. A word of warning, it is the author's contention that the hidden priesthood has suppressed information, pertaining to the history of mankind. In particular, releasing misinformation to the general public through the School Curriculum and University Publications. The secret societies also control the new age media, so caution once again should be exercised when looking at 'alternative' historical and mythical interpretations of the angelic lineage. Here however is a list of publications I do recommend:

David Icke
A much maligned author whose research is an excellent source of information on the cultic symbolism of the snake and its relationship between the ancient world and modern political structures. David is perhaps the first author to provide a 'unified world view theory' of the snake and its juxtaposition within politics, religion and the media.

David Icke: The Biggest Secret, Bridge of Love, USA, 1999

David Icke: Children of the Matrix, Bridge of Love, USA, 2001

David Icke: Alice in Wonderland and the World Trade Center Disaster, Why the Official Story is a Monumental Lie, Bridge of Love, USA, 2002

David Icke: Tales from the Time Loop, Bridge of Love, USA, 2003

David Icke: Infinite Love is the Only Truth Everything Else is Illusion, Bridge of Love, USA, 2005

Neil Hague
Britain's most important visionary artist since William Blake. Neil is a prolific illustrator known for his collaboration with David Icke. Neil is also an excellent researcher and has written and edited many books and articles on the ancient myths of the snake. His writing provides the first real alternative history of art, focusing on hidden symbolism of the Illuminati.

Neil Hague: Through Ancient Eyes, Seeing Hidden Dimensions, Exploring Art and Soul Connections, Quester Publications, UK, 2002

Neil Hague: Journeys In the Dreamtime, Keys to Unlocking the Imagination, Exposing the Untold History of Art, Quester Publications, UK, 2006

Matthew Hurley (Editor Neil Hague): The Alien Chronicles, Compelling Evidence For UFOs and Extraterrestrials Encounters In Art & Text Since Ancient Times, Quester Publications, UK, 2003

Robert Temple

Robert Temple brought attention to the connection between Sirius and the traditions of amphibian beings. Formative and influential, the book is currently one of the most authoritative texts written in English on the Nommu and Dagon deities. For anyone interested in the symbolism of the snake and fish, this is an absolute must!

Robert Temple: The Sirius Mystery, Century, London, 1976 (Updated Edition 1998)

Ralph Ellis

For scholars interested in the ancient tongues and their etymological relationship to the hieroglyphs, Ellis' work is definitely worth seeking out. A very thorough and methodical author, he draws comparisons between biblical and Egyptian theology. Ellis' detailed survey of the Semitic languages and dialects is ground breaking - Without question, a first-rate title - Superb!

Ralph Ellis: Eden in Egypt, A Translation of the Book of Genesis out of the Original Egyptian Text, Edfu Books, UK, 2005

Alan F. Alford

One of Britain's leading Egyptologists, an excellent scholar on Egyptian and classical mythology, his work is comprehensive in scope. A highly original thinker, he deserves to be on anyone's reading list - Outstanding!

Alan F. Alford: The Midnight Sun, Eridu Books, UK, 2004

Ian Ross Vayro

Vayro is very good at linking Egyptian and Masonic traditions together. His historical survey of the Bible and the creation of early Christianity effectively demolishes conventional thinking on the development of the Roman Church.

Ian Ross Vayro: Tears in Heaven, Joshua Books, Australia, 2008

Andrew Collins

Well researched, 'From the Ashes of Angels' provides a lot of occult material about the Watchers and their origins in the Middle East and Kurdistan. With Temple's book 'The Sirius Mystery', this is a very good place to start your investigation into the angelic bloodline.

Andrew Collins: From the Ashes of Angels, The Forbidden Legacy of a Fallen Race, Michael Joseph, London, 1996

Badar Azimabadi

A very obscure text (in the UK), *'The World of Angels'* is an excellent commentary on angels in Islamic theology. Azimabadi outlines a lot of useful information that is simply unheard of in the Western world. For example, a Muslim should not eat garlic when going to the mosque, as it is harmful to angels. His historical citation of the battle of Badr is insightful. People killed by the angelic troops of Allah possessed blows above their necks and strange marks on their fingertips that resembled burns - an example that draws comparison to the vampire tradition. Definitely a recommended read, if you can obtain a copy in the English language.

Badar Azimabadi: The World of Angels, Adam Publishers & Distributors, Shandar Market, Chitli Qabar, Jama Masjid, Delhi, 1996

Chris Everard

Controversial documentary film-maker and author, Everard examines in detail Masonic and occult symbolism. Well researched and produced, his work provides a good outline of Secret Societies, their symbolism and operations.

Chris Everard: The Illuminati II, The Antichrist Conspiracy, Enigma Motion Pictures, DVD, 2006

Chris Everard: Spirit World II, The Alien Kabbalah, Enigma Motion Pictures, DVD, 2007

Chris Everard: Secret Space II, Alien Invasion, Enigma Motion Pictures, DVD, 2007

Biographic Details
Pierre Sabak – Symbologist And Comparative Linguist

Pierre Sabak is a graduate of Fine Art (single honours) and obtained his degree from the University of Wales. He has worked as an illustrator focusing on portraiture and the figure. Exhibited extensively, Sabak has shown his work throughout the UK, including St. Martins West London, East London Design Show and the Museum of Modern Art Machynlleth Wales.

A member of the Institute for Learning (MifL), he has obtained a Postgraduate Certificate in Further and Higher Education. Sabak has taught Pre-Raphaelite Painting at the Working Men's College St Pancras London.

A symbologist and comparative linguist, he first became interested in the 'Serpent Race' after reading David Icke's seminal book 'The Biggest Secret'. Initially a sceptic, Pierre Sabak became convinced that extraterrestrials are controlling the planet after studying etymology and semiotics.

Remarkable, his own research has uncovered a universal code, demonstrating the existence of the 'Serpentigena' Latin (Serpent Race), working in conjunction with a 'Hidden Brotherhood', identified in this publication for the first time as the 'Western priesthood'. In addition, Sabak has found the same worded puns, encrypted in many of the world's scripts, validating the existence of a secret language written in symbols.

His utter frustration at not being able to find detailed information regarding the fallen angelic lineage led him to write the 'Serpentigena Series' - unique the set of books is the only comprehensive study of the djinn (jinn) currently available in the English language.

Sabak has travelled extensively around Japan and is interested in its history, language and culture. He is the first author to point out the similarity of Japanese to the Indo-European branch of languages. His research shows that Japanese is in fact a Sino-Indo-European language. In addition, Pierre Sabak's work on Sino-Nipponese symbolism suggests Mount Fuji's summit is artificially created in an engineering feat, akin to the pyramids. The truncated pyramid is found all over Japan and with the solar horns are evident throughout Asia, China and the Middle East.

Pierre Sabak can be contacted via his web site www.pierresabak.com or e-mail: pierresabak@hotmail.co.uk

Ginkakuji (Silver Temple), Kyoto, Japan. Truncated pyramid created from sand, Zen garden.

The truncated pyramid is adjoined with a smaller (feminine) version and suggests Japanese mountains are paired symbolically masculine and feminine (dragon and phoenix). The silver temple is matched with its partner Kinkakuji (Golden Temple) also found in Kyoto.

Contact Details

If you have any information which you think would be useful for Pierre Sabak or alternatively require a publication or book to be illustrated, please e-mail the author at pierresabak@hotmail.co.uk

For updates & details of forthcoming titles, please visit our website at www.pierresabak.com

Online Book Orders: Visit www. pierresabak.com

– SERPENTIGENA –
The Series

Thank you for reading **The Murder of Reality: Hidden Symbolism of the Dragon**. If you enjoyed this work or found the reference material useful, you may wish to read the following publications in the Serpentigena Series:

Volume 1:

The Murder of Reality: Hidden Symbolism of the Dragon

The most detailed book ever compiled in English on the 'Serpentigena' Latin (the Serpent Race). Pierre Sabak examines the worship of the snake and includes chapters on the 'mal'akh' (angel) and angelic host.

Published April 2010

Volume 2:

Shape-Shifter: The Serpent Unveiled

A continuation of Sabak's acclaimed book The Murder of Reality - Sabak goes one step forward and uncovers the most secret traditions of the serpent. A comprehensive study focusing on the human-angelic line (Hebrew the se'irim) and ancient accounts of shape-shifting.

Scheduled for release late 2011

Volume 3:

The Serpentigena: Offspring of the Dragon

Pierre Sabak's opus magnum the 'Serpentigena'. Detailed references include the Seraphim and Kerubim - Symbols of the mammal and snake.

Scheduled for release late 2012

Volume 4:

Brotherhood of the Snake: The Hidden Priesthood

Pierre Sabak's ultimate expose of the priesthood and the hidden networks that control this planet.

Scheduled for release late 2013

E-mail: pierresabak@hotmail.co.uk
Online Book Orders: Visit www. pierresabak.com

– SHAPESHIFTER –
The Serpent Unveiled

SERPENTIGENA VOLUME 2

Humanity has always adopted a 'them' and 'us' mentality. What people have failed to consider is the 'them' and 'us' may not actually be 'human'.

Pierre Sabak

Pierre Sabak examines demonic accounts and refers to the **'Serpentigena'** Latin **(Serpent Race)** as the **'Skin-Divers'** - a phenomenon equated with shapeshifting and black-eyed possession. Documented in the classical world as the **'Soulless Ones'**, they are known in Greek legend as the **'Aniridia' (without iris)** and are linked to the **priestess**. Overtly patriarchal, Sabak contends the priesthood at its core is matriarchal and excludes men from the highest levels of initiation. At the centre of this manipulation is the Reptilian control over the breeding female and her offspring.

A major series of books from one of the world's most controversial writers, the 'Serpentigena' **provides the definitive account of the Dragon, referred to variously as the Watcher, Angel or Jinn**. The unbelievable is made real in this devastating history of the angels and their control over humanity.

An important study and the first of its kind Pierre Sabak examines the cultic symbolism of the snake and its relationship to secret societies. Described by the author as a new academic field, **'Illuminotics' analyses (the study of the Illuminati and its signs)**.

Following on from his best selling book **'the Murder of Reality'**, Sabak finally shows the **conspiracy is really a 'snake'** - Greek **'speira' (a coil)**. Unveiled for the first time, the **'con-speira' discloses a 'secret fraternity', central to the very conspiracy!**

Online Book Orders: Visit www. pierresabak.com

490

Pierre Sabak: Online Book Orders

To order Pierre Sabak's books, please go to
www.pierresabak.com

Lightning Source UK Ltd.
Milton Keynes UK
UKHW021031241020
372160UK00003B/38